P. 100 line 9 "of" should be "or"

P. 238 Typographical Error
— line 19

Niebuhr:
"The nature and
Destiny of Man"

# Main Currents in

# Modern Political Thought

# Main Currents in

# Modern Political Thought

JOHN H. HALLOWELL

*Associate Professor of Political Science*
*Duke University*

NEW YORK: HENRY HOLT AND COMPANY

Selections from G. D. H. Cole, *A Guide To Modern Politics* have been reprinted from *A Guide To Modern Politics* by G. D. H. Cole and Margaret Cole by permission of Alfred A. Knopf, Inc. Copyright 1934 by G. D. H. Cole and Margaret Cole. Selections from C. E. M. Joad, *Guide To The Philosophy of Morals and Politics* have been reprinted by permission of Random House, Inc. Selections from Reinhold Niebuhr, *Nature and Destiny of Man, Christianity and Power Politics, Faith and History, The Children of Light and the Children of Darkness;* Étienne Gilson, *The Unity of Philosophical Experience;* and John N. Figgis, *The Will to Freedom, The Gospel of Nietzsche and The Gospel of Christ* have been reprinted by permission of Charles Scribner's Sons. Selections from *A State University Surveys the Humanities* have been reprinted by permission of The University of North Carolina Press.

TO MY STUDENTS

PAST AND PRESENT

# Preface

THIS study of modern political thought is intended primarily for the student but it is hoped that it will also be of interest to the general reader. It is intended less as a comprehensive history of modern political thought than as an interpretation and analysis of the main currents in political philosophy since the seventeenth century. Attention, accordingly, has been focused upon the more important political philosophers of the modern period and, as much as possible, I have allowed them to speak for themselves. These extensive quotations, however, are not intended to take the place of a reading of their works but to encourage such reading.

A great deal of attention has been given in previous studies of modern political theory, studies to which I am, of course, heavily indebted, to the historical context out of which modern political thought emerged and to the social and economic factors which have influenced that thought. Little attention has been given in most of these studies, however, to the philosophical premises upon which modern political theory is based and still less to the theological presuppositions. And it is that lack which I have sought, in part, to supply with this study. That there is both an intimate and logically necessary connection between one's metaphysical and theological presuppositions and his political theory, I have endeavored to illustrate in some detail in the pages which follow. If I have seemingly neglected other aspects of political thought it is not because I think them unimportant but because those aspects of political theory are better known and have been considered elsewhere both in detail and with competence. The assumption is made that the reader is already acquainted, at least in main outline, with the political philosophy which preceded that with which we are concerned here and the very brief attention which is given in an introductory chapter to classical and medieval political thought is intended only to remind the reader of what he already knows.

The organization of the material presented some difficulties. I have followed a logical and topical method rather than a strictly chronological one since the development of ideas rarely, if ever, corresponds exactly to the calendar. I have separated the discussion of liberalism from that of socialism and given special attention to the crisis of our times. Within these broad categories I have further subdivided the material topically, but with some concern for chronological developments within the framework of those topics. Not all political theories fit exactly or exclusively into these categories and it should constantly be kept in mind that trends of thought discussed, for example, under the heading of liberalism have significance for the development of socialism and vice versa. Some individual philosophers might have appropriately been discussed under two or three headings. The arrangement followed here is not entirely satisfactory but it yields, I believe, a better understanding of modern political thought than would have been gained by following a strictly chronological sequence.

In the presentation of these philosophies I have striven, and I hope with success, for objectivity. I do not understand by objectivity, however, indifference to the meaning and implication of ideas, nor have I undertaken this task under the illusion that my own thought is free from presuppositions. Although we are not always conscious of them, all of us, of necessity, begin our thinking from certain presuppositions. And the presuppositions from which this book is written are those of the classical Christian tradition, as I understand it.

I am indebted in this study, of course, to the works of a great many scholars, a debt I have sought inadequately to discharge by reference to their works in the footnotes. And I am indebted, too, to many friends and colleagues who have given generously of their time and assistance. My colleague, Professor R. Taylor Cole, of the Department of Political Science, Duke University, has been especially generous of his time and helpful in his assistance. He has read the manuscript in its entirety, both in its first draft and in page proof, and his constructive criticism and friendly encouragement at every stage of preparation were largely responsible for bringing this work to a successful conclusion. Helmut Kuhn, now Professor of Philosophy at the University of Erlangen, Germany, has inspired large portions of the manuscript through his writings and personal friendship. He, too, has read the manuscript in its entirety and saved me from many errors. Professor Calvin B. Hoover of the Economics Department at Duke University has read the chapters on Karl Marx and on the Soviet Union and given me the benefit of his special knowledge of these subjects. Professor Franklin W. Young of the Duke Divinity School has read the manuscript and I am indebted to him for many useful suggestions and corrections. To other friends and colleagues, at Duke and elsewhere, who have read portions of the manuscript or discussed these problems with me, I am grateful for their interest and assistance. It has not always been possible for me, however, to incorporate in the manuscript all of the suggestions which have been made to me and, as a consequence, all errors of fact and mistakes in judgment which remain are entirely my own.

I wish also to express my gratitude to the Duke University Research Council and to the Carnegie Foundation for financial assistance and to the administrative officers of my department and of Duke University for the grant of sabbatical leave which provided me with the time necessary to prepare this study for publication. The excellent clerical assistance of Mrs. Glenn Anglin has greatly facilitated the preparation of the manuscript and I am grateful for her services. Last, but not least, I am indebted to my wife, not only for her patience and understanding, but for her encouragement and devotion.

This book is the outgrowth of a course in modern political thought which I first gave at the University of California at Los Angeles and for the past several years at Duke University and it is dedicated to my students in that course because their interest and lively criticism was probably the greatest single stimulus to my writing it.

J.H.H.

*Durham, North Carolina*
*April, 1950*

# Table of Contents

xi

# THE REVOLUTION OF NIHILISM

# THE CRISIS OF OUR TIMES

# Main Currents in

# Modern Political Thought

CHAPTER I

# Introduction to Political Philosophy

MAN lives, not for the sake of existence alone, but that he may live well. It is characteristic of his nature that he is constantly seeking a justification for his existence and for his behavior. Man feels himself to be under the judgment of something beyond himself, a part of a reality that transcends his physical nature. For man is conscious not only of what he is, but of what he ought to be and may become. In ethics, he seeks rationally to define and understand the nature of the good which he ought to seek. In politics, however frustrated he may be by himself and by others, he seeks the implementation of that good in social life; and, to assist in the implementation of that good is, as I see it, the major function of political science.

The only rational motive for seeking to understand political institutions and behavior is the human benefit that may possibly be derived from such a study. If our interest in politics is unrelated to human welfare and to such concepts as justice and freedom, there is, of course, no reason why we should seek to describe political behavior in ethical terms. But if our interest in politics is motivated by an interest in human welfare, it becomes not only our right, but our responsibility, to detect corruption, to identify injustice and tyranny, to unmask sophistry, and to guide men along the paths most likely to yield happiness and freedom. With Aristotle, I believe that the social sciences can be most useful to our society when they are deliberately, consciously, and rationally directed toward making men better human beings—when they seek to discover the principles that make for a free and just society and encourage men by the best means at their disposal to put those principles

I

into practice. If that involves hortatory appeals to the conscience of men, then what our society needs, now more than ever, are clearer and stronger appeals. I vigorously dissent from the view that "good government" is, as some social scientists contend, "a matter of each man's private definition." If that were so, there could be no government at all. The social sciences are not so much in need of new research techniques, as some suppose, but of convictions based upon rational principles. If they have become sterile, as some contend, it is not because they are lacking in adequate research techniques, but because they are hesitant about affirming unequivocally the principles upon which a free and just society can be based. A social science that is not committed to the search for freedom and justice has already signed its own death warrant.

Research, however dispassionate and detached in its methods, achieves meaning and can lay claim to truth only by transcending itself, only by relating itself to something of significance beyond its immediate concern. Political science achieves meaning only by presupposing that the fruits of its research are of value to human beings who have a capacity to reason, to choose alternative modes of behavior, to differentiate good from bad, and who have a destiny that transcends the demands of time and place. If we deny these attributes of humanity, we deny at the same time any possibility of understanding political behavior rationally, i.e., the possibility of political science. It would, indeed, simplify the task of political science if man were an automaton controlled by forces completely outside his own control—except that there would then be no political scientists to understand the mechanism.[1]

## A Definition of Politics

WHAT is politics? The answer that most readily suggests itself, because it is the one most commonly accepted today, is that politics is the struggle for power. Politics, our modern "realists" tell us, is concerned primarily with the means of acquiring and keeping power. So widely accepted is this conception of politics that many regard it as a self-evident truth. Yet, a little reflection and analysis will reveal that it is far from self-evident and much less adequate as a definition than, at first glance, it appears to be.

What is the nature of this power which is everywhere so avidly sought? Is it a thing? Does it have positive dimensions in time and space? The so-called realist talks as though power were something substantive, as though it were a thing which could be stored up, manipulated, seen. But if power were something substantive, if it were a thing, we could feel it, touch it, see it—yet, no one has ever seen, felt, or touched it—though all of us have, indeed, felt the *effects* of power. Power itself eludes our grasp for the reason that it is not a substantive thing.

What do we mean when we say that a person is powerful? We mean that he has the ability to dominate someone else. Power, then, in a political sense first of all involves human beings and presupposes the existence of two or more persons. A hermit could have no power in a political sense. Power, therefore, is not the name of a thing but it is a concept describing a relationship between two or more persons. Because it is not a substantive thing but *a relational concept*, power may take many forms, of which brute force is only one. It may take the form of superior knowledge, wealth, reputation or any number of other forms. Power implies a relationship between wills whereby one will or several wills are acknowledged to be superior to other wills. Since what is spoken of as power implies a *relationship* between wills, it implies that power cannot exist except in terms of a relationship in which there is an *acknowledgment* of superiority of one kind or another. The fact of acknowledgment is essential to the concept of power. Power, in other words, depends upon the acceptance of something as power and it is the acceptance of that something which makes it power, not the claim to possession of power as a substantive thing. A person cannot will to become more powerful, though he may, indeed, become more powerful by willing to do certain things that others regard as a mark of superiority. In every power relationship there is an element of *consent*, an element which may be implicit or explicit. The power relationship is a two-way, not simply a one-way, relationship. The element of consent may be large or small but it is always present to some degree.

It is the value which men attach to material wealth that makes the man of wealth a powerful person, it is the value which men attribute to knowledge that makes the man of knowledge powerful in his influence. The man of knowledge exercises no power among people who do not value knowledge —his power depends not only upon the possession of knowledge but also upon the value attributed by others to knowledge. It might be said that, while this appears to be true in these instances it is not true in the case of power exercised in the form of brute force. Where is the element of consent in a situation in which one man is threatened by another with a revolver? There is, I think, an element of consent even in such a situation. The man threatened may refuse to yield to the demands of the person with the revolver in which case the man with the revolver will be thwarted in his attempt to impose his will on the other. The person must *consent* to yield even in such a situation. The man with the revolver may, of course, decide to kill his victim but he will not succeed in that way in imposing his will upon the other person for the simple reason that you cannot make a dead man do what you want him to do. It is certainly true that some men in such a situation would choose to yield rather than resist and risk death but that does not alter the fact that they *choose* to yield. In every power situation, then, even when resort is made to brute force, there is an element of consent. It is always a two-way and never entirely a one-way relationship.

A person who claimed to be powerful but never gave any indication of his ability to dominate others would soon lose the reputation for being powerful. Power must be exercised in order to exist. Power manifests itself only in action. Only by *doing* something, only by acting in some way, can a person demonstrate the power he claims to possess. If men must act in order to demonstrate the power they claim to have, they must, of necessity, do something specific; they must act with some purpose in mind. One cannot will to do nothing; if he wills, it must be something which he wills. A will without purpose is absurd. If power is a relational concept rather than a substantive thing, if it exists only in purposeful action, it can never be a self-sufficient end but only a means toward the attainment of purposes or ends more ultimate than power itself.[2]

One of the inadequacies of the definition of politics as a struggle for power is that it obscures, if it does not obliterate, the *purposes* in terms of which power is used and the conflict of purposes out of which politics emerges. For it is the conflict of purposes, of aims and objectives, that characterizes politics —not the struggle for a "power" divorced from all purposeful motivation. It is the specific purposes in terms of which particular men act that should concern the student of politics rather than the analysis of an abstract will to achieve an abstract "power." An abstract will is a nonexistent will.

Politics is concerned with the wills and interests of particular individuals and with the inevitable conflict between these individual interests and wills. Politics is successful when it succeeds in reconciling them, when it succeeds in formulating policies that are mutually acceptable. The end of politics is policy—the integration of conflicting interests in terms of certain interests and values which are held in common. The statesman differs from the ordinary politician in that he is able to envisage and inspire support for policies that are in the long-run, best interests of the most people and thus we think of him as the politician *par excellence*. To the extent that the ordinary politician is motivated by narrow, sectional, group or personal interests we think of him as a failure and the more narrow his vision and selfish his aim the greater the failure.

Although politics comes into being as a result of the conflict of wills and interests it presupposes the existence of certain interests and values in common, for without this basis for reconciliation there could be no politics. Politics has sometimes been defined as the technique of compromise. This is both true and false. It is false if the end of politics is thought to be compromise for its own sake, but it is true to the extent that compromise presupposes some agreement upon principles in terms of which compromise may take place. No one likes compromise for its own sake and no political society could be based on love of compromise. Persons are willing to make compromises only because they value some things more than they do the things which they are compromising. When a society no longer values common interests above personal interests the society disintegrates, compromise is no longer possible and politics ceases. And war, international or civil, generally signalizes the breakdown of politics and the end of compromise.[3]

Since politics presupposes the existence of certain interests and values which are held in common the relationship between politics and ethics is an intimate one. For morality is the embodiment of those things which are commonly valued and the science of morality is ethics. This relationship was more clearly recognized in other ages than our own. For Plato and Aristotle, the founders of political science and philosophy, politics was conceived as the application of ethical principles to social problems.[4] This conception of politics seems to me, in the light of what has been said above, to be a clearer and more realistic one than that advanced in the name of modern "realism." It recognizes that politics is purposeful, that it aims at the reconciliation of conflicting interests and that it is dependent upon the existence of certain principles in terms of which reconciliation may take place.

The principles in terms of which the reconciliation of conflicting individual purposes may take place are dependent upon the conceptions which we hold concerning the nature and destiny of man. For in order to answer the question: what is good for men?, what is in the best interest of human beings?, we must first answer the question: what is man?, what ought he to be? The answers which we give to those questions will profoundly affect the answer which we give to the former question.

Although a study of the techniques by means of which the reconciliation of conflicting wills and interests may be facilitated is a large and legitimate part of the study of politics, it is not the whole of politics nor its most fundamental part. If we would penetrate beyond the techniques of effecting compromise to the purposes in terms of which compromise is made possible, if we would look behind the institutions to the ideas and purposes that they embody and seek to realize in practical affairs, we must concern ourselves not only with such problems as the nature of the good but with such problems as the nature of man and of the universe he inhabits. But before we discuss the nature of political philosophy it might be well to ask, as we did in the case of politics, what is philosophy?

## A Definition of Philosophy

PHILOSOPHY is the search for meaning, it seeks to synthesize our knowledge in terms of some rational, meaningful pattern. Unlike natural science which is concerned with answering the question "how?", philosophy is concerned with answering the question "why?". This question does not by its very nature yield the same kind of more or less definite answers that can be obtained by asking the question "how" and, as a consequence, philosophy must be framed in more imaginative and poetic language. It is most at home in the language of metaphor and analogy. For this reason philosophy is sometimes dismissed as an impractical endeavor. Yet, a little reflection will reveal that however more difficult it is to obtain answers to the question "why," that question is of fundamental importance to the understanding of ourselves and of the universe in which we live. No one setting out on a journey would be content with a knowledge of the means by which he might make his trip, he would want to know his destination. Our journey through life is the most important journey we shall ever take and we will not have an opportunity to retrace our steps and to start over again. It is essential, therefore, that we begin our journey with the best information available about ourselves and our destination. Probably this is the most real information there is.

Underlying our ordinary discourse there are certain presuppositions which all of us take for granted. Not all of us have the same presuppositions but all of us take some things for granted, regard certain ideas as self-evidently true. These are the premises, what someone has called the "inarticulate premises," from which all our thinking begins. These are our fundamental beliefs which, of necessity, influence our observations and our conclusions. Until they are pointed out to us, however, we are generally unconscious of their existence. A contemporary English philosopher, R. G. Collingwood, has pointed out that it is one of the principal tasks of philosophy to uncover these basic presuppositions or beliefs.[5] Philosophy, he has said, seeks "to bring belief to a self-consciousness of itself." The aim of philosophy is not the increase of our knowledge but the increase of our understanding. It seeks to impart not knowledge, in the sense of facts, but wisdom. The philosopher has succeeded, not when he makes us say: "now I know something I never knew before," but rather, when we say: "now I understand what I dimly perceived but did not really understand before." As Georg Simmel once facetiously remarked: "A philosopher articulates what everybody else knows." The philosopher does not tell us something we never knew before but helps us to understand better what we already knew. This aim of philosophy was clearly revealed in the method employed by the founders of philosophy, Socrates and Plato. Both taught by the method of questioning, seeking to elicit by rational discussion, truths already known but dimly perceived and obscured by false reasoning.

The principal branches of philosophy are: metaphysics (the nature of ultimate reality), epistemology (the form of knowledge), logic, and ethics. Political philosophy is most directly and intimately related to ethics, since the reconciliation of conflicting purposes can only be brought about by a prior commitment to an objective good that transcends subjective desire and it is one of the functions of ethics to determine what that objective good is. For the Christian, the supreme good which orders all lesser goods in the ascending hierarchy of goods is God. This supreme good he knows not only by the light of his natural reason but by faith. Since an ethic must of necessity be grounded upon knowledge of reality, political philosophy cannot avoid concern with epistemological, metaphysical, and theological problems. This concern may be explicit or implicit but it is never totally absent.

## Political Philosophy

IT IS one of the principal tasks of political philosophy to bring men's political beliefs to self-consciousness and to subject them to the scrutiny of reason. Political philosophy is not so much concerned with political institutions as it is with the ideas and aspirations that are embodied in institutions. It looks behind the surface of political events and institutions in an effort to discover the underlying motives, beliefs, and aspirations that brought those events and institutions about. It looks behind the superficial struggle for power in an effort to determine why this struggle is taking place and where it is leading. It is not so much interested in how things occur as it is in what occurs and why. It is less interested in the efficiency of political techniques and institutions than it is in their legitimacy.

The relationship between ideas and institutions is an intimate and reciprocal one. All thinking about political problems takes place in particular historical periods, within the framework of specific sociological and economic conditions and is undertaken by intellectuals with a personal stake in the society to which they belong. Yet, while the environment (intellectual, political, social and economic) conditions, it does not determine what will be thought.[6] While the environment provides materials about which to think and necessarily circumscribes the vision of the thinker, it does not, as is sometimes erroneously supposed, prescribe the answers that will be found. No situation in itself embodies a self-evident meaning that is projected into the realm of ideas without some intellectual activity on the part of the observer. Every situation requires conceptualization, i.e., it must be intellectually recognized and identified, before it can exert any influence.

There are some persons under the influence of an economic determinism who will insist that political ideas are nothing more than a kind of mental reflection of economic conditions and of one's personal relationship to the prevailing economic mode of production. But the contention that all political and social change is caused by economic conditions ignores the fact that economic conditions also have a cause. To say that economic changes are brought about by "dialectical necessity" is simply to resort to a verbal subterfuge. It leaves the question: what causes changes in economic conditions unanswered. How men will *interpret* prevailing economic conditions, how they will conceive of their relation to the prevailing economic

mode of production, will depend as much upon their philosophical premises as upon the economic facts of the situation.
Facts do not present themselves to even the most impartial and
dispassionate observers with labels already attached to them,
but individuals seek facts and the kind of facts they find depend
in large part upon the conceptual presuppositions from which
they begin their search. Facts become meaningful only after
we have fitted them into some pattern of meaning, a pattern
of meaning derived, of necessity, from something beyond the
facts themselves. The Russian Revolution of 1917 took the
course it did, not simply because of the economic conditions
then prevailing in Russia, but because an intellectual by the
name of Karl Marx developed the *theory* of economic change
and revolution that he did. Economic conditions, changes in
the techniques of economic production, may give rise to widespread discontent but the way in which that discontent will
be conceived, the way in which it will express itself politically,
will depend upon *theories* about it. Exploitation must be conceived as exploitation, injustice must be recognized as injustice, before it has any political or social significance. In
other words, what you and I *think* about any situation in which
we find outselves is more important politically than the situation itself—the situation comes into being as a particular situation only when we are able rationally to identify it. Theory,
hence, is of paramount importance since it puts into words,
into ideas, that which before were only vague feelings or subjective insights and it permits us to communicate and share
those feelings and insights with others.

While all theory is born of a particular environment it
achieves significance and greatness to the extent that it transcends its environment. Just as the greatness of any work of art
depends upon the ability of the artist to transcend the limitations of his environment with a message of universal and eternal significance, so the greatest political philosophies are those,
which, although written in former centuries under conditions
much different from ours, still have something significant to
say to us about our own problems and our own times. The
greatness of Shakespeare does not lie in what he took from the
Elizabethan age but rather in his use of the materials of that

age in order to say something significant about universal and eternal human problems. The greatness of Plato lies not so much in what he had to say about political conditions in the fourth century before Christ but in his discovery of certain truths about human nature and politics which are as meaningful and as valid today as they were at the time they were written.

The environment imposes a limitation which no thinker, however great, can ever completely transcend and hence, no political theory is ever completely valid or completely applicable to the problems of other times and places. This is not to say, as some would say, that all truth is relative but rather to say that all truth is partial. Because of the limitations of perspective imposed by a particular environment and because of the corruption of the human will which perverts even reason in the service of passion truth will always be mixed with error. Yet the fact that no individual can ever know the truth completely and infallibly does not invalidate the partial truth which he does know and shares with others. Each generation has the task imposed upon it of thinking through its own particular problems and of finding proximate solutions to them. Wise men will seek the counsel of those who have grappled with similar problems before, they will cherish the truth that has already been discovered and they will learn from their mistakes.

We live in times when political problems are uppermost in men's minds. The political events of recent years have focused our attention upon the more fundamental problems of political philosophy. What is the state? For what purposes does it exist? Do I owe it unqualified obedience? Do I have obligations which transcend those imposed upon me by my membership in the state? What do we mean by individual rights? The questions could be multiplied many times. They are the questions political philosophy ever since the time of Plato has sought to answer. The answers have, of course, reflected the environment in which they were framed—some have transcended the limitations of environment better than others.

We shall be concerned in this book primarily with an analysis of the answers that have been given in modern times, i.e., with political theory since the sixteenth century. But in order that modern political theory may be seen and placed within the perspective of the Western political tradition as a whole some brief attention in the introductory chapters will be given to political philosophy prior to that time. Our attention will be focused throughout upon the thought characteristic of the Western world since the crisis we are now experiencing is primarily a crisis in Western civilization.

Considerable attention will be given to the philosophical premises and the general intellectual climate of opinion out of which modern political theory emerged since, ultimately, the political problem resolves itself into the more fundamental question: what is the nature and destiny of man? The way in which men have answered that question has profoundly influenced their political philosophies, as I shall endeavor to illustrate in the pages which follow.[7]

CHAPTER 2

# The Background of Modern Political Thought

MODERN political thought may conveniently be said to have had its origins in the climate of opinion that was produced by the Renaissance and the Reformation, yet its more remote origins extend as far back as the sixth century before Christ. We shall be concerned in this book primarily with political philosophy since the sixteenth century but it is well to remember that two thousand years of political speculation preceded that with which we shall be concerned here, and that earlier thought has had a profound influence not only upon the so-called Middle Ages but also upon modern political theory and institutions. "At the outset," a great scholar reminds us,

it is worth remembering that our very word "political" comes from the Greek *polis*. It was the Greek city-state that furnished the data for the first systematic thought of our race on "civil relations." It conditioned the thinking of some of its most powerful and penetrating minds upon the perennial and still unsolved problems involved in these relations; and even today, after the lapse of more than two thousand years of development and change, we can think of these in large part only in the terms that Plato and Aristotle formulated. . . . Whatever our modern laws may be, Rome is the source of our jurisprudence, and whatever our form of government, Greece has furnished us the main outlines of our political science. And the fact that the details of government under modern conditions have become so different from those peculiar to Aristotle only serves to bring into stronger relief their essential identity.[1]

Perhaps the greatest legacy which ancient Greece has bequeathed to the modern world is philosophy itself. For it was

13

with Thales in the sixth century before Christ that Western man began to speculate in a rational way about himself and the universe in which he found himself. Early philosophical speculation was necessarily crude as men sought gropingly to discover the underlying principle of reality. Water, air, and fire were alternately suggested to be the ultimate reality from which everything else had its origin. But, however crude the conclusions reached by pre-Socratic thinkers they set in motion speculation about the reality that lies behind the appearance of things that enabled Plato and Aristotle to reach more profound truths.

There were numerous teachers in ancient Greece, as there are in modern times, who dismissed such speculation as irrelevant, useless or impossible. There is no truth, they said, but only opinion. One opinion is as good or as bad as another. There are no absolute moral principles, they said, but only social conventions and whatever is, is right. The only knowledge possible is that derived from sense-perception and such knowledge is relative, particular, and ever-changing. Against the contentions of these Sophists Plato argued that there is a reality behind the appearance of things which is more real than that which outwardly appears to be real. Behind the constant flux of Becoming there is permanence and universality. The objects of sense perception are particular manifestations of universal ideas, indeed, it is the existence of these universal categories of thought that gives meaning to the objects of sense perception and enables us to identify them. The so-called "facts" of sense perception do not present themselves to individuals with neat labels attached, but individuals seek facts and the kind of facts they find depends upon the conceptual presuppositions from which they begin their search for them. It is the existence of such universal categories as Goodness, Truth and Beauty that is the key which unlocks the door to understanding and wisdom. Knowledge is not the acquisition of new facts but the recollection of ideas already present in the mind. The mind needs only to be reawakened and education consists, in a sense, of stimulating the memory. Because man is predisposed to virtue, virtue can be taught. We can demonstrate the existence of moral principles just as we can demonstrate the axioms of geometry—neither can be "proved" since both are *a priori*. The proof consists in the demonstration of their existence. The task of philosophy is the re-awakening of men's consciousness to those principles which animate the universe and by means of which they may lead happy, harmonious lives.

Against the contention of the Sophists that morality is simply social convention and that "might makes right," Plato and Aristotle argued that there are certain universal and absolute principles of goodness and justice which man, by virtue of his reason, can discover if he will. Man is by nature a moral and social being—to be moral is to be human, to be human is to be moral—and the state is simply the individual "writ large." The good man and the good citizen are identical in the good state. The state comes into existence in order to satisfy needs which the individual apart from other individuals could not supply for himself and it continues in existence in order that men may be guided toward moral perfection. Just as the good man is the one who combines Wisdom, Temperance, and Courage in harmonious accord, so the most just state, Plato taught, is the one in which the classes of society representing each of these virtues are harmoniously united. The most just state is that which enables each individual to perform that social function for which he is best fitted by capacity and virtue. Or, as Aristotle expressed it, justice is giving to each man his due. The end of politics, Aristotle said, "is concerned with nothing so much as with producing a certain character in the citizens, or in other words, with making them good." [2]

Plato and Aristotle differed in their thinking in many ways but they agreed that (1) man is a rational, moral being; (2) that he is also a social being who cannot live apart from his fellows; (3) that man exists in order to lead the good life and (4) the attainment of that good life is the primary purpose of the state. The intellectual battle which both philosophers waged against the Sophists is an ever-continuing one and each generation has had to fight it all over again but with the advantage that it could wage the battle with intellectual weapons forged by two of the greatest philosophers of all times.

Both Plato and Aristotle thought that men could find happiness and self-sufficiency only within the state, a life apart from the state was to them, if not inconceivable, undesirable. With the disintegration of the Greek city-states and the coming of the Alexandrian and later the Roman empires, a number of schools of thought arose which sought to explain how individuals could achieve happiness and self-sufficiency apart from the state. All these post-Aristotelian schools of thought agreed in separating ethics from politics—the search for the good life for the individual was no longer associated with the search for the just state. It was man as an individual, not man as a citizen, that engaged their attention and it was individual self-sufficiency that became the ideal. Man became conscious of himself as a particular soul with a life and destiny of his own.

Of the many schools of thought which arose in this period one in particular, Stoicism, exerted an influence that was to have profound consequences for Western civilization. For it was through Stoicism that much of Greek philosophy was transmitted to Western Europe in the early centuries before Christ. Stoicism flourished for a period of about five hundred years, from the time of its founder, Zeno (340–265 B.C.), to the death of the Roman emperor Marcus Aurelius (121–180 A.D.) who was one of the last and most renowned of its representatives.

For the Stoics the ultimate reality was matter animated by reason. Nature was conceived as being materialistic, all pervasive, containing everything in causal connectedness, and permeated by cosmic Reason. God was described as the "Fiery Reason of the cosmos" and was equated with the universal law of reason or the "Mind in matter." Man's constitution was conceived as being similar to that of the universe. Just as the universe is held together by cosmic Reason so the soul of man which is a part of this cosmic Reason holds the body together. The universe is governed by natural laws of reason which are immanent in nature and the individual achieves happiness and serenity by comprehending the inevitability of natural causation.

The Wise Man "lives according to nature," i.e., he allows his reason to guide his conduct and restrain his emotions and thus cooperates with natural necessity. The Foolish Man is a creature of impulse driven this way and that by every emotional whim and thus he acts contrary to nature and nature's laws. The Wise Man by obeying the dictates of reason and suppressing all feeling and emotion achieves a harmonious relationship to the universe, i.e., serenity. Apathy, understood as resignation to rational necessity, was, according to the Stoics, the highest virtue and the supreme good. Man may obey the universal law of reason through blind compulsion or by willing acquiescence but it is only by means of the latter that he becomes free—when he freely wills that which reason decrees. An act is good if reason controls the action, it is bad if emotion controls the action—nothing else is good or bad. Self-control through reason is the supreme virtue.

Not only did Stoicism exalt the life of reason but it emphasized the essential equality of all men. Although individuals may differ in wealth, social position, reputation and in other respects, they are, nevertheless, essentially equal since all are equally endowed with reason and equally able, if they will, to comprehend the laws of natural necessity which direct the destinies of each. The mass of men are foolish but they could be wise if they would.

For the ancient *polis* which was being swallowed up in great empires the Stoics substituted the concept of the *cosmopolis* and for the first time man could be conceived as a citizen not of a particular city-state but as a citizen of the world. There was thus born a concept of the brotherhood of man that the self-sufficiency of the early Greek city-state had obscured. Man was linked to man by a common necessity to obey the universal law of reason and in the life of reason each could find equal freedom. Man simply as man, achieved a new significance and a new status. These two concepts: (1) the universal brotherhood of man and (2) the universal law of reason were the principal contributions of Stoicism to Western civilization.

It was through Stoicism, rather than through Platonism, that Greek philosophy was introduced into the Roman world.

The Stoic doctrine of the brotherhood of man and the citizenship of the world was not ill-suited to a state that seemed destined to bring all races within its political control, nor was the Stoic belief in a universal law binding upon all entirely strange to a people under whose eyes the *pax Romana* was already growing by leaps and bounds towards its ultimate inclusion of all the known western civilized world and more.[3]

It was in the writings of Cicero that Stoicism was best exemplified in the Roman world and through him passed into Roman jurisprudence. "True law," Cicero taught,

is right reason consonant with nature, diffused among all men, constant, eternal; which summons to duty by its command and hinders from fraud by its prohibition, which neither commands nor forbids good men in vain nor moves bad ones by either. To make enactments infringing this law, religion forbids, neither may it be repealed even in part, nor have we power through Senate or people to free ourselves from it. It needs no interpreter or expounder but itself, nor will there be one law in Rome and another in Athens, one in the present and another in time to come, but one law and that eternal and immutable shall embrace all peoples and for all time, and there shall be as it were one common master and ruler, the god of all, the author and judge and proposer of this law. And he who obeys him not shall flee from himself, and in spurning the nature of human kind by that very act he shall suffer the greatest of torments, though he escapes others which men consider pain.[4]

This is the conception of natural law which is to dominate Western political thought for at least eighteen hundred years. Not until the nineteenth and twentieth centuries have men seriously challenged the idea of the existence of a law of reason which is eternal, absolute, universal and immutable. For centuries men have distinguished between this law and the laws which are enacted by men insisting that the latter is only truly law when it conforms in principle and content to the dictates of right reason. Justice, hereafter, is conceived as the expression of this natural law of reason.

According to Cicero, and to Roman thought generally, this law which is common both to God and to men is also the foundation of the state since it existed "before any written laws or any state had been founded." The state is nothing more nor less than "a partnership in law" (*juris societas*), it is "an assemblage of men associated in consent to law." [5]

Unlike the political philosophy of ancient Greece which had

difficulty conceiving of man apart from the state, Roman political thought conceived of man as prior to the state and of the state as being founded not simply upon natural necessity but upon mutual consent. It is doubtful if Roman political thought contained the idea of an actual agreement or compact but it did contain a doctrine of consent which could in time develop into the idea of a social contract. The modern doctrine that government rests upon the consent of the people had its origins in the political philosophy of Rome. It was not until the seventeenth century that that doctrine was reinforced with the right of revolution but the latter doctrine could not have emerged without the former. The idea of a universal law and the idea of the state being founded upon consent together laid the foundation for the conception of individual rights—a conception which was lacking in ancient Greek political thought. These ideas were passed on to the Middle Ages through the medium of the writings of the great Roman jurists. It was in the sixth century A.D. that a commission appointed by the Emperor Justinian compiled and published a *Digest of Roman Law*. Three other important works were published at about the same time: the *Institutes*, a handbook of law; the *Codex*, a codification of all the laws then in force; and the *Novellae*, an appendix to the Codex containing the most recent decrees of Justinian. Together these four works comprised the *Corpus Juris Civilis*. This was the final and classic expression of Roman law and after its rediscovery in the eleventh century it exerted a profound influence upon Western European political thought and institutions. "Jurisprudence," we read in the *Digest*, "is the knowledge of things divine and human, the perception of the just and the unjust. . . . The precepts of law are these: to live uprightly, to injure no one, to render to each his right." [6]

## *The Emergence of Christianity*

THROUGH Greek philosophy Western man discovered that man is a moral being endowed with reason by means of which he may aspire to truth. He was also taught that the universe is a rational one and that at its center there is a cosmic Reason holding and directing all. By following the dictates of reason man acquires human dignity and finds his freedom. But despite the grandeur of its vision and the nobility of its sentiments an air of melancholy hung over it all. The Greeks could conceive of history as nothing but an unending series of recurring cycles, a view that reduced history to meaninglessness. The very exaltation of man as a rational animal obscured, moreover, the existence of man as a passionate creature. The optimistic belief of the Greeks that wisdom is synonymous with virtue, that the wise man is the good man, obscured the corruption of human nature that perverts even reason in the service of passion. "That which I would not I do, and that which I do, I would not."

It was through Judaism that Western man learned to recognize his suffering as a judgment of God upon his unrighteousness. History was no meaningless and repetitious cycle but the revelation and judgment of One who is the perfect embodiment of Righteousness. Man is the creature of God, personally responsible to Him and dependent upon Him for his existence and salvation. God has revealed His will for man, in part at least, in the law which He handed down to Moses in the form of the Ten Commandments. The Jewish prophets called men to repentance in order that they might be prepared for the coming of the Messiah and the establishment on earth of the Kingdom of God. Whereas, the Jewish prophets, however, looked to the coming of a Messiah who would lead them, the Jews, to the Promised Land and serve as King, He who came as the Messiah recognized no such narrow mission but came to establish the Kingdom of God in the hearts and minds of all who would turn to Him in love, whether Jew or Gentile.

In Jesus, at first only a few and later many, came to recognize the Christ of whose coming the Jewish prophets had foretold and they called Him the Son of God. They recognized one who was perfectly God and perfectly man who through his life, death, and Resurrection had reconciled man to God in love and suffering. They recognized one who was the perfect embodiment in human form of perfect love and perfect wisdom. His disciples who were plunged into despair as He lay dying in agony upon the Cross condemned by the world for his innocence hastened later when He appeared to them in life to bring this good news to all who would listen.

At first Christianity was but one religion among many and for three hundred years those who professed to being Christians were subjected to persecution. When sun worship, represented by the cult of Mithra, was declared to be the official religion of the Roman Empire by the Emperor Aurelian in the second half of the third century every possible effort was made to stamp out Christianity by the most ruthless kind of violence and persecution. But that effort failed and with the conversion of the Emperor Constantine in the fourth century A.D. Christianity became the official religion of the Empire.

Christianity as a body of thought merged the teachings of Greek philosophy with those of the Jewish prophets and added the Incarnation of the Word. Prepared by the Greeks to conceive of God as the embodiment of cosmic Reason and by the Jews to conceive of God as the embodiment of perfect Righteousness, Western man was prepared to recognize in Jesus the incarnation of perfect wisdom and perfect justice.

Christianity taught that man is the creature of God, that essentially he is a spiritual being with a nature and destiny that transcends time and space. Beyond the kingdom of man there is the Kingdom of God and if an individual would enter that kingdom he must surrender his will to God and put an end to his rebellion. Thus, there is introduced into life a duality unknown in the Greek world—man is not only a citizen of the world (the kingdom of man) but is also, potentially at least, a member of the Kingdom of God. Man is confronted for the first time with a dual loyalty—a loyalty to Caesar and a loyalty to God. He is admonished to render unto Caesar that which is rightfully his but unto God that which belongs to Him and if there is a conflict of loyalties he must choose, if he would be saved, that which is God's. The concept of natural law developed by the Stoics and perpetuated by the Roman jurists is retained by Christianity and identified as a species of divine law. The law as conceived both by the Greeks and as conceived by the Jewish prophets is not abrogated but transcended by the principle of love—justice is recognized as an imperfect manifestation of God's love for man and hence-

forth men are enjoined to temper justice with mercy, to administer justice with the compassionate knowledge that the
sins of others are our own sins and that in their sinning we sin
as well.

The Stoic conception of the universal community in which
all men are brothers was given spiritual content by the Christian conception of the Kingdom of God. All men are brothers
because all men have a common Father and the Kingdom of
God knows neither male nor female, freeman or slave, Gentile
or Jew, Greek or barbarian. This Kingdom is not a partnership of law but a partnership of love. It is through love of God
that men learn to love one another. Repentance for one's sins,
a change of heart, the reorientation of one's will and thoughts
from self to God, is the only requirement for entrance into the
Kingdom of God which, unlike the kingdom of man, endures
forever.[7]

## The Middle Ages

ONE of the greatest figures of the early Middle Ages was St.
Augustine (354–430 A.D.). Having lived as a young man a life
of dissipation in which he experimented with practically every
philosophy of life and religion then known, he turned in middle life to Christianity, became a priest and finally a bishop
in North Africa. Of all the works of the early Church fathers
his *City of God* is probably the most important. Writing at the
time of the disintegration of the Roman Empire and of the
fall of Rome to the barbarians he sought to explain in Christian terms the significance of what was happening. But he
was more than a philosopher of history, he was one of the
most eminent theologians of all times.

As a theologian he emphasized something which earlier
philosophy had overlooked. The acquisition of truth, he
taught, is an activity not only of the intellect but of the will—
the direction of our will directs our reason. We learn and know
only that which we want to learn and know. Because we are
sinful our wills, until touched by the grace of God, are misdirected by the passions to which men as sons of Adam are

heir. When St. Augustine says that men are sinful he means that men have been tempted by pride to believe themselves self-sufficient, self-sustaining, self-important. Thus, until released from sin by the power and pardon of God, i.e., the grace of God, they live in a state of rebellion against God denying that they owe their existence to Him who created not only them but the universe in which they move. God created men as free beings since He would not compel their love (love compelled is not love at all) but men have chosen of their own free will to believe themselves independent of God and to act as though masters of their own destiny. That is the "original sin" from which all other sins arise. By attributing to himself the wisdom that is God's man has brought misery and suffering to himself and his children.

Because man has fallen away from that state of innocence in which he was created, external coercion is necessary as a partial remedy for the consequences of sin. Because men apart from the grace of God do not and will not love one another as brothers it is necessary to establish by coercion just relations among them, that they may not harm one another and may live orderly, if not entirely peaceful, lives. Were men motivated solely by love there would be no need for law and the state, but since men will not love God and cannot, therefore, love each other, law and the state are necessary in order to bring about that condition of earthly justice which is an approximation of God's love for man. By the law which holds men together in civil society St. Augustine understood not simply the law of reason of which Cicero spoke but the law of God. The institutions of property and of slavery were explained by St. Augustine, likewise, as the consequence of man's sinfulness. Professor A. J. Carlyle explains the medieval conception of property in this way:

To the Fathers the only natural condition is that of common ownership and individual use. The world was made for the common benefit of mankind, that all should receive from it what they require. . . . They admit, however, that human nature being what it is, avaricious and vicious, it is impossible for men to live normally under the condition of common ownership. This represents the more perfect way of life, and this principle was represented in the organization of monastic life, . . . [but] For mankind in general, some organization of ownership became necessary, and this was provided by the State and its laws. . . . Private property is therefore practically the creation of the State, and is defined, limited, and changed by the State. While, however, the Fathers recognize the legal right of private property, as a suitable and necessary concession to human infirmity . . . they are also clear that from the religious and moral standpoint the position of private property is somewhat different. . . . Whatever conventional organization may be found necessary for practical adjustment of human affairs, the ultimate nature of things still holds good. Private property is allowed, but only in order to avoid the danger of violence and confusion; and the institution cannot override the natural right of man to obtain what he needs from the abundance of that which the earth brings forth. This is what the Fathers mean when they call the maintenance of the needy an act of justice, not of mercy; for it is justice to give to a man that which is his own, and the needy have a moral right to that which they require.[8]

St. Augustine saw in history the conflict between the City of God (*civitas dei*) and the City of Man (*civitas terrena*), a conflict that would continue until the Day of Judgment when Christ would appear again in glory to judge both the living and the dead. These two cities correspond approximately but not exactly to the institutions of Church and State. For St. Augustine the Church was the community of all believers in Christ—not everyone outside the visible Church, however, was necessarily excluded from the City of God nor was everyone within the visible Church necessarily included in that Kingdom. Only on the Last Day would the truly faithful be known.

The relationship between Church and State, between ecclesiastical and secular authority, was one of the principal problems with which the Middle Ages were concerned. It was Pope Gelasius I in the fifth century who framed the problem, according to Professor Carlyle, in these terms:

. . . the spiritual and the temporal powers are intrusted to two different orders, each drawing its authority from God, each supreme in its own sphere, and independent, within its own sphere of the other . . . [but] while each is supreme in its own sphere, each is also subordinate in relation to the other sphere. The king is subject to the bishop in spiritual matters, the bishop to the king in temporal matters.[9]

Of the two obligations that of the bishops is the greater since "they shall render account to God for the kings of men themselves." In the later Middle Ages extreme positions concerning this relationship were sometimes taken especially when to the problem of the proper relationship of ecclesiastical and secular authority there was added the problem of the proper relationship of the Pope to the Church.

Perhaps the most significant political contribution of the Middle Ages to Western civilization was its conception of kingship and the supremacy of law for in these conceptions lie the origins of modern constitutional government. A king is only truly a king, it was affirmed in the Middle Ages, when he rules according to the laws of God, of reason and according to the principles of immemorial custom to which the people by their acquiescence have given their assent. A king who fails to rule justly is no king but a tyrant, an instrument not of God but of the devil. This distinction between true kingship and tyranny runs throughout the political literature of the Middle Ages and, as Professor McIlwain declares "a nobler conception of kingship . . . has seldom been expressed." [10] Practice, however, frequently fell short of theory and "the main defect of the time was not a lack of principles, but an almost total absence of any effective sanction for them. . . . Though the king was under the law in theory, there was little effective machinery in existence to make this theory a practical reality." [11] It remained for modern times to discover the effective means by which kings might be securely bridled to the law.

Throughout the Middle Ages law was thought of as principles which one discovered, not as something which was made. To the Hebraic-Stoic-Christian notion of law as the embodiment of reason and the revelation of God's will for man there was added between the fifth and ninth centuries the Germanic conception, brought in by the invaders of the Roman Empire, that law is the immemorial custom of the tribe. While Roman law lived on throughout the early Middle

Ages as custom, it was not until the eleventh and twelfth centuries that it was completely rediscovered. Medieval thought
found its greatest and most complete expression in the works
of St. Thomas Aquinas (1225–1274). It was not until the
middle of the twelfth and the beginning of the thirteenth
centuries that the complete works of Aristotle became known
to the Western world, at first through translations from the
Arabic and then directly through translations from the Greek.
It was through the Moslems by way of Spain that Aristotle
was first reintroduced into the Western world.

With the recovery of Aristotle's philosophy, Christian theology was stimulated to the undertaking of a new task—the
synthesis of Aristotle's philosophy of man and nature with
Christian conceptions. The greatest of those who undertook to
synthesize these two was St. Thomas and the name generally
applied to that endeavor is scholasticism. It might be called
the birth of Christian philosophy since it involved the application of philosophical methods to theological problems. Henceforth, the problem of the relationship between reason and
faith, although anticipated by such early Church fathers as
St. Augustine, was to become one of the central problems of
Christian theology.

Perhaps the central thought of St. Thomas' philosophy is
the idea that *"grace does not annul nature but perfects it,"* by
which he means that the world of faith while distinct from
the world of nature is yet a continuation of it. In the soul of
man the two are united. The knowledge which we have and
seek concerning the world of nature is not contradictory to
that which we have and seek concerning the world of grace
but there are truths peculiar to each and common to both.
It is through reason (philosophy) that we acquire knowledge
of the world of nature; it is through revelation (theology) that
we acquire knowledge of the world of grace. While distinct
modes of acquiring knowledge each may assist the other in
finding answers to problems that are common to both. One
essential difference between theology and philosophy is the
perspective from which each starts, for, according to St.
Thomas,          .

the two sciences do not proceed in the same order. With philosophy, which regards creatures in themselves, and from them draws on into a knowledge of God, the first consideration is in regard to the creatures and the last is as to God. But in the science of faith, which views creatures only in their relationship to God, the first consideration is of God, and the next of the creatures.[12]

Philosophy can demonstrate the existence, unity, goodness and rationality of God but only theology relying upon revelation and authority can know God as the Trinity of Persons.

Since grace does not annul nature, but perfects it, natural reason should serve faith, even as the natural inclination conforms itself to love (*caritas*). Hence sacred science (theology) uses the philosophers also as authority, where they are able to know the truth through natural reason. It uses authorities of this kind as extraneous arguments having probability. But it uses the authorities of the canonical Scriptures arguing from its own premises and with certainty. And it uses the authorities of other doctors of the Church, as arguing upon its own ground, yet only with probability. For our faith rests upon the revelation made to the Apostles and Prophets, who wrote the canonical books; and not upon the revelation, if there was any, made to other doctors.[13]

Some earlier Christian theologians had accepted the formula *credo ut intelligam* (I believe in order that I may know), others had relied upon the formula *intelligo ut credam* (I know in order that I may believe) but St. Thomas thought that both were true, that faith sustains reason while, at the same time, reason sustains faith.

In the realm of political philosophy St. Thomas accepted as true most of Aristotle's ideas concerning the origin, nature and function of the state but argued that although the state had natural origins, temporal ends and functions the state could never be self-sufficient and its purposes must always be secondary to the higher end of spiritual salvation for individuals whose ultimate destiny was not in this world. Earthly happiness is a good but not the supreme good, for salvation entails a beatitude beside which happiness upon earth is but a pale reflection. Unlike St. Augustine who explained the origin of the state in terms of man's sinfulness and ascribed to

the state functions which were conceived primarily in negative terms, St. Thomas explained the origin of the state in
terms of man's innate social nature and needs and ascribed
to the state functions that were primarily positive.

But perhaps St. Thomas' greatest contribution to political
theory was his conception of law. "A law (*lex*)," he says, "is
an ordinance of reason for the common good promulgated by
him who has the care of the community." [14] Since the universe is governed by God who is the embodiment of reason
and since all men are his creatures whom he loves, it follows
that the ultimate source of all law is God. Since God, moreover, is eternal the source of all law must be *eternal law*. The
eternal law is the law as it exists in the mind of God, it is
God's plan for the universe. God has revealed a portion of
that law in the form of *divine law* of which the Ten Commandments is the best illustration. Since man as a rational creature
participates in the eternal reason that governs the universe he
may by the light of natural reason discover some additional
principles of the eternal law and this law which he defines as
"the participation of a rational creature in the eternal law"
is *natural law* (*lex naturalis*).[15] Since man is a fallible and sinful
creature he can never know the eternal law in its completeness though he may know large portions of it through divine
and natural law. Reasoning from the premises of natural law
as to how these principles are to be applied to specific situations of time and place we derive positive *human law* (*leges
humanae*). Such laws will of necessity be fallible and relative to
changing human situations and needs—hence, they require
sanctions enforced by a ruler whose duty it is to promulgate
them. But "it is necessary that the will concerning the things
commanded be a will controlled by some reason if it is to
bear the character of a law. . . . Otherwise the will of the
prince would be iniquity, rather than law." [16] Thus, he perpetuates the usual medieval distinction between a true prince
and a tyrant. Since a true law must be "an ordinance for the
common good" the authority to establish law must belong
either to the whole people or to that person who has the care
of the whole people.

Thus through the writings and thought of St. Thomas

Aquinas there was perpetuated the political philosophy not only of the Greek world, as represented especially by Aristotle, but also the Christian thought of the early Middle Ages. By demonstrating their compatibility and clarifying the relationship of their respective truths he contributed greatly to the civilizing of Western man.

## Summary and Conclusion

FROM a primitive belief in the daemonic forces of nature compelled by a blind and meaningless fate Western man was gradually led through Greek philosophy, Hebrew prophecy and the revelation of God's nature in Jesus to understand himself as a rational creature of God, created in His image and destined by God's grace for heavenly beatitude. Man came to understand that it was Providence and not fate which controlled his destiny and he lost the fear of the daemonic when he came to recognize the evil in the world as the result of his own sinful rebellion against God and beheld the promise of reconciliation in the love and suffering of God's only begotten Son, Jesus Christ.

The conception of man as a rational personality of infinite and absolute worth was discovered only after long and painful thought and experience. But the exaltation of human nature, the discovery of the glorious potentiality that is man, had necessarily to be accompanied by the revelation of Christ that man is essentially a sinner in need of redemption if the potentialities of human nature were not to be lost in vain illusions as to the source of all creative power. It was only when man learned humility that he learned both how miserable were his motives and how great were his possibilities. It was only when he learned to recognize himself as the rebellious creature of God that he discovered the source of all power in the universe and was enabled by repentance to share in it. He learned to recognize suffering not as tragedy but as opportunity and to know love as the balm which heals even the most fatal of wounds. He learned that he was not only a rational creature but a passionate one and that only when passion was directed in love to God and guided by reason that it could be trusted.

It was only gradually that the idea of justice was discovered to be both the embodiment of reason and of the will of God— the imperfect expression upon earth of God's love for man. The idea of justice slowly crystallized into the conception of law, the ultimate authority for which was the will of God and the ultimate sanction the consent of the people exercised through the force of the ruler. The state was envisaged both as arising out of natural necessity and as a correction for man's sinfulness and continuing in existence in order both that men might achieve the good life upon earth and attend in peaceful relations with one another to the attainment of everlasting happiness in a life beyond the grave.

All this means that gradually Western man became civilized. There was mediated to him not only wisdom concerning his ultimate nature and destiny but, through the death and passion of Christ, grace, by means of which he might hope and pray and work for the eternal salvation of his soul.

CHAPTER 3

# The Transition to Modern Times

THE period from the fall of Constantinople (1453 A.D.) to about the end of the seventeenth century, is frequently spoken of as the Renaissance. Some historians would extend the initial period, others would limit the term to a much shorter period of time. The important thing about it, however, is not the precise length of its duration but the gradual change in the climate of opinion which took place between the time of St. Thomas Aquinas and that of John Locke. It is difficult precisely to date the Renaissance since there were indications as early as the eleventh and twelfth centuries that the climate of opinion was changing and there were many elements of medieval thought still lingering in the seventeenth.

Intellectually, the period was characterized by a progressive interest in things secular and temporal and a waning interest in things spiritual and eternal. Thought became more and more man-centered, less and less God-centered. Even the Church did not entirely escape the predominantly secular character of the thought of the period. A revival of interest in the Greek and Roman classics stimulated a new humanism that revived the thought of the pre-Socratic Protagoras that "Man is the measure of all things." Poetry, music, art and literature flourished under the spell of the illusion that man is his own master and the most appropriate object of adulation. Words were hardly adequate to describe, nor the skill of the artist great enough to do homage to the magnificence of man's body, the nobility of his features, the "agony" of his romantic love. Some artists saw all this as the reflected glory of God but most saw only the glory and lost sight of the source

31

from which it was reflected. The skill which had previously been directed to the building of magnificent cathedrals proclaiming the glory of God was now directed to singing the praises of men. And as the object of worship changed so did the media and forms of expression become increasingly humanistic.

The period was characterized socially by the breakdown of feudalism, the revival of commerce, the creation of new forms of wealth, the rise of towns and of a new social class that lived by carrying on trade. Though still predominantly an agricultural economy the new burghers soon began to challenge the ascendancy of the nobility and to demand political and social reforms that would improve their status and their business, freedom from such economic restrictions as the medieval notion of the "just price," from the condemnation of lending and borrowing money at interest, from the taxes that constituted barriers to free trade.

Politically, the period witnessed the rise of large centralized territorial states. The rising commercial class and the great princes collaborated in breaking the declining power of feudal ties which were an obstacle to the establishment of territorial hegemony. Let us examine in more detail the significance of these developments.

## The Intellectual Climate

INTELLECTUALLY, the later Middle Ages were divided over the issue of realism vs. nominalism. Stated somewhat simply, the issue involved the nature of the relationship between universal conceptions to particular experience. The realist maintained, in the Platonic tradition, that the particular experience was only an imperfect manifestation of the reality of universal ideas, while the nominalist (there were many kinds of nominalists, however) generally maintained that the universal was only a name (*nomen*) or an abstraction, and that reality inhered in the particular thing. This issue had profound consequences both for theology and philosophy since the position of the nominalists, if carried to its ultimate and logical con-

clusion, could lead to a relativism and a denial of the efficacy
of reason in the search for truth that would be destructive
both of theology and of philosophy. Although framed in different conceptions the issue resembled that which divided
Plato from the Sophists.

One of the earliest nominalists was Roscellinus (d. about
1100) who launched a vigorous attack against the orthodox
conception of the Trinity in defense of the doctrine that the
Godhead was composed of three separate and distinct substances. Since this amounted to a defense of polytheism he was
declared a heretic. The issue smoldered for a long time. For
a time it seemed to have been resolved by St. Thomas but
broke out again in the fourteenth century with renewed vigor.

Whereas St. Thomas had sought to reconcile philosophy
and theology attributing to each separate and legitimate functions in the search for truth, the period following his death
witnessed more and more demands for a more complete separation of theology from philosophy. One of those who pressed
this demand was Duns Scotus (c. 1265–1308), a Franciscan
who taught, for the greater part of his life, at the University
of Oxford. Theology, he argued, is a practical rather than a
speculative science. Theology and philosophy, he declared,
rest upon very different principles and the truth embodied in
theology has nothing to do with the kind of truth derived from
philosophical speculation, but, since he used the metaphysical
dialectic to make this point it tended to weaken his position.
What he actually did, as H. O. Taylor points out, was "to
produce a metaphysical counterfeit, wherein theology, founded
on revelation and church law, should present a close parallel
to what it would have been, had its controlling principles been
those of metaphysics." [1] It is the will rather than the intellect,
he contended, that raises man above nature. It is the will not
the intellect that leads man to happiness and heavenly beatitude. Only the will is free—it uses, but is not controlled by,
the intellect. The Scriptures apparently are a revelation to our
will, rather than to our intellect, and theology is essentially a
practical study of the means of relating this revelation to our
life. But how this revelation is understood apart from intellectual cognition is never made entirely clear.

William of Occam (c. 1300–1349) carried on where Duns
Scotus left off. Taylor says:

> More unreservedly than Duns he interdicts the testing of theology
> by reason: and goes beyond him in restricting the sphere of rationally
> demonstrable truth, denying, for instance, that reason can demon-
> strate God's unity, infinity, or even existence. Unlike Duns, he
> would not attempt to erect a quasi-scientific theology, in the place
> of the system he rejects. To make up for this negative result, Occam
> asserted the verity of Scripture unqualifiedly, as Duns also did. With
> Occam, Scripture, revelation, is absolutely infallible, neither requir-
> ing nor admitting the proofs of reason . . . The provinces of science
> and faith are different. Faith's assent is not required for what is
> known through evidence; science does not depend on faith. Nor
> does faith or theology depend on *scientia*. And since, without faith,
> no one can assent to those verities which are to be believed (*veri-
> tatibus credibilibus*), there is no *scientia propria dicta* respecting them. So
> the breach in the old scholastic, Thomist, unity was made utter and
> irreparable. Theology stands on the surest of bases, but isolated,
> unsupported; philosophy, all human knowledge, extends around and
> below it, and is discredited because irrelevant to highest trust.[2]

With Occam nominalism was carried farther toward its ultimate conclusion and resulted in what philosophers have called
*terminism*. Anticipating the ultra-modern science of semantics
and those contemporary philosophers who would restrict the
legitimate concern of philosophy to the study of symbolic
logic, Occam maintained that the individual is the real and
the universal is but a symbol (*signa* or *temini*) whose existence
is confined to the mind. It was a philosophy which "severed
the connection between Reason and Revelation, destroyed
the idea of an ascent from Nature to supernature and the carefully graded theory of the connatural and supernatural end
for which humanity has been created. It intensified psychological self-analysis by its appeal to experience" and changed
the theory of the sacraments by arguing that "the sacraments
do not convey a supernatural life, but they impart the righteousness which belongs to human nature by right, but which
has been lost by sin." [3] The unity which Thomism saw between natural and divine law was destroyed as revelation was

divorced completely from reason. "This reinstatement of logic," moreover, as Taylor points out, "as the instrument and means of all knowledge was to be the perdition of emptier-minded men, who felt no difference between philosophy and the war of words." [4] Scholasticism lost its creative genius and decayed rapidly into logic-chopping inanity. In the light of the inanities to which nominalism led it is not difficult to understand why the followers of Duns Scotus were frequently called *dunces* nor difficult to understand why the word still lives on.

According to a great scholar of the Middle Ages, Étienne Gilson, medieval philosophy

. . . died, primarily, of its own dissensions, and these dissensions multiplied as soon as it began to take itself for an end, instead of serving the Wisdom which was at once its end and source. Albertists, Thomists, Scotists, Occamists, all contributed to the ruin of mediaeval philosophy in the exact measure in which they neglected the search for truth to exhaust themselves in barren controversies about the formulae in which it was to be expressed. The multiplicity of these formulae would have constituted no drawback . . . if the Christian spirit that kept them in unity had not been too often obscured, sometimes lost. When this happened mediaeval philosophy became no more than a corpse encumbering the soil it had dug and on which alone it could build. . . . Failing to maintain the organic unity of a philosophy at once truly rational and truly Christian, Scholasticism and Christendom crumbled together under their own weight.[5]

With the severance of reason from faith, with the assertion of the primacy of will over intellect and with the rediscovery of man as an individual with interests and a will peculiar to himself, the man of the Renaissance groped about in his new found "freedom" for new knowledge, new methods of acquiring knowledge, and new standards with which to evaluate the new knowledge newly acquired. He re-read the ancient classics in his search for the solution to his dilemma, rested for a time in Platonism, forsook Plato for Aristotle, experimented with Epicureanism, yielded to Stoicism, flirted with scepticism and sought to combine them all in a new eclecticism to which many have applied the name Humanism. In some ways these intellectual efforts resembled those of the post-Aristotelian period with the important difference, however, that whereas men were groping then for a more complete revelation of the truth, the man of the Renaissance was experimenting with the possibility of "freeing" himself from that revelation. Captivated by the intellectual audacity of the astronomer Copernicus whose theory of the universe overturned the cosmological hypothesis which had been held for several centuries, the Italian philosopher Giordano Bruno (1548–1600) was led to exclaim that "By the stars we are moved to discover the infinite effect of an infinite cause, the true and living marks of infinite power, and to contemplate the Deity not as outside of, apart from, and distant from us, but as in ourselves and more within us than we are in ourselves." [6] Wavering between Christianity and pantheism he typified the philosophical thought of the sixteenth century.

It was not, however, as Gilson points out, "modern science . . . that destroyed Christian philosophy" for "when modern science was born there was no longer any living Christian philosophy there to welcome and assimilate it. The architect of peace had died of war; and the war came of the revolt of national egoisms against Christendom, and this revolt itself, which Christian philosophy should have prevented, came of the internal dissensions that afflicted it because it had forgotten its essence, which was to be Christian. Divided against itself, the house fell." [7] As men turned increasingly away from the revelation of Scripture and the authority of the Church they turned more and more, but not as quickly as some suppose, to the contemplation of nature as the revelation of God and the embodiment of His being. Philosophy discredited yielded its place to science. The intellectual revolution, for such it was, began with the publication in 1543 of Copernicus' *De revolutionibus Orbium Celestium* and reached its climax with the publication of Newton's *Principia* in 1687. It embraced the work of Galileo, Leonardo da Vinci, Bacon, Kepler, Descartes and Leibnitz, and culminated in the publication of two works of vast importance for modern political thought, John Locke's

*Essay Concerning Human Understanding* in 1690, and his *Treatises of Civil Government* which appeared in the same year.

## The Birth of Modern Philosophy

THROUGHOUT the Middle Ages all the branches of knowledge, metaphysics, logic, ethics, politics and economics were held together in one coherent whole through the mediation of the "queen of the sciences," Theology. In the monumental work of St. Thomas Aquinas in the thirteenth century the realm of nature and the realm of grace, the knowledge yielded by natural reason and the knowledge yielded by revelation, were conceived as complementary. But in the fifteenth and sixteenth centuries the authority of the Church, the guardian of theology, was challenged by nationalistic and intellectual forces with which it was unable successfully to cope. The massive, coherent structure raised by Aquinas had already been attacked within the Church by men like Duns Scotus and William of Occam, and the Church itself lacked the moral authority necessary to harmonize the new intellectual forces with the old. With the repudiation of the authority of the Church and the disintegration of Scholasticism the medieval edifice of thought collapsed—the keystone of its arch, theology, discredited. This revolt against authority, which characterized the period of the Renaissance, necessitated the search for some substitute method of arriving at knowledge and the intellectual activity of the fifteenth, sixteenth, and seventeenth centuries was directed toward the search for that new method.

But if the Church and its system were repudiated, what could take its place? If a man's thoughts and purposes were no longer to take their start from the only tradition available, where could they begin? And the only possible answer was "with himself." If a man was not going to start as a member of a system, accepting that system and his own place in it, then he must start with his isolated self. Of course he would submit to the authority of conscience, but it would be *his* conscience. He would submit to the Voice of God as he heard it, but it would be as *he* heard it. So the modern movement was bound to be a movement of individualism. We owe to it the distinctive blessings of modern life, but also its distinctive ills.

This strong assertion of the individual as the source or medium of the authority to which he must bow found its spiritual expression when Martin Luther, standing alone for truth as he knew it before the Diet of Worms, declared *Hier steh' ich; ich kann nichts anders*. It found its intellectual expression in the course of meditation with which René Descartes occupied his leisure in that stove which is the birthplace of modern philosophy.[8]

The characteristic feature of modern philosophy is the emphasis which it places upon the individual as the ultimate source or medium of authority. Repudiating all traditional authority, modern philosophy proclaims the autonomy of human reason.

According to one authority on this period:

Philosophically, the Renaissance marks a change in the manner of conceiving truth and knowledge generally. The epistemological transition to be inferred from the scientific attitude of such minds as da Vinci and Galileo is, briefly, from one of unquestioning conviction that truth ultimately relates to a reality transcendent and inaccessible to mind, to an active faith in the essential sufficiency of human powers to discover truth, precisely because knowledge is not ultimately of a transcendent reality. Or, as M. Brehier puts it: "truth is not disclosed in the form of a systematic and total vision of the universe (whether the vision be due to revelation or reason or both) but is, so to say, distributed in a multitude of propositions." [9]

The thought of the Renaissance is characterized not only by the rejection of the authority of the Church but in its later phase by the rejection of Aristotle as well. Roger Bacon in the thirteenth, Peter Ramus in the sixteenth, and Francis Bacon in the early seventeenth all attacked the Aristotelian logic. According to Francis Bacon: "The method of discovery and proof according to which the most general principles are first established, and then intermediate axioms are tried and proved by them, is the parent of error and the curse of all science." [10] For the demonstration of truth Francis Bacon would substitute a method of discovering truth. The "discovery" of that new method, however, was largely the work of a Frenchman, Descartes.

Probably the most influential philosopher of the Renaissance, René Descartes (1596–1650), has been called the "father of modern rationalism." With Descartes the philosophical tradition of Realism which dominated philosophical speculation from Thales to William of Occam was first seriously challenged. For until the fifteenth and sixteenth centuries it was nowhere seriously disputed that knowledge is a knowledge of real objects. It is not the external world of real objects which is the starting point of modern philosophical speculation but rather the individual mind or experience. Although there are numerous suggestions of a changed perspective before Descartes, it is with Descartes that the proclamation of the autonomy of human reason becomes explicit.

Descartes describes in his *Discourse on Method* (1637) how he determined to reject all traditional principles and doctrines and to rely solely upon his own reason to discover the truth.

I was then in Germany, to which country I had been attracted by the wars which are not yet at an end. And as I was returning from the coronation of the Emperor to join the army, the setting in of winter detained me in a quarter where, since I found no society to divert me, while fortunately I had also no cares of passions to trouble me, I remained the whole day shut up alone in a stove-heated room, where I had complete leisure to occupy myself with my own thoughts . . .

As regards all the opinions which up to this time I had embraced, I thought I could do no better than endeavour once for all to sweep them completely away, so that they might later on be replaced, either by others which were better, or by the same, when I had made them conform to the uniformity of a rational scheme . . .

I did not wish to set about the final rejection of any single opinion which might formerly have crept into my beliefs without having been introduced there by means of Reason, until I had first of all employed sufficient time in planning out the task which I had undertaken, and in seeking the true Method of arriving at a knowledge of all the things of which my mind was capable.

The "true method" of arriving at knowledge was suggested to him by geometry and algebra and could be reduced, he believed, to four basic principles:

The first of these was to accept nothing as true which I did not clearly recognize to be so; that is to say, carefully to avoid precipitation and prejudice in judgments, and to accept in them nothing more than what was presented to my mind so clearly and distinctly that I could have no occasion to doubt it.

The second was to divide up each of the difficulties which I examined into as many parts as possible, and as seemed requisite in order that it might be resolved in the best manner possible.

The third was to carry on my reflections in due order, commencing with objects that were the most simple and easy to understand, in order to rise little by little, or by degrees, to knowledge of the most complex, assuming an order, even if a fictitious one, among those which do not follow a natural sequence relatively to one another.

The last was in all cases to make enumerations so complete and reviews so general that I should be certain of having omitted nothing.[11]

Commenting upon these principles, William Temple declares:

. . . it would be hard to conceive a more complete programme for the scientific era. Descartes lays down all its leading principles; here is set out the method of analysis which has carried us through molecules to atoms, through atoms to protons, electrons, and neutrons, and now threatens to dissolve these in mere measurements which are measurements of nothing; here too is the conviction that the simple contains the explanation of the complex, which leads to the denial of objective reality to aesthetic and moral qualities because these only appear at a stage of higher development and advanced complexity. But it is noticeable that the first precept is ambiguous. Descartes will never accept as true what he does not clearly know to be such; and this he paraphrases as meaning that he will never include anything in his affirmations which is not presented to his mind so clearly and distinctly that he could have no occasion to doubt it. But does this include Isaiah's vision? or such a flaming apprehension of God as is recorded in Pascal's celebrated fragment? And if not, why not? To the subjects of these experiences there was nothing about them either confused or questionable. Why is my perception that $2 + 2 = 4$ to be regarded as either more clear and distinct, or more compelling of acceptance, than Isaiah's perception of the Holiness of God? The truth is that in order to make his method work at all, Descartes was obliged to state its first principle in terms which covered much more than he intended; for if he had limited his terms

to the scope of his intention, he would have been driven to assert a
unique claim to truth on behalf of mathematics, and would have
drawn upon himself the contradiction of all who dispute that claim.
His position has plausibility because his fundamental precept is so
stated as to be unexceptionable, but is then without notice so restricted in interpretation and application as to make the second and
third precepts appropriate successors to it.[12]

Descartes explains how he resolved to reject as false everything which it was possible to doubt.

For a long time I had remarked that it is sometimes requisite in
common life to follow opinions which one knows to be most uncertain, exactly as though they were indisputable, as has been said
above. But because in this case I wished to give myself entirely to the
search after Truth, I thought that it was necessary for me to take an
apparently opposite course, and to reject as absolutely false everything as to which I could imagine the least ground of doubt, in order
to see if afterwards there remained anything in my belief that was
entirely certain. . . . I rejected as false all the reasons formerly accepted by me as demonstrations. And . . . I resolved to assume that
everything that ever entered into my mind was no more true than
the illusions of my dreams. But immediately afterwards I noticed
that whilst I thus wished to think all things false, it was absolutely
essential that the "I" who thought this should be somewhat, and
remarking that this truth "I think, therefore I am" was so certain
and so assured that all the most extravagant suppositions brought
forward by the sceptics were incapable of shaking it, I came to the
conclusion that I could receive it without scruple as the first principle of the Philosophy for which I was seeking.[13]

Not a true sceptic, Descartes employed doubt as a methodological device. His "doubting," therefore, had an element of
artificiality about it. He employed it, he said, as an "Ar-
chimedean fulcrum."

While we thus reject all that of which we can possibly doubt, and
feign that it is false, it is easy to suppose that there is no God, nor
heaven, nor bodies, and that we possess neither hands, nor feet, nor
indeed any body; but we cannot in the same way conceive that we
who doubt these things are not; for there is a contradiction in conceiving that what thinks does not at the same time as it thinks, exist.
And hence this conclusion, *I think, therefore I am*, is the first and most

certain of all that occurs to one who philosophizes in an orderly way.[14]

Descartes' fundamental axiom (I think, therefore I am) is described by the Baron von Hügel as being "dangerously inadequate" for:

We thus take for granted . . . what is demonstrably non-existent: *I think* instead of *I think such and such realities*, or at least, *I think such and such objects*. The subject and object, always interconnected in man's actual experience and hence to be assumed in this their interconnexion, were thus severed from each other, in the very starting point of philosophy; and then this severance and quite artificial separateness could hardly any more be bridged over—the object could hardly be recovered, since man (after all) is in fact restricted, and is here rightly recognised as restricted, to the analysis of what actually exists, and to what he really experiences. The appeal here to its experience and to its analysis was, then, right: what was wrong was the exclusion, before any and all investigation, and without any justification, of one entire third of every living experience. For all experience is always threefold: it is always simultaneously experience of the subject, of the object, and of the overbridging thought; indeed, clear consciousness always first concerns the object, and only much later on the subject. And thus, through that artificial abstraction, there promptly arose such sheer figments of the brain as knowledge, not of objects at all, but of subjective states alone; and (stranger still), knowledge that objects exist, and that they all have an inside, but an inside which is never actually revealed to us by the qualities of those objects; and (culminating miracle of strangeness) that this inside abides ever essentially unknowable by us, and yet, all the same, we absolutely know that it contradicts all these appearances. Man thus, though well within the universe, isolates himself from it; he imprisons himself in his own faculties, and, as to anything further, knows only that objects exist as to which these faculties essentially and inevitably mislead him.[15]

Having rejected everything except this one axiom he then sought to erect an entire philosophy upon this one certain truth. From this ultimate intuition he argued for the existence of God and from the existence of God for the existence of an external world. He regarded intuition and deduction as the most certain routes to knowledge. Descartes employed three arguments for the existence of God, one of which was that

God must exist to create the thinker and sustain him in his existence. He then argued that God would not deceive the thinking beings whom He had created and that as a consequence there must be some real world revealed to us through our perceptions. Otherwise our sense-perceptions would be mere illusions. But how are we to distinguish that which is an illusion from that which is real? And Descartes declares that it is only that which can be apprehended "clearly and distinctly" which is to be regarded as real. As regards material things only extension and motion, he further argues, are clear and distinct; such qualities as color and smell are not essential features of material things for they are not, he declares, clear and distinct. They belong not to the things themselves but are a part of the subjective experience of the person perceiving them.

Body and mind are conceived by Descartes as two separate and distinct things. The essential feature of mind is thought or consciousness, the mind is a kind of "thinking substance." The body is an "extended substance" and independent of the mind. The interconnection between body and soul which the Christian tradition emphasized is thus explicitly denied. But if the mind is independent of the body and the body of the mind, how, then, do the two manage to work together. And Descartes' only answer is that God so constituted the world that they do. God is thus brought in at the last moment to retrieve his system from collapse but without any rational explanation of how this is so. Mind is reduced to a kind of immaterial spirit and man has become, as Santayana has rather aptly expressed it, "the clumsy conjunction of an automaton with a ghost."

Modern philosophy since Descartes has followed two main currents: rationalism and empiricism. On the European continent Descartes' rationalism was further elucidated by philosophers like Spinoza (1632–1677) and Leibnitz (1646–1716). In England an empirical tradition developed through Locke (1632–1704), Berkeley (1685–1753), and Hume (1711–1776). The effect of the separation by Descartes of mind and matter was the emphasis upon one to the exclusion of the other leading in philosophy either to idealism or materialism. Despite the brilliant efforts of the eighteenth-century German philosopher Kant to reconcile the two, contemporary philosophy is still puzzled by the apparent insolubility of the problem, as that problem emerged from Descartes' initial hypothesis. The divorce of reason from Being, the severance of reason from faith and the subsequent proclamation of the autonomy of human reason, has had its culminating effect in the twentieth-century in the repudiation of reason itself. Thus the movement which was designed to liberate reason from the "bondage" of authority has had the effect of destroying confidence in reason itself.

## The Birth of Modern Science

ACCORDING to the Ptolemaic cosmology which was accepted throughout the Middle Ages, the universe was a large, finite sphere consisting of concentric spheres. At the center of this hollow sphere was the earth and at the periphery fixed stars, and within the spheres the planets revolved about the earth with the sphere or heaven of which they were a part. The last sphere was Paradise or "the abode of the blessed." Although medieval astronomers were enabled by this hypothesis to predict eclipses it was, we know now, a very crude picture of physical reality. Copernicus (1473–1543) accepted this cosmological theory but put the sun at the center instead of the earth; Kepler (1571–1630) demonstrated that, contrary to the previously accepted theory that the planets move in perfect circles, actually planets move in ellipses, moving more rapidly the nearer they are to the sun. Another brilliant insight enabled him to frame a formula whereby the movements of the planets in relation to one another might be mathematically computed with exactitude. These three great laws to which his name has been attached laid the foundations for modern astronomy. Galileo (1564–1641) not only substantiated, by the use of the telescope, the hypotheses put forth by Copernicus and Kepler but he laid the foundations for modern physics. Not only did he first formulate the law that "if two bodies move in equilibrium their movements in distance are in inverse proportion to their weights," and that starting at zero "the speed of a falling body increases at an even rate," but, he was among the first, if not the first, to lay down the principles of modern scientific *method*.

One of the maxims Galileo laid down was that knowledge of nature can be obtained by observation and experimentation and framed in mathematical terms. "Philosophy," he wrote, "is written in that great book which ever lies before our eyes; but we cannot understand it if we do not first learn the language and characters in which it is written. This language is mathematics, and the characters are triangles, circles, and other geometrical figures." [16] Yet, it was not simply that he saw that physical reality could be expressed in mathematical terms, for Plato reveals a similar belief in his *Timaeus*, but rather that he had found a method of measuring free movement. The Aristotelian physics was incapable of explaining free movement and Galileo's achievement was to replace for this purpose the Aristotelian teleology with mathematically defined relations. All knowledge of nature must start with the perceptual observation of particular objects in their quantitative aspects from which observation we may proceed to derive mathematical hypotheses which, if found by further observation and experimentation to explain physical phenomena not previously observed, we may regard as laws of nature.

He was careful to point out that no such law, however, ever corresponds exactly to actuality but is, in a sense, an ideal law made possible by *abstraction*. Although we may state as a law that all planets move in the form of an ellipse, no particular planet ever moves in a perfect ellipse, but, we can calculate the forces which disturb its regular elliptic motion by knowing in advance the form its movement would take if there were no disturbing forces. In effect Galileo said that we can measure that which is measurable and describe mathematically that which lends itself to mathematical description, but he did not say, as some people thought and think, that *all* phenomena are measurable. It is only by abstracting out of the totality of phenomena that which is measurable in quantitative terms that physical science is made possible.

There is both gain and danger in this abstraction from the

whole. By abstraction from the whole we gain a more detailed knowledge of the part but the danger is that we may mistake the part for the whole. We may easily fall into the error which A. N. Whitehead has called the "fallacy of misplaced concreteness" and "mistake the abstract for the concrete." According to Whitehead:

The answer . . . which the seventeenth century gave to the ancient question of the Ionian thinkers, "What is the world made of?" was that the world is a succession of instantaneous configurations of matter. . . . We cannot wonder that science rested content with this assumption as to the fundamental elements of nature. The great forces of nature, such as gravitation, were entirely determined by the configurations of masses. Thus the configurations determined their own changes, so that the circle of scientific thought was completely closed. This is the famous mechanistic theory of nature, which has reigned supreme ever since the seventeenth century. It is the orthodox creed of physical science. Furthermore, the creed justified itself by the pragmatic test. It worked. Physicists took no more interest in philosophy. They emphasized the anti-rationalism of the Historical Revolt. But the difficulties of this theory of materialistic mechanism very soon became apparent. The history of thought in the eighteenth and nineteenth centuries is governed by the fact that the world had got hold of a general idea which it could neither live with nor live without. . . . It is at once evident that the concept of simple location is going to make great difficulties for induction. For, if in the location of configurations of matter throughout a stretch of time there is no inherent reference to any other times, past or future, it immediately follows that nature within any period does not refer to nature at any other period. Accordingly, induction is not based on anything which can be observed as inherent in nature. Thus we cannot look to nature for the justification of our belief in any law such as the law of gravitation. In other words, *the order of nature cannot be justified by the mere observation of nature.* For there is nothing in the present fact which inherently refers either to the past or to the future. It looks, therefore, as though memory, as well as induction, would fail to find any justification within nature itself.[17]

While the abstraction of the mechanical aspect of nature from the whole of reality has yielded significant knowledge about the universe and brought forth discoveries of considerable value in terms of human welfare there was and is the dan-

ger that mistaking the part for the whole we may be led back
to paganism and the worship of nature as God. But every gain
in knowledge is a temptation. Since man first tasted the fruit
of the tree of knowledge, he has had no alternative but the
pursuit of knowledge—knowledge that might lead him away
from God as well as toward God. That is the price he has to
pay for his rebellion. The Renaissance was both a gain and a
temptation. It would be foolish, indeed, to deprecate the
great intellectual achievements and the advantages in terms
of human welfare which are the product of the birth of modern
science, but it would be equally unwise to overlook the great
temptations to misuse that knowledge in the service of evil.
Those who live in fear and terror of the atom bomb will have
no difficulty understanding this.

Modern science differs from science as known to the Greeks
(1) by being "directed . . . upon the laws and not upon the
ends, or events in nature," and (2) by expecting to find, and
finding, "these laws realized perfectly and without exception
in the world of material nature itself; they are statements of
the ways in which natural objects not *ought* to, but *must* act."
Now these principles "are the consequences of the doctrine
that the material world is the work not of a Demiurge" as the
Greeks thought, "but of an omnipotent Creator." "Every
science of nature," Foster points out, "must depend upon
presuppositions about nature which cannot be established by
the methods of science itself. . . . It was the method of physics, or Descartes' conception of it, to proceed by demonstration, like the mathematician, from self-evident premises. But
the possibility of thus extending the methods of mathematics
to the science of nature depends upon a presupposition about
nature which cannot itself be demonstrated, namely, that
nature is a homogeneous material substance, determined
throughout by subjection to universal and necessary laws. To
assert the truth of what natural science presupposes is not
science of nature but philosophy of nature" and every philosophy of nature will necessarily depend upon theology for
there is "no doctrine of God which does not . . . contain or
imply a doctrine of the world." It is Foster's well-reasoned
contention that the modification of the Greek philosophy of

nature "necessitated by the peculiarities of Christian theology is precisely that presupposed by the peculiarities of modern natural science."[18] By preserving the principle that God's will is governed by his reason without sacrificing the principle of his omnipotence, Christianity enabled the scientist "by the use of his reason alone to enter into the reason of God, or, in Kepler's phrase 'to think God's thoughts after him'; and because God has made nature to conform to his thoughts, what the scientist discovers by this process will be in fact the laws of nature."[19] Thus the modern scientist could find intelligible law where the Greek scientist could only find the imperfect approximation to an intelligible idea.

The cardinal principle of theological rationalism that God produces the world rationally, and not by generation, involves the conclusion that the will to produce it must be arbitrary in the sense of being undetermined by his reason. It follows from this . . . that the existence of nature as a whole is contingent; but not that there is contingency in any natural existent or event, if the existence of nature be granted. This philosophy of nature does not involve the introduction of an empirical element into the methods of natural science itself, but it entails the consequence that the truth of all demonstrations of science depends upon a condition which cannot itself be demonstrated. . . . This is the Cartesian philosophy of nature and of natural science. The existence of a material world cannot itself be demonstrated . . . But once its existence is granted, no further element of contingency is held to belong to the nature of particular material things, and consequently the science of them can rely upon the method of demonstration alone.

The method of Galileo was the method of testing *a priori* reasoning by experience and the validity of that method

depends upon the assumption that induction can give rise not merely to the formation by imagination of a general idea, but to the discovery by reason of an intelligible reality. Because it is intelligible it is capable of (genuine, not merely "nominal") definition. The fact that . . . verification is possible . . . presupposes that the definition is the apprehension of the intelligible element constitutive of the being of real things. If it were merely nominal, no subsequent empirical verification could serve either to refute or to confirm it.[20]

Christianity provided the theological presuppositions without which the birth of modern science could not have taken place by (1) distinguishing between God and nature, (2) by distinguishing in the doctrine of the Trinity between God's activity as Creator (technical production) and His activity as Father (generation), (3) the doctrine that God's activity is an activity of reason, that God's reason governs his will.[21] Christianity provided that conception of nature which enabled modern science to be born. The relationship between nature and supernature did not become a problem, however, until Aristotle's philosophy was recovered late in the Middle Ages. It was the inability of Aristotle's physics to explain the free movement of objects in space that was the immediate stimulus to the birth of modern science. And it was the unwillingness of the late Scholastics to abandon Aristotle's physics that discredited their attempts to preserve his metaphysics.

The impact of modern science upon the intellectual climate generally need not have been so controversial had philosophy been prepared to meet it. Metaphysics need not have yielded its legitimate speculation concerning the totality of experience but, discredited and rendered impotent by the late scholastics, it was unprepared to assert its rightful claims to be heard. There was no great philosopher prepared to challenge the usurpation of philosophy by the new science of nature.

As a consequence, then as now, many philosophical claims hostile to Christianity were advanced by individuals in the name of science, although they were of a metaphysical nature and had nothing to do with science itself. Early scientists like Kepler, Galileo and Newton held more or less orthodox Christian beliefs and conceived of their scientific work as demonstrating the glory of God. Nevertheless, many Churchmen failed to understand the significance of what was happening and in their ignorance condemned many of the new hypotheses as heresy. Galileo condemned by the Roman Inquisition was forced to sign a formal recantation, obliged to recite daily a number of Psalms praising God in penance and confined to his home. Such actions added more fuel to the flames of controversy and the opposition of Churchmen had the unfortunate effect of framing the controversy in terms of religion vs.

science and of authority vs. reason. Thereafter, the claims of natural science were advanced in the name of enlightened reason and the authority of the Church came to be regarded as synonymous with obscurantism. In time, the Church itself recanted but not soon enough to avoid the suspicion of many that it was motivated by an opportunistic acceptance of the inevitable rather than by a sincere acknowledgment of error.

"Whosoever appeals to authority," Leonardo da Vinci wrote, "applies not his intellect but his memory. . . . While nature begins from causes and ends in experience, we must follow a contrary procedure, that is, begin with experience and from that discover causes." [22] Now whereas philosophy traditionally since the time of Plato had thought of the search for truth as a process of awakening the memory, the man of the Renaissance would discard memory in favor of the sensations of immediate experience. But it is doubtful if the scientist actually freed himself completely from the memory he scorned since he relied for the ordering of his sensations, of necessity, upon mathematical assumptions derived not from experience but from memory. What he actually sought to discard was not memory but *certain* memories, e.g., the memory that the scientist was also a creature with a nature and destiny transcending his physical existence and movements. It is a curious fact that while certain Renaissance movements emphasized the humanity of man the preponderant thought was moving in a direction that was increasingly obscuring the memory of man's humanity.

One might characterize this intellectual revolution by describing it as the birth of modern science, as the secularization of human culture, or as the proclamation of the autonomy of human reason for it was all and each. Whitehead has characterized the seventeenth and eighteenth centuries as "an age of reason based upon faith" in contrast to the Middle Ages which he describes as "an age of faith based upon reason." [23] The faith of the age, however, was not faith in Christ as "the way, the truth, and the life" but faith in nature as self-sufficient, self-contained, self-governing. Many dreamed of applying the methods and concepts of the physical sciences to areas traditionally thought to be beyond nature in an effort to

explain "naturally" what had formerly been explained super-
naturally. The perspective has shifted from God to man, from
things spiritual to things secular, from the eternal and universal to the temporal and relative. Science promises in the
minds of many to penetrate in time the ultimate mysteries and
to provide man with the tools by which he may assert his
divinity. Not content with a status "a little lower than the
angels" the man of the Renaissance seemingly aspired to be
God. "The true and lawful goal of the sciences," Francis
Bacon declared, "is none other than this: that human life be
endowed with new discoveries and powers." [24] Science will
unleash the power which will make men the "masters and
possessors of nature." According to Descartes:

It is possible to attain knowledge which is very useful in life, and
instead of that speculative philosophy which is taught in the Schools,
we may find a practical philosophy by means of which, knowing the
force and the action of fire, water, air, the stars, heavens, and all
other bodies that environ us, as distinctly as we know the different
crafts of our artisans, we can in the same way employ them in all
those uses to which they are adapted, and thus render ourselves the
masters and possessors of nature. [25]

The change in the climate of opinion brought about by the
Newtonian revolution is described by Professor Burtt in these
words:

Just as it was thoroughly natural for mediaeval thinkers to view
nature as subservient to man's knowledge, purpose, and destiny; so
now it has become natural to view her as existing and operating in
her own self-contained independence, and so far as man's ultimate
relation to her is clear at all, to consider his knowledge and purpose
somehow produced by her, and his destiny wholly dependent on
her. [26]

The poet Pope, in a couplet designed as an epitaph for
Newton's tomb, expressed the impact of modern science upon
the intellectual climate generally in these words:

Nature and Nature's laws lay hid in night;
God said, 'Let Newton be,' and all was light.

## Political Theory of the Renaissance

THE political theory of the early Renaissance is probably best typified in the writings of Niccolo Machiavelli (1469–1527). Born a citizen of Florence, Machiavelli entered public life in 1494 holding various secretarial positions, serving in diplomatic capacities, and organizing a Florentine militia. When the Florentine republic came to an end in 1512, with the rise to power of the party of the Medici, Machiavelli lost his position in the government and was exiled. The following year he participated in an unsuccessful conspiracy and was sentenced to prison. A few months later he was released through the intervention in his behalf of Cardinal Julian de Medici, but thereafter he retired from public life and spent the remainder of his days in farming and writing. The work by which he is best known, *The Prince*, although completed in 1513 and circulated privately during his lifetime, was published posthumously in 1532. Less well known, but equally important to an understanding of his political theory were his *Discourses on the First Ten Books of Titus Livius* begun about the time *The Prince* was completed. He also wrote a *Life of Castruccio* (1520), a work on the *Art of War* (1520), a *History of Florence* (1525) and is credited with the authorship of a number of plays of which the *Mandragola* is the best known.

He wrote at a time when the personal loyalties of the feudal age were disappearing, when the moral restraints of the Middle Ages were felt less keenly, and Italy was ruled by a number of petty tyrants. He wrote in an age in which compassion was scorned as weakness, when justice was no more than a name for the will of the stronger, and when treachery was regarded as synonymous with diplomacy. Civic loyalty, as a consequence, was practically nonexistent and the tyrants had to rely upon foreign troops and ruthless tactics in order to sustain their power. The focus of attention had shifted from God to man and greater emphasis, as a consequence, was laid upon temporal security than upon eternal salvation. The distinction between a "higher" and a "lower" world tended to be obliterated as attempts were made to explain all phenomena "naturally." Concerned with politics as it "is" rather than with politics as it "ought to be," Machiavelli laid the foundations for a modern political science and anticipated the attempts of the nineteenth-century positivists to found a natural science of politics. He was not so much immoral as he was non-moral.

It is in this sense that *The Prince* is to be understood, i.e., as a technical treatise on the means of gaining and keeping power. Machiavelli is less concerned with the uses to which power is to be put, with the ends in terms of which power is to be sought, than he is with the technical means of acquiring and keeping it. In *The Prince*, especially, he is concerned primarily with that which is politically expedient, the morality of the policy or action being a matter of indifference. In a chapter concerning "In What Manner Princes Should Keep Their Faith" Machiavelli declares:

It must be evident to everyone that it is more praiseworthy for a prince always to maintain good faith, and practice integrity rather than craft and deceit. And yet the experience of our own times has shown that those princes have achieved great things who made small account of good faith, and who understood by cunning to circumvent the intelligence of others; and that in the end they got the better of those whose actions were dictated by loyalty and good faith. You must know, therefore, that there are two ways of carrying on a contest; the one by law, and the other by force. The first is practised by men, and the other by animals; and as the first is often insufficient, it becomes necessary to resort to the second.

A prince then should know how to employ the nature of man, and that of the beasts as well . . . It being necessary then for a prince to know well how to employ the nature of the beasts, he should be able to assume both that of the fox and that of the lion; for whilst the latter cannot escape the traps laid for him, the former cannot defend himself against the wolves. A prince should be a fox, to know the traps and snares; and a lion, to be able to frighten the wolves; for those who simply hold to the nature of the lion do not understand their business.

A sagacious prince then cannot and should not fulfill his pledges when their observance is contrary to his interest, and when the causes that induced him to pledge his faith no longer exist. If men were all good, then indeed this precept would be bad; but as men are naturally bad, and will not observe their faith towards you, you must, in the same way, not observe yours to them; and no prince ever yet lacked legitimate reasons with which to color his want of good faith.[27]

He goes on to say that the prince should learn how to be a "hypocrite"; he should know, for instance, how to "seem to be merciful, faithful, humane, religious, and upright, and should even be so in reality; but he should have his mind so trained that, when occasion requires it, he may know how to change to the opposite." The prince must be able to change "as the winds and changes of fortune bid him" for he will often be obliged "for the sake of maintaining his state, to act contrary to humanity, charity, and religion." Machiavelli clearly holds human nature in low esteem and if a prince would be successful in the "maintenance of his state" it is better to appear to have good qualities than it is to observe them in every situation. The maintenance of the state appears in Machiavelli's thought to override all other considerations. In an age of violence and political instability he would appear to value stability above justice, not understanding, apparently, that genuine order is a product of justice. "Putting all other considerations aside," he wrote, "the only question should be, what course will save the life and liberty of the country?"

In the concluding chapter of *The Prince*, Machiavelli addresses himself, in language that is curiously impassioned for one who professes moral indifference, to the house of Medici to deliver Italy from foreign barbarians.

You must not, then, allow this opportunity to pass, so that Italy, after waiting so long, may at last see her deliverer appear. Nor can I possibly express with what affection he would be received in all those provinces that have suffered so long from this inundation of foreign foes!—with what thirst for vengeance, with what persistent faith, with what devotion, and with what tears! What door would be closed to him? Who would refuse him obedience? What envy would dare oppose him? What Italian would refuse him homage? This barbarous dominion of the foreigner offends the very nostrils of everybody!

Let your illustrious house, then, assume this task with that courage and hopefulness which every just enterprise inspires; so that under your banner our country may recover its ancient fame . . .[28]

In these words the spirit of nationalism comes to life for the first time, destined to be both a blessing and a scourge to countless generations of humanity.

Above all else Machiavelli was a patriot and a patriot with a vision—he longed to see Italy united in a state of peace and security. In this sense he was an early precursor of such nineteenth-century Italian nationalists as Mazzini, Garibaldi, Cavour, and Victor Emmanuel. Yet he was torn between two attitudes: he did not see how the Italy of his day could become united except through the employment of ruthless and immoral tactics (the Medici he regarded as the most likely to bring about the desired result); but, on the other hand, as he makes clear in his *Discourses*, he believed that a republican form of government is best, that "the rule of a people is better than the rule of a prince." Despotism, he thought, was justified only to bring a state into existence or to reform a corrupt one. Contrary to the opinion which maintains that popular rule is inconsistent and imprudent, Machiavelli declares in the *Discourses*

. . . as regards prudence and stability, I say that the people are more prudent and stable, and have better judgment than a prince; and it is not without good reason that it is said, "The voice of the people is the voice of God" . . . if we compare the faults of a people with those of princes, as well as their respective good qualities, we shall find the people vastly superior in all that is good and glorious. And if princes show themselves superior in the making of laws, and in the forming of civil institutions and new statutes and ordinances, the people are superior in maintaining those institutions, laws and ordinances, which certainly places them on a par with those who established them.[29]

A corrupt people must, of necessity, be ruled by a prince or a tyrant since it is incapable of governing itself but a virtuous people can be self-governing in a republic. When possible a free state or a republic is to be preferred to the rule of a prince. This is the argument of the *Discourses*.

I say that both governments of princes and of the people have lasted a long time, but both required to be regulated by laws. For a prince who knows no other control but his own will is like a madman, and a people that can do as it pleases will hardly be wise. If now we compare a prince who is controlled by laws, and a people that is untrammeled by them, we shall find more virtue in the people than in the prince; and if we compare them when both are freed from such control, we shall see that the people are guilty of fewer excesses than the prince, and that the errors of the people are of less importance, and therefore more easily remedied . . . The follies which a people commits at the moment of its greatest license are not what is most to be feared; it is not the immediate evil that may result from them that inspires apprehension, but the fact that such general confusion might afford the opportunity for a tyrant to seize the government. But with evil-disposed princes the contrary is the case; it is the immediate present that causes fear, and there is hope only in the future; for men will persuade themselves that the termination of his wicked life may give them a chance of liberty. Thus we see the difference between the one and the other to be, that the one touches the present and the other the future. The excesses of the people are directed against those whom they suspect of interfering with the public good; whilst those of princes are against apprehended interference with their individual interests.[30]

A reading of the *Discourses* reveals that Machiavelli did not depart so radically from the Western political tradition as is commonly supposed by those whose reading of him is confined to *The Prince*. Yet he did, of course, introduce some conflicting, new elements into that tradition. He was one of the first, if not the first, to recognize the nature of the new secular state which was emerging at the time of the Renaissance and he sought to provide a theory appropriate to it. A new body politic seemed, to Machiavelli, to be emerging from sheer force and such a body politic could only be maintained by force. And the distinctively "modern" characteristic of his theory was his attempt to divorce the foundation of the state from all theological and ecclesiastical considerations. In Machiavelli's theory "all the previous theocratic ideas and ideals are eradicated root and branch" and although religion is retained by him as "one of the necessary elements of man's social life" it can no longer "claim any absolute, independent, and dogmatic truth. Its worth and validity depend entirely on its influence on political life." [31] In the twelfth chapter of the first book of the *Discourses* Machiavelli discusses "The importance of giving religion a prominent influence in a state" and argues that "Princes and Republics who wish to maintain themselves free from corruption must above all things preserve the purity of all religious observances, and treat them with proper reverence; for there is no greater indication of the ruin of a country than to see religion contemned." [32] But, religion is conceived by him as a means toward a more ultimate end and while religion is assigned an important role *within* the state it is not above the state nor even equal with it. Its value is instrumental only and relative to secular ends. Speaking of the foundation of Rome, Machiavelli declares in the *Discourses:*

Although the founder of Rome was Romulus, to whom, like a daughter, she owed her birth and her education, yet the gods did not judge the laws of this prince sufficient for so great an empire, and therefore inspired the Roman Senate to elect Numa Pompilius as his successor, so that he might regulate all those things that had been omitted by Romulus. Numa, finding a very savage people, and wishing to reduce them to civil obedience by the arts of peace, had recourse to religion as the most necessary and assured support of any civil society; and he established it upon such foundations that for many centuries there was nowhere more fear of the gods than in that republic, which greatly facilitated all the enterprises which the Senate or its great men attempted . . . And whoever reads Roman history attentively will see in how great a degree religion served in the command of the armies, in uniting the people and keeping them well conducted, and in covering the wicked with shame. So that if the question were discussed whether Rome was more indebted to Romulus or to Numa, I believe that the highest merit would be conceded to Numa; for where religion exists it is easy to introduce armies and discipline, but where there are armies and no religion it is difficult to introduce the latter . . . Considering, then, all these things, I conclude that the religion introduced by Numa into Rome was one of the chief causes of the prosperity of that city; for this religion gave rise to good laws, and good laws bring good fortune, and from good fortune results happy success in all enterprises. [33]

Religion, as Ernst Cassirer points out,

has become a mere tool in the hands of the political rulers. It is not the foundation of man's social life but a powerful weapon in all po-

litical struggles. This weapon must prove its strength in action . . .
Religion is only good if it produces good order; and good order is
generally attended with good fortune and success in any undertaking. Here the final step has been taken. Religion no longer bears
any relation to a transcendent order of things and it has lost all its
spiritual values. The process of secularization has come to its close;
for the secular state exists not only *de facto* but also *de jure;* it has found
its definite theoretical legitimization.[34]

With Machiavelli politics is separated from all its previous
metaphysical and ethical roots and the state is declared to be
an autonomous entity. The implications of the declaration of
that autonomy did not emerge clearly until our own day but
with the destruction of the natural rights theory, which for
several centuries obscured the dangers latent in this autonomy,
"there was no longer any great intellectual or moral power to
check and counterbalance Machiavellism."[35] Perhaps the
kernel of Machiavelli's teaching is best found in Book III,
Chapter 41 of the *Discourses* when he declares that "where the
very safety of the country depends upon the resolution to be
taken, no considerations of justice or injustice, humanity or
cruelty, nor of glory or of shame, should be allowed to prevail.
But putting all other considerations aside, the only question
should be, What course will save the life and liberty of the
country?"[36] The existence of a state is its own justification.

Machiavelli's thought, however, like that of many of his
Renaissance contemporaries, wavered between Christianity
and paganism so that he was not clearly one thing nor the
other. This wavering between the pagan and Christian conception of virtue is especially apparent in Chapter 26 of Book
I of the *Discourses*. Here he says that a prince conquering a city
or a province "should destroy the old cities and build new
ones, and transfer the inhabitants from one place to another;
in short, he should leave nothing unchanged in that province,
so that there should be neither rank, nor grade, nor honor, nor
wealth, that should not be recognized as coming from him."
But he adds: "Doubtless these means are cruel and destructive
of all civilized life, and neither Christian nor even human, and
should be avoided by every one. In fact, the life of a private
citizen would be preferable to that of a king at the expense of

the ruin of so many human beings. Nevertheless, whoever is unwilling to adopt the first and humane course must, if he wishes to maintain his power, follow the latter evil course." [37] Although Machiavelli would appear in passages like this one to accept the Christian conception of virtue, he speaks of virtue, for the most part, as a combination of those qualities enabling a man to achieve power and fame, what the great historian of the Renaissance, Burckhardt, describes as "a compound of force and intellect." And Machiavelli is clearly on the side of paganism when he rejects the Christian conception of Providence for the pagan idea of Fortune, a capricious, irresistible, and incalculable power with which men must wrestle if they would win the world. It is not, as the Stoic-Christian tradition taught, by willing submission to the law that virtue is acquired but by an assault upon Fortune.

   . . . I judge that it may be assumed as true that Fortune to the extent of one half is the arbiter of our actions, but that she permits us to direct the other half, or perhaps a little less, ourselves. I compare this to a swollen river, which in its fury overflows the plains, tears up the trees and buildings, and sweeps the earth from one place and deposits it in another. Every one flies before the flood, and yields to its fury, unable to resist it; and notwithstanding this state of things, men do not when the river is in its ordinary condition provide against its overflow by dikes and walls, so that when it rises it may flow either in the channel thus provided for it, or that at any rate its violence may not be unchecked, nor its effects prove so injurious. It is the same with Fortune, who displays her power where there is no organized valor to resist her, and where she knows that there are no dikes or walls to control her . . .

   I conclude, then, inasmuch as Fortune is changeable, that men who persist obstinately in their own ways will be successful only so long as those ways coincide with those of Fortune; and whenever these differ, they fail. But, on the whole, I judge impetuosity to be better than caution; for Fortune is a woman, and if you wish to master her, you must strike and beat her, and you will see that she allows herself to be more easily vanquished by the rash and violent than by those who proceed more slowly and coldly.[38]

Most men, because they believe their fate to be in the hands of Fortune, will not seek to resist her power by erecting "dikes and walls" but this is a mistake for Fortune determines but

"one half . . . of our actions" and she can be subdued, at
least in part, by those with sufficient courage and audacity to
scorn her dominion and chart their own course. Life, for
Machiavelli, appears as a kind of warfare against the decrees of
Fortune. And since, for Machiavelli, man is not destined, as
Christianity teaches, to a supernatural end, his actions cannot
be judged either in terms of the divine or of natural law.[39] For
Machiavelli the only values that really matter are those of
greatness, power, and fame. In this sense Machiavelli is truly
typical of the Renaissance and truly modern. Here are laid the
foundations of *Realpolitik* or "power politics." Such a conception is made possible only by divorcing politics from its foundation in metaphysics and ethics. Politics conceived as a self-
sufficient end in itself is the distinctive "contribution" of
Machiavelli to modern political thought.

## The Protestant Reformation

THE Protestant Reformation might be said to have begun
when Martin Luther nailed his ninety-five theses against the
misuse of indulgences upon the Church door at Wittenberg on
October 31, 1517. Thus was begun a movement that started as
a reformation within the Church and ended in revolution and
secession. The causes of the Reformation were complex and
while Luther struck the match that kindled a widespread discontent with many of the practices of the Church, that discontent was already latent in the later Middle Ages. The search
for a more personal relationship with God had already manifested itself with the growth of mysticism in the fourteenth and
fifteenth centuries. The Conciliar movement of the fifteenth
century had already attempted to convert the Papacy into a
constitutional monarchy and failed. That the Church had
been corrupted and was in need of reform almost everyone except the more profligate of the Renaissance Popes recognized.
The spirituality of the Church was almost lost in secular and
temporal ambitions and the Church appeared to be much
more concerned about the increase of its revenues than it did

about the salvation of individual souls. The sale of indulgences by licensed vendors and the wide-spread popular belief that such indulgences removed the guilt of sin were the immediate target of Luther's criticism but his reforms went much deeper. In his attack upon the veneration of relics, the adoration of images, the practice of making pilgrimages to holy places and formal, ritualistic practices there was an attempt to purge the Church of pagan, superstitious practices and to bring people back to a conception of Christian piety that such practices obscured.

In an effort to emphasize the total dependence of man upon God, Luther preached the doctrine of salvation by faith alone. Man by his own efforts or works can never merit salvation, salvation is by the grace of God alone. Man is totally depraved. He wrote:

There are two kinds of believing, first, a believing about God which means that I believe that what is said of God is true. This faith is rather a form of knowledge than a faith. There is, secondly, a believing in God which means that I put my trust in Him, give myself up to thinking that I can have dealings with Him, and believe without any doubt that He will be and do to me according to the things said of Him. Such faith, which throws itself upon God, whether in life or in death, alone makes a Christian man.[40]

Justification is a personal experience requiring neither priesthood nor Church for its mediation. According to a prominent Protestant scholar:

The essential element in this new conception of grace is this: that grace is no longer a mystical miraculous substance, to be imparted through the sacraments, but a Divine temper of faith, conviction, spirit, knowledge and trust which is to be appropriated; in the Gospel and in the Love and Spirit of Christ towards mankind it can be discerned as the loving will of God which brings with it the forgiveness of sins . . . This does not mean that it ceases to be a miracle. But the miracle now consists in the fact that man in his weakness, rebellion, despair, and impurity can grasp such an idea from the Gospel; it is so entirely beyond the reach of his natural powers, and the religious idea of redemption is so far removed from the natural intellectual sphere, that only through the miracle of predestination can it come to pass. It is an inner miracle of faith in the Gospel and in Christ, not an interior-external miracle of the hierarchical-sacramental impartation of grace, which produces the power to do good works and to acquire merit.[41]

This idea of grace led Luther to a second doctrine—the priesthood of all believers. Scripture, he argued, makes no distinction between the priesthood and the laity and all believers "are worthy to appear before God, to pray for others, to teach each other mutually the things that are of God." [42] This conception emphasized the direct responsibility of each individual for his own salvation and emphasized the fact that through prayer and the reading of the Scripture the individual might have direct access to God without relying upon any intercession in his behalf by a special priesthood.

Both ideas, justification by faith and the priesthood of all believers, placed a new emphasis upon Scripture. The Reformers believed that if the Scriptures were made available to the people in the vernacular they could hear God speaking to them directly and personally. They seemed to believe that the Scriptures were more or less self-evident in meaning and it has been said with some justification that the Protestant Reformers sought to replace an infallible Church with an infallible Book. Yet, what the Reformers were most anxious to teach was that the word of God is a personal rather than a dogmatic revelation. Too much concern with theological and philosophical problems, they believed, obscured this fact: that salvation depends upon personal trust in a personal Savior. The question remained as to how the Scriptures were recognized, by what authority established as Scripture? Having denied both the authority of the Church and the authority of reason the Reformers were forced into the position of claiming that the Scriptures were "self-authenticated." Thus Calvin wrote:

Let it be considered, then, as an undeniable truth that they who have been inwardly taught of the Spirit feel an entire acquiescence in the Scripture, and that it is self-authenticated, carrying with it its own evidence, and ought not to be made the object of demonstration and arguments from reason; but that it obtains the credit which it deserves with us by the testimony of the Spirit.[43]

Now,

If the whole value of man consists in a right attitude of faith and trust towards God in the Word, then this general spirit also forms the basis of the standard for the ethical consequences to which it gives rise. Henceforth there is no ecclesiastical, authoritative, moral law; the Church does not shoulder the responsibility for the individual; the only rule for conduct is the impulse of the individual conscience. "Good works" exist no longer; all that matters is the general spirit and attitude of the individual . . . everything hinges on whether the new life is checked and hindered or allowed to develop freely. The system of future rewards and punishments has disappeared, and all that remains is the blessedness of the new creation, out of which all that is good will arise spontaneously.[44]

In this connection the Protestant Reformers emphasized the sacredness of every man's vocation or "calling" pointing out that it was not by leading a life of detachment from the world that one best served God but in mutual service to one's fellow-man through the conscientious pursuit of whatever vocation God happened to call him. "There is no longer any room for the conception of 'Supernature' at all; the whole idea of a gradated system, leading from Nature up to Supernature, from secular morality to that which is spiritual and super-natural has faded away." [45] Instead we find the notion that human nature is totally depraved and that redemption consists not in perfecting nature but in restoring it to its pristine condition before the Fall.

This means . . . that the idea of evolution has disappeared in its Catholic form of an ascent from Nature to Grace, which Catholicism had combined with the Aristotelian doctrine of the steady process of the development of latent potentialities into actualities, or of the whole process of Nature as a struggle towards perfection. Man does not ascend from the Primitive State to a supernatural perfection which had already been prepared by Nature; the universe and the earth did not evolve from Nature into the realm of Grace; Society is not linked with a natural basis in order that there may be continuity between it and the supernatural fellowship of Grace. In the Protestant theory everything is complete in a moment . . . the Fall means the removal of Nature, and Redemption is its restoration.[46]

For the Reformers Christ is the *only* revelation of God which we have and theology, to the extent that it survives at all, is converted into Christology.[47] "Christ is not called Christ," Luther wrote, "because He had the two Natures. What does that matter to me? He bears this glorious name because of His Office and Work which He has undertaken." [48] It is not Christ as God nor Christ as man but Christ as comforter and mediator which is the central fact and thus in Protestantism the doctrine of Atonement is given a centrality of emphasis which overshadows its organic relation to such doctrines as that of the Incarnation and the Resurrection.

Throughout the Middle Ages the Church had been conceived to be both a fellowship of all believers, the Communion of the Saints, and a divine institution established upon earth by Christ Himself for the mediation of God's grace through the apostles and a priesthood especially ordained for that purpose. With the Reformation only the former conception is retained by Protestantism. "The Church," Luther said, "is the company of people who believe in Christ." [49]

The doctrine of total depravity did not always have the effect, as some suppose, of making the person holding the doctrine feel gloomy or morbid for it could be interpreted, and frequently was, as one writer has pointed out, to emphasize "the love of God in redemption" rather than "His justice in condemnation." [50] If all men are totally depraved then *any* man, however bad, may hope for salvation. Professor Haller points out that "The concept of universal depravity, by leveling all superiority not of the spirit, enormously enhanced the self-respect of the ordinary man. If none were righteous, then one man was as good as another. God chose whom he would and the distinctions of this world counted for nothing. The concept of free grace still further heightened his confidence. If the only real aristocracy was the aristocracy created by God, then nothing really counted but character and inner worth. . . . If election were manifested not by outward conformity to an imposed law but by the struggle of the spirit within against the weakness and disobedience of the flesh, then any man might find reason for hope within his own breast. If all this was pre-destined, then there could be no fear concerning the issue of life's ordeal. 'If God be with us, who can be against us?' " [51] Professor Hoxie Neale Fairchild has brought considerable evidence together to demonstrate a rather paradoxical fact: that "the believer in total depravity" actually "was the champion of human goodness and power." In a study which will take several volumes, of which three have already appeared, Professor Fairchild has developed a very interesting and suggestive thesis, namely, that seventeenth-century Protestantism contains religious ideas and feelings which easily degenerate into the eighteenth-century religion of sentiment and thus prepare the way for nineteenth-century Romanticism. It is impossible to do justice to his thesis by quoting a sentence or two but something of what he seeks to prove, and in my opinion, with considerable success is this: "Under the rationalistic influences of the Enlightenment the Calvinist's formal beliefs decay more rapidly than his inward religious emotions. He loses most of his creed, but he retains, in a blurred and softened form, the emotions which his creed had both reflected and fostered. The God above him becomes more shadowy than the God within him, until at last he is left with the basic attitude of sentimentalism—a sense of inward virtue and freedom which must somehow find corroboration in the nature of the universe. Just enough brimstone remains to tinge his optimism with melancholy, just enough other-worldliness to make him shrink at times from the civilization he has built. It is fitting that Jean-Jacques should have been reared in Geneva." [52]

## Political Consequences of the Reformation

MARTIN LUTHER was excommunicated by the Pope in 1520 and the following year the Emperor Charles V issued an edict of outlawry against him. But despite this action many German princes and cities espoused Luther's cause and until his death in 1546 Luther was engaged in organizing his new Church. The Emperor was preoccupied with a war in Italy and it was not until 1544 that he returned to Germany determined to crush the new religious movement. A civil war broke out that ended in a compromise embodied in the Peace of Augsburg (1555). The formula embodied in this peace—*cuius regio, eius religio*—was destined to have profound consequences for all of Europe. Henceforth, it was agreed that the people of each territory should take the religion of their ruler. With the adoption of this principle the idea of a single Church disappears and instead of the Church determining the legitimacy of political rule, political rulers, in effect, if not in theory, determine the religion of the people. The Church is subordinated to the state.

While the Lutheran Church was being established in northern Germany, John Calvin was establishing a similar movement in Switzerland with its center in Geneva. Calvinism soon spread to other countries. One of his most ardent followers was the Scottish reformer, John Knox, and under his influence large numbers of the Scottish nobility became Calvinists. Soon the Calvinist Church became the official church of Scotland where it was called the Presbyterian Church. In France the Calvinists were known as the Hugenots and constituted a small but vigorous minority. In 1534 by an act of Parliament the king of England was made the supreme head of the English Church which retained many Catholic practices and doctrines and sought to steer a middle course between Roman Catholicism on the one hand and Protestantism on the other.

A Counter-Reformation began within the Roman Catholic Church led by a new religious society known as the Order of the Jesuits (1534) whose work was particularly notable in the field of education. The Inquisition was established in Rome in 1542. In 1545 a great Church council was called and met at Trent. A new statement of Catholic doctrine was adopted here and the doctrines advanced by the Reformers were explicitly declared to be heretical. A number of corrupt practices among the clergy were condemned.

The conflict between Protestants and Catholics was a bitter one and each, when able, persecuted the other. Civil and international war was widespread throughout the sixteenth and early seventeenth centuries as each side tried by violence to subdue the other. The Thirty Years War (1618–1648) was the last religious war and ended in the Peace of Westphalia. By this Treaty the boundaries between Protestant and Catholic Europe were fixed. France, Spain, Italy, southern Germany, the Spanish Netherlands and part of Switzerland remained Catholic. The map of Europe remained substantially as drawn by this Treaty until the time of the French Revolution. But after the Treaty of Westphalia the religious question ceased to be an important factor in international relations. It marked the inauguration of the era of absolute monarchies and the birth of the modern nation state.

## The Modern Nation State

IN THE Middle Ages there was no separation of private and public spheres of activity. There was no "state" in the modern sense of that word and hence, no distinction between "state" and "society." Feudalism as a system of reciprocal rights and duties was based upon personal, legal relationships organized hierarchically. Thus the distinction between political authority and personal rights was blurred. With the disintegration of the feudal order, prerogatives of rulership, which had earlier been thought of as a species of private property, were gradually transferred from the ruler to the sphere of public administration. The extension of political authority along territorial lines necessitated the introduction of general systems of taxation, the creation of bureaucracies and the employment of standing armies. Thus, gradually the prerogatives of rulership became impersonalized. When there was attached to these phenomena the concept of *raison d'état*, the idea of the modern state emerged.

The modern nation state was the product of many forces principally: (1) the individualistic climate of opinion that characterized the Renaissance and Reformation; (2) the collapse of the universal authority of the Church; (3) the desire of the rising commercial classes for uniform trade regulations, the abolition of feudal obstacles to trade and for conditions under which trade could be carried on peacefully and profitably; (4)

the desire for order and tranquility in an age marked by bloodshed, violence and intolerance; (5) the personal ambitions of monarchs who allied themselves with the rising commercial class in opposition to the more powerful feudal lords.

Something else was required before the modern nation state could come into existence—the doctrine of territorial sovereignty. This was supplied most notably by Jean Bodin (1530–1596) in his *Six Livres de la République* (1576), an enlarged Latin edition of which appeared in 1586. In the eighth chapter of the first book he says that *"maiestas est summa in cives ac subditos legibusque soluta potestas"*—sovereignty is the highest power over citizens and subjects unrestrained by the laws. The chief characteristic of sovereignty is the "power to give law to citizens generally and individually and . . . not necessarily with the consent of superiors, equals or inferiors." Sovereignty, moreover, is perpetual, i.e., not limited by time, and unconditional, i.e., "this power is given to the prince without any charges or conditions attached." In practice, sovereignty manifests itself in the ability to declare war and make peace, to commission magistrates, to act as a court of last resort, to coin money and to levy taxes.

When Bodin declared that the sovereign was *legibus solutus*, unrestrained by the laws, he did not mean, however, that the sovereign was unrestrained by *all* law but only that he was, by definition, unrestrained by the laws of his own making. For, as Bodin says, "If we should define sovereignty as a power of being free from all law no prince could be found to have sovereign rights; for all are bound by *divine law* and the *law of nature* and also by that *common law of nations* which embodies principles distinct from these." The Bodinian prince is specifically free from (1) the imperial and papal order, (2) the Roman law, and (3) the Coutume. He is bound by (1) the divine law, (2) the natural law, (3) the common law of nations, (4) the *lex Salica* and other provisions of the national constitution. Bodin perpetuates the medieval distinction between the true prince and the tyrant. If subsequent interpreters of Bodin placed more emphasis upon the phrase *legibus solutus* than is justified by the context in which it appears this is because the idea was new and it was this idea that they wanted to emphasize. One writer points out:

> The doctrine of sovereignty offered the national king the most convenient theoretical weapon with which to combat the claims of rival feudal or ecclesiastical authorities, refractory estates or competing systems of law. The idea of one unified legal scheme affording order, consistency, and certainty in the governing of all social relations within a given national area, overriding all contradictory rules and injunctions, and flexible enough to be modified at the command of a single sovereign will, made a strong appeal. . . . With Hobbes this theory reached its climax. Sovereignty thenceforth had merely to be transferred by Rousseau, Bentham and Austin from the king to a parliament, an electorate or some other determinate body or bodies of men, in order to give dynamic vogue to ideas of "parliamentary supremacy" or even "popular sovereignty." [53]

## Political Theory of the Sixteenth Century

THE period of the Reformation and Counter-Reformation produced no distinctively Protestant or Catholic political theory. Although absolute monarchy was the chief and immediate beneficiary of the fierce strife between Protestants and Catholics the sixteenth century did give rise to theories upon which resistance to absolutism might later be justified. At the same time theories were advanced which could lead to an assertion of the divine right of kings.

Both Luther and Calvin preached a doctrine of passive submission to the established political order [54] but many of their followers finding themselves in a minority in a country ruled by a Catholic felt that the circumstances justified a doctrine of resistance. One of the earliest expressions of such a doctrine was the *Vindiciae contra Tyrannos* (The Vindication of Rights against Tyrants) published in 1579 and ascribed to Duplessis-Mornay, a Hugenot pamphleteer. Here we find one of the first explicit statements of the contractual nature of government. The author of the pamphlet conceives of the king as being bound both by a contract with God and by a contract with his subjects.

In the first covenant or pact, piety comes under the bond; in the second, justice. In the one the king promises dutifully to obey God; in the second, justly to rule the people: in the one, to provide for the glory of God; in the other, to maintain the welfare of the people. In the first the condition is, if you observe my law; in the second, if you secure to each his own. Failure to fulfil the first pact is properly punishable by God; failure to fulfil the second, legitimately by the whole people, or by the magnates of the realm (*regni proceres*) who have undertaken to watch over the whole people.[55]

The author asks the question whether it is right for princes to intervene in behalf of people in neighboring countries who are oppressed because of adherence to the true religion and answers the question in the affirmative.

The very same year that the *Vindiciae* appeared in France, a similar doctrine made its appearance in Scotland in George Buchanan's *De Iure Regni apud Scotos* (On The Law of the Realm among the Scots) but Buchanan went much further than the author of the *Vindiciae* and reached the conclusion that under certain circumstances a tyrant might be assassinated with impunity.

Doctrines similar to both of these were advanced by a Spanish Jesuit, Juan de Mariana in *De Rege et Regis Institutione* (On Kingship and the Education of a King) published in 1599. Unlike the earlier writings that appeared in nations where the writer was a member of a minority group this book appeared in a country (Spain) where the Catholic faith held undisputed sway. Mariana drew the usual distinction between a true prince and a tyrant and like Buchanan concluded, after advancing a doctrine of popular sovereignty, that under certain circumstances tyrannicide was justified. The tyrant should first be warned by an assembly of the people but if this assembly is prevented from taking place or the warning goes unheeded the private citizen is justified in taking the life of the tyrant.

On the other hand the sixteenth century brought forth the first systematic and at the same time the most extreme statement of the doctrine of the divine right of kings. Shortly before he came to the throne of England James I published *The True*

*Law of Free Monarchy* (1598) designed to answer the thesis propounded by Buchanan. Against the contention of Buchanan
that kings are established by the people and responsible to
them, James argued that whatever may have been the origin of
monarchy in its infancy, in Scotland and in England monarchy
was established by conquest. Once established, the king's right
to rule descends upon his heirs by inheritance. He repeated
Bodin's conception of sovereignty but the only limitation he
would recognize was the law of succession to the throne—if
the king had obtained his throne by legitimate succession his
power was absolute and unlimited. Resistance to a lawful king
is illegal, contrary to human reason, to the law of God and to
Scripture. "A wicked king," he declared, "is sent by God for
a curse to his people and a plague for their sins. . . . Patience,
earnest prayers to God and amendment of their lives are the
only lawful means to move God to relieve them of their heavy
curse." [56] "Kings," he wrote, "are breathing images of God
upon earth" and without a king the people are simply a "head-
less multitude." Since "it is atheism and blasphemy to dispute
what God can do . . . so it is presumption and high contempt
in a subject to dispute what a king can do." In the final analysis, as James was to declare in 1616, the quality of kingship is a
"mystery" and "that which concerns the mystery of the king's
power is not lawful to be disputed; for that is to wade into the
weakness of princes, and to take away the mystical reverence
that belongs unto them that sit in the throne of God." [57] The
theory of the divine right of kings was the last desperate attempt of the House of Stuart to defend its absolutism against
the revolution that threatened to put the king under the law
by force if necessary. The extreme language in which the theory was framed was a manifestation, however, of weakness
rather than of strength.

It was in the British Isles in the seventeenth century that the
conflict between absolutism and liberalism was first resolved
in favor of the latter and that modern constitutional government was born. But before analyzing the philosophy of liberalism some attention should be given to the political philosophy of an Englishman who is difficult to classify but whose

influence has extended well beyond the century in which his philosophy was first formulated, i.e., the philosophy of Thomas Hobbes.

## *Thomas Hobbes (1588–1679)*

HOBBES was born near Malmesbury in 1588, the son of a vicar. He demonstrated unusual intellectual ability as a child and became exceptionally well versed in Latin and Greek. He attended the university at Oxford but was disappointed in his experience there. Upon leaving Oxford he became the tutor to the son of William Cavendish, who was later to become Earl of Devonshire. He traveled extensively on the continent of Europe and spent a great deal of time there. For two years he served as tutor to the Prince of Wales (who was later to become Charles II) while he was in exile in France. Hobbes' sympathies in the English Civil War were with the royalists but his writings often displeased them and it is doubtful if their immediate influence was very great. It was not until his ideas were revived by the Utilitarians and especially by John Austin in the nineteenth century that they exerted considerable influence in a practical way. His most important works include: *Elements of Law* (completed in 1640 but not published until 1650), *De Cive* (1642), *Leviathan* (1651), *De Corpore* (1655) and *De Homine* (1659). The most influential and most widely read of these is the *Leviathan*.

One of the first modern exponents of what we have since called "naturalism," Hobbes endeavored to formulate a doctrine of man and a theory of the state wholly upon naturalistic assumptions. In his introduction to the *Leviathan*, he says:

Nature, the art whereby God hath made and governs the world, is by the *art* of man, as in many other things, so in this also imitated, that it can make an artificial animal. For seeing life is but a motion of limbs, the beginning whereof is in some principal part within; why may we not say, that all *automata* (engines that move themselves by springs and wheels as doth a watch) have an artificial life? For what is the *heart*, but a *spring;* and the *nerves*, but so many *strings;* and the *joints*, but so many *wheels*, giving motion to the whole body, such as was intended by the artificer? *Art* goes yet further, imitating that rational and most excellent work of nature, *man*. For by art is created that great **Leviathan, called a Commonwealth, or State,** in Latin **Civitas,** which is but an artificial man; though of greater stature and strength than the natural, for whose protection and defense it was intended. . . .[58]

It was on these naturalistic grounds that Hobbes proceeded to justify the institution of absolute monarchy which the Stuarts sought to defend by "divine right." It was for that reason that they were not too well pleased with his endeavors in their behalf. But if his defense of absolutism did not please the royalists neither, of course, did it please the opponents of absolutism. His treatise, as a matter of fact, transcended the demands of propaganda and therein lies its importance.

A thorough-going materialist, Hobbes argued that whatever exists is matter and that whatever changes is motion. Underlying everything is matter in motion. Our thoughts are but motions in our brains. It was upon this underlying assumption, derived, Hobbes believed, from natural science that he sought to erect a doctrine of man and a theory of the state.

An empiricist, he argued that "there is no conception in a man's mind, which hath not at first, totally, or by parts, been begotten upon the organs of sense. The rest are derived from that original." [59] Anticipating modern behavioristic psychology he argued that it is physical stimuli "pressing" upon our sensory organs which give rise to mental impressions in some automatic fashion. All the different phenomena of sensation can ultimately be explained in terms of the fundamental laws of motion, i.e., in terms of physics or of a kind of physiological psychology. Just as the cognitional attributes of man's nature can be explained in physical terms so also can his volitional activities. Good he equates with pleasure, and evil with its absence.

. . . because the constitution of a man's body is in continual mutation, it is impossible that all the same things should always cause in him the same appetites, and aversions: much less can all men consent, in the desire of almost any one and the same object.

But whatsoever is the object of any man's appetite or desire, that is it which he for his part calleth *good:* and the object of his hate and aversion, *evil:* and of his contempt, *vile* and *inconsiderable.* For these words of good, evil, and contemptible, are ever used with relation to the person that useth them: there being nothing simply and absolutely so; nor any common rule of good and evil, to be taken from the nature of the objects themselves. . . .[60]

Good and evil are matters of individual taste, that which we happen to like or dislike. We are not attracted to something because it is good but "good" is the name we call that to which we are attracted. Men are naturally selfish because they are naturally attracted to that which they desire. When their desires conflict they are at war with one another and being at war with one another is the natural condition of man.

Nature hath made men so equal, in the faculties of the body, and mind; as that though there be found one man sometimes manifestly stronger in body, or of quicker mind than another; yet when all is reckoned together, the difference between man, and man, is not so considerable, as that one man can thereupon claim to himself any benefit, to which another may not pretend, as well as he.[61]

From this equality of ability there arises equality in the hope of attaining our desires. This equality of hope makes enemies of men especially when they desire something which they cannot both enjoy. We find in the nature of man, Hobbes says, three principal causes of quarrel among men: competition, diffidence, and glory.

The first maketh men invade for gain; the second, for safety; and the third, for reputation. The first use violence, to make themselves masters of other men's persons, wives, children, and cattle: the second, to defend them; the third, for trifles, as a word, a smile, a different opinion. . . .

Hereby it is manifest, that during the time men live without a common power to keep them all in awe, they are in that condition which is called war; and such a war, as is of every man, against every other man.[62]

Thus in a condition of nature, prior to the establishment of civil society, man is at war with man seeking to gratify his own desires, to keep what he has or to preserve his reputation. In such a condition men live in "continual fear" and in "danger of violent death," the "life of man" in such a condition being "solitary, poor, nasty, brutish and short." [63] In this war of every man against every man there is nothing just nor unjust, right or wrong, but force and fraud everywhere prevail. It is not until men enter society that such a thing as justice is possible for "where there is no common power, there is no law: where no law, no injustice." [64]

Confronted with such a condition man is impelled partly by his passions, partly by his reason to seek peace by entering society. "The passions that incline men to peace, are fear of death; desire of such things as are necessary to commodious living; and a hope by their industry to obtain them. And reason suggesteth convenient articles of peace, upon which men may be drawn to agreement. These articles, are they, which otherwise are called the Laws of Nature." [65] But what Hobbes means by the "laws of nature" is something quite different from what has traditionally been called "natural law." This becomes evident when Hobbes distinguishes between natural right and natural law and defines natural right solely as the right of self-preservation. "The Right of Nature . . . ," Hobbes declares, "is the liberty each man hath, to use his own power, as he will himself, for the preservation of his own nature; that is to say, of his own life; and consequently, of doing anything, which in his own judgment and reason, he shall conceive to be the aptest means thereunto." [66] This "natural right" has no moral content for Hobbes, it is simply a statement of how men do in fact, in Hobbes' opinion, act. It is a description of what is, not a principle of what ought to be.

For Hobbes a law of nature is not a moral law but a counsel of prudence, for, he says, "a law of nature . . . is a precept or general rule, found out by reason, by which a man is forbidden to do that, which is destructive of his life, or taketh away the means of preserving the same." There are three principal laws of nature: (1) "that every man ought to endeavor peace, so far as he has hope of obtaining it; and when he cannot obtain it, that he may seek, and use, all helps, and advantages of war"; (2) "that a man be willing, when others are so too . . . to lay down this right to all things; and be contented with so much liberty against other men, as he would allow other men against himself," and (3) "that men perform their covenants made." [67]

Commenting upon Hobbes' conception of the "laws of nature," Professor Sabine declares: "All his efforts were bent toward interpreting them in accordance with the principles of his own psychology while retaining, it must be admitted, the occasional advantage of talking as if he meant by them something rather like what others meant. In fact they were quite different. The laws of nature really meant for Hobbes a set of rules according to which an ideally reasonable being would pursue his own advantage, if he were perfectly conscious of all the circumstances in which he was acting and was quite unswayed by momentary impulse and prejudice. Since he assumes that in the large men really do act in this way, the laws of nature state hypothetical conditions upon which the fundamental traits of human beings allow a stable government to be founded." [68]

The basis of Hobbes' system is not justice but utility, it is not a question of doing what we ought to do but of doing that which is to our own personal advantage. We seek peace, agree with other men to give up our liberty of doing as we please, and keep this agreement once made not because we ought to but because it is the only way we can escape from the anarchy of the state of nature which constantly threatens our existence. It is not love and a desire for justice that impels us to take these steps but fear of death and a calculated prudence. Duty, in Hobbes' system, very fortunately, it must be said, coincides with self-interest. There is no moral "problem" for Hobbes because he denies that there is any conflict between what is and what ought to be. Men will in fact, he says, and with considerable optimistic assurance, seek peace because they will realize that it is to their personal advantage to do so. The "laws of nature," therefore, are not, for Hobbes, moral obligations imposed upon men by Reason or God, but rather statements of how men motivated by fear of death will in fact act if prudent. Nevertheless, Hobbes does realize that unless men do keep their promises, unless "men perform their covenants made," men will still be in a condition of war. It is this "law of nature," he declares, which is the fountain of justice and "when a covenant is made, then to break it is *unjust;* and the definition of injustice, is no other than the *not performance of covenant*." [69] Here, it seems to me, Hobbes shifts his ground and suggests that there is some kind of moral obligation to keep one's promises, something more than calculated self-interest, something dictated not by the reasonings of individuals but by Reason itself. But the very conception of moral obligation is opposed to his underlying naturalistic assumptions and to his basic conception of human nature and has no legitimate, logical place in his system. What he does, it seems to me, is surreptitiously to borrow from the tradition of natural law that support for his system which his own premises do not provide. By referring to the keeping of covenants as a "law of nature" he invokes the memory and sanctions of the natural law tradition although the basic premises of his own philosophy repudiate that tradition. Be that as it may, we are now prepared to examine his theory of the state.

The state or the commonwealth comes into existence, Hobbes believes, as the result of a contract or agreement in which every man covenants with every other man to give up his natural right of governing himself to some designated sovereign person or assemblage of persons. It is as though each man said: "I authorize and give up my right of governing myself, to this man, or to this assembly of men, on this condition, that thou give up thy right to him and authorize all his actions in like manner. This done, the multitude so united in one person, is called a **Commonwealth**." [70] A commonwealth, then, "is one person, of whose acts a great multitude, by mutual covenants one with another, have made themselves every one the author, to the end he may use the strength and means of them all, as he shall think expedient, for their peace and common defense." [71] This person, or assemblage of persons, is called Sovereign. This Sovereign, it should be noted, is not a party to the contract and his power is not conditioned by any obligation on his part. Once having transferred their right of governing themselves to a sovereign, moreover, the subjects (as they now become) "cannot lawfully make a new covenant, amongst themselves, to be obedient to any other, in any thing whatsoever, without his permission." [72] The power of the sovereign is unlimited and absolute—"there can happen no breach of covenant on the part of the sovereign; and consequently none of his subjects, by any pretence of forfeiture, can be freed from his subjection." [73] If a man should seek to withdraw his consent from the covenant he then becomes in "the condition of war he was in before; wherein he might without injustice be destroyed by any man whatsoever." [74] Nor can any man accuse the sovereign of acting unjustly since justice is, by definition, what the sovereign wills. Tyranny does not refer to any objective reality but is simply a name which individuals use when they "are discontented under monarchy." Similarly when they are displeased with *aristocracy* they "call it *oligarchy:* so also, they which find themselves grieved under a *democracy,* call it *anarchy.*" [75]

There is only one liberty which Hobbes believes to be consistent with the unlimited power of the sovereign and that is the liberty which individuals retain "to defend their own bodies, even against them that lawfully invade them." "If the sovereign command a man, though justly condemned, to kill, wound, or maim himself; or not to resist those that assault him; or to abstain from the use of food, air, medicine, or any other thing, without which he cannot live; yet hath that man the liberty to disobey." [76] This seems to amount to no more, however, than that a man cannot be commanded to take his own life. This would appear to be a dubious kind of "right," and certainly not a very substantial one. "As for other liberties," Hobbes declares, "they depend on the silence of the law. In cases where the sovereign has prescribed no rule, there the subject hath the liberty to do, or forbear, according to his own discretion. And therefore such liberty is in some places more, and in some less; and in some times more, in other times less, according as they that have the sovereignty shall think most convenient." [77]

Hobbes will permit no distinction to be drawn between the state and society, the state and government or between law and morality. All authority and all power reside in the Sovereign whom Hobbes appropriately called a "mortal God." The sovereign is the supreme legislator and is not himself bound by the law since the law is what he declares it to be. "It is manifest," Hobbes wrote, "that law in general, is not counsel, but command; nor a command of any man to any man; but only of him, whose command is addressed to one formerly obliged to obey him. . . . Civil law, is to every subject, those rules, which the commonwealth hath commanded him, by word, writing, or other sufficient sign of the will, to make use of, for the distinction of right, and wrong; that is to say, of what is contrary, and what is not contrary to the rule." Because the laws of nature are not properly called laws but are simply "qualities that dispose men to peace and obedience" there can be no conflict between the civil law and the law of nature and as a matter of fact "the law of nature and the civil law, contain each other, and are of equal extent." [78] With Hobbes, the limitations upon sovereignty envisaged by Bodin, disappear completely. The medieval distinction between a true prince and a tyrant likewise disappears. But Hobbes is unperturbed

. . . because the name of tyranny, signifieth nothing more, nor less, than the name of sovereignty, be it in one, or many men, saving that they that use the former word, are understood to be angry with them they call tyrants; I think the toleration of a professed hatred of tyranny, is a toleration of hatred to commonwealth in general, and another evil seed, not differing much from the former. For to the justification of the cause of a conqueror, the reproach of the cause of the conquered, is for the most part necessary: but neither of them necessary for the obligation of the conquered.[79]

It follows from Hobbes' conception of sovereignty that the church is and of logical necessity must be subordinate to the state. A church he defines as "a company of men professing Christian religion, united in the person of one sovereign, at whose command they ought to assemble, and without whose authority they ought not to assemble." And, he adds, "because in all commonwealths, that assembly, which is without warrant from the civil sovereign, is unlawful; that Church also, which is assembled in any commonwealth that hath forbidden them to assemble, is an unlawful assembly." There can be no such thing as a universal Church "because there is no power on earth, to which all other commonwealths are subject. . . . *Temporal* and *spiritual* government, are but two words brought into the world to make men see double, and mistake their *lawful sovereign.*" The "chief pastor" among all

pastors within a commonwealth cannot be anyone else than
"the civil sovereign." [80] There is no inconsistency between
obedience to God and obedience to the civil sovereign, Hobbes
declared, because if the sovereign is a Christian he will allow
men to believe that Jesus is the Christ (the only article of
religion, Hobbes says, necessary for salvation) and he will require "obedience to all the civil laws; in which also are contained all the laws of nature, that is all the laws of God: for
besides the laws of nature and the laws of the Church, which
are part of the civil law (for the Church that can make laws is
the commonwealth), there be no other laws divine. Whosoever
therefore obeyeth his Christian sovereign, is not thereby
hindered, neither from believing, nor from obeying God."
On the other hand, if the sovereign be not a Christian "every
one of his own subjects, that resisteth him, sinneth against
the laws of God (for such are the laws of nature), and re-
jecteth the counsel of the apostles, that admonisheth all
Christians to obey their princes, and all children and servants
to obey their parents and masters in all things. And for their
*faith*, it is internal and invisible; they have the license that
Naaman had, and need not put themselves into danger for
it. But if they do, they ought to expect their reward in heaven,
and not complain of their lawful sovereign; much less make
war upon him. For he that is not glad of any just occasion of
martyrdom, has not the faith he professeth, but pretends it
only. . . ." [81] Although Hobbes devotes the entire third of his
*Leviathan* to the discussion of Christianity and of a Christian
Commonwealth and clearly thinks that religion has its "uses"
he is not himself concerned with defending orthodox Christianity. He is more concerned with avoiding civil war engendered by religious differences than he is with the truth of
religion. It is, he says, "with the mysteries of our religion, as
with wholesome pills for the sick; which swallowed whole,
have the virtue to cure; but chewed, are for the most part
cast up again without effect." [82] The only laws of God that
we can be compelled to obey are those promulgated by that
person "whose commands have already the force of laws,"
that is to say, by the civil sovereign.

For if every man should be obliged, to take for God's law, what particular men, on pretence of private inspiration, or revelation, should obtrude upon him, in such a number of men, that out of pride and ignorance, take their own dreams, and extravagant fancies, and madness, for testimonies of God's spirit; or out of ambition pretend to such divine testimonies, falsely, and contrary to their own consciences, it were impossible that any divine law should be acknowledged.[83]

In a commonwealth of Christians, the authority of the church and the authority of the commonwealth are one and the same for it is "called a *commonwealth*, because it consisteth of men united in one person, their sovereign; and a *church*, because it consisteth in Christian men, united in one Christian sovereign." If the church be not identical with the commonwealth then it has no authority at all, can neither command nor do anything at all. For all practical purposes, Hobbes seems to be saying, the will of God and the will of the civil sovereign must be regarded as identical.

Hobbes is enmeshed in a problem here which is to plague all modern thought, namely, what is the nature and ultimate source of authority? He rejects like most modern thinkers the authority of God, except as that authority *may* be reflected in the "natural reason" of individuals, and must, therefore, seek some other authority as a substitute. Like others of his times he hits upon the idea of a social contract as the way out of his dilemma and it is the will of individuals transferred to an absolute and unlimited sovereign that is for him the ultimate authority, the source of right and wrong, of truth and error, and of justice and injustice. Here we have in an embryonic form the beginnings of the modern totalitarian state, the State substituted for God as the ultimate arbiter and absolute master of man's destiny.

Although Hobbes is generally said to have a very pessimistic, if not cynical, view of human nature, actually his conception of the way in which men may overcome the predicament in which they find themselves is extremely optimistic, for it is solely a matter of mutual agreement. Since Hobbes does argue that all individuals are basically selfish, that the desire for self-satisfaction is the supreme law of all human actions, it requires considerable optimism to assert at the same time that such individuals will agree with all other individuals to transfer their individual wills to one sovereign will. If such an agreement, moreover, is to have any effective binding force men would have to be differently constituted than Hobbes asserts that they are.

It is man's isolation from man that for Hobbes is the real predicament of mankind, not, as Christian thinkers have insisted, a defect of human nature itself. Although I cannot agree with him in all of his conclusions Oakeshott, I believe, has stated the matter aptly when he says that for Hobbes, "Man is, by nature, the victim of solipsism; he is an *individua substantia* distinguished by incommunicability." [84] The predicament from which men require deliverance is not sin but the lack of any authority among men. The trouble lies not in individuals themselves but begins when they come in contact with one another. This is not only Hobbes' problem but the problem posed by individualism itself. And the root of the problem goes back to that nominalism from which it sprang. According to Professor Oakeshott:

Individualism as a gospel has drawn its inspiration from many sources, but as a reasoned theory of society it has its roots in the so-called nominalism of late mediaeval scholasticism, with its doctrines that the reality of a thing is its individuality, that which makes it *this* thing, and that both in God and man will is precedent to reason. Hobbes inherited this tradition of nominalism, and more than any other writer passed it on to the modern world. His civil philosophy is based . . . on a philosophy for which the world is composed of *individuae substantiae*. . . . The human being is first fully an individual, not in respect of self-consciousness, but in the activity of willing. Between birth and death, the self as imagination and will is an indestructible unit, whose relations with other individuals are purely external. Individuals may be collected together, may be added, may be substituted for one another or made to represent one another, but can never modify one another or compose a whole in which their individuality is lost. *Even reason is individualized, and becomes merely the reasoning of an individual without power or authority to oblige acceptance by others:* to convince a man is not to enjoy a common understanding with him, but to displace his reason by yours. . . .

Whatever community exists must be generated by the individual acts of will directed upon a single object, that is, by agreement: the essence of agreement is, not a common will (for there can be no such thing) but a common object of will. . . . . The agreement must be for each to transfer his right of willing to a single artificial Representative, who is thenceforth authorized to will and to act in place of each individual. There is in this society no concord of wills, no common will, no common good; its unity lies solely in the singleness of the Representative, in the *substitution*, by individual acts of will, of his one will for the many conflicting wills.[85]

Since Hobbes denies the authority of God and of Reason, the only way out of his predicament is the substitution of an *artificial* authority created by individual acts of will and embodied in an Absolute Sovereign Will. Although Hobbes uses this theory to defend absolute monarchy, it is essentially the same solution to the problem of authority posed by individualism which is adopted by liberalism. Hobbes, however, already anticipates the conclusions which liberalism must ultimately reach in theory, once it has abandoned its Christian conscience, and which, in fact, it does reach in the twentieth century.

# Liberalism

CHAPTER 4

# The Rise of Liberalism

LIBERALISM was a product of the climate of opinion that emerged at the time of the Renaissance and the Reformation. As the political expression of the new individualism it was a political declaration of faith in the autonomy of human reason and the essential goodness of man. Both a mode of thought and a way of life it reflected the political, social, religious, and economic aspirations of the rising commercial class. Individual freedom was its major premise and its goal.

It was the Renaissance that produced the concept of the autonomous individual or the "masterless man." No longer was God the focal point of thought and life, but man. No longer was it a question of discovering that which was in conformity to God's will but rather that which was in conformity to human nature and to a human nature conceived more in Greek than in Christian terms. While the new concept of individuality drew heavily upon ancient Greece, and especially Stoicism, for its inspiration it was not simply a reiteration of Greek ideas about man but, indeed, a new conception. Professor Reinhold Niebuhr has emphasized the novelty of this idea:

If Protestantism represents the final heightening of the idea of individuality within terms of the Christian religion, the Renaissance is the real cradle of that very unchristian concept and reality: the autonomous individual. . . . Ostensibly Renaissance thought is a revival of classicism, the authority of which is either set against the authority of Christianity or used to modify the latter. Yet classic thought has no such passion for the individual as the Renaissance betrays. The fact is that the Renaissance uses an idea which could have grown only upon the soil of Christianity. It transplants this idea to the soil of classic rationalism to produce a new concept of individual autonomy, which is known in neither classicism nor Christianity.[1]

And Professor Sabine says:

. . . convinced that it must start from what was self-evident, modern philosophy could find nothing apparently so solid and indubitable as individual human nature. The individual human being, with his interests, his enterprise, his desire for happiness and advancement, above all with his reason, which seemed the condition for a successful use of all his other faculties, appeared to be the foundation on which a stable society must be built. Traditional differences of status already began to seem precarious. Not man as a priest or a soldier, as the member of a guild or an estate, but man as a bare human being, a "masterless man," appeared to be the solid fact.[2]

The individual seemed the proper starting point for many reasons. First of all, the early liberals lived in a cultural climate that was still essentially Christian in inspiration if not in intellectual conviction. The idea of the supreme worth of the individual, of all individuals everywhere, was a Christian concept derived from the idea that all men are equal in the sight of God and that all men are brothers since they all have a common Father. When the Reformation destroyed the concept of an intervening hierarchy or priesthood between the individual and God and set man and God immediately in one another's presence, individual personality acquired even greater significance. For when the Reformation posited the Church as "a fellowship of believers, each the direct concern of God, each directly responsible to God, *each guided by the illumination of God in his own heart and conscience,*" [3] responsibility for salvation became a very personal and individual matter. Never had the individual had so much responsibility thrust upon him, never were the opportunities nor the perils greater.

This notion of the absolute moral worth of human personality was coupled with the belief in the individual's powers of creation. With the rediscovery of his ego the man of the Renaissance became conscious, in a way in which man had never been in the Middle Ages, of his individual will and of his power to create things for their own sake and for his own pleasure. Everywhere he looked he saw individuals creating things by what appeared to be their own will and their own power; not only in the realm of science but in the realms of art, of politics, of economy. Individual initiative seemed particularly creative in the economic realm. Here a new order was rising upon the ruins of an old one by what appeared to be the sheer will and adventurous daring of individuals. With the introduction of private enterprise and the replacing of a rigid system of status by a more flexible system based on contracts, individual initiative was given wider scope than had been possible in the Middle Ages. And the fetters of privilege based on birth and social position were being rent asunder by the sheer will of rebellious individuals. As men turned increasingly from a theistic conception of God to a deistic conception (in which God was conceived as the Creator but no longer as the Regent of the universe) it was possible to attribute even greater freedom of will and power to individuals. Knowledge, Francis Bacon had said, is power and everywhere the man of the Renaissance looked he saw new knowledge challenging old authority. The knowledge of nature yielded by the new science tempted many to believe that by an extension of those methods and by his own reason man might dispense with God except perhaps as a metaphysical abstraction or a logically necessary premise.

The doctrine of individual equality was given further support by the new science. Just as the natural scientist regarded atoms, so the political philosopher regarded individuals as irreducible, self-sufficient entities deriving their nature from themselves rather than from their relationships. Having returned to an atomistic conception of reality in the physical sciences the man of the Renaissance sought to apply similar conceptions to social phenomena. As A. D. Lindsay says:

> The great prestige of the new physical sciences produced continuous attempts to apply their method to the study of man in his social relations. Such a scientific study of society will tend to treat individuals as independent units. Each will be regarded as an atom, something having its own nature complete in itself. If they are to be scientific units they will have to be atoms identical in qualitative character. Because the theory will be interested mainly in the laws of the combination of such units it will tend to regard the units as equal.[4]

But the doctrine of "human equality," he points out, "is in one sense not a scientific doctrine." For it rests essentially upon an ethical and spiritual basis, and although the scientific method, as applied to the study of social relationships, tended to give assurance to the affirmation of equality, it did not originate the concept. Rather, "the assumptions of scientific method . . . confirmed a doctrine whose real origin was in religious and not in scientific individualism." [5]

The rising commercial class began to talk about rights peculiar to individuals as human beings. They spoke of the right to possess things which they had acquired by their own labor, of the inviolability of the human body, of the freedom to speak and to write, of the right to a fair trial, of freedom from arbitrary imprisonment and cruel punishment, of the right of petition and assembly and of freedom to worship God as they saw fit. They insisted upon having a greater share in the formulation and administration of governmental policy. They were opposed to an aristocracy of birth not simply as *parvenues* but as a matter of principle. This was not, as has been suggested by some, simply a convenient doctrine, convenient though it may have been, but it was one which actually reflected their way of life, their mode of thinking, their aspirations. It was at once an intellectual doctrine derived logically from the premises of the new individualism and a reaction against specific abuses and injustices perpetrated by an absolutist political, social and religious order.

The new individualism emphasized not only the absolute moral worth of each personality but also individual autonomy. Now if individuals are conceived to be of equal moral worth and equally autonomous it follows of necessity that no individual can submit to the will of any other individual. If each individual is to be able to realize his potentialities as a human being, to realize his full moral value as an individual personality and enjoy the respect to which he is entitled as a human being, he can not submit to any will that is capable of acting capriciously or arbitrarily, for such submission would be a denial of his moral autonomy and equality. Liberalism, as the embodiment of this new individualism, accordingly, espouses individual freedom as its goal. Freedom from what?

Freedom from every authority that is capable of acting capriciously or arbitrarily. Freedom for what? Freedom for the individual to develop all of his potentialities as a human being endowed with reason.

Freedom, however, logically implies responsibility. In order for each individual to have freedom, all individuals must recognize some common authority, some common responsibility. If such authority is not to deny the essential postulate of equality, however, it must be impersonal, calculable, objective. And liberalism arose as a specific answer to this problem: How can the notion of individual autonomy be reconciled with the necessity for political authority? How can individuals conceived as having absolute and equal rights submit to political authority without denying the absoluteness or equality of their claims?

The problem of freedom was, indeed, an intellectual one but at the same time it was more than a theoretical problem. The individual of the seventeenth century was in fact hedged in and restrained politically, socially, economically by arbitrary, personal authority. This restraint not only impeded the expansion and development of free private economic enterprise but it was also incompatible with the dignity of human personality. It was the rising commercial class that felt these restraints most keenly and liberalism was its challenge to political absolutism. At first, it is true, it supported the absolute monarchs and without its support absolute monarchy probably could not have been established. But as the commercial class became stronger and more self-assertive it chafed under the arbitrary restraints imposed by the monarchy it had helped to create. Commercial activity could flourish only under conditions that were predictable, calculable, and stable. Self-confident, eager for conquest, adventurous, it found these restraints incompatible with its economic, social, religious, political and intellectual convictions and aspirations. Arbitrary control was unpredictable and unstable.

In order to realize their conception of individual freedom, and in order successfully to challenge the pretensions of absolutism the commercial classes needed such freedoms as freedom of expression, freedom of assembly, freedom from arbitrary imprisonment. They needed a voice in the shaping of governmental policy. But if civil liberties and representative government were tactically essential they were also a logical expression of the burgher philosophy. In their own minds they did not separate, as some interpreters of their philosophy are inclined to do, their social and economic motives from their intellectual convictions. Their attitude was at once the product of logical derivation from philosophic presuppositions about the nature and destiny of man and of their social and economic interests. It was at one and the same time a theoretical intellectual attitude and a practical expression of rebellion against concrete restraints and specific injustices. Liberalism was the embodiment of the demand for freedom in every sphere of life—intellectual, social, religious, political, and economic—and it is doubtful if the burgher prized one more highly than the other or even considered that he might enjoy one kind of freedom without the other. If the commercial class rebelled with vehemence against arbitrary economic restraints, it protested with equal fervor and conviction against arbitrary political power, Star chamber proceedings, *lettres de cachet*, cruel punishment, and restrictions on freedom of expression and of worship. The liberties which it demanded were not abstract liberties, not freedom in some vague sense, but specific liberties, for the rising commercial classes were rebelling not against injustice in the abstract but against specific injustices.

The central problem with which liberalism is concerned is the relation between the individual and authority. But if the individual, because of the absolute value of human personality, cannot submit to any personal authority capable of acting capriciously and arbitrarily, to what authority can he submit? And the liberal answered: He can submit only to the authority of law; it alone can command and restrain him. Accordingly, liberalism advocates freedom from every form of social control except law. As Voltaire was to put it succinctly: "Freedom consists in being independent from everything but law." [6]

The authority, which had necessarily to be impersonal, objective, and independent of will, could be nothing else than the law. The law, moreover, had to be conceived as eternal, universal, immutable and rational. If the authority was not to be arbitrary, it could not emanate from any personal will that was capable of acting capriciously; it could not change from day to day or place to place; it must be predictable and hence rational.

Merged by the force of historical circumstance into one doctrine, there are latent in liberalism as originally conceived, however, two self-sufficient and logically independent theoretical systems. As its fundamental premise liberalism postulates the absolute value and equality of human personality. Conceiving as the essence of human individuality a God-given soul it espouses individual equality in a spiritual sense and upon that basis demands equality of opportunity. Individuals are never means but always ends in themselves. Accordingly, liberalism champions individual freedom from all arbitrary compulsion since compulsion is incompatible with human dignity and equality. The individual is conceived to be free, however, not to do anything he pleases but free only to follow the dictates of "right reason." For it is freedom and not license that the liberal espouses. As its ideal, therefore, liberalism posits freedom under the impersonal rule of law, the law being conceived as filled with certain eternal, universal and objective truths and values discoverable by natural reason. The existence of such truths is regarded as self-evident.

Liberalism, on the other hand, conceived of society as being composed of atom-like, autonomous individuals with wills and interests peculiar to themselves. But how is it certain that the individual will not will that which is subjectively desired rather than that which is objectively demanded? There is no certainty. Only a conscientious sense of duty bids the individual to follow the dictates of reason rather than those of personal interest. For, ultimately, *liberalism acknowledges no limitation upon individual will except that imposed by individual conscience.* Order, then, is potentially embodied in the existence of objective truth discoverable by reason; but, in the final analysis, it is conscience *alone* that bids the individual to reason objectively, to discover the content of true law, to translate this potential order into actuality. The whole obligation for realizing order rests upon the individual, and more specifically, upon individual conscience. *Conscience is the keystone of the whole liberal structure.* Order is potentially embodied in truths transcending individuals but only dispassionate, objective reason can translate this order into actuality. The law is an ideal requiring concrete wills and concrete actions to be realized; it is a form ready to be filled in by individual wills. Only conscience bids the individual to follow the dictates of reason rather than those of interest and upon the conscientiousness of individuals alone rests the choice between order and anarchy. Con-science, as the word itself indicates, is not regarded as some vague feeling of preference, not some instinctive intuition, but rather is a *common knowledge* of truths and values transcending individuals. The true law, accordingly, to which individuals owe obedience, the law under which freedom is assured, is that law whose content is found in individual conscience. It is in obedience to that law that the individual finds his real freedom and secures the dignity of his existence as a human being.

Two logically independent notions of law, then, are embodied in integral liberalism. First of all, there is the notion that law is the product of individual wills and the expression of subjective, personal interests. In this view it is the irrational compulsion behind the law which makes the individual submit to it. On the other hand, there is the notion that the law is the embodiment of truths and values transcending individual will and interest—that law is found, not made. In this view it is the rational recognition of the inherent justice of the law that imposes obligation. The source of law is thought of, in the first instance, as individual wills; in the second, as reason, nature, or the "order of things." The validity of law, in the first case, rests simply upon the fact that the competent authority, possessed of superior coercive power, has prescribed it. In the second case, the validity of law rests upon the inherent rightness and rationality of its content. The bases of validity are, on the one hand, *formal,* and on the other, *substantive.* The link between the subjective will of the individual and the objective order transcending the individual is reason guided by individual conscience.

Integral liberalism, thus, was based upon an uneasy compromise between two conflicting principles: the idea of the autonomy of individual will and the idea of a higher law. The appeal to conscience that was supposed to reconcile these two conflicting principles proved to be without weight or sanction. At best, it was an appeal to a Christian ethic that could not survive the repudiation of the Christian religion. For the conscience that was to reconcile the two conflicting principles was essentially the Christian conscience and that conscience could not survive the separation of reason from faith and the repudiation of the authority of the Church. What appeared to be "self-evidently" true to the seventeenth-century mind that was still close to the medieval, Christian tradition was destined to appear increasingly less self-evident as the mind of man "freed" itself progressively from the Christian revelation and the authority of the Church.

So long as, and to the extent that, liberals retained the substantive, as well as the formal, conception of law (that is, so long as liberals believed that law should embody certain substantive truths and values transcending individual will and interest), liberalism retained its integral character. When, however, as eventually and inevitably happened, the formal conception of law alone was retained, liberalism became decadent, preparing the way for its own demise. For the sloughing off of objective truths and values under the impact of nineteenth-century positivism left only the subjective and anarchical elements of liberal thought; will was left without any substantial limitation.

The "higher law" which integral liberalism posited as the foundation of positive law was a secularized version of the medieval, Christian natural law. This secularization of the natural law was the work primarily of the great Dutch jurist and father of international law, Hugo Grotius.

## Grotius and the Secularization of Natural Law

GROTIUS (1583–1645) was born in the city of Delft in the Netherlands. He displayed prodigious powers of learning as a youth and entered the University of Leyden at the age of eleven. Four years later he was chosen to accompany a number of Dutch officials on an official visit to Paris. While he was there he took a doctor's degree at the University of Orleans. The following year he took a law degree at Leyden and entered upon the practice of the law in The Hague at the age of sixteen. He subsequently held a number of important public and diplomatic positions including the chief magistracy of the city of Rotterdam. It was in that position that he became involved in a quarrel between the Arminians and the Gomarists.[7]

He published a number of works in many fields but those most widely read today are the treatises he wrote in the field of international law; the most important of which is *De Jure Belli ac Pacis Libri Tres* (1625)—The Law of War and Peace in Three Books. It is in the *Prolegomena* or introduction to that work that the fundamental principles of his political theory are to be found.

Hugo Grotius wrote at a time when, as he declared in his dedication to Louis XIII, "hearts, wearied with strifes" longed for peace. Everywhere warfare was chronic—Catholics battled Protestants, Protestants warred among themselves, dynastic rivalries flourished and were nourished in blood, the rising national states fought among themselves for territory, power, and commercial interests. Grotius saw "partisan passions, fired by hatreds . . . blaze more fiercely day by day." Observing "throughout the Christian world . . . a lack of restraint in relation to war, such as even barbarous races should be ashamed of" he undertook to demonstrate "that there is a common law among nations, which is valid alike for war and in war." [8] In order to make this demonstration he had, of necessity, to examine first the nature and origin of law itself.

"I have made it my concern," he wrote, "to refer the proofs of things touching the law of nature to certain fundamental conceptions which are beyond question, so that no one can deny them without doing violence to himself." [9] Grotius sought to find that authority which could bind Protestant and Catholic alike and he believed that he had discovered that authority in a natural law derived not from revelation but from human nature itself. "The principles of that law," he thought were such that they "are in themselves manifest and clear, almost as evident as are those things which we perceive by the external senses." [10]

In the Aristotelian tradition Grotius declared that "among the traits characteristic of man is an impelling desire for society, that is, for the social life—not of any and every sort, but peaceful, and organized according to the measure of his intelligence, with those who are of his own kind." [11] The source of law, accordingly, is man's innate or instinctive desire for social order. "To this sphere of law belong the abstaining from that which is another's, the restoration to another of anything of his which we may have, together with any gain which we may have received from it; the obligation to fulfil promises, the making good of a loss incurred through our fault, and the inflicting of penalties upon men according to their deserts." [12] Man is not only a social animal but a rational being who "within the limitations of human intelligence" is able to judge between agreeable and harmful alternatives without yielding unduly to fear, "the allurement of immediate pleasure," or to "rash impulse." [13]

In addition to the social nature of man there is another source of law and "that is, the free will of God to which beyond all cavil our reason tells us we must render obedience." [14] Man's desire for the social life and all that that implies is a trait implanted in him by God. Expediency, moreover, reinforces the law of nature "for the Author of nature willed that as individuals we should be weak, and should lack many things needed in order to live properly, to the end that we might be the more constrained to cultivate the social life." [15] Men are driven by their social instinct to associate with one another and by their intelligence and recognition of their mutual dependence to band together by *agreement* into a political community. The basis of civil society is a contract. And "since it is a rule of the law of nature to abide by pacts (for it was necessary that among men there be some method of obligating themselves one to another, and no other natural method can be imagined), out of this source the bodies of

municipal law have arisen." [16] The mother of the law of
nature is the social nature of man but "the mother of municipal law is that obligation which arises from mutual consent;
and since this obligation derives its force from the law of
nature, nature may be considered, so to say, the great-grand-
mother of municipal law." [17] Similarly pacts made by mutual
consent between states are the foundation of the law of nations, the ultimate source of which is nature itself. Municipal
law and international law are conceived to be at once the
product of individual wills, consent, and the embodiment of
natural justice. Obligation to obey the municipal law derives
both from the force of the wills that have consented to it and
from the recognition by individual conscience of its inherent
rightness.

The importance of Grotius' conception of natural law was
methodological. The content he attributed to it was precisely
the content attributed to it by earlier writers. What Grotius
endeavored to do, and in the eyes of his contemporaries with
success, was to provide a *new method* of arriving at this content,
a method that did not depend upon revelation but was, in
seventeenth-century terms, *scientific*. The law of nature he defined as "a dictate of right reason, which points out that an
act, according as it is or is not in conformity with rational
nature, has in it a quality of moral baseness or moral necessity; and that, in consequence, such an act is either forbidden
or enjoined by the author of nature, God." [18] Although reference is made here to God actually it adds nothing essential to
the definition. Grotius makes this clear, when, a little later,
he declares:

The law of nature . . . is unchangeable—even in the sense that
it cannot be changed by God. Measureless as is the power of God,
nevertheless it can be said that there are certain things over which
that power does not extend. . . . Just as even God, then, cannot
cause that two times two should not make four, so He cannot cause
that which is intrinsically evil be not evil. This is what Aristotle
means when he says: "Some things are thought of as bad the moment
they are named." For just as the being of all things, from the time
that they begin to exist, and in the manner in which they exist, is not
dependent on anything else, so also the properties, which of necessity

characterize that being; such a property is the badness of certain acts, when judged by the standard of a nature endowed with sound reason.[19]

A rational system of law, Grotius thought, could be constructed from certain self-evident or axiomatic social principles just as geometry was based upon propositions regarded as axiomatic. Anticipating the formulation of "scientific method" by Descartes, Grotius insisted that we must start our thinking with "those things which we perceive by the external senses," and proceed cautiously to entertain only those simple ideas which "are in themselves manifest and clear." [20] "Because of the prevalence of this idea of good method," Professor Sabine declares, "the seventeenth century became the era of 'demonstrative' systems of law and politics, the purpose being to assimilate all sciences, the social as well as the physical, as much as possible to a form which was believed to account for the certainty of geometry. . . . The reason for the authority which this method acquired lay largely in the fact that it was believed to parallel the processes by which the physical sciences made dazzling progress in the interval between Galileo and Newton." [21]

One reason why Grotius' conception of the law was so readily accepted by his contemporaries was that there was more or less general agreement in the seventeenth century as to what was morally self-evident. Catholics were separated from Protestants over questions of religious forms and authority and there were important theological differences between them but both affirmed essentially the same moral values—what appeared morally axiomatic to the one would appear morally axiomatic to the other. Both would agree, for example, that an obligation to be binding must be freely assumed by the persons bound and that once a promise is made it should be kept. Both would agree as to the intrinsic value of human personality and to the ultimate equality of all individuals. But much of what Grotius and his contemporaries regarded as self-evident was actually a product of the Christian conscience. Although Grotius' appeal was theoretically and ostensibly an appeal to "sound reason" much of what he had to say was acceptable as "sound reason" because it appealed not only to the reason in men but to their Christian conscience. That much of what he had to say appears less reasonable to many persons in the twentieth century than it did in the seventeenth century is due not to the fact that the man of the twentieth century is more reasonable than his seventeenth century ancestors, but that his conscience is less firmly rooted in Christian convictions.

Not only did Grotius secularize the conception of natural law but he developed a conception of natural rights which was to have a profound influence upon all subsequent political thought. Throughout the Middle Ages the reign of law was directed primarily to the preservation of the *status quo* but with the seventeenth century the end of law was conceived more and more in terms of the enabling of individuals to *do* things and to *possess* things. Law was conceived to have more of a dynamic function. A right, Grotius defines as "a moral quality of a person, making it possible to have or to do something lawfully."[22] Although there was some idea of rights peculiar to corporations and groups in the Middle Ages, the idea of natural rights peculiar to individuals first emerged as a definite concept in the seventeenth century, and Grotius was one of the first to define them. These rights which are recognized by natural law and demonstrable by reason belong to individuals by virtue of their humanity—they are qualities inherent in persons and since they belong to an individual because of his nature as a human being they are called "natural" rights. It remained for John Locke to formulate them even more precisely, but with Grotius the conception emerges with definiteness.

## John Locke (1632–1704)

JOHN LOCKE was born at Wrington, North Somerset, England in 1632. His father was a Puritan lawyer who had served as a captain in the Parliamentary army. John Locke was sent to Christ Church, Oxford, where he received his degree in 1658 and was given an appointment as a tutor in Greek, rhetoric and philosophy. Under the influence of Cartesian philosophy and through his friendship with Robert Boyle, the physicist, who was one of the founders in 1663 of the "Royal Society of London for improving natural knowledge," Locke became more and more attracted to the natural sciences and decided to devote himself to the study of medicine.

It was this interest that brought him in contact with Lord Ashley, the founder of the Whig Party, who was later to become Earl of Shaftesbury and Lord Chancellor. He was invited in 1667 to become Lord Ashley's personal physician and went to live with him in London. He was destined to spend the next fifteen years of his life in his company. Locke became more and more interested in Lord Ashley's political activities and came eventually to serve him in a secretarial capacity. Due to poor health he left his service for a period of about four years (1675–1679) when he traveled abroad. When the Earl of Shaftesbury fell under grave political suspicion and was forced to leave England Locke felt himself to be under suspicion and decided like his patron to seek asylum in Holland. He left England in 1683 not to return until 1689 after the downfall of James II. It was during his exile that he first made his appearance as an author. Although he began to publish his works late in life (he was 54 years of age when he began), it was a fruitful and prolific period. He wrote in the fields of science, theology, education, philosophy, and economics as well as politics. His most important philosophical work was his *Essay Concerning Human Understanding* (1690); his most important theological work *The Reasonableness of Christianity* (1695); and his most important political works the *Two Treatises of Civil Government* (1690) and the *Letters on Toleration* (1689).

## Locke's Theory of Knowledge

IN HIS *Essay Concerning Human Understanding* Locke launched a vigorous attack upon the rationalist belief in the existence of innate ideas—a belief common to philosophy since the time of Plato. "It is an established opinion amongst some men," Locke says in the opening sentence of his *Essay*, "that there are in the understanding certain *innate principles;* some primary notions . . . characters, as it were stamped upon the mind of man; which the soul receives in its very first being, and brings into the world with it." [23] That this is an erroneous belief Locke then attempts to demonstrate. "To ask, at what *time* a man has first any ideas, is to ask, when he begins to perceive;—*having ideas*, and *perception*, being the same thing." [24] The human mind at birth, Locke says, is a *tabula rasa*, it is like a white sheet of paper on which nothing has been written.

Let us then suppose the mind to be white paper, void of all characters, without any ideas; how comes it to be furnished? Whence comes it by that vast store which the busy and boundless fancy of man has painted on it with an almost endless variety? Whence has it all the materials of reason and knowledge? To this I answer in one word, from experience: in that all our knowledge is found, and from that it ultimately derives itself, our observation, employed either about external sensible objects, or about the internal operations of our minds perceived and reflected on by ourselves, is that which supplies our understandings with all the materials of thinking. These two are the fountains of knowledge from whence all the ideas we have or can naturally have, do spring.[25]

From experience alone the mind derives its content. The source of our ideas are sensation and reflection. Sense data are partly revelations of external things in their mathematical relations and partly sensations which these evoke within us. The first, he calls primary qualities and identifies them with the "essential qualities of matter" and the sensations he calls "secondary or derived qualities." The primary qualities, such as extension, solidity, position in time, motion, are always present when matter is present; the secondary qualities, such as the sensations of color, odor and sound "are in truth nothing in the objects themselves, but powers to produce various sensations in us" and depend upon the primary qualities. From this Locke draws the conclusion that "the ideas of primary qualities of bodies are resemblances of them, and their patterns do really exist in the bodies themselves, but the ideas produced in us by these secondary qualities have no resemblance of them at all. There is nothing like our ideas, existing in the bodies themselves. They are, in the bodies we denominate from them, only a power to produce those sensations in us: and what is sweet, blue, or warm in idea is but the certain bulk, figure and motion of the insensible parts, in the bodies themselves, which we call so." [26] It follows from this that "the mind . . . hath no other immediate object but its own ideas" and that knowledge is "nothing but *the perception of the connexion of and agreement, or disagreement and repugnancy of any of our ideas.*" [27] Knowledge is simply the perception of the agreement of disagreement of two ideas. Commenting upon Locke's theory of knowledge, Bertrand Russell declares:

In all this, Locke assumes it known that certain mental occurrences, which he calls sensations, have causes outside themselves, and that these causes, at least to some extent and in certain respects, resemble the sensations which are their effects. But how consistently with the principle of empiricism is this to be known? We experience the sensations, but not their causes; our experience will be exactly the same if our sensations arise spontaneously. The belief that sensations have causes, and still more the belief that they resemble their causes, is one which, if maintained, must be maintained on grounds wholly independent of experience. The view that "knowledge is the perception of the agreement or disagreement of two ideas" is the one that Locke is entitled to, and his escape from the paradoxes that it entails is effected by means of an inconsistency so gross that only his resolute adherence to common sense could have made him blind to it.[28]

That experience, in the sense of perception, is the source of all knowledge was a new and a revolutionary doctrine. New, because it denied a philosophical tradition established by Plato and perpetuated throughout the Middle Ages and revolutionary because it exalted individual experience as the *ultimate* source of all knowledge. As Alfred North Whitehead explains Locke's theory:

. . . The primary qualities are the essential qualities of substances whose spatio-temporal relationships constitute nature. The orderliness of these relationships constitutes the order of nature. The occurrences of nature are in some way apprehended by minds, which are associated with living bodies. Primarily, the mental apprehension is aroused by the occurrences in certain parts of the correlated body, the occurrences in the brain, for instance. But the mind in apprehending also experiences sensations which, properly speaking, are qualities of the mind alone. These sensations are projected by the

mind so as to clothe appropriate bodies in external nature. Thus the
bodies are perceived as with qualities which in fact are purely the
offspring of the mind. Thus nature gets credit which should in truth
be reserved for ourselves: the rose for its scent: the nightingale for
his song: and the sun for his radiance. The poets are entirely mistaken. They should address their lyrics to themselves, and should
turn them into odes of self-congratulation on the excellency of the
human mind. Nature is a dull affair, soundless, scentless, colourless;
merely the hurrying of material, endlessly, meaninglessly.[29]

While this theory, as Whitehead points out, has been without
rival in the modern world "as the guiding principle of scientific studies" it is far from satisfactory, since, although useful
for dealing with certain aspects of nature, "it is quite unbe-
lievable." [30] There is always the danger that we may mistake
for a concrete reality that which is a high abstraction. In
Locke's theory of knowledge, Whitehead declares:

The seventeenth century had finally produced a scheme of scientific thought framed by mathematicians, for the use of mathematicians. The great characteristic of the mathematical mind is its
capacity for dealing with abstractions; and for eliciting from them
clear-cut demonstrative trains of reasoning, entirely satisfactory so
long as it is those abstractions which you want to think about. The
enormous success of the scientific abstractions, yielding on the one
hand *matter* with its *simple location* in space and time, on the other
hand *mind*, perceiving, suffering, reasoning, but not interfering, has
foisted onto philosophy the task of accepting them as the most concrete rendering of fact. . . . [But] thereby, modern philosophy
has been ruined. It has oscillated in a complex manner between
three extremes. There are the dualists, who accept matter and mind
as on an equal basis, and the two varieties of monists, those who put
mind inside matter, and those who put matter inside mind. But this
juggling with abstractions can never overcome the inherent confusion introduced by the ascription of *misplaced concreteness* to the
scientific scheme of the seventeenth century.[31]

## Locke's Political Philosophy

IN LOCKE's *Two Treatises of Civil Government*, and especially in
the second of these, liberalism finds perhaps its most detailed

and lucid expression. The treatises have sometimes been described as a rationalization of the English Revolution of 1688 and Locke himself says in his Preface that they were written

to establish the throne of our great restorer, our present King William; to make good his title in the consent of the people; which being the only one of lawful governments, he has more fully than any other prince in Christendom; and to justify to the world the people in England, whose love of their just and natural rights, with their resolution to preserve them, saved the nation when it was on the brink of slavery and ruin.

Yet it might be said that the events of 1688 did as much to justify Locke's treatise as his treatise did to justify the events. If his work was rationalization it was rationalization in the best sense of that word.

Starting from the assumption that men are "by nature all free, equal, and independent" it follows, Locke declares, that no one can be "subjected to the political power of another, without his own consent." So that

the only way by which any one divests himself of his natural liberty and puts on the bonds of civil society is by agreeing with other men to join and unite into a community for their comfortable, safe, and peaceable living one amongst another, in a secure enjoyment of their properties, and a greater security against any that are not of it. . . . When any number of men have so consented to make one community or government, they are thereby presently incorporated, and make one body politic, wherein the majority have a right to act and conclude the rest.[32]

Like many of his contemporaries Locke posited a "state of nature" in which men lived prior to the establishment of civil society. Much argument has exhausted itself over the question whether this state of nature was posited as a convenient intellectual hypothesis or as an historical fact, but actually it makes little difference so far as the conclusions derived from it are concerned. Whether regarded as historical fact or not it is certainly true that it was a convenient hypothetical proposition. In some ways the seventeenth century conception of a "state of nature" was simply a secularization of the Christian "myth" of the Garden of Eden. But whereas the latter sought to depict man as he was originally created by God, the former concept sought to examine the nature of man apart from his divine origin. It looked upon man simply as a creation of nature and sought to lay bare the attributes and characteristics with which "nature" had endowed him.

This examination, performed under the guise of describing the "state of nature" in which man originally lived before civil society came into existence, yielded very different conclusions depending upon the presuppositions about man with which the individual philosopher began his analysis. For Thomas Hobbes, for example, the state of nature was characterized as a "war of all against all" in which life was "nasty, brutish and short."[33] For Rousseau, the state of nature far from being a fearful existence was an idyllic one. For Locke, the state of nature was neither idyllic nor fearful.

For him the state of nature was "a state of perfect freedom" in which each man ordered his actions and disposed of his possessions and person as he thought fit "within the bounds of the law of nature," but "without asking leave, or depending upon the will of any other man." It was a state not only of freedom but of equality "wherein all the power and jurisdiction" was "reciprocal, no one having more than another."[34] It was a state of freedom, not of license, and had

a law of nature to govern it; which obliges every one; and reason, which is that law, teaches all mankind who will but consult it, that, being all equal and independent, no one ought to harm another in his life, health, liberty, or possessions. . . . Everyone, as he is bound to preserve himself, and not to quit his station willfully, so, by the like reason, when his own preservation comes not in competition, ought he, as much as he can, to preserve the rest of mankind, and not, unless it be to do justice on an offender, take away or impair the life, or what tends to the preservation of the life, the liberty, health, limb, or goods of another.[35]

But if the law of nature "which willeth the peace and preservation of all mankind" exist in the state of nature why should anyone want to leave it? "If man in the state of nature be so free, as has been said, if he be absolute lord of his own person and possessions, equal to the greatest, and subject to

nobody, why will he part with his freedom, this empire, and
subject himself to the dominion and control of any other
power?" [36] Several weaknesses characterize this state of perfect freedon and equality: (1) there is lacking "an established,
settled, known law, received and allowed by common consent
to be the standard of right and wrong, and the common
measure to decide all controversies between them. For though
the law of nature be plain and intelligible to all rational creatures; yet men, being biased by their interest, as well as ignorant for want of study of it, are not apt to allow of it as a law
binding to them in application of it to their particular case." [37]
(2) The state of nature lacks a definite and impartial judge
"with authority to determine all differences according to the
established law." Every one is "both judge and executioner"
and we know that a man is not the best judge in his own case.[38]
(3) There is no "power to back and support the sentence when
right, and to give it due execution." [39]

For these reasons, notwithstanding all the advantages of the
state of nature, men are "quickly driven into society." The
basis for the establishment of society is a contract or an agreement whereby individuals "give up the equality, liberty, and
executive power they had in the state of nature into the hands
of the society" but only so far as it is necessary the better to
protect their natural rights to life, liberty and property. Upon
entering society, the individual gives up the right of judging
and executing the law of nature but retains all of the other
rights which he enjoyed in the state of nature. Society, as a
matter of fact, exists solely for the purpose of preserving and
perpetuating these rights.

It is not clear from Locke's argument whether government
comes into being as a result of the contract which established
society or whether a separate contract brings government itself into existence. Most interpreters of Locke believe that he
posited two contracts; one which established society and another which created government. This two-fold contract,
however, is implicit rather than explicit in Locke's argument.
In any case the agreement to form a society leads to the creation of "one body politic, wherein the *majority* have a right to
act and conclude the rest." [40] The agreement to form a com-

munity must, of necessity, Locke argues, include an agreement to submit one's will to the will and determination of the majority "for where the majority cannot conclude the rest, there they cannot act as one body, and consequently, will be immediately dissolved again." [41]

Locke makes it clear, however, that the majority acts only on behalf of the individual and in accordance with "the obligations of the law of nature." Since no one in the state of nature has absolute arbitrary power over himself and since "nobody can transfer to another more power than he has in himself" the legislative power can never claim the right to act in an arbitrary or absolute manner.[42] For

the law of nature stands as an eternal rule to all men, legislators as well as others. The rules that they make for other men's actions must, as well as their own and other men's actions, be conformable to the law of nature, i.e., to the will of God, of which that is a declaration, and the fundamental law of nature being the preservation of mankind, no human sanction can be good or valid against it.[43]

The legislative power may not rule by arbitrary decrees but "by established and promulgated laws; that both the people may know their duty and be safe and secure within the limits of the law; and the rulers too kept within their due bounds. . . ." [44] Nor can the legislative power be transferred or delegated to any one else since such delegation would be a breach of the contract whereby the people established the legislative power. Nor must the legislative power "raise taxes on the property of the people without the consent of the people, given by themselves or their deputies," [45] since the government exists solely for the preservation of the people's "lives, liberties, and fortunes."

That the legislative power of the commonwealth is not absolute Locke makes even more clear in his discussion of the right of revolution in Chapter XIX of the *Second Treatise*. And here, perhaps, is his most original contribution to political theory. That the power of government is restrained by the natural law is an idea long established in the Western political tradition. Locke provided a means of making such restraint *effective* by justifying the right of revolution.

Whensoever, therefore, the legislative shall transgress this fundamental rule of society, and either by ambition, fear, folly, or corruption, endeavor to grasp themselves or put into the hands of any other an absolute power over the lives, liberties, and estates of the people, by this breach of trust they forfeit the power the people had put into their hands, for quite contrary ends, and it devolves to the people, who have a right to resume their original liberty, and by the establishment of the new legislative (such as they shall think fit) provide for their own safety and security, which is the end for which they are in society.[46]

When a government abrogates the natural rights of men for the preservation of which government was established the people have not only the right but the responsibility to revolt and to empower a new government.

But if they who say it lays a foundation for rebellion mean that it may occasion civil wars or intestine broils, to tell the people they are absolved from obedience when illegal attempts are made upon their liberties or properties, and may oppose the unlawful violence of those who were their magistrates when they invade their properties contrary to the trust put in them, and that therefore this doctrine is not to be allowed, being so destructive to the peace of the world: they may as well say upon the same ground that honest men may not oppose robbers or pirates because this may occasion disorder or bloodshed. If any mischief come in such cases, it is not to be charged upon him who defends his own right, but on him that invades his neighbor's. If the innocent honest man must quietly quit all he has for peace's sake to him who will lay violent hands upon it, I desire it may be considered what a kind of peace there will be in the world which consists only in violence and rapine, and which is to be maintained only for the benefit of robbers and oppressors. Who would not think it an admirable peace betwixt the mighty and the mean when the lamb without resistance yielded his throat to be torn by the imperious wolf? Polyphemus's den gives us a perfect pattern of such a peace and such a government, wherein Ulysses, who was a prudent man, preached up passive obedience, and exhorted them to a quiet submission by representing to them of what concernment peace was to mankind, and by showing the inconveniences which might happen if they should offer to resist Polyphemus, who had now the power over them.

The end of government is the good of mankind, and which is best for mankind, that the people should be always exposed to the boundless will of tyranny, or that the rulers should be sometimes liable to be opposed when they grow exorbitant in the use of their power, and employ it for the destruction and not the preservation of the properties of their people? [47]

No doctrine of Locke's had more influence than this doctrine of revolution. It is embodied in our own Declaration of Independence and it provided a justification for the overthrow of tyrants that had long been sought but imperfectly envisaged. It gave substance to the doctrine of popular sovereignty and a means of enforcing the contractual basis of government.

## Locke's Theory of Property

ACCORDING to liberalism there exists a sphere of rights belonging to individuals by virtue of their humanity for the preservation of which the state exists and beyond which the state may not penetrate. These rights, Locke describes, as the natural right to "life, liberty, and property." The greatest of these is property for without property there exists neither life nor liberty. Property is an essential attribute of personality since "every man has a property in his own person." [48] When Locke uses the word property he uses it in a manner very different from current usage. We would come closer to capturing Locke's essential meaning if we translated the phrase "life, liberty, and property" to read "life, liberty, and the fruits of one's own labor." He recognized that to be clothed with substance liberty must include some measure of economic security. But whereas we would say "economic security" Locke says "property."

When God made the world he gave it in common to all mankind "for the support and comfort of their being." He gave it to men for their enjoyment and use but since only individual men can enjoy and use the fruit of the earth there must have been some means provided for its appropriation by individuals. The way individuals appropriate the fruit of the earth for their use is by means of their labor. And it is in this way that property comes about. Property is simply that with which one has mixed his labor.

Whatsoever, then, he [i.e., man] removes out of the state that nature hath provided and left it in, he hath mixed his labor with, and joined to it something that is his own, and thereby makes it his property. . . . For this labor being the unquestionable property of the laborer, no man but he can have a right to what that is once joined to, at least where there is enough and as good left in common to others.[49]

It is the labor expended upon something that makes that thing one's own.

Locke combines with this labor theory of value a theory of limitation based upon man's ability effectively to use that which he has appropriated for his needs. "As much as any one can make use of to any advantage of life before it spoils, so much he may by his labor fix a property in; whatever is beyond this is more than his share, and belongs to others. Nothing was made by God for man to spoil or destroy." [50] Kept "within the bounds, set by reason, of what might serve for his use," Locke believed, there could be "little room for quarrels or contentions about property so established." [51]

Although in the beginning labor established a man's title to property it was by mutual consent, Locke argues, that men surrendered their "natural common right" to property and "by positive agreement, settled a property amongst themselves in distinct parts and parcels of the earth." [52] The use of money as a medium of exchange came into being since it is a "lasting thing that men might keep without spoiling" and which "by mutual consent, men would take in exchange for the truly useful and perishable supports of life." [53] It was this consent to the use of money that gave "men possessions in different proportions." [54] It is thus that men "by a tacit and voluntary consent" have found a way whereby

a man may fairly possess more land than he himself can use the product of, by receiving in exchange for the overplus, gold and silver, which may be hoarded up without injury to any one: these metals not spoiling or decaying in the hands of the possessor. This partage of things in an equality of private possessions men have made practicable, out of the bounds of society, and without compact, only by putting a value on gold and silver, and tacitly agreeing in the use of money. For in governments the laws regulate the right of property, and the possession of land is determined by positive constitutions.[55]

Locke endeavors to argue that property is both, at one and the same time, a natural and a legal right, an attribute of personality and a product of mutual consent. He does not draw all the implications which might be drawn from the labor theory of value—although at a later date many socialist economists were to do so. He does not justify an unlimited right to property and insists that a man has a right only to that which he can make use of before it spoils. But while he does not justify the unlimited appropriation of land he has no objection to the hoarding of money which does not spoil. He did not apparently see any difficulty or any inconsistency in these attitudes. Commenting upon Locke's theory of property Professor Thomas I. Cook declares: "It is interesting . . . that Locke, starting with the idea of the earth held in common and with individuals getting a right to property in consumers' products from their labor in acquiring them and from their ability and need to consume them, ended with the idea of property as a legal and social matter. . . . The astounding fact . . . is that a careful reading of Locke's treatment of the subject shows no real connection between his theory of land ownership in a simple society and his doctrine of a legal right of property in a complex one, where the law rests on consent. Save for his comments on the convenience of money and the utility of deferred consumption, Locke developed no theory of civilized property. He in no sense justified the ownership of capital, in land, or otherwise, beyond the ability of the owner to consume its products and to produce them by his own labor; nor did he justify inequality in a world where there is no longer plenty for all. His doctrine was used, and was intended to justify, individual property as a fundamental right. Though in his mind that right rests on work and ability to consume, his theory served as the justification of 'using' capital effectively or profitably, a very different meaning of 'use' from his original one. Locke ended with the technically correct concept of property as a legal structure, as distinct from physical possession. He also ended with the implication that actual property in an advanced society is largely a social creation

and a matter of social concern: and he concluded that it was
subject to such regulation of use and title as the community
might consent to." [56]


## *The Criteria of Integral Liberalism* [57]

THE word Liberal did not come into use until early in the
nineteenth century and it was not until around 1839 that
the Whig Party in Great Britain came to be referred to as "the
Liberal Party." But liberalism as a political philosophy finds
classic expression in the writings of Hugo Grotius and John
Locke and it was a modified version of this philosophy which
was adopted as the program of the English Liberal Party.
Liberalism defies succinct definition and rather than attempting to express its tenets within the framework of a brief formula
we shall rather seek to identify it by enumerating the attributes which distinguish it. Integral liberalism is characterized
by the following beliefs:

(1) A belief in the absolute value of human personality and the
    spiritual equality of all individuals.
(2) A belief in the autonomy of individual will.
(3) A belief in the essential rationality and goodness of man.
(4) A belief in the existence of certain inalienable rights peculiar
    to individuals by virtue of their humanity. They are commonly
    spoken of as the natural rights to "life, liberty, and property."
(5) A belief that the state comes into existence by mutual consent
    for the sole purpose of preserving and protecting these rights.
(6) A belief that the relationship between the state and individuals
    is a contractual one and that when the terms of the contract
    are violated individuals have not only the right but the re-
    sponsibility to revolt and establish a new government.
(7) A belief that social control is best secured by law rather than
    by command. The law is conceived as being at once the prod-
    uct of individual will and the embodiment of reason. The law
    alone can command and restrain the individual and "govern-
    ment under the law" is the liberal ideal.
(8) A belief that "the government which governs least governs
    best." The government is conceived as having primarily neg-
    ative functions, the protection of the individual in his rights

and freedom in order that he may be free to follow the "dictates of conscience," and the laws of nature.

(9) A belief in individual freedom in all spheres of life (political, economic, social, intellectual and religious). Freedom is conceived as freedom from all authority that is capable of acting capriciously or arbitrarily, freedom to act in accordance with the dictates of "right reason," i.e., with the dictates of natural law as it is revealed to men through natural reason.

(10) A belief in the existence of a transcendental order of truth which is accessible to man's natural reason and capable of evoking a moral response. It is an order requiring both individual thought and will for its realization, i.e., it is a potential order requiring individual thought and will for its translation into actuality. Through his autonomous reason and in the light of his conscience the individual avoids anarchy by translating the principles of this natural order into practice. The choice between order and anarchy devolves upon the individual, and more particularly, upon individual conscience. Thus conscience is the keystone of the liberal doctrine.

Not all of these beliefs are peculiar to liberalism and many of them have a long heritage in the history of Western civilization. The beliefs, for example, in the absolute moral worth of the individual, in the spiritual equality of individuals, and in the essential rationality of man are a heritage from the Middle Ages and have their roots deep in Christian and Greek thought. The ideal of individual freedom under the impersonal rule of law is not a peculiarly modern or liberal ideal. It has a long heritage in Western political thought extending at least as far back as the Stoics in ancient Greece if not even further into the past. There are suggestions of it in Homer.

One of the attributes which distinguishes liberalism from this earlier tradition is the emphasis which it places upon the *autonomous individual*. The passion for the individual which characterizes the climate of opinion ushered in by the Renaissance has no counterpart in classical or medieval thought. It is an outgrowth of the Christian concern for the salvation of individual souls but it is not synonymous with that concern. The idea of man as a "masterless man" is an entirely novel conception. Although God still looms in the thought of classical liberals like Grotius and Locke it is not God who is the starting point of speculation but man, and more particularly, the individual. God tends to be retained more as a logically necessary premise than as the Creator and Preserver of mankind upon whom man is totally dependent for his existence. Having substituted individual experience for revelation, the methods of scientific empiricism for theological speculation, the liberal believed that man must begin his search for order with his own unaided reason and in the Cartesian formula—I think, therefore I am—there is vividly expressed a completely new point of departure for speculation. It is true that the content yielded by this method, at least for the early liberal, was not very different from that yielded by the method of theology so that he could feel secure in a knowledge that was still essentially Christian, although he repudiated the Christian method of illumination. It was his own unaided, natural reason, he believed, which derived the conclusions which in essence were those of the Christian conscience. In its espousal of the *autonomy of human reason* liberalism departs radically from the medieval tradition in which faith sustained reason and gave it direction.

Liberalism also differs from the earlier tradition in its emphasis upon the essential goodness of man. There was little, if any, room for the Christian conception of sin, and the liberal tended to deny, or at least to minimize, the passionate side of man's nature and the corrupting influence of self-centeredness. He tended to equate evil with ignorance and to envisage its cure through education. Through the reform of political institutions, moreover, he believed that the environment could be made more congenial to the expression of man's essentially good will. It was the institutions of men, rather than men themselves that needed reform.

The liberal emphasis upon the *inalienable* rights of the individual was also new. For although the conception of rights implies correlative duties, liberalism tends to emphasize the inalienable nature of these rights rather than the duties which these rights imply. As a matter of fact, the liberal endeavor to ground these rights in the empirical nature of man, in an effort to divorce them from any dependence upon theological considerations, ignored the fact, which soon became apparent, that such rights are not empirically demonstrable. In reality, the rights of man derive not from the empirical nature of man but from the fact that man is a spiritual being created in the image and likeness of God. Men have rights because they have responsibilities which transcend the demands of the natural world. Because these rights are correlative to such responsibilities they are never absolute but relative to the way in which such responsibilities are carried out. One example may illustrate this distinction. The liberals declared that individuals have an absolute and inalienable right to property, a right which under *no* condition can be taken away or curtailed. The Christian tradition, on the other hand, recognized that men have a right to property but declared that that right is relative to the way in which it is used. A man, it said, has a right to property only so long as he serves the common good and shares the use of that property with others. For liberalism the right was regarded as an end in itself.

It was not long, moreover, before tension developed within liberalism as a result of the logical incompatibility of the idea of inalienable rights and the idea of popular sovereignty, especially when that sovereignty was conceived as absolute and unlimited. It was not until the nineteenth century that that tension became acute but it was an inevitable and logical consequence of liberalism's original attempt to combine two contradictory principles.

Liberalism, moreover, sought to erect the state upon the subjective claims of individuals rather than upon objective reality. The atomistic conception of society upon which liberalism erects its theory minimizes, if it does not ignore, the organic nature of the human community and the fact that individuals *of necessity* require one another. The only basis of civil society which the liberal can conceive is a contract or an agreement. "No other natural method can be imagined," Grotius declared, whereby individuals may be obligated to one another. Although, as Locke said, reason "teaches all mankind who will but consult it, that . . . no one ought to harm another in his life, health, liberty or possessions" it is only by an act of will, of consent, that the teachings of reason become practically binding. The individual is conceived as *choosing to assume* this obligation not to harm another by entering into a contract whereby civil society is established. Although impelled by reason the decision is a pure act of will. Conceivably, by another act of will he might repudiate this decision. This possibility is not contemplated by Locke because he cannot envisage man acting contrary to the dictates of natural reason. Men might decide to revolt against a tyrannical government but it is inconceivable to Locke that they would decide to establish a government contrary to the dictates of reason and destructive of natural rights.

Here, then, is another distinctive feature of liberalism. The state is regarded not as a natural necessity arising out of men's needs and social nature with a purpose transcending the subjective wills of individuals but as an artificial instrumentality based on the claims of individuals.[58] Here again is a radical and revolutionary departure from the political tradition that began with Plato and Aristotle. The state exists, not, as Aristotle believed, to make men good, to enable them to live the "good life" but to satisfy their *claims* and to reflect their *will*. This conception did not appear dangerous in any way to the early liberal for it was inconceivable to him that the will of men could be anything other than good or their claims anything other than legitimate. We have witnessed the rise of states in the twentieth century, however, in which the will of men which they reflected was anything but good and the claims they advanced anything but legitimate. And the rise of these states was made possible partly by the conception of the state which was embodied in integral liberalism. The conception of the state as an instrumentality of the will of men contains in itself no limitation upon the way in which that will shall be employed. Without the conception of a final end or purpose for which the state exists the will of men can rapidly degenerate, as it did in fact degenerate, into an irresponsible one.

The logical structure of liberalism may be diagrammatically represented as in the figure which appears on page 115. Now, so long as conscience retains a valid role in the scheme of things liberalism retains its integral character, but with the disintegration of conscience and the denial of the existence of eternal truth and justice the liberal is driven by his own logic to either of two conclusions: to make the sovereign absolute

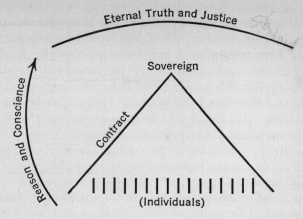

(tyranny) or to make the individual absolute (anarchy). With the acceptance of a positivistic point of view which denies the existence of objective truth and justice the relationship between individuals and the sovereign can no longer be regarded as a contractual one since no means of interpreting the contract are left. With the rejection of metaphysics the positivist rejects at the same time any possibility of evaluating the acts of the sovereign in terms of justice or injustice for justice is a metaphysical concept. Since for the positivist the only rights of individuals are those secured by the positive law, he cannot evaluate the acts of the sovereign in terms of the observance or violation of individual rights. All basis of obligation as a matter of fact disappears. Compulsion is substituted for obligation and the coercive force behind the law becomes the distinguishing characteristic of legality. Thus, ultimately, the liberal who accepts the positivistic perspective has no choice but to make either the sovereign or the individual absolute and his own logic forces him, whether explicitly or not, to an espousal either of tyranny or of unbridled subjectivism.

## *Constitutional Government* [59]

LIBERALISM found practical political expression in the struggle for constitutional government. It was in England that liberalism achieved its earliest and perhaps its greatest victory. It was the commercial middle class that had supported Tudor absolutism in the sixteenth century that led the revolutionary battle in the seventeenth and succeeded in establishing the supremacy of Parliament and eventually of the House of Commons. The distinctive feature of modern constitutionalism was not its insistence upon the idea that the king is subject to the law (although this is an essential characteristic of all constitutionalism) since this was a principle already well established in the Middle Ages, but the distinctive feature of modern constitutionalism was the establishment of effective, political means of control whereby the rule of law might be enforced. When the political doctrine that government rests upon the consent of the government found effective expression in the practice of representative government, modern constitutionalism was born. It was through the "power of the purse" that modern constitutional government came into being. "The principle that 'supply and redress of grievances go hand-in-hand' is the key," Professor McIlwain declares, "to modern constitutional development, and when it was accompanied by the decline of the king's feudal revenues, the growth of representative institutions, and a feeling of national solidarity, it tended to make real and effective the limited, as well as the national, character of kingship." [60]

Perhaps there is no more effective way to illustrate the issues of the Revolution of 1688 than to quote some excerpts from the Bill of Rights of 1689:

(1) That the pretended power of suspending laws, or the execution of laws, by regal authority, without the consent of parliament is illegal.

(2) That the pretended power of dispensing with laws, or the execution of laws, by regal authority, as it hath been assumed and exercised of late, is illegal.

(3) That the commission for erecting the late court of commissioners for ecclesiastical causes, and all other commissions and courts of like nature, are illegal and pernicious.

(4) That levying of money for or to the use of the crown by pretense of prerogative, without grant of parliament, for longer time or in other manner than the same is or shall be granted, is illegal.

(5) That the rights of the subjects to petition the king, and all commitments and prosecutions for such petitioning are illegal.

(6) That the raising or keeping a standing army within the kingdom in time of peace, unless it be with consent of parliament, is against law.

(7) That the subjects which are Protestant may have arms for their defense suitable to their conditions, and as allowed by law.

(8) That election of members of parliament ought to be free.

(9) That the freedom of speech, and debates and proceedings in parliament, ought not to be impeached or questioned in any court or place out of parliament.

(10) That excessive bail ought not to be required, nor excessive fines imposed, nor cruel and unusual punishments inflicted.

(11) That jurors ought to be duly impaneled and returned. . . .

(12) That all grants and promises of fines and forfeitures of particular persons before conviction are illegal and void.

(13) And that for redress of all grievances, and for the amendment, strengthening, and preserving of the laws, parliament ought to be held frequently.[61]

The Revolution was fought not simply to protect the rights of property in a narrow sense but to establish those liberties which the liberal believed essential to human dignity and moral worth. The "rights of man" established by the Revolution of 1688 and enumerated in the Bill of Rights of 1689 gradually were proclaimed beyond the confines of England, notably in the American Declaration of Independence of 1776[62] and in the French Declaration of the Rights of Man of 1789.

The eighteenth century witnessed the emergence of constitutional government in the United States of America and in France, and the nineteenth century saw its extension to Germany, Italy and other nations of the Western world. In every instance peculiar national conditions shaped the particular form which constitutional government took in each of these countries but everywhere throughout the Western world constitutionalism in one form or another and to some degree triumphed over the earlier absolutist regimes.

CHAPTER 5

# The Age of Enlightenment

THE eighteenth century has long been characterized as the Age of Enlightenment. In an essay on the meaning of Enlightenment published in 1784 the German philosopher Immanuel Kant declared that:

Enlightenment is the liberation of man from self-imposed tutelage. Tutelage is the incapacity of using one's own understanding except under the direction of another. This tutelage is self-imposed when its cause lies not in the lack of understanding but in a lack of resolution and of courage. . . . Dare to use your own understanding! That is the motto of Enlightenment.[1]

To be enlightened, Kant declared in another place, is to think for one's self and to think for one's self means "to seek the highest touchstone of truth in one's self, i.e., one's own reason."[2] And the late Professor Ernst Cassirer declared that:

The basic idea underlying all the tendencies of enlightenment was the conviction that human understanding is capable, by its own power and without any recourse to super-natural assistance, of comprehending the system of the world and that this new way of understanding the world will lead to a new way of mastering it.[3]

The leaders of the movement regarded their intellectual labors as the emancipation of men from prejudice, superstition, convention, and tradition. It was an age marked by a passionate avowal of the self-sufficiency of human reason and by a faith in the capacity of men to establish paradise on earth by their own powers and in their own image. Rejecting the orthodox Christian trinity, the enlightened intellectual of the eighteenth century proclaimed his faith in the new trinity of Reason, Nature, and Humanity.

Although it proclaimed itself to be uniquely an Age of Reason it was a particular kind of reason that it exalted. Reason, of course, was not unknown in former centuries nor was the appeal to its authority unique with the eighteenth century. Life in accordance with reason was an ancient ideal long before discovered by the Greeks and passed on as part of their heritage to Western civilization. Nor had reason, as some erroneously suppose, been repudiated by Christianity. The Christian religion teaches that it is through faith in Christ as the embodiment of the reason that governs the universe, that human reason directed in love to God can be trusted to lead men to the truth. St. John speaks of Christ as the Word made flesh, the Incarnation of Wisdom. Christianity does not repudiate reason but subordinates it to the revelation of God's nature in Jesus Christ, thus securing its integrity and giving it direction.

Since a life in accordance with reason was an ideal shared by the ancient Greeks and the Christians, since the appeal to its authority was not unique with the eighteenth century, that century might be more correctly characterized as the Age of Scientific Rationalism, than as the Age of Reason. For the reason to which appeal was made as the ultimate authority, was a reason "freed" from the revelation of God in Christ but bound by the truths of Nature as revealed by the methods of scientific empiricism. It was not that the eighteenth century substituted reason for faith, as some suppose, but that it exchanged one kind of faith for another, a faith in the methods of scientific empiricism for those of theology.

To be "enlightened" was to be freed from God's revelation in Christ, to dispense with "the revelation through Holy Writ and Holy Church." This was indeed, a prominent historian of the eighteenth century, Carl Becker, declares:

the whole point of their high, offensive gesture. Renunciation of the traditional revelation was the very condition of being truly enlightened; for to be truly enlightened was to see the light in all its fulness, and the light in its fulness revealed two very simple and obvious facts . . . the fact that the supposed revelation of God's purposes through Holy Writ and Holy Church was a fraud, or at

best an illusion born of ignorance, perpetrated, or at least maintained, by the priests in order to accentuate the fears of mankind,
and so hold it in subjection. The other fact . . . that God had re-
revealed his purpose to men in a far more simple and natural, a far
less mysterious and recondite way, through his works. To be enlightened was to understand this double truth, that it was not in
Holy Writ, but in the great book of nature, open for all mankind to
read, that the laws of God had been recorded. This is the new revelation, and thus at last we enter the secret door of knowledge.[4]

The eighteenth century, however, did not begin by repudiating the tenets of orthodox Christianity but by converting
them into a "reasonable" religion acceptable to minds enlightened by the new science. Anticipated by Archbishop
Tillotson's writings in the seventeenth century the establishment of a natural theology was given impetus by John Locke's
essay on *The Reasonableness of Christianity* (1695) and his *Discourse on Miracles* (1706). In the place of the traditional creeds
Locke would substitute as the "indispensable conditions" for
salvation: (1) the belief that Jesus is the Messiah, and (2) a
good life.[5] What is the relationship between revelation and
reason? Locke explains it in this way:

A great many things which we have been bred up in the belief of,
from our cradles, and are notions grown familiar (and, as it were,
natural to us) under the gospel, we take for unquestionable obvious
truths and easily demonstrable; without considering how long we
might have been in doubt or ignorance of them, had revelation been
silent. And (thus) many are beholden to revelation, who do not
acknowledge it. It is no diminishing to revelation, that reason gives
its suffrage too, to the truths which revelation has discovered. But
it is our mistake to think, that because *reason confirms* them to us, we
had the first certain knowledge of them from reason and in that
clear evidence we now possess them. The contrary is manifest, in
the defective morality of the Gentiles before our Saviour's time; and
in the want of reformation in the principles and measures of it, as
well as in its practice. Philosophy seemed to have spent its strength,
and done its utmost; or if it should have gone farther (as we see it
did not) and from undeniable principles given us ethics in a science
(like mathematics) in every part demonstrable; this yet would not
have been so effectual to man in this imperfect state, nor proper for
the cure.[6]

Religion adds supernatural sanction and motivation to what natural reason acknowledges to be true and good. Revelation confirms what reason could but did not discover for itself.

It is too hard a task for unassisted reason, to establish morality in all its parts, upon its true foundations; with a clear and convincing light. And it is at least a surer and shorter way, to the apprehensions of the vulgar and the mass of mankind, that one manifestly sent from God and coming with visible authority from him; should, as a king and law-maker, tell them their duties and require their obedience; than leave it to the long, and sometimes intricate deductions of reason, to be made out to them. Such strains of reasoning the greatest part of mankind have neither leisure to weigh; nor (for want of education and use) skill to judge of.[7]

Leslie Stephen, summarizing Locke's views on Christianity, declares:

Here, then, is the thesis laid down by the typical thinker of the age, to be incessantly attacked and defended through the next century. Locke's view of Christianity entirely ignores the aspects of the faith which have in other days been most prominent. A rationalist to the core, he does not even contemplate as possible an appeal to any authority but that of ordinary reason. The truth of Christianity was to be proved like the truth of any historical or philosophical theory. It was simply a question of evidence, and especially of the overwhelming evidence of the Christian miracles. The fact, indeed, that those miracles were wrought in confirmation of a perfect system of morality, made it possible to accept them. But the excellence of that system appeared not from its transcending the limits of human knowledge, but from its entire coincidence with the teaching of the unassisted intellect. Christianity is regarded less as the revelation of the true relation of man to his Maker than as a new promulgation of the moral law. It makes notorious to all men the sanctions by which that law is enforced, and which they had previously dimly conjectured rather than decidedly believed. It regulates the mode in which men are to approach their Creator, and promises assistance in obeying him; but though regulating and systematising the dictates of common sense, it does not—nay, it is its very glory and the proof of its supreme excellence that it does not—run counter to them or materially alter them. No visible outward guardian of the sacred mysteries, and no sublime internal faculty of insight into heavenly things, is necessary to maintain this prosaic but thoroughly sensible religion.[8]

In his discussion of Christianity Locke emphasizes the encouragement which it gives to "a virtuous and pious life." He points out that "virtue and prosperity do not often accompany one another" and that "it is no wonder" that virtue attracted few "in a state where the inconveniences that attended her were visible and at hand, and the rewards doubtful and at a distance." [9] Though men believed vaguely in a future existence beyond the grave before the coming of Jesus Christ *"a perfect complete life of an eternal duration* after this, was what entered little into their thoughts and less into their persuasions. And they were so far from being clear herein, that we see no nation of the world publicly professed it, and built upon it; no religion taught it, and it was nowhere made an article of faith, and principle of religion—till Jesus Christ came: of whom it is truly said, that he at his appearing, 'brought life and immortality to light.' "[10] It is only upon a firm belief in the reality of heaven attested to by Christ's Resurrection and Ascension that "morality stands firm; and may defy all competition. This makes it . . . worth all our aims and endeavours." [11] Thus, in the last analysis, Locke would seem to be arguing that the test of the truthfulness of Christianity is its social utility, i.e., that it provides a foundation for morality that otherwise would not exist. It remained, however, for William Paley, writing at the close of the eighteenth century, to state this conclusion bluntly: virtue consists in "the doing good to mankind in obedience to the will of God and for the sake of future rewards." [12] Or, as it was put more cynically by Voltaire, "if God did not exist, it would be necessary to invent him."

Following Locke's death numerous writings appeared that repeated and extended his arguments on behalf of the reasonableness of Christianity. They argued that Christianity contained nothing contrary to natural reason but defended the "necessity of some particular revelation, to give men full assurance of the truth of those great motives of religion, the rewards and punishments of a future state, which, notwithstanding the strongest arguments of reason, men could not yet forbear doubting of." [13] This "religion of reason," to which the name Deism has been attached, had no enthusiasm for the traditional creeds of Christianity. Doctrine and religious ritual were increasingly regarded as having little or nothing to do with moral conduct and moral conduct was regarded as the sole *raison d'être* of religion. "For modes of faith," the poet Pope declared:

> . . . let graceless bigots fight;
> He can't be wrong whose life is in the right.

The creed of the typical Deist is easily stated. It consisted of three propositions: (1) there exists an omnipotent God, (2) it is His will that men should live virtuous lives, and (3) in a future life He will reward the virtuous and punish the wicked. "To such a pass had the Newtonian world brought the great Christian tradition, with all its passionate feeling and yearning for God," Professor Randall declares, that:

It had become merely a philosophical system appealing to the cool and deliberate reason of the man of common sense, and the inner experience of the presence of the divine, the immediate vision of God's living reality, was condemned as unwholesome "enthusiasm" —the worst sin during the Age of Reason. It is no wonder that mystics heard again the voice of God within the heart, and that the same century saw the great revivals of mediaeval faith that became Pietism in Germany and Wesleyan Evangelicalism in England. But such things were not for the intelligent man, or the middle class; they spread among the lower classes.[14]

Emptied of its spiritual content Christianity was retained, if retained at all, by the typical intellectual of the eighteenth century as a convenient safeguard of morality.

But soon Christianity itself came under direct attack. The pretense of retaining its "essential" elements, while discarding those elements that were extraneous, was dropped. And "natural religion" was proclaimed to be sufficient unto itself requiring neither Christ nor the Gospels as support. Respectful attention was paid to Jesus as a noble man, at least at first, but his Messiahship was denied. "Every man of sense, every good man," the Frenchman Voltaire declared, "ought to hold the Christian sect in horror."

The great name of Deist, which is not sufficiently revered, is the only name one ought to take. The only gospel one ought to read is the great book of Nature, written by the hand of God and sealed with his seal. The only religion that ought to be professed is the religion of worshipping God and being a good man. It is as impossible that this pure and eternal religion should produce evil as it is that the Christian fanaticism should not produce it.[15]

His contemporary Diderot wrote in a letter to a friend, if not for publication:

The Christian religion is to my mind the most absurd and atrocious in its dogmas; the most unintelligible, the most metaphysical, the most intertwisted and obscure, and consequently the most subject to divisions, sects, schisms, and heresies; the most mischievous for the public tranquility, the most dangerous to sovereigns by its hierarchic order, its persecutions, its discipline; the most flat, the most dreary, the most Gothic, and the most gloomy in its ceremonies; the most puerile and unsociable in its morality, considered not in what is common to it with universal morality, but in what is peculiarly its own, and constitutes evangelical, apostolic, and Christian morality, which is the most intolerant of all. Lutheranism, freed from some absurdities, is preferable to Catholicism, Protestantism (Calvinism) to Lutheranism, Socinianism to Protestantism, Deism, with temples and ceremonies, to Socinianism.[16]

Deism perched precariously between orthodox Christianity on the one hand and atheism on the other could not long retain this impossible position. And it was not long before Deism gave way to skepticism and eventually to atheism.

## Skepticism and Atheism in the Eighteenth Century

AT THE end of the seventeenth century Locke had endeavored to combine a belief in "the reasonableness of Christianity" with an empirical theory of knowledge. But despite his arguments it is by no means clear how he could derive the tenets of Christianity from an empirical theory of knowledge. For if, as he contended, there are no innate ideas and all ideas are ultimately but reflections of sensory experience how could he accept, as he did, the miracle of the Incarnation of which he had no direct sensory experience? Although he attacked the theory of innate ideas, he retained certain theological presuppositions for which he was able to provide no adequate theological explanation. This confusion was perpetuated by the eighteenth century but gradually it came to be recognized as confusion and denounced as such. When the inconsistency between the empirical theory of knowledge and the theological presuppositions which Locke had grafted on to it became apparent there was no alternative for those who accepted the empirical theory of knowledge as valid but to discard the theological presuppositions.

It was David Hume (1711–1776) in England who most notably and successfully performed this intellectual operation. We shall have occasion to return to Hume in a later chapter but it may be said here that by adhering strictly to the empirical theory of knowledge formulated by Locke, Hume demonstrated that that theory leads, of necessity, to skepticism. In his own words, he sums up his conclusions in this way:

If perceptions are distinct existences, they form a whole only by being connected together. But no connections among distinct existences are ever discoverable by human understanding. We only feel a connection or determination of thought to pass from one object to another. It follows, therefore, that the thought alone feels personal identity, when, reflecting on the train of past perceptions that compose a mind, the ideas of them are felt to be connected together and naturally introduce each other.

However extraordinary this conclusion may seem, it need not surprise us. Modern philosophers seem inclined to think that personal identity *arises* from consciousness, and consciousness is nothing but a reflected thought or perception. The present philosophy, therefore, has a promising aspect. But all my hopes vanish when I come to explain the principles that unite our successive perceptions in thought or consciousness. I cannot discover any theory which gives me satisfaction on this head. . . .

In short, there are two principles which I cannot render consistent, nor is it my power to renounce either of them; viz., *that all our distinct perceptions are distinct existences, and that the mind never perceives any real connection between distinct existences*. Did our perceptions either inhere in something simple or individual, or did the mind perceive some real connection among them, there would be no difficulty in the case.[17]

The mind, in other words, can never know anything outside itself. Hence, no "comparison of ideas" can ever prove a matter of fact. As a further consequence there are no "necessary connections" between matters of fact but only empirical correlations. All of our reasoning about matters of fact is based upon the theory of cause and effect but this theory, Hume says, has no empirical basis. Convenient though it may be, the notion that there is a *necessary* connection between cause and effect is in reality a fictitious one. All that anyone can say by relying upon empirical observation alone is that one event precedes another or that one event follows another. The moment we label one of these events the "cause" and the other the "effect" we are indulging in metaphysical speculation for which there is no adequate empirical evidence. No one has ever seen one event cause another. What happens is that we observe the conjunction in time of two successive events and from this *infer* a causal relationship. The validity of this inference, however, can never be proven by empirical methods. "In a word, then," Hume declared, "every effect is a distinct event from its cause. It could not, therefore, be discovered in the cause; and the first invention or conception of it, *a priori*, must be entirely arbitrary." [18]

In simple and blunt terms Hume's theory amounted to this: the empirical theory of knowledge does not permit us to penetrate the nature of any ultimate reality. It gives us no real knowledge of the external world. It follows that any knowledge of God, such as Locke insisted was entirely conformable to what could be discovered by "natural reason," is impossible. Since the empirical theory of knowledge neither permits us to prove or to disprove the existence of God it can only lead to skepticism. But if Hume's demonstration of the implications which follow from a thorough-going empirical method do not permit us to accept even the simple propositions of the Deist no more does it provide a satisfactory foundation for natural science. The first part of this was more readily recognized than the latter. Yet in time the devastating character of Hume's

criticism as it applied to natural science had to be recognized
if not resolved. For, according to A. N. Whitehead, "If the
cause in itself discloses no information as to the effect, so that
the first invention of it must be entirely *arbitrary*, it follows at
once that science is impossible, except in the sense of establishing *entirely arbitrary* connections which are not warranted
by anything intrinsic to the natures either of causes or effects." [19] Hume had shown that a method that could be used
to destroy the traditional theological conceptions could be
used with equal efficacy to destroy the "rational" and "natural" concepts which the eighteenth century had sought to
substitute for them. Hume's arguments could give little intellectual comfort to the Deist for he not only attacked the traditional Christian presuppositions but also the presuppositions
of the Deist. In effect, Hume challenged the very foundations
of eighteenth-century scientific rationalism.

Toward the end of the century some sought a refuge from
futility in materialistic atheism. The most extreme expression
of this materialism in the eighteenth century was the Baron
d'Holbach's (1723–89) *Système de la Nature* which was published pseudonymously in 1770. Rejecting the traditional conception of God, denying the immortal soul in man, he sought
an explanation for all things in terms of matter in motion.
Newtonian physics, he believed, contained all that any one
needed to know or could know about man and the universe.
"We cannot go beyond this aphorism," he wrote, "*Matter acts
because it exists, and exists to act.* If it be inquired how, or why
matter exists? We answer, we know not; but reasoning by
analogy of what we do not know, by what we do, we should
be of opinion, it exists necessarily, or because it contains
within itself a sufficient reason for its existence." [20] It is
enough, he says, to know that the world of nature exists. To
inquire why it exists or how it comes into existence is to ask
something that cannot be answered. He "solves" the problem,
if it can be called a solution, by denying that any problem
exists. He argues that it is "more natural and more intelligible to derive everything which exists from the bosom of
nature, whose existence is demonstrated by every one of our

senses . . . than to attribute the formation of things to an unknown force." That nature itself is self-evidently intelligible he assumes without question.

Yet for all his denial of divinity the Baron d'Holbach could not rest content without a God of some sort. Having rejected God as revealed in Jesus Christ he found him in Nature. Personifying Nature and putting these words in Nature's "mouth," the Baron exhorts us to the life of virtue by exclaiming:

> O thou, who following the impulse I have given you, during your whole existence, incessantly tend towards happiness, do not strive to resist my sovereign law. Labor to your own felicity. . . . Dare . . . to affranchise yourself from the trammels of superstition, my self-conceited, pragmatic rival, who mistakes my rights; denounce those empty theories, which are usurpers of my privileges; return under the dominion of my laws, which, however severe, are mild in comparison with those of bigotry. It is in my empire alone that true liberty reigns. Tyranny is unknown to its soil, slavery is forever banished from its votaries; equity unceasingly watches over the rights of all my subjects, maintains them in the possession of their just claims; benevolence, grafted from humanity, connects them by amicable bonds; truth enlightens them; never can imposture blind them with his obscuring mists. . . . Deserter, trace back thy wandering steps to Nature! She will console thee for thine evils; she will drive from thy heart those appalling fears which overwhelm thee. . . . Enjoy thyself, and cause others also to enjoy those comforts, which I have placed with a liberal hand for all the children of the earth, who all equally emanate from my bosom. These pleasures are freely permitted thee, if thou indulgest them with moderation, with that discretion which I myself have fixed. Be happy, then, O man! [21]

The adoration which the Christian reserves for God, the Baron d'Holbach bestows upon Nature. In a hymn of praise whose language is curiously passionate for an age which had repudiated prayer and expressed a marked disdain for "enthusiasm" the Baron offers up these words of homage:

> O Nature, sovereign of all beings! and ye, her adorable daughters, Virtue, Reason and Truth! remain forever our revered protectors! it is to you that belong the praises of the human race; to you apper-

tains the homage of the earth. Show us then, O Nature! that which man ought to do, in order to obtain the happiness which thou makest him desire. Virtue! animate him with thy beneficent fire. Reason! conduct his uncertain steps through the paths of life. Truth! let thy torch illumine his intellect, dissipate the darkness of his road. Unite, O assisting deities! your powers, in order to submit the hearts of mankind to your dominion. Banish error from our mind; wickedness from our hearts; confusion from our footsteps; cause knowledge to extend its salubrious reign; goodness to occupy our bosoms.[22]

The Baron was not so much of an atheist as he supposed. Reason, Nature, and Humanity were the deities he worshipped and the greatest of these was Nature. For the revelation of Holy Writ and Holy Church he would substitute the revelation of Science. With the poet Pope he could say:

> All are but parts of one stupendous whole,
> Whose body Nature is, and God the soul;
> . . . . . . . . . . . . . . . . . . . . . . . . . . . . . . . . . . .
> All Nature is but Art, unknown to thee,
> All Chance, direction, which thou canst not see;
> All discord, harmony not understood;
> All partial evil, universal good:
> And, spite of pride, in erring reason's spite,
> One truth is clear, whatever is, is right.[23]

## *The Religion of Humanity*

HAVING either "watered down" or dispensed with the Christian religion, the Age of Enlightenment sought to find refuge from chaos and nihilism in the religion of humanity. Most of the thinkers of the eighteenth century refused to go as far as Hume had gone; they refused to embrace the skepticism which he insisted was the only logical conclusion to be derived from the empirical theory of knowledge. Skepticism could not satisfy their passions and although they proclaimed themselves to be free of passion they could not deny in fact that they were men; men who were more than thinking machines —men who could and would, love and hate. But having analyzed God as a Personal Being out of existence, having dispensed with the Comforter and Mediator as but a noble example of a "good man" they had no one to worship but themselves. Thus was born the religion of humanity. "For the love of God," Carl Becker says, "they substituted the love of humanity; for the vicarious atonement the perfectibility of man through his own efforts; and for the hope of immortality in another world the hope of living in the memory of future generations." [24]

Man was not, as Christianity had taught, predisposed to evil but, in the words of Rousseau, "good naturally, and . . . by institutions only . . . debased." The remedy for this evil lies not in repentance and a new life but in education and political reform. It is not sin, as the Christians taught, that blocks his path to happiness but ignorance and a faulty environment. Let man but discover the laws of Nature and live in accordance with them and he will find happiness. The "laws of Nature," very conveniently it must be said, were thought to impel the same moral conduct that had for centuries been associated with the Judeo-Greek-Christian tradition. The Golden Rule was discovered to be a law of man's nature. He could no more repudiate it than he could repudiate the law of gravitation for it rested upon the very same foundation. In the words of Bishop Butler:

> Mankind has various instincts and principles of action, as brute creatures have; some leading most directly and immediately to the good of the community, and some most directly to private good. Man has several which brutes have not; particularly reflection or conscience, and approbation of some principles or actions, and disapprobation of others. . . . Self-love and benevolence, virtue and interest, are not to be opposed, but only to be distinguished from each other. . . . There are as real indications in human nature, that we were made for society and to do good to our fellow-creatures, as that we were intended to take care of our own life and health and private good. . . .[25]

Or as Hume declared:

> It appears that a tendency to public good, and to the promoting of peace, harmony, and order in society, does always, by affecting

the benevolent principles of our frame, engage us on the side of the social virtues. And it appears, as an additional confirmation, that these principles of humanity and sympathy enter so deeply into all our sentiments, and have so powerful an influence, as may enable them to exite the strongest censure and applause.[26]

"The essential articles of the religion of the Enlightenment," Carl Becker declares, "may be stated thus: (1) man is not natively depraved; (2) the end of life is life itself, the good life on earth instead of the beatific life after death; (3) man is capable, guided solely by the light of reason and experience, of perfecting the good life on earth; and (4) the first and essential condition of the good life on earth is the freeing of men's minds from the bonds of ignorance and superstition, and of their bodies from the arbitrary oppression of the constituted social authorities. With this creed," moreover

the "constant and universal principles of human nature," which Hume tells us are to be discovered by a study of history, must be in accord, and "man in general" must be a creature who would conveniently illustrate these principles. What these "universal principles" were the Philosophers, therefore, understood before they went in search of them, and with "man in general" they were well acquainted, having created him in their own image. They knew instinctively that "man in general" is natively good, easily enlightened, disposed to follow reason and common sense; generous and humane and tolerant, more easily led by persuasion than compelled by force; above all a good citizen and a man of virtue, being well aware that since the rights claimed by himself are only the natural and imprescriptable rights of all men, it is necessary for him voluntarily to assume the obligations and to submit to the restraints imposed by a just government for the commonweal.[27]

This belief in the essential goodness and benevolence of man coupled with a faith in Science as the true liberator of man's creative capacities, gave birth to the idea of Progress. This idea, a secularized version of the Christian concept of Providence, was one of the dominant ideas of the Age of Enlightenment. Science at last had provided the certain means whereby man by his own efforts might successfully assert his own divinity, achieve the perfection of his being and the establishment of the perfect society on earth. The dream was as old as Adam but never did it seem as likely of realization as it did toward the close of the eighteenth century. That confidence was bequeathed to the nineteenth century as possibly the greatest legacy which the eighteenth century could bestow upon the nineteenth.

Many writers contributed to the fashioning of the idea of progress but none were more successful than the Frenchman, Condorcet (1743–1794). In his *Outline of an Historical View of the Progress of the Human Mind*, published in 1795, he divided history into ten great epochs in which he depicted history as the record of Man's slow but sure struggle against the forces of ignorance and superstition culminating in the Age of Enlightenment and the French Revolution. Are not the French and the Anglo-Americans, he asks, "the most enlightened, most free, most exempt from prejudices" of present-day people? [28] Is it not likely that in time peoples throughout the world might achieve the same state of civilization? What could be more perfect or more desirable? "Such is the object of the work I have undertaken," Condorcet writes, that it will show

. . . from reasoning and from facts, that no bounds have been fixed to the improvement of the human faculties; that the perfectibility of man is absolutely indefinite; that the progress of this perfectibility, henceforth above the control of every power that would impede it, has no other limit than the duration of the globe upon which nature has placed us. The course of this progress may doubtless be more or less rapid, but it can never be retrograde; at least while the earth retains its situation in the system of the universe, and the laws of this system shall neither effect upon the globe a general overthrow, nor introduce such changes as would no longer permit the human race to preserve and exercise therein the same faculties and find the same resources.[29]

Condorcet looks forward with confidence to a future state of humanity in which there will no longer be any inequality among nations nor, indeed, any inequalities within one and the same nation. There are no limits to the improvement which we can, from the past history of man, confidently predict for his future. The perfectibility of man is absolutely indefinite and can never be retrogressive. "If man can predict,

almost with certainty, those appearances of which he understands the laws; if, even when the laws are unknown to him,
experience of the past enables him to foresee, with considerable probability, future appearances: why," Condorcet asks,
"should we suppose it a chimerical undertaking to delineate,
with some degree of truth, the picture of the future destiny
of mankind from the results of its history?

The only foundation of faith in the natural sciences is the principle
that the general laws, known or unknown, which regulate the
phenomena of the universe, are regular and constant; and why
should this principle, applicable to the other operations of nature,
be less true when applied to the development of the intellectual and
moral faculties of man? In short, as opinions formed from experience,
relative to the same class of objects, are the only rule by which men
of soundest understanding are governed in their conduct, why
should the philosopher be proscribed from supporting his conjec-
tures upon a similar basis, provided he attribute to them no greater
certainty than the number, the consistency, and the accuracy of
actual observations shall authorize? [30]

Guided by pure science and experimentation "without a mixture of superstition, prejudice, and authority" we may
eventually arrive at "the moment in which the sun will observe in its course free nations only, acknowledging no other
master than their reason; in which tyrants and slaves, priests
and their . . . instruments will no longer exist but in history
and upon the stage." [31] With the abolition of religious superstition and political tyranny "the means of health and
frugality will be increased, together with the instruments in
the arts of production, of procuring commodities and manufacturing their produce, without demanding the sacrifice of
one enjoyment by the consumer." [32] And as the human race
marches inexorably toward the goal of perfection it may not,
Condorcet believes, be unreasonable to expect that death itself may be postponed indefinitely if not completely eliminated. Is it unreasonable, he asks

to suppose that a period must one day arrive when death will be
nothing more than the effect either of extraordinary accidents, or
of the slow and gradual decay of the vital powers; and that the

duration of the middle space, of the interval between the birth of man and his decay, will itself have no assignable limit? [33]

It is this dream of mankind "marching with sure steps on the road to truth, virtue, and happiness" that "consoles the philosopher for the errors, the crimes, the injustices that still soil the earth, and of which he himself is often the victim.

It is in the contemplation of this picture . . . that he finds his true recompense for virtue. The contemplation of this picture is an asylum in which the memory of his persecutors does not follow him, an asylum in which, living in imagination with mankind re-established in its rights and in its true nature, he can forget mankind corrupted and tormented by greed, fear, envy. It is in this asylum that he truly lives with his fellows, in a *heaven* which his reason has created, and which his love of humanity embellishes with the purest joys.[34]

A note of melancholy creeps into the idea of Progress as the philosopher seeks the consolation of the vision of posterity to obscure his vision of a "mankind corrupted and tormented by greed, fear, envy."

Christian in inspiration the idea of progress was anti-Christian in implication. In contrast to the ancient pagan belief that history is but a meaningless repetition of events in an endless cycle the Jewish and Christian faiths regarded history as having both a beginning and an end. But if the modern world "has assimilated the Christian perspective toward a goal and a fulfillment" it has "at the same time . . . discarded the living faith in an imminent *eschaton*," [35] i.e., the belief in God's judgment and the reality of heaven and of hell. Thus the idea of progress, although derived from "the Christian hope and Jewish expectation" is anti-Christian in implication and consequence. Professor Löwith points out that there is "a basic difference between Christianity and secular futurism," that for the Christian

the pilgrim's progress is not an indefinite advance toward an unattainable ideal but a definite choice in the face of an eternal reality and that the Christian hope in the Kingdom of God is bound up with the fear of the Lord, while the secular hope for a "better world" looks forward without fear and trembling. They have in common, nonetheless, the eschatological viewpoint and outlook into the future as such. The idea of progress could become the leading principle for the understanding of history only within this primary horizon of the future as established by Jewish and Christian faith, against the "hopeless," because cyclic, world view of classical paganism. All modern striving for improvements and progresses, in the plural, is rooted in that singular Christian progress from which the modern consciousness has emancipated itself because it cannot be known and demonstrated by reason as a natural law but only by hope and faith as a gift of grace.[36]

The idea of progress is bound up with the idea that time itself is redeeming, that in time man must *inevitably* become more reasonable, freer, happier, and better. Man himself is no longer conceived as standing before the judgment of God or in need of redemption. Man is impelled by the "laws" of Nature or of History to an end that depends in no sense upon his choices nor his actions. His freedom is an illusion.

## The Science of Political Economy

THE liberalism that found political expression in the political theory of John Locke and in the rise of constitutional government found economic expression in a new "science of political economy." Originated in France by a group of thinkers who were known as the Physiocrats it found classic expression in Adam Smith's *Wealth of Nations* (1776). Like the political liberalism of which it was the counterpart the new science of economics reflected the aspirations and way of life of the merchant and manufacturing middle class. A reaction to Mercantilism it advocated economic freedom—especially freedom from the governmental regulation fostered by the mercantilist theory.

Physiocracy, which means the "rule of nature," was the designation first used by Dupont de Nemours to describe what he defined as "the science of the natural order." [37] Sharing with their contemporaries in the eighteenth century a view of the natural order which was derived from Newtonian physics they "maintained that all social relations into which men enter, far from being haphazard, are, on the contrary, admirably regulated and controlled. To those who took the trouble to think, the laws governing human associations seemed almost self-evident, and the difficulties they involved no greater than the difficulties presented by the laws of geometry. So admirable were these laws in every respect that once they were thoroughly known they were certain to command allegiance." [38] What are these self-evident laws? According to Dupont de Nemours, they

. . . are the rules of justice, of morality, of conduct, useful to all and to each. Neither men nor governments *make* them nor can *make* them. They recognize them as conforming to the supreme reason which governs the universe; they declare them; they present them to the obedience of good men, even to the conscience of the wicked. . . . These laws are irrevocable, they pertain to the essence of men and things; they are the expression of the will of God; and the more one reflects, the more one reveres them. [39]

This natural order is simply "the physical constitution which God Himself has given the universe." [40] It is, it should be noted, a Providential order, "the work of a kind Providence, which desires that the earth should be peopled by happy human beings." [41] By discovering its laws and living in accordance with them one achieves the happiness ordained for him by God. It is a transcendental order, divine in origin, immutable and universal. It is the same for all men in all times and in all places.

Liberty is inseparable, the Physiocrats taught, along with Locke, from property, and the preservation of property is one of the primary duties of the state. "The social laws established by the Supreme Being," according to Dupont de Nemours, "prescribe only the preservation of the right of property; and of that liberty which is inseparable from it.

The ordinances of sovereigns which we call positive laws can be only *acts declaratory of these essential laws of the social order*. If the ordinances of sovereigns were contradictory to the laws of the social order, if they prohibited the respect of property, if they commanded men to burn crops, if they prescribed the sacrifice of little children, they would not be *laws*, they would be insane acts obligatory upon no one. Thus there is a natural judge, a court of final appeal, for the ordinances of sovereigns themselves, and this judge is the evidence of their conformity or their opposition to the natural laws of the social order.[42]

The function of government was simply stated: to secure the individual's natural right to liberty and property. The government should refrain from any interference with the economy since such interference could not but be an arbitrary and unnecessary interference with the laws of the natural order. *Laissez-faire, laissez-aller, le monde va du lui-même*—was their slogan. Let things alone *because* the world is *self-regulating*. As Baudeau said, "Remove all useless, unjust, contradictory, and absurd laws, and there will not be much legislative machinery left after that." [43] Let the state be a policeman, guarding, protecting, punishing but not interfering with the harmonious functioning of Nature.

Unlike Locke and Montesquieu who advocated a separation of governmental powers, the Physiocrats favored a strong absolute monarch combining executive and legislative powers in his own person. They did not favor, however, as some interpreters of their theory suppose, a personal despotism for they insisted that the king should be a law-giver not a law-maker. It is difficult to see in the absence of any practical checks upon the power of the monarch how the absolute monarchy which they advocated could be prevented from degenerating into tyranny but that is quite a different matter from saying that they espoused tyranny. They were, no doubt, naïve in believing that "the personal despotism will only be the legal despotism of an obvious and essential order" but it was their belief that the law not the person was supreme and absolute. Mercier de la Rivière declared that

In legal despotism the obviousness of a law demands obedience before the monarch enjoins it. Euclid is a veritable despot, and the geometrical truths that he enunciates are really despotic laws. The legal and personal despotism of the legislator are one and the same. Together they are irresistible.[44]

As Baudeau explained it: "This supreme will which exercises supreme power is not, strictly speaking, a human will at all.

It is just the voice of nature—the will of God." [45] Like Locke they believed that the law is sovereign, unlike him they saw no necessity for constitutional checks upon the power of the sovereign. Their philosophy basically was not much different from that of the political liberals like Locke and in some ways was more liberal since they followed the tenets of liberalism to their logical conclusion so that the difference between them and political philosophers like Locke and Montesquieu was a difference not in the ends envisaged but in the means best adapted to secure those ends. Their naïveté was not something peculiar to them alone but a consequence of following too literally some of the naïve assumptions latent in liberalism itself. It was Locke's common sense that prevented him from drawing the simple conclusions drawn by the Physiocrats.

The new science of political economy conceived by the Physiocrats culminated in the classic economic liberalism of Adam Smith (1723–1790). His two most important works are his *Theory of Moral Sentiments* (1759) by which he first gained a great reputation and his *Wealth of Nations* (1776). The Physiocrats believed that if individuals were left alone to follow their own enlightened self-interest, economic prosperity would result. Adam Smith shared this optimistic view since he believed, Gide and Rist point out, that "Natural economic institutions are not merely good; they are providential. Divine Providence has endowed man with a desire to better his own condition . . . so that man, following where this desire leads, is really accomplishing the beneficent designs of God Himself." [46] In the spirit of the Age of Enlightenment Adam Smith "discovered" that self-interest and benevolence were in pre-established and harmonious accord. By seeking one's own interest one promotes, by some mysterious process, the welfare of all. The mysterious process is the "invisible hand" of Providence for, as Adam Smith explained it, man, by pursuing his own interest, "is in this as in many other cases led by an invisible hand to promote an end which was no part of his intention." [47] The older commandment: "Thou shalt love the Lord thy God with all thy heart and thy neighbor as thyself" is now amended to read: "Love thyself with all thy heart and God will love thee and look out for thy neighbor." By seeking one's own interest one becomes both the obedient servant of God and a benefactor of one's fellow man. There is no conflict between individual self-interest and social welfare.

Like the Physiocrats, Adam Smith believed that the government which governs least governs best. The state is not suited by its nature to the management of economic affairs. "No two characters seem more inconsistent than those of trader and sovereign," he wrote.[48] There are numerous reasons why this is so. Governments are always spendthrifts, using money earned by others in a wasteful and lavish manner. They are too far removed from the centers of industry to give them the attention which they require. Finally, the agents of government, being paid out of public funds, are generally inefficient administrators. He predicted that if the administration of land should pass into the hands of government that not a fourth of the present produce would be raised because of "the negligent, expensive, and oppressive management" that would ensue.[49]

"Every man, as long as he does not violate the laws of justice," Smith believed, ought to be "left perfectly free to pursue his own interest his own way, and to bring both his industry and capital into competition with those of any other man, or order of men." Accordingly he would restrict the activities of the State to three legitimate functions: (1) "the duty of protecting the society from the violence and invasion of other independent societies"; (2) "the duty of protecting, as far as possible, every member of the society from the injustice and oppression of every other member of it, or the duty of establishing an exact administration of justice"; and (3) "the duty of erecting and maintaining certain public works and certain public institutions which it can never be for the interest of any individual, or small number of individuals, to erect and maintain," because it would be unprofitable.[50]

It should be emphasized that the freedom of economic enterprise which Smith advocated was essentially *individual* economic enterprise. He would have tolerated few of the modern corporations which since his time have largely replaced the individually owned and operated business. Banks, insurance companies, and public utilities were the only kind of joint-stock companies which he believed were desirable, because necessary.[51] He was vigorously opposed to any kind of monopoly, whether corporate or individual. "The whole of Smith's work," Gide and Rist declare, "is a plea for the economic freedom of the individual. It is an eloquent appeal against the Mercantilist policy and a violent attack upon every economic system inspired by it." [52]

Smith was not unmindful of the fact that individuals might often be tempted to conspire against the public good. "People of the same trade seldom meet together," he wrote, "even for merriment and diversion, but the conversation ends in a conspiracy against the public, in some contrivance to raise prices." [53] If the entrepreneur is motivated by personal interest and his actions are checked by competition, however, Smith believed there is no danger to the public in private enterprise.

Commenting upon the influence of Adam Smith's *Wealth of Nations*, Gide and Rist declare:

> To pass a criticism on the labours of Adam Smith would be to review the economic doctrines of the nineteenth century. That is the best eulogy one can bestow upon his work. The economic ideas of a whole century were, so to speak, in solution in his writings. Friends and foes have alike taken him as their starting-point. The former have developed, extended, and corrected his work. The latter have subjected his principal theories to harsh criticism at every point. All with tacit accord admit that political economy commenced with him. . . . Smith persuaded his own generation and governed the next.[54]

## The Science of Government

WITH the possible exception of Rousseau, the greatest political philosopher produced by France in the Age of Enlightenment was Montesquieu (1689–1755), born Charles Louis de Secondat at the Château de la Brède near Bordeaux. Born into the ranks of the lesser nobility he enjoyed a quiet life of ease devoted to scholarship, to writing and to the dispensing of justice in Bordeaux. When he was 27 years of age he inherited from an uncle the title of Baron de la Brède et de Montesquieu, a large fortune and an important judicial office in Bordeaux. His first published work, the *Persian Letters*, were issued anonymously in 1721. Consisting of satirical comments on the customs of his day and society, they earned him a reputation as a wit. He wrote a number of other things including a philosophy of history published in 1734 but his greatest and most lasting work was *L'Ésprit des Lois* (The Spirit of the Laws) published after a life-time of study in 1748. He records the fact that it took him nineteen years to write it. In the preface to this work he says: "I have not drawn my principles from my prejudices, but from the nature of things. . . . Every nation will find here the reasons on which its maxims are based."

Born in an age that was captivated by the success of the Newtonian physics in dispelling the mysteries of the universe he was one of the first to envisage the possibility of a natural science of government. In that sense he anticipated the historical and evolutionary schools of political thought of the nineteenth century and was a harbinger of the positivistic climate of opinion that was destined to become the dominant one in the centuries that followed. His method of analysis resembled that which today we would call "sociological," and it is this method which many think is his greatest contribution.

As a political philosopher he endeavored to do for France what Locke had done for England in the seventeenth century. A liberal, his first concern was with individual freedom and he endeavored to discover the checks on political authority by means of which it might be secured. To this end he developed a theory of the separation of powers which has had far-reaching influence.

Montesquieu begins his treatise on *The Spirit of the Laws* by declaring that the entire universe is regulated by laws: "all beings have their laws: the Deity His laws, the material world its laws, the intelligences superior to man their laws, the beasts their laws, man his laws." Laws, he says, in the broadest sense of the word, "are the necessary relations arising from the nature of things." [55] There is nothing capricious or arbitrary about the universe, it is governed by invariable laws of cause and effect, for if it were not so "it would inevitably perish."

Behind positive law there are principles of justice to which positive law ought to conform if it is to be truly law. "To say that there is nothing just or unjust but what is commanded or forbidden by positive laws, is the same as saying that before the describing of a circle all the radii were not equal. We must therefore acknowledge relations of justice antecedent to the positive law by which they are established. . . ." [56] But the world of man is not as well governed as is the physical universe because, although the laws of the world of man are just as invariable as physical laws, man does not conform to them "so exactly" as things conform to physical laws. "This is because, on the one hand, particular intelligent beings are of a finite nature, and consequently liable to error; and on the other, their nature requires them to be free agents." [57] The greater man's knowledge the better he will be governed by nature's laws. Ignorance is the greatest obstacle to real freedom.

Before men lived in society they lived in a state of nature. In this state man had no knowledge but only the potentiality for learning. Feeling weak and impotent, gripped by excessive fears man was like a savage "trembling at the motion of a leaf, and flying from every shadow." His first concern, as a consequence, would be security and "peace would be the first law of nature." The second concern of man in the pre-social state of existence would be the satisfaction of his wants. "Hence another law of nature would prompt him to seek for nourishment." And "the attraction arising from the difference of sexes" would lead him, also, to seek the association of others and this "natural inclination . . . would form a third law." A fourth law of nature results from man's social predisposition, the desire fostered by reason in the light of these other laws, to live in society.[58]

But as soon as man enters society (Montesquieu says nothing about a contract) "he loses the sense of his weakness; equality ceases, and then commences the state of war." This war breaks out not only between individuals but between different nations. As a consequence of this strife three kinds of law arise: political law, governing the relations of the governors to the governed; civil law, governing the relations of one individual to another; and the law of nations, governing the relations between nations.[59] The desire for self-preservation interpreted in the light of reason is the foundation of all these laws. "Law in general is human reason" and "the political and civil laws of each nation ought to be only the particular cases in which human reason is applied." Such laws "should be adapted . . . to the people for whom they are framed" since what is suitable for one people may not be suitable for another. Moreover, "they should be in relation to the climate of each country, to the quality of its soil, to its situation and extent, to the principal occupation of the natives . . . they should have relation to the degree of liberty which the constitution will bear; to the religion of the inhabitants, to their inclinations, riches, numbers, commerce, manners, and customs." [60]

Montesquieu then proceeds to delineate in some detail the "spirit of the laws" appropriate to different societies. He distinguishes three species of government: republican, monarchical, and despotic. The republican form of government may be either democratic or aristocratic, it is republican when the supreme power is lodged in the people or a part of the people. When it is possessed by the entire body of the people it is democratic, when the supreme power is lodged in only a part of the people it is aristocratic. A monarchy is a government "in which a single person governs by fixed and established laws"; and a despotic government is "that in which a single person directs everything by his own will and caprice." [61] Each of these forms has its own peculiar structure and is animated by a particular virtue or principle peculiar to it.

It is a fundamental maxim of democracy that the people should choose their magistrates but it does not follow that every citizen should be regarded as qualified for public office. "As most citizens have sufficient ability to choose, though unqualified to be chosen, so the people, capable of calling others to an account for their administration, are incapable of conducting the administration themselves." [62] The great danger in democracy is that the people may forget this fact: that although all are qualified to choose not all are qualified to be chosen. Hence, in a democracy virtue must be the animating principle for

when virtue is banished, ambition invades the minds of those who are disposed to receive it, and avarice possesses the whole community. The objects of their desires are changed; what they were fond of before has become indifferent; they were free while under the restraint of laws, but they would fain now be free to act against law; and as each citizen is like a slave who has run away from his master, that which was a maxim of equity he calls rigor; that which was a rule of action he styles constraint; and to precaution he gives the name of fear. Frugality, and not the thirst for gain, now passes for avarice. Formerly the wealth of individuals constituted the public treasure; but now this has become the patrimony of private persons. The members of the commonwealth riot on the public spoils, and its strength is only the power of a few, and the license of many.[63]

By virtue Montesquieu says he means "love of the republic" and by love of the republic he means love of equality and of frugality.

The love of equality in a democracy limits ambition to the sole desire, to the sole happiness, of doing greater services to our country than the rest of our fellow-citizens. They cannot all render equal services, but they ought to serve her with equal alacrity. . . . The love of frugality limits the desire of having to the study of procuring necessaries to our family, and superfluities to our country. Riches give a power which a citizen cannot use for himself, for then he would be no longer equal.[64]

Well-regulated democracies, therefore, will foster by their laws, institutions and education love of equality and of frugality. They will seek to prevent extremes of wealth and poverty not in order to establish exact equality but to prevent gross inequality.

Although virtue is desirable in an aristocracy it is not "absolutely requisite." Virtue is certainly necessary in the body of the people who govern but since the entire people do not have the same power which they have in a democracy it is not so necessary for the entire body to possess virtue. "The nobles form a body, who by their prerogatives, and for their own particular interest, restrain the people; it is sufficient that there are laws in being to see them executed." But how are the nobles to restrain themselves? It is clear that they can be restrained only by "moderation . . . founded on virtue." [65] "The spirit of moderation is what we call virtue in an aristocracy; it supplies the place of the spirit of equality in a popular state." [66] An aristocracy will be characterized by "modesty and simplicity of manners." "In aristocratic governments there are two principal sources of disorder: excessive inequality between the governors and the governed; and the same inequality between the different members of the body that governs. From these two inequalities, hatreds and jealousies arise, which the laws ought ever to prevent or repress." [67]

In a monarchy the animating principle is honor. The ambition which "is pernicious in a republic" has in a monarchy "some good effects" if it is an ambition stimulated by a desire for that which is honorable.

It is with this kind of government as with the system of the universe, in which there is a power that constantly repels all bodies from the centre, and a power of gravitation that attracts them to it. Honor sets all the parts of the body politic in motion, and by its very action connects them; thus each individual advances that public good, while he only thinks of promoting his own interest. . . . There is nothing so strongly inculcated in monarchies, by the laws, by religion and honor, as submission to the prince's will; but this very honor tells us that the prince never ought to command a dishonorable action, because this would render us incapable of serving him. . . .

There is nothing that honor more strongly recommends to the nobility than to serve their prince in a military capacity. And, indeed, this is their favorite profession, because its dangers, its success, and even its miscarriages are the road to grandeur. . . .

It insists also that we should be at liberty either to seek or to reject employments, a liberty which it prefers even to an ample fortune.

Honor, therefore, has its supreme laws, to which education is obliged to conform. The chief of these are, that we are permitted to set a value upon our fortune, but are absolutely forbidden to set any upon our lives.

The second is, that when we are raised to a post or preferment, we should never do or permit anything which may seem to imply that we look upon ourselves as inferior to the rank we hold.

The third is, that those things which honor forbids are more rigorously forbidden, when the laws do not concur in the prohibition; and those it commands are more strongly insisted upon, when they happen not to be commanded by law.[68]

When writing on the monarchy as a form of government Montesquieu sometimes seems to be writing with his tongue in his cheek as when he declares, for example, that "The laws ought to favor all kinds of commerce consistent with the constitution, to the end that the subjects may, without ruining themselves, be able to satisfy the continual cravings of the prince and his court." [69]

A despotism, being one in which a single person directs everything according to his own will and caprice, knows neither virtue nor honor. "As virtue is necessary in a republic, and in a monarchy honor, so fear is necessary in a despotic government." [70] Motivated generally by wrath or vengeance, a tyrant has no notion of true honor or glory. The preservation of the state means nothing more than the preservation of his person.

Politics, with its several springs and laws, must here be very much limited; the political government is as simple as the civil.

The whole is reduced to reconciling the political and civil administration to the domestic government, the officers of the state to those of the seraglio. . . .

As fear is the principle of despotic government, its end is tranquility; but this tranquility cannot be called a peace; no, it is only the silence of those towns which the enemy is ready to invade.

Since strength does not lie in the state, but in the army that founded it, in order to defend the state the army must be preserved, how formidable soever to the prince. . . .

After what has been said, one would imagine that human nature should perpetually rise up against despotism. But, notwithstanding the love of liberty so natural to mankind, notwithstanding their innate detestation of force and violence, most nations are subject to this very government. This is easily accounted for. To form a moderate government, it is necessary to combine the several powers; to regulate, temper, and set them in motion; to give, as it were, ballast to one, in order to enable it to counterpoise the other. This is a masterpiece of legislation, rarely produced by hazard, and seldom attained by prudence. On the contrary, a despotic government offers itself, as it were, at first sight; it is uniform throughout; and as passions only are requisite to establish it, this is what every capacity may reach.[71]

As virtue reigns in republican forms of government, honor in monarchical, so terror reigns in those that are despotic. Montesquieu gives considerable attention, following Bodin, to the influence of climate upon forms of government and reaches the conclusion that despotism and slavery are more common to southern climates than to northern ones.[72]

Although Montesquieu is generally said to have had no preference for one form of government over another, that that government is best which is best adapted to the people for whom it is designed, nevertheless he was not indifferent to the *end* which all governments ought to serve. For like all liberals he was a partisan of liberty and was concerned to discover the most appropriate means by which that liberty might be secured. Although he points out that people in different times and places have conceived of liberty in very different ways, that "they have all applied the name of liberty to the government most suitable to their own customs and inclinations" and sought to identify liberty with the particular form of government they have happened to have or preferred, nevertheless, liberty has a *meaning* which is the same for all.

In a philosophic sense "liberty consists in the free exercise of the will"; [73] in a political sense it consists of the power of doing what we ought to will and in not being constrained to do what we ought not to will. "Political liberty does not consist in an unlimited freedom . . .," Montesquieu declares, but "is a right of doing whatever the laws permit. . . ." [74] Although "all governments have the same general end. . . . One nation there is . . . in the world that has for the direct end of its constitution political liberty." [75] That nation he believed was England. And he believed that he had discovered there the principle on which this liberty is founded: the prin-

ciple of the separation of powers. Although the Revolution of
1688 had established the supremacy of Parliament it had not
established the separation of powers which Montesquieu
professed to discern in the new constitution but if he was
confused about it so were many others, including many
Englishmen. In any case he propounded a theory of the separation of powers which, whether descriptive of actual conditions in England or not, was destined to play a prominent role
in political theory and practice thereafter.

In an oft quoted passage from Book XI of his treatise he
describes this theory in this way:

In every government there are three sorts of power: the legislative;
the executive in respect to things dependent on the law of nations;
and the executive in regard to matters that depend on the civil law.

By virtue of the first, the prince or magistrate enacts temporary or
perpetual laws, and amends or abrogates those that have been already enacted. By the second, he makes peace or war, sends or receives embassies, establishes the public security, and provides against
invasions. By the third, he punishes criminals, or determines the
disputes that arise between individuals. The latter we shall call
the judiciary power, and the other simply the executive power of
the state.

The political liberty of the subject is a tranquility of mind arising
from the opinion each person has of his safety. In order to have this
liberty, it is requisite the government be so constituted as one man
need not be afraid of another.

When the legislative and executive powers are united in the same
person, or in the same body of magistrates, there can be no liberty;
because apprehensions may arise, lest the same monarch or senate
should enact tyrannical laws, to execute them in a tyrannical manner.

Again, there is no liberty, if the judiciary power be not separated
from the legislative and executive. Were it joined with the legislative,
the life and liberty of the subject would be exposed to arbitrary control; for the judge would be then the legislator. Were it joined to the
executive power, the judge might behave with violence and oppression.

There would be an end of everything, were the same man or the
same body, whether of the nobles or of the people, to exercise those
three powers, that of enacting laws, that of executing the public
resolutions, and of trying the causes of individuals.[76]

The legislative power should reside in the whole body of the people but it should be exercised by representatives who have a capacity for the discussion of public affairs. Representative government is preferable to pure democracy since the people collectively are not properly qualified to partake of this discussion. Yet everyone should have "the right of voting at the election of a representative, except such as are in so mean a situation as to be deemed to have no will of their own." [77] Though a man himself may not be qualified to serve as a representative he is able to choose those who are better qualified. The legislative power, moreover, ought to be exercised by a bicameral body consisting of representatives chosen by the people and of persons distinguished by "birth, riches, or honors." Each will act as a check upon the other; the one checking "the licentiousness of the people," the other checking "any encroachment of their freedom." But since the hereditary nobility might be tempted to disregard the interests of the people "they should have no other share in the legislation than the power of rejecting, and not that of resolving," i.e., the veto power upon acts established by the representatives of the people.[78]

Montesquieu would place the executive power in the hands of a monarch "because this branch of government, having need of dispatch, is better administered by one than by many." To entrust the executive power to persons selected from the legislative body would be the end of liberty, he believed. Actually, of course, this is what happened in England but not with the loss of liberty.

The judicial power ought

to be exercised by persons taken from the body of the people at certain times of the year, and consistently with a form and manner prescribed by law, in order to erect a tribunal that should last only so long as necessity requires. By this method the judicial power, so terrible to mankind, not being annexed to any particular state or profession, becomes, as it were, invisible. People have not then the judges continually present to their view; they fear the office, but not the magistrate.[79]

The importance of Montesquieu's theory of the separation of powers lies not so much in the details with which he elaborated it as in the idea itself and with the compelling arguments he provided for its adoption in practice. The idea of mixed government was an ancient one and Locke, too, had spoken of the separation of powers but Montesquieu's contribution was the idea that this separation of powers should be provided for constitutionally with a system of checks and balances. It was in America, however, rather than in England that that system was adopted as a part of the constitutional fabric of the state.

## Political Philosophy in America in the Eighteenth Century

LIBERALISM in America, although generally and rightly associated with the names of Tom Paine, Thomas Jefferson and Benjamin Franklin had its origins in the philosophies of men like Thomas Hooker, Roger Williams and John Wise.[80] The transition from the era of Puritan theocracy to liberal constitutionalism was a gradual one. There was no sharp break between the two periods but the one developed out of the other as the idea of consent latent in the orthodox Puritan conception of the Church gradually overshadowed in importance the Calvinistic idea of foreordination and the doctrine of the elect.

The first stirrings of liberalism in America might be said to have found specific expression in the *Survey of the Summe of Church Discipline* (1648) written by Thomas Hooker (1586–1647), the founder of Connecticut. Hooker was no religious radical but one who accepted without question the Calvinist theology and ethics. But unlike many orthodox Puritans he did not believe that the Calvinist doctrine of predestination implied the establishment of a theocracy. It is known only to God, he insisted, who will be saved. No one can claim with any assurance to being among the elect, hence no one can claim to be better qualified than anyone else to decide policy on earth. Certainly no one can claim to have a mandate from God to do so.

He then presented arguments for the democratic organization of the Church, arguments that anticipated in many striking ways the political theory of John Locke forty years later. The orthodox Puritans defined a church as "a company of people combined together by covenant for the worship of God." Implicit in this definition is the doctrine of consent, i.e., the idea that the church is an instrument of the people created by them for purposes shared by each. Even when the doctrine of the elect overshadowed the more democratic elements in this conception of the church it was admitted in theory, at least, by the orthodox Puritans that although their authority came from God their power rested upon the consent of the governed.

It was the doctrine of consent latent in the orthodox Puritan conception of the church that Hooker emphasized. According to him, "Every spiritual or ecclesiastical corporation receives its being from a spiritual combination." It is the will of each member to combine with others in a mutual undertaking that furnishes "the cement which solders them all." "There is no man constrained to enter into such a condition, unless he will; and he that will enter, must also willingly bind and engage himself to each member of that society to promote the good of the whole, or else a member he is not." [81] According to Hooker the distinguishing mark of the church covenant is the fact that it is based upon freedom of the will and it is the voluntary nature of the agreement to combine for the worship of God that not only authorizes the association but sets limits to it. In a sermon delivered on May 31, 1638, he said: "the choice of public magistrates belongs unto the people by God's own allowance." But he emphasized that the privilege of electing magistrates should not be "exercised according to their humors, but according to the blessed will and law of God." "Mutual subjection," he declared, "is, as it were, the sinew of society, by which it is sustained and supported." It follows as a consequence that the people have "the power to appoint officers and magistrates" and "to set the bounds and limitations" of the power entrusted to these officers.[82]

Desirous of putting these principles into practice Thomas Hooker left Massachusetts Bay Colony in order to establish a new society in Connecticut. One of his first acts was the draw-

ing up of a constitution, the now famous Fundamental Orders
of Connecticut (1639) which have been called "the first
written constitution of modern democracy." The Orders dispensed with the usual property and religious qualifications for
voting, and provided for town-meeting government and for
popularly elected assemblies.

The struggle with the autocratic theocracy which Hooker
began, Roger Williams (1603–1684) continued. So disturbing
did the leaders in Massachusetts Bay find him that he was
banished from the colony in 1635 and shortly thereafter
founded a new colony in Providence, Rhode Island. From
there he carried on a heated controversy by pen with John
Cotton, his most important writings consisting of *The Bloudy
Tenent of Persecution for Cause of Conscience* (1644) and *The
Bloudy Tenent yet more Bloudy* (1652). Three major ideas dominated his writings: (1) the contractual nature of government,
(2) the separation of church and state, and (3) the need for
religious toleration.

Government, he taught, rests upon consent; it is established
by mutual agreement although ordained by God to conserve
peace and to protect the people's bodies and goods. Established by the people for definite ends government is consequently limited in what it can do. "Every lawful magistrate
whether succeeding or elective, is not only the Minister of
God, but the Minister or servant of the people also (what
people or nation soever they be all the world over), and that
Minister or Magistrate goes beyond his commission who inter-
meddles with that which cannot be given him in commission
from the people. . . ." [83] "The Sovereign power of all civil
authority is founded in the consent of the People that every
Commonwealth hath radically and fundamentally. The very
Commonweales, Bodies of People . . . have fundamentally
in themselves the Root of Power, to set up what Government
and Governors they shall agree upon." [84]

Church and state should be separate, each has its own peculiar function and the weapons appropriate to it. Since the
true church is spiritual in nature its weapons should be exclusively spiritual; it should not expect or demand the state to
use its power for its support and preservation. God does not

require uniformity of religion. He does not require that any civil government enforce any particular religious creed or practice and any attempt to enforce such uniformity will ultimately lead to civil war. The church is a corporate body with corporate rights and its legal status is no different from that of any other corporate body. The state is no more concerned with the character of its membership or with the purposes that unite the members than it is concerned with those of other corporations.

It is the will and command of God, that . . . a permission of the most Paganish, Jewish, Turkish, or Antichristian consciences and worships be granted to all men in all nations and countries and they only are to be fought against with that Sword which is only (in Soul matters) able to conquer, to wit, the Sword of God's Spirit, the Word of God. True civility and Christianity may both flourish in a state or Kingdom, notwithstanding the permission of divers and contrary consciences, either of Jew or Gentile.[85]

It was John Wise (1652–1725) who was the first successfully to attack the New England theocracy from within the borders of Massachusetts Bay. That he was able to remain in Massachusetts Bay was an indication that the theocracy there was already in decline. As a Congregational minister in Ipswich he waged unrelenting intellectual warfare upon the Presbyterianism of Cotton Mather. An advocate of ecclesiastical democracy he sought to justify the principle of Congregationalism by using arguments derived from political theory. Most of his arguments he got from Pufendorf's *De Jure Naturae et Gentium* (1672) rather than from Locke whose writings he seems not to have known. In 1710 Wise published his *Churches Quarrel Espoused* and a few years later his *Vindication of the Government of New England Churches* (1717).

All men are free by natural right, he argued.

Every man ought to be conceived to be perfectly in his own power and disposal, and not to be controlled by the authority of any other. And thus every man must be acknowledged equal to everyman, since all subjection and all command are equally banished on both sides; . . . every man has a prerogative to judge for himself, namely what shall be most his behoof, happiness, and well-being.

Does this mean that men are free from *all* authority? No; for all men are subject to the authority of God and to those ordinances of reason which are the embodiment of God's will. Men should be freed from all arbitrary and personal compulsion in order that they might be free to follow the dictates of reason. For by giving men the faculty of reason "God has provided a rule for men in all their actions, obliging each one to the performance of that which is right, not only as to justice, but likewise as to all other moral virtues, the which is nothing but the dictates of right reason founded in the soul of man."

Now, "if every man could secure himself singly, it would be great folly for him to renounce his natural liberty" but since each man cannot secure himself he finds it necessary to band together with others for the protection of his rights. Hence "the end of all good government is to cultivate humanity and promote the happiness of all and the good of every man in his rights, his life, liberty, estate and honor without injury or abuse to any." [86]

In an effort to discover which form of government "can with the best show of reason be predictable of the church of Christ on earth" Wise then examines monarchy, aristocracy and democracy. Which is best: the monarchial form as exhibited in episcopacy, the aristocratic form as found in Presbyterianism, or the democratic form as embodied in Congregationalism? The monarchial form he dismisses as being self-evidently contrary to reason—"God and wise nature were never propitious to the birth of this monster." The aristocratic form, that is, government by a "select company of choice persons," might be justified if "we could be assured that they would make the Scripture, and not their private will the rule of their personal and ministerial actions" but, in practice, he thought, we can have no such assurance.[87] Democracy is a much safer form of government since each man is a better guardian of his own liberty than others would be for him. Democracy, accordingly, he finds consonant with God's purpose and the dictates of right reason.

While Wise was primarily concerned with democratizing church government he used arguments that were to prove fruitful and useful in the establishment of more democratic civil government. It is a short step from the philosophy of Wise to that of Jefferson and the Declaration of Independence.

The Declaration of Independence which reads, it has been said, like a transcript of Locke's second *Treatise of Civil Government* was not original in its ideas nor intended to be. Its author, Thomas Jefferson, writing to Lee in 1825 said:

I did not consider it as any part of my charge to invent new ideas altogether and to offer no sentiment which had ever been expressed before. . . . Not to find out new principles, or new arguments, never before thought of, not merely to say things which had never been said before; but to place before mankind the common sense of the subject, in terms so plain and firm as to command their assent. . . . Neither aiming at originality of principles or sentiments, nor yet copies from any particular and previous writing, it was intended to be an expression of the American mind. . . . All its authority rests then on the harmonizing sentiments of the day, whether expressed in conversation, in letters, in printed essays, or the elementary books of public right, as Aristotle, Cicero, Locke, Sidney, etc.[88]

Premised upon the presuppositions of the Age of Enlightenment the Declaration of Independence declares:

We hold these truths to be self-evident, that all men are created equal, that they are endowed by their Creator with certain unalienable Rights, that among these are Life, Liberty and the pursuit of Happiness. That to secure these rights, Governments are instituted among Men, deriving their just powers from the consent of the governed, That whenever any Form of Government becomes destructive of these ends, it is the Right of the People to alter or to abolish it, and to institute new Government, laying its foundation on such principles and organizing its powers in such form, as to them shall seem most likely to effect their Safety and Happiness.[89]

Following this Declaration of Independence from Great Britain the various colonies having become independent states adopted constitutions defining and limiting the powers of government. Explicitly or implicitly all of them emphasized the voluntary character of government and the doctrine of popular sovereignty. Thus, the Massachusetts Constitution of 1780 declares: "The body-politic is formed by a voluntary association of individuals; it is a social compact by which the whole people covenants with each citizen and each citizen with the whole people that all shall be governed by certain laws for the common good."

The period following the American Revolution was a turbulent one which seemed to many contemporary observers to border on anarchy. "There are combustibles in every State," Washington wrote in 1786, "which a spark might set fire to. Good God! Who, besides a Tory, could have foreseen, or a Briton predicted them?" The Revolution had unleashed passions which were not easily bridled and the newly United States found themselves seriously threatened with disunity. Political leaders began to call attention to the weaknesses of the Articles of Confederation which had been adopted by the Continental Congress in 1777 (it was ratified and put into effect in 1781) "the better to secure and perpetuate mutual friendship and intercourse among the people of the different states." Since the Articles actually provided for a league of sovereign states rather than for one general government of the entire people and since the central government which it created had no power to enforce its decisions however limited in scope, to levy taxes or to regulate commerce between the states, there was much talk of amending the Articles and some suggestion that an entirely new government was required to cope with the situation. Hence it was that in 1787 delegates representing the states were selected to attend a Convention in Philadelphia for the purpose of considering the defects of the Articles and proposing remedies.

The adoption of the Constitution and its subsequent ratification by the state conventions to which it was submitted might with reason be characterized as the "second American Revolution" or, at least, as the second phase of the American Revolution. For its adoption and ratification was a revolutionary act—the Articles of Confederation were not amended but replaced, the government established by the Articles being dissolved rather than reformed.

The events of the times had converted many of the Revolutionary radicals to a more conservative point of view and it was in this light that the Constitution was framed. Yet for all its conservatism the Constitution is still loyal to the basic liberal principles that inspired the Revolution—if less enamored of democracy in a radical sense than many of the Revolutionary leaders had been, the framers of the Constitution still retained a sincere and deep respect for the dignity of the individual and for his rights as a man. Although originally the Constitution contained no written bill of rights because many of the framers thought that the existence of such rights was so self-evident as not to require enumeration, nevertheless a Bill of Rights was added to the Constitution by the first Congress after popular criticism of the Constitution on these grounds had threatened its successful ratification.

The political theory of the Constitution finds, perhaps, best expression in *The Federalist*, a collection of essays written in support of the Constitution at the time the Constitution was being submitted to the states for their approval. Originally published under pen-names, these essays were the work of Hamilton, Madison and Jay.

Certain leading ideas, implicitly or explicitly, are contained in the Constitution of the United States: (1) government rests upon the consent of the governed, ultimately all political power resides in the people; (2) all government is limited government, there are some things which no government has the right to do; (3) as a safeguard against tyranny the functions of government ought to be divided between separate branches of government—executive, legislative, and judicial—each branch of government having its own distinct personnel and no branch having the right to delegate its power to another; (4) as an additional safeguard against tyranny the powers of government are divided on a geographical basis as between the central government on the one hand and the state governments on the other—each, presumably, supreme in its own jurisdiction.

Whether the framers of the Constitution took their idea for the separation of powers directly from Montesquieu or not (and there is considerable doubt on that score), they agreed with his theory and found ample support for it in their own experience. The principle of federalism (the division of power on a geographical basis) was one of the framers' original contributions to political theory and practice and, at the same time, destined to be a source of controversy for the life of the Republic. Dual sovereignty is a logical contradiction and that contradiction did not long escape being recognized and debated. While the Civil War presumably settled the issue for all practical purposes by establishing the supremacy of the federal government it still smolders as an issue both in American theory and in practice.

## Conclusion

LIBERALISM sought to effect a compromise between two conflicting principles. On the one hand, it insisted upon the absolute value of human personality, the autonomy of human reason and of the individual will. On the other hand, it insisted that there is a fundamental law, binding upon individual will, which is eternal, universal, and rational. It sought to effect a compromise between these contradictory principles by an appeal to the Christian conscience. But the Christian conscience, freed from the authority of the Church and progressively divorced from revelation, soon degenerated into a mere cult of sentiment, without weight or sanction, and the will of the individual was left without any substantial limitation. As the tenets of the orthodox Christian faith were gradually abandoned, one by one, the "religion of justification by faith" was soon converted into "a religion of justification by self-esteem." And "at last, in the eighteenth-century, self-love achieves its broadest, most satisfying rationalization: the conception of a universal harmony in which God, man, and nature are pantheistically interfused. In this 'closed system of benevolence,' man shares immanent divinity with nature. Self-love, social love, and divine love are indistinguishable. Nature's God has confirmed man's longing to find goodness, wisdom, and creative power in the depths of his heart." [90]

## CHAPTER 6

# The Romantic and Conservative Reaction

E VER since the Renaissance the dominant voice in the
Western world has been that of the Cartesian rationalist
but from the very beginning it has been accompanied by the
antiphonic protest of a minority. That protest which could be
heard only as a murmur of dissent in the seventeenth and early
eighteenth centuries swelled to mighty proportions in the late
eighteenth and nineteenth. In all reactions of this kind there
is both gain and danger, but of that we shall say more later.

## Giambattista Vico

ONE of the earliest voices to be raised in protest against Cartesian rationalism was that of the Italian poet, jurist, philologist
and philosopher, Giambattista Vico (1668–1744).[1] Ignored by
his contemporaries it was not until the nineteenth century that
his monumental work the *New Science* (1725) received the
attention it deserved and not, indeed, until the nineteenth
century that many of his manuscripts were published.

Unlike those of his contemporaries who believed in the
autonomy of human reason and the capacity of the human
mind ultimately to comprehend all things, Vico was impressed
with the limitations of the human mind and the dependence
of human reason upon God for the truth which it was able to
discover.

Truth is simply fact, what is made. In God there is the first truth,
because He is the first maker (factor); infinite truth, because He is
the maker of all things; absolutely accurate truth, because He has

present to Himself all the elements, both external and internal, of things, seeing that He contains them. To know (*scire*) is to combine the elements of things, and thence it follows that thought (*cogitatio*) belongs to the human mind, but intelligence to the divine mind; for God keeps before Him all the elements, whether external or internal, of things, because He contains them and disposes of them. But the human mind, because it is limited, and because, as to all things external to and apart from itself, it can only reach their outward conditions, never can combine all the elements of things, and so, although it can think of things, it cannot intellectually comprehend them; wherefore the human mind participates in reason, but does not possess it. I may illustrate these statements by a comparison. Divine truth is a solid image of things, as it were a moulded figure or statue; human truth is a linear sketch, a plane image, like a picture: and just as divine truth is what God in the act of knowing disposes of and produces, so human truth is what man in knowing composes and makes. Thus science is the knowledge of the form or of the mode in which a thing is produced, and by which the mind, because in knowing a thing it combines its elements, makes the thing,—God the solid whole, because He comprehends all elements; man a plane, because he comprehends only externals.[2]

In endeavoring to know things man must divide them into their parts and "human science," therefore, "is a kind of anatomy of the works of nature."

. . . to illustrate this by examples, it has dissected man into body and soul, and soul into intellect and will; and it has selected, or, as it is termed, abstracted from the body figure and movement, and from these, as from all other things, it has drawn being and unity. Metaphysics considers being, Arithmetic the unit and its multiplication, Geometry figure and its dimensions, Mechanics motion without thought, Physics motion from the centre, Medicine the body, Logic reason, and Moral Science the will.[3]

But things divided are things diminished and any anatomical dissection must of necessity alter the whole. Yet it is this defect of the human mind which can only know by dissecting and abstracting that is at the same time the foundation of science. "We may conclude," Vico declares, "that the criterion of truth, the rule by which we may certainly know it, is *to have made it*. Hence the clear and distinct idea of our mind not only cannot be the criterion of truth in general, but not even of that of the mind itself; for while the mind apprehends itself, it does not make itself, and because it does not make itself it is ignorant of the form or mode in which it apprehends itself." [4] Absolute, perfect knowledge is possible only where there is absolute creative power and since absolute creative power belongs only to God, human knowledge must always fall short of perfection. God is the truth which embodies all other truths and by which all human truth must be judged. The knowledge of truth and the making of truth are inseparable.

In mathematics the process of human knowledge is in an eminent, and almost exclusive sense, a process of production; in this ideal region the mind possesses a constructive and creative power vastly greater than in the real world; it can form for itself, by abstraction and definition, the few simple elementary conceptions which are postulated by geometry, arithmetic, algebra, etc., and can, then, by its own purely intellectual action, so combine and dispose these conceptions as to form innumberable truths. Accordingly, instead of attributing, as Descartes did, the superiority of mathematical over other knowledge to the greater clearness and distinctness of the successive steps of mathematical demonstration, Vico deemed it of much more importance to refer this the clearness and distinctness of mathematical demonstration to its being entirely the mind's own work. The mind knows what itself does, and in mathematics the mind does everything. Mathematical truth being the only truth which the mind of man wholly makes, is the only truth which that mind perfectly knows, or knows in essentially the same way as the Divine Mind knows all truth. [5]

Science can never be a knowledge of the essence of a thing but is a knowledge of the way in which a thing is made, a knowledge of causes. Science can never take the place of metaphysics, as the Cartesian system of physics endeavored to do. It can explain how material things obey physical laws but it cannot explain the things or the laws themselves. "Give me extension and motion," Descartes had boasted, "and I will construct the universe." But "neither can be given," Vico replied, "for both need to be themselves explained; what you ask to account for the formation of the world, is a world already formed." [6] But if physics cannot do the work of metaphysics neither can metaphysics do the work of physics. Thus Aristotle, he thought, had erred in his way as much as Descartes had in his.

But if there is no foundation for a certain science of nature is there any area in which men can have certain knowledge? In Vico's opinion, there is such an area and that is the historical world created by men.

. . . in the night of thick darkness enveloping the earliest antiquity, so remote from ourselves, there shines the eternal and never-failing light of a truth beyond all question: that the world of civil society has certainly been made by men, and that its principles are therefore to be found within the modifications of our own human mind. Whoever reflects on this cannot but marvel that the philosophers should have bent all their energies to the study of the world of nature, which, since God made, He alone knows; and that they should have neglected the study of the world of nations or civil world, which, since men have made it, men could hope to know.[7]

The "new science" he envisages is the science or philosophy of history. It is in the realm of languages, laws, and customs that Vico looks for certain knowledge. The philosophers, he says, have not yet contemplated God's providence

in respect of that part of it which is most proper to men, whose nature has this principal property; that of being social. In providing for this property God has so ordained and disposed human affairs that men, having fallen from complete justice by original sin, and while intending almost always to do something quite different and often quite contrary—so that for private utility they would live alone like wild beasts—have been led by this same utility and along the aforesaid different and contrary paths to live like men in justice and to keep themselves in society and thus to observe their social nature. It will be shown in the present work that this is the true civil nature of man, and thus that law exists in nature. The conduct of divine providence in this matter is one of the things whose rationale is a chief business of our Science, which becomes in this respect a rational civil theology of divine providence.[8]

The key to the understanding of history, the method of the "new science," is Providence.

Our new Science must . . . be a demonstration, so to speak, of the historical fact of Providence, for it must be a history of the forms of order which, without human discernment or intent, and often against the designs of men, providence has given to this great city of the human race. For though this world has been created in time and particular, the orders established therein by providence are universal and eternal.[9]

Vico apparently conceives of God as manifesting his will for men completely "in the natural course of history" and "by natural means," [10] and "represents the plan of history at once as a plan which God has ordained and which man realizes." [11] Through the study of history we may be led to the discovery of the principles whereby God governs the world and determines its destiny.

Anticipating the work of modern historians like Spengler and Toynbee, Vico believed that civilizations are the proper unit of historical study and emphasized the contemporaneity of particular historical developments. Using an ancient Egyptian myth Vico conceived of history as passing through three stages: the age of the gods, the age of the heroes, and the age of men. Corresponding to these three stages are three kinds of human nature and government, three kinds of languages and natural laws. The passage from one stage to another is a kind of progress from anarchy to order, from barbarism to civilization but it is a progress without end or fulfillment. For every civilization ends in decadence and a new barbarism, but it is by lapsing into barbarism that mankind recovers "piety, faith and truth." Describing the condition of a people who have succumbed to the new barbarism, Vico says:

For such peoples, like so many beasts, have fallen into the custom of each man thinking only of his own private interests and have the extreme of delicacy, or better of pride, in which like wild animals they bristle and lash out at the slightest displeasure. Thus in the midst of their greatest festivities, though physically thronging together, they live like wild beasts in a deep solitude of spirit and will, scarcely any two being able to agree since each follows his own pleasure or caprice. By reason of all this, providence decrees that, through obstinate factions and desperate civil wars, they shall turn their cities into forests and the forests into dens and lairs of men. In this way, through long centuries of barbarism, rust will consume the misbegotten subtleties of malicious wits, that have turned them into beasts made more inhuman by the barbarism of reflection than the first men had been made by the barbarism of sense. For the latter displayed a generous savagery, against which one could defend oneself or take flight or be on one's guard; but the former, with a base savagery, under soft words and embraces, plots against the life and fortune of friends and intimates. Hence peoples who have reached this point of premeditated malice, when they receive this last remedy of providence and are thereby stunned and brutalized, are sensible no longer of comforts, delicacies, pleasures and pomp, but only of the sheer necessities of life. And the few survivors in the midst of an abundance of the things necessary for life naturally become well behaved and, returning to the primitive simplicity of the first world of peoples, are again religious, truthful and faithful. Thus providence brings back among them the piety, faith and truth which are the natural foundations of justice as well as the graces and beauties of the eternal order of God.[12]

Although history, in Vico's view, is a repetition of cycles it is not without meaning, for "the cyclic recurrence provides for the education and even 'salvation' of mankind by the rebirth of its social nature. It saves man by preserving him. This alone, but not redemption, is the 'primary end' and providential meaning of history. The recurrence of barbarism saves mankind from civilized self-destruction." [13]

It was not until the nineteenth century in the work of men like Schelling, Hegel, Grimm and Savigny that the voice of Vico could be heard above that of the Cartesian rationalist but in the work of Vico the foundations were laid upon which this protest could be made.[14]

## Romanticism

ROMANTICISM defies precise definition and there is little agreement as to its proper use as a label. It is the name, however, generally used to describe the reaction to the scientific rationalism of the Age of Enlightenment. That reaction took many diverse forms, some of which were Christian in inspiration and direction and some of which were frankly pagan. Although not always agreeing in their positive affirmations the Romantics were unanimous in their protest against the mechanical conception of nature fostered by Newtonian physics and Cartesian philosophy and against the conception of man as an intricate calculating machine. Man, they said, is a creature of passion impelled more by sentiment than by reason. He is a creature with the capacity to love and to hate, and to neglect this side of his nature is to neglect that which is essential to the understanding of human nature. As a consequence, they protested against the unrealistic attempts of the political philosophers of the Age of Scientific Rationalism to reduce all political and social phenomena to mathematically inspired formulae. The problems of politics and of morality, the Romantics declared, are not analogous to the problems of geometry and physics. They cannot be solved simply by drawing the proper conclusions from self-evident axioms.

To the mechanical concept of nature they opposed the concept of organic growth anticipating in many striking ways the nineteenth-century concept of evolution. To the scientist's dull and meager description of the cosmos they opposed the poet's vision. They rejected the mathematical equality of individuals and emphasized individual differences and the particularity of individual personality and experience. Neither man nor the universe is a machine—neither can be fully comprehended in a mathematical formula. Man abhors a spiritual vacuum and since reason chained to scientific empiricism left no room for the spirit of man to dwell in the Romantic was determined to fashion a home for the spirit if only by artificial means. Romanticism emphasized the transcendent nature of man but made feeling, rather than reason, the link between man and God or the Absolute.

In its emphasis upon the transcendent nature of man, in its emphasis upon the passionate side of human nature, in its recovery of the importance of the particularity of individuality, Romanticism recovered truths obscured by scientific rationalism but the way in which those truths were recovered threatened their integrity. Feeling may be directed, as it was in the Christian pietism of the nineteenth century, to God but without the discipline and direction of reason, feeling alone, even when it is directed to God, is rarely trustworthy except perhaps in the case of the unusual mystic. Feeling undisciplined by reason can lead us anywhere and if the Romantic proclamation of the autonomy of feeling led some to God it led many more to the worship of Self.

For the Romantic recovery of the unique importance of the individual, when that uniqueness was divorced from the reason which is the image of God in man, could only lead to a relativity that must end in anarchy or be overcome by the submergence of the self in some mythical collectivity such as the race or the nation. Thus, what begins as the recovery of individuality ends in a loss of individuality even more disastrous than the loss of individuality in the affirmation of mathematical equality. If the Cartesian rationalist limited the function of reason to the description and understanding of that which could be abstracted from the whole and mathematically defined, at least he retained more of the image of God in man than did the Romantic who allowed his feelings to overwhelm his reason.

But, as I have said, there were many kinds of Romantics. Some, like Burke, sought to counter the liberal, rationalist pretensions concerning the autonomy and self-sufficiency of human reason by emphasizing the organic nature of human society, the primacy of sentiment, and the importance of tradition, authority and custom in the shaping of human institutions. Others, like Rousseau, rejected all tradition, authority and custom in the glorification of the sacred ego and the cult of primitivism. Thus Burke represents Romanticism at its best, Rousseau at its worst.

One writer describes Romanticism as the "religious eviction of reason and its works, the sacred unbridling of sensation, the holy parade of self, and the adoration of primitive natural instinct, pantheism as theology, and emotional stimulus as the rule of life." [15] Whether this is an accurate description of all Romantics, and I am inclined to think it is too strong a statement when applied to all who might be subsumed under that label, it is certainly an accurate statement of the kind of Romanticism that is found so vividly in Rousseau. In Rousseau we find the glorification of sensory experience for its own sake, the assertion of the sacred ego which denies the necessity for any discipline or authority in order to be itself, the affirmation that God to the extent that he exists at all exists in and through Nature alone, the assertion of the primacy of the feelings over reason and the belief that man is a harmless animal whose every natural impulse is good.

The supernaturalism of medieval Christianity gives way to naturalism. Although we find men like Locke as late as the seventeenth century defending the reasonableness of revelation as an aid to morality it is this very Deism which prepares the way for the pantheism of Rousseau. As Irving Babbitt explains it:

The strict Christian supernaturalist had maintained that the divine can be known to man only by the outer miracle of revelation, supplemented by the inner miracle of grace. The deist maintains, on the contrary, that God reveals himself also through outer nature which he has fitted exquisitely to the needs of man, and that inwardly man may be guided aright by his unaided thoughts and feelings (according to the predominance of thought or feeling the deist is rationalistic or sentimental). Man, in short, is naturally good and nature herself is beneficent and beautiful. The deist finally pushes this harmony in God and man and nature so far that the three are practically merged. At a still more advanced stage God disappears, leaving only nature and man as a modification of nature, and the deist gives way to the pantheist who may also be either rationalistic or emotional.[16]

Communion with nature replaces communion with God as the source of inspiration and true enlightenment. The truth is to be found neither in the Church nor in Science but in Nature understood not in terms of mathematics and physics but as "pure spirit."

> One impulse from a vernal wood
> May teach you more of man,
> Of moral evil and of good,
> Than all the sages can.
> Sweet is the lore which Nature brings;
> Our meddling intellect
> Mis-shapes the beauteous forms of things:
> —We murder to dissect.[17]

## Jean-Jacques Rousseau
### (1712–1778)

BORN at Geneva, Switzerland, on June 28, 1712, Jean-Jacques Rousseau left home at the age of sixteen filled with a wander-lust that was never to be satisfied. Restless, impulsive, unstable he embraced the career of a vagabond as others might enter upon a profession. At Turin he became a Catholic convert with the same impulsive abandon with which he embraced susceptible women, engaged in petty thievery and accused another of the theft, and at the age of twenty-eight sought temporary refuge in the home and embraces of Madame de Warens, a divorcée and pensioner of the King of Sardinia. The next twelve years he spent by her side until she wearied of his attentions and turned her favor toward the gardener.

The Madame de Warens was only the first of a succession of such patronesses. In 1741 Rousseau turned up in Paris. Momentarily without a patroness he devoted himself to literary hack-work just barely managing to keep alive. He sought out the acquaintance of the literary great, met Diderot and d'Alembert and agreed to write a piece at their suggestion for the Encyclopedia. He took as his mistress an illiterate laundress, Thérèse Levasseur, who remained with him throughout his life despite his other attachments and whom he eventually married in 1770. She bore him five children all of whom he abandoned and sent to an institution for foundlings.

In the *Mercure de France* of October, 1749, there appeared an announcement which attracted Rousseau's attention. The Academy of Dijon would give a prize, it was announced, for the best essay on the theme: "Has the restoration of the sciences contributed to purify manners?" Rousseau won the prize with an essay entitled *Discourse on the Sciences and Arts* (1751) in which he elaborated the theme, which he said came to him in a dream, "That man is naturally good and that our social institutions alone have rendered him evil." Having thus successfully launched a career as a writer he proceeded to turn out other essays and books, the most important of which are his: *Discourse on Inequality* (1754), *New Heloise* (1761), *Social Contract* (1762), *Émile* (1762), *Confessions* (1765–1770) and *The Reveries of a Solitary Walker* (1778). Gradually lapsing into deeper and deeper insanity he died of a stroke on July 2, 1778.

How can we reconcile a life of debauchery with writings of high moral tone? How can we reconcile Rousseau's shameless exhibition of moral degradation with his fervent moral indignation? How can we reconcile the adulterer with the eloquent defender of the sanctity of the family and the home? What role does reason play in the life of such a man? It plays a twofold part.

Sometimes it serves passion, and then it displays a prodigious talent for sophistry. This is the moralizing, stoical, plutarchian Jean-Jacques, pompous with virtue, censor of the vices of his age, the Rousseau of the *Discours* . . . and the *Contrat Social.* Sometimes reason, like an ineffectual light, watches the intoxications of evil desire and sees clearly the harm in them. But it takes care not to interfere. . . .

That is the Jean-Jacques of the "weak-soul," the "indolent" Jean-Jacques, the true Jean-Jacques, who resists no allurement, who weakens and yields, who surrenders to pleasure. He sees that he does ill, and keeps his eyes raised to the image of the good; and he delights at the same time in the good he loves but does not, and the evil he does and hates not. . . .[18]

But is Rousseau so different from other men? Do they not, too, love the good but do the evil? Is it possible to pass judgment on Rousseau without, at the same time, passing judgment on all men? It is, of course, impossible and it is just because "he bares humanity in us and in himself" that he arouses our sympathy. But the question is, "whether he does not lead us to sympathize with just the lowest parts of our soul and what is most vitiated in the taste of our senses." [19]

It is sometimes said in Rousseau's behalf that "at least he was sincere." Did he not himself acknowledge the moral inconsistencies and contradictions in his life? Rousseau not only acknowledged them but, what is quite different, he gloried in them. It is one thing to confess one's sins in a spirit of repentance and to God and quite another thing to glorify them and publish them abroad. Rousseau was quite certain that his sins were no worse than those of other men and, indeed, that he was a better man than most. In his *Confessions* he wrote:

Let the trumpet of the last judgment sound when it will, I shall come to appear before the sovereign judge with this book in my hand. I shall say boldly: This is what I have done, what I thought, what I was. I have told with equal candour good and ill . . . have shown myself just as I was; contemptible and vile, when I was so;

good and generous and sublime, when I was so; I have revealed my
heart as it was in Your eyes, eternal Being. Gather round me the
countless multitude of my fellow creatures; let them hear my confessions, let them lament my infamies, let them blush for my mean-
nesses. Let each of them in his turn disclose his heart at the foot of
Your throne with the same sincerity, and then let but one of them
say, if he dare, *I was better than that man.*[20]

There is a vast difference between acknowledging the evil in
ourselves in order that, by the grace of God, we may purge
that evil from our souls, and accepting that evil as something
to which one has no alternative but resignation. Rousseau's
"sincerity" "consists in never meddling with what you find in
yourself at each moment of your life, for fear of perverting
your being" thus tainting all moral endeavor "from its source
and by definition, with pharisaical hypocrisy." But "it is a
wicked sophistry," Jacques Maritain points out, "to confuse
skill in appearing what one is not, with zeal to *be* more vigorously (that is, more spiritually), and to bring the great riot of
what is less in us under the law of what is more." [21]

In his *Confessions* Rousseau speaks of his "warmth of heart,"
his "keenness of sensibility," his "innate benevolence for his
fellow creatures," his "ardent love for the great, the true, the
beautiful, the just," and of the "melting feeling, the lively and
sweet emotion" experienced "at the sight of everything
that is virtuous, generous and lovely," and concludes this
portion of his confession by adding: "And so my third child
was put into the foundling hospital." [22] If Rousseau is a hypocrite at least it must be said that he was the first victim of his
own hypocrisy for his is a duplicity that springs from the heart
and not the head. In an usually apt phrase Maritain has described his most striking characteristic as the "mimicry of
sanctity." [23] Mistaking candor for confession, ignorant of the
meaning of shame and of the healing balm of repentance, he
exalts his moral weakness as other men take pride in their
righteousness. Feeling overwhelms his reason and as he sinks
into the voluptuous enjoyment of the pleasurable moment he
seeks to hallow his life by claiming that feeling is the beginning
and end of all existence. "I am convinced," he wrote to M. de
Malesherbes, "that of all the men I have known in my life none

was better than I." [24] "The religious enjoyment of self" is what he offers as a substitute for Christianity to an age that had thought that it could dispense with religion now that it had Science. The love for which the Age of Enlightenment had no object, the intuitions of the heart for which the *philosophes* had nothing but scorn, assert themselves in Rousseau in a perverted religiosity of feeling that seeks to satisfy man's hunger for God by feeding him upon "the fruit of the knowledge of evil."

It was by spreading the contagion of that perverted religiosity over so many souls, that he gave the modern world one of its characteristic aspects. . . . Rousseau plunged the heart into *endless* uneasiness, because he *hallows the denial of grace*. With the philosophers he rejected Him who first loved us, but yet he makes an outlet for religious feeling. He turns our hunger for God towards the sacred mysteries of sensation, towards the infinite of matter. . . . Present-day thought, where it is diseased, still hangs on him. As the search for mystical enjoyment in things which are not God is an endless search, it can stop nowhere. . . .

The desire enkindled by Rousseau casts the intelligence into an infinite world of perceptions, tastes, spiritual experiences, refinements, and ecstasies—sad as death, when all is said, but real for the moment—which are disclosed to us only in sin. There is a spirituality of sin more treacherous than the vulgar attraction for pleasure of the senses. What holds the descendants of Jean-Jacques is the *spiritual savour* of the fruit of the knowledge of evil. . . .

Rousseau aims not at our heads, but a little below our hearts. He quickens in our souls the very scars of the sin of nature, he summons the powers of anarchy and weakness which lie dormant in each of us. . . . He profits by all the inadequacies of reason, manifested in such terrible aggravation in the modern world, to hand our distress over to the action not of grace, but of our lower nature. Above all, he has taught our eyes to take pleasure in ourselves and to connive at what they thus see, to discover the charm of those secret bruises of the most individual sensitiveness which less impure ages left with trembling to the eyes of God. "All the veils of the heart have been rent," said Mme. de Stael of the *Nouvelle Heloise*. "The ancients would never have made novels of their souls in this way." It will be a grievous business for modern literature and thought, thus wounded by him, to find again the purity and uprightness once known by an intelligence turned towards Being. [25]

## Rousseau's Political Theory

DESPITE the inconsistencies and contradictions that characterize Rousseau's political theory one central theme runs through
it all, the theme which he first expressed in his *Discourse on the
Arts and Sciences* (1749), namely: man is by nature good and
only by institutions is he debased. It was in that *Discourse* that
he offered up this prayer: "Almighty God! thou who holdest
in Thy hand the minds of men, deliver us from the fatal arts
and sciences of our forefathers; give us back ignorance, innocence and poverty, which alone can make us happy and are
precious in Thy sight." [26] In his *Discourse on the Origin of Inequality* (1753) this theme is further elaborated. Speaking of
the pre-social "state of nature" he says:

. . . The more we reflect on it, the more we shall find that this state
was . . . altogether the very best man could experience; so that he
can have departed from it only through some fatal accident, which,
for the public good, should never have happened. The example of
savages . . . seems to prove that men were meant to remain in it
. . . and that all subsequent advances have been apparently so
many steps towards the perfection of the individual, but in reality
towards the decrepitude of the species.

So long as men remained content with their rustic huts, so long as
they were satisfied with clothes made of the skins of animals and
sewn together with thorns and fishbones, adorning themselves with
feathers and shells, and continued to paint their bodies different
colours, to improve and beautify their bows and arrows and to make
with sharp-edged stones fishing boats or clumsy musical instruments;
in a word, *so long as they undertook only what a single person could accomplish*, and confined themselves to such arts as did not require the
joint labour of several hands, *they lived free, healthy, honest and happy
lives*. . . . But from the moment one man began to stand in need of
the help of another . . . equality disappeared, property was introduced, work became indispensable, and vast forests became smiling
fields, which man had to water with the sweat of his brow, and where
slavery and misery were soon to germinate and grow up with the
crops.[27]

There is a superficial resemblance between this description of
the pre-social state of nature and the Christian conception of

the Garden of Eden but it is a "purely natural paradise" in which Nature is assigned the role attributed by Christianity to grace. Man is naturally good, he has no predisposition to do evil—his salvation consists not in responding to the will of God but in following his own pure natural instincts. Moreover, it is man's dependence upon man that is the root of evil; so long as man could remain a solitary, self-sufficient individual he was free, healthy, honest and happy. The self-sufficiency which in Christian thought is associated with original sin is proclaimed by Rousseau to be the hallmark of innocence. Christianity teaches us that only by serving one another can we find happiness but Rousseau declares that "from the moment one man began to stand in need of the help of another" slavery and misery was man's lot. All restraint upon man's natural impulses Rousseau believes is bad—goodness consists in being liberated from law, from discipline, from authority, from the obligations imposed by God and our fellowmen. All that we need to know Nature teaches us, all that we need to do is to follow our natural impulses, and happiness will be ours. "Our wisdom," Rousseau writes, "is slavish prejudice, our customs consist in control, constraint, compulsion. Civilised man is born and dies a slave. . . . All his life long man is imprisoned by our institutions. Fix your eyes on nature, follow the path traced by her." [28]

Education, as Rousseau explains it in *Émile* (1762), should consist "not in teaching virtue or truth," but in preserving the child's natural innocence. Words like "duty," "obligation," "obey," and "command" should be purged from his vocabulary. Experience, not law, must be his guide, instinct not wisdom. "Let us lay it down as an incontrovertible rule that the first impulses of nature are always right." [29] Anticipating the modern school of progressive education Rousseau laid down a number of maxims which its adherents would find congenial to their way of thinking:

Keep the child dependent on things only. Let his wishes meet with physical obstacles only, or the punishment which results from his own actions. . . .

Keep this truth ever before you—Ignorance never did anyone any harm, error alone is fatal. . . .

Let the senses be the only guide for the first workings of reason. No book but the world, no teaching but that of fact. . . .

Let him know nothing because you have told him, but because he has learnt it for himself. If ever you substitute authority for reason he will cease to reason. . . .

If he goes wrong let him alone, do not correct his mistakes; hold your tongue till he finds them out for himself and corrects them, or at most arrange something, as opportunity offers, which may show him his mistakes. . . .

It is not your business to teach him the various sciences, but to give him a taste for them and methods of learning them when this taste is more mature. . . .

Our real teachers are experience and emotion, and man will never learn what befits a man except under its own conditions. . . . etc.[30]

In short, true education consists in not teaching the child anything but in allowing the child to learn from his own experience what Nature will teach him. That experience requires no interpretation Rousseau apparently believes—or rather, he believes that it will teach what he teaches.

In the *Social Contract* (1762), his most important work, he continues to talk of an idyllic state of nature in which men were ignorant and happy, but he is now more concerned with explaining how natural liberty can be reconciled with the necessity for political authority. "Man is born free," he declares, "and everywhere is in chains. One thinks himself the master of others, and still remains a greater slave than they. How did this change come about? I do not know. What can make it legitimate? That question I think I can answer."[31] Political society is a fact—what can make it legitimate?

The attempt to explain political obligation in terms of force, as Hobbes endeavored to do, actually explains nothing. "Force," he says, "is a physical power and I fail to see what moral effect it can have. To yield to force is an act of necessity, not of will—at the most, an act of prudence. In what sense can it be a duty?" Until might is transformed into right there is no obligation. Force creates no right for

if force creates right, the effect changes with the cause: every force that is greater than the first succeeds to its right. As soon as it is possible to disobey with impunity, disobedience is legitimate; and, the strongest being always in the right, the only thing that matters is to act so as to become the strongest. But what kind of right is that which perishes when force fails? [32]

Now if men are by nature free, if no one has any authority over his fellow, and if force establishes no right then what is the basis of legitimate authority? "The problem," as posed by Rousseau, "is to find a form of association which will defend and protect with the whole common force the person and goods of each associate, and in which each, while uniting himself with all, may still obey himself alone, and remain as free as before." [33] How can a man obey but himself alone and at the same time submit to the authority of society? And Rousseau answers: by a convention or social compact. But "it is an empty and contradictory convention that sets up, on the one side, absolute authority, and, on the other, unlimited obedience," [34] hence the task he sets himself is the discovering of the means whereby men can submit to authority without losing their liberty. He believes that he has discovered the magic formula in the conception of the general will. If, he says, we discard what is nonessential in the idea of the social compact we find that it reduces itself to this simple proposition: "*Each of us puts his person and all his power in common under the supreme direction of the general will, and, in our corporate capacity, we receive each member as an indivisible part of the whole.*" [35]

Unlike Locke who argued that the establishment of society necessitated only the giving up of the right of interpreting and enforcing the law of nature, Rousseau argues that, under the terms of the original compact, each individual gave himself and his rights up completely and unreservedly to the community as a whole. Like Locke he retains the conception of consent but rejects the idea that the individual retains any natural and unalienable rights, "for, if the individuals retained certain rights, as there would be no common superior to decide between them and the public, each, being on one point his own judge, would ask to be so on all; the state of nature would thus continue. . . ." [36] Like Hobbes he argues that upon entering society the individual alienates himself completely but unlike Hobbes does not believe that the individual gives up his rights to any particular person or ruler. This, he thinks, is the advantage of his conception of the original compact over those propounded by Hobbes and by Locke: since everyone gives himself up absolutely under conditions that are the same for all equality is preserved and since "each man, in giving himself to all, gives himself to nobody" liberty is preserved. (But is it really a solution to the problem to argue that in giving one's self up to everybody one gives one's self to "nobody?" Does this amount to anything more than a verbal subterfuge?)

The social compact, Rousseau argues, creates "a moral and collective body," a "public person," "body politic" and "Sovereign." [37] The individual having agreed under the terms of the compact to identify his will with the general will of the community in all matters of public concern, the body politic now acts in the place of the individual personality of each contracting party. The body politic being nobody in particular and everybody in general can never act contrary to the real interests of those who created it. In the act of agreeing to the terms of the compact the individuals became citizens and as citizens identified their interests and wills with the interests and wills of all other citizens. But what if the individual as a man, i.e., as distinct from a citizen, wants to do something which is contrary to or different from the general will, what if his particular interest as a man conflicts with his common interest as a citizen? In that case Rousseau says: "whoever refuses to obey the general will shall be compelled to do so by the whole body." And he adds, "This means nothing less than that he will be forced to be free. . . . In this lies the key to the working of the political machine; this alone legitimises civil undertakings, which, without it, would be absurd. . . ." [38] Sovereignty, for Rousseau, is identical with liberty. "The Sovereign, being formed wholly of the individuals who compose it, neither has nor can have any interest contrary to theirs." [39] The Sovereign is absolute, indivisible, inalienable, and infallible.

The idea of "the general will" lies at the center of Rousseau's political theory yet no where is it precisely defined, probably because being a "mystical" conception it defies precise description. He does endeavor to draw a distinction between "the will of all" (*volonté des tous*) and "the general will" (*volonté générale*)—the latter is concerned only with those interests which are common, while the former "takes private interest into account, and is no more than the sum of particular wills: but take away from these same wills the pluses and minuses that cancel one another, and the general will remains as the sum of the differences." [40] Since man is naturally good, since his will is uncorrupted, it follows, Rousseau declares: that "*the general will is always right and tends to the public advantage.*" [41] The people may be deceived but they are never corrupt, they may be misled but their *will* is always good. For practical purposes, moreover, the will of the majority may be taken as indicative of the general will. Rousseau explains it by saying:

There is but one law which, from its nature, needs unanimous consent. This is the social compact. . . . If there are opponents when the social compact is made, their opposition does not invalidate the contract, but merely prevents them from being included in it. They are foreigners among citizens. When the State is instituted, residence constitutes consent; to dwell within its territory is to submit to the Sovereign.

Apart from this primitive contract, *the vote of the majority always binds all the rest.* . . . But it is asked how a man can be both free and forced to conform to wills that are not his own. How are opponents at once free and subject to laws they have not agreed to?

I retort that the question is wrongly put. The citizen gives his consent to all the laws, including those which are passed in spite of his opposition, and even these which punish him when he dares to break any of them. The constant will of all the members of the State is the general will; by virtue of it they are citizens and free. When in the popular assembly a law is proposed, what the people is asked is not exactly whether it approves or rejects the proposal, but whether it is in conformity with the general will, which is their will. Each man, in giving his vote, states his opinion on that point; and the general will is found by counting votes. When, therefore the opinion that is contrary to my own prevails, this proves . . . that I was mistaken, . . . If my particular opinion had carried the day I should have achieved the opposite of what was my will; and it is in that case that I should not have been free.

*This presupposes, indeed, that all the qualities of the general will still reside in the majority:* when they cease to do so, whatever side a man may take, liberty is no longer possible.[42]

It follows, accordingly, that the attributes which he assigns to the Sovereign belong *for all practical purposes* to the majority. The will of the majority, practically speaking, is absolute, indivisible, inalienable, and infallible. Sovereignty theoretically resides in the people as a whole but for all practical purposes it expresses itself in the will of the majority.

Now what is the law? The law is a decree of the General Will and

we see at once that it can no longer be asked whose business it is to make the laws, since they are acts of the general will; nor whether the prince is above the law, since he is a member of the State; nor whether the law can be unjust, since no one is unjust to himself; nor how we can be both free and subject to the laws, since they are but registers of our wills.[43]

Here is born a conception of law which is radically modern and absolutely contrary to the Judaeo-Christian tradition. It is not God who is the ultimate author of law but "the people" and this is true whether the form of government be democratic, aristocratic, or monarchical. It is not a question of which form of government is best (which is quite another question) for Rousseau says that no government is legitimate unless it be "republican" by which he understands "not merely an aristocracy or a democracy, but generally any government directed by the general will, which is the law. To be legitimate, the government must be, not one with the Sovereign, but its minister. In such a case even a monarchy is a Republic." [44] This is something more, it should be noted, than the doctrine of popular sovereignty for Rousseau is not arguing here that the ultimate power should reside with the people but that all *authority* ultimately and legitimately springs from the General Will. And if, for practical purposes, the General Will expresses itself in the will of the majority it follows that, for practical purposes, the source of all authority ultimately is the will of the majority. Justice and right thus tend to be equated with that will and law proceeds not from reason but from numbers. The test of true law is not its conformity to reason but its emanation from the will of the people and "it can no longer be asked," as Rousseau pointed out in the quotation above, "whether the law can be unjust," for justice is whatever the majority of the people will.

It is one thing to argue that all political power ought ultimately to be exercised by the people, but it is quite another matter to argue that all *authority* emanates from the people; it is one thing to say that in the long run and generally speaking the majority is more likely to render wise decisions in matters of common policy than is a minority, and quite another thing to say that the majority is always right. It is one thing to submit to the superior *reasoning* and deliberation of the majority and quite another to submit to its will because it is quantitatively larger. Only if the majority will represents the reasoned judgment of the people as a whole can it impose obligations upon us to submit, for it is reason that obliges us and not will, and reason that stands in judgment not only over our own will but over that of the majority also. The confusion in Rousseau's thought between Democracy as a desirable form of government and Democracy as a spiritual principle is a confusion that remains to plague our thinking on the subject today.

By arguing that the whole is greater than the sum of its parts, by regarding the body politic as a separate entity with a will of its own, the moral worth of the individual tends to be submerged in the abstract "good" of an abstract "public." When it is further contended that the individual can be compelled to obey the General Will in order to realize his own true "freedom" we have a conception entirely congenial to tyranny. The good and freedom of the individual is identified with the good and freedom of a mythical entity.

Up to a certain point there is a great deal in the *Social Contract* that appears rational and reasoned yet beneath it "is just as mad as the mysticism of sentiment and passion which we find in *Émile* and the *Nouvelle Heloise*." [45] In Chapter VII Rousseau declares:

In order to discover the rules of society best suited to nations, a superior intelligence beholding all the passions of men without experiencing any of them would be needed. This intelligence would have to be wholly unrelated to our nature, while knowing it through and through; its happiness would have to be independent of us, and yet ready to occupy itself with ours; and lastly, it would have, in the march of time, to look forward to a distant glory, and, working in one century, to be able to enjoy in the next. . . .[46]

Since Rousseau rejects the idea that man is by nature a social creature, since he rejects the Aristotelian idea that man is by nature fitted and destined for life in society, he must argue that

He who dares to undertake the making of a people's institutions ought to feel himself capable, so to speak, of changing human nature, of transforming each individual, who is by himself a complete and solitary whole, into part of a greater whole from which he in a manner receives his life and being; of altering man's constitution for the purpose of strengthening it. . . . He must, in a word, take away from man his own resources and give him instead new ones alien to him, and incapable of being made use of without the help of other men. *The more completely these natural resources are annihilated,* the greater and the more lasting are those which he acquires, and *the more stable and perfect the new institutions;* so that if each citizen is nothing and can do nothing without the rest, and the resources acquired by the whole are equal or superior to the aggregate of the resources of all the individuals, it may be said that legislation is at the highest possible point of perfection.[47]

Rousseau's conception of the General Will whereby man's nature is to be transformed is, as Maritain says, his "finest myth" and "the most religiously manufactured."

We might call it the myth of political pantheism. The *General Will* . . . *is the Common Self's own will, born of the sacrifice each has made of himself and all his rights on the altar of the city.*
Truth to tell, here there is a question of a kind of immanent God mysteriously evoked by the operation of the pact, of whose decrees the majority of votes is only a sign, a sacred sign which is only valid under certain conditions—particularly, Rousseau teaches, under the condition that no partial society exist in the whole.
Immanent social God, common self which is more I than myself, in whom I lose myself and find myself again and whom I serve to be free—that is a curious specimen of fraudulent mysticism.[48]

There are Christian insights in Rousseau's thought but those insights are corrupted and debased. In Rousseau Christianity becomes *naturalized* and Nature is assigned the role that

Christianity attributes to grace, to the power and pardon of God. Rousseau finds, for example, the essential characteristic of man to consist not in his reason but in his feelings and passions.

Not only . . . is there no original sin of which we bear the guilt at our birth and still keep the wounds, not only is there in us no seat of concupiscence and unhealthy proclivities to incline us to evil, but, further, the state of suffering and hardship is one essentially *opposed to nature* and started by civilization, and our nature demands that we should, at all cost, be freed from it.[49]

The Christian doctrine that man was created good but fell through pride into sin is converted by Rousseau into the anti-Christian dogma of natural goodness. The Christian doctrine of equality in the sight of God, the idea that each of us are equally dependent upon God for our existence, becomes in Rousseau the doctrine that we are each equally independent of one another and subordinate only to a common Self. Christianity holds out to men the hope of the Kingdom of God and His righteousness. But the price exacted of men for this kingdom is repentance, the conversion of one's will with the aid of Christ to the will of God. Rousseau expects this kingdom to be realized through Revolution "in the very conditions of the present life and . . . from the strength of man."[50]

"If we wish to see the psychology of Rousseau writ large," Irving Babbitt declares, "we should turn to the French Revolution.

That period abounds in persons whose goodness is in theory so superlative that it overflows in a love for all men, but who in practice are filled like Rousseau in his later years with universal suspicion. There was indeed a moment in the Revolution when the madness of Rousseau became epidemic, when suspicion was pushed to such a point that men became "suspect of being suspect." One of the last persons to see Rousseau alive at Ermenonville was Maximilien Robespierre. He was probably a more thoroughgoing Rousseauist than any other of the Revolutionary leaders. Perhaps no passage that could be cited illustrates with more terrible clearness the tendency of the new morality to convert righteousness into self-righteousness than the following from his last speech before the Convention at the very height of the Reign of Terror. Himself devoured by suspicion, he is repelling the suspicion that he wishes to erect his own power on the ruins of the monarchy. The idea, he says, that "he can descend to the infamy of the throne will appear probable only to those perverse beings who have not even the right to believe in virtue. But why speak of virtue? Doubtless virtue is a natural passion. But how could they be familiar with it, these venal spirits who never yielded access to aught save cowardly and ferocious passions? . . . Yet virtue exists as you can testify, feeling and pure souls; it exists, that tender, irresistible, imperious passion, torment and delight of magnanimous hearts, that profound horror of tyranny, that compassionate zeal for the oppressed, that sacred love for one's country, that still more sublime and sacred love for humanity, without which a great revolution is only a glittering crime; it exists, that generous ambition to found on earth the first Republic of the world; that egoism of unregenerate men who find a celestial voluptuousness in the calm of a pure conscience and the ravishing spectacle of public happiness. You feel it at this moment burning in your souls. I feel it in mine. But how could our vile calumniators have any notion of it? . . . etc.[51]

This was the Robespierre who kept the guillotine permanently employed during the Reign of Terror which he dared to call the "Dictatorship of Virtue"; the Robespierre who wrote: "Virtue, apart from which terror is baneful; terror, apart from which virtue is powerless." Thousands were slaughtered by the man who believed himself to be the incarnation of Virtue out of "compassionate zeal for the oppressed" and "that still more sublime and sacred love for humanity."

In the concluding chapter (VIII) of the *Social Contract* Rousseau discusses what he calls "civil religion," which, "making country the object of the citizens' adoration, teaches them that service done to the State is service done to its tutelary god. It is a form of theocracy, in which there is no pontiff save the prince, and no priests save the magistrates. To die for one's country then becomes martyrdom; violation of its laws, impiety; and to subject one who is guilty to public execration is to condemn him to the anger of the gods."[52] It was this kind of religion that some men tried to establish in France during the Revolution. Church bells, spoken of as "trinkets of the Eternal Father," were melted into coins and cannon, the belfries, "which by their height above other buildings seemed to contradict the principles of equality" were dismantled, parodies of the Holy Communion were staged in public theaters, a Revolutionary Calendar was proposed abolishing Saints days and Sundays and substituting civic festivals, a Festival of Reason "to celebrate the triumph won by Reason . . . over the prejudices of eighteen centuries" was held in the Cathedral of Notre Dame renamed for the occasion, the Temple of Reason.[53] To restore a more "genuine" religion Robespierre inaugurated the Festival of the Supreme Being. A prominent historian of the French Revolution describes the scene.

Robespierre, in his blue coat, which had already attained something like celebrity, and with tricolour plumes waving in his hat, presided over the proceedings first at the Tuileries, and then on the Champs-de-Mars. From the platform—pulpit or throne—he spoke a lengthy rhapsody. . . . This done, a hundred thousand voices chanted the praises of the Lord. Incense was burnt the while on the summit of the symbolic Mountain on which Maximilien stood, and concealed him in its clouds. For one moment this most prudent man forgot his caution; his face, usually grave, was brightened by a smile of triumph. For a moment the Vicar of God fancied he was himself God![54]

## The Conservative Reaction

THE Enlightenment had its culmination politically in Revolution. The English Revolution of 1688 had succeeded in establishing a constitutional government, the French Revolution of 1789 began by espousing liberalism and ended by embracing Caesarism. As a prominent historian of European liberalism declares: "the Liberalism of 1789 was stifled by the democracy of 1793" for this "democracy of 1793 was a true butcher of liberties . . .

In order to maintain itself it was compelled to suppress one by one all the liberties previously proclaimed: freedom of thought, freedom of the press, property, at any rate for those who did not share ideas of the new dictators, personal security, and freedom of worship. The individual was completely at the mercy of the crushing power of the Convention. And the Convention, in its turn, after making the world tremble, itself trembled before Robespierre. . . . With Robespierre comes Caesarism. . . . It is a maxim of classical wisdom that the tyranny of the many breeds the tyranny of one. Anti-Liberalism has run its course to the predestined end.[55]

The Caesarism of Robespierre was overthrown only eventually to be replaced by the Caesarism of Napoleon Bonaparte, a less brutal dictatorship, perhaps, but one no more enamored of political liberty than that which had gone before. Frightened and disgusted by the excesses of license to which the political liberty of 1789 had degenerated the liberal bourgeoisie turned in the hope of finding security of person and property to Bonaparte.

The Enlightenment produced one kind of Romantic reaction the nature and effects of which we have just examined. But it produced another kind that, while equally vehement in its rejection of the excessive claims made for reason, emphasized the importance of authority, tradition and custom. That reaction we generally call Conservatism.

## *Edmund Burke (1729–1797)*

PERHAPS the most influential, and certainly the most eloquent, spokesman for the Conservative reaction to the Age of Enlightenment was Edmund Burke, whom someone has called not inappropriately "the prophet of political common sense." Born in Ireland and educated at Trinity College, Dublin, he went to London in 1750 to study law. The law failed to engage his interest and he soon abandoned its study in favor of a literary career. As a young author he came under the influence of Samuel Johnson and joined the circle of which he was a leader. His earliest published work was an essay entitled *A Vindication of Natural Society* which appeared anonymously in 1756. It was a satirical imitation of the writings of Lord Bolingbroke and was so successful that many mistook it for a posthumous work of that author. Burke endeavored to show in this essay that the same kind of wit which Bolingbroke used to discredit Christianity could be used with equal efficacy to demolish the foundations of civil society. The witticism is an impartial instrument and can be turned in any direction. A few months later Burke published *A Philosophical Inquiry into the Origin of our Ideas on the Sublime and the Beautiful*, an essay in the field of aesthetics. Both essays demonstrated his unusual talents as a thinker and a stylist.

Following these literary ventures Burke returned for a short time to Ireland as a companion to William G. Hamilton who had been appointed secretary to the Lord Lieutenant of Ireland. Anxious to exploit Burke's genius, Hamilton sought to bind the young Burke to his service for life but Burke rebelled against being "considered as a piece of his household stuff" and after six years in his service left it to become private secretary to Lord Rockingham in England. On December 26, 1765, Burke became a member of the House of Commons and served his country faithfully in that capacity until his retirement in 1794. He served in the British Parliament during one of the most critical periods in its history (the period from just before the American to the close of the French Revolution) but while he soon became an influential member of the Whig party he never became its acknowledged leader. Hazlitt says:

> The truth is that he was out of his place in the House of Commons; he was eminently qualified to shine as a man of genius, as the instructor of mankind, as the brightest luminary of his age: but he had nothing in common with that motley crew of knights, citizens, and burgesses. He could not be said to be "native and endued unto that element." He was above it; and never appeared like himself, but when, forgetful of the idle clamours of the party, and of the little views of little men, he appealed to his country, and the enlightened judgment of mankind.[56]

Burke's political ideas are not contained in any systematic political treatise but are found scattered here and there through a number of books, pamphlets, letters and speeches which he wrote in response to particular political events. In addition to the two essays already mentioned his most important works are probably *Thoughts on the Cause of the Present Discontents* (1770); *Reflections on the French Revolution* (1790); *Appeal from the New to the Old Whigs* (1791) and *Letters on a Regicide Peace* (1796). Of his numerous speeches the most important are the ones which he delivered in Bristol in 1774, his speech on moving his resolutions for conciliation with the American colonies delivered on March 22, 1775, and the speech on the Nabob of Arcot's debts of February 28, 1785.[57]

After the wild metaphysical speculation in which men like Rousseau had indulged it is no wonder that Burke had an aversion to metaphysics and scorn for all abstract theory. His very first essay was directed against a kind of teaching that had much in common with that of Rousseau and from that time to his death he never ceased to expose the dangers latent in abstract speculation. It is dangerous to begin our thinking with *a priori* assumptions that have no roots in reality for such "thinking" is nothing more than wish-fulfillment and when it is presented as the "truth" it renders us helpless in contact with reality. It encourages us to indulge in vain illusions that must sooner or later be shattered, it is better to face the facts of life now rather than later. A truly rational man never did govern himself by abstractions. The rules of morality have none of the rigidity of mathematics but they must be adapted to particular circumstances. Logic, in the realm of morality, is not enough.

The lines of morality are not like ideal lines of mathematics. They are broad and deep as well as long. They admit of exceptions; they demand modifications. These exceptions and modifications are not made by the process of logic, but by the rules of prudence. Prudence is not only first in rank of the virtues political and moral, she is the director, the regulator, the standard of them all.[58]

It is not reason which Burke opposes, as some interpreters of his writings have said, but *abstract* reason, i.e., reason divorced from the totality of experience. It is the "reason" of the *philosophes* he rejects, not the reason of an Aristotle. Aristotle distinguished between the theoretical and the practical use of reason, between theoretical and practical science. The end of theoretical science is knowledge, the end of practical science is action. Theoretical science is concerned with what is absolute and invariable, practical science with what is accidental and contingent. The realm of nature is characterized by universality and necessity, hence a theoretical science of nature is possible; but in the realm of practical, human affairs where there is neither universality nor necessity, where we are concerned with the voluntary actions of particular human beings, there can be no science of human affairs such as is possible in dealing with nature. Politics, hence, is a practical science. With Aristotle, Burke believed that the primary qualification for a statesman is not philosophy but practical wisdom, for to know what is the right thing to do in a particular, human situation is a matter not of science but of judgment. This judgment is acquired, much as an artist attains artistic judgment, by moral discipline, practice, and experience.

The science of constructing a commonwealth, or renovating it, or reforming it, is, like every other experimental science, not to be taught *a priori.* Nor is it a short experience that can instruct us in that practical science; because the real effects of moral causes are not always immediate, but that which in the first instance is prejudicial may be excellent in its remoter operation, and its excellence may arise even from the ill effects it produces in the beginning. The reverse also happens; and very plausible schemes, with very pleasing commencements, have often shameful and lamentable conclusions. . . . The science of government being, therefore, so practical in itself, and intended for such practical purposes, a matter which requires . . . even more experience than any person can gain in his whole life, however, sagacious and observing he may be, it is with infinite caution that any man ought to venture upon pulling down an edifice which has answered in any tolerable degree for ages the common purposes of society, or on building it up again without having models and patterns of approved utility before his eyes.[59]

There are some who contend that Burke's conception of man is pessimistic; actually it is neither pessimistic nor optimistic, it is, I venture to suggest, realistic. It overlooks neither men's propensities to do evil nor their potentialities for good. Nowhere can we find in Burke's writings an explicit statement of this conception but it underlies all of his writing and must be extracted by inference. Man is a rational animal, a compound of reason and passion. Man is an affectionate creature capable of "love, veneration, admiration . . . attachment." To deny, as the *philosophes* endeavored to do, that man is a creature of love and of sentiment is to deny that he is a person. Man's reason does not operate in a vacuum but is motivated and given direction by his passions, by his loves and fears. Man is also a creature of habit and by acquiring habits he becomes civilized, i.e., socially and historically conditioned. Through our habits and our "prejudices" (which Burke uses in a special sense to mean the more or less imperfect intuitions of the truth embodied in sentiment and crystallized in institutions) our loves and fears become channelized in directions that are socially beneficent. "Naked reason" can never impel us to action but "prejudice, with the reason involved . . . has a motive to give action to that reason, and an affection which will give it permanence. . . . Prejudice renders a man's virtue his habit, and not a series of unconnected acts. Through just prejudice, his duty becomes a part of his nature." Because the individual's "own private stock of reason . . . is small" and not entirely trustworthy "individuals would do better to avail themselves of the general bank and capital of nations and of ages." [60] Locke and the French *philosophes* had exalted the individual reason of the individual man, Burke would subordinate such reason to the accumulated wisdom of the ages, to the "collected reason" of men of all nations and of all times.

Burke discarded the social contract theory of government as an over-simplified fiction thought up by men who sought to find a mathematically clear explanation of society. It is not so simple.

Society is, indeed, a contract . . . but the state ought not to be considered as nothing better than a partnership agreement in a trade of pepper and coffee, calico or tobacco, or some other such low concern, to be taken up for a little temporary interest, and to be dissolved by the fancy of the parties. It is to be looked on with other reverence; because it is not a partnership in things subservient only to the gross animal existence of a temporary and perishable nature. It is a partnership in all science, a partnership in all art, a partnership in every virtue and in all perfection. As the ends of such a partnership cannot be obtained in many generations, it becomes a partnership not only between those who are living, but between those who are living, those who are dead, and those who are to be born. Each contract of each particular state is but a clause in the great primeval contract of eternal society, linking the lower with the higher natures, connecting the visible and invisible world, according to a fixed compact sanctioned by the inviolable oath which holds all physical and all moral natures each in their appointed place. This law is not subject to the will of those, who by an obligation above them, and infinitely superior, are bound to submit their will to that law. The municipal corporations of that universal kingdom are not morally at liberty at their pleasure, and on their speculations of a contingent improvement, wholly to separate and tear asunder the bands of their subordinate community, and to dissolve it into an unsocial, uncivil, unconnected chaos of elementary principles. It is the first and supreme necessity only, a necessity that is not chosen, but chooses, a necessity paramount to deliberation, that admits no discussion, and demands no evidence, which alone can justify a resort to anarchy.[61]

It is not man but God who is the "Master, Author, and Founder of society." It is "His will which is the law of laws, and the sovereign of sovereigns" and it is He who willed the state as the necessary means for the perfection of human nature. Unlike Rousseau, Burke argued that "without . . . civil society man could not by any possibility arrive at the perfection of which his nature is capable, nor even make a remote and faint approach to it." [62] Man is born into society and that fact alone imposes obligations upon him; these obligations do not require his formal consent but arise out of a relationship which is an essential and not a voluntary one. The relation of man to society is like the relation of parent and child, our moral duties arise from a relationship which is not a matter of choice but a matter of fact. "The place of every man determines his duty." Society, in short, is not an artificial creation of men, is not an invention of their reason and an instrument of their desires, but it is a living organism, with a destiny that transcends the interests of individuals. It is a product not of man's will but of God's will.

Burke does not deny the existence of natural rights, but he is less concerned with arguing their existence, which few, if any, of his contemporaries doubted, than he is in pointing out that they can never be realized as perfectly in practice as they can in theory.

Government is not made in virtue of natural rights, which may and do exist in total independence of it; and exist in much greater clearness, and in a much greater degree of abstract perfection; but their abstract perfection is their practical defect. Government is a contrivance of human wisdom to provide for human *wants*. Men have a right that these wants should be provided for by this wisdom. Among these wants is to be reckoned the want, out of civil society, of a sufficient restraint upon their passions. Society requires not only that the passions of individuals should be subjected, but that even in the mass and body, as well as in the individuals, the inclinations of men should frequently be thwarted, their will controlled, and their passions brought into subjection. This can only be done *by a power out of themselves;* and not, in the exercise of its function, subject to that will and to those passions which it is its office to bridle and subdue. In this sense the restraints on men, as well as their liberties, are to be reckoned among their rights. But as the liberties and restrictions vary with times and circumstances, and admit of infinite modifications, they cannot be settled upon any abstract rule; and nothing is so foolish as to discuss them upon that principle.[63]

Experience, not abstract reason, must determine what measure of liberty it is good for men to have. Although "incapable of definition" the rights of man are "not impossible to be discerned" but it is to experience and not theory that we must look for guidance in determining what these rights are. Liberty cannot be secured by fiat, but is a product of social growth.

Burke saw in the British Constitution established by the Revolution of 1688 the best possible reconciliation of liberty and authority. King, Parliament and the courts deriving their authority from the law and custom of the land check and balance one another and prevent any one principle from being carried to excess.

Our constitution is a prescriptive constitution, it is a constitution whose sole authority is that it has existed time out of mind. . . . Your king, your lords, your judges, your juries, grand and little, all are prescriptive. . . . Prescription is the most solid of all titles, not only to property, but, which is to secure that property, to government. . . . It is a presumption in favor of any settled scheme of government against any untried project, that a nation has long existed and flourished under it. It is a better presumption even of the *choice* of a nation, far better than any sudden and temporary arrangement by actual election. Because a nation is not an idea only of local extent,

and individual momentary aggregation; but it is an idea of continuity, which extends in time as well as in numbers and in space. And
this is a choice not of one day, or one set of people, not a tumultuary
and giddy choice; it is a deliberate election of the ages and of generations; it is a constitution made by what is ten thousand times better
than choice, it is made by the peculiar circumstances, occasions,
tempers, dispositions, and moral, civil, and social habitudes of the
people, which disclose themselves only in a long space of time.[64]

Burke saw that constitution threatened in his own day by
George III's attempt systematically to break down the cabinet
system of government. In an effort to break through the limitations established by the Revolution of 1688, in a desire to
rule as well as to reign, George III encouraged the faction-
alism that already existed within the Whig party in order to
divide its strength and build up a personal following in the
House of Commons by every corrupt means, but chiefly
through the use of the patronage. After the Revolution of
1688, it had been the custom for the king to choose as Ministers men acceptable to Parliament. However, with the
accession of George III to the throne in 1760, an effort
was made to make Parliament subservient to the king by
choosing Ministers from the ranks of the "King's men." That
disregard for the rights of Parliament encouraged a similar
disregard for the rights of the people. This was graphically
illustrated in the case of John Wilkes. In 1763 Wilkes was
expelled from the House of Commons and sentenced to imprisonment for daring to launch a series of attacks upon the
King's favorite, and prime minister, Lord Bute. Since Wilkes
was in France at the time of the sentence, he was outlawed.
Later he returned to England and was elected to Parliament
by the voters of Middlesex but again he was expelled and
again he was re-elected. This occurred three times. He was
re-elected a fourth time by an overwhelming majority of
votes but again the Crown used its influence and the House
of Commons declared his opponent to be the lawful representative. Burke protested with vehemence and eloquence
against this violation of the constitution, against "this unnatural infusion of a *system of favouritism* into a government
which in a great part of its constitution is popular." [65] Pro-

testing the "shocking and shameless pretence" which led to the expulsion of Wilkes, he said:

The House of Commons can never be a control on other parts of government, unless they are controlled themselves by their constituents; and unless these constituents possess some right in the choice of that House, which it is not in the power of that House to take away. If they suffer this power of arbitrary incapacitation to stand, they have utterly perverted every other power of the House of Commons.[66]

Some argued that these abuses could only be cured by extending the suffrage, by holding more frequent elections, by abolishing the rotten boroughs, by limiting the duration of Parliaments. (Cures which, in fact, were later to be employed.) Burke, however, did not believe that these "cures" really got to the heart of the disease. He was afraid that they would only transfer arbitrary power from the king to the people and since it was arbitrary power that was the real danger it was better to return to the principles of 1688, to the principle of mixed government and a balanced constitution. The important thing, he insisted, is the *character* of the men who represent the people and the conception which they hold of the nature of their office. A true representative will regard himself, Burke insisted, not as an instrument of somebody else's will—whether it be the will of the King or the will of the electorate—but as a man answerable to Providence for his opinions and his judgment. In a famous speech which he made to the electors of Bristol in 1774 he said, speaking of his opponent for the seat in Parliament:

My worthy colleague says his will ought to be subservient to yours. If that be all, the thing is innocent. If government were a matter of will upon any side, yours, without question, ought to be superior. But government and legislation are matters of reason and judgment, and not of inclination; and what sort of reason is that, in which the determination precedes the discussion; in which one set of men deliberate, and another decide; and where those who form the conclusion are perhaps three hundred miles distant from those who hear the arguments?

To deliver an opinion is the right of all men; that of constituents is a weighty and respectable opinion, which a representative ought always to rejoice to hear; and which he ought always most seriously to consider. But *authoritative* instructions; *mandates* issued, which the member is bound blindly and implicitly to obey, to vote, and to argue for, though contrary to the clearest conviction of his judgment and conscience,—these are things utterly unknown to the laws of this land, and arise from a fundamental mistake of the whole order and tenor of our Constitution.

Parliament is not a *congress* of ambassadors from different and hostile interests; which interests each must maintain, as an agent and advocate, against other agents and advocates; but Parliament is a *deliberative* assembly of *one* nation, with *one* interest, that of the whole; where, not local purposes, not local prejudices, ought to guide, but the general good, resulting from the general reason of the whole.[67]

## Representatives have obligations not only to their constituents but to God.

Certainly, gentlemen, it ought to be the happiness and glory of a representative to live in the strictest union, the closest correspondence, and the most unreserved communication with his constituents. Their wishes ought to have great weight with him; their opinion, high respect; their business, unremitted attention. It is his duty . . . to prefer their interest to his own. But his unbiased opinion, his mature judgment, his enlightened conscience, he ought not to sacrifice to you, to any man, or to any set of men living. These he does not derive from your pleasure; no, nor from the law and the Constitution. They are a trust from Providence, for the abuse of which he is deeply answerable. Your representative owes you, not his industry only, but his judgment; and he betrays instead of serving you, if he sacrifices it to your opinion.[68]

The lobbies, special interest groups, and blocs that play such a prominent role in the modern legislative process; the use of public opinion polls as oracles of wisdom and as weapons with which to coerce legislators into action; the sycophancy that characterizes so many modern politicians in their relations with their constituents and their demogogic tactics in securing election, Burke would regard as a sign of parliamentary decadence. To the extent that deliberation is replaced by will, to the extent that the search for justice is replaced by the search for the best means of gratifying desires, legislation degenerates into arbitrary commands and obligation gives way to force.

Like James Madison in America, Burke feared the rise of factions and warned against them. A political party, Burke said, in what has become a classic definition: "is a body of men united, for promoting by their joint endeavors the national interest, upon some particular principle in which they are all agreed."

Speaking of the French Revolution, Burke declared:

> I cannot conceive how any man can have brought himself to that pitch of presumption, to consider his country as nothing but *carte blanche* upon which he may scribble whatever he pleases. A man . . . may wish his society otherwise constituted than he finds it; but a good patriot and a true politician always considers how he shall make the most of the existing materials of his country. A disposition to preserve and an ability to improve, taken together, would be my standard of a statesman.[69]

Burke is not opposed to change, he is not opposed to reform, but he is opposed to the radical presumption that it is possible to start *de novo* without concern for history or tradition. There is a middle ground, he insists, between "absolute destruction" and "unreformed existence" and it is the task of the statesman to find that middle ground. "To innovate is not to reform." [70]

Burke is sometimes thought to be inconsistent in his defense of the American and his condemnation of the French Revolution. He would explain this apparent inconsistency by saying that, in his opinion, the American Revolution preserved more than it destroyed while the French Revolution destroyed more than it preserved. The Americans were fighting for the preservation of the ancient liberties which Englishmen themselves had fought to establish but "in order to prove that the Americans have no right to their liberties," he said to his colleagues in Parliament on March 22, 1775,

> we are every day endeavouring to subvert the maxims which preserve the whole spirit of our own. To prove that the Americans ought not to be free, we are obliged to deprecate the value of freedom itself and we never seem to gain a paltry advantage over them in debate without attacking some of the principles or deriding some of those feelings for which our ancestors have shed their own blood.[71]

Liberty can be a blessing or a curse depending upon how it is used. "The effect of liberty to individuals is, that they may do what they please; we ought to see what it will please them to do, before we risk congratulations." [72] The French revolutionists, Burke thinks, used that liberty not to reform the state but to establish a tyranny. "I am amazed," he wrote, "at the morbid strength or the natural infirmity of . . . mind" that "can contemplate the result of this complete innovation" and "call it, *reform*." [73]

For the Reason worshipped by the *philosophes* Burke substituted custom and tradition and he cautioned those who would pin their hopes upon "the mere designs of men" not to delude themselves into thinking that they could resist "the decrees of Providence."

By a constitutional policy working after the pattern of nature, we transmit our government and our privileges, in the same manner in which we enjoy and transmit our property and our lives. The institutions of policy, the goods of fortune, the gifts of Providence, are handed down to us, and from us, in the same course and order. Our political system is placed in a just correspondence and symmetry with the order of the world, wherein, by the disposition of a stupendous wisdom, moulding together the great mysterious incorporation of the human race, the whole, at one time, is never old, or middle-aged, or young, but, in a condition of unchangeable constancy, moves on through the varied tenor of perpetual decay, fall, renovation, and progression. Thus, by preserving the method of nature in the conduct of the State, in what we improve, we are never wholly new; in what we retain, we are never wholly obsolete. [74]

Burke's conservatism is not, as some would say, *simply* a veneration of the past, a worship of tradition for the sake of the tradition alone, but an appreciation for what is good in the past and a hope that that good may be perpetuated into the future. When we stand upon the shoulders of those who have gone before us we increase our vision. It is presumptuous as well as foolish to think that our reason and our experience are the only things that matter. If each generation literally insisted upon the "right" to make over the social order in its own image we should have chaos instead of continuity. The newest is not necessarily the best nor the latest necessarily the truest.

The *philosophes* had an unbounded confidence in man's ability to be persuaded by reason to establish a just social order. Burke emphasized a truth which they had neglected—that sentiment plays an even larger role in social life than reason, that "naked reason" unmotivated by the love of what is good, will be turned not only against the good but against reason itself. Political problems are not like problems in geometry nor can we proceed to construct a social order from a set of *a priori* assumptions. The materials with which the statesman must work are not counters which can be pushed this way and that in accordance with some preconceived plan but are passionate human beings, capable of cooperation with the good but capable also of rebellion against it. Sentiment, or love, therefore, must always be reckoned with and it is only by inculcating habits of veneration through institutions that the passions of men can be channelized into socially beneficent action.

Undoubtedly Burke placed greater reliance upon the redemptive power of history as such than history can or does warrant. He conceived of God as a kind of divine immanence working in history for the redemption of mankind but he neglected the conception of God as a transcendent Being confronting each one of us here and now. The Church, he conceived more in terms of its utility as a social institution than as a divine institution for the mediation of grace.

It was not Burke's intention, however, to develop either a systematic political philosophy or a theology. His ideas were formulated in response to specific political events, in the heat of battle and in his role as statesman. If he transcended the role of statesman to utter some truths of timeless quality we may be grateful, that, however unsystematic as a thinker, he combined the talents of a politician with the wisdom of a philosopher. And that was as rare a combination in his day as it is in ours.

Burke laid the foundations for nineteenth-century idealism and more systematic philosophers were destined to develop theories that in Burke were undeveloped insights. "What

Burke had taken for granted," Professor Sabine declares, "Hegel tried to prove: that the apparently fragmentary social tradition can be placed in a general system of social evolution. He added what Burke had not thought of: that the rational form of this evolution might be made into a method generally applicable to philosophy and social studies." [75]

CHAPTER 7

# *Utilitarianism*

LIBERALISM as originally conceived regarded the state as existing for the primary purpose of protecting the individual's natural rights to "life, liberty, and property." The link between objective order (embodied in natural law) and subjective reality (individual will) was individual conscience. It was by following the dictates of conscience that the ideal of freedom under the law was to be realized. But with the destruction of the liberal conception of natural law, notably by Hume, liberalism in the nineteenth century was forced to seek a new foundation for freedom. The typical liberal of the nineteenth century believed that he had discovered this new foundation in the principle of utility. Utility, accordingly, was substituted for conscience as the link between objective order and subjective will. Freedom was conceived less and less as a natural right and more and more as a social utility. Happiness, in the sense of pleasurable sensation, was conveniently discovered to coincide with moral duty so that the moral problem was "solved" by denying its existence. The state was now justified less and less in moral terms and more and more in hedonistic terms; its function was no longer conceived as the protection of man's natural rights but as the promotion of "the greatest happiness of the greatest number."

Utilitarianism was an attempt to establish ethical and political theory upon a thoroughgoing scientific empiricism. The place occupied by philosophy in the eighteenth century was now destined to be occupied more and more by the methods and concepts of the natural sciences. Held together in an uneasy harmony in the seventeenth and eighteenth centuries philosophy all but abdicated to the natural sciences in the nineteenth. Valiant attempts were made to rescue philosophy from oblivion by the idealists; but more shall be said of that endeavor in another place. Associated primarily with the names of Jeremy Bentham, James Mill and his son, John Stuart Mill, Utilitarianism had its roots in the skepticism of David Hume and found early expression in the writings of the Frenchman, Helvetius.

## David Hume (1711–1776)

BORN in Edinburgh, Scotland, on April 26, 1711, David Hume was destined for a quiet life as a man of letters. He abandoned the study of the law in favor of philosophy after having tried for a short intervening period the career of a merchant. Supported by a small allowance from his family and "resolved to make a very rigid frugality supply" his "deficiency of fortune," he embarked permanently upon a literary career. In 1734 he went to France and three years later, at the age of twenty-six, produced what future generations were to regard as his greatest work, the *Treatise of Human Nature*. But Hume was frustrated in his first literary venture for it had no immediate success, having fallen, according to its author, "dead-born from the press."

In 1741 he published a collection of *Essays on Moral and Political Subjects*, a second volume of which appeared the following year. These ran through several editions and brought him his first fame as a writer. He then tried unsuccessfully to secure a position as a professor at the University of Edinburgh and his failure to do so was a great personal disappointment. It was undoubtedly the unorthodox and skeptical nature of his views which constituted the barrier to a professorship. Subsequently, Hume obtained positions as a tutor, a secretary, a librarian and in 1765 served as secretary to the British Embassy in Paris. He retired to Edinburgh in 1769 where he remained until his death on August 25, 1776.

It was in 1748 that he published his *Enquiry Concerning the Human Understanding* and in 1751 his *Enquiry Concerning the Principles of Morals*. Although he still clung in these works to the basic beliefs espoused in his first *Treatise* he did modify some of the ideas which he said he was "carried away by the heat of youth to publish too precipitously." It was in 1754 that he published the first volume of his *History of England* a work which, although probably his poorest intellectual and literary achievement, brought him considerable fame and financial prosperity. It was probably read more widely during his lifetime than anything else which he had written. In addition to these works he wrote a number of essays and books attacking the foundations of religion, the most important of which were his *Dialogues on Natural Religion*, published posthumously in 1779.

In his *Treatise of Human Nature* which was written, Hume said, "to introduce the experimental method of reasoning into moral subjects" he launched a frontal assault upon the presuppositions of eighteenth-century rationalism. We have already seen, in an earlier chapter, how he carried Locke's empirical theory of knowledge to its logical conclusion and ended in a skepticism that permitted little, if any, certain knowledge about anything. It remained for Kant to rescue, with some success, both science and morality from the impossible morass in which Hume had left them, but others sought to establish morality upon the shifting sands left by Hume's analysis.

The empirical method fostered by Locke was extended by Hume to destroy the medieval Christian elements still lingering in Locke and joined precariously to his empirical theory of knowledge. We have already seen how Hume denied the possibility of establishing any necessary connection between matters of fact by relying solely upon an empirical theory of knowledge. Since the mind can know nothing outside itself the realm of "fact" is completely divorced from the realm of "ideas." Reason can tell us something about the necessary relations between ideas but it can tell us nothing about "relationships between matters of fact." The idea of cause and effect, however useful it may be, is, in the last analysis, a fiction. Hume then proceeded from this point to examine the ethical and political theory which had been premised upon the assumption that there is a necessary connection between things and that reason can discover it.

Locke, in the ancient tradition, had contended that there are rational principles of justice which reason can discover and called these principles the laws of nature. But there is no such thing, Hume countered, as reasonable conduct. The so-called moral "laws of nature" are as fictitious as are the so-called physical "laws" of cause and effect. Reason by itself dictates no particular way of acting; it can tell how to achieve some desired end but it cannot tell us whether that end is good or bad. Some ends may be *conventionally* more worth while than others but no end is *necessarily* better than another. There is no such thing, therefore, as a reasonable or unreasonable desire. "Since reason alone can never produce any action or give rise to volition," Hume wrote, "I infer that the same faculty is as incapable of preventing volition or of disputing the preference with any passion or emotion. . . . Reason is, and ought only to be, the slave of the passions, and can never pretend to any other office than to serve and obey them." [1] It follows, in this view, that the rules of morality are not derived from deductions of reason, but, at best, that they are useful conventions.

Reason is the discovery of truth or falsehood. Truth or falsehood consists in an agreement or disagreement either to the *real* relations of ideas, or to *real* existence and matter of fact. Whatever, therefore, is not susceptible of this agreement or disagreement is incapable of being true or false, and can never be an object of our reason. Now, it is evident our passions, volitions, and actions, are not susceptible of any such agreement or disagreement. . . . It is impossible, therefore, they can be pronounced either true or false, and be either contrary or conformable to reason.[2]

(It also follows, if, as Hume has contended in other places, there is no necessary correspondence between ideas and matters of fact, that there is no possibility of discovering the truth about anything, including the truth of his own theory. Not only does he undermine the rational basis for morality but he undermines any possibility of establishing by rational means the truth about *anything*.)

Having denied the necessary existence of laws of nature and rules of morality he then proceeds to explain on a "purely" empirical basis how morality arises. He starts from the assumption that "the distinguishing impressions by which moral good or evil is known are nothing but *particular* pains or pleasures" [3] and reaches the conclusion *"that it is only from the selfishness and confined generosity of man, along with the scanty provision nature has made for his wants that justice derives its origin."* [4] It does not matter, he says, whether we regard human nature as good or bad: "For whether the passion of self-interest be esteemed vicious or virtuous, it is all a case, since itself alone restrains it; so that if it be virtuous, men become social by their virtue; if vicious, their vice has the same effect." [5] Men learn from experience that in order to satisfy their selfishness and their limited generosity society is necessary and hence "they are *naturally induced* to lay themselves under the restraint of such rules as may render their commerce more safe and commodious." [6] It is by no means clear, however, how men who are naturally selfish can be "naturally induced to lay themselves under the restraint of such rules." Hume simply says that

When . . . men have had experience enough to observe that, whatever may be the consequence of any single act of justice performed by a single person, yet the whole system of actions concurred in by the whole society is infinitely advantageous to the whole and to every part, it is not long before justice and property take place. Every member of society is sensible of this interest; every one expresses this sense to his fellows along with the resolution he has taken of squaring his actions by it, on condition that others will do the same. No more is requisite to induce any one of them to perform an act of justice, who has the first opportunity. This becomes an example to others; and thus justice establishes itself by a kind of convention or agreement, that is, by a sense of interest, *supposed* to be common to all, and where every single act is performed in expectation that others are to perform the like. . . . Taking any single act, my justice may be pernicious in every respect; and it is only upon the supposition that others are to imitate my example that I can be induced to embrace that virtue; since nothing but this combination can render justice advantageous, or afford me any motives to conform myself to its rules. [7]

This assumes "a sense of interest . . . common to all" but does not explain whence it arises or how it is to be enforced if others do not "imitate my example." If there are no principles of justice which reason can discern as being in the common interest of all, and if selfish interest alone motivates men to submit to convenient and mutually advantageous "rules," there can be no reason for abiding by these "rules" and no moral obligation. In place of moral obligation derived from a rational apprehension of the good Hume would substitute a kind of moral sentiment based upon a psychological principle of association. Any sense of duty which men have derives not from nature but from "human conventions."

Men are born, Hume declares, with an instinctive capacity for *sympathy*, and it is this sympathy which makes society possible. But the word sympathy is used by him in a very ambiguous way and explained quite differently in the *Treatise* than it is in his later *Enquiry Concerning the Principles of Morals*. In the *Treatise* the word sympathy is used to mean the capacity to *feel*, but not necessarily to sympathize with, the emotions of others. Perhaps the word "empathy" would explain better what he means. Sympathy is produced through the "association of ideas." The similarity of other individuals to ourselves makes it possible for us, through the association of ideas, to entertain the idea of another's emotion and the entertainment of the idea may give rise to the same emotion in ourselves. Speaking of this conception in Hume a prominent historian of utilitarianism declares:

> This aspect of Hume's system, in its earlier form, is the more confusing for the reason that he never seriously attempts to state the relation between our derived "sympathy" and our fundamental self-regarding tendency. The result is a degree of theoretical confusion that can only be appreciated by those who have read the *Treatise* with considerable care. It should be observed that one does not here refer to the inevitable ambiguity of the words "egoism" and "altruism," as ordinarily used, but rather the fact that Hume professes to explain—almost in the sense of explaining away—what we ordinarily understand by (general) "sympathy," without anywhere, telling us exactly what he claims to have reduced it to.[8]

In the *Enquiry* he makes no attempt to define sympathy but uses it in its more usual meaning as a general benevolent tendency. Speaking of this "general benevolence" or "sympathy," he says: "I assume it as real from general experience, without any other proof." [9] In his conclusion to the *Enquiry* he states that "Whatever contradiction may vulgarly be supposed between the *selfish* and *social* sentiments or dispositions, they are really no more opposite than selfish and ambitious, selfish and revengeful, selfish and vain. It is requisite that there be an original propensity of some kind, in order to be a basis to self-love, by giving a relish to the objects of its pursuit; and none more fit for this purpose than benevolence or humanity." [10] This feeling of "benevolence and friendship, humanity and kindness," he says, "is sweet, smooth, tender, and agreeable" and "besides, attended with a pleasing consciousness or remembrance" that makes it possible for us "to keep in humour with ourselves as well as others, while we retain the agreeable reflection of having done our part towards mankind and society." [11] Moreover, it gives us a "good reputation." Benevolent actions give pleasure not only to ourselves but to others, hence there is no conflict between selfish and social sentiments. Utility alone explains the approbation which is attached to benevolent actions. So sure was Hume of the validity of his reasoning that he wrote:

> It may justly appear surprising that any man in so late an age should find it requisite to prove by elaborate reasoning that Personal Merit consists altogether in the possession of mental qualities, *useful* or *agreeable* to the person himself or to *others*. It might be expected that this principle would have occurred even to the first rude, unpracticed enquirers concerning morals, and been received from its own evidence without any argument. Whatever is valuable in any kind, so naturally classes itself under the division of *useful* or *agreeable* . . . that it is not easy to imagine why we should ever seek further or consider the question as a matter of nice research or inquiry . . . the complete delineation or description of merit seems to be performed as naturally as a shadow is cast by the sun or an image is reflected upon water.[12]

Hume himself pointed out one difficulty with this theory. What about the generally accepted maxim that "honesty is the best policy?" What are we to say to the man who argues that by following this maxim he is the loser? What about the man who argues that "he . . . conducts himself with most wisdom who observes the general rule and takes advantage of all the exceptions?" And Hume says: "I must confess that, if a man think that this reasoning much requires an answer, it would be a little difficult to find any which will to him appear satisfactory and convincing." The best answer Hume can formulate is to say that "inward peace of mind, consciousness of integrity, a satisfactory review of our own conduct—these are circumstances very requisite to happiness, and will be cultivated by every honest man who feels the importance of them." [13] But, here, he shifts the basis of morality from utility to an innate moral consciousness and

this appeal to our moral consciousness hardly meets the theoretical difficulty—the self-imposed difficulty of eighteenth-century individualism—which was to show that morality was for the advantage of the moral agent, not as a social thing, with no interests wholly separate from those of society, but rather as an isolated centre of self-interest. The only logical solution, from that point of view, was that of the so-called "Theological Utilitarians," who frankly depended upon the doctrine of rewards and punishments after death. [14]

(Typical of the thought of the Theological Utilitarians was William Paley's famous definition of virtue as "the doing good to mankind, in obedience to the will of God, and for the sake of everlasting happiness." [15])

Utilitarianism finds classic expression in Jeremy Bentham but before examining his formulation of the creed it might be well to give some brief attention to the ideas of the Frenchman, Helvetius, whose influence upon Bentham was considerable.

## *Helvetius (1715–1771)*

BENTHAM declares that it was from the French philosopher, Helvetius, that he obtained the principle that government should promote "the greatest happiness of the greatest number." Helvetius also anticipated Bentham by unequivocally stating that

The springs of action in man are corporeal pains and pleasures. Pleasure and pain, are, and always will be, the only principles of action in man. . . . Corporeal pleasure and pain are the real and only springs of all government. We do not properly desire glory, riches and honors, but the pleasures only of which glory, riches, and honors are representatives. . . . In man all is sensation. . . . All our desires, and all our passions . . . are nothing more in us than the application of self-love to particular objects. . . . Self-love makes us totally what we are.[16]

The assumption from which he starts is that man is essentially a physical organism, and that his ideas are no more than the remembrance and association of physical sensations. Judgment is nothing more than the memory that one sensation is more pleasant than another. Moral conduct is simply explained as being motivated by a desire to seek that which is pleasurable and avoid that which is painful. Every act is motivated ultimately by self-interest—we are generous, kind, self-sacrificing, because it will give us a good reputation and make us feel comfortable. But why the motive of self-interest should make us kind and self-sacrificing rather than cruel and selfish Helvetius does not really say. To say, as he does, that a hero is a person who enjoys being heroic does not explain anything about heroism nor does it explain why some persons are heroic and others are not. But the significant thing is that he thought it explained a great deal. Helvetius, along with other utilitarians, believed that he had discovered that the Golden Rule—do unto others as you would they should do unto you—was simply the embodiment of enlightened self-interest anchored in the physical constitution of man himself.

Helvetius had, like all utilitarians, to offer some explanation how man as a self-loving and self-seeking individual could be inspired to promote the happiness of others. He believed that society, by providing rewards for socially beneficent behavior and punishment for socially destructive behavior, could make morality attractive. Men are not born with "innate principles of virtue" or with "natural compassion" but they can be made to approximate them by means of education and legislation. (Where "society" gets its ideas of what is socially beneficent he does not say or how "society" acts and thinks apart from individuals.) Education "is capable of effecting everything," it "makes us what we are," [17] and "the virtues and vices of a nation are always necessary effects of its legislation." [18] The inequalities among men are the result of differences in experience, education, and environment for Nature, he says, "never made a dunce." He believed, Kingsley Martin says, that "under a good system of education and laws, therefore, creative ability can be manufactured." [19] "*It is certain*," Helvetius wrote, "*that great men, who now appear haphazard, will in the future be produced by legislature*, and the abilities and virtues of the citizens in great empires need not be left so much to chance: by really good education they may be infinitely multiplied." [20] No more striking and clear statement of the liberal's faith in education could be found than this. That "creative ability" derives not from the Creator of all things and of all men but from the legislature is, indeed, a novel idea; that it can be "manufactured" is a typical liberal belief that springs from a fundamental fallacy concerning the autonomy of human nature.

Government, in Helvetius' view, ought to have no "other object than the happiness of the majority." Since happiness is a personal matter the State should promote the freedom which is essential to each individual's search for happiness. What if my personal happiness consists in doing something that is socially undesirable? In that case, I must be taught by an appropriate system of rewards and punishments administered by the State to find my happiness in that which promotes the social well-being. "If the right penalties are attached to unsocial conduct, men will freely seek virtue. The right laws will ensure both happiness and righteousness." [21]

Although he believed in representative government Helvetius would exclude from participation in that government the uneducated and the poor. "Have not the poor," he asked, "too many wants to be virtuous?" [22] "Without education or property a man could not be expected to see any advantages in moral conduct; indeed Helvetius admitted that the poor were necessarily immoral, and argued that private property was an essential without which a man 'had no country.' " [23]

Helvetius hoped that "these principles" might be "adopted by an enlightened and benevolent prince" and accordingly dedicated one of his essays to Catherine II of Russia. "If I could demonstrate," he wrote, "that man is indeed but the product of his education, I should undoubtedly have revealed a great truth to the nations. They would then know that they hold within their own hands the instrument of their greatness and their happiness, and that *to be happy and powerful is only a matter of perfecting the science of education.*" [24] It remained for Bentham, the disciple of Helvetius, to elaborate upon these ideas and to render them popular.

## *Jeremy Bentham (1748–1832)*

JEREMY BENTHAM was born in London, England, in 1748. He was a precocious child and entered Queen's College, Oxford, at the age of thirteen. He was unhappy there and pronounced all formal education to be a waste of time. He was motivated by a family interest in the law to undertake that career and it absorbed his interest so completely that he devoted a lifetime to its study. Economically independent by virtue of an inheritance he could devote himself to what interested him most, the theory rather than the practice of law. He was a prolific writer and his collected works comprise twenty-two volumes but despite that fact he never seemed to be able to complete what he began, so that the works which he published during his lifetime consist primarily of introductions to and fragments from larger projected treatises. His writings cover a wide range of interests including ethics, theology, psychology, logic, economics, penology but his main interest and a constantly recurring one is the law. His first important publication was an essay entitled *A Fragment on Government* (1776) consisting of a criticism of Sir William Blackstone's Introduction to his Commentaries on the Laws of England. Published at first anonymously it was credited to a number of different eminent men of the time. In 1785 Bentham set out on an extended tour of Europe spending nearly two years in Russia. In 1789 he published his *Introduction to the Principles of Morals and Legislation* on which he had been at work for fifteen years. It was intended to be an introduction to a series of works on the principal branches of the law but Bentham was never able to execute the project he had planned. Shortly after the publication of this book he tried to obtain a seat in Parliament but failed and henceforth abandoned any idea of becoming active in politics. He then became absorbed in a plan for a model prison, but, although Parliament passed a bill in 1794 authorizing the establishment of such a prison the plan was never carried out, due, it is said, to the opposition of George III. He participated during his lifetime in many reform movements and was a partner of Robert Owen in the model factory village of New Lanark. His supreme ambition was to draft a scientific code of laws which he could persuade some government to put into effect. When the French revolutionists showed little interest in his project he turned to the United States but his proposal was received there with equal coolness. In 1823 he founded the *Westminster Review* to which James Mill and later John Mill frequently contributed. He died in June, 1832, in his eighty-fifth year.

In the opening paragraph of his *Introduction to the Principles of Morals and Legislation* Bentham states clearly the presuppositions upon which his ethical theory is based:

Nature has placed mankind under the governance of two sovereign masters, *pain* and *pleasure*. It is for them alone to point out what we ought to do, as well as to determine what we shall do. On the one hand the standard of right and wrong, on the other the chain of causes and effects, are fastened to their throne. They govern us in all we do, in all we say, in all we think; every effort we can make to throw off our subjection, will serve but to demonstrate and confirm it. . . . The *principle of utility* recognises this subjection, and assumes it for the foundation of that system, the object of which is to rear the fabric of felicity by the hands of reason and of law.[25]

To prove the validity of this principle, Bentham says, is as unnecessary as it is impossible. It must be assumed as self-evidently true. There is no such thing as a moral sense or conscience, all a person means when he says that his moral sense approves of something is that he prefers it. There are no eternal and immutable rules of right, no Law of Reason, no moral Law of Nature, no Natural Justice. Unnatural never means anything more than infrequent.[26]

"But is it never, then, from any other considerations than those of utility, that we derive our notions of right and wrong?" I do not know: I do not care. Whether a moral sentiment can be originally conceived from any other source than a view of utility, is one question: whether upon examination and reflection it can, in point of fact, be actually persisted in and justified on any other ground, by a person addressing himself to the community, is a third. The two first are questions of speculation: it matters not, comparatively speaking, how they are decided. The last is a question of practice: the decision of it is of as much importance as that of any can be.[27]

To those who would refer the question of right and wrong to the will of God, Bentham replies that "God does not, he confessedly does not now, either speak or write to us. How are we to know what is his pleasure? By observing what is our own pleasure, and pronouncing it to be his." [28] As far as the will of God revealed in the sacred writings is concerned, Bentham says that "this is a system which nobody ever thinks of recurring to at this time of day." [29]

Goodness and badness, Bentham claims, have nothing whatsoever to do with motives. If "pleasure is in itself a good: nay, even setting aside immunity from pain, the only good: pain is in itself an evil; and, indeed, without exception, the only evil. . . . It follows, therefore, immediately and incontestibly, that *there is no such thing as any sort of motive that is in itself a bad one*." [30] It is simply a question of their effects, motives are good if they produce pleasure, bad if they produce pain, but no motive is good or bad in itself. Lust, cruelty, and avarice, Bentham claims, do not refer to any reality but are simply words which are used to describe the "bad" effects of motives which in themselves are neutral or indifferent. Something of Bentham's reasoning on this subject may be gathered from one illustration:

To the pleasures of wealth corresponds the sort of motive which, in a neutral sense, may be termed pecuniary interest: in a bad sense, it is termed, in some cases avarice, covetousness, rapacity, or lucre . . . in a good sense, but only in particular cases, economy and frugality; and in some cases the word industry may be applied to it. . . .

1. For money you gratify a man's hatred, by putting his adversary

to death. 2. For money you plough his field for him.—In the first case your motive is termed lucre, and is accounted corrupt and abominable: and in the second, for want of a proper appellation, it is styled industry; and is looked upon as innocent at least, if not meritorious. Yet the motive is in both cases precisely the same: it is neither more nor less than pecuniary interest.[31]

Having rejected the revealed will of God as a standard of right and wrong, and having rejected all systems of morality based upon man's natural reason as being nothing more nor less than subjective evaluations actually based on the principle of utility, Bentham is anxious to provide some *objective*, external, standard by means of which right and wrong can be decided. He believes that he has discovered this standard, or rather a method of computing the utility of an action, in what is called the *calculus of pleasure*. It is his contention that pleasure and pain can be mathematically measured and that the decision as to the utility and, hence, in his view, the rightness of an action, can be reduced to a problem in arithmetic.

In estimating the amount of pleasure and pain in any particular action we have but to measure seven factors: its (1) intensity, (2) duration, (3) certainty or uncertainty, (4) propinquity or remoteness, (5) fecundity, (6) purity, and (7) extent, that is the number of persons to whom it extends or who are affected by it.[32] We then proceed as follows:

Sum up all the values of all the *pleasures* on the one side and those of all the pains on the other. The balance, if it be on the side of pleasure, will give the *good* tendency of the act upon the whole, with respect to the interests of that *individual* person; if on the side of pain, the *bad* tendency of it upon the whole.

Take an account of the number of persons whose interests appear to be concerned; and repeat the above process with respect to each. *Sum up* the numbers expressive of the degrees of *good* tendency, which the act has, with respect to each individual, in regard to whom the tendency of it is *good* upon the whole: do this again with respect to each individual, in regard to whom the tendency of it is *bad* upon the whole. Take the *balance:* which, if on the side of *pleasure*, will give the general *good tendency* of the act, with respect to the total number or community of individuals concerned; if on the side of pain, the general *evil tendency*, with respect to the same community.[33]

He conceives of pleasures and pains as being of two general kinds: simple and complex. He lists fifteen simple pleasures among which are the pleasures of sense, wealth, amity, power, piety, benevolence, malevolence and imagination. He lists eleven simple pains among which are the pains of sense, privation, awkwardness, enmity, piety, benevolence, malevolence and imagination. Complex pleasures and pains are combinations of these.[34] All pains and pleasures are effects produced by external causes but individuals do not experience the same quantity of pleasure or pain from the same cause and this is because they differ in sensitivity, or to use Bentham's word, sensibility. Bentham lists some thirty-two factors which he says influence sensibility and these have to be taken into account in any computation of the total amount of pleasure or pain involved in any given act. Among the factors he lists are: health, quantity and quality of knowledge, intellectual capacity, steadiness of mind, moral sensibility, religious sensibility, pecuniary circumstances, sex, age, rank, climate, lineage, and government.[35]

The apparent simplicity of Bentham's ethical theory disappears under analysis and the simplicity is seen for what it is, namely, naïveté. Pleasure is arbitrarily defined as good and pain as evil; no proof of this is offered despite the fact that we can all think of pleasures that are bad for us if pursued immoderately or to the exclusion of other things and we all know that under some circumstances it is a good thing to endure pain rather than to avoid it. The greatest contributions which have been made to our civilization were made (and are being made) by men and women who endured pain for the sake of something they valued more than pleasure. The reference of all moral questions to pleasure and pain is a gross oversimplification of the moral problem. But Bentham refuses to acknowledge that there *is* any moral problem for he says that pleasure and pain not only should be our guide in making moral decisions but that they actually *determine* what we will think, do and say. In that case there is no conflict between what we ought to do and what we actually do, so the moral problem is neatly "solved" by denying that it exists. The constitution of man is such that he cannot help but do that which he ought to do. But we all know from our own experience that that simply is not true.

The calculus of pleasure with which Bentham supplies us turns out to have no practical significance at all. He provides no scale of values with which to measure the various factors and no way of determining the relative importance of the factors he lists. How actually could we measure the fecundity or purity of a pleasure? Should we prefer greater purity to greater duration, or greater duration to greater intensity? Bentham does not tell us and he does not tell us for the good reason that he cannot. He assumes, moreover, that the only end is pleasure and that the only variations that matter are quantitative. But there are obvious qualitative differences between things which are pleasurable and the choice between them must be made on other grounds than that of the amount of pleasure yielded. In fact, the kind of pleasure which we derive from one kind of activity is not the same kind of pleasure we get from another—pleasure is not something external to activity but inheres in the activity itself and differs in kind depending upon the kind of activity in which we are engaged. The pleasure we receive from eating cake and ice cream is different in kind from the pleasure we receive from listening to a symphony by Beethoven. The pleasure we get from playing a game of tennis is different in kind from the pleasure we experience from a performance of Hamlet. These pleasures are neither comparable nor are they susceptible to mathematical evaluation.

The search for pleasure alone, moreover, can never result in happiness for the reason that our pleasures are insatiable. The more we are in bondage to our appetites the more they demand and the less easily are they satisfied. The wise man learns to restrain his desires and to seek his pleasure in moderation, the foolish man yields to every desire and finds himself eventually the slave of his appetites. Self-indulgence rather than leading to happiness leads to misery. As a matter of fact, as Aristotle pointed out in the tenth book of his *Nicomachaean Ethics*, to pursue pleasure directly is to lose it, for pleasure is not something that can be sought for directly, it is a by-product of activity that has some more ultimate object in view than pleasure itself. Pleasure perfects the activity which it accompanies but it is not a part of that activity nor its end.

Bentham's political theory is simply an extension of his ethical theory. It is nonsense, he says, to talk of the interest of the community apart from the interests of those who compose it: "The interest of the community . . ." is nothing more nor less than "the sum of the interests of the several members who compose it." [36] Since a thing is said to promote the interest of an individual when it adds to the sum total of his pleasures or diminishes the sum total of his pains, the task of government is to promote the greatest happiness of the greatest number.[37]

Bentham conceives of government as having primarily negative functions.

Every law is an evil, because every law is a violation of liberty; so that government . . . can only choose between evils. What should be the aim of the legislator when making this choice? He should satisfy himself of two things: *First*, that in all cases the events which he strives to prevent are really evils; and, *secondly*, that these evils are greater than those he is about to employ as the means of prevention.[38]

The happiness of the body politic consists in Subsistence, Abundance, Equality, and Security and these are the objects which the law should promote. Liberty is not included in this list, Bentham says, because "if we would avoid confusion we must regard it as a branch of 'security.' " [39] If there is any conflict between these ends "security" must be regarded as of paramount importance. Speaking of the role which government should play in relation to the economy Bentham wrote: "the general rule is, that nothing ought to be done or attempted by government. . . . With few exceptions, and those not very considerable ones, the attainment of the maximum enjoyment will be most effectually secured by leaving each individual to pursue his own maximum of enjoyment, in proportion as he is in possession of the means." [40] Each one knows best what serves his own interest and no one will serve that interest better than the individual himself.

In a work entitled *Anarchical Fallacies*, Bentham subjected the French Declaration of the Rights of Man of 1789 to a critical examination, article by article, premised upon the assumption that there are no natural rights and that the reasoning in the Declaration is fallacious. For example, Article II of that Declaration states that "The end in view of every political association is the preservation of the natural and imprescriptable rights of man. These rights are liberty, property, security, and resistance to oppression." And Bentham says:

More confusion—more nonsense. . . . The words can scarcely be said to have a meaning. . . . There are no such things as natural rights, no such things as rights anterior to the establishment of government,—no such things as natural rights opposed to, in contradistinction to, legal . . . the expression is merely figurative. . . . *Natural rights* is simply nonsense . . . rhetorical nonsense,—nonsense upon stilts.[41]

There are no natural rights but only legal rights; a man has no rights by virtue of his humanity but only by virtue of the law. Properly speaking rights are only concessions made by the state and which, being concessions, the state may withdraw at will. A person may be said to have a "right" only "in proportion as it is . . . advantageous to the society in question" and "there is no right which, when the abolition of it is advantageous to society, should not be abolished." [42]

Bentham likewise rejected the social contract theory of government, as of course, "nonsense" (one of his favorite words). Men obey the laws of government not because they have consented to do so, not because the laws embody principles of justice to which their reason inclines them to render obedience, but because "the probable mischiefs of obedience are less than the probable mischiefs of resistance." [43] It is a matter of calculated self-interest, of utility. What is political society? —simply a number of persons habitually obeying other persons, "When a number of persons (whom we may style *subjects*) are supposed to be in the *habit* of paying obedience to a person, or an assemblage of persons, of a known and certain description (whom we may call *governor* or *governors*) such persons altogether (*subjects* and *governors*) are said to be in a state of *political* society." [44] Law is simply the expression of a will in the form of a command.[45] Since neither nature nor reason can be said to have a will neither can be said to be the source of law. The law must be the reflection either of the will of God or of the will of man. Since the will of God is obscure, if it can be said to exist at all, it follows that law must be the expression of the will of man, and not, of course, of man in general but of particular men for only they have wills. The particular man or men whose will is habitually obeyed is sovereign and there are no definite, assignable boundaries to sovereign power. To say that the supreme body in a state cannot do something, to say that its acts can be illegal or void, to speak of its exceeding its authority is, Bentham says once again, nonsense and "an abuse of language." [46] The only conceivable restraint upon the sovereign power is the practical consideration of how far it can go without arousing resistance to its commands. Political power is necessarily unlimited and undefined. The only distinctions Bentham will admit between a despotic government and a free one is the manner in which the supreme power is distributed; the ease and frequency with which "changes of condition between governors and governed" may be brought about "whereby the interests of the one class are more or less indistinguishably blended with those of the other"; the extent to which the governed are informed of the reasons for "every act of power"; the degree of freedom of the press that exists and the extent of freedom of "public association." In other words a "free" government is one in which the people possess greater opportunities for registering complaints and practicing "every mode of opposition short of actual revolt, before the executive power can be legally justified in disturbing them." [47]

Bentham's formula—the greatest happiness for the greatest number—has been accepted widely as a standard by means of which to measure good government. Yet despite its apparent simplicity it is much less satisfactory than, at first, it appears to be. Given two possible courses of action should we prefer that which yields the greater amount of happiness or that which would give some happiness to more people? The formula does not help us to decide such a question and that situation reveals a fundamental contradiction in the formula itself. Take this situation: $x$ is capable of producing 100 units of happiness for 10 people ($100 \times 10 = 1000$); $y$ is capable of producing 10 units of happiness for 100 people ($10 \times 100 = $

1000)—which should we choose to do in terms of Bentham's formula? But there is an even more serious objection to it. As a guide in practical affairs it is not only more abstract than the concept of justice (which it is intended to replace) but it may actually be used to lend a semblance of justification to acts that in fact are unjust. Why should the happiness of the greatest *number* be preferred to the happiness of all and of each? Would it be right (if it were possible) for the overwhelming majority of the people to purchase its happiness at the expense of unhappiness and injustice to the minority? Is it all right to confine a minority of individuals to concentration camps if such action is deemed necessary in order to provide for the happiness of the majority? Would it be all right to enslave a minority of the population in order that the majority might be "happy?" According to Bentham's formula, apparently it would. The formula is one that can be made congenial to tyranny so long as the tyrant can make his actions appear to serve the greatest happiness of the greatest number. For without a conception of justice there is no way in which his acts of injustice can be identified as such, no way in which the rights of the minority can claim a priority over the "happiness" of the majority.

Bentham makes it abundantly clear that no individual has any rights by virtue of his humanity and that the sovereign power is absolute and unlimited in the exercise of its powers. It is limited only by the practical consideration of how far it can go without arousing resistance—hence, if it can develop techniques of propaganda and coercion to reduce the possibility of resistance (as the modern totalitarian states have done) it can do just about as it pleases. The liberalism of Locke which arose to combat tyranny is converted by Bentham, unwittingly it may be, into a liberalism that is congenial to tyranny.

# John Stuart Mill (1806–1873)

JOHN STUART MILL's father, James Mill (1773–1836) was an ardent disciple and intimate friend of Bentham. As an editor, essayist, historian, and economist he achieved considerable fame and although he added little to what Bentham had already said he sought to provide additional historical, economic and psychological data with which to buttress the utilitarian theory. His *Elements of Political Economy* (1821) was one of the first English textbooks in economics and supported Ricardo. His *Analysis of the Human Mind* (1829) was an elaboration upon the doctrine of the association of ideas. James Mill planned his son's education with meticulous care and tutored him himself. John Mill was studying Greek at the age of three, was reading Hume at the age of eight, reading Aristotle in the original Greek at twelve and attending John Austin's lectures in jurisprudence at fifteen. When he was seventeen years of age he entered the India Service as a clerk and the next thirty-five years were spent in that Service. He retired on a pension in 1858 and served in Parliament for three years (1865–1868) during which time he advocated such unpopular measures as proportional representation, woman suffrage, and the reduction of the national debt.

Under the direct influence of his father and of Bentham, Austin, and Ricardo it was practically predetermined that he should become an ardent supporter of utilitarianism. He dedicated his intellectual energies to the propagation of that creed and was instrumental in founding the Utilitarian Society in 1822. He wrote extensively in many fields and was a frequent contributor to the *Westminister Review*. His principal works include his *Logic* (1843), *Political Economy* (1848), *The Subjection of Women* (1869), and a number of essays. The most important of his essays include *Utilitarianism*, first published in a magazine in 1861; *On Liberty* (1859); *Considerations on Representative Government* (1861) and three posthumous essays on *Nature*, *The Utility of Religion*, and *Theism*.

Some attention will be given in a later chapter to Mill's "Logic of the Moral Sciences" and we shall concentrate our attention here upon his ethical and political theory. It is enough to point out here that Mill was an empiricist who believed that all experience could be reduced to sensations, which, when combined by the laws of association, constitute our knowledge, and our only knowledge, of the world about us. He denies that we know anything *a priori;* all knowledge consists ultimately of inductions from experience. Even mathematics, which Hume's radical empiricism had left immune from doubt, is no exception Mill insisted. "By driving empiricism to its extreme limit," Guido de Ruggiero declares, "Mill succeeded better than any criticism in revealing the absurdity of its thesis." [48] Reality is reduced by Mill to nothing more than the "possibilities of sensation."

. . . in fact, according to him not only is external reality resolved into these possibilities, but so is the sentient subject. The belief that my spirit exists when it does not feel or think, and has no consciousness of its own existence, is reduced to the belief in a permanent possibility of these states. Yet here Mill stops short, unwilling to tread forbidden ground. What is really incomprehensible, he says, is that a thing which has ceased to exist, should nevertheless be able to be in some manner present: that a series of feelings of which the greater part lies in the past or the future could be incorporated, so to speak, in a present sensation, accompanied by the belief in its reality. "I think," he adds, "by far the wisest thing we can do, is to accept the inexplicable fact, without any theory of how it takes place."

Thus the incomprehensible finishes by being the whole of Mill's theory. His sensations are a sort of shadows that do not come to be and do not perish, but only appear together and disappear together in a mysterious manner, independently of any consciousness, and arrange themselves in groups in order to produce consciousness: a process which . . . resembles the naturalistic theory of the production of sensation by means of the movements of matter.[49]

In his essay on Utilitarianism Mill begins by accepting the Benthamite conception without, apparently, any reservation.

The creed which accepts as the foundation of morals, Utility, or the Greatest Happiness Principle, holds that actions are right in proportion as they tend to promote happiness, wrong as they tend to produce the reverse of happiness. By happiness is intended pleasure, and the absence of pain; by unhappiness, pain, and the privation of pleasure . . . pleasure, and freedom from pain, are the only things desirable as ends; and . . . all desirable things . . . are desirable either for the pleasure inherent in themselves, or as means to the promotion of pleasure and the prevention of pain.[50]

Yet a few paragraphs further on it becomes clear that Mill is accepting a modified form of the Benthamite theory for he

says that "It would be absurd that while, in estimating all
other things *quality* is considered as well as quantity, the esti-
mation of pleasures should be supposed to depend on quantity
alone." [51] Bentham had argued that all that mattered was the
quantity of pleasure but Mill says that "it would be absurd"
not to take quality into account as well. Some pleasures, he
argues, are qualitatively superior to others—the pleasures of
the intellect, for example, are superior intrinsically to those of
the palate.

> . . . there is no known Epicurean theory of life which does not
> assign to the pleasures of the intellect, of the feelings and imagination,
> and of the moral sentiments, a much higher value as pleasures than
> to those of mere sensation. It must be admitted, however, that utili-
> tarian writers in general have placed the superiority of mental over
> bodily pleasures chiefly in the greater permanency, safety, uncostli-
> ness, etc., of the former—that is, in their circumstantial advantages
> rather than in their intrinsic nature. . . . It is quite compatible with
> the principle of utility to recognize the fact, that some kinds of pleas-
> ure are more desirable and more valuable than others.[52]

But is it "quite compatible" with the principle of utility to
argue that some pleasures are *intrinsically* more desirable and
more valuable than others? To say that one kind of pleasure
is in itself more desirable and valuable than another kind is
to introduce, surreptitiously it may be, some other standard
than that of pleasure to differentiate between them. If it is
not the amount of pleasure which makes one kind more desirable than another then it is something else which is not
pleasure which makes one kind more desirable than another.
What this "something else" is, Mill does not tell us but it is
clear, at any rate, that this supposed modification of utilitarianism actually amounts to its repudiation. For it is logically
impossible to hold *both* that pleasure is the only thing desirable and that pleasures can differ in quality.

Pressed for an answer to the question: how are we to know
which pleasures are more desirable intrinsically than others?
Mill answers in this fashion: consult those persons who are
best qualified to judge. How are we to identify those persons?
And he answers: by the fact that they prefer superior pleasures.

. . . it is an unquestionable fact that those who are equally acquainted with, and equally capable of appreciating and enjoying,
both, do give a most marked preference to the manner of existence
which employs their higher faculties . . . no intelligent human
being would consent to be a fool, no instructed person would be an
ignoramus, no person of feeling and conscience would be selfish and
base, even though they should be persuaded that the fool, the dunce,
or the rascal is better satisfied with his lot than they are with their . . .

From this verdict of the only competent judges, I apprehend there
can be no appeal. On a question which is the best worth having of
two pleasures . . . the judgment of those who are qualified by
knowledge of both, or, if they differ, that of the majority among
them, must be admitted as final.[53]

There is contained in this quotation a remarkable indication
of the conception of human nature held by Mill; "no intelligent human being," he says, "would consent to be a fool";
"no person of feeling and conscience would be selfish and
base." Surely this is an overly optimistic view of human nature, for we need only consult our own experience to know
that intelligent people are often fools and that persons of
feeling and conscience often act in a selfish and base way. Even
more curious for one who is a professed utilitarian is the occurrence of words like "conscience," "selfish" and "base."
What possible meaning can the word "conscience" have to
one who claims that right is synonymous with pleasure and
wrong with pain? How can the word "selfish" be used, as it is
in this context, in a derogatory manner by one who claims
that one both does and ought to be guided by his own interests and desires? The truth of the matter is that Mill is not
a thoroughgoing utilitarian but since he claims to be one his
theoretical position is severely damaged by the surreptitious
introduction of standards other than those of utility into his
theory, particularly when those standards are never made
explicit.

In the fourth chapter of his essay on *Utilitarianism* Mill
tackles the crucial problem which confronts all utilitarians:
how can individuals who are conceived as being motivated
solely by the desire to experience pleasure and avoid pain
desire the happiness of others? Why should I prefer the happiness of others to my own pleasure? And Mill answers:

No reason can be given why the general happiness is desirable, except that each person, so far as he believes it to be attainable, desires his own happiness. This, however, being a fact, we have not only all the proof which the case admits of, but all which it is possible to require, that happiness is a good: that each person's happiness is a good to that person, and the general happiness, therefore, a good to the aggregate of all persons.[54]

Commenting upon this statement a contemporary English philosopher declares:

> The argument is a bad one. What Mill is, in effect, saying is that, if A's pleasure is a good to him, B's pleasure a good to him and C's pleasure a good to him, and so on, then the aggregate pleasures of A, B, and C will be good to all three of them taken together. Therefore, they will be a good to each one taken separately.
>
> But the pleasures of A, B and C are no more to be moulded into a single whole than are their persons. Nor is it clear why, even if they should be so moulded, the resultant aggregate should, on the basis of Mill's hedonist premises, appear desirable to any of them singly. . . . The philosopher F. H. Bradley . . . justly observed that the aggregate of all persons is nobody, yet every good must, on Mill's premises, be a good for somebody; therefore, again in Mill's premises, the good of all, being the good of nobody, cannot be good at all.[55]

Mill tends to assume that what will give pleasure to A will also give pleasure to B and to C yet, in actuality, it may very well happen that what A finds pleasurable B finds painful and that A, therefore, can realize his pleasure only by giving pain to B. But Mill says that in the event of conflict between my own happiness and the happiness of the greatest number I should prefer the latter to the former. "In the golden rule of Jesus of Nazareth, we read the complete spirit of the ethics of utility. To do as you would be done by, and to love your neighbour as yourself, constitute the ideal perfection of utilitarian morality." [56] Commenting upon this the same philosopher quoted above says:

> The conclusion derived . . . is . . . that a man ought to pursue something other than his own pleasure, namely the greatest happiness of the greatest number, and furthermore that he ought to pursue it even if it conflicts with his own pleasure.

Now it may be argued that though this is giving up one form of the hedonist position—the form, namely, which asserts that a man *can* only desire his own pleasure, it is not giving it up in the form in which it asserts that pleasure is the sole good; for by insisting that he ought to promote the greatest happiness of the greatest number, Mill is still maintaining that pleasure is the only thing that ought to be pursued, although the pleasure in question is no longer that of the agent.

But in maintaining that the individual ought not to pursue his own pleasure always, but other people's pleasure even at the cost of his own, we are admitting that the individual can and ought to desire something which may have no relation to his own pleasure, namely, the good of the community. Now there is no necessary relation between the good of the community and the individual's pleasure.

Hence Mill implicitly admits that the individual ought to desire at least one thing besides his own pleasure, namely, the good of the community to which he belongs.[57]

Mill clings to the utilitarian vocabulary and thinks that he is defending utilitarianism but in effect he introduces elements into the theory that cannot be explained on hedonistic premises so that what is offered as a qualification of Benthamite utilitarianism turns out to be its repudiation.

In the concluding section of his essay on *Utilitarianism* Mill declares that there are "certain social utilities which are vastly more important, and therefore more *absolute* and imperative, than any others are as a class . . . and which, therefore, *ought to be*, as well as naturally are, guarded by a sentiment not only different in degree but also in *kind;* distinguished from the milder feeling which attaches to the mere idea of promoting human pleasure or convenience, at once by the more definite nature of its commands, and by the sterner character of its sanctions."[58] "Justice," he says is "the appropriate name" for these social utilities. Although in what sense they can be spoken of as "absolute," or why they "ought to be" desired, or by what kind of "sentiment" they are guarded is not clear, nevertheless, it is significant that Mill believes that there are "social utilities" of such an absolute nature that they should be guarded by a sentiment different in kind from "the milder feeling which attaches to the mere idea of promoting human pleasure or convenience." Perhaps the sentiment to which Mill refers is conscience but, if so, he nowhere specifically says so.

Among the higher social utilities which men ought to prefer, Mill declares, is liberty and in his essay on *Liberty* we have one of the most eloquent defenses of individual freedom in the English language. His arguments on behalf of freedom of thought and discussion are justly famous. They may be briefly summarized, in part, with a few quotations:

(1) All silencing of discussion is an assumption of infallibility.

(2) Complete liberty of contradicting and disproving our opinion is the very condition which justifies us in assuming its truth for purposes of action; and on no other terms can a being with human faculties have any rational assurance of being right.

(3) Very few facts are able to tell their own story, without comments to bring out their meaning.

(4) It is not the feeling sure of a doctrine (be it what it may) which I call an assumption of infallibility. It is the undertaking to decide that question *for others*, without allowing them to hear what can be said on the contrary side.

(5) Men are not more zealous for truth than they often are for error, and a sufficient application of legal or even of social penalties will generally succeed in stopping the propagation of either.

(6) There is a class of persons . . . who think it enough if a person assents undoubtingly to what they think true, though he has no knowledge whatever of the grounds of the opinion, and could not make a tenable defense of it against the most superficial objections . . . to shut out discussion entirely is seldom possible, and when it once gets in, beliefs not grounded on conviction are apt to give way before the slightest semblance of an argument.

(7) If a person is to be able to judge wisely between opposing doctrines or opinions, "He must be able to hear them from persons who actually believe them; who defend them in earnest, and do their very utmost for them. He must know them in their most plausible and persuasive form; he must feel the whole force of the difficulty which the true view of the subject has to encounter and dispose of; else he will never really possess himself of the portion of truth which meets and removes that difficulty."

(8) Truth, in the great practical concerns of life, is so much a question of the reconciling and combining of opposites, that very few have minds sufficiently capacious and impartial to make the adjustment with an approach to correctness, and it has to be made by the rough process of a struggle between combattants fighting under hostile banners.[59]

Mill's eloquent and fervent defense of liberty of thought and expression was prompted by fear of social tyranny. The struggle for liberty was first conceived, he wrote, as a struggle against political tyranny and two means were employed to safeguard liberty against encroachment by a tyrant: (1) the formulation of a doctrine of rights the infringement of which constituted grounds for rebellion, and (2) "the establishment of constitutional checks, by which the consent of the community . . . was made a necessary condition to some of the more important acts of the governing power." [60] But with the growing demand for more popular participation in government, limitations on the power of government were thought to be less important as a safeguard of liberty than the identification of power with the will of the people.

What was now wanted was, that the rulers should be identified with the people; that their interest and will should be the interest and will of the nation. The nation did not need to be protected against its own will. There was no fear of its tyrannising over itself. Let the rulers be effectually responsible to it, promptly removeable by it, and it could afford to trust them with power of which it could itself dictate the use to be made. . . . This mode of thought, or rather perhaps of feeling, was common among the last generation of European liberalism, in the Continental section of which it still apparently predominates.[61]

Despite the excesses of the French Revolution, he says, it is a belief commonly held, especially on the European continent. Now that "self-government" has been widely established it is possible to see that the identification of the will of the people with the will of the sovereign is not alone as adequate a safeguard of liberty as was at first supposed by the advocates of democracy.

It was now perceived that such phrases as "self-government," and "the power of people over themselves," do not express the true state of the case. The "people" who exercise the power are not always the same people with those over whom it is exercised. . . . The will of the people . . . practically means the will of the most numerous or the most active *part* of the people; the majority, or those who succeed in making themselves accepted as the majority; the people, consequently *may* desire to oppress a part of their number; and precautions are as much needed against this as against any other abuse of power. The limitation of the power of government over individuals loses none of its importance when the holders of power are regularly accountable to the community . . . and in political speculations "the tyranny of the majority" is now generally included among the evils against which society requires to be on its guard.[62]

But although, he says, we have begun to appreciate the necessity of checking abuses of power by the majority we generally think of that danger as arising from the government itself and we overlook, as a consequence, the tyranny which *society* may exercise over individuals.

Society can and does execute its own mandates; and if it issues wrong mandates instead of right, or any mandates at all in things with which it ought not to meddle, it practises a social tyranny more formidable than many kinds of political oppression, since, though not usually upheld by such extreme penalties, it leaves fewer means of escape, penetrating much more deeply into the details of life, and enslaving the soul itself. Protection, therefore, against the tyranny of the magistrate is not enough; there needs protection also against the tyranny of the prevailing opinion and feeling. . . . There is a limit to the legitimate interference of collective opinion with individual independence: and to find that limit, and maintain it against encroachment, is as indispensable to a good condition of human affairs, as protection against political despotism.[63]

To this problem, then, Mill especially addresses himself in his essay. It was the standardization of opinion that Mill regarded as the greatest single threat to individual liberty in his day. Variety, he argued, is essential to the development of the human mind; uniformity can only render it sterile.

Many of the arguments in Mill's essay on *Liberty* are derived from the German liberal Wilhelm von Humboldt's *The Sphere and Duties of Government* (1792). "Few persons, out of Germany," Mill wrote, "even comprehend the meaning of the doctrine which Wilhelm von Humboldt, so eminent both as a *savant* and as a politician, made the text of a treatise—

. . . that "the end of man, or that which is prescribed by the eternal or immutable dictates of reason, and not suggested by vague and transient desires, is the highest and most harmonious development of his powers to a complete and consistent whole"; that, therefore, the object "towards which every human being must ceaselessly direct his efforts, and on which especially those who design to influence their fellow-men must ever keep their eyes, is the individuality of power and development"; that for this there are two requisites, "Freedom, and variety of situations"; and that from the union of these arise "individual vigour and manifold diversity," which combine themselves in "originality." [64]

Mill was probably as extreme an individualist as can be found anywhere. "The sole end for which mankind is warranted, individually or collectively, in interfering with the liberty of action of any of their number," Mill wrote, "is self-protection.

. . . the only purpose for which power can be rightfully exercised over any member of a civilised community, against his will, is to prevent harm to others. His own good, either physical or moral, is not a sufficient warrant. He cannot rightfully be compelled to do or forbear because it will be better for him to do so, because it will make him happier, because, in the opinion of others, to do so would be wise, or even right. These are good reasons for remonstrating with him, or reasoning with him, or persuading him, or entreating him, but not for compelling him, or visiting him with any evil in case he do otherwise. . . . The only part of the conduct of any one, for which he is amenable to society, is that which concerns others. In the part which merely concerns himself, his independence is, of right, absolute. Over himself, over his own body and mind, the individual is sovereign. [65]

Mill would allow, however, certain exceptions to this general rule, namely: children and young persons below the legal definition of adulthood, the backward and undeveloped races of mankind, and persons deficient in mind or body. "Despotism is a legitimate mode of government in dealing with barbarians, provided the end be their improvement, and the means justified by actually effecting that end." Liberty, as a principle, is applicable only to that portion of mankind which is "capable of being improved by free and equal discussion." [66]

In the tradition of *laissez-faire* Mill would restrict the activities of government to the bare minimum. Government interference, even when it does not infringe individual liberty, is objectionable on three counts: (1) Most things can be done better by individuals than they can by government. "Speaking generally, there is no one so fit to conduct any business, or to determine how or by whom it shall be conducted, as those who are personally interested in it"; (2) "In many cases, though individuals may not do the particular thing so well, on the average, as the officers of government, it is nevertheless desirable that it should be done by them, rather than by the government, as a means to their own mental education—a mode of strengthening their active faculties, exercising their judgment, and giving them a familiar knowledge of the subjects with which they are thus left to deal"; and (3) "The third and most cogent reason for restricting the interference of government is the great evil of adding unnecessarily to its power." [67]

Mill's conception of freedom is stated most succinctly in these words: "The only freedom which deserves the name, is that of pursuing our own good in our own way, so long as we do not attempt to deprive others of theirs, or impede their efforts to obtain it." [68] Granting for the sake of argument (although it is by no means self-evidently true) that it is desirable for each individual to pursue his own good in his own way, *who* is to determine when my exercise of liberty deprives other persons of theirs and *on what basis?* At this point Mill becomes vague. The early liberal had less difficulty with this question since he could reply that ultimately the basis for such a decision was individual conscience or "right reason." Since Mill denies the existence of a natural law discoverable by reason, since he denies the efficacy of individual conscience as an arbiter, he cannot appeal either to reason or to conscience. If the basis for decision is utility, as presumably in Mill's theory it is, how can we be sure that individual liberty will always be regarded as one of the higher social utilities? Mill does not doubt that it always will be but recent political experience, if nothing else, should be proof enough that liberty is not necessarily nor always regarded as socially desirable. Who, moreover, is to decide what is socially desirable and what is not? Presumably Mill might answer: society. But society is no person and possesses no mind, is capable of no judgment, which means that although we designate society as the arbiter we actually leave the decision to certain undetermined individuals who will speak in the name of society. For one, moreover, who was as conscious as Mill was of the possibility of society tyrannising over the individual the designation of society as the arbiter of freedom is curious, if not contradictory. The problem never looms large in Mill's thought for the reason that he never considered it likely or even possible that "society" might find a large measure of individual liberty undesirable.

In his essay on *Representative Government* Mill undertook to describe the criteria of good government and reached the conclusion that the ideally best form of government is a representative one

in which the sovereignty, or supreme controlling power in the last resort, is vested in the entire aggregate of the community; every citizen not only having a voice in the exercise of that ultimate sovereignty, but being, at least occasionally, called on to take an actual part in the government, by the personal discharge of some public function, local or general.[69]

In order better to protect the rights of the minority Mill advocated proportional representation based on Hare's *Treatise on the Election of Representatives* (1859) and in order to "counterpoise the numerical weight of the least educated class" he proposed the establishment of plural voting. "Democracy is not the ideally best form of government . . . unless it can be so organised that no class, not even the most numerous, shall be able to reduce all but itself to political insignificance, and direct the course of legislation and administration by its exclusive class interest." [70] He would exclude no one from the suffrage except those who were unable to read, write, or perform the common operations of arithmetic, but he would give two or more votes to those persons who had a university education or its equivalent as attested by examination or the nature of the profession in which they were engaged.

In his discussion of the proper functions of the representative assembly he reached the conclusion that

Instead of the function of governing, for which it is radically unfit, the proper office of a representative assembly is to watch and control the government; to throw the light of publicity on its acts: to compel a full exposition and justification of all of them which any one considers questionable; to censure them if found condemnable, and, if the men who compose the government abuse their trust . . . to expel them from office, and either expressly or virtually appoint their successors.[71]

Since "every branch of public administration is a skilled business" the knowledge of which "does not come by intuition" the representative assembly should refrain from deciding matters that properly belong to administration for such judgment "at its best, . . . is inexperience sitting in judgment on experience, ignorance on knowledge." [72] The actual preparation of laws would be the function of a special Commission on Legislation drawn from the ranks of the civil service although the actual enactment of the laws would remain the function of Parliament.

The Commission would only embody the element of intelligence in their construction; Parliament would represent that of will. No measure would become a law until expressly sanctioned by Parliament: and Parliament, or either House, would have the power not only of rejecting but of sending back a Bill to the Commission for reconsideration or improvement. Either House might also exercise its initiative, by referring any subject to the Commission, with directions to prepare a law. . . . Once framed . . . Parliament should have no power to alter the measure, but solely to pass or reject it. . . . The Commissioners should be appointed by the Crown, but should hold their offices for a time certain, say five years, unless removed on an address from the two Houses of Parliament, grounded either on personal misconduct . . . or on refusal to draw up a Bill in obedience to the demands of Parliament.[73]

A plan very much like this one proposed by Mill is now in operation in Switzerland and in all modern representative governments there is a tendency (which some deplore and others praise) for more and more legislation to originate in the executive branch of government and for parliaments to confine themselves increasingly to the consideration of general principles and broad policies.

In this proposal Mill was attempting to combine the principle of quantity with the principle of quality; the principle of popular sovereignty with the necessity for skill and intelligence in the actual direction of governmental affairs. In a word he was attempting to combine the principles of democracy with those of an aristocracy. As he explained it:

Nothing but the restriction of the function of the representative bodies within these rational limits, will enable the benefits of popular control to be enjoyed in conjunction with the no less important requisites (growing ever more important as human affairs increase in scale and complexity) of skilled legislation and administration. There are no means of combining these benefits except by separating the functions which guarantee the one from those which essentially require the other; by disjoining the office of control and criticism from the actual conduct of affairs, and developing the former on the representatives of the Many, while securing for the latter, under strict responsibility to the nation, the acquired knowledge and practised intelligence of a specially trained and experienced Few.[74]

Some brief attention should be given in conclusion to Mill's ideas on political economy. According to Professors Gide and Rist the economic writings of John Stuart Mill mark both the apogée and the decline of the Classical school of economics. "With him," they declare, "Classical economics may be said in some way to have attained its perfection, and with him begins its decay."

What makes his personality so attractive is his almost dramatic appearance, and the consciousness that he was placed between two schools, even between two worlds. To the one he was linked by the paternal ties which bound him to the Utilitarian school, wherein he was nurtured; the other beckoned him towards the new horizons that were already outlined by Saint-Simon and Auguste Comte. During the first half of his life he was a stern individualist; but the second found him inclined to socialism, though he still retained his faith in liberty. His writings are full of contradictions; of sudden, complete changes, such as the well-known *volte-face* on the wages question. Mill's book exhibits the Classical doctrines in their final crystalline form, but already they were showing signs of dissolving in the new current.[75]

Unlike the Physiocrats who tended to think of the "natural laws" of economics as normative and providential the Classical school conceived of them as exactly analagous to the physical laws that govern the universe. "They may prove useful or they may be harmful, and men must adapt themselves to them as best they can. To say that political economy is a 'dismal science' because it shows that certain laws may have unfortunate results is as absurd as it would be to call physics a 'dismal science' because lightning kills." [76] If economics is to be a science it must concern itself not with man as such but with "economic man," i.e., man as he is motivated by economic self-interest. It is only by abstracting the economic interests and actions of man from the totality of his interests and life that the study of these economic interests and actions can be scientific, i.e., that permanent and universal laws of economic behavior can be discovered.

The Classical school of economics posited seven laws of this kind: (1) the law of self-interest, (2) the law of free competition, (3) the law of population, (4) the law of demand and supply, (5) the law of wages, (6) the law of rent, and (7) the law of international exchange.[77] John Stuart Mill accepted all of these laws with some modifications. As a utilitarian, Mill believed that the individual is impelled by a desire to further his own happiness and is the best judge of his own interests. He also believed that "Every restriction of competition is an evil" and that "every extension of it is always an ultimate good." [78] Yet, he could also write that "co-operation is the noblest ideal," and that it "transforms human life from a conflict of classes struggling for opposite interests to a friendly rivalry in the pursuit of a good common to all." [79]

Fearful, like Malthus, of the disastrous social effect of a large population Mill would go even further than Malthus in proposing restrictions upon the propagation of the human race. It is one of the worst features of the Christian religion, Mill thought, that it encourages people to have large families in the belief that they will be cared for by the Providence of God. "Little improvement can be expected in morality, until the producing of large families is regarded with the same feelings as drunkenness or any other physical excess," he wrote.[80] And although zealous in defense of most kinds of liberty he declared that "the laws which in many countries on the Continent forbid marriage unless the parties can show that they have the means of supporting a family, do not exceed the legitimate powers of the State. . . . They are not objectionable as violations of liberty." [81] On the other hand, he believed that limitations upon the number of public houses "for the express purpose of rendering them more difficult of access and diminishing the occasions of temptation, . . . is suited only to a state of society in which the labouring classes are avowedly treated as children or savages. . . ." [82]

Mill made a distinction between the laws which govern economic production and those which govern distribution. Only the former partake of the nature of physical laws, the latter are conventional laws subject to change by human legislation. "The laws and conditions of the production of wealth," he wrote, "partake of the character of physical truths. There is nothing optional or arbitrary in them. . . . It is not so with the distribution of wealth. This is a matter of human institution solely. The things once there, mankind, individually or collectively, can do with them as they like." [83] So "contrary to the opinion of the Classical school, he tries to show that wages, profits, and rent are not determined by immutable laws against which the will of man can never prevail," but that they can be changed if men want to change them.[84] The laws of production are immutable but the legislator is given free rein in the field of distribution to institute whatever reforms he thinks best.

And Mill himself proposed certain far-reaching reforms. "(1) Abolition of the wage system and the substitution of a cooperative association of producers. (2) The socialization of rent by means of a tax on land. (3) Lessening of the inequalities of wealth by restriction on the rights of inheritance." [85] Such reforms, he thought, far from imposing restrictions upon individual freedom would actually extend it. "If mankind is to continue to improve," he wrote, the wage system must even-

tually be replaced by an "association of the labourers themselves on terms of equality, collectively owning the capital with
which they carry on their operations, and working under
managers elected and removable by themselves." [86] Since rent
represents the appropriation of something which is not earned
and is contrary to the principle that an individual should have
only the fruits of his own labor, it would be desirable to levy a
tax on land to absorb the rent. Nor should individuals be
allowed contrary to the principle of free competition to gain
an unequal advantage by the accident of birth. "Were I framing a code of laws according to what seems to me best in itself,
without regard to existing opinions and sentiments," he wrote,
"I should prefer to restrict, not what anyone might bequeath,
but what anyone should be permitted to acquire by bequest or
inheritance. Each person should have power to dispose by will
of his or her whole property; but not to lavish it in enriching
some one individual beyond a certain maximum." [87]

In this way Mill laid the foundations for socialism while
claiming to uphold the principles of Classical economics.
Socialism, rather than being a contradiction of liberalism, is a
logical outgrowth of it.

CHAPTER 8

# Idealism

PHILOSOPHICALLY, idealism was an attempt to rescue knowledge from the hopeless predicament in which Hume's extension of Locke's empirical theory of knowledge had left it. Since Hume had reached the conclusion that no certain knowledge about anything is possible there was room, if one accepted the empirical theory of knowledge, neither for science nor for philosophy as methods of gaining true knowledge about reality. Ethically, idealism sought to rescue man's moral consciousness from the attempts which had been made to reduce this consciousness to nothing but utilitarian self-interest and politically it was the embodiment of a reaction to the extreme individualism that denied the reality of man as a social being and of a community welfare that transcended the rights of individuals and was more than the sum of their individual interests.

Idealism found classic expressions in the writings of the German philosophers Johann Gottlieb Fichte (1762–1814), Friedrich Wilhelm von Schelling (1775–1854) and Georg Wilhelm Friedrich Hegel (1770–1831). Anticipated in part by the "transcendental idealism" of Immanuel Kant (1724–1804) their idealism embodied conclusions that he would have found unacceptable. Kant insisted with some measure of justification that his philosophy could also be described as "empirical realism." Idealism found expression in England, principally through the influence of Hegel, in the philosophical writings of Thomas Hill Green (1836–1882), Francis H. Bradley (1846–1924) and Bernard Bosanquet (1848–1923) and in the United States in the writings of the New England transcendentalists

235

and later in the work of philosophers like William T. Harris (1835-1909) and Josiah Royce (1855-1916).

## Immanuel Kant (1724-1804)

BORN in Königsberg, East Prussia, of humble parentage on April 22, 1724, Kant attended the University of Königsberg where he made a brilliant record as a student. He was appointed an instructor in that university in 1755 and remained there as a professor of logic and metaphysics until his death in 1804. It was not until he was fifty-seven years of age that he published his monumental *Critique of Pure Reason* (1781), a work which brought him international fame. This was followed soon after by the *Critique of Practical Reason* (1788) and the *Critique of Judgment* (1790). His moral and political philosophy is contained principally in his *Fundamental Principles of the Metaphysic of Morals* (1785) his *Metaphysical Foundations of the Philosophy of Law* (1797) and in a famous essay entitled *Eternal Peace* (1795).

Kant was particularly concerned with the problem of knowledge, a problem that since the time of Hume had become acute. It will enable us better to understand Kant's "solution" of the problem if we recall briefly what the problem was and how it arose.

With the rise of Newtonian science the universe was conceived as a vast machine in perpetual motion in which "every event in it can be deduced mathematically from the fundamental principles of its mechanical action; the discovery of these mathematical relations" being "the goal of science. The universe is one great harmonious order; not as for Thomas and the Middle Ages, an ascending hierarchy of purposes, but a uniform mathematical system." [1] Descartes, who first systematically formulated this philosophy of nature, believed that we can discover the laws that define these mathematical relations in the same manner in which we solve a problem in geometry, i.e., by using a few, simple and self-evident axioms which we know intuitively. But if the universe is nothing more than a mathematical system how can we explain the mind and thought of man? What is the relation between mind and matter, between thought and reality? If we eliminate all purpose from experience, of what then does experience consist? Professor Randall declares:

Here we reach one of the most perplexing and difficult paradoxes in the history of thought. The conceptions and methods which the special scientific investigators were employing to win vast new continents of facts and laws, whatever their ultimate and theoretical foundation, have indisputably been supremely successful in enabling men to manipulate and control their physical environment. Yet these methods practically forced reflective men to raise the question of what this new scientific knowledge was really knowledge of, and what its actual relation was to the world it purported to describe . . . the very age that has seen so impressive a growth in scientific knowledge has also been profoundly troubled by the thought that it seems very difficult to understand how in any intelligible sense such a science is possible of attainment by the human mind. This paradox may be somewhat explained if we realize that scientists were attempting to discover a *kind* of knowledge which their very methods made it impossible for them to arrive at; by modern scientific methods of investigation they were trying to reach an absolute system of truth quite independent of any limitations of the mental powers of the essentially imperfect and biological creature that man seems to be. In a word, they were trying to arrive at that complete and perfect understanding and explanation of the universe that only God could possess. . . . Their ideal was still a *system of revelation*, though they had abandoned the *method* of revelation. They found knowledge, and valid knowledge, to be sure; but it gradually and painfully dawned upon them that the knowledge they could find and have been finding is a different sort of knowledge from that which they thought they were finding. Just what sort of knowledge it is, men are even today by no means agreed. . . .[2]

After Descartes' unsuccessful attempt to solve the problem John Locke sought to bridge the chasm between the mind of man and the world described by science by insisting that the only reality is *in* the mind of man through which the sensations of experience are filtered. But

This naturally created an insoluble problem. How can the mind get outside itself to a physically and mathematically real world when it is forever shut up inside its own walls? How can we get from sensations to physics? Too honest to claim a solution when there was none, Locke became hopelessly confused in the impossible attempt to reconcile the conception of the method of knowledge as starting inside the mind with his Cartesian ideal of an independent and certain mathematical physics that described nature. His provisional conclusion was that such a science was unattainable, and that man could at best arrive at probable knowledge. . . .[3]

Hume, by carrying Locke's empirical theory of knowledge to its ultimate logical conclusion, reached the point of saying that we can never know the certain truth about anything and that the foundation of science, the law of cause and effect, is nothing more nor less than a hypothetical fiction, a conventional and habitual way of speaking. The empirical theory of knowledge thus ended in complete scepticism about everything including science itself.

It was to this problem that Kant addressed himself. He sought to effect a synthesis between rationalism on the one hand and empiricism on the other and to establish by means of this synthesis a sure foundation both for natural science and for morality. The Cartesian rationalists had erred, he believed, by trying to establish a theory of knowledge upon the *a priori* insights of reason which were conceived to be independent of sense. The empiricists had erred, on the other hand, by trying to establish a theory of knowledge wholly upon sensation. Human knowledge, Kant insisted in the realistic tradition, depends upon both reason and sense, knowledge is a joint product of mind and matter. But at the same time Kant was sufficiently under the influence of Cartesian philosophy to argue that we can never know "things-in-themselves" except through the faculty of our moral will. His philosophy, therefore, embodied subjectivistic tendencies inherited from Descartes which he could not quite overcome and which his followers exploited.

## The Philosophy of Kant

KANT endeavored to solve the problem presented to him by his predecessors by bifurcating the universe. He divided the universe into two: the world of things as they appear to us to be, and, the world of things as they really are in themselves. Men gain knowledge in three ways: through the senses, through the intellect, and through the moral will. The knowledge which we gain through the senses and the intellect is knowledge of the world of things as they appear to us to be. It can never be knowledge of the world of things as they really are for the reason that in seeking knowledge through the senses and the intellect we necessarily impose upon the things themselves forms of intuition (space and time) and categories (such as quality, quantity, substance, causality) which exist not in the things themselves but in our own minds. Nature can only answer the questions which we put to it and its answers must conform to the way in which we frame the question. Kant explained it in this way:

When Galileo caused balls which he had carefully weighed to roll down an inclined plane . . . a new light broke on the mind of the scientific discoverer. It was seen that reason has insight only into that which it produces after a plan of its own, and that it must itself lead the way with principles of judgment based upon fixed laws, and force nature to answer its questions. Even experimental physics, therefore, owes the beneficial revolution in its point of view entirely to the idea, that, while reason can know nothing purely of itself, yet that which it has itself put into nature must be its guide to the discovery of all that it can learn from nature.[4]

It is reason which devises the experiment from which the scientist learns from nature. The relation between the scientist and nature is a relation, however, not like that of pupil to teacher but like that of judge and witness. Commenting upon this Lindsay declares:

Something of what Kant is after is plain enough. We can never attain knowledge without asking the right questions, and the rightness of the question depends as much on us as on the things. Mere apprehension of facts never made a science. Facts have to be made intelligible, and the conditions of their intelligibility are in the mind. "Teacher and scholar," "judge and witness," are, of course, but similes: but the judge learns more of his witness than the scholar of his teacher, because the judge's mind is prepared and he has got his questions ready. And he learns more in spite of the fact that his questions limit and condition the witness's replies. He may miss something important which the witness has to tell him, because he has not asked the right question, but without his theory, which dictates his question and limits the answer, there would be no understanding of the facts at all. This is the truth which Kant is going to express later in the sentence: "Concepts without intuitions are empty, intuitions without concepts are blind. . . ."

It may be objected to all this that the simile is being pushed too far. Facts and things cannot answer. What can possibly correspond in science to the answering of a witness? Are not facts just there to be apprehended and understood or not? But this is precisely what Kant denies. He does think that knowledge is always a joint product, of the form prescribed by the mind and the matter supplied by the object; that without this joint process there can be no knowledge whatever and that, therefore, there is a sense in which we must think of the mind and its objects as being as independent of and indispensable to one another as are judge and witness, and yet in such a relation that the objects have to submit to the conditions prescribed by the mind.[5]

Kant likened his theory to the Copernican revolution. It has always been assumed before, Kant declared, that all our knowledge must conform to objects. But all attempts to extend our knowledge of objects by establishing something in regard to them *a priori*, by means of concepts, have ended in failure. Perhaps we would have more success if we supposed that objects must conform to our knowledge.

Our suggestion is similar to that of Copernicus in astronomy, who, finding it impossible to explain the movements of the heavenly bodies on the supposition that they turned round the spectator, tried whether he might not succeed better by supposing the spectator to revolve and the stars to remain at rest. Let us make a similar experiment in metaphysics with *perception*. If it were really necessary for our perception to conform to the nature of objects, I do not see how we could know anything of it *a priori;* but if the sensible object must conform to the constitution of our faculty of perception, I see no difficulty in the matter.[6]

If the "faculty of perception" be the same for all individuals, as Kant demonstrated it was, then the laws of nature which science discovers are a kind of valid and objective knowledge in the sense that they are both universal and permanent. But since "reason can know nothing" except what "it has itself put into nature" this knowledge must always be knowledge of the world as it appears to us to be. We can never attain through the senses and the intellect, through science, knowledge of the world as it really is, for we can never "know" through our senses and intellect the things-in-themselves. This world of things as it appears through the forms of intuition and the categories of understanding to be, Kant calls the world of *phenomena*. The world of things as they are in themselves and of which we can have no knowledge through our senses and intellect is the world of the *noumena*. The world of phenomena is the proper domain of science and through its method we obtain an accurate description of the world as it appears to be. But science can never tell us anything about the world of the *noumena*, about the world as it really is.

There is one way and one way only that we can have contact with the world as it really is and this is through our moral will. As creatures of desire we belong to the phenomenal world and are subject in this world to the empirical law of cause and effect, our actions, so long as they are dictated by desire, being completely determined. This is our "empirical Self." But there is another Self, the moral or "transcendental Self" that is capable of legislating for itself. It is this Self which is free and able to transcend the phenomenal world and to bring us into contact with the real or noumenal world. All of us are conscious of moral obligation, of a conflict between "what is" and "what ought to be." This consciousness of moral obligation cannot be accounted for empirically because it is not a consciousness of what is but of what ought to be. No empirical analysis can ever reveal what ought to be, it can only bring to light what is. Ought, Kant says, expresses a kind of necessity which is found nowhere else in the whole of nature. We cannot say that anything in nature ought to be other than it actually is. When we have the course of nature alone in view, "ought" has no meaning whatever. Nevertheless, in deciding how we should act we have to transcend the realm of what is and act in terms of some principle prescribing how we ought to act. It is in moral action, in the act of deciding to do this rather than that, that we experience freedom. The consciousness of moral obligation, Kant says, is inextricably bound up with the consciousness of freedom, since one knows that one can act because one is conscious that one ought and thus one knows in one's self the freedom which, without the moral law, had remained unknown. The moral law is not something imposed from without but from within.

Moral behavior is action in conformity with the idea of a law; we act as moral beings when we will to do that which our reason prescribes as our duty. A person may do something which has the appearance of moral behavior because it is to his advantage to do so but we do not, Kant says, regard such behavior as being truly moral. We regard as truly moral behavior, behavior which is dictated not by any personal advantage or self-interest but behavior which is impelled by a consciousness of duty. It is not the effect of behavior, its success or failure, that matters so much as it is the *will* of which it is the expression. There is nothing that can be called good without qualification except a "good will."

The commands of reason which impel our will Kant calls imperatives. There are two kinds of imperatives: hypothetical and categorical. A hypothetical imperative is one which tells us to do something if we want to reach some particular end. It directs us to act in a certain way not because of any intrinsic value which that action may have, but, because it is the best means to attain a desired objective. A categorical imperative is one which directs us to act in a certain way because of the intrinsic value of that way of acting. It commands that kind of conduct which is objectively necessary without regard to any personal advantage, desire, or more ultimate goal. And Kant declares that there is only one such imperative: Act so that the maxim of your act might be made a universal principle.

The consciousness of moral obligation belongs to man by virtue of his nature as a moral being, but since it belongs to the world of noumena it cannot be explained in the sense in which things in the phenomenal world can be explained. There can be no "explanation" of the noumena. Science, accordingly, belongs to the realm of the phenomenal (the world of things as they appear to be) and morality belongs to the realm of the noumenal (the world of things as they really are). Kant at-

tributes ultimate reality to the noumenal world but denies that
it can ever be known through the senses and the intellect.
Thus, Kant "saves" morality (and religion) from the criticism
of Hume by denying that it has any sensory or intellectual
reality. This has some of the earmarks of a tactical retreat
rather than of a genuine reconciliation, but it was, and is by
some still, hailed as the only possible solution. If one starts with
the problem as that problem was formulated by the predecessors of Kant then Kant's solution is probably the best, if not the
only solution, possible. The question is whether it is the real
problem. The difficulty would seem to lie not in Kant's attempted solution but in the way in which that problem was
first posed by Descartes and later by Locke.

In Kant's theory reason is rendered powerless to explain the
existence of God, it can entertain conceptions of God but cannot prove his existence. The existence of God, accordingly, is
regarded as a possibility which we may hold only as a postulate
upon the grounds of faith or "practical reason." Kant retains
God as a necessary postulate of moral action but demolishes all
of the traditional proofs for the existence of God as no proofs
at all. Kant wrote:

From the critical point of view the doctrine of morality and the
doctrine of science may each be true in its own sphere; which could
never have been shown had not criticism previously established our
unavoidable ignorance of the real world, and limited all that we can
*know* scientifically to mere phenomena. I have, therefore, found it
necessary to deny *knowledge* of *God*, *freedom*, and *immortality*, in order
to find a place for *faith*.[7]

According to Lindsay:

Kant was equally determined to defend the integrity of moral
experience and the integrity of science. But that is only possible, he
was convinced, by some doctrine of the limitations of the insight of
science into the nature of reality. Unless he could maintain that the
fact that a principle was valid in science did not show that it held
of the real, he could have found no way of reconciling the determinism of science with the freedom of morality. The distinction
"transcendentally ideal and empirically real," or the distinction in
some form or other of phenomena and things in themselves, was vital

to him. But he was quite capable of holding on to the necessity of that distinction without making it in itself intelligible, as he was capable of proposing various ways of explaining it.

The consequence was that Kant's system proved far more unstable than he had supposed. For even if it be regarded as in substance sound . . . there are various difficulties in it which needed clearing up. It was always possible to suggest a way of clearing up any one of these difficulties at the cost of giving up one or other of the positions which Kant would have insisted on holding on to. Those who came after him, trying to clear up the difficulties which he had left, and not having the firm determination to hold on to each of the different fundamentals of his system, developed Kantianism along different lines into something very un-Kantian.[8]

Although Kant did not believe that speculative reason could demonstrate the existence of a moral world in which the will of man was free he believed that the existence of such a world was a necessary postulate of the practical reason of man. The existence of such a world is presupposed in the moral actions of men, when they act *as if* they were free, *as if* there were a God, and *as if* they were concerned with purposes transcending the concerns of time and space. Although this dualism involves us in metaphysical difficulties we cannot escape it—our interests and desires bind us to the sensible world of nature in which we are determined by the laws of causality but at the same time our rational will binds us to a transcendent moral world in which our actions are free.

In an eloquent passage at the end of the *Critique of Practical Reason* Kant declares:

Two things fill the mind with ever new and increasing admiration and awe, the oftener and the more steadily we reflect on them: *the starry heavens above and the moral law within.* I have not to search for them and conjecture them as though they were veiled in darkness or were in the transcendent region beyond my horizon; I see them before me and connect them directly with the consciousness of my existence. The former begins from the place I occupy in the external world of sense, and enlarges my connexion therein to an unbounded extent with worlds upon worlds and systems of systems, and moreover into limitless times of their periodic motion, its beginning and continuance. The second begins from my invisible self, my personality, and exhibits me in a world which has true infinity, but which is traceable only by the understanding, and with which I discern that I am not in a merely contingent but in a universal and necessary connexion, as I am also thereby with all those visible worlds. The former view of a countless multitude of worlds annihilates, as it were, my importance as an *animal creature*, which after it has been for a short time provided with vital power, one knows not how, must again give back the matter of which it was formed to the planet it inhabits (a mere speck in the universe). The second, on the contrary, infinitely elevates my worth as an *intelligence* by my personality, in which the moral law reveals to me a life independent of animality, and even of the whole sensible world—at least so far as may be inferred from the destination assigned to my existence by this law, a destination not restricted to conditions and limits of this life, but reaching into the infinite.[9]

The great achievement of Kant is his critical method, a method which "does not proceed either deductively or inductively" but "interrogates the conditions of experience in general to ascertain principles presupposed in its possibility."[10] With the discovery of this method philosophy was given a renewed vitality and a task which it had lost with the repudiation of Scholastic logic. Some of its effects were unfortunate, for it tended to give priority to epistemology over metaphysics and to concentrate philosophical attention accordingly upon "how we know" to the neglect of "what we know."

It has been said, with some truth, that what Hume gave to Kant as a problem Kant handed back unchanged as the solution. William Temple is of the opinion that Kant's failure to effect a genuine reconciliation was due to the fact that Kant "never discarded the fatal Cartesian hypothesis that the mind deals directly not with objects known throughout as objects, but with its own ideas which have to be related to the real world by a special act."[11] The failure of modern philosophy as a whole, he thinks, is due to "the inherent error of its initial assumption that in knowledge the mind begins with itself and proceeds to the apprehension of the external world by way of construction and inference."[12]

## *Kant's Ethical Theory*

KANT's ethical theory may be briefly summarized in a number of propositions: (1) "Nothing in the whole world . . . can possibly be regarded as good without limitation except a *good will*"; [13] (2) "Man's will is good, not because the consequences which flow from it are good, nor because it is capable of attaining the end which it seeks, but it is good in itself, or because it wills the good"; [14] (3) "Duty is the obligation to act from reverence for law"; (4) "The supreme good which we call moral can therefore be nothing but the *idea of law* itself, in so far as it is this idea which determines the will, and not any consequences that are expected to follow." [15] It is man's capacity to experience moral obligation that removes him, when he does experience it, from the realm of things as they appear to be. It is then and then only that he becomes a real being in contact with the world as it really is. Acting in accordance with the idea of moral law he acts in accordance with the law of his own being. Only then is he *free*, only then does he transcend the world of cause and effect. Nothing can be said by way of explanation of this consciousness of moral obligation except that it is what distinguishes man as a moral being from other animals.

The moral law to which Kant refers has no specific content, it is not a legal or moral code, it prescribes only that we should act in such a way that our conduct is not self-contradictory. "There is," Kant wrote, "but one categorical imperative, which may be stated thus: Act in conformity with that maxim, and that maxim only, which you can at the same time will to be a universal law." [16] From this single imperative, he believed, all particular imperatives can be derived. Legislate for yourself, he said, as if you were a sovereign making laws for the universe—do only that which you would prescribe as universally binding conduct. Presupposing that human beings are "ends in themselves," that they possess an absolute worth, Kant adds an additional maxim deduced from the nature of the moral law which he calls the practical imperative: "Act so as to use humanity, whether in your own person or in the per-

son of another, always as an end, never as merely a means." [17]
A third practical principle is that one should act as though he
were a member of an ideal *kingdom of ends*. Kant wrote:

By kingdom I mean the systematic combination of different rational beings through the medium of common laws. Now, laws determine certain ends as universal, and hence, if abstraction is made
from the individual differences of rational beings, and from all that
is peculiar to their private ends, we get the idea of a complete
totality of ends combined in a system. . . .[18]

In such an ideal kingdom every person would act in accordance with the categorical imperative and in accordance with
the conduct of every other person. As a consequence, the laws
of such a kingdom would be willed by everyone and obeyed by
everyone.

Morality, then, consists in the relation of all action to the system
of laws which alone makes possible a kingdom of ends. These laws
must belong to the nature of every rational being, and must proceed
from his own will. The principle of the will, therefore, is that no
action should be done from any other maxim than one which is
consistent with a universal law. . . . *Autonomy* thus is the foundation
of the moral value of man and of every other rational being.[19]

In the moral order, as distinct from the natural order of causality, man is both sovereign and subject. Here he is truly *free*—
he is restrained by no other law than that of his own will.

The existence of moral obligation presupposes the conditions necessary to its realization, namely, immortality, freedom, and the existence of God.

The *first* rests upon the practically necessary condition, that existence
should continue long enough to permit of the complete realization
of the moral law. The *second* arises from the necessary presupposition
of man's independence of the world of sense, and his capability of
determining his will in conformity with the law of an intelligible
world, that is, the law of freedom. The *third* depends upon the
necessity of presupposing a supreme, self-existent good, that is, the
existence of God, as the condition under which the highest good
may be realized in such an intelligible world.[20]

These Kant calls the necessary "postulates of practical reason." Rather than morality being derived from the existence

of God, the existence of God is derived from the existence of moral obligation.

It has been said, in criticism of Kant's ethical theory, that it is not very useful in a practical way however formidable it may be theoretically. To tell us that we ought to do what we ought to do is not very helpful in making practical moral decisions. As finite, fallible and imperfect beings how can we possibly legislate as though we were legislating for the universe—only God in his infinite wisdom and power can do this. If, moreover, we can derive no moral principles from our senses and intellect how are we to understand and put into practice the dictates of our "will?" How can our will influence our "empirical selves"? Is it not contradictory to conceive of two "selves?"

## Kant's Political Theory

KANT's political theory is less important in the history of thought than is his critical method and ethical theory. The political problem for Kant is simply the ethical problem stated in practical terms; how can my freedom be reconciled in practice with the like freedom of every other individual? This, of course, is the same problem that has engaged the attention of most political philosophers since the seventeenth century. Kant endeavored to answer it in the same way in which he "solved" the moral problem. "Every action is *right* which in itself, or in the maxim on which it proceeds, is such that it can co-exist along with the Freedom of Will of each and all in action, according to a universal Law." [21] An action is wrong if it hinders the exercise of freedom of will according to universal law and any compulsion or restraint which is necessary to remove this hindrance is right. The State exists to promote the exercise of freedom in accordance with universal law; it is an instrument through which the voluntary actions of individual persons may be harmonized in accordance with the universal law of freedom.

The state is founded upon three principles:

(1) No one has a right to compel me to be happy in the peculiar way in which he may think of the well-being of other men; but

everyone is entitled to seek his own happiness in the way that seems to him best, if it does not infringe the liberty of others in striving after a similar end for themselves when their Liberty is capable of consisting with the Right of Liberty in all others according to possible universal laws.

(2) Every member of the Commonwealth has rights against every other that may be enforced by compulsory laws, from which only the Sovereign or Supreme Ruler of the State is excepted, because he is regarded not as a mere member of the Commonwealth, but as its Creator or Maintainer; and he alone has the Right to compel without being himself subject to compulsory law.

(3) All right . . . depends on the laws. A public law, however, which determines for all what is to be legally allowed or not allowed in their regard, is the act of a public Will, from which all right proceeds, and which therefore itself can do no wrong to anyone. For this, however, there is no other Will competent than that of the *whole* people, as it is only when all determine about all that each one in consequence determines about himself . . . The fundamental law thus indicated, which can only arise out of the universal united will of the people, is what is called the *Original Contract*.[22]

The original contract or social compact is not regarded by Kant as an "actual fact" but rather as "an idea of Reason," it is a necessary and logical presupposition but not an historical fact. This compact is

the coalition of all the private and particular wills of a people into one common and public Will, having a purely juridical legislation as its end . . . it ought to bind every legislator by the condition that he shall enact such laws as might have arisen from the united will of a whole people; and it will likewise be binding upon every subject, in so far as he will be a citizen, so that he shall regard the law as if he had consented to it of his own will.[23]

Since "no one can prescribe for another as to what he shall find happiness in" there is no principle based on happiness that could be universally applied and serve as a guide to the legislator. The function of the state is not to promote happiness but to establish and preserve those conditions of freedom which will leave "the individual . . . undisturbed in his right to seek his happiness in whatever way may seem best to him, if only he does not infringe the universal liberty secured through the law, by violating the rights of other fellow-subjects." [24] Reason, not utility, should be the legislator's guide. When the sovereign, even acting with the best of intentions, endeavors to legislate on the basis of the principle of happiness and "determines to make the people happy according to his notions . . . he becomes a despot" and the people who "will not give up their common human claim to what they consider their own happiness become rebels." [25]

Professor de Ruggiero summarizes Kant's political theory by saying:

The State controlled the sphere of legality, the sphere of actions in their outward conformity to law; it had nothing to do with the sphere of morality, which lay wholly in the conscience of the individual; for no authority except that of conscience could either create or judge the inner morality of human acts. . . .

The State is a strictly legal organization, whose chief care is to ensure the possibility of an ordered co-existence of individuals; it personifies that universal law in which the free will of each may be reconciled with that of all others. But the single individuals enabled by the State to co-exist are not its creation; they have their own autonomous ground, and their claim to existence forms the primary right belonging to every man simply as man. . . .

Kant explains the origin of the State by a social contract in virtue of which all, *omnes et singuli*, give up their outward liberty in favour of the community, to receive it again, converted into civil liberty, in their capacity as members of a political organization. In this exchange the individual does not sacrifice part of himself to a greater whole; by giving up a savage and lawless liberty, he finds the whole of his liberty in legal dependence, that is, in the legal state.[26]

Here we have what seems to be simply a restatement of the liberal theory of the state as propounded by Grotius and Locke. But there is a significant difference. For Grotius and Locke the natural law binding sovereign and subject was a law with a *specific content*, for Kant the natural law has no specific content; for Grotius and Locke the natural law was grounded in the empirical nature of man, for Kant its basis is the nature of man as a moral being but man as a moral being is not, for him, an empirical fact but a logical postulate.

Kant, moreover, could discover no right of resistance such as Locke found, for the original contract in Kant is not based upon consent and limited by specific obligations but its basis is simply abstract reason and it cannot be dissolved without destroying the law. No distinction is made in Kant's theory between society and the state and rebellion against the state, therefore, is rebellion against society itself. "Even if the Supreme Power . . . ," Kant wrote, "were to violate the original contract, and thereby in the judgment of the subject . . . lose the right of making the laws, yet as the Government has been empowered to proceed even thus tyrannically, no right of resistance can be allowed to the subject as a power antagonistic to the State." He endeavors to explain it in this way:

The reason of this is that in the actually existing Civil Constitution the people have no longer the right to determine by their judgment how it is to be administered. For suppose they had such a right, and that it was directly opposed to the judgment of the actual Head of the State, who would there be to decide with which of them the right lay? Evidently neither of them could do this, as it makes them judges in their own cause. There would therefore have to be another sovereign Head above the sovereign Head to decide between it and the people, but this is a contradiction. Nor can some supposed *right of necessity* . . . come in here as a lever for the removal of the barrier thus limiting the voluntary power of the people. For the Head of the State may just as well think to justify his hard procedure against the subjects by the fact of their obstinacy . . . , as they justify their revolt by complaining against him about their undue suffering. Who is to decide between them? It is only he who is in possession of the supreme public administration or right, or who is otherwise the Head of the State, who can do this; and no one in the commonwealth can have the right to contest his possession of the power to do it.[27]

In an essay entitled *Idea of a Universal History* (1784) Kant elaborated a theory of progress but, unlike some of the eighteenth-century theories of progress that were based upon a belief in the perfectibility of human nature, Kant was fully cognizant of the evil propensities of human nature. He believed, however, that Nature used these evil propensities as well as those for good in order to achieve an end that transcended man's will although entirely compatible with the dictates of his "practical reason." He thus "discovered" man's practical reason to be in accord with the teleology of nature and found a harmony between what "is" and what "ought to be" that is not at first apparent. In a later essay entitled *Eternal Peace* (1795) Kant declared that Nature reveals a teleology that guarantees "to produce harmony from the very disharmony of men even against their will."[28] "How," he asks, "does nature guarantee that what men ought to do according to the laws of freedom, but does not do, will be made secure regardless of this freedom by a compulsion of nature which forces him to do it?"[29] And he explains this by saying that men are driven by nature, by war, to seek security in legal relationships and thus nature decrees what man's reason imposes as a duty. "In short," Kant wrote, "we can say that nature *wants* that law achieve superior force. If one neglects to do this, it will be accomplished anyhow, albeit with much inconvenience."[30] Just as individuals are driven by "the mechanism of nature" to submit to the rule of law within a given territory so eventually nations will be similarly impelled to submit to the rule of a world federation of constitutional governments.

Nations may be considered like individual men which hurt each other in the state of nature, when they are not subject to laws, by their very propinquity. Therefore each, for the sake of security, may demand and should demand of the other to enter with him into a constitution similar to the civil one where the right of each may be secure. This would be a *union of nations* (*Völkerbund*) which would not necessarily have to be a *state of nations* (*Völkerstaat*). . . .[31]

It is both a duty, i.e., a dictate of "practical reason" and a decree of Nature that man should work for eternal peace through the establishment of a league of nations.

If it is a duty, and if at the same time there is well-founded hope that we make real a state of public law, even if only in an infinitely gradual approximation, then the *eternal peace* which will take the place of the peacemakings, falsely so-called because really just truces, is no empty idea, but a task which, gradually solved, steadily approaches its end, since it is to be hoped that the periods within which equal progress is achieved will become shorter and shorter.[32]

Kant suggested six conditions that, in a practical way, would be desirable in order to implement the establishment of lasting peace:

(1) No treaty of peace shall be held to be such, which is made with the secret reservation of the material for a future war.

(2) No state having an independent existence, whether it be small or great, may be acquired by another state, through inheritance, exchange, purchase or gift.

(3) Standing armies shall gradually disappear.

(4) No debts shall be contracted in connection with the foreign affairs of the state.

(5) No state shall interfere by force in the constitution and government of another state.

(6) No state at war with another shall permit such acts of warfare as must make mutual confidence impossible in time of future peace: such as the employment of assassins, of poisoners, the violation of articles of surrender, the instigation of treason in the state against which it is making war, etc.[33]

On the positive side he suggested that "the civil constitution in each state should be republican," that "the law of nations should be based upon a federalism of free states," the elimination of imperialism and wars of conquest, and the cultivation of the feeling that injustice done anywhere is an injustice suffered everywhere.

The liberal faith in the intelligence of man and in political institutions to overcome the self-seeking propensities of human beings is nowhere more vividly illustrated than in Kant's essay on *Eternal Peace*. In a remarkable passage in the first supplement to that essay Kant declares that "the problem of the formation of the state . . . is not insoluble, *even for a race of devils*, granted that they have intelligence." [34]

"Given a multitude of rational beings who, in a body, require general laws for their own preservation, but each of whom, as an individual, is secretly inclined to exempt himself from this restraint: how are we to order their affairs and how establish for them a constitution such that, although their private dispositions may be really antagonistic, they may yet so act as to check upon one another, that, in their public relations, the effect is the same as if they had no such evil sentiments?" Such a problem must be capable of solution. For it deals not with the moral reformation of mankind, but only with the mechanism of nature; and the problem is to learn how this mechanism of nature can be applied to men, in order so to regulate the antagonism of conflicting interests in a people that they may even compel one another to submit to compulsory laws and thus necessarily bring about the state of peace in which laws have force.[35]

What is needed, Kant believes, is "a good political constitution." Such a constitution, however, "is not to be expected as a result of progress in morality; but rather, conversely, the good moral condition of a nation is to be looked for, as one of the first fruits of such a constitution." [36] Through "the good organization of the state . . . each individual is compelled to be, if not a morally good man, yet at least a good citizen." [37]

## Georg Wilhelm Friedrich Hegel (*1770–1831*)

BORN in Stuttgart in 1770 Hegel attended the University of Tübingen where he devoted himself primarily to theological studies in preparation for the Lutheran ministry. Unable to accept the orthodox tenets of Christianity Hegel abandoned the career upon which he had been launched by his parents and upon leaving the university secured a position as a tutor. When Schelling, who had been a student at Tübingen with Hegel, was appointed to the chair of philosophy at the University of Jena left vacant by Fichte's retirement in 1800, Schelling used his influence to secure Hegel's appointment as an instructor at that university. The disastrous battle of Jena in 1806 disrupted the German universities and in 1807 Hegel found himself forced by financial considerations to leave the university. He served for a short time as an editor of a newspaper and for several years as the head of a boys' school in Nuremberg. In 1816 he received a call to a professorship at the University of Heidelberg and in 1818 was called to the University of Berlin as "the one man who could fill with credit the chair of philosophy that had been vacant since the death of Fichte." [38] He remained there until his death in a cholera epidemic in 1831.

His principal works include the *Phenomenology of Mind* (1807),

*Science of Logic* (1816), the *Encyclopedia of the Philosophical Sciences* (1817), the *Philosophy of Right* (1821) and a number of works published posthumously including his very important *Philosophy of History* (1837). Hegel's philosophy, like that of Kant, is abstruse and, as a consequence, there are many conflicting interpretations concerning what he really meant. Perhaps the most distinctive feature of Hegel's philosophical system is his dialectical method which Josiah Royce has described as the "logic of passion." The dialectical method is as old as Socrates but in the hands of Hegel it is given a universal validity and application that is both novel and profound.

## Hegel's Dialectical Method

HEGEL's philosophy starts from the assumption that the real is rational and the rational real. And it is the unique task of philosophy to comprehend what is. It is philosophy which enables us to reconcile "what lies between reason as self-conscious mind and reason as an actual world before our eyes" and "to recognize reason as the rose in the cross of the present and thereby to enjoy the present, that is the rational insight which reconciles us to the actual." [39] It is through philosophy that God reveals Himself as an ideal system of thought. Essentially God or the Absolute is Thought and Thought is the ultimate reality.

When we understand that Thought is Life and Life is Thought we have grasped the key that unlocks the door to understanding. But we must also understand that thought is something which changes, grows and develops. Until finally reconciled in the Absolute which is both Thought and Will, Reason and Spirit, thought must pass through successive stages of affirmation, destruction, and reconstruction. The movement of thought is dialectical. Every truth is the synthesis of two contradictory elements. Affirmation always leads to negation and only through the synthesis of these two opposed "truths" does truth emerge. Affirmation leads to dogmatism, negation to scepticism, and only through the synthetic mediation of mysticism can the real truth emerge. [40]

In his *Science of Logic* Hegel points out that the affirmation of
the existence of something necessarily leads to the affirmation
of what it is not, so that all affirmation implies a negation. The
antithesis between "what is" (being) and "what is not" (not-
being) gives rise to a synthesis (becoming) that includes both
and yet something new in addition. Professor Loewenberg
explains it by saying that:

The governing idea of the dialectic . . . involves at once analysis
and synthesis. From the point of view of analysis, dialectic is a
method whereby each concept may be seen to imply its own opposite as a necessary and inseparable part of itself. Taken merely as a
mode of analysis the dialectical method is productive of a situation
which is logically absurd, showing as it does that any concept is
burdened with a meaning antithetical to it. This situation can be
relieved only by synthesis, by the admission of a wider idea in which
the original concept and its generated antithesis are reconciled.
Synthesis or federation of antithetical categories is what the dialectical logic is designed to accomplish. This repetitive pattern—mutual
antagonism and consequent reconciliation—is the fate to which *all*
concepts must submit. Such a pattern provides a scheme for their
combination into a single hierarchical system, demanding and
justifying an ultimate distinction between "lower" and "higher"
categories. This in brief is what Hegel is supposed to mean by his
doctrine that all concepts are "dialectically" related: concepts advance in meaning from lower to higher by an inherent rhythm of
logical opposition and unison.[41]

According to Hegel, the dialectic is the only way in which the
human mind can arrive at the truth about anything. As human beings we formulate a doctrine about something. That
doctrine will contain elements of truth but also, since all human beings are passionate, self-centered, fallible, and limited
by their particular historical perspective, elements of error.
Other individuals perceiving the error in that doctrine will
formulate a doctrine which is precisely the opposite. Their
doctrine will contain elements both of truth and error. We
cannot say that one doctrine is right and the other wrong for
both contain elements of right and wrong. A third doctrine is
necessary in order to preserve what is true in both, only a syn-

thesis can reconcile the thesis and its antithesis. But when analyzed this third doctrine will be found to be far from adequate as a complete statement of the truth. The third doctrine becomes then a new thesis subject to self-contradiction and we are faced with the problem again of constructing a new synthesis out of this third doctrine and its antithesis. This process presumably continues indefinitely although each synthesis is thought to be closer to the absolute truth than each preceding synthesis. It is not "bloodless concepts," however, that Hegel sets in opposition to one another but "passionate conceptions."

Different emotional and reflective views of life—sensuous and intellectual, emotional and reflective, practical and theoretical, mystic and philistine, sceptical and dogmatic, empirical and speculative, conservative and radical, selfish and social, religious and secular— are here induced to voice the will to believe in their own exclusive reasonableness. And reasonable each does appear from the point of view of its own perspective. But, alas, each human attitude in the process of contending for mastery always finds its claim to power rebuked and impugned. For there is no human view or belief without its rival. . . . Life, as Hegel conceives it, is an incessant strife of partisan views. They are partisan because they are particular. . . . Whatever is particular—a particular art, a particular religion, a particular philosophy—is self-absorbed and self-centered and hence never free from bias. The truth is that every particular point of view ineluctably suffers from a warped perspective. The unavoidable tendency of everything particular to emphasize its own particularity Hegel discerns to be the source of all the fatal collisions that render human life so everlastingly unstable. The dialectical method, taken merely as a mode of analysis, simply consists in laying siege to every typical attitude or belief by rendering its partisan claims logically ridiculous.[42]

Since all "points of view" are partial and particular it would follow that only in their entirety are they "true." "Absolute knowledge is the insight that 'the truth is the whole.' " [43] Now absolute knowledge implies an absolute knower and the ultimate reality must be an Absolute Mind, which religion, Hegel says, popularizes as God. For Hegel the dialectic is not simply a method of acquiring knowledge, it is reality itself—thought and being are one—and the ultimate reality can be nothing but the ultimate knowledge of this process embodied in the Absolute.

## Hegel's Philosophy of History

HISTORY, for Hegel, is the manifestation of Reason realizing itself as will, it is the dialectical unfolding of the will of God or the Absolute. It is not the realization of this particular idea or of that particular idea but of the Idea or Reason in general. Hegel declares:

The only Thought which Philosophy brings with it to the contemplation of History, is the simple conception of *Reason;* that Reason is the Sovereign of the World; that the history of the world, therefore, presents us with a rational process. . . . On the one hand, Reason is the *substance* of the Universe; viz., that by which and in which all reality has its being and subsistence. On the other hand, it is the *Infinite Energy* of the Universe; since Reason is not so powerless as to be incapable of producing anything but a mere ideal, a mere intention—having its place outside reality, nobody knows where. . . . It is the *infinite complex of things*, their entire Essence and Truth. It is its own material which it commits to its own Active Energy to work up. . . . It supplies its own nourishment, and is the object of its own operations. While it is exclusively its own basis of existence, and absolute final aim, it is also the energising power realizing this aim; developing it not only in the phenomena of the Natural, but also of the Spiritual Universe—the History of the World. That this "Idea" or "Reason" is the *True*, the *Eternal*, the absolutely *powerful* essence; that it reveals itself in the World, and that in the World nothing else is revealed but this and its honour and glory—is the thesis which . . . has been proved in Philosophy, and is here regarded as demonstrated.[44]

Herbert Marcuse, in a recent analysis of Hegel's philosophy, explains Hegel's philosophy by saying:

Man alone has the power of self-realization, the power to be a self-determining subject in all processes of becoming, for he alone has an understanding of potentialities. . . . His very existence is the process of actualizing his potentialities, of molding his life according to the notions of reason. . . . Reason presupposes freedom, the power to act in accordance with knowledge of the truth, the power to shape reality in line with its potentialities. The fulfillment of these ends belongs only to the subject who is master of his own development and who understands his own potentialities as well as those of the things around him. Freedom, in turn, presupposes reason, for it is comprehending knowledge, alone, that enables the subject to gain and to wield this power. . . .

The life of reason appears in man's continuous struggle to comprehend what exists and to transform it in accordance with the truth comprehended. Reason is also a historical force. Its fulfillment takes place as a process in the spatio-temporal world, and is, in the last analysis, the whole history of mankind. The term that designates reason as history is mind (*Geist*) which denotes the historical world viewed in relation to the rational progress of humanity—the historical world not as a chain of acts and events but as a ceaseless struggle to adapt the world to the growing potentialities of mankind.[45]

History is the process of working out the knowledge of that which it is potentially. The universal divine reason is not, for Hegel, an abstraction but a vital principle. To the extent that human beings follow the dictates of their reason they participate in the realization of this vital principle in history; to the extent that they are motivated by particular interests and desires they put obstacles in the way of its realization. But men cannot completely thwart the realization of divine reason and their very efforts to do so will only prove ultimately that "the real is rational and the rational real." There is a Reason immanent in history that is greater than the reason of any single individual and the dialectical process will vindicate that Reason over the particular reasons of particular individuals. Hegel declares:

The History of the World begins with its general aim—the realization of the Idea of Spirit—only in an *implicit* form that is, as Nature; a hidden, most profoundly hidden, unconscious instinct; and the whole process of History . . . is directed to rendering this unconscious impulse a conscious one. Thus appearing in the form of merely natural existence, natural will—that which has been called the subjective side,—physical craving, instinct, passion, private interest, as also opinion and subjective conception,—spontaneously present themselves at the very commencement. This vast congeries of volitions, interests and activities, constitute the instruments and means of the World-Spirit for attaining its object; bringing it to consciousness, and realising it. And this aim is none other than finding itself—coming to itself—and contemplating itself in concrete actuality. But that those manifestations of vitality on the part of individuals and peoples, in which they seek and satisfy their own purposes, are, at the same time, the means and instruments of a higher and broader purpose of which they know nothing,—which they realize unconsciously—might be made a matter of question. . . . But on this point I announced my view at the very outset, and asserted our hypothesis . . . that Reason governs the world, and has consequently governed its history. . . . The Union of Universal Abstract Existence generally with the Individual,—the Subjective— that this alone is Truth, belongs to the department of speculation and is treated in this general form in Logic. But in the process of the World's History itself,—as still incomplete,—the abstract final aim of history is not yet made the distinct object of desire and interest. While these limited sentiments are still unconscious of the purpose they are fulfilling, the universal principle is implicit in them, and is realizing itself through them. The question also assumes the form of the union of *Freedom* and *Necessity;* the latent abstract process of Spirit being regarded as *Necessity* while that which exhibits itself in the conscious will of men, as their interest, belongs to the domain of *Freedom*.[46]

In this way Hegel believes that he has succeeded in reconciling the subjective will of man with the objective order of the universe, freedom with necessity. History uses the instincts, passions and interests of men to fulfill purposes of which men are unconscious; by becoming conscious of this Reason in history men become free, for true freedom is the identification of one's own reason with universal Reason.

In what sense can it be said that Hegel's conception of history embodies the Christian conception of Divine Providence? Hegel himself sought to answer this question by saying that there is a sense in which Divine Providence presides over the events of the world "for *Divine* Providence is Wisdom, endowed with an infinite Power, which realises its aim, viz., the absolute rational design of the World." But, he adds, that "a difference—rather a contradiction—will manifest itself, between this belief and our principle. . . ." [47] Christians believe that the general plan of Providence is hidden from men's view, that it will only become evident on the Last Day when history comes to an end, and that it is folly, if not presumption, to endeavor to scrutinize that which is inscrutable. Hegel, on the contrary, argues that the revelation of God in Christ imposes upon us the *duty* of seeking as much knowledge about God as we can since "He is no longer a concealed or secret existence . . .

And this possibility of knowing Him, . . . renders such knowledge a duty. God wishes no narrow-hearted or empty heads for his children; but those whose spirit is of itself, indeed, poor, but rich in the knowledge of Him; and who regard this knowledge of God as the only valuable possession. That development of the thinking spirit, which has resulted from the revelation of the Divine Being as its original basis, must ultimately advance to the *intellectual* comprehension of what was presented in the first instance, to *feeling* and *imagination*.[48]

Hegel believes that he has discovered the general plan of Divine Providence in the dialectical interpretation of History which he himself calls a theodicy or "a justification of the ways of God" to men "so that the ill that is found in the World may be comprehended and the thinking Spirit reconciled with the fact of the existence of evil." [49] There is another significant way in which Hegel's philosophy of history differs from the orthodox Christian conception of Providence. For the orthodox Christian, God's will is revealed in the world but God Himself is a Personal Being who transcends the world; for Hegel, God is immanent in the world and coextensive with its history—history is not a revelation of God's will but *is* God's will. Moreover, God reveals himself *only* in the dialectical unfolding of Universal Reason. In the Hegelian system of philosophy God as a Personal Being is absorbed, if not obliterated, in the Absolute—God becomes the "Idea." There is no room in the Hegelian system either for prayer or for grace. In a recent interpretation of this aspect of Hegel's thought, Foster declares:

The "Weltgeist," in a word, represents a Providence, but the Providence of a divine Demiurge, not of a divine Creator. Thus the human agent through which it works is related to it as tool to artificer; thus, above all, it works by purpose to an end, so that the process which it directs is a teleological one, and the end, as in every product of a demiurge, can be discriminated in thought from the means by which it is achieved or the matter in which it is realized.

Hegel himself claims that his doctrine of the "Weltgeist" is the philosophical, and therefore adequate apprehension of the same truth which is represented imaginatively and therefore inadequately in the religious doctrine of Providence. He regards it as a sign of the inadequacy of the religious imagery that those who hold it, while they assert that there is a plan of Providence, deny that the plan is knowable, and he claims it as the business of philosophy to penetrate the mysteries which religion thus maintains to be inscrutable. But in this instance Hegel perverts the truth which he purports to be "translating into the concept." To say that the plan of Providence is inscrutable is, no doubt, an inadequate expression, but the truth which it expresses inadequately is not that God's plan is knowable, but that, as Creator and not Demiurge, God does not act according to a *plan* at all. Hegel is not really replacing religious imagery by conceptual apprehension of the truth which it contains; he is replacing the Christian idea of Creation by the Greek one of Techne.[50]

From the point of view of man history is full of evil and frustration, and it appears to end in defeat; but, from the point of view of God, a super-human mind that is omniscient and omnipresent, history is good and rational. History, you might say, has a logic of its own that is superior to the logic of individuals. Freedom is the recognition of historical necessity. In the Hegelian system history is not merely the revelation of God's will but it *is* God. It is in the historical process and in that alone that God is revealed. Moreover, history is the final court of appeal, the final arbiter of right and wrong, truth and falsehood—from history there is no appeal. Out of the historical process, "out of this dialectic rises the universal Spirit," Hegel wrote, "the unlimited World-Spirit, pronouncing its judgment—and its judgment is the highest—upon the finite nations of the world's history; for *the history of the world is the world's court of justice.*" [51]

## Hegel's Conception of the State

THE ultimate reality, for Hegel, is history understood as the dialectical unfolding of Reason and the state as the embodiment of "rational freedom" is the principle means through which history manifests itself. The state is the incarnation of the "spirit of the world," it is the "Divine Idea as it exists on earth." As Hegel explains it:

> The state is the actuality of the ethical Idea. It is ethical mind *qua* the substantial will manifest and revealed to itself, knowing and thinking itself, accomplishing what it knows and in so far as it knows it. The state exists immediately in custom, mediately in individual self-consciousness, knowledge, and activity, while self-consciousness in virtue of its sentiment towards the state finds in the state, as its essence and the end and product of its activity, its substantive freedom . . .
>
> The state in and by itself is the ethical whole, the actualization of freedom; and it is an absolute end of reason that freedom should be actual. The state is mind on earth and consciously realizing itself there . . . The march of God in the world, that is what the state is. The basis of the state is the power of reason actualizing itself as will. In considering the Idea of the state, we must not have our eyes on particular states or on particular institutions. Instead we must consider the Idea, this actual God, by itself. On some principle or other, any state may be shown to be bad, this or that defect may be found in it . . . But since it is easier to find defects than to understand the affirmative, we may readily fall into the mistake of looking at isolated aspects of the state and so forgetting its inward organic life. The state is no ideal work of art; it stands on earth and so in the sphere of caprice, chance, and error, and bad behaviour may disfigure it in many respects. But the ugliest of men, or a criminal, or an invalid, or a cripple, is still always a living man. The affirmative life, subsists despite his defects, and it is this affirmative factor which is our theme here.[52]

Freedom consists in willing to make my natural self (composed of my particular interests and passions) conform to my thinking self (my reason). I realize my freedom when I submit to the law, to the rules of social morality and to the institutions of the national State. The State is the highest and most perfect embodiment of social morality; it both sustains my personality as a being with freedom of will and transcends my personality by compelling me to contemplate a good beyond my own personal interests.

According to Kant, freedom consists in obedience to my moral will, but according to Hegel, freedom consists in obedience to the dictates of Social Morality, to the moral will of the *community*. Hegel would agree with Kant in saying that freedom consists in obedience to the dictates of universal reason but he would identify the dictates of universal reason with Social Morality, rather than with the isolated moral will of the individual. The State, for Hegel, is the crystallization of this Social Morality, it is the embodiment of the moral will of the community and, as such, it has a will, personality, and purpose of its own. It includes but transcends the purposes of individuals. The State includes not only those individuals living today but those who lived in the past and those who will live in the future under its jurisdiction—hence it has a destiny of its own which is superior to the destiny of any particular individuals. It is not an abstraction or an ideal but a living entity, an organism with a life of its own.

Individual conscience cannot, as Kant believed, be the final court of judgment because individual consciences do not always agree. Individual conscience can tell us that there is a right and a wrong but it cannot tell us what is eternally and universally right and wrong. Individual consciences, moreover, change from time to time and from place to place. Because the community conscience is more likely to be right than the individual conscience, true morality consists in obedience to the dictates of Social Morality. What is this Social Morality or Social Righteousness? An English philosopher explains it by saying:

Social Righteousness is both within and without. It is without, because it is the spirit of a society precipitated in custom, opinion, belief and law. It is within, because it is also present in our hearts prompting us to respond, and by responding to contribute to the spirit of society. When, therefore, we cheerfully perform our functions and loyally observe the duties appropriate to our station in society, we are recognizing and obeying a moral law which has a more real, because a more concrete, authority than either the purely subjective prescriptions of the Kantian good-will, or the purely objective injunctions and prohibitions of the law of the State. Now this concrete moral authority, which is instinct in the notion of Social Righteousness cannot be a mere floating sanction unlocalized and unanchored. Like Rousseau's General Will, it must belong to, it must be vested in, something; and this something which is at once the fount and the repository of Social Righteousness is, for Hegel, the State.[53]

Hegel rejected the conception of natural rights, and, of course, the contract theory of government. Since the State is a moral organism apart from which the individual can be said to have no spiritual reality, it is not the creation of individual wills but the actualization of universal Reason. Rights are commensurate with duties and duties are prescribed by the State, the true rights which an individual has are those which are dictated by the rational will of the State. Although Hegel never uses this expression he would appear to be substituting a conception of "social rights" for "natural rights." Whatever rights an individual has, he has not by virtue of his humanity but by virtue of his relationship to the social organism.

According to Hegel the state is "the absolute power on earth" and only history can pronounce judgment upon its actions.

The nation state is mind in its substantive rationality and immediate actuality and is therefore the absolute power on earth. It follows that every state is sovereign and autonomous against its neighbours. . . . It is as particular entities that states enter into relations with one another. Hence their relations are on the largest scale a maelstrom of external contingency and the inner particularity of passions, private interests and selfish ends, abilities and virtues, vices, force, and wrong. All these whirl together, and in their vortex the ethical whole itself, the autonomy of the state, is exposed to contingency. The principles of the national minds are wholly restricted on account of their particularity, for it is in this particularity that, as existent individuals, they have their objective actuality and their self-consciousness. Their deeds and destinies in their reciprocal relations to one another are the dialectic of the finitude of these minds, and out of it arises the universal mind, the mind of the world, free from all restriction, producing itself as that which exercises its right—and its right is the highest rule of all—over these finite minds in the "history of the world which is the world's court of judgment." [54]

He argues, however, that "world history is not the verdict of mere might" but rather the judgment of Reason itself. The nation, he speaks of, as "a moment of the Idea" and sees the conflict between nations as a working out of the dialectical movement of thought. "All actions, including world-historical actions, culminate with individuals as subjects giving actuality to the substantial. They are the living instruments of what is in substance the deed of the world mind and they are therefore directly at one with that deed though it is concealed from them and is not their aim and object." [55] Nations are the unconscious tools and organs of the world mind at work within them.

Warfare and conflict between States is an aspect of the working out of the dialectical process that is history. War demonstrates the limited character of all national perspectives. According to Hegel:

> War is the state of affairs which deals in earnest with the vanity of temporal goods and concerns—a vanity at other times a common theme of edifying sermonizing. This is what makes it the moment in which the identity of the particular attains its right and is actualized. War has the higher significance that by its agency, as I have remarked elsewhere, "the ethical health of peoples is preserved in their indifference to the stabilization of finite institutions; just as the blowing of the winds preserves the sea from the foulness which would be the result of a prolonged calm, so also corruption in nations would be the product of prolonged, let alone, perpetual, peace."
> . . . successful wars have checked domestic unrest and consolidated the power of the state at home. Other phenomena illustrate the same point: e.g., peoples unwilling or afraid to tolerate sovereignty at home have been subjugated from abroad, and they have struggled for their independence with the less glory and success the less they have been able previously to organize the powers of the state in home affairs—their freedom has died from the fear of dying. . . .[56]

A state, Hegel says, is an individual and individuality essentially implies negation. Hence, even if a number of states could succeed in making themselves one, this group, as an individual, would of necessity engender an opposition. War, Hegel says, is an evil but not an absolute evil. War is an aspect of reality which must be accepted as such. It is only when we understand that the apparently "accidental" is "necessary" that we are able to transform it into the ethical, to give it an ethical content. Even if a federation of States, such as Kant proposed, were to be established it would not bring about the "eternal peace" for which he hoped because such a federation must eventually and inevitably create an opposition and so beget an enemy.

In any particular epoch, Hegel declares, there is only *one* nation that is truly representative of the World-Spirit.

This nation is dominant in world history during this one epoch, and it is only once that it can make its hour strike. In contrast with this its absolute right of being the vehicle of this present stage in the world mind's development, the minds of the other nations are without rights, and they, along with those whose hour has already struck, count no longer in world history. The history of a single world-historical nation contains (a) the development of its principle from its latent embryonic stage until it blossoms into the self-conscious freedom of ethical life and presses it upon world history; and (b) the period of its decline and fall, since it is its decline and fall that signalizes the emergence in it of a higher principle as the pure negation of its own. When this happens, mind passes over into the new principle and so marks out another nation for world-historical significance. After this period, the declining nation has lost the interest of the absolute; it may indeed absorb the higher principle positively and begin building its life on it, but the principle is only like an adopted child, not like a relative to whom its ties are immanently vital and vigorous. Perhaps it loses its autonomy, or it may still exist, or drag out its existence, as a particular state or group of states and involve itself without rhyme or reason in manifold enterprises at home and battles abroad.[57]

There is no judge between states and although there may be an arbitrator or mediator his efficacy depends upon the particular wills of those who are parties to the dispute. International law always is "ideal" law because its application depends upon different wills, each of which is sovereign. Hegel explains this by saying that:

The fundamental proposition of international law (i.e., the universal law which ought to be absolutely valid between states, as distinguished from the particular content of positive treaties) is that treaties, as the ground of obligations between states, ought to be kept. But since the sovereignty of a state is the principle of its relations to others, states are to that extent in a state of nature to each other. . . . This universal proviso of international law therefore does not go beyond an ought-to-be, and what really happens is that international relations in accordance with treaty alternate with the severance of these relations. There is no Praetor to judge between states; at best there may be an arbitrator or a mediator, and even he exercises his functions contingently only, i.e., in dependence on the particular wills of the disputants. Kant had an idea for securing "perpetual peace" by a League of Nations to adjust every dispute. It was to be a power recognized by each individual state, and was to arbitrate in all cases of dissension in order to make it impossible for disputants to resort to war in order to settle them. This idea presupposes an accord between states; this would rest on moral or religious or other grounds and considerations, but in any case would always depend ultimately on a particular sovereign will and for that reason would remain infected with contingency. It follows that if states disagree and their particular wills cannot be harmonized, the matter can only be settled by war. . . . The fact that states reciprocally recognize each other as states remains, even in war—the state of affairs when rights disappear and force and chance hold sway—a bond wherein each counts to the rest as something absolute. Hence in war, war itself is characterized as something which ought to pass away. It implies therefore the proviso of the *jus gentium* that the possibility of peace be retained (and so, for example, that envoys must be respected), and, in general, that war be not waged against domestic institutions, against the peace of family and private life, or against persons in their private capacity.[58]

It was not Hegel's purpose to exalt war, as some interpreters of his philosophy insist, but to justify it. For those who think that war is never justified then this, of course, amounts to glorification; but Hegel was simply asking this question: if war is a real aspect of history in what sense can it be said to have an ethical purpose? To say that war can have an ethical purpose is not to deny that it is an evil, and to recognize its reality is not the same thing as advocating it. Hegel was not advocating war but trying to explain it.

## Hegel's Conception of Civil Society

THE state, for Hegel, is an organic whole composed not of isolated, separate individuals but of individuals grouped into classes, estates, guilds and local communities. The individual in his economic and civil relations Hegel designates as "civil society" and marks this realm off from that of the State proper. It is this distinction between State and society which is one of the novel features of Hegel's philosophy and it is a distinction which has been perpetuated by other writers ever since. Suggestions of such a separation can be seen implicitly in Locke's political philosophy but generally speaking it is not a distinction which is found in English political thought prior to its "discovery" by Hegel.

Marcuse explains his conception by saying that:

Hegel bases his analysis of civil society on the two material principles of modern society: (1) The individual aims only at his private interests, in the pursuit of which he behaves as a "mixture of physical necessity and caprice"; (2) Individual interests are so interrelated that the assertion and satisfaction of the one depends upon the assertion and satisfaction of the other. This is so far simply the traditional eighteenth-century description of modern society as a "system of mutual dependence" in which every individual, in pursuit of his own advantage, "naturally" also promotes the interest of the whole. Hegel, however, follows the negative rather than the positive aspects of this system. The civil community appears, only to disappear at once in a "spectacle of excess, misery, and physical and social corruption." We know that from the beginning Hegel maintained that a true society, which is the free subject of its own progress and reproduction, can only be conceived as one that materializes conscious freedom. The complete lack of such within civil society at once denies to it the title of a final realization of reason. Like Marx, Hegel emphasizes the fact that the integration of the private interests in this society is the product of chance and not of free rational decision. The totality appears, therefore, not as liberty "but as necessity." [59]

The inner dialectic of civil society is such, Hegel declares, that it creates the accumulation of wealth, on the one hand, and the "creation of a penurious rabble" or proletariat on the other. According to Hegel:

When civil society is in a state of unimpeded activity, it is engaged in expanding internally in population and industry. The amassing of wealth is intensified by generalizing (a) the linkage of men by their needs, and (b) the methods of preparing and distributing the means to satisfy these needs, because it is from this double process of generalization that the largest profits are derived. That is one side of the picture. The other side is the subdivision and restriction of particular jobs. This results in the dependence and distress of the class tied to work of that sort, and these again entail inability to feel and enjoy the broader freedoms and especially the intellectual benefits of civil society.

When the standard of living of a large mass of people falls below a certain subsistence level—a level regulated automatically as the one necessary for a member of the society—and when there is a consequent loss of the sense of right and wrong, of honesty and the self-respect which makes a man insist on maintaining himself by his own work and effort, the result is the creation of a rabble of paupers. At the same time this brings with it, at the other end of the social scale, conditions which greatly facilitate the concentration of disproportionate wealth in a few hands.[60]

This contradiction was resolved, Hegel believed, in the formation of three estates or classes: (a) the peasantry, or agricultural class, (b) the business class composed of merchants, manufacturers, and craftsmen, and (c) the bureaucracy or class of civil servants. The peasantry since it is dependent upon the variability of nature "remains one which owes comparatively little to reflection and independence of will." [61] "The business class has for its task the adaptation of raw materials, and for its means of livelihood it is thrown back on its work, on reflection and intelligence, and essentially on the mediation of one man's needs and work with those of others." [62] The class of civil servants "has for its task the universal interests of the community. It must therefore be relieved from direct labour to supply its needs. . . ." [63] "The question of the particular class to which an individual is to belong is one on which natural capacity, birth, and other circumstances have their influence, though the essential and determining factors are subjective opinion and the individual's arbitrary will. . . ." [64] The administration of justice, the police and the corporation emerge to safeguard the security of person and property for "the growing antagonisms of civil society increasingly make the social organism a blind chaos of selfish interests and necessitate the

establishment of a powerful institution to control the confusion." [65] Civil society is driven by its own dialectic to establish government. He denies that civil society is characterized
by a "natural harmony" such as economists like Adam Smith
posited but insists rather that it is characterized by conflict that
can only be resolved by an organic ordering of the individuals
who compose the society, by an organic hierarchy that culminates in the State. "The dialectical analysis of civil society had
concluded that society was not capable of establishing reason
and freedom of its own accord. Hegel therefore put forward a
strong state to achieve this end and tried to reconcile that state
with the idea of freedom by giving a strong constitutional
flavoring to monarchy." [66]

## Hegel's Theory of Government

FOR the traditional classification of governmental powers
(executive, legislative, and judicial) Hegel substitutes the
monarchic, the administrative, and the legislative. What is
called judicial power in the traditional classification is subsumed under the monarchic and administrative powers. Hegel
does not propose or envisage the separation of these powers in
distinct agencies. The legislative power enacts general laws
which the administrative power applies to specific cases. The
details of legislation should be left to the discretion of the administrative power. It is the function of the monarch to harmonize the administrative and legislative powers and with him
rests the final decision. But it is the office of the monarch not
his person which is the pinnacle of the State. To the objection
that the monarch may be uneducated or unworthy of his
power, Hegel replies that "he has only to say 'yes' and dot the
'i' because the throne should be such that the significant thing
in its holder is not his particular make-up." [67] It is a constitutional monarchy that Hegel envisages, not the personal government of an individual. The function of the monarch is
simply to say "I will" in the name of the State; the content of
that will presumably being determined by the administrative

and legislative powers. The people are represented in the legislature not numerically but through the different classes or estates.

One class is especially well fitted for governing and this is the landed aristocracy because it is economically independent and has a "naturally ethical character."

This class is more particularly fitted for political position and significance in that its capital is independent alike of the state's capital, the uncertainty of business, the quest for profit, and any sort of fluctuation in possessions. It is likewise independent of favour, whether from the executive or the mob. It is even fortified against his own wilfulness, because these members of this class who are called to political life are not entitled, as other citizens are, either to dispose of their entire property at will, or to the assurance that it will pass to their children, whom they love equally, in similarly equal divisions. Hence their wealth becomes inalienable, entailed, and burdened by primogeniture. The right of this section of the agricultural class is thus based in a way on the natural principle of the family.[68]

The landed aristocracy is represented in the legislature "by birth without the hazards of election." The deputies of civil society enter politics through election but not as instructed delegates.

Regarded as a mediating organ, the Estates stand between the government in general on the one hand and the nation broken up into particulars (people and associations) on the other . . . the significance of their position is that, in common with the organized executive, they are a middle term preventing both the extreme isolation of the power of the crown, which otherwise might seem a mere arbitrary tyranny, and also the isolation of the particular interests of persons, societies, and Corporations. Further, and more important, they prevent individuals from having the appearance of a mass or an aggregate and so from acquiring an unorganized opinion and volition and from crystallizing into a powerful *bloc* in opposition to the organized state.[69]

Hegel distinguished in his *Philosophy of History* three principal historical stages in the development of freedom: the Oriental, the Greco-Roman and the Germanic-Christian.

The Orientals have not attained the knowledge that Mind—man *as such*—is free; and because they do not know this, they are not free. They only know that *one is free*. But on this very account, the freedom of that one is only caprice. . . . That *one* is therefore only a Despot, not a freeman. The consciousness of freedom first arose among the Greeks, and therefore they were free; but they, and the Romans likewise, knew only that *some* are free—not man as such. . . . The Greeks, therefore, had slaves; and their whole life and the maintenance of their splendid liberty, was implicated with the institution of slavery. . . . The German nations, under the influence of Christianity, were the first to attain the consciousness, that man as man, is free: that it is the *freedom* of Mind which constitutes its essence.[70]

Corresponding to these three historical stages in the development of freedom are three forms of government; (1) despotism, (2) democracy and aristocracy, and (3) monarchy. Constitutional monarchy represents the most perfect form of government since "In monarchy . . . there is one lord and no serf, for servitude is abrogated by it; and in it Right and Law are recognized; it is the source of real freedom. Thus in monarchy, the caprice of individuals is kept under, and a common gubernatorial interest established." [71] Marcuse explains this by saying that:

Hegel does not mean to say that the Oriental world knew only despotism, the Greco-Roman world only democracy, and the German world only monarchy. His scheme rather implies that despotism is the political form most adequate to the material and intellectual culture of the Orient, and the other political forms respectively to the other historical periods. He then proceeds to assert that the unity of the state is conditioned by the prevailing national culture; that is, the state depends on such factors as the geographical location, and the natural, racial, and social qualities of the nation. This is the purport of his concept of national mind (*Volksgeist*). The latter is the manifestation of the world mind (*Weltgeist*) at a given stage of historical development; it is the subject of national history in the same sense as the world mind is the subject of universal history. "Each particular National genius is to be treated as only one individual in the process of Universal History." The history of a nation has to be judged according to its contribution to the progress of all mankind towards the self-consciousness of freedom. . . . Every form of state must be evaluated according to whether it is adequate to the stage of historical consciousness that mankind has reached. Freedom does not and cannot mean the same thing in the different periods of history, for in each period one type of freedom is the true one. . . . The German world, through the Reformation, produced in its course that kind of freedom which recognized the essential equality of men. Constitutional monarchy expresses and integrates this form of society. It is for Hegel the consummation of the realization of freedom.[72]

## The Implications of Hegel's Philosophy

LIKE KANT, Hegel believed that freedom consists in bringing one's own reason into conformity with the dictates of universal Reason, in the self-conscious recognition of a universal and eternal moral order. But unlike Kant who believed that one discovered this moral order in one's own moral will, Hegel believed that one discovered this moral order in the dialectical process that is History. For Hegel, moreover, the individual is less important than the social group to which the individual belongs, in fact, for Hegel, the individual has no real existence apart from his social relations. It was, indeed, only in the life and form of the State, the culminating unity of man's social relationships, that the individual found his real freedom and his true existence. For Hegel an individual has no abstract, natural rights but only those rights which are correlative to the social duties imposed by his particular relationship to existing social groups. Hence it is the social group and ultimately the State which looms large in Hegel's philosophy rather than the individual.

As a corrective to the extreme individualism of the seventeenth and eighteenth-centuries the Hegelian philosophy emphasizes the organic nature of society and the fact that individuals have not only rights as over against other individuals but duties as well. But Hegel apparently is able to perform this correction only by the dangerous and blasphemous expedient of substituting loyalty to the State for loyalty to God. So closely does Hegel identify the State with God that he may justly be accused of raising false idols in the name of Him who

is truly God and of substituting nationalism as the true religion for Christianity. That that nationalism is justified in
the name of God does not make it less blasphemous, but, if
anything, more blasphemous. There is no nobler conception
of nationalism than that expounded by Hegel, a nationalism
dedicated to the realization of freedom and of God's will in
history, but it is for that reason all the more dangerous for it
attracts the passions of men to an entity (the nation) that
cannot possibly satisfy those passions and is unworthy of their
absolute devotion. It raises men above their selfish and particular interests but it does not raise them far enough. It is
not Hegel's exaltation of the Prussian monarchy of his time
which is the most dangerous feature of his political philosophy
but the deification of the State itself.[73]

Even more important than Hegel's political philosophy is
his philosophy of history. The notion that History is the final
court of appeal lingers in many men's minds today long after
they have forgotten the philosopher who first formulated it
and many who verbally repudiate Hegel's influence cling to it
as a self-evident truth. As the founder of Historicism Hegel's
influence still lives on in the contemporary world. That there
is a design or plan in history that dwarfs the petty plans and
designs of individuals, that all things work for good to those
who do good, that justice must ultimately triumph over the
evil of the world, many of us, with good reason, believe, but it
is one thing to wait humbly upon the judgment of God and
quite another to assume that history is governed by an inexorable dialectic. It is one thing to believe that God knows the
final outcome of human history and quite another to believe
that the details of human history are predetermined. The
orthodox Christian belief in God's Providence does not free
the individual from responsibility for his actions, but Historicism does. Historicism borrows the hope which springs from
the Christian belief in Providence without taking over the
repentance and self-sacrifice that is the price demanded for
that hope. Historicism, it is true, does not gloss over the evil
and misery in the world but it cannot identify it for what it is
and although Hegel preferred to think of his philosophy of
history as a Theodicy, it sometimes appears to be a Demon-

odicy, a justification not of the ways of God but of the devil. Loewenberg speaks of Hegel as "a comic genius of the first water." For he says:

Without the beatific vision of the all-encompassing Absolute it is ultimately intent upon, his philosophy retains the value of a *human* comedy more comprehensive and more diversified than any of its kind. It is a tragi-comic biography of human experience. . . . In an altogether unique way, it sums up the myriad attempts of mankind, recurring rhythmically as do the seasons, to adapt an obdurate universe to certain preferential ideas and interests . . . genuine comedy neither preaches nor does it scold: it emanates from a realistic conception that human follies are patterns of behavior not of today or of yesterday. What inspires and directs all great comedy is the shrewd observation of a repetitive rhythm in human delusions and contradictions. Of this Hegel's dialectic is a singular expression. With all its abstruseness and obfuscation it is an ingenious instrument of comic art. When all the technical trappings are laid aside Hegel emerges as a comic genius of the first water. He is the laughing philosopher, but his laughter is sober, his laughter is sad.[74]

Historicism leads either to fanatical activism or to indifferent quietism. Those who believe themselves and their doctrine to be the spearhead of history may be led by a belief in the inevitable righteousness and triumph of their cause to the most brutal and ruthless undertakings. They will usually "justify" their tactics by an appeal to "history" and speak much of the necessity of sacrificing the individual to more ultimate and more abstract goals. On the other hand, historicism may be invoked to obscure man's role as an active participant in history and to encourage the notion that he is simply a spectator whose individual thoughts and actions can in no way influence the ultimate and inevitable course which history must take. In this form the historical situation in which we find ourselves is presented to us less as a challenge to action than as a particular moment in a stream of history which will carry us forward irrespective of our action. So that instead of asking: what ought we to do? we are more inclined to ask: what is likely to happen?

There is a sense in which history may be regarded as the revelation of God's judgment upon man but this is a different matter from saying that history is the final court of appeal and the ultimate judge of right and wrong. For history is not a person and pronounces no judgment. History may, indeed, be the medium through which God's judgment is revealed but it is God who is the judge, God who pronounces the judgment, not history. The temporal process that is history, time alone, will never solve any problem nor arbitrate any dispute; it is only when that which is eternal and universal is introduced into time that judgment is possible—it is only when that which occurs in time is viewed from a perspective that is timeless that judgment is possible. Since the Absolute which Hegel seeks to substitute for God finds its complete manifestation and fruition only *in* time it cannot provide any standard for evaluating that which occurs in time; we can only know what is right at the very end of time when it will be too late to make use of that knowledge or to amend our ways in the light of it. There is the grave danger that in waiting upon time to decide what is right and wrong we may abdicate the responsibility for deciding what is right and wrong now and in our particular situation. There is the danger, of course, that in attempting to decide now what is right we may mistake our own particular conception of what is right for what is universally and eternally right but only when our love of truth is greater than our fear of error can we live as responsible beings in the world. We may with genuine humility defer the final decision of what is right to God's judgment recognizing the fallibility and imperfection of our own reason but that does not relieve us of the responsibility for using our reason to the very best of our ability and seeking, in a spirit of repentance and contrition, as unperverted a view of the truth as God's grace may enable us to find. It is not our reason that we should distrust but ourselves.

## *Thomas Hill Green (1836–1882)* 19th cent.

THE idealist philosophy founded by Kant and Hegel found expression in Great Britain in the teaching and writings of Thomas Hill Green, F. H. Bradley, and Bernard Bosanquet. We shall examine the philosophy of Green in some detail with brief mention of his successors. Born in Yorkshire in 1836, the son of a clergyman in the Church of England, Green graduated from Oxford in 1858. He spent his entire life there and was chosen Whyte Professor of Moral Philosophy in 1878. He died at the early age of forty-six. He was most influential during his lifetime as a teacher and it was not until after his death that his most important works were published. These included a *Prolegomena to Ethics* (1883) and his *Lectures on the Principles of Political Obligation* which were first delivered in the winter of 1879–1880.

In his general philosophy Green was influenced both by Kant and Hegel but drew more heavily, perhaps, upon Kant than upon Hegel. Since we have already examined those philosophies in some detail it is not necessary to repeat what has already been said. It is enough to point out that for Green "reason and will, even as they exist in men, are one in the sense that they are alike expressions of one self-realizing principle." [75]

By "practical reason" we mean a consciousness of a possibility of perfection to be realized in and by the subject of consciousness. By "will" we mean the effort of a self-conscious subject to satisfy himself. In God, so far as we can ascribe reason and will to Him, we must suppose them to be absolutely united. In Him there can be no distinction between possibility and realization, between the idea of perfection and the activity determined by it. But in men the self-realizing principle, which is the manifestation of God in the world of becoming, in the form which it takes as will at best only *tends* to reconciliation with itself in the form which it takes as reason. Self-satisfaction, the pursuit of which is will, is sought elsewhere than in the realization of that consciousness of possible perfection which is reason. In this sense the object of will does not coincide with the object of reason. On the other hand, just because it is self-satisfaction that is sought in all willing, and because by a self-conscious and self-realizing subject it is only in the attainment of its own perfection that such satisfaction can be found, the object of will is intrinsically or potentially, and tends to become actually, the same as that of reason. It is this that we express by saying that man is subject to a law of his being which prevents him from finding satisfaction in the objects in which under the pressure of his desires it is his natural impulse to seek it. [76]

Like Kant, Green believed that the only good thing is a good will. Freedom consists not simply in the absence of restraint but in the pursuit of those objects which "good will" presents to us, it consists in obeying the law of our own moral being. Hence freedom is not a negative thing but something positive. It is achieved not by annihilating our "natural impulses" but by uniting them with higher interests, in the realization in one's self of "an idea of perfection." It is through seeking self-perfection or self-improvement that true freedom is to be found.

But self-perfection, Green tells us, can never be realized apart from other individuals. Social institutions are necessary in order that individuals may achieve this self-perfection. There can be no individual well-being apart from social well-being.

> The value . . . of the institutions of civil life lies in their operation as giving reality to these capacities of will and reason, and enabling them to be really exercised. In their general effect, apart from particular aberrations, they render it possible for a man to be freely determined by the idea of a possible satisfaction of himself, instead of being driven this way and that by external forces, and thus they give reality to the capacity called will: and they enable him to realize his reason, i.e., his idea of self-perfection, by acting as a member of a social organization in which each contributes to the better-being of all the rest.[77]

Individuals derive their conception of what constitutes self-improvement from social morality, from a conception of a common good that is embodied in that morality. That conception of common good changes as civilization progresses and changes; Green thinks, progressively for the better. What binds individuals in society, then, is never simply fear, much less physical compulsion, but the will to do that which they conceive to be in their own and in the common interest. Society teaches us to prefer that which we ought, to that which we would like.

> Morality and political subjection thus have a common source. . . . That common source is the rational recognition by certain human beings—it may be merely by children of the same parent—of a

common well-being which is their well-being, and which they conceive as their well-being whether at any moment any one of them is inclined to it or no, and the embodiment of that recognition in rules by which the inclinations of the individuals are restrained, and a corresponding freedom of action for the attainment of well-being on the whole is secured.[78]

The social contract theory of government, Green says, is simply a confused way of stating this truth. He rejects that theory because it suggests that the foundation of society rests upon voluntary consent. At the same time he rejects the suggestion that society rests upon force. The basis of the state is not "consent" neither is it force but it is *will*. This conception of his becomes clearer when he analyzes Austin's definition of sovereignty. Austin defined sovereignty in these words: "If a determinate human superior, not in the habit of obedience to a like superior, receive habitual obedience from the bulk of a given society, that determinate superior is sovereign in that society and the society (including the superior) is a society political and independent." [79] What is the basis of that "habitual obedience" which "the bulk of a given society" render unto a "determinate superior?" It cannot be explained simply in terms of the coercive power of the "determinate superior" for no ruler, however, absolute or despotic, could long command the obedience or allegiance of the bulk of society by force alone. And Green concludes that

That which determines this habitual obedience is a power residing in the common will and reason of men, i.e., in the will and reason of men as determined by social relations, as interested in each other, as acting together for common ends. It is a power which this universal rational will exercises over the inclinations of the individual, and which only needs exceptionally to be backed by coercive force.[80]

This general will, which is the basis of political society, Green describes in rather vague terms as "that impalpable congeries of the hopes and fears of a people, bound together by common interests and sympathy." [81]

The State, for Green, is the highest form of society, the completion of the idea of society. There are many societies of men inferior to the State, of which the family is the most fundamental.

It is a mistake then to think of the state as an aggregation of individuals under a sovereign; equally so whether we suppose the individuals as such, or apart from what they derive from society, to possess natural rights, or suppose them to depend on the sovereign for the possession of rights. A state presupposes other forms of community, with the rights that arise out of them, and only exists as sustaining, securing, and completing them.[82]

It is not the existence of supreme coercive power that makes a state but "supreme coercive power exercised in a certain way and for certain ends . . . viz., exercised according to law, written or customary, and for the maintenance of rights." [83] The state maintains through a system of law the possibility of freedom that otherwise would not exist. Hence, apart from the state the individual can really be said to have no existence as a person.

To ask why I am to submit to the power of the state, is to ask why I am to allow my life to be regulated by that complex of institutions without which I literally should not have a life to call my own, nor should be able to ask for a justification of what I am called on to do. For that I may have a life which I can call my own, I must not only be conscious of myself and of ends which present to myself as mine; I must be able to reckon on a certain freedom of action and acquisition for the attainment of those ends, and this can only be secured through common recognition of this freedom on the part of each other by members of society, as being for a common good.[84]

Far from being a necessary evil the state is a positive good, since it is only through the state that I may realize my reason as will.

Green speaks frequently of individual rights but his conception of such rights is quite different from that of Locke for, in the last analysis, he regards such rights as concessions granted by society rather than as rights belonging to individuals by virtue of their humanity. A right, Green says, is "on the one hand a claim of the individual, arising out of his rational nature, to the free exercise of some faculty; on the other . . . a concession of that claim by society, a power given by it to the individual of putting the claim in force." [85] The two aspects cannot be separated. We can speak of such rights as "natural" only in the sense that they are claims that the state *should* recognize because there is a "common consciousness" that an individual ought to have such rights; they are not natural facts but *ideals*. Such rights vary from time to time and from place to place in accordance with the moral consciousness of the community. With the growth of moral consciousness, with that moral progress which Green assumes as inevitable, certain rights which were once regarded as "natural" will no longer be so regarded and other claims may come to be regarded as "natural." Every right that an individual has is "dependent on" the "social judgment of its compatibility with general well-being." [86] In the last analysis it is the well-being of the community rather than the humanity of the individual that determines his "rights." Does an individual have any rights against society or the state? Green answers this question by saying:

A right against society as such, a right to act without reference to the needs or good of society, is an impossibility, since every right depends on some social relation, and a right against any group of associated men depends upon association on some footing of equality with them or with some other men . . . if we regard the state as the sustainer and harmoniser of social relations . . . the individual can have no right against the state: . . . its law must be to him of absolute authority . . . *no exercise of a power, however, abstractedly desirable for the promotion of human good it might be, can be claimed as a right unless there is some common consciousness of utility shared by the person making the claim and those on whom it is made.* It is not a question whether or no it ought to be claimed as a right; it simply cannot be claimed except on this condition.[87]

In another place Green declares that "A right is a power of acting for his own ends,—for what he conceives to be his good,—secured to an individual by the community, on the supposition that its exercise contributes to the good of the community." [88] The individual as such has no inherent, unalienable rights which are always and everywhere the same. What Green has done is to reduce all so-called natural and unalienable rights to *one* right, namely, the right to pursue one's own good so long as that good is recognized by the society, in which one happens to find one's self, as compatible with the common good of all. A man is entitled to that degree of freedom, and that degree only, that is socially approved as desirable. "The right to free life rests on the common will of the society." [89] Ideally, we may speak of rights antecedent to the state but they become *real* rights only when recognized and enforced by the State. Conceivably we could challenge the State in the name of certain ideal rights but the presumption is always against such resistance to the will of the state. Since such resistance is liable to result in general anarchy and since "such a destruction of the state would mean a general loss of freedom," it is necessary carefully to weigh the possibility of anarchy against the ideal freedom desired.[90]

The right to property rests upon the same basis, Green explains, as other rights: "The rationale of property . . . is that everyone should be secured by society in the power of getting and keeping the means of realizing a will, which in possibility is a will directed to social good." [91] It is no argument against the right of property that that right is often abused for so are other rights and freedoms abused.

It is not then a valid objection to the manner in which property is possessed among us, that its holders constantly use it in a way demoralising to themselves and others, any more than such misuse of any other liberties is an objection to securing men in their possessions. Only then is property held in a way inconsistent with its idea, and which should, if possible, be got rid of, when the possession of property by one man interferes with the possession of property by another; when one set of men are secured in the getting and keeping the means of realising their will, in such a way that others are practically denied the power. In that case it may truly be said that "property is theft." The rationale of property, in short, requires that everyone who will conform to the positive condition, viz., respect for it as possessed by others, should, so far as social arrangements can make him so, be a possessor of property himself, and of such property as will at least enable him to develop a sense of responsibility, as distinct from mere property in the immediate necessaries of life.[92]

In other words, if private property is necessary in order that individuals may have the means of realizing their "will . . . to social good" then the system of private property must be such that all individuals have the same opportunity of obtaining those means necessary to the realization of their wills. It is not necessary that property be equally divided but that all individuals have the opportunity of obtaining some property above that necessary for existence. Only "if an inequality of fortunes . . . necessarily results in the existence of a proletariat, practically excluded from such ownership as is needed to moralise a man," would there be "a contradiction between our theory of the right of property and the actual consequence of admitting the right according to the theory." [93] Green defends freedom of inheritance and freedom of trade.

"To buy in the cheapest and sell in the dearest market" is a phrase which may no doubt be used to cover objectionable transactions, in which advantage is taken of the position of sellers who from circumstances are not properly free to bargain. It is so employed when the cheapness of buying arises from the presence of labourers who have no alternative but to work for "starvation wages." But in itself it merely describes transactions in which commodities are bought where they are of least use and sold where they are of most use. The trader who profits by the transaction is profiting by what is at the same time a contribution to social well-being. . . .

The same principle which forbids us to limit the degree to which a man may provide for his future, forbids us to limit the degree to which he may provide for his children, these being included in his forecast of his future. . . . Of course the possessor of any estate, who has contributed nothing by his own labour to its acquisition, may yet by his labour contribute largely to the social good, and a well-organised state will in various ways elicit such labour from possessors of inherited wealth. Nor will it trust merely to encouraging the voluntary fulfillment of social functions, but will by taxation make sure of some positive return for the security which it gives to inherited wealth.[94]

The question must still be considered, however, whether the freedom of unlimited accumulation of wealth by individuals and complete freedom of bequest on their part necessarily means the existence of a proletariat, i.e., persons who are "nominal owners of their powers of labour," but who, in fact, are "obliged to sell these on such terms that they are owners of nothing beyond what is necessary from day to day for the support of life, so that, as regards the moral functions of property, they may be held to be not proprietors at all." [95] Green argues that the freedom enjoyed by one man to accumulate wealth without limit does not in any way diminish a like freedom on the part of other individuals, because the stock of wealth is not fixed and because "the wealth of the world is constantly increasing in proportion as the constant production of new wealth by labour exceeds the constant consumption of what is already produced." [96] Capital is constantly being distributed through wages and profits and there is nothing "in the fact" that "labour is hired in great masses by great capitalists to prevent them from being on a small scale capitalists themselves." [97] Laborers have every opportunity to become small scale capitalists, especially when they are encouraged by education and self-discipline. What then accounts for "the multiplication in recent times of an impoverished and reckless proletariat?" [98] What accounts for the fact that so many men in our society are forced to sell their labor so cheaply that they seldom have the means to save? "It is certain . . . ," Green declares, that this situation has "no necessary connection with the maintenance of the right of individual property and consequent unlimited accumulation of capital." [99] It is due, he thinks, not to the institution of private property but to one aspect of it, namely, landed property. Property in the form of land is unique in its nature and in its origin. Property in land was established not by the expenditure of labor upon it but by force. "The original landlords have been conquerors." [100] Moreover, the supply of land is limited and no one can acquire more land without taking it from others. Because of this some persons have been landless. The modern proletariat is simply the spawn of the feudal serfdom. Historical developments have been such as to favor the accumulation of land as property in the hands of a few and the law has been such as to entail the land in certain families and at the same time allowed the individual landlords to do with the land as they pleased, irrespective of the social consequences. It is not capitalism that is to blame for the existence and condition of the proletariat, but the "arbitrary and violent way in which the rights over land have been acquired and exercised." [101] He does not think that this necessitates preventing private property in land but only a special control over the exercise of such rights. He rejects the proposal to tax the "unearned increment" in the value of land as being too complicated and too liable to lessen "the stimulus to the individual to make the most of the land." [102]

The social problems that loomed large in Green's thought were the problems of: education, temperance, and of property in land. In these matters he favored considerable intervention and regulation by the state. In other words, the three greatest obstacles to freedom as he saw it, were ignorance, drunkenness and poverty. It is the function of the state to remove such obstacles. Classical liberalism, he thinks, went wrong in regarding freedom simply in negative terms; freedom is positive. Thus Green laid the intellectual foundations for the modern social welfare state, for old age pensions, unemployment insurance, health insurance, and all the other legislative schemes designed to promote "social security." Green would not have gone as far, probably, as we have gone today in this direction but he helped to provide the philosophical justification upon which that development has taken place. Commenting upon Green's political philosophy Sabine declares:

> Green's general principle, that a liberal government ought to legislate in any case where the law can remove an obstacle to the highest moral development of its citizens, provided at least the framework for a wholly different conception of government from that held by the older liberalism. In place of *laissez-faire* and freedom of contract it opened the way, in the name of positive freedom, for any degree of social legislation that could be justified as practically effective in improving the standard of living. . . . What Green added to liberal theory was the conception of collective well-being as a precondition of individual freedom and responsibility. . . . Thus in principle Green's revision of liberalism closed up the gap which *laissez-faire* had placed between politics and economics and put on government the duty of regulating the economic system when it fails to produce humanly satisfying results.[103]

A more Hegelian conception of the State finds expression in the writings of two other British idealists, F. H. Bradley (1846–1924) and Bernard Bosanquet (1848–1923). Bradley wrote very little on political subjects, his principal contribution in this field being an essay entitled "My Station and its Duties" which appeared in his *Ethical Studies* (1876). The State, according to him, is a moral organism—"it is not put together, but it lives; it is not a heap nor a machine; it is no mere extravagance when a poet talks of a nation's soul. It is the objective mind which is subjective and self-conscious in its citizens; it feels and knows itself in the heart of each. It speaks the word of command and gives the field of accomplishment, and in the activity of obedience it has and bestows individual life and satisfaction and happiness." The individual has no real existence apart from the state for it is the means of realizing the true idea of man. "What we call an individual man is what he is because of and by virtue of community." [104]

In *The Philosophical Theory of the State* (1899) Bosanquet carried Green's philosophy to the Hegelian limit. For him the State

includes the entire hierarchy of institutions by which life is determined, from the family to the trade, and from the trade to the Church and the University. It includes all of them, not as the mere collection of the growths of the country, but as the structure which gives life and meaning to the political whole. . . . It follows that the State, in this sense, is above all things, not a number of persons, but a working conception of life. [105]

He finds in Rousseau's conception of the general will "the key to the whole problem of self-government and freedom under law." [106] In submitting to the general will of the community the individual is submitting to his own real and rational will and thus, submitting to himself. Hence, a man is more free when he submits to the dictates of the General Will than when he yields to his own momentary impulses or desires. The General Will is embodied in the State and in the laws laid down by the State; hence true freedom is to be found in loyalty to the State and submission to its laws. The State exists to promote the good life but it is not the agent of society so much as it is its highest and most perfect embodiment. It "is itself the supreme community; the guardian of a whole moral world, but not a factor within an organized moral world." [107] The moral terms which we use to identify certain actions of individuals, such as murder, theft, etc., cannot be applied to the State for the state is not limited by morality, it *is* morality.

The Nation-State . . . is the widest organization which has the common experience necessary to found a common life. This is why it is recognized as absolute in power over the individual, and as his representative and champion in the affairs of the world outside. It is obvious that there can be but one such absolute power in relation to any one person . . . and . . . his discharge from one allegiance can only be effected by his acceptance of another. . . .

The Nation-State as an ethical idea is, then, a faith or a purpose— we might say a mission, were not the word too narrow and too aggressive. . . . The modern nation is a history and a religion rather than a clear cut idea. [108]

CHAPTER 9

# Positivism

DURING the nineteenth century the physical sciences achieved an unprecedented prestige. By stimulating inventions, by improving the methods of economic production, by adding greatly to the physical stature of man and to his technological skill, the physical sciences added greatly to the material prosperity, comfort and security of an ever-increasing number of people. To many, the practical application of scientific discoveries seemed to herald the dawn of the "millennium." The eighteenth-century promise of an earthly utopia seemed definitely within reach of man's power. The method had been found: paradise on earth waited only upon the proper execution of the plan to be discovered in the truths and with the methods of the natural sciences. It was to Science that the nineteenth century turned for understanding and salvation as men in the Middle Ages had turned to theology and the Church.

Technical efficiency and mechanical certainty were the ideals of the nineteenth century, and they were the ideals, not only of the scientists, but of the socially dominant and materially satiated bourgeoisie, whose primary desires, unlike those of their seventeenth-century progenitors, were for certainty, security, and stability. Hoping to achieve for the study of human phenomena the same calculable certainty that characterized the physical sciences, students of social phenomena accepted with eagerness the perspective of positivism.

Positivism is an attempt to transfer to the study of social and human phenomena the methods and concepts of the natural sciences in the belief that human phenomena, like physical phenomena, obey certain laws of nature which can be inductively discovered by the empirical examination of successive events. These laws do not transcend experience, according to the positivist, but are found immanently in the things themselves, and behind them is the compulsion of nature, which, independent of individual will or reason, determines the course of human events. With the rise of positivism in the nineteenth century the only task left to social science and jurisprudence is the description of events and the induction from these events of general laws of causality—the evaluation of the goodness or badness, justice or injustice, of particular events being regarded not only as irrelevant but as being incompatible with scientific methods and "ideals." In an effort to confine himself to the "pure" description of empirically observable "facts," the positivist substitutes the inductive reasoning of the physical scientist for the "right reason" of the seventeenth-century philosopher. In a word, positivism is an attempt to substitute an immanent conception of order for the earlier transcendental conception; an attempt to substitute the physical laws of nature for the natural law of reason. Positivism is an outgrowth of the natural sciences but it is not, indeed, synonymous with them. As an intellectual perspective, it is more commonly found among social scientists than among natural scientists.

Guido de Ruggiero defines positivism as "a philosophical tendency oriented around natural science and striving for a unified view of the world of phenomena, both physical and human, through the application of the methods and the extension of the results whereby the natural sciences have attained their unrivalled position in the modern world." It represents the complete victory of empiricism and "calls 'positive' the facts and things of immediate perception as well as the relations and uniformities which thought may discover without transcending experience." It regards as metaphysical "every inquiry which claims to go beyond the sphere of the empirical and seeks either hidden essences behind phenomenal appearances, or ultimate efficient and final causes behind things, as well as any attempt to attribute reality to species, ideas, concepts or the mind's logical 'intentions' in general." [1] It is an attempt to repudiate all metaphysical speculation and ethical evaluation in the interest of "scientific objectivity."

Positivism became, in the nineteenth century, the dominant climate of intellectual opinion and only very recently has it been seriously challenged. The name of positivism is intimately associated with that of Auguste Comte for he was one of the first to use the term.

## *Auguste Comte (1798–1857)*
### *Founder of Sociology*

A DISCIPLE of Saint-Simon, Comte devoted his intellectual energies to the formulation of "A Plan for the Scientific Work Necessary to Reorganize Society," the title of one of the early essays which brought him his first recognition as a writer. His most important works include his *Course of Positive Philosophy* (1830–1842) in six volumes, *System of Positive Polity* (1851–1854) in four volumes and *The Catechism of Positivism* (1852).

One of Comte's fundamental theories is what he called "the law of the three stages." According to this "law" the history of human thought can be divided into three stages: theological, metaphysical, and positive. In the first stage man attempted to explain everything in terms of supernatural causes, progressing from animism to polytheism to monotheism. This stage extended from the most primitive times down through the Middle Ages. Gradually it was replaced by the *metaphysical* stage which is characterized by the substitution of abstractions for a personal God or gods. In this stage Nature is frequently substituted for God, and "fictions" such as the "social contract," "natural rights" and "the sovereignty of the people" appear in the social philosophy of this period. The eighteenth-century, according to Comte, best exemplifies this stage. The third and ultimate stage Comte calls *positive*. This is the age of Science when man discards all abstractions and metaphysical concepts and confines himself to the empirical observation of successive events from which he induces natural laws. This is the stage toward which all other stages have been "progressing" and the stage in which mankind may look forward with confidence to the establishment, with the aid of scientific methods, of perfect order and social harmony.[2]

Before this order can be realized, however, a new science is needed, namely: a science of society, which Comte first called "social physics" and later renamed "sociology." Sociology will be the queen of the sciences, playing a role in the modern world which theology played in the Middle Ages. Comte arranged the sciences in hierarchical order claiming that this order represented not only the order in which each science historically appeared but also their logical order (from the most simple to the most complex), namely: mathematics, astronomy, physics, chemistry, biology, and sociology.

He distinguished between *social statics* which deals with the mutual interaction of ideas, customs and institutions in any particular time and place, and *social dynamics* which is concerned with describing the development of society in terms of the law of three stages. The one emphasizes order, and the other, progress. Social dynamics reveals, according to Comte, that the warfare which was so prevalent in the theological stage will disappear in the positive stage and with industry triumphant economic problems will also be solved.

Human activity, as I have long since shown, passes successively through the stages of Offensive warfare, Defensive warfare, and Industry. The respective connection of these states with the preponderance of the theological, the metaphysical, or the positive spirit leads at once to a complete explanation of history. It reproduces in a systematic form, the only historical conception which had become adopted by universal consent: the division, namely, of history into Ancient, Mediaeval, and Modern.

Thus the foundation of social science depends simply upon establishing the truth of this theory of development. We do this by combining the dynamic law which is its distinctive feature, with the statical principle which renders it coherent; we then complete the theory by extending it to practical life. . . . The Positive spirit, so long confined to the simpler inorganic phenomena, has now passed through its difficult course of probation. It extends to a more important and more intricate class of speculations, and disengages them for ever from all theological or metaphysical influence. . . . A firm objective basis is consequently laid down for that complete coordination of human existence towards which all sound Philosophy had ever tended, but which the want of adequate materials has hitherto made impossible.[3]

"The true Positive spirit," Comte declares, "consists in substituting the study of the invariable laws of phenomena, for that of their so-called Causes, whether proximate or primary; in a word, in studying the *How* instead of the *Why*." [4]

Not only does the positive stage of man's development require a new science (sociology) but it requires a new religion. Religion is necessary in order to harmonize man's intelligence and his heart, "the individual can attain his highest perfection and happiness only in so far as he is, at once and by virtue of the same principle, in harmony with the world, with his fellowmen, and with himself." [5] But man can obtain this harmony only by surrendering himself to something outside himself and to which he is necessarily related. This object outside himself must be a power superior to himself and one capable of commanding his affections.

Submission and love are both necessary to religion, for if we have merely the former, the utmost we can feel is resignation to a fatality; and this, though it involves a certain limitation of the selfish tendencies, can never overcome them, or substitute a new motive for them. To retain the energy of egoism and combine it with resignation to a power greater than ours, we must love that power to which we submit. Finally, this submission and self-surrender must be consistent with a certain relative sense of independence, for no feeling is really powerful which does not result in action. . . . Only thus, when veneration for that which is above us, is combined with love for that which is the constant source of good to us and with benevolence towards that which needs our help, can we rise above the unreal and imperfect unity of selfishness into the perfect unity of religion." [6]

Since science, Comte insists, does not permit us to worship God in the traditional Christian sense we must manufacture a new religion to take the place of Christianity and the religion Comte proposes to put in its place is the Religion of Humanity. For the worship of God Comte would substitute the worship of Humanity "the real author of the benefits for which thanks were formerly given to God." [7] For the Holy Trinity of the

Christian religion Comte would substitute a new trinity—the Great Being (Humanity), the Grand Fetich (the earth) and the Grand Medium (space). Hymns should be composed praising humanity and public services conducted for her worship; private meditations on the deeds and lives of great men should take the place of prayer; the Christian calendar should be replaced by a Positivist calendar of thirteen months, each month named for a great man and each day of the week for another; and a special priesthood trained in all branches of science will support the faith and direct the intellectual energies of scientists into socially beneficent channels. Women are to have an especially exalted role in Comte's positive society for "When the mission of Woman is better understood, and is carried out more fully, she will be regarded by Man as the most perfect impersonation of Humanity." [8] Only by learning to worship Woman can men be taught to worship Humanity —"in a word," Comte declares, "Man will in those days kneel to Woman, and to Woman alone." [9] What Comte seems to want is the church without Christianity or as someone has declared "Catholicism without Christianity." The religion Comte offers us is an artificial one. He seems to say, as Edward Caird, an eminent Scottish philosopher, has explained it, that

We have derived from the experience of our own past and of the past of humanity, a clear idea of what religion should be: and we also know from the same experience that, without a religion, we cannot have that fulness of spiritual life of which we are capable. Go to, let us make a religion, as nearly corresponding to the definition of religion as modern science will permit. . . . God, the Absolute Being, is hidden from us, but Humanity will serve for a "relative" or "subjective" kind of God; or rather not Humanity, but the selected members of the race, whose services entitle them to our recognition, and whom therefore *we* incorporate in the "Great Being." And as for the inscrutable fatality that bounds all our views, and on which in the last resort the fate of humanity must depend, to *it* we can but submit; or (since such a separation of submission from love is so far irreligious) we can invoke the powers of imagination to hide it from our eyes. To Humanity, as represented to us by the good and wise of the past, we can present the old offerings of praise and prayer, in a spirit that is perfectly disinterested; for we have no reason to believe that *they* exist except in our memory of them, or that the "Great Being," in whom they are incorporated, has any gift to bestow upon us in the future except a similar life in the memory of others. For, after all, the "Great Being," who alone makes things work together for our good and whom alone we can love, is not absolute or objective; and of the real Absolute Being or Principle of the Universe, we know nothing, except perhaps that He or It is not what men call good.[10]

Now, such a religion, Caird declares, "is no religion at all: it is at best a morality, trying to gather to itself some of the emotions which were formerly connected with religious belief. . . . And the religion of Comte could scarcely become more than a pious aspiration, unless the poetic license of worship were carried to the point of self-deception." [11] Comte, in his latest works, seemed bent upon just this kind of self-deception for he wrote:

The logic of religion when freed from scientific empiricism, will not restrain itself any longer to the domain of hypotheses which are capable of verification, though these alone were compatible with the Positive preparation for it. It must in the end find its completion in the domain, much wider and not less legitimate, of those conceptions which, without offending reason, are peculiarly suited to develop the feelings. Better adapted to our moral wants, the institutions of true Poetry are as harmonious as those of sound Philosophy with the intellectual conditions of the relative synthesis. They ought therefore to obtain as great extension and influence in our efforts to systematize our thoughts; and Positivism permits their doing so without any danger of confusion between the two distinct methods of thinking, which it openly consecrates, the one to reality and the other to ideality.[12]

Commenting upon this statement Caird asks:

Is it possible to express more clearly a desire to combine the advantages of believing, with the advantages of disbelieving, in the accordance of objective reality with our highest feelings and aspirations? But a worship of fictions, confessed as such, is impossible. Art, indeed, is kindred with Religion; and Art, as Plato said, is "a noble untruth." This, however, means only that Art is untrue to the immediate appearances of things, in order that it may suggest the deeper reality that underlies them. But, in Comte's view, the service of imagination is to supply wants of the heart, which *cannot* be supplied by reality, either in its superficial or in its deeper aspect; it is to nurture our moral nature on conceptions that are purely fictitious. It is not difficult to prophesy that the schism of the head and the heart thus introduced must end in the sacrifice of the one or of the other . . . which will separate, not only man from the world, but also the individual from the race; and which must ultimately reduce Humanity from an object of worship into a subjective moral ideal.[13]

Comte sought to combat the emotional sterility of scientific empiricism with a poetic illusion. The human perfectibility of which the eighteenth-century *philosophes* dreamed appeared to Comte in the nineteenth century to be realizable through the methods of natural science motivated by the worship of Humanity.

## On the Logic of the Moral Sciences

THE application of scientific methods to the study of human and social phenomena was given added impetus by the writing of John Stuart Mill, especially his section "On the Logic of the Moral Sciences" in his *System of Logic* (1843). Although he differed from Comte in many significant ways he approved generally of Comte's philosophy, especially his law of three stages. The presuppositions upon which Mill looks forward confidently to the establishment of a natural science of man and of society are these:

All phenomena of society are phenomena of human nature, generated by the action of outward circumstances upon masses of human beings; and if, therefore, the phenomena of human thought, feeling, and action are subject to fixed laws, the phenomena of society can not but conform to fixed laws, the consequence of the preceding. There is, indeed, no hope that these laws, though our knowledge of them were as certain and as complete as it is in astronomy, would enable us to predict the history of society, like that of celestial appearances, for thousands of years to come. *But the difference of certainty is not in the laws themselves, it is in the data to which these laws are to be applied.* . . .

But . . . an amount of knowledge quite insufficient for prediction, may be most valuable for guidance. The science of society would have attained a very high point of perfection if it enabled us, in any given condition of social affairs, in the condition, for instance, of . . . any European country at the present time, to understand by what causes it had, in any and every particular, been made what it was; whether it was tending to any, and to what, changes; what effects each feature of its existing state was likely to produce in the future; and by what means any of those effects might be prevented, modified, or accelerated, or a different class of effects superinduced. There is nothing chimerical in the hope that general laws, sufficient to enable us to answer these various questions for any country or time with the individual circumstances of which we are well acquainted, do really admit of being ascertained. . . . Such is the object of Social Science.[14]

The principle obstacle to the establishment of a natural social science, as Mill sees it, is the lack of sufficient data. He examines some of the scientific methods by means of which the laws of social phenomena might be discovered and rejects the experimental method as being inappropriate for the study of human beings. He also rejects what he calls the geometrical method because "the phenomena of society do not depend, in essentials, on some one agency or law of human nature, with only inconsiderable modifications from others." [15] Social science, he concludes, should be modeled after "the more complex physical sciences" and the method most appropriate to it he calls the "Concrete Deductive Method," of which astronomy, he contends, furnishes the most perfect example. This method consists "in finding general propositions which express concisely what is common to large classes of observed facts; and these are called the empirical laws of the phenomena." [16] Statistics may be used to yield some of the data from which such general propositions may be deduced but the best source of data is history. "Up to the present time," Mill said, "the only known example of the study of social phenomena according to" his conception of "the Historical Method" was the work of Auguste Comte.[17] We may not be able to agree completely with all of Comte's conclusions

But whatever decision competent judges may pronounce on the results arrived at by any individual inquirer, the method now characterized is that by which the derivative laws of social order and of social progress must be sought. By its aid we may hereafter succeed not only in looking far forward into the future history of the human race, but in determining what artificial means may be used, and to what extent, to accelerate the natural progress in so far as it is beneficial . . . and to guard against the dangers or accidents to which our species is exposed from the necessary incidents of its progression. Such practical instructions, founded on the highest branch of speculative sociology, will form the noblest and most beneficial portion of the Political Art.[18]

Mill's confidence in the possibility of establishing a natural social science was predicated upon the presupposition that:

The actions and feelings of human beings in the social state, are, no doubt, entirely governed by psychological and ethological laws: whatever influence any cause exercises upon the social phenomena, it exercises through these laws. Supposing therefore the laws of human actions and feelings to be sufficiently known, there is no extraordinary difficulty in determining from those laws, the nature of the social effects which any given cause tends to produce.[19]

Psychology, he thought, had reached such an advanced stage that there was little more to discover about the laws of the mind. All that remained to be done was to translate these empirical laws into "the causal laws which explain them." This was to be the function of a new "science of the formation of character" which Mill called "ethology."[20] This science will discover "what makes one person, in a given position, feel or act in one way, another in another." This science, moreover, "may be called the Exact Science of Human Nature; for its truths are not, like the empirical laws which depend on them, approximate generalizations, but real laws."[21] Unlike psychology which is principally a science of observation and experimentation, Ethology will be a deductive science. The data for such a science are already abundant.

Excepting the degrees of uncertainty which still exist as to the extent of the natural differences of individual minds, and the physical circumstances on which these may be dependent (considerations which are of secondary importance when we are considering mankind in the average, or *en masse*) I believe most competent judges will agree that the general laws of the different constituent elements of human nature are even now sufficiently understood to render it possible for a competent thinker to deduce from these laws, with a considerable approach to certainty, the particular type of character which would be formed in mankind generally by any assumed set of circumstances.[22]

Education consists of the application of the laws of Ethology to particular individuals. By knowing what factors in the environment produce what effects upon human character we can mold human nature through education to conform to what—? Mill does not say explicitly what his standard of a "good" human nature would be, but by implication we may gather that a "good man" is the typical "gentleman" of nineteenth-century England. Through education mankind, then, can be made over, following the principles of Ethology, in the image of the English aristocracy. That this is an improvement over earlier attempts to make man over in the image of God, Mill presumably believes. Mill did not, and no one has yet, developed the science of Ethology which he presupposed as the basis of a natural social science but that failure has not deterred many from attempting to found one. In fact, most social scientists today are preoccupied with that endeavor; some would insist that they had succeeded.

## The Doctrine of Evolution

IF WE mean by evolution the progressive development in Nature of plants and animals from lower stages to higher ones then the theory is as old as Aristotle. If we mean that life is characterized by ceaseless flux and change then the idea is as old as Lucretius and Heracleitus. Modern theories of evolution differ from older theories in that they seek to explain progressive change in purely naturalistic terms, they find the causes of change immanent in the process itself rather than outside the process. It was in the eighteenth century, rather than in the nineteenth century, that the modern theory of evolution first made its appearance. And it was the German philosopher, Leibnitz (1646–1716), who anticipated that theory in the seventeenth century.

The ultimate reality, according to Leibnitz, consists of "monads" which are percipient, self-acting beings. They have neither extension, parts, or figure but are centers of force, the action of each being independent of every other. "The essential characteristics of the universe are for him plenitude, continuity, and linear gradation. The chain consists of the totality of monads, ranging in hierarchical sequence from God to the lowest grade of sentient life, no two alike, but each differing from those just below and just above it in the scale by the least possible difference." [23] For the mechanical conception of nature envisaged by Descartes, Leibnitz substituted a *dynamic* conception.

But "it was in the eighteenth century that the conception of the universe as a Chain of Being, and the principles which underlay this conception—plenitude, continuity, gradation—attained their widest diffusion and acceptance. . . . Next to the word 'Nature,' 'the Great Chain of Being' was the sacred phrase of the eighteenth century, playing a part somewhat analogous to that of the blessed word 'evolution' in the late nineteenth." [24] It was a common assertion in the eighteenth century that there is a principle of continuity extending, in Bolingbroke's words, "almost from nonentity up to man." Indeed, Bolingbroke declared

Man is connected by his nature, and therefore, by the design of the Author of all Nature, with the whole tribe of animals, and so closely with some of them, that the distance between his intellectual faculties and theirs, which constitutes as really, though not so sensibly as figure, the difference of species, appears, in many instances, small, and would probably appear still less, if we had the means of knowing their motives, as we have of observing their actions. [25]

Although some writers dwelt upon the superior reasoning power of man, the distinctiveness of human nature was progressively minimized. Soame Jenyns (1704–1787), an English poet and author, wrote:

Animal life rises from this low beginning in the shell-fish, through innumerable species of insects, fishes, birds, and beasts, to the confines of reason, where, in the dog, the monkey, and chimpanzee, it unites so closely with the lowest degree of that quality in man, that they cannot easily be distinguished from each other. From this lowest degree in the brutal Hottentot, reason, with the assistance of learning and science, advances, through the various stages of human understanding, which rise above each other, till in a Bacon, or a Newton it attains the summit.

Yet, he adds that "The superiority of man to other terrestrial animals is as inconsiderable in proportion to the immense plan of universal existence, as the difference of climate between the north and south end of the paper I now write upon." [26] It was a commonplace assumption of the eighteenth century that, as the *Encyclopédie* put it, "everything in nature is linked together." The discovery by Trembley in 1739 of the fresh-water polyp *Hydra* seemed to fill the gap between the animal and vegetable worlds and to suggest that the gap between the vegetable and mineral kingdoms might eventually be closed by similar discoveries. Zoologists set about seeking the "missing link" between man and the animal kingdom. A Swedish botanist, Linnaeus, was not only the first to lay down the principles for defining genera and species, but suggested the *homo troglodytes* as the "missing link" and spoke of the apes as "the nearest relations of the human race." [27] And such interest in man's possible descent from the anthropoids was by no means uncommon at this time.

In the seventeenth and early eighteenth centuries the principles of plenitude and continuity, however, "were invoked primarily as a support for the doctrine of the essential logicality of the world. They were designed to justify the belief in the rationality, the perfection, the static completeness, the orderliness and coherency of reality." Yet, as Professor Lovejoy points out, "they were at heart ideas profoundly antipathetic to the simple rationalism of the Enlightenment; the ultimate effect of their vogue was to introduce subtly and gradually into the European mind several of those tastes and those philosophical presuppositions which at the end of the century took form in a conscious and aggressive revolutionary movement in thought, that to which the name of Romanticism is commonly applied." [28] Gradually through the work and writings of men like Charles Bonnet (1720–1793) and George Buffon (1707–1788) the idea of fixed species was abandoned,

the unique nature of man challenged, and a vitalistic principle substituted for the earlier mechanical explanation. First
botany and later biology came to take the place of Newtonian
physics as a pattern for thought about the universe. It is this
revolution in thought patterns which clearly marks off the
nineteenth century from the eighteenth.

It was a French naturalist, Jean Lamarck (1744–1829) expanding upon Buffon's ideas, who was one of the first to express clearly the idea of the mutability of species and to suggest an hypothesis "explaining" it. In a work published in
1809 Lamarck summarized his theory by saying:

> Great changes in environment bring about changes in the habits
> of animals. Changes in their wants necessarily bring about parallel
> changes in their habits. If new wants become constant or very last-
> ing, they form new habits, the new habits involve the use of new
> parts, or the disuse of old parts, which results finally in the produc-
> tion of new organs and the modification of old ones.[29]

He also proposed a theory of the biological inheritance of
acquired characteristics. "All that has been acquired, im-
printed, or changed in the organization of the individual during the course of its life is preserved by generation and transmitted to the new individuals that descend from the individual
so modified." [30] Interest in his theory was not great during his
lifetime and his theory was greeted in many quarters with
scorn. Somewhat similar ideas were arrived at independently
by Dr. Erasmus Darwin (1731–1802) in England at about the
same time. It remained for his grandson Charles Darwin
(1809–1882) to systematize the doctrine of organic evolution
and to popularize it. The doctrine of evolution did not originate with Charles Darwin's *Origin of Species* (1859) but that
work marked the culmination of a long development.

Perhaps the most distinctive feature of the *Origin of Species*
is Darwin's conception of "natural selection." According to a
biologist, the Darwinian theory of natural selection may be
briefly stated in this way:

> No two animals—or plants—are exactly alike. There are always
> slight differences or variations in size, colour, shape, and intelligence.
> Owing to the rate at which all living forms tend to increase, there is

a continual *struggle for existence* in the competition for food and shelter. The variations in form that have proved advantageous will increase their possessor's chances of survival. In this way there is a *natural selection* where the "weakest go to the wall" and the "fittest" survive, ultimately to reproduce and transmit their heritable variations to their offspring.[31]

The popularity of Darwin's theory is to be accounted for, at least in part, by the fact that it suited the times in which it was formulated, it confirmed many individuals in believing what they already wanted to believe. As Jacques Barzun declares, it "captivated a generation of thinkers whose greatest desire was to get rid of vitalism, will, purpose, or design as explanations of life, and to substitute for them an automatic material cause."[32]

The transference of biological terminology to the description of social phenomena, however, was largely the work of Herbert Spencer (1820–1903) and it was Spencer who had already coined the phrase "survival of the fittest" in essays entitled "The Development Hypothesis" (1852) and "Progress—Its Law and Cause" (1857). It was Spencer who converted the eighteenth-century idea of progress, conceived by Comte as the historical law of three stages, into a *biological* law. Thus, for a time at least, the idea of progress was given greater "scientific" validity than it had ever possessed before.

## *The Philosophy of Herbert Spencer (1820–1903)*

BORN in Derby, England, in 1820, Herbert Spencer was brought up in humble surroundings and had very little formal education. When he was seventeen years of age he went to work for the London and Birmingham Railway as an engineer. Ten years later he became an editor of *The Economist*. He gave up that position in 1853 and spent the rest of his life writing and lecturing. He was a prolific writer and at the age of thirty had already written one of his most important works, *Social Statics* (1850). Spencer believed that the time had come to synthesize all the knowledge that the particular natural sciences had discovered and that it was possible to arrive at a conception of evolution that would apply universally from the stars and the planets to human government, art, language and morality. Accordingly, he announced in 1860 his intention of writing a Synthetic Philosophy that would bring all scientific knowledge together in a unified whole and from 1860 to 1893 worked continuously at this task. He revised for this series an earlier work entitled *Principles of Psychology* (1855) and added other volumes in the fields of biology, ethics and sociology. His more important political works included the *Social Statics*, mentioned earlier, and a series of articles published under the general title of *Man versus the State* (1884). A book entitled *First Principles* (1864) contains his general philosophy and underlying presuppositions.

In *First Principles* he contends that the ultimate nature of reality is unknowable and assigns to religion the realm of the unknowable and to science the realm of the knowable, thus effecting, he thought, a happy reconciliation between science and religion. "If Religion and Science are to be reconciled, the basis of reconciliation must be this deepest, widest, and most certain of all facts—that the Power which the Universe manifests to us is utterly inscrutable." [33] But ultimate scientific ideas, such as matter, motion, space, time, etc.,

are all representative of realities that cannot be comprehended. After no matter how great a progress in the colligation of facts and the establishment of generalizations ever wider and wider . . . the fundamental truth remains as much beyond reach as ever. The explanation of that which is explicable, does not bring out into greater clearness the inexplicableness of that which remains behind. Alike in the external and the internal worlds, the man of science sees himself in the midst of perpetual changes of which he can discover neither the beginning nor the end.[34]

The human mind can conceive only the limited, and the conditionally limited, all its knowledge must necessarily be relative.

By a rather ingenious piece of reasoning Spencer manages to restore to the "ultimate scientific ideas," however, a reality he apparently denied them at first. A little later on in his exposition he defines reality as "persistence in consciousness" [35] and says that "Reality then . . . being nothing more than persistence in consciousness, the result must be the same to us whether that which we perceive be the Unknowable itself, or an effect invariably wrought on us by the Unknowable."

If, under the constant conditions furnished by our constitutions, some Power of which the nature is beyond conception, always produces some mode of consciousness—if this mode of consciousness is as persistent as would be this Power were it in consciousness; the reality will be to consciousness as complete in the one case as in the other. Were Unconditioned Being itself present in thought, it could but be persistent; and if, instead, there is present Being conditioned by the forms of thought, but no less persistent, it must be to us no less real.[36]

Scientific knowledge, however, is always partial knowledge and some principle, which only philosophy can supply, is necessary to unify the knowledge of the several particular sciences. For

no number of analytical truths, will make up that synthesis of thought which alone can be an interpretation of the synthesis of things. . . . To have ascertained the laws of the factors is not at all to have ascertained the laws of their co-operation. The question is, not how any factor, Matter or Motion or Force, behaves by itself, or under some imagined simple conditions; nor is it even how one factor behaves under the complicated conditions of actual existence. The thing to be expressed is the joint product of the factors under all its various aspects. Only when we can formulate the total process, have we gained that knowledge of it which Philosophy aspires to.[37]

Now Spencer believed that he had found the formula that would bring about the complete unification of the various sciences and that was the doctrine of evolution.

Evolution is conceived by Spencer as movement from uniformity and incoordination to diversity and coordination or as he expressed it in his own words:

Evolution is an integration of matter and concomitant dissipation of motion; during which the matter passes from a relatively indefinite, incoherent homogeneity to a relatively definite coherent heterogeneity; and during which the retained motion undergoes a parallel transformation.[38]

All such movement has a beginning and an end in space and time and eventually the process comes to an end in equilibrium. *Dissolution* is the opposite of evolution, i.e., movement toward homogeneity, incoherence, and indefiniteness, and inevitably follows the attainment of equilibrium. Whether the universe itself evolves, Spencer says, it is impossible to say. But the principle of evolution applies to all finite phenomena: to the solar system, to the geological development of the earth, to all plant and animal organisms, to human beings, and to human societies. "So understood, Evolution becomes not one in principle only, but one in fact. There are not many metamorphoses similarly carried on; but there is a *single* metamorphosis universally progressing. . . ."[39]

Sociology, for Spencer, is a kind of social biology and society he likened to a biological organism. Both social and biological organisms exhibit significant similarities:

(1) both exhibit phenomena of growth, they begin as small aggregations and gradually increase in size;

(2) in the process of growth both exhibit differentiation of structures and functions—at first, both are simple in structure, if not indeed, structureless, but in the course of growth they become more complex with different parts of the organism assuming special functions;

(3) both are composed of units—in the case of biological organisms, cells, and in the case of society, individuals;

(4) in their undeveloped states both manifest scarcely any mutual dependence of parts but gradually in the process of growth their parts acquire mutual dependence, the life and activity of one part depending upon the life and activity of other parts:

(5) both have a special sustaining system—an alimentary system in the case of biological organisms and in the case of society, agriculture and industry;

(6) both have a special distributive system—a vascular and circulatory system in the case of biological organisms and arteries of transportation, commerce, and exchange, in the case of society;

(7) both have a special regulatory system—the nervous system in biological organisms and the governmental system in the case of society.

There are also some dissimilarities:

(1) Societies have no specific external forms such as biological organisms have;

(2) The units of biological organisms are physically continuous but the units of society are dispersed persons:

(3) The living elements of biological organisms are mostly fixed in their relative positions but the units of society are capable of moving from place to place;

(4) In biological organisms only a special tissue is endowed with feeling, in a society all the members are so endowed.

(5) In a biological organism consciousness resides in the brain and not in its individual cells but in society there is no mind or consciousness except that which resides in its individual members.

These dissimilarities are not significant enough, Spencer thought, to destroy the validity of his analogy. His elaboration of this analogy led him to draw some fantastic comparisons between biological organisms and societies. He explained the evolution of the factory, for example, as analogous to the clustering together of cells in the biological organism to form the liver; he likened the military class in society to the defensive weapons of biological organisms; he compared the alternate increases and decreases of traffic to the pulsations of the blood-flow in the vascular system and he likened the lines and fences that mark off railways and roads from the surrounding countryside to the walls through which the blood courses in the arterial system of biological organisms. Even more fantastic comparisons including the attribution of sexual characteristics to the State were to be made at a later date by a Swiss Professor J. K. Bluntschli. Spencer made the fatal mistake, which many continue to make, of transferring concepts that are appropriate to one science to another where the phenomena are quite different.

The end of social evolution according to Spencer is perfect harmonious adaptation or equilibrium. Evolution is purposive, it is teleological. A hedonist in ethical theory Spencer adapted the ethics of utilitarianism to his concept of evolution. Biological laws confirm utilitarian ethics since, in general,

pleasurable sensations are attached to those acts which promote survival and unpleasant sensations attach themselves to
acts that are inimical to survival. Moral obligation stems from
the preference for future pleasures to more immediate ones
but as men learn to take pleasure in the actions which promote survival and adaptation moral conduct will, in the
process of evolution, become simply natural conduct. As duty,
in other words, becomes more and more pleasurable the sense
of duty will disappear. Similarly, the apparent conflict between altruism and egoism will disappear for as society evolves
toward perfect equilibrium and adaptation men will increasingly find pleasure in altruistic acts over egoistic ones.

Two biological laws govern the evolution of society: (1) individuals who do not adapt themselves to the social environment will be exterminated—the fittest will survive either because of attributes with which they were born or because of
attributes which they acquired in the process of adaptation;
(2) Individuals who survive will transmit their characteristics
(including those which they have acquired during their lifetime) to the next generation and society, thus, will become
increasingly better. Spencer relies on Lamarck's theory of the
inheritance of acquired characteristics for this assurance of
progress, and progress is thus asserted to be a biological law.

The ultimate stage of social evolution will be characterized
by an industrial economy in which there is employment and
food for everyone and no one will require much if any assistance from anyone else. It will be an age of peace and plenty
and men instead of being cruel, brutal and treacherous as
they were required to be under more primitive social conditions will now be kindly, friendly and charitable. Voluntary
cooperation will progressively replace coercion and all the
nations and races of the world will live in harmonious accord.
What will happen then? Presumably, since no process of
evolution continues forever and every process must eventually
give way to dissolution the process will begin to work backward but since we have not yet achieved the ultimate stage
of social evolution we need not worry about that now—we
have several hundred, if not thousand, years of social evolution ahead of us. Although Spencer talked at times as though

he thought we were upon the very threshold of ultimate equilibrium.

Spencer's political theory is an application of these ideas and since he believed that social progress is assured by virtue of the operation of immanent laws of nature he tended to think of the state as a temporary necessary evil that in time would disappear. Meanwhile its functions should be confined to the bare minimum necessary to preserve order. What he regarded as the bare minimum was considerably less than even the most ardent advocates of *laissez-faire* had dreamed possible. Individuals must be left alone in order that the process of evolution may occur without hindrance, in order that the laws of nature may operate freely and without the interference of arbitrary, human legislation. But why is government necessary at all? Spencer explains it in this way:

It is clear that any being whose constitution is to be moulded into fitness for new conditions of existence, must be placed under those conditions. This granted, it follows that as man has been, and is still, deficient in those feelings which prevent the recurring antagonisms of individuals and their consequent disunion, some artificial agency is required by which their union may be maintained. Only by the process of adaptation itself, can be produced that character which makes social equilibrium spontaneous. And hence, while this process is going on, an instrumentality must be employed, firstly, to bind man into the social state, and secondly to check all conduct endangering the existence of that state. Such an instrumentality we have in government.[40]

Government is necessary because men still have some of the predatory instincts inherited from primitive existence. As these, however, are gradually eliminated through evolution government will become increasingly unnecessary. The function of government is to maintain as far as possible a condition under which each individual experiences the good effects and suffers the evil effects of his own nature and conduct. The duties of government are of two kinds: defense against external attack and the protection of individual rights. The mention of individual rights seems inconsistent for, presumably, if the state is to protect the rights of individuals this means the rights of the unfit as well as those of the fit. Is this not an artificial hindrance to evolution and an obstacle to progress? Spencer endeavors to explain it in this way:

If each, having freedom to use his powers up to the bounds fixed by the like freedom of others, obtains from his fellowmen as much for his services as they find them worth in comparison with the service of others—if contracts uniformly fulfilled bring to each the share thus determined, and he is left secure in person and possessions to satisfy his wants with the proceeds; then there is maintained the vital principle alike of individual life and of social life. Further, there is maintained the vital principle of social progress; inasmuch as, under such conditions, the individuals of most worth will prosper and multiply more than those of less worth. So that utility, not as empirically estimated, but as rationally determined, enjoins this maintenance of individual rights; and, by implication, negatives any course which traverses them.[41]

Reduced to its simplest terms, Spencer wrote, "every proposal to interfere with citizens' activities further than by enforcing their mutual limitations, is a proposal to improve life by breaking through the fundamental conditions of life."[42] As a consequence, he was opposed to many governmental undertakings that others regarded as essential; he was opposed, for example, to public education, to poor relief, to legislation regulating conditions of work, to a state controlled monetary system, to a governmentally operated postal system and to sanitary legislation and regulation.

## Spencer's Doctrine in America

HERBERT SPENCER's ideas found a welcome reception in many intellectual quarters in the United States. Perhaps the most important single writer who was instrumental in introducing Spencer's ideas in America was John Fiske (1842–1901). In a four volume work entitled *Outlines of Cosmic Philosophy* published in 1874 he rendered a faithful account of his master's teaching. In another book *Through Nature to God* (1899) he pursued the theme that evolution is the instrumentality of a benevolent God. Unlike Spencer who remained agnostic,

Fiske interpreted evolution as a divine plan for the production of human happiness.

The story shows us man becoming more and more clearly the image of God, exercising creative attributes, transforming his physical environment, incarnating his thoughts in visible and tangible shapes all over the world, and extorting from the abysses of space the secrets of vanished ages. From lowly beginnings, without breach of continuity, and through the cumulative action of minute and inconspicuous causes, the resistless momentum of cosmic events has tended towards such kind of consummation; and part and parcel of the whole process, inseparably wrapped up with every other part, has been the evolution of the sentiments which tend to subordinate mere egoism to unselfish and moral ends. . . .

Though in many ways God's work is above our comprehension, yet those parts of the world's story that we can decipher well warrant the belief that while in Nature there may be divine irony, there can be no such thing as wanton mockery. . . . The moral sentiments, the moral law, devotion to unselfish ends, disinterested love, nobility of soul—these are Nature's most highly wrought products, latest in coming to maturity; they are the consummation, toward which all earlier prophecy has pointed.[43]

Through natural evolution, he thought, humanity would one day be "purified and redeemed."

Fiske was not much interested in the political application of Spencer's doctrine. That task was most notably performed in America by a Yale professor of sociology, William Graham Sumner (1840–1910). The most vigorous advocate of *laissez-faire* policies in the United States, Sumner opposed with vehemence such early regulatory measures as the Sherman Anti-Trust Act and the Interstate Commerce Act of 1887 and, more consistently than some advocates of *laissez-faire*, opposed the American policy of protective tariffs. "The social order," he wrote, "is fixed by laws of nature precisely analogous to those of the physical order. The most that man can do is by ignorance and self-conceit to mar the operations of social laws." Let nature alone and eventually she will cure, through competition and by weeding out the unfit, the evils that now plague society. "Let it be understood," Sumner wrote, "that we cannot go outside of this alternative: liberty, inequality, survival of the fittest; non-liberty, equality, survival of the un-fittest. The former carries society forward and favors all its best members; the latter carries society downwards and favors all its worst members." But why, as we asked in the case of Spencer, should government, then, protect the rights of property and of person as Sumner insists it should? And Sumner explains it in much the same way as Spencer did:

What civil liberty does is to turn the competition of man with man from violence and brute force into an industrial competition under which men vie with one another for the acquisition of material goods by industry, energy, skill, frugality, prudence, temperance, and other industrial virtues. Under this changed order of things the inequalities are not done away with. Nature still grants her rewards of having and enjoying, according to our being and doing, but it is now the man of the highest training and not the man of the heaviest fist who gains the highest rewards.[44]

"What the notions of 'form' and 'harmony' were to Plato," Whitehead has written,

that the notions of "individuality" and "competition" were to the nineteenth century. God had placed his bow in the skies as a symbol; and the strip of colours, rightly read, spelt "competition." The prize to be competed for was "life." Unsuccessful competitors died; and thus, by a beautiful provision of nature, ceased from constituting a social problem.[45]

A very different conclusion claiming, however, to be equally scientific was reached by another American sociologist, Lester F. Ward (1841–1913). An ardent opponent of *laissez-faire* he helped lay the ideological foundations for the twentieth-century social-welfare state and was an early intellectual harbinger of the Rooseveltian New Deal. His most important works include his *Dynamic Sociology* (1903) intended as a reply to Spencer's *Social Statics, Applied Sociology* (1906), and a six volume work entitled *Glimpses of the Cosmos* (1918). As the editor of *The Iconoclast* published by the National Liberal Reform League which Ward helped to organize in 1869 he declared:

Science is the great Iconoclast. Our civilization depends wholly upon the discovery and application of a few profound scientific and philosophical principles, thought out by a few great minds who hold the shallow babble of priests in utter contempt, and have no time to dabble in theology.[46]

A disciple of Comte, and to some extent of Spencer, although he reached radically different conclusions, Ward believed that science was the salvation of society and sociology the queen of the sciences. "Not content with the conquest of nature and the subjection of its laws to human uses," Ward wrote, "man resolved to find out what he was, whence he came and what was to be his destiny. He proceeded to interrogate nature at all points, and the thousand conflicting and commingled answers that he got, all rolled together, when closely listened to, were found to spell out the talismanic word: 'Evolution.' "[47] For Ward, however, evolution does not take place in a straight line but proceeds in a zig-zag fashion, upward and downward, backward and forward.

The ultimate reality for Ward is matter eternally evolving and manifesting itself as energy.

The distinction between materials and forces disappears entirely upon analysis. It is no longer metaphysical to say that we know nothing of matter except through its properties. It is only its reactions that affect men's senses, only its properties that are utilized. But no line of demarcation can be drawn between the properties of matter and physical forces. . . . Matter is causality. Matter is power. . . . Matter is dynamic and every time that man has touched it with the wand of reason, it has responded by satisfying a want. That is the true philosophical basis of that "historical materialism" of which we hear so much in these days.[48]

Everything in existence is a product and embodiment of this basic energy including life itself and the human mind which Ward regards as Nature's greatest achievement although, presumably, it was produced by chance and with no particular intention or purpose. But with the emergence of the human mind there was provided for the first time a means by which the basic energy of the cosmos could be directed into socially beneficent channels. It is Science, a product of the human mind, that makes it possible for men to harness the forces of nature to his desires. Through Science men can give a direction to nature which without scientific control it does not itself possess. It is by no means clear from Ward's account how a mind capable of transcending and controlling the nature of which it is itself the product and embodiment could emerge but it is clear that to Ward it is no mystery. He thinks it enough to say that the mind emerged to preserve the organism from destruction but does not explain why men are especially endowed with a capacity which other organisms lack and presumably perpetuate themselves without. The only lacuna in Science is a knowledge of the laws of thought. When these are finally discovered, as Ward was confident they would be, no further obstacle will remain blocking man's complete and ultimate control of himself and his society.

"Just as reason, even in early man, rendered instinct unnecessary," Ward wrote, "so further intellectual development and wider knowledge and wisdom will ultimately dispense with both religion and ethics as restraints to unsafe conduct, and we may conceive of the final disappearance of all restrictive laws and of government as a controlling agency." [49] But the world is still far from this ideal state and meanwhile we must work for the establishment of a *sociocracy* (a word he borrowed from Comte). Economic competition rather than being a good, is an evil.

The evils of society are due to the competitive system in a state of artificial inequality of intelligence, and as this state has always existed it is supposed that it must always exist. The world has scarcely begun to reflect upon the possibility of any other system. . . . There are many other things to compete for besides money or wealth . . . part of it is intellectual, and consists of rivalry in achievement. On this higher plane, competition takes the form of honorable emulation.[50]

That intellectual competition involves none of the pride, envy, or jealousy that is involved in economic competition Ward apparently believed. Education is the great panacea for it is through education that intelligence may be equalized and when intelligence is equalized then the economic opportunities of men will be equalized. In *Dynamic Sociology* Ward gave the following synopsis of his philosophy:

(A) *Happiness* is the aim of man; the excess of pleasure over pain. . . .

(B) *Progress* is the state by which happiness is increased; the success in harmonizing natural phenomena with human advantage; the direct means to happiness, and the primary means to the ultimate end:

(C) *Dynamic Action* is the right action which leads to happiness; the employment of the intellect or the inventive and indirect method; the direct means to progress and the secondary means to the ultimate end;

(D) *Dynamic Opinion* is the correct view of the relation of man to the universe; the direct means to dynamic action, and the third means to the ultimate end. . . .

(E) *Knowledge* is correct opinion; acquaintance with the environ-ment; the direct means to dynamic opinion, and the fourth means to the ultimate end;

(F) *Education*, the universal distribution of extant knowledge is the direct means to knowledge and the initial means to the ultimate end.[51]

By knowledge Ward means, of course, scientific knowledge. Through the acquisition of knowledge Ward was confident that man can make both nature and the environment serve himself. Rather than man being adapted to his environment, as Spencer urged, the environment should be adapted to man. Mankind has made the progress it has not by letting nature alone but by gradually extending its control over nature, by making nature serve the purposes of men. Ward wrote:

It is not the doctrine of inactivity, of the folding of the arms that naturally and legitimately flows from a full comprehension of the law of evolution, but a gospel of action . . . of man as a great and po-tent cause in the world.

Nature is first to be observed, but, having been learned, the laws of nature become the property and servants of man, and he is not to imitate the methods by which nature accomplishes results, but must direct the forces of nature into channels of his own advantage, and utilize for his own good all powers of the universe.

The true crown of a system of scientific philosophy is not an ethics which seeks to restrain and circumscribe activity, but a sociology which aims at the liberation of action through the directive agency of intelligence.[52]

It is only through social cooperation that individual freedom can be achieved and the history of mankind is nothing more than the history of the effort on the part of man to escape the tyranny of nature and its law of competition. "Every artificial form that serves a human purpose, is a triumph of mind over the physical forces of nature in ceaseless and aimless competition." [53] Not individualism but collectivism is the natural social process.

Against men like Sumner, Ward urged the use of government to bring about more effective social regulation and planning. The distrust of government, he said, is irrational and "not only makes it worse than it otherwise would be, but, so far as this is possible it tends to give it the character it is accused of possessing." [54] If government would, it could find a solution to the problem of poverty and all similar social problems for man's intelligence is capable of solving any problem it wants to solve. Ward predicted the establishment in the near future of what he called a *sociocracy* to replace our present political democracy. In such an ideal state legislatures "will doubtless need to be maintained, and every new law should be finally adopted by a vote of such bodies, but more and more this will become merely a formal way of putting the final sanction of society on decisions that have been carefully worked out in what may be called the sociological laboratory.

Legislation will consist in a series of exhaustive experiments on the part of true scientific sociologists and sociological inventors working on the problems of social physics from the practical point of view. It will undertake to solve not only questions of general interest to the State, . . . but questions of social improvement, the amelioration of the condition of all the people, the removal of whatever privations may still remain, and the adoption of means to the positive increase of the social welfare, in short the organization of human happiness.[55]

Government will become the "organization of human happiness" through the science of sociology. No social problems are incapable of solution by the application of intelligence; it is simply a matter of allowing government to become the instrument of social experimentation under the direction of social scientists. When the mass of people become convinced that their salvation lies in science then we shall enter upon the last stage of evolution, the stage that will bring about everlasting social peace and harmony.

## Ludwig Gumplowicz (1838–1909)

also on P. 574 under "national expansion"

A CLOSE friend of Lester Ward's was the Austrian Polish sociologist Ludwig Gumplowicz whose sociological theory was based upon the assumption that the state originates in the conflict of racial groups. The group has always been more significant than the individual for:

It is not man himself who thinks but his social community; the source of his thoughts is in the social medium in which he lives, the social atmosphere which he breathes, and he can not think aught else than what the influences of his social environment concentrating upon his brain necessitate. . . .[56]

Human progress is the result of the conflict between groups, a conflict in which the fittest necessarily survive and dominate the less fit. To these primitive groups which have existed from the dawn of history Gumplowicz applies the name "race."

Every political organization, and hence every developing organization, begins when one group permanently subjects another. Subjection of some to the others is the source of political organization, is the condition essential to social growth. This proposition constitutes the cornerstone of the author's theory.[57]

Primitive existence was marked by chronic warfare between these "racial" groups and it was out of these conflicts that such social institutions as the family, private property, slavery and eventually the state emerged. It is absurd, he argued, to say that the state has its existence in a mandate from God and equally absurd to say that the state came into existence as the result of a social contract, nor is the state a consequence of man's social nature—the state originates in armed conquest, ultimately its basis is not consent but force. Recalling the doctrine of Thrasymachus in Plato's *Republic* Gumplowicz declared that:

The state . . . during the first stages of its existence, is a social institution, forced by a victorious group of men on a defeated group, with the sole purpose of regulating the dominion of the victorious group over the vanquished. . . .[58]

There are no natural rights belonging to individuals by virtue of their humanity and antecedent to the state but rather "every right is a true reflection of the state, to which it owes its existence." [59] The idea of natural rights is "overthrown, dead, and buried."

That man is a free being is pure imagination. . . . The premises of "inalienable human rights" rest upon the most unreasonable self-deification of man and overestimation of the value of human life, and upon a complete misconception of the only possible basis of the existence of the state. This fancied freedom and equality is incompatible with the state and is a complete negation of it.[60]

But the state far from being an evil is a necessary good. Without the state there could be no organized social life, no culture, no industry, no science. The only alternative to "the state with its necessary servitude and inequality" is "anarchy," for there can be no return to primitive existence. Since "anarchy raises infinitely the evil which is unavoidable in the state without affording even the least of its advantages" it is not difficult to choose between "the state and anarchy." [61]

Coupled with this doctrine is the notion that every nation despite its appearance of homogeneity is actually composed of conflicting social and economic classes. The history of any nation is the history of class conflict within it, a conflict in which, again, the fittest necessarily survive and dominate the less fit. Superficially, there is an attempt made to assimilate the various classes and ethnic groups especially through the myth of nationalism but in reality each group "has its own interests which it represents, its own power which it strives to increase, and each bears down upon the others according to its strength and their resistance." [62] Each group strives to become the controlling group within the nation and "the struggle between social groups, the component parts of the state, is as inexorable as that between hordes or states. The only motive is self-interest." [63] Political history is a reflection of the compe-

tition between biological species for survival, the class struggle
and the conflict between states is simply the biological struggle
for existence on the human and social plane.

No matter what the outward form of government, government is always rule by the few, who, since they are on top as a
result of conflict, must be the best, for in "the subjection of one
social group by another and the establishment of sovereignty
. . . the sovereign body is always less numerous." But numerical inferiority "is supplemented by mental superiority." [64]
Neither the creation of parliamentary forms of government
nor the existence of universal suffrage alters this fact. No matter what political or economic reforms are made the state will
always be "the organized control of the minority over the
majority." [65]

In short, Gumplowicz declared "my doctrine is that justice
is the interest of the stronger." [66] All human civilization and
culture, he thought, is the product of the inexorable conflict
of human groups:

> Out of frictions and struggles, out of separations and unions of
> opposing elements, finally come forth as new adaptation products
> the higher socio-psychical phenomena, the higher cultural forms,
> the new civilizations, the new state and national unities . . . and
> this merely through social action and reaction, entirely independent
> of the initiative and will of individuals contrary to their ideas and
> wishes and social striving. [67]

## Summary and Conclusions

SOME Social Darwinists like Ward believed that social telesis
(planning) is superior to natural genesis but this meant only
that men were capable of *accelerating* the natural process by
conscious control of natural forces. It represents no abandonment of the belief in a naturally immanent order. It was the
belief of men like Ward and Gumplowicz that Nature operates
through groups rather than through individuals, by means of
social cooperation (according to Ward), by means of social conflict (according to Gumplowicz), rather than by means of individual competition (Spencer and Sumner). But this amounts

to no more than a substitution of collective determinism for individual determinism. All believe in inevitable Progress although they differ as to the means which Nature, as revealed by the methods of science, uses to control the destinies of men. Each claims, of course, to have discovered the *true* scientific answer from the empirical observation of social phenomena.

Now truth is regarded by the positivist simply as that which can be described inductively from the empirical observation of successive events. But in actuality, as the positivist's belief in inevitable progress illustrates, metaphysical speculation, far from being abandoned, is indulged in unconsciously and uncritically. By claiming that their conclusions are scientifically rather than metaphysically derived, the positivists remove their conclusions from the scrutiny and criticism of reason. And surreptitious metaphysical speculation and ethical evaluation are then promulgated as the latest discovery of "science." Thus science is used, or rather misused, to lend prestige to ideas whose origin is not in nature or in science but in the uncritical mind of the person promulgating them. The imagination of the individual is thus given free rein to indulge in any kind of metaphysical speculation, unchecked by any consideration of objective, rational principles. That this has often been done in the sincere belief that one is being scientific does not mitigate the error though it may, indeed, excuse the person who is ignorant of the fallacy to which he has fallen an unconscious victim.

The positivist who claims that his conclusions are true, and, of course, all positivists make this claim, must necessarily transcend the empirical observation of successive events. The positivist starts, as Whitehead has demonstrated, from "an instinctive faith that there is an Order of Nature which can be traced in every detailed occurrence," and tends to believe that the reason for his faith is "the apprehension of its truth." But, as Whitehead cautions, "the formation of a general idea —such as the idea of the Order of Nature—and the grasp of its importance and the observation of its exemplification in a variety of occasions are by no means the necessary consequences of the truth of the idea in question." [68] The world as the positivist sees it "exhibits . . . an involution of paths and a concatenation of circumstances which have arisen entirely by change. We can describe what has happened, but with that description all possibility of knowledge ends." [69] But to claim truth for this description the positivist must transcend the methods of science. As one writer has put it succinctly and well:

> To retain . . . the distinction of truth and falsity *even for science alone* we have to enlarge the scientific world, and in enlarging it to modify it deeply, for what is added is not something of the same order but something different in kind, not having even an analogy with the rest. Knowing, the process that has to other events the unique relation of apprehending them, is above the causal order, in the sense that, although in it, it also knows it. Science as knowing transcends the scientific world; its claim to be true lifts it above the type of order its content depicts. Deny the claim and the content is worthless; admit the claim and the content is set in a larger context. Science can explain things naturally, but never itself. It cannot be true in a purely scientific world. [70]

It is only by transcending its own method that science achieves meaning and the positivist can ascribe meaning to his own observations only by engaging in the kind of speculation he denounces as improper.

The inadequacy of positivism as the most valid perspective in which to achieve a description and understanding of physical and social phenomena is proven by this fact: that the positivist cannot avoid engaging in the metaphysical speculation he claims to have dispensed with. His belief in a causal order, as Hume pointed out, does not rest upon empirical observation, for all that empirical observation alone reveals is that one event follows another. The moment the observer labels one of these events the cause and the other the effect he is indulging in metaphysical speculation which is essentially and by its nature beyond empirical observation or proof.

The positivist insists that he is concerned only with "facts" and with the stubborn "reality" of the "world of fact." But it can easily be demonstrated that the most detached observer actually does something more than record "facts" that are brought to his attention by means of his sense organs. That thought involves a great deal more than the sensory awareness of one's physical and social environment should be obvious to anyone who thinks. Perception itself involves selection and choice. No individual, however detached or however dedicated to the methods of natural science, is equally aware of all the possible data that may be brought to his attention by means of his sense organs. If he were, he would *perceive* nothing, since his environment would appear as a chaos of sensations, unintelligible and meaningless. The recognition of facts requires not only sensory awareness but judgments as to value and significance. As a matter of fact, it is only by fitting the data made available to him by means of his senses into some preformulated conceptual scheme that the individual is able to perceive facts at all. Actually, then, when the positivist insists that to be properly scientific we must confine ourselves to a description of "positive facts" that can be observed without transcending our immediate sensory experience, he is insisting upon the impossible.

By eliminating the rational from the real positivism eliminates at the same time any possibility of adequately explaining, at least in rational terms, the reality it seeks to describe. As Morris R. Cohen has pointed out, positivism

. . . begins with a great show of respect for "fact" as the rock of intellectual salvation. On it we are to escape from the winds of dialectic illusion. But as science critically analyzes the "facts," more and more of them are seen to be the products of old prejudices or survivals of obsolete metaphysics . . . the "facts" of science are admittedly checked and controlled by theoretic considerations—for they are characterized by rational or mathematical relations. Hence the empiricism which has an anti-intellectual animus consistently turns from the rational scientific elaboration of specific facts to a mystical pure experience in which all clear distinctions are eliminated as the conceptual fictions of the mind. Thus does the worship of fact become the apotheosis of an abstraction devoid of all the concrete characteristics of fact.[71]

Nor can positivism, by seeking to reduce logic to psychology (as some neo-positivists have attempted to do), succeed by that technique in eliminating all normative considerations. For again, as Morris Cohen observes:

. . . the attempt to make psychology identical with the whole field of science or philosophy can lead only to confusion. This is certainly the case when in the interests either of positivism or of psychologic idealism we deny the distinction between logic and psychology. . . . To me the greatest absurdity of all is the fundamental premise . . . that logic should be a description of the way we actually think. *Granted that all thinking goes on in individual minds, it does not follow that a psychologic description of reasoning as a mental event can determine whether the resulting conclusion is true.* All sorts of variations in imagery or motive may take place in the minds of those who come to the same conclusions as to the multiplication table, but these considerations are irrelevant to the truth or validity of what is asserted. . . . A psychologic description of what goes on in my mind as I deal with an ethical or practical problem will not determine the correctness of the solution arrived at; and psychology can no more include the whole of logic and ethics than it can the whole of technology.[72]

Positivism can achieve meaning for the facts which it describes only by engaging in the kind of metaphysical speculation it denounces as improper; or it can insist, as some neo-positivists do, that the facts have no meaning. In the latter instance, it leads directly to the conclusion that, as one of the intellectual harbingers of Nazi tyranny, Oswald Spengler, declared, "in the historical world there are no ideals but only facts—no truths, but only facts. There is no reason, no equity, no final aim, but only facts." [73] And it follows, as well, that "Life has no 'aim.' Mankind has no 'aim.' . . . Life is the beginning and the end . . . life has no system, no program, no reason; it exists for itself and by itself . . . it cannot be dissected according to good or bad, right or wrong, useful and desirable." [74] It leads to nihilism in thought and to anarchy in practice; and anarchy manifests itself politically as tyranny.

## The Impact of Positivism upon Liberalism

WHEN liberal ideas were focused from the perspective of positivism they underwent a significant change in content, if not in form. The positivist retained the liberal vocabulary but what he meant is something quite different from what the classical liberal meant. He continued to talk about a natural order, about freedom, about individual rights but these concepts had a different meaning for him than they had for classical liberalism.

For the transcendent order potentially embodied in reason and conscience, the positivist liberal substituted the conception of an immanent order of nature. For the natural law of reason the positivist sought to substitute social laws exactly analogous to the physical laws of the universe. The transcendent, potential order of classical liberalism required individual effort (the will to do that which was dictated by reason to be morally right) for its realization; the immanent order substituted for it was conceived as being already in existence and hence requiring neither reason (except in a technological sense) nor moral effort for its actualization. Freedom as conceived by classical liberalism was freedom to act in accordance with the dictates of right reason; freedom as conceived by the positivist liberal, was freedom to act in accordance with the immutable laws of nature. In the first instance it is necessary for the individual to will to act in accordance with reason; but in the second instance the individual has no choice but to act in accordance with the laws of nature—he may temporarily obstruct their operation but their operation does not depend upon either his will or his reason. Individuals could, it was believed, discover the laws of the natural order by the methods of natural science but these laws would remain in operation whether discovered or not. Their efficacy did not depend upon their discovery although men might be enabled to accelerate the natural process if they used the methods of science to discover them. The natural law as conceived by classical liberalism could never be realized except through its discovery and application by men. When the methods of science were substituted for conscience, the result was that, whereas the former might increase the vista of men's knowledge, that knowledge, unlike that yielded by conscience, was not necessary to the attainment of social order. No matter what men might think, believe, or do, the immanent laws of "nature" or of "history" would control their destiny and compel them to a progress entirely independent of the initiative and will of individuals and even contrary to their ideas and wishes. Thus the individual is relieved of all responsibility for social progress and freedom, for all practical purposes, degenerates into license. It was comfortable to believe that the laws of nature controlled men's destinies especially when there was linked to that belief the never-explained metaphysical assumption that these laws inevitably and automatically impel men along the road of progress. It led to a smug complacency that has only very recently been shattered.

When the classical liberal theory of law was subjected to the positivist's scrutiny, as we shall see in more detail in the chapter which follows, only the subjective part of that theory survived. It will be remembered that the classical liberal theory of law merged two self-sufficient theories of law: on the one hand, the theory that law is the product of individual will, its ultimate sanction consisting of the force behind it; and, on the other hand, the theory that law is the embodiment of principles discoverable by reason, the obligation to obey it derived from the inherent justness of its content. When focused from the perspective of positivism only the former, subjective theory remained. Justice, being a metaphysical concept, was discarded as being empirically worthless. Since reason was denied the capacity of discovering the principles of justice, its function was confined to an analysis of the existing law in the belief that positive law is the only true law. The criteria of law became the manner of enactment and the force behind it. Any command that issued from a legislature or other organ of government empowered to issue commands in accordance with a prescribed procedure with sufficient force behind it to compel obedience was law and the only true law. Freedom under the law was retained by the positivist liberal as an article of his liberal faith but it came to mean something quite different from what it had meant originally. Originally it meant that a man could not be compelled to do anything contrary to reason or conscience, that the test of a law was its justness. Under the influence of positivism, the concept came to mean that a man could not be compelled to do anything except by a law enacted in accordance with a prescribed procedure (any prescribed procedure) with sufficient force behind it to compel obedience. Now there is a great difference between freedom from *unjust* compulsion and freedom from *illegal* compulsion. When the test of legality, moreover, is ultimately conceived as the force behind the law, freedom from illegal compulsion amounts to no more than freedom to do whatever the state does not forbid. This is a conception of freedom much more congenial to tyranny than to the preservation of the inalienable rights of man.

But the conception of the inalienable rights of man no more survived the scrutiny of positivism than did the concept of justice. Viewed from the perspective of positivism the rights of man were conceived no longer as natural rights but as legal rights. Properly speaking, according to the positivist view, man has no rights at all; what the liberals have traditionally called rights are actually only concessions granted by the state or society. Whatever rights men have are those guaranteed by the law and since the rights are the product of the law they are not, properly speaking, rights at all but concessions to claims which the individual makes and the state recognizes. As concessions, it follows, of course, that they can be withdrawn to the extent that the state deems such withdrawal of its recognition compatible with the interests of the "general welfare."

Of the many factors which have contributed to the decline of liberalism in the modern world no single factor has been more important than the rise of positivism and its infiltration into every sphere of thought. For it was the liberal, positivistic jurists long before Hitler who taught (explicitly or implicitly) that might makes right and that rights are not attributes which individuals have by virtue of their humanity but simply claims which the state may or may not choose to recognize. Unwittingly, it may be, such liberals prepared the way for Lidice and Dachau. When the liberals were finally confronted with totalitarian dictatorship most of them could not find words of condemnation. For how can you condemn a tyrant as unjust when you have purged the word justice from your vocabulary? How, indeed, can you recognize tyranny when it arises? How can you complain of the loss of freedom when you have forgotten what it means? The liberals who were under the influence of positivism had neither the convictions nor the will to identify injustice or to combat it. It was not because they were any less courageous than their liberal predecessors but because their liberal convictions were less firmly and deeply rooted. The liberal vocabulary and slogans alone remained, emptied, by positivism, of all substantive content.

## CHAPTER 10

# Changing Concepts of Law in the Nineteenth and Twentieth Centuries

THE modern theory of law emerged most clearly in the writings of Hugo Grotius. Conceiving of the law as a "dictate of right reason" grounded in the nature of man, Grotius severed the conception of the law from all theological considerations, the validity and efficacy of the law no longer being dependent upon the existence of God nor a necessary reflection of His commandments. And throughout the seventeenth and eighteenth centuries, "jurists believed that a complete and perfect system of legal precepts could be built upon principles of natural law discoverable by reason and derived from the ideal of the abstract man." [1] Although Grotius and his immediate successors believed that the eternal truths embodied in the natural law were immutable, either by man or God, at the same time they believed that these eternal truths had their source in human nature and that they depended for materialization upon the exercise of creative reason and conscience. "The mother of natural law," Grotius wrote, "is human nature itself." [2] Right is what is in accordance with reason and since man is endowed with reason by virtue of his being human, even if there were no God, the realization of right would rest entirely upon individuals. The link between the subjective will of the individual and objective truth is individual reason and conscience. The responsibility for realizing the potential order embodied in human reason depends upon the *willingness* of individuals to reason rightly, to follow the dictates of reason rather than the impulses of subjective and particular desire.

Gradually, as we have seen, there was a growing tendency (under the influence of empiricism) to substitute an immanent conception of order for the earlier transcendental conception. In the early nineteenth century, history and philosophy were combined to produce a philosophical-historical jurisprudence that retained the notion that law is found and not made but looked for its content in history rather than in human nature. Roscoe Pound describes the historical school by saying:

It did not think of a law which had always been the same but of a law which had grown. It sought stability through establishment of principles of growth, finding the lines along which growth had proceeded and would continue to proceed, and it sought to unify stability and change by a combination of historical authority and philosophical history. Utilizing the idea of authority, it sought to put a historical foundation under the seventeenth—and eighteenth—century theory of law as only declaratory of something having a higher authority than the pronouncement of legislator or judge as such. Law was not declaratory of morals or of the nature of man as a moral entity or reasoning creature. It was declaratory of principles of progress discovered by human experience of administering justice and of human experience of intercourse in civilized society; and these principles were not principles of natural law revealed by reason, they were realizings of an idea, unfolding in human experience and in the development of institutions—an idea to be demonstrated metaphysically and verified by history. All this body of doctrine did not develop at once. But such was the creed of the school which was dominant in the science of law throughout the century, and in one form or another, this creed may be identified in all the varieties of juristic thinking during the century, even in schools which professed a different method.[3]

## The Historical School of Jurisprudence

UNDER the influence of Romanticism and Idealism historical jurisprudence found one of its earliest and most distinctive expressions in the writing of the German jurist, Frederick von Savigny (1779–1861). Just as Arnim and Brentano found the embodiment of the folk spirit in popular songs, as the brothers Grimm found it in fairy tales and in language, so Savigny found the folk spirit embodied in law. Law, he declared, is peculiar to particular places, peoples, and times; it is the product of a particular folk-mind or folk-spirit. Law, essentially, is *Volksrecht* or custom. "In the earliest times to which authentic history extends," he wrote, "the law will be found to have already attained a fixed character, peculiar to the people, like their language, manners and constitution. Nay, these phenomena have no separate existence, they are but the particular faculties and tendencies of an individual people, inseparably united in nature, and only wearing the semblance of distinct attributes to our view. That which binds them into one whole is the common conviction of the people, the kindred consciousness of an inward necessity, excluding all notion of an accidental and arbitrary origin." [4] For Savigny the development of the law, however, was an organic and not a progressive one, it was simply the unfolding of that idea of the law which was contained in embryonic form in the very beginning of a peoples' history. Kant's idea of a transcendent universal principle was merged with an idealistic interpretation of history. Both the philosophical and historical schools

. . . postulated an ideal law. One sought to discover this ideal law through history, the other sought to find it through logical development of an abstract form. . . . Philosopher and historian were agreed that law was found, not made. One found it by deduction from a metaphysical principle, the other found it by historical study. Each, one need not say, found an ideal development of the principles of existing law; the historian because he so interpreted history, the philosopher because he was seldom a lawyer and got his facts and illustrations from the historian.[5]

Each supplemented the other. From metaphysical deductions one found the form of law, from history the content of law.

Law, for Savigny, is inseparably bound up with nationality. "Law grows with the growth, and strengthens with the strength of the people, and finally dies away as the nation loses its nationality." [6] The historical perspective, he insisted, protects us from "self-delusion," particularly from the self-delusion that that which is peculiar to a particular people is common to human nature in general.

When we lose sight of our individual connection with the great entirety of the world and its history, we necessarily see our thoughts in a false light of universality and originality. . . . History . . . is ever a noble instructress. . . . For only through her can a lively connection with the primitive state of a people be kept up; and the loss of this connection must take away from every people the best part of its spiritual life.[7]

History, from Savigny's viewpoint, is a kind of morality which informs us not only what we have become through the experience of the past but what we can look forward to in the future as our destiny. He declares:

The sum . . . of this theory is, that all law is originally formed in the manner, in which, in ordinary but not quite correct language, customary law is said to have been formed: i.e., that it is first developed by custom and popular faith, next by jurisprudence,—everywhere, therefore, by *internal* silently-operating powers, not by the arbitrary will of a law-giver.[8]

In a similar manner G. F. Puchta (1798–1846) describes the law as the product of the particular genius of a particular people.

All human Right presupposes a common Consciousness as its source. A principle of Right becomes a fact by being recognized as such in the common conviction of those to whom it is applicable. . . . Through this common consciousness of Right, as by a common Language and a common Religion, the members of a people are bound together in a definite union. This union rests upon a certain relationship of body and mind; it extends beyond the intimacy of the inner family bond, and arises out of an actual division of the race of mankind. The consciousness which permeates the members of a people in common, is born with them and makes them spiritually members of one whole. It constitutes, in a word, the national mind or spirit of the people; and it is the source of human or natural Right, and of the convictions of Right which stir and operate in the minds of the individuals.[9]

Just as there are peculiarities of language differentiating one people from another so there are peculiarities in their conception of justice. It is, indeed, the existence of these peculiarities that distinguishes one nation from another. Justice is not something which is fixed and always the same but "It develops with the People. It attaches itself to the national character at its different stages of culture; and it adapts itself to the changing wants and requirements of the People." [10] Justice, however, he insists, is not something arbitrary for it has its content fixed in the character of the particular people from the very beginning and "the People at the beginning and at the end of their historical career, are the same people, though they may present differences here and there. In like manner, their system of Right becomes different, and yet it is always the Right of the same people." [11]

The historical school of jurisprudence represents a reaction to the rationalism of the eighteenth century.

It was a reaction from two phases of the natural-law thinking in its last stage, namely, from the paper-constitution making and confident disregard of traditional political institutions and conditions of time and place which characterized the era of the French Revolution and from the belief in the power of reason to work miracles in legislation and consequent no less confident code-making of the end of the eighteenth and beginning of the nineteenth century.[12]

Puchta, for example, declares that "reason is not the principle of freedom" but an element antagonistic to it. Freedom as it unfolds in history is a more reliable guide to law than abstract reason:

Freedom is the foundation of right, which is the essential principle of all law. Hence we do not reach right as the principle of law by setting out from the notion of reason. . . . For if the bad, as being evil, is the irrational, then freedom, which includes the possibility of evil, cannot be deduced from reason and *vice versa*. It would be much more in accordance with reason that the good should be realized of necessity. On the other hand it is contrary to mere reason that it comes through freedom, which does not exclude the possibility of evil. Thus reason is not the principle of freedom but is rather an element in human nature antagonistic to freedom; and it has shown itself to be such from the beginning.[13]

It follows from this reasoning that every law is an evil since every law is a restriction upon freedom. Thus a French jurist declares:

Every rule of law in itself is an evil, for it can only have for its object the regulation of the exercise of rights, and to regulate the exercise of a right is inevitably to limit it. On the other hand every rule of law which sanctions a right, which preserves it from infringement which protects it from a peril, is good because in this way it responds to its legitimate end. Thus if law is an evil it is a necessary evil.[14]

Reform is not only impossible, it is undesirable. It is better to let the historical process work itself out without help or hindrance.

In England the historical school of jurisprudence found classic expression in the writings of Sir Henry Sumner Maine (1822–1888). According to Dean Pound, Maine's theory at bottom is Hegelian.

The idea which is realizing is liberty—free individual self-assertion. The way in which it is realizing is a progress from status to contract. It is a progress away from legal institutions and legal rules and legal doctrines in which one's legally recognized claims and legally enforced duties flow from a condition in which he is put or in which he finds himself without reference to his will and of which he cannot divest himself by any manifestation of his will. It is a progress toward legal institutions and rules and doctrines in which legally recognized claims flow from personality, from being a conscious free-willing human individual, and legally enforceable duties with respect to others are consequences of willed action, either in assuming the duties by some legally recognized form of undertaking or by willed culpable action or by willed action culpably carried on.[15]

Maine depicted history as a process leading from status to contract, from a situation in which the position of individuals was determined by the group in which they happened to find themselves to a situation in which their relative positions were determined by contractual arrangements to which they had voluntarily consented. For the abstract theorizing of the social contract philosophers Maine would substitute "sober research into the primitive history of society and law." [16] Historical research can reveal the real nature of law in a way in which abstract reason cannot, for, Maine insisted, such research is verifiable and empirical.

In the United States the historical school of jurisprudence found expression in the writings of James C. Carter. A student of Savigny's, Carter insisted in his early writings that the whole judicial process "consists in a search to find a rule" and "that the field of search is the habits, customs, business, and manners of the people, and those previously declared rules which have sprung out of previous similar inquiries into habits, customs, business and manners." [17] Even in his later writing he closely associated custom with justice.

> In associating Custom with Justice . . . we do not dethrone the latter, but seat Custom beside her. Justice is the felt necessity of doing that which secures order and peace. Custom furnishes the rule which answers to that necessity. . . .
> Justice is, therefore, not an absolute but a relative virtue, finding its play in that field of our conduct which, according to the division I have employed, relates to our dealings and intercourse with each other in society, and enforcing in that field the things necessary to the existence of society . . . justice consists in the compliance with custom in all matters of difference between men. . . . This accords with the definition of the Roman law—*constans et perpetua voluntas suum cuique tribuendi*. To each his due; but as we know the due of each only from the common feeling of what is due, and this is dependent upon custom, the identity of justice with conformity with custom is implied.[18]

According to the historical school, law is neither an arbitrary creation of human will nor a product of nature but a product of history and the manifestation of the particular genius of a particular national consciousness. For the "dictates of right reason" it substitutes inexorable principles of historical development. Several implications follow from this conception of the law: (1) law is relative to time and place and to particular peoples, (2) since law is found not in reason or in conscience but in the historical process, the individual has little or no responsibility for shaping the content of law, (3) the idea of individual natural rights is replaced by the idea of the historic rights of Englishmen, Frenchmen, Germans, etc., (4) reform is impossible, it is better to allow the historical process to work itself out without hindrance, (5) the idea of a transcendent natural order is replaced by the idea of an order immanent in the historical process, (6) the sanction of the law is conceived less in terms of the inherent justice of the rule and more in terms of the social pressure behind it.

Throughout the greater part of the nineteenth century the notion prevailed that society was evolving toward a certain predetermined end. The end was thought to be dictated by reason and verified by history. The process was thought to be inevitable, irreversible, and independent of individual will or desire. The limitation imposed upon arbitrary will was conceived to be "the spirit of history," the *Volksgeist*, or custom. As a consequence men believed that the less legislation there was the better. It was best to let the historical process work itself out unaided and unhindered.

The dominant tone of the period was optimistic. As Whitehead observes: "The political, liberal faith of the nineteenth century was a compromise between the individualistic, competitive doctrine of strife and the optimistic doctrine of harmony. It was believed that the laws of the Universe were such that the strife of individuals issued in the progressive realization of a harmonious society. In this way, it was possible to cherish the emotional belief in the Brotherhood of Man, while engaging in relentless competition with all individual men." [19] Historical jurisprudence reflected a mentality that was buttressed by "science." The doctrine of evolution seemed to confirm their own conclusions.

But there was implicit in their thinking ideas which other men might use to refute them. If law is the product of the community, if it is peculiar to time and place, it might easily be regarded as a social instrument. Moreover, if society could change in character one might assume that the content of the law could also change. If the sanction of law is thought of as residing in the common "convictions" or "consciousness" of a people, this might, moreover, be taken to imply that a law which does not satisfy the wants and desires of a people is not really law at all. Rather than being an end in itself the law might more validly be conceived as a means to an end.

In part, then, as a reaction to the historical school and in part as a result of the method which they employed a new school of jurists arose to posit the law as a means to an end;

these were the utilitarians. The shift in emphasis from the normative to the explanatory, already observable in the historical school, is carried further by the utilitarians and with this shift in emphasis the concept of society itself underwent a change. Society became, as Talcott Parsons points out,

. . . the mechanism whereby individual wants, conceived to vary at random with no common standard, could be satisfied in the greatest possible degree under the existing conditions of human life. Social relations were thus reduced to the level of means to individual satisfactions. All idea of essentially normative control was abandoned; but on the other hand an element of determinism of a different sort was introduced by the analysis of the nature and extent of the limitations imposed by the conditions, the external environment and man's inherited nature under which it took place. Pushed to its final logical conclusion this determinism in terms of conditions ended up in the positivism of the later nineteenth century completely eliminating the relativism of the earlier utilitarians.[20]

The historical school of jurisprudence was born of a merger of history and philosophy. When history (under the impact of empiricism) was severed from philosophy, the historical school gave way to the analytical school.

## The Analytical School of Jurisprudence

UNLIKE the historical school which thought of law as something which was found and not made, the analytical jurists regarded the law as something which was consciously made by the lawgiver. Whereas, the historical jurists saw the social pressure behind the law as the sanction of the law, the analytical jurists saw primarily force and constraint. Thus, for the latter, there could be no law apart from some agency capable of enforcing it. Law was embodied most typically for the historical jurists in custom, it was embodied most typically for the analytical jurists in statutory law. Whereas, the philosophical basis of historical jurisprudence was idealistic and principally Hegelian, the philosophical basis of analytical jurisprudence was utilitarianism.

Bentham, we may remember, discarded all conceptions of

"natural law" as fictitious and argued that "the primitive sense of the word *law*, and the ordinary meaning of the word, is—the will or command of a legislator." [21] The object of the law, according to Bentham, is to promote the greatest happiness of the greatest number. Utility is the foundation of the legislator's reasoning. All laws are evil because all laws are an infraction of liberty, hence, the legislator should carefully weigh the evils he hopes to prevent against the evil he employs to prevent them. In deciding what he should do the legislator should employ the calculus of pleasure which Bentham provided. The task of the legislator is thus reduced to something resembling the calculations of an automatic calculating machine.

The real founder of the English analytical school of jurisprudence was a disciple of Bentham, John Austin (1790–1859). According to Austin all laws are a species of commands.

But, being a *command*, every law properly so called flows from a *determinate* source, or emanates from a *determinate* author. In other words, the author from whom it proceeds is a *determinate* rational being, or a *determinate* body or aggregate of rational beings. . . . Every sanction properly so called is an eventual evil *annexed to a command* . . . every positive law . . . is a direct or circuitous command of a monarch or sovereign number in the character of political superior . . . to a person or persons in a state of subjection to its author. And being a *command* (and therefore flowing from a *determinate* source), every positive law is a law proper, or a law properly so called.[22]

Law is what is commanded by a definite body of political superiors, nothing more and nothing less. Positive law is the only true law. It is the form of the law, moreover, not its substance which is the distinguishing element of law. What constitutes a definite body of political superiors—what is sovereignty? Austin answered by saying:

If a *determinate* human superior, *not* in the habit of obedience to a like superior, receive *habitual* obedience from the *bulk* of a given society, that determinate superior is sovereign in that society, and the society (including the superior) is a society political and independent.[23]

With the crucial question—what underlies "habitual obedience"?—Austin was not much concerned. He was content to
"explain" it in terms of Bentham's pleasure-pain formula and
to ground obedience ultimately in force. Men obey the law
out of fear of the consequences which will arise from not obeying it. Actually he has no theory of obligation, he assumes it
as a "fact" but does not explain it. Austin's conception of
sovereignty is more absolute than that of Bodin for he discards the limitations upon sovereignty which Bodin specifically
enumerated. In essence, his philosophy resembles that of
Hobbes.

In Germany jurisprudence was transformed into a formal
science of law through the work of men like Gerber, Laband,
and Jellinek. Under the influence of positivism the study of law
was confined to an analytical examination of the existing body
of positive law in an effort to establish a *Staatsrechtwissenschaft*
or "science of law" which would exclude all consideration of
political and moral ends or purposes. Justice was discarded as
a meta-juristic concept and compulsion was substituted for
justice as the criterion of law. Having denied that there was
any other law than positive law, having denied the existence
of a transcendent order of law, these jurists were forced to conclude that the source of the law is the will of the state.

They conceived of the state as a juristic person with a will
of its own. Theoretically this subordinated the monarch to the
rule of law and they were able, abstractly at least, to distinguish the will of the state from the will of the monarch. As
Gerber expressed it: "The State's power to will, political
power, is the law of the State." [24] The will of the state was the
will of all individuals united politically, it was not any particular individuals but all of them. For practical purposes, he
admitted however, that "the monarch formally absorbs the
personality of the State into his own personality" but he insisted that the will of the state nevertheless was a real and not
a fictitious one because "this power to will is something existing in and for itself." [25] This distinction between the will of the
state and the will of the monarch is a highly tenuous one and
for practical purposes they are indistinguishable. To say,
therefore, that the source of law is the will of the state as a
juristic person and to say at the same time that it is only made

manifest through the will of the monarch, is to say, for practical purposes, that the source of law is the will of the monarch.

Gerber argued, however, that since the power of the state to will was limited by the ends which it pursued, the State's power was not absolute but limited. Since, according to his theory however, the State itself determines what ends it shall pursue, it also determines what it wills. To say that will is *limited* by purpose is meaningless for there can be no will where there is no purpose to act. The fact that one must will something in order to will at all does not constitute a limitation upon will but simply describes the act of willing. The limitation which Gerber would impose upon the will of the State is (for all practical purposes), no limitation at all.

The fiction of the State as a juristic person, somehow apart from the governmental organs through which its will is made manifest, was accepted by Laband. Only the State, he argued, can enforce rules which are binding on individuals; it alone can demand compliance, suggest or prohibit action on the part of its citizens. This is the thing which distinguishes the State from other organizations and persons. Its rules are the only law because the distinguishing aspect of law is its binding force and only the state has this power to compel obedience. "The specific activity of the power of the State," he wrote, "appears not in the production of the content of law, but only in sanctioning the validity of law, in equipping a legal prescript with power to bind, with outer authority." [26] The content is not what distinguishes law but the form in which it appears. "The sanction is the heart of the whole process of legislation; everything that precedes it in the way of legislation is only preparation for it, fulfillment of necessary conditions." [27] Another jurist of the same school, Philipp Zorn, put it even more directly:

The sanction is that public law which perfects the law. In the sanction lies the command in law: *whoever issues the command is the legislator*. The sanction is the highest and true act of legislation; therefore the right of sanction belongs only to the bearer of sovereignty. [28]

There would appear to be no limitation upon the arbitrary will of the sovereign but the analytical jurists contended that this was not so. According to Laband:

The imperium in the modern civilized State is no arbitrary power, but one determined by legal prescriptions. It is the characteristic of the *Rechtsstaat* that the State can require no performance and impose no restraint, can command its subjects in nothing and forbid them in nothing, except on the basis of a legal prescription.[29]

The whole crux of the matter depends upon what is meant by a "legal prescription." Since, as we saw above, Laband believed that "a legal prescript with power to bind" could only be issued by the state it would appear that the only limitation upon the will of the state would be the will of the state. In other words the only limitation is self-limitation. Laband wrote:

It is not disputed that there must be a supreme and highest power, which is subordinated to no other earthly power, and which is in truth the *potestas suprema*. The criterion of supreme and highest power exists in the fact that it is determined only by itself and can receive no legally binding prescriptions from any other power.[30]

In similar fashion Georg Jellinek declared that "a power to rule becomes legal by being limited. Law is legally limited power. The potential power of the community is greater than its actual power. Through auto-limitation it achieves the character of legal power." [31] To say that "law is legally limited power" is like saying "law is limited by law" which means nothing. Under analysis Jellinek's conception of "auto-limitation" turns out to be no limitation at all. He defined sovereignty as "the exclusive capacity of the power of the State to give its ruling will a universally binding content, to determine its own legal order in every direction" and "the impossibility of being legally restrained by any other power against its own will." [32] The logical implication from this is that the state, potentially at least, is omnipotent. The State can make any content binding that it desires. Irked by critics who contended that the effect of his theory was to make the State omnipotent, Jellinek declared that sovereignty, as he defined it,

is not State omnipotence. It is legal power and bound by the law. To be sure, it suffers no legal limits: the State can rid itself of every self-imposed limitation, but only within the forms of law and by creating new limits. Not the individual limit but the fact of limitation is the permanent factor. As little as the absolutely restricted State exists, so little does the State with absolutely boundless sovereignty.[33]

In effect, Jellinek declares that the legality of an action depends not upon the content of an action but upon the *form* which it takes. Anything can be done if it is done in accordance with some prescribed legal procedure. And even the procedure can be changed so long as some new procedure is substituted. The limitation he envisages, therefore, is purely formal, technical and procedural. He recognizes no substantive limitations to the power of the State. Jellinek would agree with Laband when he declared that "there is no idea which could not be made into a law." [34] Such a theory of the law and of the State would appear to be more congenial to despotism than to the preservation of freedom but the analytical jurists did not think so because they put their faith in procedural limitations. They could not, apparently, envisage a situation in which that procedure might be used to give an illiberal content to the law.

Conceiving of individual rights as concessions granted by the State the analytical jurists contended that "whatever rights a person has he has not by virtue of being an individual but because the State itself sets certain auto-limitations to its power." [35] There can be rights against the State only when the individual and the State are both subordinated to the same order of law. But when the State is conceived as the source of law, and hence above the law, there can be no rights against it. Individual rights can only be thought of as concessions and if they are concessions they can, theoretically as well as practically, be granted or withdrawn at will. They are not absolute rights secured transcendentally but relative rights secured immanently in a particular legal system. Such rights are not conceived as being antecedent to the state but as depending upon the state for their existence. "Only as a member of the State," Jellinek declared, ". . . is man the bearer of rights." "Personality," in fact, he wrote, "is *juris publici*." [36] The slave, he argued, possessed no personality until he was freed by the State.

It is not correct, in any case, Jellinek contended to speak of individual liberties but only of individual liberty. All so-called rights can, in reality, be reduced to one right because "all freedom is simply freedom from illegal compulsion." [37] The individual cannot be commanded to do anything except by law, his freedom can be limited only by legal prescription. Whereas, classical liberalism declared that the individual ought to be free from all *unjust* compulsion, the analytical jurists argue that an individual can claim freedom only from *illegal* compulsion. The two things are not necessarily the same. The one conception emphasizes the content of the law, the other merely the form of the command. If the command is formally prescribed, no matter what its content, it is legal. Individual freedom in this view is a formal freedom not a substantive one and the dividing line between the sphere of state activity and individual freedom becomes a shifting, relative, and purely formal one.

In effect, the analytical jurist says that the legality of an action depends not upon the content of the action but upon the form of the action. Not *what* is done but *how* it is done is the crucial consideration. Such a theory, however much a jurist like Jellinek may have doubted it, and he did, prepares the way for despotism. With such a theory despotism may, indeed, be legislated into existence—as it was in Germany in 1933. The legislature may decide, as the German *Reichstag* did, to legislate itself out of existence and to adopt a new procedure for the enactment of legal prescriptions that dispenses with its services as a deliberative body altogether. If the State itself determines its own competency, the extent of its own power and the content of its own law, who, indeed, is to say that the State is wrong? By abolishing from jurisprudence all conceptions of right and wrong, justice and injustice, Jellinek and the other analytical jurists might consistently answer that the question is invalid and irrelevant. From *their* point of view the question is invalid and irrelevant; from the point of view of the classical liberals, however, the question is not only relevant but crucial.

It is a short step from the conception of law as the product of the will of the state, whether the state be conceived as an instrument for the satisfaction of human desires (utilitarianism) or whether conceived as the personification of the good life (idealism) to the notion that law is the command of the stronger. When the distinguishing criterion of law is the form the command takes rather than the content which it embodies justice soon degenerates into being nothing more than the will of the stronger. Since the will of the state has no reality apart from the will of individuals who act in the name of the state the identification of the law with the will of the state amounts in practice to the identification of the law with the will of those who act in the name of the state.

## *Jurisprudence in the Twentieth Century*

BY THE end of the nineteenth century jurists had split into two opposing schools: the Neo-Hegelians and the Neo-Kantians. The formalism of Gerber, Laband and Jellinek was carried to its logical conclusion by the Neo-Kantians in an effort to create a "pure" science of law divorced completely from all political and social reality. Regarding jurisprudence as being essentially a normative science concerned with "what ought to be" rather than with "what is," they removed jurisprudence by definition to a "pure" realm of theory beyond actuality. By emphasizing norms to the exclusion of the wills that must exist in actuality in order to realize them, the Neo-Kantians postulated a realm that may have had logical but certainly no actual existence. At any rate they assumed the existence of this realm apart from social reality and acted for the purposes of constructing a "pure theory of law" "as if" it actually existed.

Repelled by this highly abstract and formal endeavor the Neo-Hegelians rejected all normative criteria of law and emphasized the conception of law as a social product and instrument. Positivism had led to a complete separation of fact and standard, will and norm. It was necessary after the emergence of positivism to make one or the other absolute. The result of this separation and the focusing of attention upon either fact or standard to the exclusion of the other was to divorce the concept of law completely from any absolute idea of justice in the form of eternal and universal truths transcending individuals. The Neo-Hegelians focused their attention upon legal content to the exclusion of all normative considerations, the Neo-Kantians focused their attention upon the normative elements in law to the exclusion of all consideration of legal content. Both schools of thought, as a consequence, fostered irresponsibility; the Neo-Kantians, individual irresponsibility, and the Neo-Hegelians, irresponsibility on the part of the State. In the final analysis both placed the law beyond the boundaries of good and evil. Any action was lawful, according to the Neo-Kantians, if it conformed to certain formal, procedural requirements. As the criterion of law they substituted the manner of enactment for the content of action. The Neo-Hegelians, on the other hand, distinguished the law by the physical coercion behind it irrespective of the form which that coercion took. By separating will and norm, interest and ideal, fact and standard, and by emphasizing one of these as the criterion of law to the exclusion of the other, responsibility is made impossible for the idea of responsibility requires both notions. A will, unrestrained by a recognition of transcendent standards, is limited only by its physical capacity and by the might of a stronger will. A norm, without a will to actualize it, is equally devoid of imposing responsibility, for the notion of responsibility necessarily implies *willing* to do or not to do something specific. In the last analysis justice is equated with might. Coercibility rather than morality is the thing which distinguishes law. Whether this coercion springs from a parliamentary majority or a well-organized armed party machine is immaterial when the distinguishing criterion of law is conceived as being nothing more than the force behind it. When the form of law alone is considered significant there can be no substantive limitation to arbitrariness; there can be no guarantee of freedom as classical liberalism understood it.

## The "Pure" Theory of Law

THE separation of law from political and social reality, begun by jurists like Laband and Jellinek, was completed by the

Neo-Kantians. In an effort to establish a "pure" science of law, jurists like Rudolph Stammler and Hans Kelsen sought to find the *a priori* principles which underlie all law regardless of its content. They sought to isolate, in a Platonic sense, the "idea" of law, which was universal from the content of law which was variable. They adopted for this purpose the critical method of Kant, a method which ignores historical development and psychological motivation in favor of a deductive search for the universal and formal elements of knowledge. They sought to find the pure forms of law, the universal elements that are found in all law. They assume, of course, that the content of law is ever changing and that the form of law alone is eternal and immutable.

According to Stammler "The pure forms—are nothing but conceptual methods of ordering."

The old endeavor to obtain an ideal law with limited content is entirely futile. It is not possible to conceive of a law which would really have a content limited in subject matter but which yet would hold good for all times and peoples. *Absolute* validity of conceptions can, in *legal* questions, also, be attributed only to the *pure forms*, in which we arrange *legal* experience according to a fixed and uniform plan.[38]

Here is an explicit assertion that it is not the content of law which distinguishes it from non-law but the form. Belief in eternal and universal truths transcending individuals is abandoned completely, it is only the "idea of law" which is transcendent, which possesses "absolute validity." "There are certainly," Stammler contends, "pure forms of juristic thought which are unconditionally necessary as ordering principles *for any content of law whatsoever*." [39] It is these formal, universal elements that are the distinguishing criteria of law. According to Rupert Emerson "the unity of the pure ideas of law" is, for Stammler, "only the unity of procedure by which conditioned legal prescriptions are to be determined in an identical fashion, that is, the formal unity of law is for him the unity of the method of intellectual apprehension or thinking of law." [40]

Stammler explains the "notion of law" in the following manner:

By the combination of the purposes of a number of men an external regulation is implicitly imposed upon them. They are, however, subjected to this either in an *objectively* enduring way or else according to *subjective whim* from one time to another. . . . Not until we have the *objectively* enduring type of social combination do we get the "notion of law." Law appears thus as a necessary part of the system of pure principles for ordering consciousness. . . . The law . . . signifies *inviolable, sovereign, combining will.*[41]

Stammler sees a social will binding men together for the purpose of achieving ends common to them all. Law is an expression of this will. It is not a creation of this will, it *is* that will. He is vague, however, about the binding nature of law, for he says:

Law presents itself as an external regulation of human conduct. By this we understand the laying down of norms which are quite independent of the person's inclination to follow them. It is immaterial whether a person obeys them because he regards them as right, submitting out of respect for the law; or whether his obedience is due to a selfish motive of some sort, fear of punishment, or hope of reward; or, finally, whether he thinks about it at all, or acts from mere habit.[42]

Having discarded the notion of a law "whose content shall be unchangeable and absolutely valid" in favor of a "universally valid formal method, by means of which the necessarily changing material of empirically conditioned legal rules may be so worked out, judged, and determined that it shall have the quality of objective justice," [43] he has placed himself in the position of discarding natural law at the outset and then letting it in again through the back door under a different name. He repeatedly speaks of "just law" and of a "community of free-willing men" as the social ideal by means of which the justness of positive law may be determined.[44]

Stammler postulates as the "idea of justice" a harmony of wills, the bringing of "all possibilities of desire into one harmonious realm of the will." "The content of a particular aspiration," he writes, "is then *fundamentally* right if it fits harmoniously, so far as one can see, into that totality of aims." That is only possible when the individual "directs his will in the sense of what is *universally valid*, guided by the idea of perfect harmony with all other will contents." [45] But his idea of justice is a purely formal idea having no specific content. "The only thing which can serve as an absolutely valid standard for all possible striving," Stammler declares, "is a *purely formal* method of guidance in the shape of an ideal object of thought which directs one's judgment." [46] Professor Hocking explains Stammler's view in these words:

Each individual must recognize (and to some extent does recognize) the fact that his own particular ends are particular, and therefore not absolutely valid; each one conceives a condition in which he would be free from the domination of such partial objects, in view of a completely legitimate and imperative object which his purified will would seek. And if the ideal condition of purity of will were reached by all, then (as we all dimly recognize) the business of bringing about social solidarity would likewise be ideally simplified; for there would be no disposition to use any member as a means, beyond the point at which he is himself served by the union, so that the united willing becomes means to his ends. And this ideal of "pure community" is the ideal which more or less blindly stands over each actual will and constitutes the element of "right" which it recognizes in the concrete agencies of social control.

Commenting on this theory, Hocking continues:

Clearing this notion of Stammler's verbiage, it seems rather an empty one—so empty indeed as to be perhaps slightly perverse. For what else does it amount to than the proposition that the whole valid end of a community is the *existence* of a community; or, that communities have nothing else to work for, in their notions of right, than simply *to be communities* in the perfect sense of that term—working out in all their arrangements the principle of consent which is involved in any free union of wills? [47]

It is difficult to see how Stammler's conception of a "pure community" of will imposes any substantive limitations upon individual will. For there is no such thing as a will without content or aim. And where there is no common affirmation of truth there can be no common will. Without a community of interests and of values the will of the community becomes for all practical purposes the will of the strongest individuals within the community. There can be no moral responsibility where there is no objective good. Because he denies the existence of absolute truth and justice he provides no substantive limitations which might restrain the community of will from acting arbitrarily. It is just this lack of content in his theory that makes it impossible to conceive of any obligation because obligation means that you ought to do *certain* things or refrain from doing *certain* things. In order to will you have to will something specific; in order to will rightly you have to know what it is that you ought to will. No formal method, such as Stammler suggests, can tell us this. When the criteria of obligation are emptied of all content, when *any* content can be filled in, there exists no moral obligation and hence no limitation upon will except that imposed by force.

Stammler emptied the criteria of obligation of all substantive content but Hans Kelsen went even further in an effort to create a "pure theory of law." Kelsen is concerned only with the form of the law and, unlike Stammler, has no concern at all for the will behind the law. As Rupert Emerson observes:

Not even the factual source of the content of the norm interests him. Law can be produced—i.e., logically derived—from law; if the norms of law are set by the despot, the absolute monarch, the parliament, this means, from Kelsen's standpoint, that there is logically supposed a norm authorizing these persons to fix the content of law. . . . We are in fact told no more than that, given a legal norm, we can find its logical presuppositions. The original norm at which Kelsen arrives is not to be traced back to any will; it is a purely formal concept which can be filled with any content; it is only a necessary aid to thought.[48]

Kelsen distinguishes legal norms from other social norms by the coercive force behind the former, and conceives the law as a coercive norm prescribing certain human behavior. As he states it:

Legal norms are coercive norms. In order to bring about the desired behavior, the norm threatens the person disobeying it with a coercive act which he deems as evil. . . . Thus the specific structure of a legal norm is revealed as the typical rule of law; it connects two facts; a certain fact, as the condition, with another fact—the coercive act—as the consequence. The simplest example is the norm of criminal law. If some one commits larceny, he shall be punished. It is one of the most important contentions of the Pure Theory of Law that the whole material of positive law can be rendered in rules of this fundamental form.[49]

The "legal order" consists of "a plurality of norms forming one system" and the unity of this order is found in the fact "that all the norms constituting this order have the same ground of validity, i.e., they can be traced back to one and the same basic norm." [50]

The norms of a particular legal order acquire validity for Kelsen as they are derived from this basic norm but the question immediately arises as to the nature and validity of the basic norm itself. What *is* this basic norm? Kelsen is rather vague and ambiguous in his answer.

The basic norm of the legal order is the one which determines in what way the norms belonging to the order are to be created. All these norms are valid because, and insofar as, they have been created in the way prescribed by the basic norm. . . . The supreme basic norm cannot be "created" in the same sense as the norms of the legal order whose unity is founded upon it. This basic norm is not created by the organs of the legal order, but is presupposed by legal cognition; the basic norm is therefore not a positive but a hypothetical norm.[51]

How is the validity of this basic norm determined? Kelsen refuses to answer, dismissing the question as irrelevant because it raises considerations which he regards as metajuristic. In the final analysis he assumes the validity of the basic norm *a priori*. Commenting upon his theory, Hans Lauterpacht declares:

The norm which lies at the basis of his system, although not arbitrary, is purely relativist and hypothetical. There is in it no such absolute element which it would necessarily contain if it were grounded in a material ethical value, for instance, in that of justice. The initial hypothesis is an act of human intelligence. It is not a dictate of a higher power. It is not a deduction from an immutable principle of justice; it is an assumed hypothesis glorying in its realistic relativism. Kelsen claims for his initial hypothesis that it trans-

forms might into law. However, this claim is in itself morally indifferent. Frequently such transformation will prove ethically re-
pugnant. The fundamental norm is a methodological instrument
pure and simple. It certainly substantiates Kant's dictum of "the
method creating its objects." [52]

Kelsen's theory envisages procedural limitations only upon
the will which gives the law its content. According to Kelsen

*Any content whatsoever can be legal; there is no human behavior which could
not function as the content of a legal norm.* A norm becomes a legal norm
only because it has been constituted in a particular fashion, born
of a definite procedure and a definite rule. Law is valid only as
positive law; that is, statute (constituted) law.[53]

The content may be good or bad, just or unjust; it may be
supplied by a parliament or a despot—so far as the Pure
Theory of Law is concerned these are matters of complete
indifference.

Since Kelsen identifies the state with the legal order it follows that all of its acts must necessarily be legal. It cannot act
illegally. As stated by Kelsen:

The Pure Theory of Law views the State as a system of human behavior, an order of social compulsion. This compulsive order is
not different from the legal order for the reason that within one
community only one and not two compulsive orders can be valid
at the same time. *Every expression of the life of a State, every act of State,
is a legal act.*[54]

Since he regards the State as being essentially a system of
norms he tends to ignore or minimize the human agencies and
organs through the medium of which the will of the State is
made manifest. "A human act," he contends, "is only designated an act of State by virtue of a legal norm which qualifies
it as such." [55] He tends to assume that the will of the state is
somehow predetermined, somehow embodied in the legal
order itself. Rupert Emerson explains this aspect of his theory
by saying:

The physical or psychical acts of the State's organs are juristically
irrelevant: they are only material for attribution. The will of the

State is, then, only a juristically constructed attribution point. In consequence the person of the State, like all other legal personality, is merely the personification of legal norms . . . the State, as wholly a legal construction, has no other content than that given it by law and no acts attributed to it which are not foreseen by law.[56]

According to Kelsen himself:

Wherever anyone alleges that he acts for the State, he must be able to fall back upon a legal prescription which allows this act to appear as willed by the State and, therefore, attributable to the State. An act of a State organ not founded on a legal prescription or statute is unthinkable in the modern *Rechtsstaat*.[57]

It is significant that for Kelsen a *Rechtsstaat* is simply any state that issues its commands in the form of legal prescriptions. Every state in this view, therefore, is a *Rechtsstaat*. But if every state is a *Rechtsstaat* it is by no means clear what, if anything, is meant by that designation. That procedural limitations such as those envisaged by Kelsen constitute no bulwark to tyranny the rise of National Socialism in Germany in 1933 has amply demonstrated. The Hitlerian dictatorship was created by the Enabling Act in accordance with the letter, if not the spirit, of the Weimar Constitution and Hitler even went through the formality of having it renewed periodically by the Reichstag.

Although Kelsen gives no attention to the will behind the law he does accept positive law as the only true law. By doing so he tacitly, if not expressly, recognizes individual will as the sole source of the content of law. Moreover, since he believes that it is the form rather than the content of law which makes it binding he removes any substantive limitation to individual will in the determination of the content of law. By recognizing procedure alone as a limitation, by denying that the basic norm itself must have any specific content, his theory fosters individual irresponsibility in practice.

The only thing which constitutes a limitation is a sense of obligation on the part of individuals to follow a certain procedure in enacting law. But this sense of obligation is not grounded in conscience, for conscience demands the recognition of absolute truth, the existence of which Kelsen denies.

Since he does deny it he has real difficulty explaining *why* the individual ought to observe legal rules, *why* a certain procedure should be followed, *why* one norm should be derived from another more basic one. He has destroyed all criteria for obligation.

Without acknowledging it, he does resort in the final analysis, through the notion of a basic norm, to natural law concepts. He assumes that obligation is self-evident, that it is "natural." His concept of the basic norm is really the old conception of the natural law emptied of all specific content.

## The Pure Theory of Power

THE founder of the Neo-Hegelian school of jurisprudence was Josef Kohler (1849–1919). He attacked both the historical and the analytical schools of jurisprudence. But unlike the Neo-Kantians who sought refuge in abstract formalism he was acutely conscious of the changing needs of a dynamic society. Law, he argued, can only be understood as a part of a cultural pattern; law is both a product and an instrument of civilization. He conceived of culture or civilization (*Kultur*) as "the greatest possible development of human knowledge and the great possible development of human control over nature." [58] According to Dean Pound:

Every one had begun to say that law was relative. But relative to what? Kohler answers that it is relative to civilization and laws are relative to the civilization of the time and place. There is no universal body of legal institutions and legal rules for all civilizations. Instead there is a universal idea, namely, human civilization. "Different in its details," he says, law "is alike in the fundamental quest, that is, the furthering of civilization through a forcible ordering of things." Hence if there is no natural law, there is still the constant factor of the relation between law and civilization, "a relation which takes on a different content with the infinite variety in the conditions of human cultivation." But law is not only a means toward civilization, it is a product of civilization. We must look at it, therefore, in three ways: as to the past as a product of civilization, as to the present as a means of maintaining civilization, as to the future as a means of furthering civilization.[59]

Law is relative to time and place but all law, at all times
and in all places, strives to attain one goal, namely, the
"greatest possible development of human control over nature." The content of law continually changes but the goal
remains the same. The final agency entrusted with the function of carrying out the cultural ends of a particular time and
place is the State. The promotion of culture demands the
initiative of political rulers conscious of the destiny of the
nation. The distinctive thing about law is the coercion behind
it.

Law is the standard of conduct which, in consequence of the inner
impulse which urges men toward a reasonable form of life, emanates
from the whole, and is forced upon the individual. It is distinguished
from morals, customs, and religion as soon as the point is reached at
which compulsory standards are separated from those demands
that involve merely social amenity.[60]

The individual is subordinate to the culture in which he lives
and "The demands of culture often require the downfall of
existing rights." [61] History has a destiny which overrides the
destinies of individuals; "progress" often demands that the
individual be sacrificed to its needs.

It must be taken into consideration (in the errors of trial by divine
judgment) that the sacrifice of the individual secured the peace of
society. . . . Universal history often requires the individual to be
thus sacrificed: the iron tread of progress tramples thousands under-
foot. This is a terrible phenomenon which we must moderate and
ameliorate as far as possible. . . . But here we must simply accept
the ways of Divine Providence, and in the consciousness that thus
the progress of the world is accomplished.[62]

Nothing can be declared to be eternally and universally right
and wrong and human rights, like all things, are relative to
time and place.

No one who looks at the matter entirely from the standpoint of . . .
human rights will be able to appreciate slavery in its historical development. Human rights are not advantageous to every development: technical arts must advance, humanity must make progress
in industrial life, and for centuries this goes on with the sacrifice of

human life. The sacrifice to culture is the highest sacrifice that the individual can make; but it is also one that he must make.[63]

Kohler would sacrifice human life on the altar of progress in the name of culture because culture apparently is something greater and more valuable than individual lives.

How are we to know if a particular action furthers culture or not? Kohler is rather vague in the answer which he proposes.

The culture of an age is connected with the soul and spirit of a people. To fathom them is the task of folk-psychology, which, it must be admitted, still needs to be greatly developed. . . . Moods follow one another owing to psychic necessity, and owing to laws that are yet partly unknown.[64]

As Hocking says, "one must be something of a seer to catch the pulse of Culture," [65] and perhaps, only a Hitler, impressed with his own messianic mission, can actually feel the pulse of a national culture. For the ordinary legislator or judge, unimpressed with his powers as prophet, the standard supplied by Kohler would prove impracticable as a guide. As Hocking aptly observes: "the relation of the law-maker to Culture remains . . ." in Kohler's theory "that of a mystic to his deity," and, in the final analysis, "Kohler then, as well as Stammler, falls back upon intuitive judgment and upon the intuitive judgment of specially qualified minds." [66] Just as Stammler's theory fostered irresponsibility on the part of the individual, so Kohler's theory fosters irresponsibility on the part of the State.

Kohler was more temperate in his views than other Neo-Hegelians for jurists like Lasson, Berolzheimer, Kaufmann, and Carl Schmitt tended to substitute power for culture and to identify the law with the search for power. Since Kohler himself, however, thought of culture as control or power over nature it was but a short step to the identification of culture with power.

Adolf Lasson conceived of the State as the embodiment of supreme power within society, as the final arbiter between conflicting social norms. Law, for him, consists of all rules which are effective within society. The State, as the sole agency capable of coercing individuals because of its superior force, finally declares what is law by enforcing obedience to certain rules rather than others. Law is identical with the will of the State. And like Kelsen, Lasson is driven to the conclusion that every State is a *Rechtsstaat*. This is so because whatever the State does it necessarily does in the form of law.

The State can will nothing other than the law, i.e., than its own will. *Any desired content which the State wills becomes* immediately, because the State wills it, *a legal command*, and the State can will nothing other than in the form of a legal command.[67]

Although motivated by different considerations Lasson reaches the identical conclusion reached by Kelsen, namely, that "any content whatsoever can be legal" and that "every act of State is a legal act."

Freedom for Lasson means freedom from all compulsion that is not legal. Since, however, he conceives of the State as the supreme arbiter and contends that all action on the part of the State is necessarily legal, this means nothing more than that the individual is as free as the State permits him to be. Indeed, freedom might actually become slavery. There are no substantive limits to the activity and power of the State for

The State is the highest and last of all natural things, as the law which is the content of its will is the highest and last of all natural systems. The empirical individual is for the activity of the State nothing but an object serving the State's ends . . . the natural individual with his interests is sacrificed for the State as soon as it is necessary.[68]

For Erich Kaufmann the State, too, was the embodiment of power, the agency responsible for carrying out the cultural aims of a particular people in a particular time and place. The State, he wrote, is "the organization which a people gives itself, in order to thread itself into world history and to assert its peculiar genius in it." [69] Indeed, as he put it more explicitly, "*the essence of the State is the development of power*, is the will to assert itself and make itself effective in world history." [70] The ideal toward which all human striving is directed is not a community of free men, as classical liberalism believed, but the victorious war.[71] In war, Kaufmann believed, a people expresses its peculiar genius at its best; hence, war is the ultimate standard of "right."

The most extreme position among Neo-Hegelians, but one which followed logically from the presuppositions of that position, was taken by another German jurist, Carl Schmitt. It was entirely in keeping with his philosophy that he should have become the "Crown jurist" under the Nazis. In a book on the nature of politics published in 1927, Schmitt argued that politics is a species of warfare and that, as a struggle for power, the most distinctive feature of political activity is enmity. Every sphere of human thought and action, he declared, has certain categories which distinguishes it from other spheres. In ethics the distinctive categories are Good and Evil, in aesthetics they are Beautiful and Ugly, in economics Profitable and Unprofitable. Politics, as an independent sphere, is distinguished by the categories of *friend* and *enemy*. In his own words;

The specifically political distinction to which political acts and motivations may be traced back, is the distinction between *friend* and *enemy*. . . . Just as the contrast between Good and Evil is not identical with, nor reducible to, that of Beautiful and Ugly, or of Useful and Harmful, it must not be confused or mixed up with any of these other contrasts. The distinction between friend and enemy can subsist, in theory and practice, without applying, at the same time, moral, esthetic, economic or other distinctions. The political enemy need not be morally evil nor esthetically ugly; he need not appear as an economic competitor, and it may, in fact, be advantageous to do business with him. He is the other, the stranger, and his nature is sufficiently defined if he is, in an intense way, existentially different and strange; in case of conflict, he constitutes the negation of one's own kind of existence, and must therefore be repulsed or fought, in order to preserve one's own way of life. . . .

The concepts of friend and enemy are to be understood in their concrete meaning of existence, not as symbols or metaphors, nor fused with, or weakened by, economic, moral and other ideas, nor as the expression of private feelings and tendencies. They are not normative or "spiritual" contrasts. . . .

The enemy is, thus, not the competitor or opponent in general. Nor is he the private opponent whom one hates. "Enemy" is only a collectivity of men who eventually, i.e., as a real possibility, will *fight* against a similar collectivity of people. Enemy is only the public enemy, because everything that relates to such a collectivity, especially a whole nation, becomes *public*. . . .

The genuine concept of the enemy thus implies the eventual reality of a struggle. . . . The word "struggle," like the term "enemy," is to be taken here in its original meaning. It does not mean competition, nor the "intellectual" struggle of discussion, nor the symbolic struggle, which, after all, every person fights, and be it only with his inertia. The terms "friend," "enemy," and "struggle" obtain their real significance from their relation to the real possibility of physical killing.[72]

Because politics is a species of warfare which, ultimately at least, contemplates "the real possibility of physical killing," any attempt to settle political differences by compromise, discussion and persuasion, is bound to be futile. Since political conflict represents the collision of forces which have no rational or spiritual content it cannot be resolved by appeal to rational or spiritual principles. The natural solution of political conflict, in the last analysis, is war.

Thus, both Neo-Kantianism and Neo-Hegelianism led to irresponsibility—the one, to irresponsibility on the part of the individual; the other, to irresponsibility on the part of the State. One placed procedural restrictions upon individual will but left it otherwise free to do what it liked; the other subordinated individual will to the State but left the State free to pursue power for its own sake. One conceived of law as an empty form ready to be filled in with any desired content; the other conceived of law as the product and embodiment of power. Both, in somewhat different fashion, identified the State with the legal order and saw the coercive power behind the law as its distinguishing characteristic. Although some of the jurists sought to retain some connection between law and justice, the identification remained one principally of vocabulary only, for they tended, in the final analysis, to identify justice with might.

For neither school does the individual possess inviolable rights as a human being; for neither is there a sphere of individual liberty which cannot be taken away. The Neo-Kantians

would demand only that such deprivation of individual freedom be undertaken in accordance with a prescribed procedure (*any* prescribed procedure); the Neo-Hegelians would
demand only that it be done for the purpose of acquiring
greater power for the state. The Neo-Kantians are interested
solely in the formal equality of individuals; the Neo-Hegelians
are ready to sacrifice the individual, reluctantly in the case of
Kohler, willingly in the case of Schmitt, in the interest of
power. For both schools of thought equality before the law
means simply that law, whatever its content, be *applied* alike
to every individual. A *Rechtsstaat* for both schools is not a state
founded upon the natural rights of individuals to life, liberty,
and property but simply a state that issues its commands in
the form of legal prescriptions. Both schools reject the idea
that there are eternal and universal standards filled with substantive content which bind the will of individuals and of the
State. Both pay lip-service to liberalism but empty liberalism
of all the substantive content which it originally had. As a
consequence their "liberalism" is more congenial to despotism
than to freedom.[73]

## Jurisprudence in Twentieth-Century America

THE historical and analytical schools of jurisprudence found
many adherents among jurists in the United States and there
are many American jurists today who see eye to eye with
either the Neo-Hegelians or the Neo-Kantians. But perhaps
the most distinctive American "contribution" to jurisprudence in the twentieth century is a school of thought which
calls itself "realistic." Realism in American jurisprudence is
sometimes said to have had its origins in the writings of John
Chipman Gray, especially in his *Nature and Sources of the Law*
published in 1909. It was his contention that the law of the
state is composed of the rules which the courts lay down for
the determination of legal rights and duties. The law is not
an ideal but is made up of the rules for decision which the
courts lay down. Moreover, it is the fact that courts apply
rules that makes those rules law. Rather than being dis-

coverers of the law, the judges are creators of the law. The sources of law, upon which judges draw, are statutes, judicial precedents, expert opinions, customs and moral principles but these do not become law until they are embodied in judicial decisions. From Gray's suggestion that the law is what the judges *say*, his successors proceeded to derive the conclusion that law is what the judges *do* and modern realism is concerned primarily with an analysis of judicial behavior. Contemporary legal realism is associated with the names of Cook, Llewellyn and Frank [74] but it has no more illustrious adherent than the late Justice Oliver Wendell Holmes, Jr.

Holmes was appointed a justice of the United States Supreme Court in 1902 and served in that capacity until his resignation in 1932. It is not as a justice of the Supreme Court, however, but as a legal philosopher that we shall be concerned with him here. Holmes was particularly impressed with what he thought was the "danger, both to speculation and to practice, of confounding morality with law." He wrote:

For my own part I often doubt whether it would not be a gain if every word of moral significance could be banished from the law altogether, and other words adopted which should convey legal ideas uncolored by anything outside the law. We should lose the fossil records of a good deal of history and the majesty got from ethical associations, but by ridding ourselves of an unnecessary confusion we should gain very much in the clearness of our thought.[75]

A positivist and a pragmatist Holmes was skeptical of the possibility of ever arriving at the truth about anything but especially about the truth of our fundamental presuppositions. Our moral and philosophical preferences he likened to our taste for food and drink. There is no accounting for taste.

Deep-seated preferences can not be argued about—you can not argue a man into liking a glass of beer—and therefore, when differences are sufficiently far reaching, we try to kill the other man rather than let him have his way. But that is perfectly consistent with admitting that, so far as appears, his grounds are just as good as ours.[76]

In the last analysis, Holmes declares, the only arbiter of our differences when these differences are "deep-seated" is force.

All of our beliefs about what is true or morally necessary are ultimately arbitrary. Speaking of the natural law jurists who contend that men must accept certain truths as absolute if they wish to live together in peace, Holmes declares:

> I see no *a priori* duty to live with others and in that way, but simply a statement of what I must do if I wish to remain alive. If I do live with others they tell me that I must do and abstain from doing various things or they will put the screws on to me. I believe that they will, and being of the same mind as to their conduct I not only accept the rules but come in time to accept them with sympathy and emotional affirmation and begin to talk about duties and rights. But for legal purposes a right is only the hypostasis of a prophecy—the imagination of a substance supporting the fact that the public force will be brought to bear upon those who do things said to contravene it—just as we talk of the force of gravitation accounting for the conduct of bodies in space.[77]

It is not a question of duty, as the natural law jurists contend, but a matter of instinct. Men fight for their rights as dogs fight for their bones, it is not a matter of justice but of animal instinct. Man is but a complex animal and we do not know why it is, Holmes declares, that "a certain complex of energies can wag its tail and another can make syllogisms." So far as we know both dog and man serve an unknown power whose will for us is unscrutable. Life itself, the joy of living, is its own end so far as we are concerned.

We still shall fight—all of us because we want to live, some, at least, because we want to realize our spontaneity and prove our powers, for the joy of it, and we may leave to the unknown the supposed final valuation of that which in any event has value to us. It is enough that the universe has produced us and has within it, as less than it, all that we believe and love. If we think of our existence not as that of a little god outside, but as that of a ganglion within, we have the infinite behind us. It gives us our only but our adequate significance. A grain of sand has the same, but what competent person supposes that he understands a grain of sand?[78]

Life is the beginning and end of all existence, it has no final aim (so far as we know or can know) or purpose. Yet, man has within him "that unspeakable somewhat which makes him capable of miracle, able to lift himself by the might of his own soul, unaided, able to face annihilation for a blind belief." [79] No one knows this better than the soldier.

> I do not know what is true. I do not know the meaning of the universe. But in the midst of doubt, in the collapse of creeds, there is one thing I do not doubt, what no man who lives in the same world with most of us can doubt, and that is that the faith is true and adorable which leads a soldier to throw away his life in obedience to a blindly accepted duty, in a cause which he little understands, in a plan of campaign of which he has no notion, under tactics of which he does not see the use.[80]

It is man's will to believe that enables him to continue the fight for life in a world in which "the very smile of God" under the impact of science, "fades slowly out into the pale irony of the void." [81] In an address to the Bar Association of Boston on March 7, 1900, Holmes summarized his philosophy of life in these words:

> The rule of joy and the law of duty seem to me all one. I confess that altruistic and cynically selfish talk seem to me about equally unreal. With all humility, I think "Whatsoever thy hand findeth to do, do it with all thy might" infinitely more important than the vain attempt to love one's neighbor as one's self. If you want to hit a bird on the wing, you must have all your will in a focus, you must not be thinking about yourself, and, equally, you must not be thinking about your neighbor; you must be living with your eye on that bird. Every achievement is a bird on the wing.
>
> The joy, the duty, and I venture to add, the end of life. I speak only of this world, of course, and of the teachings of this world. I do not seek to trench upon the province of spiritual guides. But from the point of view of the world the end of life is life. Life is action, the use of one's powers. As to use them to their height is our joy and duty, so it is the one end that justifies itself. . . .
>
> We are all very near despair. The sheathing that floats us over its waves is compounded of hope, faith in the unexplainable worth and sure issue of effort, and the deep, subconscious content which comes from the exercise of our powers.[82]

In the tradition of historical jurisprudence Holmes sometimes likened the development of the law to the "development of a plant, each generation taking the inevitable next step, mind, like matter, simply obeying a law of spontaneous growth." [83] But it is the task of the jurist to take the law, "stunted and distorted by the dead weight" of the past, and shape it according to the social needs of the present. For it is "the first requirement of a sound body of law . . . that it should correspond with the actual feelings and demands of the community, whether right or wrong." [84] The "dogma of equality" cannot be allowed to stand in the way of community welfare and "no society has ever admitted that it could not sacrifice individual welfare to its own existence." [85] Of necessity the law must regard the individual as a means to an end rather than as an end in himself.

. . . it seems to me clear that the *ultima ratio* . . . of private persons is force, and that at the bottom of all private relations, however tempered by sympathy and all the social feelings, is a justifiable self-preference. If a man is on a plank in the deep sea which will only float one, and a stranger lays hold on it, he will thrust him off if he can. When the state finds itself in a similar position, it does the same thing.

The considerations which answer the argument of equal rights also answer the objections to treating man as a thing, and the like. If a man lives in society, he is liable to find himself so treated.[86]

It is "no sufficient condemnation of legislation that it favors one class at the expense of another; for much or all legislation does that; and none the less when the *bona fide* object is the greatest good of the greatest number.

Why should the greatest number be preferred? Why not the greatest good of the most intelligent and most highly developed? The greatest good of a minority of our generation may be the greatest good of the greatest number in the long run.[87]

In the tradition of Hobbes, Bentham and Austin, Justice Holmes conceived of the law as the command of the dominant social group. He rejected the doctrine of natural law and of natural rights and he argued that "no society has ever admitted that it could not sacrifice individual welfare to its own existence." Such thought is more congenial to despotism than it is to the preservation of individual freedom and the rights of man. It did not seem dangerous at the time it was expounded because it was linked to a faith in democratic procedure which could not envisage the use of that procedure to do things which are essentially undemocratic. It was expounded, moreover, by a man whose personal character was beyond reproach. But the recognition that Holmes was a gentleman and an ardent champion of freedom of speech and of press must not obscure the recognition that his underlying philosophy was potentially dangerous to the foundations of the democracy he thought he was defending. In a recent analysis of his philosophy one writer declares:

He loved his country dearly. He was a champion of liberty of mind and speech and press. But his basic principles lead straight to the abasement of man before the absolutist state and the enthronement of a legal autocrat—whether individual, minority or majority—a legal autocrat who may perhaps be genial as Holmes, benevolently paternalistic, perhaps grim and brutal as any Nazi or Japanese totalitarian, but none the less an autocrat in lineal succession from Caesar Augustus and Nero through Hobbes and Austin and Mr. Justice Holmes.[88]

According to Justice Holmes the law is nothing more and nothing less than "what the courts will do in fact."

What constitutes the law? You will find some text writers telling you that it is something different from what is decided by the courts of Massachusetts or England, that it is a system of reason, that it is a deduction from principles of ethics or admitted axioms or what not, which may or may not coincide with the decisions. But if we take the view of our friend the bad man we shall find that he does not care two straws for the axioms or deductions, but that he does want to know what the Massachusetts or English courts are likely to do in fact. I am much of his mind. The prophecies of what the courts will do in fact and nothing more pretentious, are what I mean by the law.[89]

From this point of view every decision is a correct one. There can be no such thing as an incorrect decision nor an unjust one. It is not the content of a decision that makes it law but the source from which it emanates. Why this source should be respected is not clear. Presumably, from what Holmes has said in other places, it is not a question of respect but fear of

the consequences of challenging it that constitutes the sanction
for obedience. Ultimately the basis of law is fear and force
rather than consent and justice.

Justice Holmes' insistence upon drawing a sharp distinction
between the *law that is* and the *law that ought to be* was carried
to even greater extremes by jurists who came after him. Contemporary realism in American jurisprudence, according to
Dean Pound, rejects any notion of the existence of a legal
order or system. To the contemporary realist law "is only a
regime in which certain persons who wield the force of a
politically organized society apply that force to or exercise
it upon others." [90] The legal realist rejects the notion that
adjudication is or should be guided by objective principles
transcending the will of the judge. Instead of looking for the
principles that do or ought to guide the judge in the adjudication of controversies, the realist looks for the "economically
determined class interest" that motivates the judge in his
decision or wades into the depths of individual psychology.[91]
Law is the judicial process itself and it makes little difference,
according to the realist, whether that process is presided over
by a judge or an administrative official.

Much of the vogue of this doctrine is due to the boast involved in
the terms real and realism. The terms imply that the political and
juristic radicals are in exclusive touch with reality while the rest of
us are groping in superstition and led astray by mythology. Their
favorite words and phrases are superstition, myth, symbol, pious
fiction and the like. The ugly and brutal features of human exercise
of political power are reality. Everything else in political and juristic
theory is illusion, self-deception, or sentimental moonshine. To
subject to judicial scrutiny the action of an administrative official
who decides against a man without hearing him is no more than
an equally arbitrary piling of one arbitrary act upon another, because the court will go through a solemn ritual of hearing both, in
arriving at its decision it will inevitably hear one only. When lawyers
point out the difference between judicial discretion exercised on
principles and a personal discretion exercised on whatever appeals
to the official for the time being in the case at hand, we are told
that they are but cloaking their own arbitrary action with hypo-
critical pretense in comparison with the frank arbitrariness of the
realist.[92]

All judicial decisions whether made by a judge or by an administrative official performing quasi-judicial functions are fundamentally arbitrary in character, according to the realist. Therefore, if we would predict decisions, and that is what lawyers are primarily interested in doing, we should concentrate our attention upon the behavior of judges and those who make decisions. Professor Walter W. Cook describes the task of realistic jurisprudence in these words:

We as lawyers, like the physical scientists, are engaged in the study of objective physical phenomena. Instead of the behavior of electrons, atoms or planets, however, we are dealing with the behavior of human beings. As lawyers we are interested in knowing how certain officials of society—judges, legislators, and others—have behaved in the past, in order that we may make a prediction of their probable behavior in the future. . . . "Right," "duty," and other names for legal relations are therefore not names of objects or entities which have an existence apart from the behavior of the officials in question, but merely terms by means of which we describe to each other what prophecies we make as to the probable occurrence of a certain sequence of events—the behavior of officials.[93]

The underlying assumption, of course, is that the behavior of human beings is determined by laws precisely analogous to those which govern the behavior of atoms. The task of the realistic student of jurisprudence is to discover those laws. The only role played by legal principles and rules is to lend a semblance of rationality to decisions which in fact are arbitrary or determined by forces beyond the conscious control of the decision maker. Why judges should feel any necessity for giving their decisions this semblance of rationality, if, in fact, men are essentially irrational, is never really explained. That judges do feel some necessity for giving "good" reasons for "bad" ones says more about the ethical consciousness and rationality of human beings than the realists really intend to concede. Nevertheless the realist argues that no reason advanced for a judicial decision is ever the real reason and any good reason is always a cloak for a bad one.

The realist first argued that the key to the understanding of judicial behavior lay in an analysis of the social and economic predilections of the judges but more recent realists have argued that the motivations lie much deeper and must be sought in the unconscious motivations that spring from the sexual experiences of childhood. In a book written under the influence of Freudian psychology, Jerome Frank declares that men seek an unrealizable certainty in the law "because they have not yet relinquished the childish need for an authoritative father and unconsciously have tried to find in the law a substitute for those attributes of firmness, sureness, certainty and infallibility ascribed in childhood to the father." [94] The fact is that judges make the law but people generally do not want to believe this because of their "childish dread of uncertainty." The legal order is a myth which many adults cling to because they cannot give up their "childish thought-ways." If we are to make progress we must rid ourselves of these "thought-ways."

Modern civilization demands a mind free of father-governance. To remain father-governed in adult years is peculiarly *the* modern sin. *The modern mind is a mind free of childish emotional drags, a mature mind.* And law, if it is to meet the needs of modern civilization must adapt itself to the modern mind. It must cease to embody a philosophy opposed to change. It must become avowedly pragmatic. . . . Until we become thoroughly cognizant of, and cease to be controlled by, the image of the father hidden away in the authority of the law, we shall not reach that first step in the civilized administration of justice, the recognition that man is not made for the law, but that the law is made by and for men.[95]

He concludes his book with a chapter on Justice Holmes whom he describes as "the completely adult jurist." It does not occur to Frank, apparently, that the father is the symbol not only of authority but a reality. Psychoanalysis is a double-edged weapon. It might be that a psychoanalytical analysis of Jerome Frank would reveal that it is he who is endeavoring to escape from reality by denying the reality of any authority to which he owes submission.[96] In any event, the effect of Frank's theory is the dogmatic assertion that all judicial decisions are arbitrarily motivated and by their nature unpredictable. As Dean Pound sees it:

The juristic absolutism, which is so widespread today as a re-inforcement of administrative absolutism, assumes . . . that in the nature of things it is psychologically impossible for the judicial process to operate objectively and impartially. Hence the apparatus of principles and rules and conceptions which for centuries men have sought to constrain the process to operate uniformly and predictably and objectively is futile. Its supposed achievement in that direction is a delusion. Our faith in it is superstition. Behind the supposed principles and rules and conceptions, the true moving forces of decision are operating independently. It is not scientific to take account of more than the individual decision itself. Thus it follows that what is done in the course of judicial decision is law because it is done, not done because it is law. The attempt to hold down the individual judge to legally prescribed paths of action is futile. Legislator, administrative official and judge may as well be left free in theory to pursue their own paths to the general good each in his own way, since in practice they will do so in any event. If we think in this fashion, the way out does seem to be a postulated all-wise leader with no limit to his power. At any rate, he can make some one conception of the general good the common objective of the many agencies of administration and adjudication.[97]

As an augury of things to come realistic jurisprudence certainly suggests that tyranny is an inevitability. For the only way out of the intellectual and moral anarchy underlying the realist's conception of the law is tyranny. If force alone, as Justice Holmes believed, is the only possible arbiter of our "deep-seated preferences," if moral judgments are nothing more than expressions of individual taste or preference, and if law, as Jerome Frank declares, is simply what men arbitrarily declare it to be, then we have no choice but to submit our differences to the arena of force. If it is an illusion to believe that there is a forum of reason and conscience to which we can submit our differences for judgment then we have no alternative but to submit them to the arena of force. In that arena it is not the best reason that will prevail but the mightiest fist.

# Socialism

## CHAPTER 11

# The Origins of Modern Socialism

SOCIALISM is the logical counterpart to liberal capitalism. Both liberalism and socialism start from a belief in the autonomy of human reason and in the perfectibility of man. Both assign redemptive powers to Nature or to History. Both have as their goal the freeing of the individual from arbitrary and capricious authority. They differ not in the presuppositions from which they begin nor essentially in the goal which they envisage but rather in the diagnosis of the problem to be solved and the best means of solving it.

Liberalism regards individuals as being primarily constrained and hampered in the full enjoyment of their freedom by arbitrary and capricious political rule. The practical problem, as the liberals see it, is to find some way of effectively bridling the political sovereign. They believe that they have found the answer to this problem in constitutionalism and representative democracy.

Socialism regards individuals as being primarily constrained in the full realization of their freedom by arbitrary and capricious economic power in the form of the private ownership of the means of production. The practical problem, as the socialists see it, is to find some way of destroying this power or transforming it. They believe that they have found the answer in the common ownership of the means of production and of exchange.

There are many varieties of socialism but all socialists agree that the principal source of evil in the world is the institution of private property and all, although in varying degrees, advocate the common ownership of the means of production as the cure. All advocate the transformation of private property into public property and the division of the income from such property in accordance with individual needs. Some socialists advocate the division of income equally but others argue only for a more equitable distribution. Capitalism, the socialist contends, inevitably involves an inequitable distribution of wealth and it is this inequitable distribution that socialism promises to overcome. While capitalism tends to concentrate upon the problem of production, leaving the problem of distribution to take care of itself "naturally," socialism tends to place its emphasis upon the problem of distribution to the neglect of the problem of production. Communism differs from socialism primarily in the means which it advocates for the transformation of capitalism into socialism. It believes that such a transformation can take place generally only by means of revolution and that the transition period must necessarily be one of dictatorship. The Socialist believes that the transformation of the economy can be brought about by democratic, peaceful means and that there is no incompatibility between a socialist economy and a democratic government.

Modern socialism emerged during the latter part of the eighteenth and the beginning of the nineteenth century. The word socialism appears to have come into use around 1830. In Great Britain it was used to describe the teachings of Robert Owen and in France the teachings of Fourier and Saint-Simon. With the rise of Marxian socialism in the middle of the nineteenth century the socialist movement came to be identified more and more specifically as a working-class movement and as a reaction to the abuses and misery that flowed in the wake of the Industrial Revolution. There are some writers who profess to see evidences of socialism in theory and in practice in ancient and medieval times but the "socialism" of those times, if socialism it was, was something quite different in nature and in scope from that of modern times. Nevertheless it may assist in better understanding modern socialism if we briefly examine the characteristics of "socialist" thought prior to the nineteenth century.

## *"Socialism" in Ancient and Medieval Times* [1]

SOME writers find evidence of socialism in practice on the
island of Crete as early as 1300 B.C. and many find evidences
of socialism in the writings of the Jewish prophets as recorded
in the Old Testament. Many of the Jewish prophets and
notably Amos, Hosea and Isaiah condemned the tyrannous
iniquity of the rich, calling down the wrath of God upon those
who were responsible for the oppression and exploitation of
the poor. None before or since have been more eloquent or
fervent in their denunciation of unrighteousness, greed, luxury
and the abuse of wealth. But they were not socialists. The
Mosaic Law clearly recognizes the existence of private property and enjoins men to respect the property of others and not
to covet that which rightfully belongs to others. The injunction
to refrain from stealing clearly implies the existence of private
property as does the injunction to refrain from coveting one's
neighbor's goods. The oppression of the poor springs not from
the institution of private property but from the covetousness
and greed of men. Hence it is the abuse of property and the
lack of charity that the Jewish prophets specifically condemned. They did not call upon the Jewish community to
establish an economy in which property would be held and
shared in common but to repentance. The cure they prescribed was spiritual. Indignation in the face of social injustice is, indeed, as old as recorded history but the moral condemnation of economic exploitation is not synonymous with
socialism although some socialists would seem to say that they
alone have discovered the abuse of wealth and condemned it.
Men have long recognized, as did the Jewish prophets, the
injustice of economic oppression but while socialism has its
roots, at least in part, in the recognition of this injustice, it is
not identical with it.

There are some writers who find evidences of socialism in the
New Testament and among them some who contend that the
gospel of Christ and socialism are identical. It is only by reading certain passages in the New Testament out of their context,
however, that this identification is made possible for, in reality,

the gospel consists of a spiritual message not an economic program. Christ enjoins men neither to defend the institution of private property nor to destroy it but rather to seek the Kingdom of God and His righteousness. When Christ, for example, declares that the rich shall have greater difficulty entering the Kingdom of God than the poor, it is a warning against the *temptations* involved in the possession of wealth rather than a condemnation of wealth itself. It will be impossible, Christ declared, for those who *trust* in riches to enter the Kingdom of God but that applies equally to the poor who think that their salvation lies in the attainment of riches as to the rich who think that, being rich, they have everything they need.

Lay not up for yourselves treasures upon earth, where moth and rust doth corrupt, and where thieves break through and steal: but lay up for yourselves treasures in heaven, where neither moth nor rust doth corrupt, and where thieves do not break through nor steal . . .

is Christ's injunction, "for where your treasure is there will your heart be also." His message is that only the love of God endures forever.

Wealth itself is a neutral thing which can be used in the service of God or of Self. Christ teaches that wealth is given us that we may satisfy man's needs; if we do not use it as it was intended to be used but for our exclusive benefit and enjoyment, then it is a curse. Christ warns against the temptations involved in the possession of wealth, and against the lack of charity that sometimes accompanies its possession, but it is the lack of charity he condemns rather than the possession of wealth itself. "Whoso hath the world's goods, and seeth his brother have need, and shutteth up his compassion for him, how dwelleth the love of God in him?" The evil lies not in the possession of wealth but in what the possession of wealth may do to our souls.

The parable of the rich young man seeking Christ's counsel is sometimes quoted as evidence of the "socialism" in the gospel of Christ. But, when read in context the parable is not an argument for socialism but an example of what one must do to attain spiritual perfection. When the rich young man asks what he should do to inherit eternal life, Christ tells him to follow the Ten Commandments. When the young man replies that he has done so and asks what *more* he should do, *then* Christ tells him: "If thou wilt be perfect, go and sell what thou hast and give it all to the poor." This is not an injunction to redistribute the wealth more equitably but to detach one's self *completely* from the things of this world. Read in context this is a counsel of perfection rather than a commandment intended to be binding upon all individuals in every circumstance. It is a counsel of perfection that is as difficult for the poor to follow as for the rich. St. Clement, one of the early Church fathers, points out in his interpretation of this parable that there is no special merit in being without riches. The real meaning of the story, he says, is that we should "banish from the soul its opinions about riches, its attachment to them, its excessive desire, its morbid excitement over them, its anxious cares, the thorns of our earthly existence which choke the seed of the true life." [2] Unless the renunciation of wealth leads us closer to the love of God there is no special merit in poverty, no more, of course, than there is in the possession of wealth. Wealth is an instrument which can be used rightly or wrongly and it is the way in which we use it that is the important consideration. Evil lies not in things but in the passions of men. It is pride, covetousness, and anxiety, that is the real evil. Men of wealth may be tempted to greater pride and covetousness than other men, they may be more anxious, but pride, covetousness and anxiety infect the poor as well as the rich. They are human infirmities and not peculiar to any one class. Essentially this is the teaching of most of the early Church fathers.

The great Christian philosopher of the Middle Ages, St. Thomas Aquinas, repeats with additional arguments drawn from Aristotle much the same thing. He distinguishes between the power to acquire and administer property and the power to use it. The first he defends on the grounds that such a power is necessary to human life and because of the imperfection of human beings. In one sense private property is an evil made necessary by the imperfection of men but it is a lesser evil than that which would exist if private property were done away with. Because of their nature, men have a right to the possession of property but its *use is common*. No one has a right to use property solely for his own enjoyment or benefit but only for the common good and the right to property obliges the owner to share it with others. The owner of property is a trustee of that property and his title remains good only so long as he uses it for the good of mankind. The giving of alms is what justifies the possession of property, the ownership of property becomes theft when it is divorced from charity. A man has a right, St. Thomas believed, only to those goods which are necessary to maintain his station in society and to discharge the obligations which that status imposes upon him. Everything beyond what he needs belongs *by right* to others.

Among some early Christians there is evidence that property was often shared and held in common. This, however, was a voluntary *renunciation* of property by individuals rather than an attempt to found a universal, permanent and obligatory social system. The motivation was an ascetic and spiritual one and it was as Christians, rather than as socialists, that they held their property in common. The same motivation was at work among the religious orders of the Middle Ages and is at work among them today. The "communism" that is characteristic of Christian religious orders is not a "communism" that springs from a desire to share property in common but from a resolution to renounce all earthly possessions in the more perfect service of God. The motivation is spiritual rather than material, ascetic rather than sensual. It is a form of self-discipline, moreover, which is not thought of as being universally possible. It is a vow of poverty, not an embracement of abundance. It seeks not a more equitable distribution of the world's goods but a *detachment from them*. In short, the renunciation of private property is regarded by the Christian Church as a vocation for the saint rather than as a discipline for the many. This is not to say that the Church regards social injustice with complacency or that it regards the institution of private property as an unqualified good but it is to say that it does not believe that private property can be abolished without first abolishing the sin that gives rise to it.

One of the earliest expressions of socialism is thought by

some writers to occur in Plato's *Republic*, but, despite the fact
that Plato declares that the guardian class in society should
not own property, Plato is not a socialist. Speaking of the
guardian class Plato says:

> . . . none of them should have any property of his own beyond
> what is absolutely necessary; neither should they have a private
> house or store closed against one who has a mind to enter; their
> provisions should be only such as are required by trained warriors,
> who are men of temperance and courage; they should agree to re-
> ceive from the citizens a fixed rate of pay, enough to meet the ex-
> penses of the year and no more; and they will go to mess and live
> together like soldiers in a camp. Gold and silver we will tell them
> that they have from God; the diviner metal is within them, and
> they have therefore no need of the dross which is current among
> men, and ought not to pollute the divine by any such earthly ad-
> mixture; for that commoner metal has been the source of many
> unholy deeds, but their own is undefiled. And they alone of all the
> citizens may not touch or handle silver or gold, or be under the same
> roof with them, or wear them, or drink from them. And this will be
> their salvation, and they will be the saviours of the state. But should
> they ever acquire homes or lands or moneys of their own, they will
> become housekeepers and husbandmen instead of guardians, ene-
> mies and tyrants instead of allies of the other citizens; hating and
> being hated, plotting and being plotted against, they will pass their
> whole life in much greater terror of internal than of external enemies,
> and the hour of ruin, both to themselves and to the rest of the state,
> will be at hand.[3]

What Plato is saying here, and elsewhere, is not that the guardians should own property in common, but that they should not
own property at all beyond what they require for their immediate and personal use. He does not advocate the common
ownership of property by the guardian class but the common
*renunciation* of property by them. He hopes in this way to divorce political power from economic interest and possession.
He believes that the rulers of a state will rule more justly and
in the interest of the welfare of all citizens if they are not tempted
by the possession of wealth to put their own economic interests above those of others. And for a similar reason he advocates a community of wives and of children for the guardian
class since he believes that in this way the guardians will be

freed from the temptation to think first of their own families. If they do not know who their wives and children are they cannot act in their special interest. The third class in Plato's *Republic*, moreover, would own property individually.

This aspect of Plato's thought has not always been clearly recognized and even Aristotle seems to have misinterpreted his meaning in his discussion of Plato's conception of property in Book II of the *Politics*. Commenting on that discussion in a recent edition of Aristotle's *Politics*, Professor Ernest Barker declares that "Aristotle here forgets, or at any rate neglects, the actual argument of the *Republic*. Plato makes it clear that the farmers own private property, and live in private or separate families." [4] Barker says

> There is . . . no common ownership in the Platonic system; there is only common consumption, and that only among the class of the guardians. The members of the farming class own, cultivate, and consume in severalty—subject only to two conditions, first that they pay a quota of their produce to the guardians, for *their* common use, and secondly that the amount of land which each may own is restricted. There is thus a sense in which it may be said that Aristotle's own formula of 'property several, use of it communal' is observed in the *Republic*.[5]

One of the earliest expressions of "socialist" thought in modern times is contained in Sir Thomas More's *Utopia* published in 1516. Yet the chief motivation in writing it was probably not a desire to establish a socialist system so much as to subject the economic conditions in sixteenth-century England to a searching criticism that would lead to real amelioration of the peasants' lot. With a savage irony More depicted the sickness of that society. Published in Latin at Louvain in France, More's *Utopia* was a political satire rather than a serious program of action. Speaking of the condition of the poor in the sixteenth century in phrases that strikingly anticipate those to be used by Karl Marx in the nineteenth, More wrote:

> Their daily wages is so little, that it will not suffice for the same day, much less it yieldeth any overplus that may daily be laid up for the relief of old age. Is not this an unjust and unkind public weal, which giveth great fees and rewards to gentlemen, as they call them,

and to goldsmiths, and to such other, which be either idle persons, or else only flatterers, and devisers of vain pleasures; and of the contrary part maketh no gentle provision for poor ploughmen, colliers, labourers, carters, ironsmiths, and carpenters: without whom no commonwealth can continue? . . . the rich men not only by private fraud but also by common laws, do every day pluck and snatch away from the poor some part of their daily living. . . . Therefore when I consider and weigh in my mind all their commonwealths, which nowadays anywhere do flourish, so God help me, I can perceive nothing but a certain conspiracy of rich men procuring their own commodities under the name and title of the commonwealth.

More's was the first in a long series of utopian writings that were to include Campanella's *City of the Sun* (1623), Francis Bacon's *New Atlantis* (1627) and Harrington's *Oceana* (1656).

## *Socialism in the Seventeenth Century*

THE seventeenth century produced many utopian and visionary schemes of social justice but it also produced the first real socialist movements. During the English civil wars two movements arose espousing radical political and economic programs: the Levellers and the Diggers. The Levellers were particularly active in the years 1647–1650 and tried to turn the liberal revolution into more radical, democratic channels than the leaders of the revolution were willing at that time to go. A numerically small group drawn from the poorer economic classes and headed by John Lilburne and Richard Overton, the Levellers agitated for a written constitution, universal suffrage, regular meetings of Parliament for definitely limited periods, and recognition of the "rights of the people." Perhaps the most significant aspect of the Leveller movement was its insistence upon the view, which was then new but now regarded as an integral part of democratic parliamentary systems, that organized opposition to the prevailing government is not necessarily disloyal but often legitimate. According to Professor Haller who has made an extensive study of the Leveller movement:

in Lilburne the oncoming democracy had developed out of its own ranks a new kind of leader, and under his leadership was developing a new kind of organization to give force to the old idea of natural law. That organization was not a sect but a party, an association of men drawn together by certain definite interests to seek certain concrete benefits by concerted political action; and what the party leaders demanded was that the consent of the people, without which no law of the state was valid, should not be assumed without their participation. This was, of course, tantamount to a fundamental change in the structure of government. . . . Presuming upon their ability to organize some hundreds of thousands of people in their support, the Levellers set themselves up to "give a rule" to the Long Parliament, and that body had either to concede their right to do so—which is to say to grant to their kind of organized opposition and complaint a place and function in the state—or repress them.[6]

The Leveller movement failed in its immediate purpose but it anticipated the typical democratic philosophy of the late nineteenth century. The Levellers were primarily interested in political reform and in the establishment of radical political equality.

Demands for more radical economic reform were made by the Diggers who sometimes described themselves as the "True Levellers." Like the Levellers, the Diggers saw an opportunity during the civil wars to turn the revolution into more radical paths. A very small group, they achieved some prominence in 1649 but were quickly dispersed by force. They appealed to the natural law in defense of their claim that land should be free to all. "None ought to be lords or landlords over another, but the earth is free for every son and daughter of mankind to live free upon." [7] They tended to see in the institution of private property the root evil of all social injustice and corruption. Their pamphlets smoldered with hatred of the landlords who were the personification in their eyes of that evil:

You Pharaohs, you have rich clothing and full bellies, you have honors and your ease; but know the day of judgment is begun and that it will reach you ere long. The poor people you oppress shall be the saviors of the land. If you will find mercy, let Israel go free; break to pieces the bands of property.[8]

One of the leaders of the Digger movement was Gerald Winstanley whose *Law of Freedom* published in 1652 was the only

important piece of writing associated with it. Winstanley envisaged a utopia in which

there shall be no buying and selling of the earth, nor of the fruits
thereof. . . . If any man or family want corn or other provisions,
they may go to the storehouse and fetch without money. If they
want a horse to ride, they may go into the fields in summer or to
the common stables in winter, and receive one from the keepers,
and when the journey is performed, bring him back. . . . As every
one works to advance the common stock, so every one shall have
free use of any commodity in the storehouse for his pleasure and
comfortable livelihood, without buying or selling or restraint from
anybody.[9]

Meantime Winstanley urged the poor to begin cultivating the
uncultivated common land (the commons, parks, etc.) from
whence the movement derived its name of Diggers. But as a
means of achieving the common ownership of land this method
proved to be but a futile gesture.

Winstanley's recognition of the intimate relationship of
property ownership to political power was more clearly expressed in the seventeenth century by another Englishman,
James Harrington, in his *Oceana* (1656). A liberal republican,
rather than a socialist, Harrington recalled the arguments of
Aristotle on behalf of a balanced economy as the most stable
basis of political order. "Domestic empire," he wrote, "is
founded upon dominion. Dominion is property, real or personal; that is to say, in lands, or in money and goods." The
form of government depends upon "the proportion of balance
of dominion or property in land," change this balance and
you change the form of government.

If one man be the sole landlord of a territory, or overbalance the
people . . . his empire is absolute monarchy. If the few or a nobility, or a nobility with the clergy, be landlords, or overbalance
the people to the like proportion, . . . the empire is mixed monarchy. . . . And if the whole people be landlords or hold the lands
so divided among them that no one man, or number of men, . . .
overbalance them, the empire . . . is a commonwealth.[10]

There can be no stable political order, he argued, without a
proper distribution of wealth which avoids both the excesses
of wealth and of poverty.

## Socialism in France

THE real home of what has come to be called Utopian Socialism, however, was eighteenth-century France. The French Revolution had destroyed the political power of the *ancien régime* and the institutions of absolute monarchy and it had brought the bourgeoisie to positions of economic and political power, but it did not go far enough in its transformation of society to satisfy some of the more radical leaders. It left untouched the institution of private property which some saw as the root of social injustice. The French Constitution of 1793 declared that "All men are equal by nature and by law" and the socialists argued that this meant not only that men should enjoy political equality but economic equality as well. They were in substantial agreement with the liberals but did not think that the liberals went far enough in their transformation of society. It is impossible to mention all of those who contributed to this line of thought and we shall single out only a few of the more prominent ones for consideration.

One of the first to advocate socialism during the Revolutionary period was Francis Noel Babeuf (1764–1797). The aim of society, he declared, consists in providing happiness for all and happiness consists of equality. "Nature has given to every man an equal right in the enjoyment of all goods." [11] To realize the goal of equality: everyone should be obliged to work; the hours of work should be fixed by law; production should be regulated by a committee elected by the people; this committee will assign work to the citizens each one taking his turn at the more disagreeable kinds of work; all commodities shall be distributed to individuals in accordance with their individual needs. He proposed a gradual process of nationalization of property to extend over a period of some fifty years at the end of which time all property would be in the hands of the State. All children would be taken from their parents at an early age and educated by the State in order to prevent any inequalities from arising. Babeuf organized a secret society to propagate these ideas and its discovery brought him to the guillotine.

With emphasis upon equality of opportunity rather than

upon absolute equality Comte Henri de Saint-Simon (1760–1825) developed a more systematic conception of socialism based less upon moral criticism of the existing order and more upon economic arguments. Gide and Rist declare:

> The socialism of Saint-Simon is not a vague aspiration for some pristine equality. . . . It is rather the naive expression of juvenile enthusiasm in the presence of the new industrial regime begotten of mechanical invention and scientific discovery. . . . It sought to interpret the generous aspirations of the new bourgeois class, freed through the instrumentality of the Revolution from the tutelage of baron and priest, and to show how the reactionary policy of the Restoration threatened its triumph. Not content, however, with confining itself to the intellectual orbit of the bourgeoisie, it sought also to define the sphere of the workers in future society and to lay down regulations for their benefit. But its appeal was chiefly to the more cultivated classes—engineers, bankers, artists, and savants. It was to these men . . . that the Saint-Simonians preached collectivism and the suppression of inheritance as the easiest way of founding a new society upon the basis of science and industry. . . .
>
> Consequently Saint-Simonianism appears to be a somewhat unexpected extension of economic Liberalism. . . .[12]

A new industrial State, Saint-Simon argued, must take the place of the Church as the supreme authority among men to bring harmony into their lives. Society ought to be reorganized on the model of the factory.

> The object of socialism is to set up a new system of society based upon the workshop as a model. The rights of society will be the customary rights of the factory. Not only will socialism stand to benefit by the existence of the industrial system which has been built up by capital and science upon the basis of technical development, but it will gain even more from that spirit of cooperation which has long been a feature of factory life, drawing out the best energy and the best skill of the workman.[13]

Society must be reorganized into a "productive association" with an economic rather than a political form of government. Representation in the government should be in terms of economic interest and occupation and the supreme task of government should be the development of the nation's economic resources. Government in the ordinary sense would become unnecessary as the state became transformed into a national "industrial enterprise." Concepts such as "liberty," "equality" and "sovereignty of the people," Saint-Simon declared were but abstract fictions with which the Liberals were deceiving themselves. In the new age of Industrialism there will be no need for such metaphysical speculation and argument. "Industry is the basis of liberty" and there is no real liberty apart from the industrial system. The development of industry is synonymous with the development of freedom.[14] In the new Industrial system there will be no class distinctions for there will be only workers and idlers, bees and drones. Among the drones he includes all nobles, priests, owners of real estate, judges and soldiers—"in a word," he says, "every one who is opposed to the establishment of the system that is most favorable to economy or liberty." [15] Eventually these "drones" must disappear from society since they perform no useful service to it.

Saint-Simon did not advocate, however, the abolition of private property but believed that capital as well as labor was legitimately entitled to remuneration. He did favor some drastic reform of ownership in the form of land. Most of his followers, however, believed that private property in the form of capital was equally as bad as private property in land. In a brochure addressed to the Chamber of Deputies in 1829 the Saint-Simonians summarized their position in these words:

The Saint-Simonians do not advocate community of goods, for such community would be a manifest violation of the first moral law, which they have always been anxious to uphold, and which demands that in future every one shall occupy a situation becoming his capacity and be paid according to his labor.

In view of this law they demand the abolition of all privileges of birth without a single exception, together with the complete extinction of the right of inheritance, which is today the greatest of all privileges and includes every other. The sole effect of this system is to leave the distribution of social advantages to a chance few who are able to lay some pretence to it, and to condemn the numerically superior class to deprivation, ignorance, and misery.

They ask that all the instruments of production, all lands and capital, the funds now divided among individual proprietors, should be pooled so as to form one central social fund, which shall be employed by associations of persons hierarchically arranged so that each one's task shall be an expression of his capacity and his wealth a measure of his labor.

The Saint-Simonians are opposed to the institution of private property simply because it inculcates habits of idleness and fosters a practice of living upon the labor of others.[16]

Property is not something sacred and inviolable but it "is a social fact which, along with other social facts, must submit to the laws of progress. Accordingly it may be extended, curtailed, or regulated in various ways at different times." [17] The Saint-Simonians predicted the abolition of the institution of private property by a process of gradual extension that would eventually include all individuals. This was to be accomplished principally through the abolition of private inheritance.

Gide and Rist comparing the Saint-Simonians with the classical school of economics, declare:

No attempt was made either by Adam Smith, Ricardo, or J. B. Say to make clear the distinction between the science of political economy and the fact of social organization. Property . . . was a social fact that was accepted by them without the slightest demur. The methods of dividing property and of inheriting it, the causes that determined its rise and the consequences that resulted from its existence, were questions that remained outside the scope of their discussions. By division of distribution of wealth they meant simply the distribution of the annual revenue between the various factors of production. . . . Their theory of distribution is simply a theory concerning the price of services. No attention was paid to individuals, the social product being supposed to be divided between impersonal factors—land, capital, and labor—according to necessary laws. . . .

For the Saint-Simonians, on the other hand, and for socialists in general the problem of distribution consists especially in knowing how property is distributed. The question is to determine why some people have property while others have none; why the instruments of production, land, and capital should be so unevenly distributed, and why the revenues resulting from this distribution should be unequal. For a consideration of the abstract factors of production the socialists are anxious to substitute the study of actual living individuals or social classes and the legal ties which bind them together. These differing conceptions of distribution have given rise to two different problems, the one primarily economic, the other social. . . .

Economists think that society ought to be organized from the point of view of the consumer and that the general interest is fully realized when the consumer is satisfied. Socialists, on the contrary, believe that society should be organized from the standpoint of the worker, and that the general interest is only fully achieved when the workers draw their full share of the social product, which is as great as it possibly can be.

There is one last element of difference which is very important. Classical writers made an attempt to reduce the apparent disorder of individual action within the compass of a few scientific laws. By the time the task was completed so struck were they with the profound harmony which they thought they had discovered that they renounced all attempts at amelioration. . . .

The Saint-Simonians, on the other hand . . . are convinced of the slowness, the awkwardness, and the cruelty with which spontaneous economic forces often go to work. Consequently they are concerned with the possibility of substituting a more conscious, carefully thought-out effort on the part of society. Instead of a spontaneous reconciliation of conflicting interests they suggest an artificial reconciliation, which they strive with all their might to realize.[18]

Almost contemporaneously with Saint-Simon, another Frenchman, Charles Fourier (1772–1837) was developing quite independently of Saint-Simon a theory of socialism that was so fantastic in its details as to convince many that he was mad. He spent most of his life as a shop clerk and traveling salesman devoting all of his spare time to writing on social problems. Comparing himself to Newton, Fourier believed that he had discovered the underlying principle of social relations in the form of mutual attraction. He describes the way in which he hit upon this discovery in these words:

Chance counts for half in the success of a man of genius. . . . I myself paid tribute to it when I discovered the calculus of attraction. . . . An apple was for me, as for Newton, a guiding compass. For this apple, which is worthy of fame, a traveller who dined with me at Fevrier's restaurant in Paris paid the sum of fourteen sous. I had just come from a district where the same kind of apples, and even superior ones, sold for a half-liard, that is to say, more than a hundred for fourteen sous. I was so struck by this difference in price between places having the same temperature, that I began to suspect there must be something radically wrong in the industrial mechanism, and

hence originated the researches, which, after four years, caused me to
discover the theory of series of industrial groups, and, consequently,
the laws of universal motion missed by Newton. . . .

I have since then noticed that we can reckon four apples as celebrated, two for the disasters which they caused, Adam's apple and
that of Paris, and two for the services they rendered to science, Newton's apple and mine. Does not this quadrille of apples deserve a
page of history?[19]

The industrial world ought to be organized on the principle of
mutual attraction and labor so organized as to make it attractive since "naturally" it is not. But when Fourier speaks of
organizing society on the principle of attraction he is not content to state it in such general terms but illustrates in detail
exactly what he has in mind.

As the basic social unit he posits the "group," a unit composed of at least seven persons bound together by similar
tastes and desiring to be united in the pursuit of some common
art, science or industry. Five or more groups would constitute
a series and a union of series a phalanx. The phalanx, composed of approximately 1600 persons, would be the largest
social unit. It would be a perfect social community and economically self-sufficient.

A company will be collected consisting of from 1500 to 1600 persons of graduated degrees of fortune, age, character, of theoretical
and practical knowledge; care will be taken to secure the greatest
variety possible, for the greater the number of variations either in the
passions or the faculties of the members, the easier it will be to make
them harmonize in a short space of time.[20]

Each phalanx should occupy about 500 acres of land, the
members of it living together in a great house to be known as
the Palace. He then sketches in some detail the actual construction of this edifice.

The central part of the Palace or Phalanstery ought to be appropriated to peaceful uses, and contain the dining-halls, halls for finance, libraries, study, etc. In this central portion are located the
place of worship, the *tour d'ordre*, the telegraph, the post-office boxes,
the chimes for ceremonials, the observatory, the winter court adorned
with resinous plants, and situated in the rear of the parade-court.

One of the wings ought to combine all the noisy workshops, such as the carpentershop, the forge, all hammer-work; it ought to contain also all the industrial gatherings very noisy in industry and even in music. This combination will obviate a great annoyance of our civilised cities, where we find some man working with a hammer in every street, some dealer in iron or tyro on the clarinet, who shatter the tympanum of fifty families in the vicinity.

The other wing ought to contain the caravansary with its ballrooms and its halls appropriated to intercourse with outsiders, so that these may not encumber the central portion of the palace and embarrass the domestic relations of the Phalanx.[21]

Division of labor ought to take place according to individual aptitude. There should be equal education for children with special training for special skills and talents. No detail is overlooked by Fourier in his graphic sketch of the perfect community. He has an elaborate plan for distributing food and says that "the variety of food which will be found upon the tables of the peoples . . . cannot be estimated at less than thirty or forty dishes, renewed by thirds every day, along with a dozen of different drinks, varied at each meal." [22] He gives considerable attention to the problem of storage and heating and says that one of the advantages of living in such a Palace would be the possibility of going "to the workshops, the dining-halls, to balls and assemblies without needing furs or boots" and "without exposing" one's self "to colds and inflammations." [23] Such "associative conditions," moreover, would have the advantage over ordinary living conditions that no elaborate and expensive precautions would need to be taken against thievery since "a people who live in ease and are imbued with sentiments of honor do not even conceive any projects for stealing. It will be shown that children, so essentially robbers of fruit, would not, in the associative state, take an apple off a tree." [24]

Fourier does not propose the abolition of private property since each Phalanx is to be organized very much like a joint-stock corporation. The profits, which he predicted would be large, would not be distributed, however, solely to those who owned stock but would be divided in this proportion: five-twelfths to labor, four-twelfths to capital, and three-twelfths to talent. The wage system would be abolished since labor would be rewarded by this share in the profits. All the members of the association, moreover, would be guaranteed a minimum as regards food, shelter, clothing and amusements. This plan he thought would unite "the three classes" (capital, labor and talent) in such a way that they

would forget their hatred; and that the more readily because the opportunities for attractive labor would put an end to the drudgery of the people and the disdain of the rich for inferiors, whose labors, now become enticing, they would share. There would be an end to the envy with which the poor regard the idle, who reap without having sown: there would no longer be any idlers, or poor, and social antipathies would disappear with the causes which produced them.

That which will charm a rich man in the associative state will be his ability to repose perfect confidence in all who surround him, to forget the cunning with which one must be armed at all points in the relations of civilization, and yet be unable to escape dupery. In the Phalanx, a rich man . . . will have no snares to fear, no importunate demands to trouble him, because the Harmonians, provided with a sufficient *minimum* have nothing in the way of personal interest to ask of anyone, assured as they are of obtaining, in every branch of attractive industry, a compensation proportioned to their labor, their capacity, and their capital, if they have any.[25]

Another advantage of this scheme, according to Fourier, is that it would do away with commerce and the merchant class since all would carry on their buying and selling directly with each other and "henceforth all the friends of commerce, the hosts of merchants, would find themselves stranded, like a string of spiders that perish in their web for lack of insects. . . . This downfall of the merchants would be the result of *free competition*, for they would not be prevented from trading; but nobody would have confidence in them. . . ."[26]

The Phalanx which Fourier envisaged may be compared, Gide and Rist say, to

a kind of co-operative hotel, belonging to an association and accommodating members of that association only. It is much more thoroughgoing than the ordinary co-operative society, which is just content to buy commodities of an association without making any real at-

tempt to practice communism. . . . The "Phalange" not content
to remain a mere consumers' association, was to attempt production
as well. . . . The Phalange was to be a small self-sufficing world, a
microcosm producing everything it consumed, and consuming—as
far as it could—all it produced.[27]

Several attempts were made to put Fourier's ideas into practice, most notably in the United States under the leadership of
men like Albert Brisbane, Horace Greeley, Charles A. Dana,
George Ripley and others. Brisbane founded *The North American Phalanx* in New Jersey, and another was founded in Wis-
consin. The most famous of all was *Brook Farm* founded at
West Roxbury, Massachusetts, in 1841, by a Unitarian minister. Cooperating in its creation were Ralph Waldo Emerson,
Nathaniel Hawthorne, Theodore Parker and other literary
figures. It was disbanded in 1846 when a fire destroyed the
"palace" and money to rebuild it was unavailable. It is estimated that some thirty of these communities were tried but
none survived more than five or six years.[28]

## Robert Owen (1771–1858)

WHILE Fourier was spinning his fantasies, an Englishman,
Robert Owen was endeavoring to put some of the principles
of a socialist society into practice. Although contemporaries,
neither seems to have known the other and neither even mentions the other. The significance of Owen's work lies more in
his life than in his writings, which are few. His parents were
poor and Owen went to work in a textile factory at the age of
eleven. His rise was rapid and at 19 he was employed as the
superintendent of a cotton factory in Manchester. Soon he was
in business for himself, and by the time he was thirty years of
age had amassed considerable wealth and achieved recognition as one of the most prominent textile manufacturers in
England. With a group of partners he decided in 1799 to buy
an entire textile village at New Lanark, Scotland. It was a
typical mill village of the time—its people (numbering some
2500) were impoverished, living under unsanitary conditions,
working seventeen hours a day at wages that barely provided

subsistence. Children of six years of age and up were employed in the mill as part of the labor force. Sickness and moral corruption were chronic conditions of life.

Owen proceeded with his partners to transform this village into a model community. He reduced the hours of work from seventeen to ten, he forbade the employment of children under ten years of age and established free public schools, he cleaned the town, installed a drainage system, built homes for the workers, abolished the prevalent practice of fines for faulty work in the shop, and raised the wages. All profits over 5 per cent were used to improve conditions for the workers. In 1806 when the Jefferson Embargo Act cut off all supplies of American cotton and he was forced to shut down his mill, Owen continued, unlike other textile employers, to pay his workers their regular wage. And although at first some of the workers had greeted his reforms with derision this act of generosity converted even the most skeptical among them. In 1824 he purchased a 30,000 acre tract of land in Indiana and established a settlement known as New Harmony there the following year. He came to the United States and was invited to deliver a talk before the assembled houses of Congress. By 1827 the settlement had dispersed due to internal dissension and Owen leased the land to private settlers. He tried another unsuccessful experiment at Orbiston, Scotland, about the same time.

Disappointment and the lack of funds caused him to abandon, at the age of 63, any further experiments and to turn his attention to winning converts to his cause by means of writing and lecturing. He was active in the trade union movement and participated in the foundation of the Rochdale cooperatives in 1844. He died at the age of 87 in 1858.

One of his earliest works was a series of essays entitled *A New View of Society* or *Essays on the Formation of Human Character* published in 1813. Here he told the story of New Lanark and urged the adoption of similar methods in other places. In these essays he declared that there is one principle that ought to be the guiding principle of legislation, namely, that "Any general character, from the best to the worst, from the most ignorant to the most enlightened, may be given to any community, even to the world at large, by the application of proper means; which means are to a great extent at the command and under the control of those who have influence in the affairs of men." [29] Character is the product of environment, improve the environment and you will improve the character of men. Evil in the world is due not to a defect in human will but to faulty reasoning. The belief that man shapes his own character is a product of false reasoning: the truth is that man is the product of his environment. If men be "rationally educated" and "their labor be usefully directed" the inhabitants of any community can be trained to lead a perfect, harmonious existence. [30]

Let it not, therefore, be longer said that evil or injurious actions cannot be prevented; or that the most rational habits in the rising generation cannot be universally formed. In those characters which now exhibit crime, the fault is obviously not in the individual, but the defect proceeds from the system in which the individual has been trained. Withdraw those circumstances which tend to create crime in the human character, and crime will not be created . . . for the worst formed disposition, short of incurable insanity, will not long resist a firm, determined, well-directed, persevering kindness. [31]

In 1817 Owen wrote a report for a parliamentary Committee on Poor Laws in which he argued that:

The immediate cause of the present distress is the depreciation of human labour; and which has been occasioned by the general introduction of mechanism into the manufactures of Europe and America, but principally into those of Britain, where the change was greatly accelerated by the inventions of Arkwright and Watt. . . .

When . . . it became necessary to contract the sources of supply, it soon proved that mechanical power was much cheaper than human labour; the former, in consequence was continued at work, while the latter was superseded; and human labour may now be obtained at a price far less than is absolutely necessary for the subsistence of the individual in ordinary comfort. [32]

Three alternative possibilities follow from this fact: (1) reduce the use of machinery, (2) leave things as they are, or (3) find some advantageous employment for the poor and unemployed working classes. The first is impracticable and the second is unthinkable because it would mean starvation for millions. The third alternative can be achieved by establishing cooperative villages averaging about 1000 persons and including both agricultural and industrial workers. Rather than spending vast sums of money on poor relief which offers "greater reward for idleness and vice than for industry and virtue" the money should be used for the establishment of cooperative villages the existence of which in time will make poor relief in any form unnecessary.[33] These communities would be self-sufficient economic units with the advantages both of city and country life. Since the spirit of brotherhood would prevail among the inhabitants, poverty and exploitation would be unknown. A Deist rather than a Christian, Robert Owen summed up his religious beliefs in these words:

Any religion that does not produce *in practice*, universal truth, justice, charity or love, among the whole family of man is spurious— is of no value to the human race. . . . Hitherto, none of the religions of the world, have, in practice, produced truth, justice, charity, or love, among any people. . . .

Man has been created with all the qualities, faculties, and powers, when they shall be directed aright from birth, to enable him to enjoy a high degree of rational happiness; and made, with all that has life upon earth, to desire the attainment and continued enjoyment of happiness.

This end and object of human existence is to be obtained only by the universal introduction and maintenance of *rational religion*, derived from the fundamental laws of humanity. . . .

Happiness can be attained only by the united feelings of charity and love among the entire population of the world.

Charity and love are, therefore, *effects*, which can *proceed only* from their natural *cause*.

Charity and love for our race can emanate only from a correct knowledge of the laws of humanity relative to the formation of man.

And this knowledge of the fundamental laws of our nature is the cause which will always create, in rational-made beings, universal charity and love for our race. . . .

This religion will make all men, trained in it from their birth, to know and practice it—to become good, wise, and happy; and to have their greatest pleasure in promoting, to the utmost of their power, the happiness of all their race. . . .

This is that religion of truth, honesty, and common-sense, which the rational system of society can and will produce over the world. . . .[34]

The older Robert Owen grew, the more radical he became and finally was convinced that only the abolition of private property and the profit system could bring about the establishment of a "rational" and happy society.

To distribute wealth justly and beneficially for all, the world, and all which it contains, must be made the property of all.

Each one will be, as it were, the possessor of the earth, for his free use and enjoyment during life; and will be far more sovereign of the world, than any one is now sovereign over any empire or nation. . . .

But before wealth can be thus, for all, justly and beneficially distributed, it must be justly and beneficially created *by* all. It is vain to expect that one part of the rational system of society can be introduced without all the others, which together constitute a rational state of existence for the human race—a state which will secure to them high intelligence and permanent happiness.[35]

Competition and the profit system go hand in hand. If we would destroy profits we must do away with competition. There must be an end to buying cheap and selling dear and to making profits "by deteriorating the qualities" of articles "for use or consumption." [36] Instead:

All articles for use or consumption will be made or produced of the best qualities that the means of society will admit. They will be stored in the best place to preserve each kind in the most perfection; and, when required, will be freely and liberally given to every one; none having any motive to misuse or waste anything.[37]

Money will be replaced by labor notes since labor is the source of all value. These notes will be distributed to workers in proportion to the hours worked and articles will be "priced" according to the number of labor hours expended upon them.

An actual attempt to try this was made with the establishment of the National Equitable Labor Exchange in London in 1832 but the experiment failed. Gide and Rist enumerate the reasons for the failure by saying:

(a) The associates, being themselves allowed to state the value of their products, naturally exaggerated, and it became necessary to . . . place the valuation in the hands of experts. But these experts . . . valued the goods in money, in the ordinary way, and then expressed those values in labor notes at the rate of 6d. for every hour's work . . . instead of the labor standard determining the selling value of the product, the money value of the product determined the value of the labor.

(b) As soon as the society began to attract members who were not quite as conscientious as those who had first joined it, the Exchange was flooded with goods that were really unsaleable. But for the notes received in exchange for these the authorities would be forced to give goods which possessed a real value . . . with the result that in the long run there would be nothing left in the depot except worthless products. In short, the Exchange would be reduced to buying goods which cost more than they were worth, and selling goods that really cost less than they were worth.

Since the notes were not in any way registered, anyone, whether a member of the society or not, could buy and sell them in the ordinary way and make a handsome profit out of the transaction. Three hundred London tradesmen did this by offering to take labor notes in payment for merchandise. They soon emptied the Exchange, and when they saw that nothing valuable was left they stopped taking the notes, and the trick was done.[38]

But despite the failure of this Exchange, Owen insisted that the principle was correct—that only by abolishing profit could a rational and equitable system of society be established. Although it was largely a by-product of his life-time effort Owen's principal contribution to socialist thought and practice was the establishment of a number of cooperative societies, many of which exist today and continue to be formed.


## Pierre-Joseph Proudhon (1809–1865)

PROUDHON's ideas are difficult to classify. Like all socialists he condemned the institution of private property yet rejected the utopian schemes of Saint-Simon, Fourier and Owen as the embodiment of "crass stupidity." A militant revolutionary he was, nevertheless, equally critical of Marxian Communism.

He has been called, with considerable justification, an anarchist.

Proudhon first received public attention with the publication in 1840 of a book entitled *Qu'est-ce que la Propriété?* (What is Property?). And to the question he propounded he had a ready answer: "Property is theft." Yet, it is not the possession of property as such that he condemned but the use of the title to property to extract rent, profit, and interest. When the possession of property entitles the proprietor to an income he has not earned by his labor, then it is "theft." Without labor both land and capital are unproductive, Proudhon argued, hence when the landowner or capitalist demands a return for the use of his land or money in the form of interest he is, in reality, insisting upon something for nothing and appropriating for himself that which actually belongs to someone else, to labor. Yet at the same time he attacked the socialists.

Property is the exploitation of the weak by the strong. Communism is the exploitation of the strong by the weak. In property, inequality of conditions is the result of force, under whatever name it is disguised. . . . In communism, inequality springs from placing mediocrity on a level with excellence. . . .

Communism is oppression and slavery. Man is willing to obey the law of duty, serve his country, and oblige his friends; but he wishes . . . to act from judgment, not by command. . . . Communism violates the sovereignty of the conscience, and equality: the first, by restricting spontaneity of mind and heart, and freedom of thought and action; the second, by placing labor and laziness, skill and stupidity, and even vice and virtue on an equality in point of comfort. For the rest, if property is impossible on account of the desire to accumulate, communism would soon become so through the desire to shirk.[39]

His principal argument is that "all capital, whether material or mental, being the result of collective labor, is in consequence, collective property" and "that the exchangeable value of a product, being measured neither by the opinion of the buyer nor that of the seller, but by the amount of time and outlay which it has cost, the property of each always remains the same."[40]

Seeking absolute equality which he equates with "liberty"

Proudhon looks forward to the establishment of "anarchy." By anarchy he does not mean disorder and chaos but "the absence of a master" and the rule of law. Reason, not will, should be sovereign. He seeks a "synthesis of communism and property," a society based upon the four principles of "equality, law, independence, and proportionality." [41]

I have accomplished my task; property is conquered, never again to rise. Wherever this work is read and discussed, there will be deposited the germ of death to property; there, sooner or later, privilege and servitude will disappear, and the despotism of will will give place to the reign of reason. What sophisms, indeed, what prejudices (however, obstinate) can stand before the simplicity of the following propositions:—

I. Individual *possession* is the condition of social life. . . . *Property* is the suicide of society. Possession is a right; property is against right. Suppress property while maintaining possession, and by this simple modification of the principle, you will revolutionize law, government, economy, and institutions; you will drive evil from the face of the earth.

II. All having an equal right of occupancy, possession varies with the number of possessors; property cannot establish itself.

III. The effect of labor being the same for all, property is lost in the common prosperity.

IV. All human labor being the result of collective force, all property becomes, in consequence, collective and unitary. To speak more exactly, labor destroys property.

V. Every capacity for labor being, like every instrument of labor, an accumulated capital, and a collective property, inequality of wages and fortunes (on the ground of inequality of capacities) is, therefore, injustice and robbery.

VI. The necessary conditions of commerce are the liberty of the contracting parties and the equivalence of the products exchanged. Now, value being expressed by the amount of time and outlay which each product costs, and liberty being inviolable, the wages of laborers (like their rights and duties) should be equal.

VII. Products are bought only by products. Now, the condition of all exchange being equivalence of products, profit is impossible and unjust. Observe this elementary principle of economy, and pauperism, luxury, oppression, vice, crime, and hunger will disappear from our midst.

VIII. Men are associated by the physical and mathematical law of production, before they are voluntarily associated by choice. Therefore, equality of conditions is demanded by justice. . . .

IX. Free association, liberty—whose sole function is to maintain equality in the means of production and equivalence in exchanges—is the only possible, the only just, the only true form of society.

X. Politics is the science of liberty. The government of man by man (under whatever name it be disguised) is oppression. Society finds its highest perfection in the union of order with anarchy.[42]

Questions of legislation and of politics ought to be matters of science and not of opinion, and the science of government ought to be entrusted "to one of the sections of the Academy of Sciences, whose permanent secretary is necessarily prime minister." [43] Government will consist of scientific analysis by departments of statistics, all decisions concerning domestic and foreign politics, being entrusted to such departments. But since "no one can substitute his will for reason—nobody is king." [44] It is appropriate that Proudhon concluded this section of his book with a prayer to an unidentified "God of liberty and equality." In impassioned phrases Proudhon pleaded with this god to:

Abridge, if possible, the time of our trial, stifle pride and avarice in equality; annihilate this love of glory which enslaves us; teach these poor children that in the bosom of liberty there are neither heroes nor great men! Inspire the powerful man, the rich man, him whose name my lips shall never pronounce in Thy presence, with a horror of his crimes; let him be the first to apply for admission to the redeemed society; let the promptness of his repentance be the ground of his forgiveness! "Then, great and small, wise and foolish, rich and poor, will unite in an ineffable fraternity; and, singing in unison a new hymn, will rebuild Thy altar, O God of liberty and equality!" [45]

He sought to find the principle of equality, as he himself expressed it, "no longer in charity and self-sacrifice . . . but in justice." [46] He appealed not to the love of God but to the dictates of reason. That the "God of liberty and equality" to whom Proudhon offered up his prayer was not, in reality, God, he makes clear in the concluding chapter of his *Philosophy of Misery*.

. . . if there is a being who, before ourselves and more than ourselves, is deserving of hell,—I am bound to name him,—it is God . . .

The first duty of man, on becoming intelligent and free, is to continually hunt the idea of God out of his mind and conscience. For God, if he exists, is essentially hostile to our nature. . . . We arrive at knowledge in spite of him, at comfort in spite of him, at society in spite of him, every step we take in advance is a victory in which we crush Divinity.

Let it no longer be said that the ways of God are impenetrable. We have penetrated these ways, and there we have read in letters of blood the proofs of God's impotence, if not of his malevolence. My reason, long humiliated, is gradually rising to a level with the infinite; with time it will discover all that its inexperience hides from it; with time I shall be less and less a worker of misfortune, and by the light that I shall have acquired, by the perfection of my liberty, I shall purify myself, idealize my being, and become the chief of creation, the equal of God.[47]

## Conclusion

THERE are many varieties of socialists. Those we have considered so far are frequently identified as Utopian socialists. They were, first of all, voluntary socialists, i.e., they believed that socialism to be effective could only be brought into existence voluntarily, and they relied chiefly upon reason, persuasion and education to convert the reluctant. Capitalism, they believed, was self-evidently unreasonable and unjust, its defects had only to be pointed out to convince reasonable men of this fact.

Most of these socialists believed that it was possible to establish, on a voluntary basis, model communities organized along socialistic lines that would serve as examples of the kind of system they hoped universally to substitute for capitalism. Through the widespread adoption of similar projects, socialism would eventually triumph throughout the nation and the world.

Most of these socialists based their case upon humanitarian and moral considerations. Capitalism, they argued, leads inevitably to human degradation and poverty. It is the embodiment of exploitation. It degrades the laboring man into a commodity to be bought and sold like every other commodity and denies the essential dignity of man. It results in a distribution of wealth that is not only unequal but inequitable. The profit system they depicted as a thinly disguised system of force and fraud whereby the laborer was robbed of the real value of his work. They proposed to substitute a system whereby each would work according to his capacity and be rewarded in accordance with his labor, or as some said, with his needs. And they derived many of these conclusions from the labor theory of value first propounded by the liberal economists. Socialism in the latter half of the nineteenth century was increasingly converted, however, into State Socialism and the argument shifted from a humanitarian and moral base to one that claimed to be "scientific."

Socialism aims at nothing less than the re-creation of a new social life through the collective reason of the community and the public ownership and administration of property. Christianity, likewise, promises the re-creation of a new social life but believes that this will be possible only if individuals through the love and worship of God become regenerate. Evil, according to socialist thought, springs primarily from the private ownership of the means of production; evil, according to Christian thought, springs primarily from the misdirected passions of men.

## CHAPTER 12

# Karl Marx and the Rise of "Scientific" Socialism

THE name most frequently associated with socialism is that of Karl Marx and among socialists he has, indeed, been the most influential. It is not, however, as we have seen, the discovery of socialism that accounts for this prominence among them but rather the fact that he sought, and his followers believe with success, to provide socialism with a "scientific" undergirding that assures the inevitable victory of socialism over capitalism. The collapse of capitalism and the coming of socialism are depicted by Marx as events of natural necessity—"natural laws" of economics and of history decree the inevitable victory of socialism over capitalism. And for many of those who have lost the apocalyptic vision of the Kingdom of God, Marx's "revelation" of the coming of the perfect Kingdom of Man has been embraced with all the fervor of religious zeal. Although Marx's vision is no less utopian than that of the socialists who preceded him, it appears to be less utopian to those who believe that the victory of socialism is decreed by History itself.

Karl Marx was born in Treves, in the Rhineland, Germany, on May 5, 1818. His father was a moderately well-to-do lawyer and both Marx's father and mother were descended of a long line of Jewish rabbis. When Karl was six years of age his father became a Protestant Christian by conversion and his children were baptized in that faith. When he was seventeen years of age Karl began the study of law at the University of Bonn but soon abandoned that study in favor of philosophy,

398

the study of which he pursued at the Universities of Berlin and Jena. He was greatly impressed with the dialectical philosophy of Hegel and became an active member of the "Young Hegelians" while still a student. He completed his doctoral dissertation at the University of Jena in 1841 on "The Difference between the Natural Philosophy of Democritus and of Epicurus."

Unable to secure a university appointment as a teacher, Marx embarked upon a career as a free-lance journalist. In 1842 he became the editor of the democratic-liberal *Rheinische Zeitung*, but it was forced to suspend publication the following year when its radicalism brought it into conflict with the Prussian authorities. About that time Marx married Jenny von Westphalen, the daughter of a Prussian aristocrat, and moved to Paris. He became associated as an editor with a magazine published by German exiles in Paris, the *Deutsch-Französische Jahrbücher*. The journal had but one issue, but it had a profound influence on Marx's life. Marx had contributed an article on the economic basis of law and the same issue contained an article by Friedrich Engels. Each was profoundly impressed with the work of the other, and as a consequence, there sprang up between them a friendship that was to last throughout Marx's lifetime. Henceforth, they collaborated not only in political activity but in much of their research and writing.

(Friedrich Engels was born in Barmen, Germany, in 1820 and died in London in 1895. His father was a wealthy textile manufacturer with mills in Barmen, Germany, and Manchester, England. Except for a short period between 1845 and 1850 Engels was actively associated with his father's business and when his father died in 1860 Engels became a partner in the firm. He sold his partnership in 1869 and moved to London where he and Marx worked closely together. He frequently extended financial assistance to Marx who had no regular employment and hence no regular income and in the 1860's began to give Marx the sum of 350 pounds a year as a kind of pension.)

Asked to leave Paris in 1845 Marx went to Brussels, where, the following year, he formed the Communist Correspondence

Committee. In 1847 a Communist League was established by Marx and Engels in London. It was in that year that the two men were commissioned by this League to prepare a statement of principles and this appeared in 1848 as the now famous *Communist Manifesto*. The year 1848 brought revolutionary uprisings throughout most of Europe and in February, 1848, a revolution broke out in France that resulted in the abdication of Louis Philippe and the proclamation of the Second French Republic. An unsuccessful attempt was made to direct the revolution along socialist lines and by 1852 through a *coup d'état* the short-lived Second Republic had succumbed to the restoration of the Empire with Louis Napoleon proclaimed as Emperor Napoleon III. Probably Marx's *Manifesto* had little or nothing to do with the actual uprisings but it was associated with them and Marx, as a consequence, was asked to leave Belgium in 1848 when the authorities there feared that he might foment revolution. He returned to Germany as the editor of the *Neue Rheinische Zeitung* but a year later the paper was suppressed and Marx was ordered to leave the country. He then went to London where he took up permanent residence for the remainder of his life. In September, 1864, Marx was active in the formation in London of the International Working Men's Association. This organization has since been called the First International and it continued in existence with annual meetings until about 1872 when its headquarters were transferred from London to New York where it soon died. After the disruption of this body Marx devoted himself exclusively to research and writing. Shortly after he moved to London he began contributing articles on the German situation to the *New York* (Herald) *Tribune* then under the editorship of Horace Greeley. His life in London was spent in poverty until the 1860's when, through the receipt of some legacies and the generosity of his friend Engels, he was able to live a more comfortable existence. He was in ill health from 1875 to his death in 1883.

He collaborated with Engels in the writing of *The Holy Family* in 1844 and both worked on the *Manifesto* of 1848. He published a polemic directed against Proudhon's *Philosophy of Poverty* (sometimes translated as the *Philosophy of Misery*) and entitled it the *Poverty of Philosophy* (1847). Marx wrote numerous articles and books but his major works are the *Critique of Political Economy* (1859) in which he formulated his economic interpretation of history and the theory of surplus value and the famous "bible" of Marxian socialism, *Das Kapital* or *Capital*, the first volume of which appeared in 1867. He was never able to complete the writing of his magnum opus, some say because of ill health, others because he had worked himself into contradictions from which he could not extricate himself.

In examining Marxian socialism we shall rely not only upon the writings of Marx but upon those of Engels as well, since they were substantially in agreement and Engels often elaborated upon aspects of the system concerning which Marx was silent.

## Basic Presuppositions

AFTER the death of Hegel a controversy arose among his followers concerning the nature of the Absolute. Does it exist independently of human minds? Does it exist incarnate in Jesus Christ? Do individuals survive death or is immortality peculiar only to the Absolute Mind? These and other questions of a similar kind were raised by the followers of Hegel and divided them into two principal groups. "The Hegelian Right" argued that Hegelian philosophy and Christianity were entirely compatible. The "Hegelian Left" or "Young Hegelians" argued that the two were essentially incompatible. Among the latter group the most prominent were David Strauss (1808–1874), Bruno Bauer (1809–1882) and Ludwig Feuerbach (1804–1872). It was with this group that Marx associated himself while a student and its influence upon him was a profound one. Applying the new methods of historical criticism in the spirit of positivism to the narratives in the New Testament, Strauss and Bauer concluded that Christianity had its origins in a myth. Ludwig Feuerbach went one step further and reached the conclusion that God Himself is but a beautiful projection of human hopes and aspirations. Religion is concerned not with the relation of man to God but of man to man and man himself is the highest of all beings. Marx greeted this hypothesis with enthusiasm.

Who has annihilated the dialectic of concepts, the war of the gods which the philosophers alone knew? Feuerbach. Who has put man in place of the old lumber, and in place of the infinite consciousness as well? Feuerbach, and no one else! Feuerbach, who completed and criticized Hegel from a Hegelian standpoint, resolving the metaphysical absolute spirit into the real man standing on the foundation of nature, was the first to complete the criticism of religion—inasmuch as, at the same time, he undertook a critique of Hegelian speculation, and thereby sketched the great and masterly outlines of all metaphysics.[1]

From Feuerbach Marx learned that it is not God who creates man but man who creates God and the discovery of this "truth" had an intoxicating effect upon him. For, if God is the creation of men there is nothing, absolutely nothing, that stands in the way of men to do what they will. Gradually Marx came to the realization that Feuerbach did not appreciate the revolutionary character of his discovery and he determined to push it beyond the frontiers that Feuerbach himself was willing to go. In the essay which appeared in the *Deutsch-Französische Jahrbücher* on Hegel's philosophy of law, Marx declared:

Man makes religion; religion does not make man. Religion, indeed, is the self-consciousness and the self-feeling of the man who either has not yet found himself, or else (having found himself) has lost himself once more. But man is not an abstract being, squatting down somewhere outside the world. Man is the world of men, the State, society. This State, this society, produce religion, produce a perverted world consciousness, because they are a perverted world. . . .

Religion is the sigh of the oppressed creature, the feelings of a heartless world, just as it is the spirit of unspiritual conditions. It is the opium of the people. . . .

The people cannot be really happy until it has been deprived of illusory happiness by the abolition of religion. The demand that the people should shake itself free of illusion as to its own condition is the demand that it should abandon a condition which needs illusion. . . .

Thus it is the mission of history, after the other-worldly truth has disappeared, to establish the truth of this world. In the next place, it is the mission of philosophy, having entered into the service of history after the true nature of the reputed sainthood of human self-estrangement has been disclosed, to disclose all the unsaintliness of this self-estrangement. Thus the criticism of heaven is transformed into a criticism of earth, the criticism of religion into a criticism of law, the criticism of theology into a criticism of politics.[2]

Religion has taught us that man is a stranger in the world, a pilgrim seeking the Kingdom of God. Feuerbach's "discovery" that God is but the creation of man frees us from this illusion. And freed from this illusion mankind can now transform the "condition which needs illusion." Now that we "know" that God does not exist except in our imagination we can look forward with the assurance of certainty to a Kingdom of Man so perfect as not to require the solace of imagination. It is the world that is wrong, it is man that is right and "the root of things is man himself." The emancipation of mankind waits only upon a "radical revolution" to be undertaken by that class which is so estranged from the rest of society that its emancipation must bring about the emancipation of mankind itself.

A radical revolution, the general emancipation of mankind, is not a utopian dream for Germany; what is utopian is the idea of a partial, an exclusively political revolution, which would leave the pillars of the house standing. Upon what does a partial, an exclusively political revolution rest? Upon this, that a part of civil society emancipates itself, and attains to general dominion; upon this, that a particular class, from a position peculiar to itself, should undertake to effect the general emancipation of society. That class can free the whole of society, but only on the proviso that the whole of society is in the position of that class. . . .

What, then, are the practical possibilities of German emancipation? Here is the answer. They are to be found in the formation of a class with radical chains, a class of civil society which is not a class of civil society: of an estate which is the dissolution of all estates; of a sphere which is endowed with a universal character by the universality of its sufferings; one which does not lay claim to any particular rights, the reason being that it does not suffer any one specific injustice, but suffers injustice unqualified; one which can no longer put forward a historically grounded title, but only a general human title; one which is not in any sort of one-sided opposition to the consequences, but only in a general opposition to the presuppositions of the German political system; and, finally, a sphere which cannot emancipate itself, without emancipating itself from all the other spheres of society—one which, in a word, has been completely deprived of its human privileges, so that it can only regain itself by fully regaining these human privileges. This dissolution of society as a particular estate is—the proletariat.[3]

In *The Holy Family* (1844) Marx carried these ideas forward in the direction of a more explicit socialism. Here he argues that "the proletariat fulfils the judgment which private property has brought upon itself by the creation of the proletariat." Because the proletariat *is* the proletariat, it is compelled "to abolish itself and therewith to abolish private property, the opposite that has determined its own existence, that has made it into a proletariat." In revolting against the unhuman conditions of life to which the institution of private property condemns the proletariat, the proletariat liberates not only itself but mankind as a whole "because, in the proletariat, the human being has lost himself, but has gained something more than the theoretical awareness of this loss, for he has gained this in addition, that it has become an imperious necessity for him to revolt against unhumanity." History is not an encounter between man and God, it is not a conflict between spirit and matter, it is not the unfolding of the spirit of the Absolute, it "is nothing else than the activity of man pursuing his own aims."[4] According to Marx

No great perspicacity is needed—setting out from the teachings of materialism regarding the primitive goodness and the equal intellectual endowments of man; regarding the omnipotence of experience, habit, education, environing conditions over man; regarding the great importance of industry, the right to enjoyment, etc., etc.,—to deduce the necessary connexion of materialism with communism and socialism. If man derives all his knowledge and his perceptions, etc., from the world of the senses and from experience in the world of the senses, it is our business to order the empirical world in such a way that man shall have truly human experiences in it, shall experience himself to be a human being. If self-interest rightly understood is the basic principle of morality, it behoves us to make sure that the private interest of the individual shall coincide with the general human interest. If man is unfree in the materialist sense (this meaning that he is free, not through the negative power of avoiding this or that, but through the positive power of fulfilling his own true individuality), it behoves us, not to punish individual offences, but to destroy the anti-social food of crime, and to give every one social space for the manifestation of his life activities. *If man is formed by circumstances, we must make the circumstances human. If man is social by nature, he can only develop his true nature in society, and we must measure the power of his nature, not by the power of the isolated individual, but by the power of society.*[5]

According to Marx, man as "a product of existing historical forms" is not the real man but man divided, incomplete, estranged. Only "in a communist society where every man can develop himself in any way he chooses" will the true nature of man be revealed. Historical man, man as he exists here and now, has, as a consequence, no absolute value. He acquires value only to the extent that he is the spearhead of the positive forces of history. Society alone can produce the "true" man but produce him, it will, in the inevitable course which history decrees. Through the social crisis that must end in revolution, the dictatorship of the proletariat and the establishment of the communist society, man finally becomes incarnate. The instrument of this incarnation is the proletariat and the means is the destruction of private property through revolution.

## Dialectical Materialism

IN THE *Theses on Feuerbach* written in 1845 but first published as an appendix to the 1888 edition of Engel's *Ludwig Feuerbach*, Marx laid the foundations for what he called dialectical materialism. A few excerpts from those "theses" illustrate the trend of Marx's thought at this time:

## I

The chief defect of all hitherto existing materialism—that of Feuerbach included—is that the object, reality, sensuousness, is conceived only in the form of the *object* or *contemplation* but not as *human sensuous activity, practice,* not subjectively. . . .

## II

The question whether objective truth can be attributed to human thinking is not a question of theory, but is a practical question. In practice man must prove the truth, i.e., the reality and power, the "this-sidedness" of his thinking. The dispute over the reality or non-reality of thinking which is isolated from practice is a purely scholastic question.

## III

. . . The coincidence of the changing of circumstances and of human activity can only be conceived and rationally understood as revolutionising activity.

## IV

Feuerbach starts out from the fact of religious self-alienation, the duplication of the world into a religious, imaginary world and a real one. His work consists in the dissolution of the religious world into its secular basis. He overlooks the fact that after completing this work, the chief thing still remains to be done. For the fact that the secular foundation lifts itself and establishes itself in the clouds as an independent realm is only to be explained by the self-cleavage and self-contradictoriness of this secular basis. The latter must itself, therefore, first be understood in its contradiction and then, by the removal of the contradiction, revolutionised in practice. . . .

## VIII

Social life is essentially *practical*. All mysteries which mislead theory to mysticism find their rational solution in human practice and in the comprehension of this practice.

## X

The standpoint of the old materialism is "civil society"; the standpoint of the new is *human* society or socialized humanity.

## XI

The philosophers have only *interpreted* the world in various ways; the point however is to change it.[6]

In the first of these theses Marx says that Reality is nothing more and nothing less than "human sensuous activity," or, rather, that this is what reality is capable of becoming and, hence, what it is. Nowhere, however, does Marx analyze the relationship between matter and mind and his refusal to examine the question in detail leads to considerable confusion concerning his real meaning. The truth of the matter is that Marx was not himself a profound philosopher. Whatever profundity his system has is a profundity borrowed from the Hegelian philosophy from which it is derived. He insisted, however, that he was neither an Idealist nor a Materialist and preferred to describe his "philosophy" as "dialectical materialism." He accepted the Hegelian dialectic (which we discussed in a previous chapter) as the key to the understanding of reality but argued that reality is not, as Hegel posited, the Idea, but matter in motion.

What Marx apparently objects to in the theses quoted above is any kind of metaphysical speculation even if that speculation leads to materialistic conclusions about the nature of ultimate reality. He draws a sharp distinction between human thought and human action and insists that only human action is important and "real." Nevertheless, he proceeds to erect a theory of revolution upon a metaphysical interpretation of history while he disclaims doing any such thing. As a consequence, there is a fundamental ambiguity and contradiction running throughout the Marxian system: it is claimed on the one hand that there is no such thing as absolute truth or absolute reality, that all judgments of truth and error, good and bad, are relative and particular judgments only, yet at the same time Marx claims to have discovered *the* absolute truth about the meaning and direction of history.

The key to the understanding of history is what he calls "dialectical materialism." But for the clearest explanation of what this is we must turn to the writings of Engels. Except for the hints contained in the "Theses on Feuerbach," Marx himself is not very explicit. Both Marx and Engels insist that their version of materialism is something radically different from what they call mechanistic materialism. The mechanistic materialists, Engels says, speak of matter *and* motion whereas "true" or dialectical materialism regards matter and motion as inseparable.

*Motion is the mode of existence of matter.* Never anywhere has there been matter without motion, nor can there be . . . at each given moment each individual atom of matter in the world is in one or other of these forms of motion. . . . All rest, all equilibrium, is only relative, and only has meaning in relation to one or other definite form of motion. . . . Matter without motion is just as unthinkable as motion without matter. Motion is therefore as uncreatable and indestructible as matter itself. . . . Motion cannot therefore be created; it can only be transferred. When motion is transferred from one body to another, in so far as it transfers itself, is active, it may be regarded as the cause of motion, in so far as the latter is transferred, is passive. We call this active motion *force*, and the passive, the *manifestation of force*. In this it is as clear as daylight that the force is equal to its manifestation, because in fact it is the *same* motion which takes place in both.[7]

The ultimate reality is matter in motion, a process. Moreover, this is a *dialectical* process, the reconciliation of opposing movements in an endless effort to achieve a more perfect harmony. Matter contains within itself the energy necessary to transform it, matter is self-moving or self-determining. The universe is self-sufficient, self-creating, self-perpetuating. Hegel explained the dialectical process as the activity of God in the world; Marx borrows the "energy" from Hegel's immanent God but disassociates it from God and locates it in matter itself. Engels declares that:

Motion itself is a contradiction: even simple mechanical change of place can only come about through a body at one and the same amount of time being both in one place and in another place, being in one and the same place and also not in it. And the continuous assertion and simultaneous solution of this contradiction is precisely what motion is.

And if simple mechanical change of place contains a contradiction, this is even more true of the higher forms of motion of matter, and especially of organic life and its development . . . life consists just precisely in this—that a living thing is at each moment itself and yet something else. Life is therefore also a contradiction which is present in things and processes themselves, and which constantly asserts and solves itself; and as soon as the contradiction ceases, life too comes to an end, and death steps in.[8]

Engels makes the jump from inorganic matter to organic "life" without any explanation and presumably regards organic "life" as nothing more than a complex form of material existence.

Engels explains the transformation of Hegel's dialectic in these words:

According to Hegel . . . the dialectical development apparent in nature and history, i.e., the causal inter-connection of the progressive movement from the lower to the higher, which asserts itself through all zigzag movements and temporary setbacks, is only a miserable copy of the self-movement of the concept going on from eternity, no one knows where, but at all events independently of any thinking human brain. This ideological reversal had to be done away with. We comprehended the concepts in our heads once more materialistically—as images of real things instead of regarding the real things as images of this or that stage of development of the absolute concept. Thus dialectics reduced itself to the science of the general laws of motion—both of the external world and of human thought— two sets of laws which are identical in substance, but differ in their expression in so far as the human mind can apply them consciously, while in nature and also up to now for the most part in human history, these laws assert themselves unconsciously in the form of external necessity in the midst of an endless series of seeming accidents. Thereby the dialectic of the concept itself became merely the conscious reflex of the dialectical motion of the real world and the dialectic of Hegel was placed upon its head; or rather, turned off its head, on which it was standing before, and placed upon its feet again.[9]

And in another place he wrote: "Dialectics is nothing more than the science of the general laws of motion and development of Nature, human society and thought." [10] Thought itself is a natural process acting upon and being acted upon by the natural environment in which it takes place. It is impossible to transcend the natural process—there are "the general laws of motion and development" and that is all. Human nature has no reality apart from this natural process, it is part and parcel of it. Reality, if the word can be used, is in a constant state of flux and change and truth is what the "general laws of motion" bring about. There is only the truth of the moment which exists to give rise to a new truth.

# The Economic Interpretation of History

ACCORDING to Engels, speaking at Marx's graveside, it was Marx's great achievement that he

discovered the law of evolution in human history; he discovered the simple fact, hitherto concealed by an overgrowth of ideology, that mankind must first of all eat and drink, have shelter and clothing, before it can pursue politics, science, religion, art, etc.; and that therefore the production of the immediate material means of subsistence and consequently the degree of economic development attained by a given people or during a given epoch, form the foundation upon which the state institutions, the legal conceptions, the art and even the religious ideas of the people have been evolved, and in the light of which these things must therefore be explained, instead of *vice versa* as had hitherto been the case.[11]

Yet nowhere in the writings of Marx do we find a systematic account of this economic interpretation of history and of its implications. We must search for it in scattered extracts and in various places and, as a matter of fact, it is Engel's speech, quoted above, that is frequently cited as one of the best summaries of that interpretation. As a consequence, there is great controversy over just what Marx's economic interpretation is and what it means. It is explained by Engels in another place in these words:

The materialist conception of history starts from the principle that production, and with production the exchange of its products, is the basis of every social order; that in every society which has appeared in history the distribution of its products, and with it the division of society into classes or estates, is determined by what is produced and how it is produced, and how the product is exchanged. According to this conception, the ultimate causes of all social changes and political revolutions are to be sought, not in the minds of men, in their increasing insight into eternal truth and justice, but in changes in the mode of production and exchange; they are to be sought not in the *philosophy* but in the *economics* of the period concerned.[12]

We find passages in *The Eighteenth Brumaire* and in *The German Ideology* in which Marx makes passing references to the economic interpretation of history but probably the best single statement by Marx himself is contained in his Preface to the *Critique of Political Economy* (1859). Here Marx states in summary form his economic interpretation of history in these words:

In the social production of their means of existence men enter into definite, necessary relations which are independent of their will, productive relationships which correspond to a definite stage of development of their material productive forces. The aggregate of these productive relationships constitutes the economic structure of society, the real basis on which a juridical and political superstructure arises, and to which definite forms of social consciousness correspond. The mode of production of the material means of existence conditions the whole process of social, political, and intellectual life. It is not the consciousness of men that determines their existence, but, on the contrary, it is their social existence that determines their consciousness. At a certain stage of their development the material productive forces of society come into contradiction with the existing productive relationships, or, what is but a legal expression for these, with the property relationships within which they had moved before. From forms of development of the productive forces these relationships are transformed into their fetters. Then an epoch of social revolution opens. With the change in the economic foundation the whole vast superstructure is more or less rapidly transformed. In considering such revolutions it is necessary always to distinguish between the material revolution in the economic conditions of production, which can be determined with scientific accuracy, and the juridical, political, religious, aesthetic, or philosophic—in a word, ideological forms wherein men become conscious of this conflict and fight it out. Just as we cannot judge an individual on the basis of his own opinion of himself, so such a revolutionary epoch cannot be judged from its own consciousness; but on the contrary this consciousness must be explained from the contradictions of material life, from the existing conflict between social productive forces and productive relationships. A social system never perishes before all the productive forces have developed for which it is wide enough; and new, higher productive relationships never come into being before the material conditions for their existence have been brought to maturity within the womb of the old society itself. . . . In broad outline, the Asiatic, the ancient, the feudal and the modern bourgeois modes of production can be indicated as progressive epochs in the economic system of society. Bourgeois productive relationships are the last antagonistic form of the social process of production . . . but the productive forces developing within the womb of bourgeois society at the same time create the material conditions for the solution of this antagonism. With this social system, therefore, the pre-history of human society comes to a close. . . .[13]

Marx is not a careful writer and for that reason his meaning is not always clear. In the passage quoted above, for example, he writes in one sentence that "The mode of production . . . *conditions* (*bedingt*) the whole process of social, political, and intellectual life." While in the very next sentence he writes that "It is not the consciousness of men that *determines* (*bestimmt*) their existence, but, on the contrary, it is their social existence that *determines* their consciousness." It is, as a consequence, of such contradictions that there is such a voluminous and conflicting literature on "what Marx really meant." Does Marx mean that the mode of production determines the whole process of social and intellectual life or only that it conditions it? Paul Barth says that he means "determines"—"There is . . . according to Marx this causal series: a determined state of technique—determined industrial form—determined property system . . .—determined political structure—determined social forms of consciousness, which are characterized as religious, artistic, or philosophical." [14] It is questionable, however, whether Marx meant by the phrase "mode of production" technique exclusively or whether he meant to include other factors of production as well.[15] There are statements throughout Marx's writings in which he very clearly identifies production with technique:

In acquiring new productive forces men change their mode of production, and in changing their mode of production, their manner of gaining a living, they change all their social relations. The windmill gives you society with the feudal lord; the steam-mill society with the industrial capitalist.[16]

The bourgeoisie cannot exist without constantly revolutionizing the instruments of production, and thereby the relations of production, and with them the whole relations of society.[17]

Relics of by-gone instruments of labor possess the same importance for the investigation of extinct economic forms of society as do fossil bones for the determination of extinct species of animals. It is not the articles made, but how they are made, and by what instruments, that enables us to distinguish different economic epochs.[18]

Technology discloses man's mode of dealing with Nature, the process of production by which he sustains his life, and thereby also lays bare the mode of formation of his social relations, and of the mental conceptions that flow from them.[19]

Yet, in other places Marx and Engels insist that it is not technology alone which is the basis of social systems but the "mode of production" or "the productive forces."

The materialist conception of history starts from the principle that production, and with production the exchange of its products, is the basis of every social order. . . . According to this conception, the ultimate causes of all social changes and political revolutions are to be sought . . . in changes in the mode of production and exchange.[20]

In the long passage quoted earlier from the *Critique of Political Economy*, Marx declared that "The aggregate . . . productive relationships constitutes the economic structure of society, the real basis on which a juridical and political superstructure arises, and to which definite forms of social consciousness correspond." M. M. Bober comments upon this particular controversy by saying:

On the one hand, certain statements by Marx and Engels and to some extent their discussion of the transition from the gens order to ancient slavery indicate that they consider technology of predominant influence in social organization. On the other hand, an examination of their concepts of production and productive forces, as well as a study of their account of the evolution of productive systems place the root causes of history in a larger light. Of these two views which one is to be chosen?

It would be better to keep both in mind. There is no reason to ignore what Marx and his colleague state repeatedly and clearly. But if a choice has to be made, it seems that the evidence and spirit of their writings combine to justify a preference for the broader interpretation. It seems that when they advance the mode of production as the controlling factor in history, "in the last instance," they refer to an organic whole characterized by the following components: (1) the organization of labor in a scheme of division and cooperation, the skills of labor, and the status of labor in the social context with respect to degrees of freedom or servitude; (2) the geographical environment and the knowledge of the use of resources and materials; and (3) technical means and processes and the state of science generally.[21]

Whichever view we choose to take, it is apparent that Marx and Engels are themselves ambiguous in their statements and often inconsistent. We can make the Marxian explanation consistent only by ignoring certain statements in preference for others. The best we can say is, that in some places Marx and Engels declare that technology determines the mode of production, while in other places they conceive of the mode of production as being determined not only by technology but by other factors including "the state of science generally."

According to Marx and Engels, the earliest economic order was a communistic one. Relying upon the investigations of the American anthropologist Lewis Morgan for his own conception of primitive society Engels believed that primitive society was best exemplified among the Iroquois Indians of North America.

It is the magnificent but at the same time the limiting feature of gens society that it had no place for domination and subjection. Within gens society there was as yet no distinction between rights and obligations; the question whether participation in public affairs, revenge for the murder of kinsmen or other expiatory act, is a right or a duty, does not exist for the Indian; it would seem to him as absurd as the question whether eating, sleeping, hunting is a right or a duty. Just as little can a division of the tribe and the gens into different classes take place. . . .

The division of labor is purely natural; it exists only between the two sexes. . . . Each owns the tools made and used by each: the man owns the weapons and the instruments for hunting and fishing, the woman the household equipment. The housekeeping is communal for several families, often a great many. Whatever is used and made in common is common property. . . . Here, therefore, and as yet only here, exists that "self-made property" falsely ascribed by jurists and economists to civilized society—the last fictitious legal subterfuge on which modern capitalist property still rests.[22]

This idyllic existence "so wonderful . . . in all its natural simplicity," however, was soon transformed by the advent of private property. But Engels does not tell us how this came about, in fact, he says: "we do not know how and when the herds passed from the common possession of the tribe or the gens into the property of the individual heads of families." [23] When the pastoral tribes separated themselves from the great mass of barbarians there took place the first great social division of labor, and from this "sprang the first great cleavage of society into two classes: masters and slaves, exploiters and exploited." [24] With the separation of handicrafts from agriculture the second great division of labor took place, with the result that "slavery, in the preceding period still coming into existence and sporadic, now became an essential part of the social system: slaves ceased to be mere auxiliaries and were driven in dozens to work in the fields and workplaces." [25] At this stage the pairing marriage gave way to monogamy, the individual family became the basic economic unit of society, and full private ownership of property came into existence. Also rich and poor first made their appearance. Engels characterizes these stages as the lower, middle and upper stages of barbarism.

With the dawn of civilization a new division of labor takes place as a result of the increased production which stimulates trade, commerce and navigation and a new class, engaged not in the production but in the exchange of products, arises—the merchant class.

Now for the first time a class arose which, without in any way participating in production, won for itself the directing role over production as a whole and threw the producers into economic subjection; a class which made itself the indispensable mediator between every two producers and exploited them both. Under the pretext of relieving the producers of the trouble and risk of exchange, and extending the sale of their products to the most distant markets . . . a class of parasites was formed, real social bloodsuckers, who as compensation for very slight actual services skimmed the cream off both home and foreign production, rapidly acquired enormous wealth and corresponding social influence, and precisely because of this throughout the period of civilization attained ever fresh honors and ever greater control of production, until it ultimately brought to light a product of its own: the periodical commercial crises.[26]

With the division of society into classes the gens organization is replaced by the state. According to Engels: the State

. . . is the product of society at a certain stage of development; it is the admission that this society has become entangled in an insoluble contradiction with itself. . . . But in order that these antagonisms, classes with conflicting economic interests, may not consume themselves and society in sterile struggle, a power apparently standing above society becomes necessary, whose purpose is to moderate the conflict and keep it within the bounds of "order. . . ." [27]

The State is characterized by the grouping of subjects on a territorial basis, the establishment of a police force and army and the ability to levy taxes and contract debts. But although "the State arose out of the need to hold class antagonisms in check" it arose at the same time in the midst of class conflict and, as a consequence, becomes the instrument of "the most powerful, economically dominant class, which by virtue thereof becomes also the dominant class politically, and thus acquires new means of holding down and exploiting the oppressed class." [28] Although the State, in other words, *appears* to be above the conflict of classes, and *appears* to hold that conflict in check, it actually is, from the very beginning, an instrument of class coercion.

We need not trace in detail the subsequent history of human society as Marx and Engels conceive of it—the main outlines are clear. The economic interpretation of history is applied by them with most confidence to the modern period of human history and their principal concern is with capitalistic society as it existed in the nineteenth century. The *Communist Manifesto* summarizes their conclusions concerning the history of human society from its earliest beginnings to the present day in these words:

The history of all hitherto existing society is the history of class struggles. Freeman and slave, patrician and plebian, lord and serf, guild-master and journeyman, in a word, oppressor and oppressed, stood in constant opposition to one another, carried on an uninterrupted, now hidden, now open fight, a fight that each time ended in a revolutionary reconstitution of society at large or in the common ruin of the contending classes.[29]

With the discovery of America, the opening up of new markets throughout the world, with the growth in navigation, commerce and industry feudalism gave way to capitalism. And under capitalism "the bourgeoisie . . . created more massive and more colossal productive forces than have all preceding generations together." [30] At the same time the rise of the bourgeoisie (capitalists) gave rise to a new social class, the industrial working class or proletariat—a class "who live only so long as they find work, and who find work only so long as their labor increases capital." [31] Labor becomes a commodity to be bought and sold like every other commodity, its fortunes "exposed to all the vicissitudes of competition, to all the fluctuations of the market." [32] Capitalism does not destroy slavery but perpetuates it in a disguised form and the wage-earner is more truly called a "wage-slave."

For a time a large middle class serves as a kind of buffer between the capitalists and the proletariat but as time goes on this middle class begins to disappear sinking gradually into the ranks of the proletariat. The proletariat sink lower and lower into poverty as the bourgeoisie become richer and richer and fewer in number. Eventually and inevitably the bourgeoisie and the proletariat become locked in deadly embrace, violent revolution breaks out, a dictatorship of the proletariat is established, and the bourgeoisie are dispossessed of their property. With state ownership of the means of production and the liquidation of the last remnants of capitalism the dictatorship of the proletariat disappears, coercion is replaced everywhere by voluntary cooperation, and the classless society toward which history has been inevitably moving comes into being.

## *Marx's Economic Theory*

ACCORDING to Engels, Marx's two great discoveries were the economic interpretation of history and the doctrine of surplus-value. Through these two discoveries Engels claims that socialism became a science. Before we can consider Marx's doctrine of surplus-value, however, we must first examine his conception of value.

Marx distinguishes at the outset, in the classical tradition, between *value in use* and *value in exchange.* Value in use is the utility of an object in terms of its ability to satisfy human wants. Value in exchange is the ratio in which commodities are exchangeable for other commodities. Nothing can have value without being an object of utility but not all objects of utility have exchange value. Bread as an article of food has value in use; when it is sold or bartered for other commodities it has another kind of value, value in exchange. This value in exchange depends, Marx argues, upon the quantity of labor expended in its production. The exchange-value is not determined by its use-value but solely upon the number of social necessary labor hours expended upon it. Marx explains it in these words:

Let us take two commodities, e.g., wheat and iron. . . . Let us suppose a ton of wheat to be equivalent to two tons of iron. What does this equation mean? It means that a common property of the same dimension exists in two different things—in a ton of wheat and also in two tons of iron. The two things are thus equal to a third, which in itself is neither the one nor the other. So far as constituting exchange values, each of the two must therefore be reducible to the third in question.

This property possessed in common cannot be a natural quality inherent in commodities. Their natural physical qualities only come under consideration at all in so far as such qualities render these commodities useful, i.e., in so far as they confer on the latter a value in use. In the exchange of commodities, abstraction is to all intents and purposes made of the value in use in such commodities. In this case one value in use is worth just as much as any other, if only it be available in the proper proportion. . . .

If we make abstraction of the value in use of commodities, they appear henceforth under one single aspect, namely as *products of labour* . . . it is quite indifferent whether the labour power in question was expended by a carpenter, a stonemason, or a spinner. All products of labour . . . merely demonstrate that human labour power has been expended in their production and that labour is accumulated in them.

The exchange value of a commodity thus only exists because, and in so far as abstract human labour is embodied in that commodity. . . .

The total labour power of society which is embodied in the sum total of the values of all commodities existing at any given moment, is to be considered as one homogeneous mass of human labour power, although it consists in the labour power of society and operates as such, i.e., in so far as it needs the working-time necessary on an average, or socially necessary, for the production of a commodity. Socially necessary is only such working-time as is required for producing a value in use under existing normal conditions of production and with the average amount of skill and intensity prevalent at the time. . . .

Thus it is only the quantity of labour or of working-time socially necessary for its production, which determines the exchange value of a commodity. . . . The value of a commodity is to the value of every other commodity as the working-time necessary for the production of one commodity to the working-time necessary for the production of others.[33]

The distinction between value in use and value in exchange is a distinction which was familiar to Aristotle and insisted upon by the classical economists. What Marx did was to divorce the two completely from one another and to deny categorically that value in use has any determining influence upon value in exchange. That the value common to all commodities consists solely of the labor expended upon them Marx nowhere really proves, but only *assumes*. But if value in use has nothing to do with exchange-value why does Marx say that "nothing can have value without being an object of utility?" [34] This can be so only if the use-value enters into the exchange-value of a

commodity. In the passage quoted above Marx declared that
"In the exchange of commodities . . . one value in use is
worth just as much as any other, if only it be available in the
proper proportion." Why must it be available *in the proper
proportion* if use-value is not of importance, and of decisive
importance, in the determination of exchange-value?

For support of the notion, however, that the exchange-value
of a commodity depends exclusively upon the labor embodied
in it Marx could, with some justification, appeal to such classical economists as Adam Smith and Ricardo. The labor theory
of value was theirs, what Marx did was to draw inferences
from that theory which they were unwilling to draw. In that
sense, his theory was only a logical derivation from economic
liberalism.

At any rate, it is upon this basis that Marx develops the
doctrine of *surplus-value.* Because the laborer does not own the
means of production he must sell his services and his labor,
therefore, becomes an object to be bought and sold like any
other commodity. Since it is a commodity the distinctions
which Marx made earlier between use-value and exchange-
value apply here, too. There is a difference between the use-
value of labor and its exchange-value; its use-value consists of
the value of the products which it produces but its exchange-
value depends solely upon the cost of the food, clothing and
shelter necessary for sustenance and physical survival. The
capitalist, Marx says, pays only for the exchange-value of labor
capacity, but aims at obtaining its use-value. The difference
between the exchange-value of labor capacity and its use-
value is *surplus-value.* This surplus-value is appropriated by the
capitalist in the forms of profit, rent, and interest and is used
by him to acquire greater quantities of surplus-value by expanding production and employing more labor. Marx explains it in these words:

> The value of labour power and the utilization of that power in the
> labour process are two different things. The capitalist had this dif-
> ference in value in view when buying the labour power. The latter's
> useful quality, i.e., the capacity for producing yarn or boots, was
> merely an indispensable secondary condition, because in order to
> create value, labour in an useful shape must be performed. What was

decisive was the peculiar value in use in this commodity, *which is a source of value, and of value greater than it possesses itself.* This is the service which the capitalist expected from it. And he acted in conformity with the eternal laws governing the exchange of commodities. For it is a fact that the vendor of labour power, like the vendor of every other commodity, obtains its exchange value and sells its value in use. The value in use of his labour power, i.e., the labour itself, belongs just as little to the vendor as the value in use in oil which has been sold belongs to the oil dealer. The capitalist has paid the daily value of labour power; consequently its use during the day, the whole day's labour belongs to him. The circumstance that the daily sustenance of labour power only costs half a working day, although such labour power can be in action the entire day—that consequently the value which its employment creates in a single day is double its own daily value; this circumstance is doubtless particularly lucky for the purchaser, but by no means an injustice towards the vendor.

Our capitalist has foreseen this state of things, which was the cause of his hilarity. The laborer therefore finds in the workshop not only the means of production necessary for working six hours, but also those necessary for working twelve hours. . . .

If we compare the process of creating value with that of creating surplus-value, we see the latter to be but the continuation of the former beyond a definite point. If the process be only carried as far as the point where the value paid by capital for labour power be replaced by an exact equivalent, then it is simply a process of producing value. But if the process be continued beyond that point, it becomes a process of creating surplus-value.[35]

The value which labor produces beyond that which is socially necessary to sustain itself is surplus-value. It is a value, Marx declares, acquired without compensation and by the work of others and hence is a form of theft. Capital, he defines, as the sum total of all the privately owned means of production employed for the acquisition of surplus value. Accordingly the essence of capital is, by definition, the exploitation of labor.

Marx divides the total capital into two kinds: *constant* capital and *variable* capital. Constant capital is "that part of the capital expended by the capitalist for procuring means of production, i.e., raw materials, machinery, buildings, etc." The value of this part, he argues, remains constant since this kind of capital is not productive of surplus-value. Variable capital is "the capital expended on buying labor power." This capital "reproduces its own value and yields a surplus-value over and above the latter." [36] Variable capital is the amount paid by the capitalist in the form of wages. In mathematical form Marx stated his theory thus: Let C stand for the total capital advanced, let c stand for the constant part and v for the variable part, then at the beginning of the process of production $C = c + v$. After the process of production is completed we have an amount of manufactured goods that can be represented by the formula $C = c + v + m$. In this formula "m" stands for the absolute surplus-value. To determine the ratio of increase in the original capital it is necessary to abstract from c, to make $c = O$, and to consider only the ratio between "m" and "v." The ratio of surplus-value is its proportion to the variable capital and may be expressed thus: $\frac{m}{v}$ or $\frac{surplus\ labor}{necessary\ labor}$. The greater the ratio the greater the exploitation of the laborer by the capitalist. In making his calculations, however, the capitalist does not divide his total capital outlay into constant and variable parts. The ratio of profit, therefore, is not the same as the ratio of surplus-value but rather is the proportion between the surplus-value and the total capital invested, or $\frac{m}{c + v}$. It follows from this, according to Marx, that the larger the variable capital expended (the larger the wage-bill) the greater the profits will be. The capitalist, therefore, will seek to keep the outlay of constant capital as small as possible while increasing the amount of variable capital employed in production. It will also be to the pecuniary interest of the capitalist to keep the labor force employed as long a time as possible, to keep the wage rate as low as possible, to employ cheap labor in the form of women and children, and to increase production by the introduction of mechanical labor-saving devices. "But here we are met with an anomaly which is the despair of all Marxian commentators, and which must have caused Marx himself some amount of embarrassment, if we may judge by the laborious demonstration which he gives." For:

If fixed capital is really unproductive, how is it that modern production is always increasing the quantity of fixed capital which it employs, until this has now become one of its most familiar features? . . . Again, how are we to account for the variation in the rates of profit in different industries according to the different quantities of capital employed, seeing that it is an axiom of political economy that under a regime of free competition with equal security for everybody the returns on different capital should everywhere be the same?

Marx replies by saying that the rate of profit is the same for all capitalists within the country, but this rate is the average of the different rates in all the different industries. In other words, it is the rate that would obtain if every industry in the country employing varying amounts of fixed and circulating capital formed a part of one whole. . . .

While admiring the ingenuity of the dialectics, we must not blind ourselves to the simple fact which Marx was so anxious to hide, but which is nevertheless implicit in all this, namely, that the rate of profit which means also the value of the goods, is regulated by competition—that is, by demand and supply—but bears no relation to the quantity of labor employed. We must also remember that the *entrepreneur*, far from seeing his profits diminish as he employs less human labor, finds them increasing. This contradiction is just one of those flaws that finally cause the downfall of the majestic edifice so laboriously raised by Marx.[37]

Despite this contradiction Marx went on to argue in this way: the larger the rate of surplus-value, the greater becomes the total amount of capital in use. A large part of this surplus-value is reinvested in constant capital so that in order to keep the same amount of profit there must be an increase in the rate of surplus-value, i.e., in the rate of exploitation. More and more machinery is introduced into the productive process in order to increase production while at the same time decreasing the number of laborers necessary to be employed. This creates a large "industrial reserve army" which brings down the exchange value of labor power.

. . . within the capitalist system all methods for raising the social productiveness of labor are brought about at the cost of the individual laborer; all means for the development of production transform themselves into means of domination over, and exploitation of, the producers; they mutilate the laborer into a fragment of a man, degrade him to the level of an appendage of a machine, destroy every remnant of charm in his work and turn it into a hated toil . . . they transform his lifetime into working-time, and drag his wife and children beneath the wheels of the Juggernaut of capital. But all the methods for the production of surplus-value are at the same time methods of accumulation; and every extension of accumulation becomes again a means for the development of those methods. It follows, therefore, that in proportion as capital accumulates, the lot of the laborer, be his payment high or low, must grow worse. The law, finally, that always equilibrates to relative surplus-population, or industrial reserve army, to the extent and energy of accumulation, this law rivets the laborer to capital more firmly than the wedges of Hephaistos did Prometheus to the rock. It establishes an accumulation of misery, corresponding with accumulation of capital. Accumulation of wealth at one pole is, therefore, at the same time accumulation of misery, agony of toil, slavery, ignorance, brutality, moral degradation, at the opposite pole.[38]

Growth in capital, and growth in poverty, go hand in hand and this is the fundamental contradiction in capitalism that must inevitably lead to its downfall. Concurrently with the overaccumulation of capital and the increasing poverty of the working class go the concentration of industries and the centralization of control. Large-scale production, accelerated by the accumulation of capital, leads to greater productivity, to greater profits and to great accumulation of capital. At the same time independent enterprises are merged into larger and larger units. Competition destroys the small capitalist and his properties and markets are taken over by the larger capitalists. Gigantic monopolies under centralized management and control are the result. Capital gravitates into fewer and fewer hands. The credit system is discovered as a new weapon of competition and "by unseen threads it . . . draws the disposable money, scattered in larger or smaller masses over the surface of society, into the hands of individual or associated capitalists. It is the specific machine for the centralization of capitals." [39]

As soon as this process of transformation has sufficiently decomposed the old society from top to bottom, as soon as the laborers are turned into proletarians, their means of labor into capital, as soon as the capitalist mode of production stands on its own feet, then the further socialization of labor and the further transformation of the land and other means of production, as well as the further expropriation of private proprietors takes a new form. That which is now to be expropriated is no longer the laborer working for himself, but the capitalist exploiting many laborers. This expropriation is accomplished by the action of the immanent laws of capitalistic production itself, by the centralization of capital. One capitalist always kills many.[40]

The accumulation and centralization of capital accelerates a fall in the rate of profit since there is an increasing rise in the amount of constant over variable capital. This leads to overproduction both of capital and of commodities. And this is what is responsible, Marx says, for the periodic economic crises which capitalism experiences. These crises are simply reflections of the contradictions inherent in capitalism and as those contradictions become more and more apparent the crises must inevitably become more frequent and more severe. These crises, moreover, are but an intimation of the final collapse of capitalism which its inherent contradictions must inevitably bring about. Unable to dispose of the surplus of goods in the home market due to the decreased purchasing power of labor the capitalist must seek foreign markets. This leads to imperialism and to war.

## The Transition to Communism

THE downfall of capitalism is heralded by the concentration of wealth and production, the growth of unemployment, the increasing misery of the working class, the greater frequency and severity of economic crises, the disappearance of the middle class and the emergence of a militant working class. As the working class (the proletariat) becomes larger and larger in numbers and as its poverty increases it becomes more and more class conscious, more and more united and disciplined, more and more militant.

Along with the constantly diminishing number of the magnates of capital, who usurp and monopolize all advantages of this process of transformation, grows the mass of misery, oppressions, slavery, degradation, exploitation; but with this too grows the revolt of the working-class, always increasing in numbers, and disciplined, united, organized by the very mechanism of the process of capitalist production itself. The monopoly of capital becomes a fetter upon the mode of production, which has sprung up and flourished along with, and under it. Centralization of the means of production and socialization of labor at last reach a point where they become incompatible with their capitalist integument. This integument is burst asunder. The knell of capitalist private property sounds. The expropriators are expropriated. . . .

. . . capitalist production begets, with the inexorability of a law of nature, its own negation.[41]

As we have seen, according to Marx, "The history of all hitherto existing society is the history of class struggles." The conflict between the capitalists and the proletariat is the class struggle to end class struggles. It is the final battle toward which all of history has been leading, it is a secularized version of Armageddon. It must end inevitably in the victory of the proletariat, for this is the end toward which the dialectical development of history has been moving.

A socialist society can never be brought into existence by persuasion for the bourgeoisie can never be persuaded voluntarily to relinquish their property and their control of the means of production. Socialism can be brought into existence only by the forceful expropriation of the bourgeoisie, by revolution. Speaking of such socialists as Saint-Simon, Fourier, and Owen, the *Communist Manifesto* declares:

The founders of these systems see, indeed, the class antagonisms, as well as the action of the decomposing elements in the prevailing form of society. But the proletariat, as yet in its infancy, offers to them the spectacle of a class without any historical initiative or any independent political movement.

Since the development of class antagonisms keeps even pace with the development of industry, the economic situation as they find it, does not as yet offer to them the material conditions for the emancipation of the proletariat. They therefore search after a new social science, after new social laws, that are to create these conditions. . . .

They want to improve the condition of every member of society, even that of the most favored. Hence, they habitually appeal to society at large, without distinction of class, nay, by preference to the ruling class. . . .

Hence, they reject all political, and especially all revolutionary action; they wish to attain their ends by peaceful means, and endeavor, by small experiments, necessarily doomed to failure, and by the force of example, to pave the way for the new social gospel.[42]

What is the aim of the Communists, then, in contrast to these "utopians"? The *Manifesto* declares:

The Communists . . . have no interests separate from and apart from those of the proletariat as a whole. They do not set up any sectarian principles of their own, by which to shape and mold the proletarian movement.

The Communists are distinguished from the other working class parties by this only: (1) In the national struggles of the proletarians of the different countries, they point out and bring to the front the common interests of the entire proletariat, independently of all nationality. (2) In the various stages of development which the struggle of the working class against the bourgeoisie has to pass through, they always and everywhere represent the interests of the movement as a whole.

The Communists, therefore, are on the one hand, practically, the most advanced and resolute section of the working class parties of every country, that section which pushes forward all others; on the other hand, theoretically, they have over the great mass of the proletariat the advantage of clearly understanding the line of march, the conditions, and the ultimate general results of the proletarian movement.

The immediate aim of the Communists is the same as that of all the other proletarian parties: formation of the proletariat into a class, overthrow of the bourgeois supremacy, conquest of political power by the proletariat. . . .

They actually express, in general terms, actual relations springing from an existing class struggle, from a historical movement going on under our very eyes. The abolition of existing property relations is not at all a distinctive feature of Communism.[43]

The last sentence does not, of course, mean that Communists do not favor the abolition of private property in the means of production (for they do) but that the advocacy of such abolition is not the *distinctive* feature of the Communist movement. The distinctive feature of the Communist movement, as Marx

envisaged it, is that it will lead the proletariat in its ultimate
and inevitable victory over the bourgeoisie. The Communist
movement, according to Marx, is not an advocate of socialism
but an instrument of history, the embodiment and spear-head
of the proletariat class-consciousness. It is not a political party
but a political *movement*, it aims not at the reform of society but
at its complete destruction and reconstitution along completely new lines. It abandons any idea of cooperation with
other "bourgeois" parties for the bourgeoisie, the arch-enemy
of the proletariat, can never be an ally. The *Communist Manifesto* closes with these words:

> The Communists disdain to conceal their views and aims. They
> openly declare that their ends can be attained only by the forcible
> overthrow of all existing social conditions. Let the ruling classes
> tremble at a Communist revolution. The proletarians have nothing
> to lose but their chains. They have a world to win.
> Working men of all countries, unite! [44]

And Marx concluded his *Poverty of Philosophy* written a year
earlier by saying:

> Would it, moreover, be a matter for astonishment if a society
> based upon the *antagonism* of classes should lead ultimately to a brutal
> *conflict*, to a hand-to-hand struggle as its final *denouement?* . . . It is
> only in an order of things in which there will be no longer classes or
> class antagonism that *social evolutions* will cease to be *political revolu-
> tions*. Until then, on the eve of each general reconstruction of society,
> the last word of social science will ever be: Combat or death; bloody
> struggle or extinction. It is thus that the question is irresistibly put.[45]

Marx, however, was never entirely consistent on this point.
As he grew older he was inclined to take a less bloody view of
the inevitable transition to socialism, at least in some countries. At a meeting of the Congress of the International at The
Hague in 1872 he declared:

> We know that the institutions, the manners and the customs of the
> various countries must be considered, and we do not deny that there
> are countries like England and America, and, if I understood your
> arrangements better, I might even add Holland, where the worker
> may attain his object by peaceful means. But not in all countries is
> this the case.[46]

And in 1891 Engels was inclined to add France to this list of countries where the revolution might be achieved by peaceful means. Yet these were clearly recognized by both men as possible exceptions to the general rule, to the general rule stated by Marx in his *Capital* (1867) that "Force is the midwife of every old society pregnant with a new one." In the same speech which Marx delivered at The Hague he declared: "It is to force that in due time the workers will have to appeal if the dominion of labor is at long last to be established." [47]

When we turn to consider Marx's ideas on the dictatorship of the proletariat and on the society which it is to establish in place of capitalism we encounter considerable vagueness. But the lack of clear "blueprints" for the future society is not accidental; for the revolution and its aftermath is not a "program" but an eschatological event and in our "pre-historic" state we are unable to know exactly what the structure of society will be like after man has become "transfigured."

## The Dictatorship of the Proletariat

THE exact form that the dictatorship of the proletariat will take, therefore, is never clearly stated. It seems to mean no more than that the proletariat will become the ruling class in place of the bourgeoisie, but how that ruling power will be exercised and through what organs neither Marx nor Engels explicitly say. In his introduction to Marx's *Civil War in France* Engels wrote:

Of late the Social Democratic philistine has once more been filled with wholesome terror at the words: Dictatorship of the Proletariat. Well and good, gentlemen, do you want to know what this dictatorship looks like? Look at the Paris Commune. That was the Dictatorship of the Proletariat. [48]

But "towards the end of his life" Marx

acknowledges in a letter that the Commune, representing the uprising of a single town, under exceptional conditions, and with most insurgents as non-socialists, could not accomplish a good deal. Evidently, in retrospect, the Commune fails to impress Marx as a model to follow, and we are left without a blueprint from his pen for the steps in the introduction of socialism.[49]

Nevertheless, it is clear that both Marx and Engels believed that some kind of political authority and organization was necessary in the transition period between capitalism and communism. The State remains as an instrument of coercion but it is used under the "direction" of the "proletariat" to liquidate the bourgeoisie. The dictatorship of the proletariat means that political power is used by the proletariat against the bourgeoisie, but just *how* the proletariat is to be represented, how its "direction" is to be given, neither Marx nor Engels say. That both regard the dictatorship as a temporary thing seems clear enough but as to how long it is to last, neither say explicitly. Both believe that it will create conditions that will eventually make coercion unnecessary and its own existence superfluous.

If Marx and Engels are vague about the way in which the dictatorship of the proletariat will be organized they are explicit enough about what it will do. According to the *Communist Manifesto:*

The proletariat will use its political supremacy to wrest, by degrees, all capital from the bourgeoisie, to centralize all instruments of production in the hands of the State, i.e., of the proletariat organized as the ruling class; and to increase the total of productive forces as rapidly as possible.

Of course, in the beginning, this cannot be effected except by means of despotic inroads on the rights of property, and on the conditions of bourgeois production; by means of measures, therefore, which appear economically insufficient and untenable, but which, in the course of the movement, outstrip themselves, necessitate further inroads upon the old social order, and are unavoidable as a means of entirely revolutionizing the mode of production.

These measures will, of course, be different in different countries. Nevertheless in the most advanced countries, the following will be pretty generally applicable:

(1) Abolition of property in land and application of all rents of land to public purposes.

(2) A heavy progressive or graduated income tax.

(3) Abolition of all right of inheritance.

(4) Confiscation of the property of all emigrants and rebels.
(5) Centralization of credit in the hands of the State. . . .
(6) Centralization of the means of communication and transport in the hands of the State.
(7) Extension of factories and instruments of production owned by the State; the bringing into cultivation of wastelands and the improvement of the soil generally in accordance with a common plan.
(8) Equal obligation of all to work. Establishment of industrial armies, especially for agriculture.
(9) Combination of agriculture with manufacturing industries; gradual abolition of the distinction between town and country, by a more equitable distribution of the population over the country.
(10) Free education for all children in public school. Abolition of children's factory labor. . . . Combination of education with industrial production.[50]

During the transition period from capitalism to Communism, i.e., the period of the dictatorship of the proletariat, labor will be remunerated in accordance with its work so that there will be differences in pay according to differences in skill. Differences in wealth, then, will still exist but they will not lead to exploitation, we are told, because the means of production will be owned by the State and not by individuals. Exploitation disappears by definition.

The family, too, will disappear along with the abolition of the private ownership of the means of production for, according to Marx, the two are inseparably bound together. Just what form relations between the sexes will take, however, he does not inform us.

Abolition of the family! Even the most radical flare up at this infamous proposal of the Communists. On what foundation is the present family, the bourgeois family, based? On capital, on private gain. In its completely developed form this family exists only among the bourgeoisie. But this state of things finds its complement in the practical absence of the family among the proletarians, and in public prostitution.

The bourgeois family will vanish as a matter of course when its complement vanishes, and both will vanish with the vanishing of capital. . . .

The bourgeois claptrap about the family and education, about the hallowed correlation of parent and child, becomes all the more disgusting the more, by the action of modern industry, all family ties among the proletarians are torn asunder. . . .

Bourgeois marriage is in reality a system of wives in common and thus, at the most, what the Communists might possibly be reproached with is that they desire to introduce, in substitution for a hypocritically concealed, an openly legalized community of women. For the rest, it is self-evident that the abolition of the present system of production must bring with it the abolition of the community of women springing from that system, i.e., of prostitution both public and private.[51]

Engels is even more explicit:

We are now approaching a social revolution in which the . . . economic foundations of monogamy will . . . disappear. . . . Monogamy arose from the concentration of great riches in a single hand—that of the man—and from the need to bequeath these riches to the children of that man and not of any other. And for this purpose the monogamy of the woman was necessary. . . .

With the transfer of the means of production into common ownership the individual family ceases to be the economic unit of society. Private house-keeping is transformed into a social industry. The care and education of children becomes a public affair; society looks after all children equally, whether they are legitimate or not.[52]

Marriage in the future, Engels declares, will have no other basis than that of "mutual affection"—it will have no religious, moral or economic significance.[53] In fact there will be no marriages as that relationship has been traditionally conceived.

The duration of an attack of sex-love for an individual is however very different for different individuals, expecially among men, and if affection comes to an end, or is supplanted by a new passionate love, this makes divorce a benefit for both partners as well as for society. The only thing people will be spared will be having to wade through the useless mire of a divorce case.[54]

Religion, too, will disappear. Religion "is the opium of the people. The abolition of religion as the illusory happiness of the people is the requirement of their real happiness." "The social principles of Christianity preach cowardice, self-contempt, abasement, submission, humility, in brief, all the attributes of the *canaille* . . . but to the proletariat, its courage, its self-confidence, its pride and its sense of independence are more essential than its daily bread." [55] According to Engels:

All religion . . . is nothing but the fantastic reflection in men's minds of those external forces which control their daily life, a reflection in which the terrestrial forces assume the form of supernatural forces. . . .
When society, by taking possession of all means of production which they themselves have produced but which now confront them as an irresistible extraneous force; when therefore man no longer proposes, but also disposes—only then will the last extraneous force which is still reflected in religion vanish; and with it will also vanish the religious reflection itself, for the simple reason that then there will be nothing left to reflect. . . .[56]

In the socialist state, according to Engels, religion "dies a natural death."

Morality in the sense of obedience to principles that are eternal, ultimate, and immutable no more survives in the socialist state than does religion. Morality is always relative to particular economic conditions; morality, in short, is always "class morality," i.e., the reflection in so-called moral terms of the economic interests of a particular class. Hence, in the socialist state "bourgeois morality" will be replaced by proletarian morality. Says Engels:

We therefore reject every attempt to impose on us any moral dogma whatsoever as an eternal, ultimate and forever immutable moral law on the pretext that the moral world too has its permanent principles which transcend history and the differences between nations. We maintain on the contrary that all former moral theories are the product, in the last analysis, of the economic stage which society had reached at that particular epoch. And as society has hitherto moved in class antagonisms, morality was always a class morality. . . . A really human morality which transcends class antagonisms and their legacies in thought becomes possible only at a stage of society which has not only overcome class contradictions but has even forgotten them in practical life. . . .[57]

What "a really human morality which transcends class antagonisms" will be like, he does not specifically say. But if this
foregoing analysis is to be taken seriously, as presumably it is,
then "a really human morality" cannot be based on an "eternal, ultimate and forever immutable moral law" nor can it
resemble the "class" moralities which preceded it in time.
This leaves us then completely in the dark as to the nature of
"a really human morality." We know that it will be different
from any morality in the past but that is all. That the traditional conceptions of morality will not survive in the socialist
state Engels makes abundantly clear. Take, for example, the
commandment: thou shalt not steal. Here is Engel's comment:

From the moment when private property in movable objects developed, in all societies in which this private property existed there
must be this moral law in common: Thou shalt not steal. Does this
law thereby become an eternal moral law? By no means. In a society
in which the motive for stealing has been done away with in which
therefore at the very most only lunatics would ever steal, how the
teacher of morals would be laughed at who tried solemnly to proclaim the eternal truth: Thou shalt not steal! [58]

According to Engels, "Men, consciously or unconsciously,
derive their moral ideas in the last resort from the practical
relations on which their class position is based—from the economic relations in which they carry on production and exchange." [59] Slavery may be right or wrong, for example, depending upon existing economic conditions and one's particular
relation to these conditions.

We should never forget that our whole economic, political, and
intellectual development has as its presupposition a state of things
in which slavery was as necessary as it was universally recognized.
In this sense, we are entitled to say: Without the slavery of antiquity,
no modern socialism. [60]

It is useless and undesirable, Engels contends, to condemn
such institutions or practices as "unjust" for the important
thing is not moral condemnation but "scientific understanding" of the process which produced such institutions and which
will eventually eliminate them. Nevertheless, the writings of
Marx and Engels are full of protests against "injustice,"

"greed," and "exploitation." And here again we encounter a contradiction, for the language they employ is frequently that of passionate moral indignation.

Like morality, law is but a reflection of the prevailing economic mode of production. "The jurist," Engels declares, "imagines he is operating with *a priori* principles, whereas they are really only economic reflexes." [61] And Marx declared:

Truly it is necessary to be entirely innocent of all historical knowledge not to know that in all times sovereigns have had to submit to the economic conditions and have never made laws for them. Legislation, political as well as civil, could do no more than give expression to the will of the economic conditions and have never made laws for them. Legislation, political as well as civil, could do no more than give expression to the will of the economic conditions.[62]

Marx believed that Montesquieu labored in vain to determine the "spirit of the laws" for the answer is quite simple: "The spirit of the laws is property." Neither Marx nor Engels tell us, however, what will happen to the law with the advent of socialism. We may infer from what they have said, however, that the more closely the socialist society approximates communism the less necessity there will be for law in any form.

## Communism

EVENTUALLY (how long, neither Marx nor Engels say) under the dictatorship of the proletariat the last traces of capitalism and of "bourgeois mentality" will be wiped out and there will be ushered in the perfect, classless society that will render any further coercion unnecessary. At this stage, the state disappears. "The government of persons," Engels declares, "is replaced by the administration of things, and by the conduct of the processes of production. The state is not 'abolished.' *It dies out.*" [63] The state as an instrument of coercion withers away but the state as an administrative apparatus controlling and managing the instruments of production remains. The state is thus destroyed by definition, rather than in fact.

In the new society, class conflict will disappear since there will be only one class, the proletariat. Here all the contradictions of history will be resolved. Exploitation will end. Everyone's wants will be satisfied. Man becomes for the first time the master of his destiny.

In the higher phase of Communist society, after the enslaving subordination of the individual under the division of labor has disappeared, and therewith also the opposition between manual and intellectual labor; after labor has become not only a means to life, but also the highest want in life; when, with the development of all the faculties of the individual, the productive forces have correspondingly increased, and all the springs of social wealth flow more abundantly—only then may the limited horizon of Capitalist right be left behind entirely, and society inscribe on its banners: "From everyone according to his faculties, to everyone according to his needs." [64]

Christopher Dawson, among others, sees in this vision of Marx a secularization of the ancient Jewish belief in the coming of the Messianic kingdom.

Karl Marx was of the seed of the prophets, in spite of his contempt for anything that savoured of mysticism or religious idealism. . . . The Messianic hope, the belief in the coming destruction of the Gentile power and the deliverance of Israel were to the Jews not mere echoes of Biblical tradition; they were burnt into the very fibre of his being by centuries of thwarted social impulse in the squalid Ghettoes of Germany and Poland. And in the same way the social dualism between the elect and the reprobate, between the people of God and the Gentile world-power, was a fact of bitter personal experience of which even the most insensitive was made conscious. . . .

Now, the Revolution and the coming of Liberalism had put an end to this state of things. . . . (But Karl Marx) could not deny his Jewish heredity and his Jewish spirit . . . the only way of escape that remained open to him was by the revolutionary tradition, which was then at the height of its prestige and popularity. In this he found satisfaction at once for his conscious hostility to bourgeois civilization and for the deeper revolt of his repressed religious instincts.

To three fundamental elements in the Jewish historical attitude— the opposition between the chosen people and the Gentile world, the inexorable Divine judgment on the latter and the restoration of the former in the Messianic kingdom—all found their corresponding principles in the revolutionary faith of Karl Marx. Thus the bourgeois took the place of the Gentiles, and the economic poor took the place of the spiritual poor of the Old Testament . . . while the Messianic kingdom finds an obvious parallel in the dictatorship of the proletariat which will reign until it has put down all rule and authority and power and in the end will deliver up its kingdom to the classless and stateless society of the future which will be all in all.[65]

## A Critique of Marxism

DID Marx contend that the economic mode of production is the ultimate cause of historical change or only one factor among many? On this question there is great controversy among interpreters of Marxian thought. The latter-day Marxians are inclined to say that Marx was entirely conscious of the non-economic factors influencing history and that he only claimed that the economic mode of production is the *primary* and most important factor. But, as Bober points out in his excellent analysis of Marx's interpretation of history, "There is hardly a perceptible difference between the claim that the mode of production overrides all other influences and in the last resort governs institutions and events." [66] The contention that the economic mode of production determines the nature of historical change, the institutions to be found in any given society, and the ideas of all the persons living in that society is obviously an over-simplification and can only be held by willfully ignoring many other factors that influence the course of history. Moreover, even if we accept Marx's contention, it does not explain what causes historical change. For, if we say with Marx that historical change is brought about by changes in the economic mode of production the question still remains: what causes changes in the economic mode of production? In answer to this question, Marx has no satisfactory reply.

It is accepted as a commonplace today that economic needs are fundamental, that men must satisfy their need for food, clothing and shelter before they can satisfy any other needs. And this leads many persons to accept the economic interpretation of history either in the Marxian form or in some variant form as self-evidently true. Yet, however commonplace the assertion of the fundamental character of men's economic needs may be, it is not self-evidently true. Our age is so predominantly concerned with economic problems and institutions that it is difficult for us to conceive of an age or society in which economic problems, occupations and institutions were or could be of secondary importance. It is no more true to say that man's need for food is his primary need, than it is to say that his need for sexual fulfillment is fundamental. If Marx is right, Freud is wrong. If Freud is right, Marx is wrong. If both are partially right, both are partially wrong. Men's physical needs, as Freud has demonstrated, are not only economic in character and it is not true that man always and in every situation prefers to satisfy his physical needs before all other needs. For man is not only, or primarily, a biological organism but a spiritual creature. Man has spiritual needs as well as physical ones, he craves spiritual nourishment as well as physical nourishment. In short, man cannot live by bread alone, and no man who ever lived has been satisfied with bread alone. Many have jeopardized the satisfaction of their physical needs because they wanted something more and many have chosen to risk death rather than to exist under conditions which were physically satisfactory but spiritually intolerable. Marx himself endured poverty for the sake of something he regarded as more important than the satisfaction of his economic needs. The more momentous changes in history have been brought about not by men whose primary aim was physical satisfaction or a greater abundance of material things, but by men who endured poverty, pain and insecurity for the sake of something they prized more highly than physical security. It has been by self-sacrifice rather than by self-aggrandizement that the progress of the world has been made when it has been made.

The mere existence of needs, moreover, tells us nothing whatsoever about the way in which men will *interpret* those needs nor the way in which they will seek to satisfy them. The religious, philosophical and moral presuppositions by means of which our experiences become meaningful will determine in large part not only how we will interpret our needs but how we will seek to satisfy them. All men have the same basic physical needs but not all men interpret them in the same way nor seek to satisfy them identically.

Marxians are quick to retort that they are not necessarily saying anything about the motivations of particular individuals but only about the motivations of men in the mass and more particularly of men as members of particular classes. I have never been able to understand how the motivations of men in the mass or of men as members of a particular "class," however, differ from the motivations of particular men. Either a mass of men and classes of men are made up of particular individuals or they are not. If they are not made up of particular individuals and if the actions of a large group of men are not determined by the actions of the particular men comprising that group then I fail to understand exactly what a "mass" or "class" is. If it is not made up of particular individuals what is its composition?

Moreover, Marxians believe that with the satisfaction of men's economic needs all conflict will cease, all crime disappear, and all men will live in perfect harmony with each other. It is a characteristic of men's physical needs, to which any one of us can attest, that they are insatiable. Only with death do we cease to want. The more we acquire, the more we want. The satisfaction of one want only leads to the multiplication of other wants. We never get "enough" of anything, except, perhaps, for very short intervals. Clearly Marx believes that with the coming of Communism it will be possible to satisfy men's wants and that no one will want more than is "enough." If the past history of the human race is any evidence, then this is an illusion. Greed, envy, jealousy, covetousness and all the other sins with which human nature is infected are not peculiar, as history testifies, to the age of capitalism alone and they are not likely to disappear with the disappearance of capitalism as an economic system. Marx expects the dialectical process of history to do what Christianity believes can only be done by God's grace and through the medium of His sacraments. Marx expects the historical process to purge human nature of its evil propensities and to transform human nature. The promise is similar to that of Christianity, but the means proposed are radically different. One expects revolution to do what the other believes can only be accomplished through repentance.

When the economic interpretation of history is applied to such phenomena as natural science, the arts and literature, its inadequacy becomes even more apparent.

To Marx and his colleague the growth of science is pre-eminently a derivative of productive requirements. Economic activity creates the needs, provides the motives, and furnishes the techniques and facilities for investigation. . . . Subsumed under the technique of production, science is, in their view, essentially an economic datum, and they do not mention science independently when citing examples of institutions and ideas as the superstructure on the economic base. Science is treated as a component of the economic substructure.

That economic problems have much to do with the career of science is scarcely debatable. But the general emphasis on needs is subject to reservations, and the unique stress on economic needs goes too far . . . the assurance that needs invariably produce scientific advances reflects a disposition to regard science as a mechanistic reaction in simple linear causation. . . .[67]

The great scientific advances rarely, if ever, have been motivated by utilitarian considerations alone and frequently utilitarian uses have been discovered only long after the scientific knowledge itself. To say that scientific investigation is conditioned by the environment in which it takes place is one thing; to say, as Marx and Engels do, that it is determined by the economic environment is nonsense.

The problems which the scientist undertakes to solve are suggested by economic factors. Galileo was stimulated by seventeenth-century engineering. Newton by the calculations of probability made by insurance societies, modern scientists by modern technology. But *the fact that scientists often deal with problems which are socially determined does not mean that the answers to those problems are also socially determined.* What the technologist wishes to do is decided by society, but the correct method of doing it is dependent upon processes of nature which remain the same under all societies. Marxists, nevertheless, declare that not only the problems of the scientist but also the natural laws which he discovers are socially determined.[68]

Not all science is applied science, as the Marxists seem to contend, and the attempt to make it such can only lead to the end of scientific progress.

Esthetic creation can no more be explained in economic terms than can science. Certainly every artist and every writer is influenced by the environment in which he lives but the environment is a point of departure not an explanation of the artist's creative genius. The environment provides the artist and the writer with materials with which to work, it does not determine how the individual artist will interpret those materials any more than it determines what physical laws the scientist will discover. As a matter of fact the greatness of an artist depends upon his ability to transcend his social and historical environment, to speak to men of all ages and times. The least important thing about Shakespeare is what he took from the Elizabethan age.

Equally untrue and equally dangerous is the Marxian denial of eternal and universal principles of moral conduct. Moral *judgments* do differ from age to age and from society to society but to recognize the relativity of moral judgments is not the same thing as to say, as Marx and Engels do, that there are no absolute, universal, and eternal *principles* of right and wrong. For these particular and relative judgments are only properly called moral when they approximate the absolute standards or principles that are the same for all societies and for all times. We are enabled, as a matter of fact, to recognize the relativity and partiality of our moral judgments only by the affirmation of a standard that is neither relative nor partial. The inability of any particular individual in any particular society to know the whole truth and nothing but the truth testifies not to the non-existence of truth but rather to the infallibility of individuals.

The doctrine that all ideas and all values are socially determined leads . . . to the destruction of individual freedom and to the tyranny of the collectivity or of its embodiment in a dictator. Only the belief in objective rational truths and moral values can preserve freedom; for it is only through the right of appeal to objective standards that men can judge the actions of their government and resist them when they believe them to be wrong. . . . If standards of right and of rationality vary in different societies, and are mere products of a social system, then the individual loses his right of appeal, the independence of his conscience is undermined, and he can be compelled to conform to whatever the state chooses to recommend. . . . This growth of moral relativism is the most alarming tendency in both the theory and the political practice of the modern world and . . . it originated . . . with the Marxists. By interpreting all cultural phenomena in terms of class struggle, by explaining all the beliefs of every individual by his role in that struggle, by proclaiming that any means whatever are justified in achieving the end, and that the only predestined historic end is the conquest of power by the proletariat, Marxism subordinates man to the march of history and ennobles tyranny, dishonesty, cruelty, and mass murder. And since the collectivity is an abstraction and only individuals are real, Marxism, by enthroning a collectivity, must also create individuals who can embody and interpret the will of that collectivity. The conquest of power by the proletariat becomes, therefore, the conquest of power by an individual whose function is to represent the march of history and to destroy the right of any other individual to criticize or oppose it.[69]

## Marxism as a Religion

THE moral relativism of Marxian thought disappears in Marxian action and historical relativism gives way to an apocalyptic determinism. And, in practice, Marxism takes on all the characteristics of a crypto-religion. This accounts for its wide appeal and for the passionate devotion with which it is embraced by its followers.

As soon as Marx turns to action all his philosophy goes by the board. . . . The exploitation of the proletariat arouses a genuinely moral indignation: he regards it not as a necessary phase in economic revolution, but as a sin that cries to heaven for vengeance. The cause of the proletariat is the cause of social justice in the most absolute sense. It is a cause for which the Communist is ready to suffer and die and to cause the suffering and death of others. All this is the fruit not of his philosophy or of his materialism but of the underlying religious impulse which finds expression in the revolutionary apocalyptic. It is a spiritual passion which has lost its theological object and has attempted to find independent justification in a purely rational theory. And the intrusion of this spiritual force falsifies Marx's whole theory by imparting to it an absolutism that is foreign to its real nature. Thus his historical relativism becomes contaminated by an apocalyptic determinism—a doctrine of the End of History—and his ethical relativism passes away before a Puritanical rigorism of a strictly dualist type. And this is why Marxism is characterized by a certain inhumanity which does not belong either to the religious apocalyptic tradition or to rationalism but which arises from the union of intense apocalyptic convictions with materialist philosophy.[70]

In theory Marxism rejects religion but in practice the passion which informs it is religious in character. The true Marxian believer accepts the dogma of Marx as a gospel of salvation. The doctrines of Marx are never held with the scientific detachment with which scientific hypotheses are held by a natural scientist but as an act of religious faith, as a doctrine without which life would have neither meaning nor direction. But as a religion it proves to be inadequate, for, as Reinhold Niebuhr declares:

Its inadequacy as a religion is due to its effort to solve the total human problem in political terms, and its limitations as a political philosophy and strategy are derived from its religio-dogmatic over-simplifications. Marxism attributes practically all ills from which the human flesh suffers to the capitalistic social order, and promises every type of redemption in a new society in which the productive process is socially owned. . . . While the Communist can be brutally realistic in discounting moral pretensions and penetrating to the actual egoistic economic motives revealed in a contemporary social situation, he gives himself to the unwarranted illusion that a new order of society will eliminate egoism and socialize men to such a degree that the problem of justice will be practically solved and eliminated. . . . His Utopianism blinds him to the perennial nature of the political problem. This problem can be briefly stated in the following form: (1) Social cooperation on a large scale requires a measure of coercion. (2) The instruments of coercion are always wielded by a particular social group, whether capitalistic industrialists or communistic oligarchs. (3) The natural force of human egoism tempts these oligarchs to use the instruments of power for their own advantage rather than that of the total society. The result is therefore always something less than perfect justice. (4) The problem is to place the most effective possible inner moral and external social checks upon the centers of social power in society in order that the perennial tendencies toward injustice in society may be retarded. . . .

The orthodox Marxian is tempted into another grave error by his faulty religion with its mistaken analysis of the problem of human sin. By attributing all injustice to the capitalistic social structure it lifts the class of rebellious victims of injustice into the category of the only redemptive and Messianic community. The proletarian class is in fact the counterpart of Messianic nation or community in the early Jewish eschatology. But the Marxian idealisation of this class represents a kind of religious primitiveness; for its claims for this class are as unqualified as were the claims of Israel, before the prophets criticised and refined this tribalism in religion. The consequence of this religious sanctification of the peculiar insights and needs of a particular class and group is the same that it has always been in history: fanaticism and brutality.[71]

There is a marked resemblance between the Marxian interpretation of history and the Christian interpretation in the sense that each believes that history is a kind of judgment and revelation and each shares an apocalyptic conception of the End of History. The Marxian, however, sees the conflict in history as a conflict between materialistic forces, the Christian sees the conflict as an essentially spiritual one. For the Marxian the end of history is found in history itself, for the Christian history is "a dialogue between God and man, and the end of history is not found in history itself but arises from the raising of history to a supertemporal plane." [72] For the Marxian conflict is resolved through the medium of class conflict and the dialectical process of history as an immanent process, for the Christian, conflict is resolved on the Cross.

. . . the mystery of the Cross which reverses the material values of history and gives a new meaning to victory and defeat. The true makers of history are not to be found on the surface of events among the successful politicians or the successful revolutionaries: these are the servants of events. Their masters are the spiritual men whom the world knew not, the unregarded agents of the creative action of the Spirit. The supreme instance of this—the key to the Christian understanding of history—is to be found in the Incarnation—the presence of the maker of the world in the world unknown to the world. And though this divine intervention in the course of history seems at first sight to empty secular history of all ultimate significance, in reality it gives history for the first time an absolute spiritual value. The Incarnation is itself in a sense the divine fruit of history—of the fullness of time—and it finds its extension and completion in the historic life of the Church.[73]

We lose sight of the real importance of Marxism, however, if we do not realize that its power resides not so much in its material promises as in its spiritual promises. It is not as philosophy, not as economic theory, not as an economic program, that Marxism attracts large numbers of the industrial working class but as a religion. For God, Marx substitutes Historical Necessity, for the Chosen People, the proletariat, and for the Messianic Kingdom, the Realm of Freedom. When these substitutions are grasped with the faith of religious conviction then the power of Marxism becomes readily apparent. The sixteenth-century Calvinistic faith in predestination was converted by liberalism into the Law of Progress, and the Law of Progress was converted by Marx into the doctrine of Historical Necessity and the inevitable victory of socialism over capitalism. The assurance which Calvin gave to the Elect that the forces of the universe were on their side, the assurance which the eighteenth-century *philosophes* gave to the bourgeoisie, Marx gave to the proletariat in the nineteenth. Marx held out a hope to the proletariat which the traditional social institutions of Western civilization apparently denied. For the proletariat not only felt itself to be but was in fact estranged from the rest of society. They felt alienated, little more than a tool. And their sense of dignity as human beings suffered as a consequence. The response which large numbers of the industrial working class have made to Marxism is less an indication of the soundness of Marx's economic interpretation of history than it is of this failure of Western social institutions to give the working class a sense of belonging, a sense of dignity and spiritual worth without which life cannot long be endured. Marx filled what was and is for the proletariat a real spiritual void and restored to large numbers of the working class a dignity of existence which capitalism had in fact denied. Whether he filled that void successfully is another matter but unless the twentieth century can find ways of reforming its social and economic institutions in such a way that the worker feels himself to be a necessary and integral part of society we can expect that the gospel of Marx will attract more and more adherents. The deepest need of the worker, like that of every human being, is not material but spiritual and it is the spiritual promise of Marxism that attracts him. More than the abundance of things, the worker wants the responsibility that is his birthright as a human being. It is not wages and hours that is his principal concern but a desire to participate creatively in a society which has long regarded him as a tool. If our present social and economic system cannot provide the worker with a creative role and that sense of dignity which all men need to live then he will turn to Marxism or some other gospel of salvation through revolution. We may reject the program of Marxism but we cannot ignore the indictment which it makes of capitalism.

## CHAPTER 13

# Socialism After Marx

AFTER Karl Marx's death in 1883, and even during his lifetime, his followers divided into conflicting schools of thought. Some of the divisions resulted from differences of opinion concerning the proper tactics to be pursued in particular countries and situations, others resulted from attempts to "revise" Marxian thought with respect to the economic interpretation of history, the labor theory of value, or the inevitability of violent revolution. Some endeavored to transform Marx's revolutionary doctrine into an evolutionary one while others seized upon the more violent aspects of his thought to the exclusion of his "program." The confusion among them was intensified by the fact that many claimed to be the "true" defenders of the faith and the orthodox interpreter of the works of the master. It is impossible here to examine in detail all the currents and cross currents of socialist thought after Marx. Instead, we shall focus out attention upon the more significant movements, leaving the developments in Russia to a separate chapter.

## Social Democracy in Germany

SOCIALISM in Germany made its appearance as early as 1848 but it was not until the 1860's that it began to assume definite political form. One of the early leaders was Ferdinand Lassalle (1825–1864) who accepted the Marxian interpretation of history but who differed from Marx in believing that political democracy (majority rule based on universal and equal suffrage) must precede the rise to power of the proletariat. Lassalle, moveover, advocated the immediate establishment of producers' cooperatives, the state to provide the capital necessary for their formation. To this end he urged the working class to form a political party so that the interests of labor might be represented in the legislative bodies of the German states and in 1863 he became the leader of a newly formed Universal German Workingmen's Association. This Association had as its immediate purpose the securing of adequate representation for labor and, in the words of its charter, "the real removal of class antagonism in society . . . by universal, equal, and direct suffrage" and "the acquisition of such suffrage by peaceable and legal means, and particularly by gaining over public opinion." [1]

After Lassalle's death the more orthodox Marxians under the leadership of men like Bebel and Liebknecht endeavored to direct the working class movement along more radical lines. At a convention in Gotha in 1875, however, they were forced to compromise with the followers of Lassalle and their statement of principles which was called the Gotha Program was subjected to criticism at many points by Marx himself. This criticism resulted eventually in the drawing up of a new program, the so-called Erfurt Program in 1891. The Erfurt Program laid more emphasis upon the economic interpretation of history, especially upon the inevitability of the transition to socialism and the monopolistic character of the capitalist economy. "The social democratic party of Germany," it declared, "does not contend for new rights or privileges for the laboring classes, but for the abolition of the rule of the classes and of the classes themselves, and for the equal rights and equal duties of all without distinction of sex or pedigree." [2] As a practical program for the present it advocated among other things: universal, direct, and equal suffrage; representation apportioned according to population; direct legislation by the people through the right of initiative and referendum; popular militia in the place of standing armies; popular referenda on the declaration of war; the abolition of the use of public funds for religious purposes; secularization of the schools;

popular election of judges with free legal counsel; abolition of capital punishment; free medical attendance; progressive income taxes; an eight hour work day; prohibition of night work and child labor and the establishment of a system of social insurance. It does not mention the formation of producers' cooperatives as the Gotha Program had done, nor does it assert as the earlier program had that labor is the source of all wealth. The Erfurt Program was the official platform of the Social Democratic Party until it was replaced by a somewhat milder platform around 1925.

Many different interpretations of the Erfurt Program followed almost immediately upon its adoption. Two groups, however, clearly emerged from this conflict of interpretation: those who called themselves "orthodox Marxists" and the so-called "revisionists." Among the revisionists the most important was Eduard Bernstein (1850–1932). In a letter which he wrote to a meeting of the German Social Democratic Party at Stuttgart in October, 1898, there are contained his principal objections to the orthodox Marxian position. They may be summarized as follows:

(1) It is a mistake to believe that the collapse of capitalism is imminent.

(2) "The enormous increase of social wealth is not accompanied by a decreasing number of large capitalists, but an increasing number of capitalists of all degrees. The middle classes change their character, but they do not disappear from the social scale." Neither the small merchant class nor the peasantry is on the point of becoming extinct.

(3) The concentration of industry is not occurring at the rate at which Marx predicted it would nor is it occurring uniformly.

(4) Through the activities of the labor movement exploitation has been retarded. "Factory legislation, the democratizing of local government, and the extension of its area of work, the freeing of trade unions and systems of co-operative trading from legal restrictions, the consideration of standard conditions of labor in the work undertaken by public authorities—all these characterize this phase of the evolution. But the more the political organization of modern nations is democratized the more the needs and opportunities of great political catastrophes are di-

minished." Socialism may be brought into existence by peaceful,
evolutionary means. If socialism were an historic necessity there
would be no point to the activities of socialist parties.

(5) "Unable to believe in finalities at all I cannot believe in a final
aim of socialism. But I strongly believe in the socialist movement, in the march forward of the working classes, who step by
step must work out their emancipation by changing society from
the domain of a commercial land-holding oligarchy to a real
democracy which in all its departments is guided by the interests
of those who work and create." [3]

Bernstein accepted the economic interpretation of history only
in a modified form and argued that non-economic factors have
greater importance than that which is attributed to them by
most Marxians. "The purely economic causes create, first of
all, only a disposition for the creation of certain ideas, but how
these then arise and spread and what form they take, depend
on the co-operation of a whole series of influences." [4] The
labor theory of value as formulated by Marx is useful he argued
as "a key . . . to the exposure and presentation of the mechanism of capitalist economy" but it is not a key that fits all
locks and "therefore it has become disastrous to nearly every
disciple of Marx." [5] As an exact measure of the rate of exploitation of the worker by the capitalist it is misleading. "A
scientific basis for socialism or communism cannot be supported on the fact only that the wage worker does not receive
the full value of the product of his work." [6] The existence of
surplus-value, he thinks, is a fact which needs no proof.

Marx's prediction that wealth would be concentrated in
fewer and fewer hands and that such a concentration was
necessarily antecedent to the coming of socialism, Bernstein
rejects as manifestly untrue.

It is . . . quite wrong to assume that the present development of
society shows a relative or indeed absolute diminution of the number
of the members of the possessing classes. Their number increases
both relatively and absolutely. . . .

If the activity and the prospects of social democracy were dependent upon the decrease of the wealthy, then it might indeed lie down
to sleep. But the contrary is the case. The prospects of socialism
depend not on the decrease but on the increase of social wealth. . . .

Whether the social surplus produce is accumulated in the shape of monopoly by 10,000 persons or is shared up in gradual amounts among half a million men makes no difference in principle to the nine or ten million heads of families who are worsted by this transaction. Their struggle for a more just distribution or for an organization which would include a more just distribution is not on that account less justifiable and necessary. On the contrary, it might cost less surplus labor to keep a few thousand privileged persons in sumptuousness than half a million or more in wealth.[7]

Bernstein was skeptical, too, of the Marxian contention concerning the increasing severity of economic crises in capitalistic economies and declared "that, at least for some time, general commercial crises similar to the earlier ones are to be regarded as improbable." [8] This was written, of course, before the worldwide economic crisis of the 1930's.

The problem of crises cannot be solved by a few well-preserved catchwords. We can only investigate what elements of modern economy work in favor of crises and what work against them. It is impossible to prejudge *a priori* the ultimate relation of these forces to one another, or their development. Unless unforeseen external events bring about a general crisis—and we have said that can happen any day—there is no urgent reason for concluding that such a crisis will come to pass for purely economic reasons. Local and partial depressions are unavoidable; general stagnation is not unavoidable with the present organization and extension of the world market, and particularly with the great extension of the production of articles of food.[8]

Unlike more orthodox Marxian socialists Bernstein believed that the trade union "has very important social tasks to fulfill for the trades, which, however, do not demand, nor are even consistent with, its omnipotence in any way." [9] He is opposed, however, to making the trade union the "mistress of a whole branch of production, the ideal of various older socialists" because it "would be only a monopolist productive association, and, as soon as it relied upon its monopoly or worked upon it, it would be antagonistic to socialism and democracy, let its inner constitution be what it may." [10]

He is opposed to the establishment of socialism through the medium of a dictatorship of the proletariat. The "universal franchise," he declared "is . . . the alternative to violent revolution." [11]

Is there any sense . . . in maintaining the phrase of the "dictatorship of the proletariat" at a time when in all possible places representatives of social democracy have placed themselves practically in the arena of parliamentary work, have declared for the proportional representation of people, and for direct legislation— all of which is inconsistent with a dictatorship? . . .

The whole practical activity of social democracy is directed toward creating circumstances and conditions which shall render possible and secure a transition (free from convulsive outbursts) of the modern social order into a higher one. . . . The dictatorship of the classes belongs to a lower civilization, and . . . it is only to be looked upon as a reversion to political atavism.[12]

Socialists should be less critical than they frequently are of the institutions and values associated with liberalism, for socialism does not aim to destroy the principles upon which liberalism is based, Bernstein contended, but to extend them. With liberalism it shares the belief in the necessity of developing freedom of personality.

Feudalism, with its unbending organizations and corporations, had to be destroyed nearly everywhere by violence. The liberal organizations of modern society are distinguished from those exactly because they are flexible and capable of change and development. They do not need to be destroyed but only to be further developed. For that we need organization and energetic action, but not necessarily a revolutionary dictatorship.[13]

Legislation is a more certain road to socialism than is violence. Violence may be quicker but legislative reforms are more lasting. Moreover, "in legislation intellect dominates over emotion . . . during a revolution, emotion dominates over intellect. . . . Where the revolution sins by overhaste, the every day legislator sins by procrastination. Legislation works as a systematic force, revolution as an elementary force." [14] The socialist movement needs not only "the fighting spirit" but co-ordinated and constructive thinking and the kind of thinkers who are able to recognize "the little plant that has grown on another soil than theirs, and who, perhaps, though not kings, are warm-hearted republicans in the domain of socialist thought." [15]

Bernstein's frank revision of Marxian doctrine was met in Germany by the opposition of the orthodox Marxians and in particular by Karl Kautsky (1854–1938). With the death of Engels in 1895, Kautsky became one of the foremost interpreters of Marxian socialism. When a split developed within the Social Democratic Party on the question of supporting the war which began in 1913, Kautsky, together with Bernstein and Hugo Haase, the President of the Party's representatives in the Reichstag, issued a manifesto in 1915 declaring that the war had become an imperialistic war of conquest and as such was not a war to which true Socialists could give their support. In 1917 he was active in the formation of an Independent Social Democratic Party on a platform of opposition to the continuance of the war. He rejoined the regular Social Democratic Party, however, after the war and became one of its principal spokesmen. In the years following World War I he was most active in his opposition to Leninism and to the Russian Revolution.

Kautsky undertook to defend the basic tenets of Marxian socialism against the criticism which had been made of them by men like Bernstein. Although many of the predictions of Marx and Engels had not come literally true, Kautsky conceded, nevertheless, "Marx and Engels were able to determine the *direction* of economic development for many decades in a degree that the course of events has magnificently justified." [16] Perhaps they were not infallible in details but they were always right in principle. The labor theory of value may not be "tangible and exactly measurable" but nevertheless "it is real." [17] The existence of a large number of small enterprises did not mean that capital was not being concentrated for a comparison of the product of the large industries with those of the smaller ones would reveal a very large concentration of capital under the control of the larger. Rather than serving as an agency for the diffusion of wealth, as Bernstein had contended, the modern corporation, Kautsky declared

. . . not only makes the control of production by a few banks and industrial combines possible; it also furnishes a means by which the smallest fortunes can be transformed into capital and thereby be made to contribute to the centralizing process of capital.

Through the corporation the savings of even the poor are placed at the disposal of great capitalists, who are enabled to use those savings as if they were a part of their great capitals. As a result the centralizing of their own great fortunes is increased still more.[18]

Kautsky and the orthodox Marxians generally rejected the statistical evidence which Bernstein had supplied to support his criticism of Marxian doctrine as "unconvincing."

The greatest controversy between the orthodox Marxians and the revisionists, however, did not take place over Marxian economics but over the question of tactics and the transition from capitalism to socialism. Should socialists work for reform or prepare for revolution?

Kautsky believed that socialism could be brought about ultimately only by revolution, nevertheless, he hoped that it could be accomplished with a minimum of violence. Universal suffrage could not, as Bernstein contended, replace the necessity for revolution but ". . . it can avert many premature, hopeless revolutionary attempts, and render superfluous many revolutionary uprisings. It creates clearness regarding the relative strength of the different parties and classes." Whether the revolution will be violent or not depends upon the kind of opposition it encounters. It need not be violent and it will be to the workers' advantage if they seek progress "through strictly legal methods alone."

For this reason Kautsky looked with favor upon the growth of the trade union movement, the extension of co-operatives, participation in parliament and legislation designed to ameliorate the workers' situation. Thus he wrote:

The slightest reform or organization may be of great significance for the physical or intellectual rebirth of the proletariat that, without them, would be surrendered helpless to capitalism and left alone in the misery that continuously threatens it. But it is not alone the relief of the proletariat from its misery that makes the activity of the proletariat in Parliament . . . indispensable. They are also of value as a means of familiarizing the proletariat with the problems and methods of national and municipal government and of great industries, as well as to the attainment of intellectual maturity which the proletariat needs if it is to supplant the bourgeoisie as the ruling class. . . . Democracy is to the proletariat what light and air are to the organism; without them it cannot develop its powers.

But he goes on to say that participation in Parliament, the growth of the trade union movement, reform legislation and the extension of co-operatives are not, in themselves, enough. These reforms are not socialism although they prepare the way for it.

To be sure, the co-operatives are increasing, but simultaneously and yet faster grows the accumulation of capital; to be sure, the unions are growing, but simultaneously and yet faster grows the concentration of capital and its organization in gigantic monopolies. To be sure, the socialist press is growing but simultaneously grows the partyless and characterless press that poisons and unnerves ever wider popular circles. To be sure, wages are rising, but still faster rises the mass of profits. Certainly the number of socialist representatives in Parliament is growing, but still more sinks the significance and efficaciousness of this institution, while simultaneously Parliamentary majorities, like the government, fall into ever greater dependence on the powers of high finance.

So beside the resources of the proletariat develop also those of capital, and the end of this development can be nothing less than a great, decisive battle, that cannot end until the proletariat has attained the victory.[19]

The orthodox Marxians were less rigidly "orthodox" in practice than they claimed to be in theory. For despite their criticism of revisionists like Bernstein, they acted in practice very much like them. They participated in politics, they collaborated with other parties and they supported much of the reform legislation which was proposed by non-socialist governments. Kautsky argued in defense of these tactics that it is the "ultimate aims" which distinguish the socialist party from other parties and not their "momentary demands."

The eight-hour day . . . is in itself no revolutionary demand; it is such within the framework of a socialist program, where it is a means for lifting up the working class and for contributing to its political and social maturity and to its capacity to take the work of liberation and reconstruction into its own hands. The same eight-hour day may be a conservative demand within the framework of the program of a social-reformist party, which is subject to the illusion that it can, by concessions, reconcile the working-class to the existing social order. . . . What holds political parties together, when they have great historical tasks to accomplish . . . is their ultimate aims, not their momentary demands.[20]

In *The Social Revolution* (1903) and *The Road to Power* (1909) Kautsky was primarily concerned with defending the Marxian conception of the class struggle against the Revisionist attempts to substitute a doctrine of gradualness and of socialism "by evolution." The ultimate revolution in his opinion need not be violent but it must be decisive. So long as the capitalist mode of production remains in existence, social peace is impossible. Only the seizure of complete political and economic power by the proletariat can end exploitation and the class war. Despite his criticism of Revisionism, however, Kautsky demonstrated an attachment for democracy and for democratic methods of change that was as strong as that of any Revisionist. This became even more apparent as time went on. In *The Dictatorship of the Proletariat* (1918) Kautsky turned his attention from the "rightist" deviations of Bernstein and the Revisionists to the "leftist" deviations of Lenin and the leaders of the Russian Revolution. While Lenin read Marx as advocating a dictatorship of the Communist Party for the proletariat, Kautsky read Marx as advocating a democratic government controlled by the proletariat through universal suffrage. Kautsky regarded the Russian dictatorship as a deviation from Marxian teachings because it tried to go faster than historical and economic developments in Russia at that time warranted and because it represented the seizure of power by a minority (the Bolsheviki) and the rule by force. Unless the proletariat represent a majority of the population no socialist revolution can be successful, and if they represent a majority no dictatorship by force is necessary. As a matter of fact, Kautsky argues, there is something more important than the social control of the means of production and that is "the abolition of every kind of exploitation and oppression, be it directed against a class, a party, a sex, or a race." Here Kautsky seems to be arguing that democracy is more important than socialism. Socialism is an indis-

pensable means to bring about the end of exploitation but it
is not a self-sufficient end. Unless it is accompanied by democratic government it cannot really succeed. Neither socialism
alone nor democracy alone can end exploitation, both are
essential—that is the core of Kautsky's teaching. Thus he
opposed both the Revisionists and the Communists, claiming
that each represented deviations from the teachings of Marx.

In 1919 Lenin wrote an answer to Kautsky's *Dictatorship
of the Proletariat* which he entitled *The Proletarian Revolution
and Kautsky the Renegade*. It was not the Bolsheviki, he argued,
who had misunderstood Marx but Kautsky. In part he said:

> The distance between Kautsky, on the one hand, and Marx and
> Engels, on the other, is as great . . . as between the bourgeois
> Liberal and the proletarian revolutionary. Pure democracy, or
> simple "democracy," of which Kautsky speaks, is but a paraphrase
> of the "free popular State," that is, a perfect *absurdity*. Kautsky
> with the learned air of a most learned arm-chair fool, or else with
> the innocent air of a ten-year-old girl, is asking: Why do we need
> a dictatorship when we have a majority? And Marx and Engels
> explain: In order to break down the resistance of the bourgeoisie;
> in order to inspire the reactionaries with fear; in order to main-
> tain the authority of the armed people against the bourgeoisie;
> in order that the proletariat may forcibly suppress its enemies!
> . . . Kautsky unwittingly commits the same little error which
> is committed by all bourgeois democrats, namely, he accepts the
> formal equality, which under capitalism is only a fraud and a
> piece of hypocrisy, at its face value as a *de facto* equality. . . .
> But the exploiter cannot be equal to the exploited. This is a truth
> which, however disgraceful to Kautsky, is nevertheless of the es-
> sence of Socialism. Another truth is that there can be, in reality,
> no *de facto* equality unless and until the possibility of exploitation of
> one class by another has been abolished . . . except in very rare
> and particular cases, the exploiters cannot be destroyed at once.
> . . . In addition, expropriation alone, as a legal or political act,
> does not by far settle the matter, since it is necessary practically to
> replace the landlords and capitalists, to substitute for theirs an-
> other, a *working class*, management of the factories and estates. . . .
> Never, except in the sentimental Utopia of the sentimental Mr.
> Kautsky, will the exploiters submit to the decision of the exploited
> majority without making use of their advantages in a last desperate
> battle, or in a series of battles. [21]

By seeking to merge the democratic tradition with the Marxian socialist doctrine, Kautsky laid the foundations for the activities of the Social Democratic Party in Germany. And although he repudiated in theory the idea of attaining socialism by a gradual process of "evolution," he appeared to be committed to that tactic in practice. He was closer to the Revisionists in fact than he appeared to be in theory. The stronger the Social Democratic Party became politically the less radical became its demands and together with the Catholic Center Party it helped to found the Weimar Republic and was one of the staunchest supporters of democratic constitutionalism. To the more radical Marxists this was a betrayal of socialism which they never forgot nor forgave. As a consequence, throughout the life of the Weimar Republic, the opposition of the Communists to the Social Democratic Party was more passionately violent than was their opposition to the more conservative parties.

## French Syndicalism

A THIRD movement, a kind of hybrid of anarchism, Marxism, and trade unionism sprang up in France, a movement which repudiated Marx's political program but retained his doctrine of revolutionary violence. The most important intellectual leader of the movement was Georges Sorel (1847–1922). The organizational heart of the movement was the General Confederation of Labor (known by the French abbreviation of the name as the *C. G. T.*), which was established in 1895. The movement came to be known as syndicalism after the French word for trade union, *syndicat*.

The task of the syndicalists is to organize the more or less class-feeling of the working men and to raise it to a clear consciousness of class interests and class ideals. This aim can be attained only by organizing the working men into syndicats. The syndicat is an association of working men of the same or of similar trades, and is held together by bonds of common interest. In this is its strength. *Of all human groupings it is the most fundamental and the most permanent*, because

men in society are interested above everything else in the satisfaction
of their economic needs. . . .

Political parties, groups of idealists, or communities possessing a
common creed are associations which cannot but be weak and
transient, in view of their heterogeneous composition and of the
accidental character of their bond of union. . . .

A working man enrolling in a syndicat is not entering a party,
not subscribing to a platform, nor accepting a creed. He is simply
entering into a relation which is forced upon him by his very position in society. . . . The syndicat is a sphere of influence which by
the volume of its suggestion and the constancy and intensity of its
action shapes the feelings and ideas of the working men after a
certain pattern. . . .

The syndicats should prefer industrial unionism to craft or trade
unionism. The separation of working men into trades is apt to develop in them a corporate spirit which is not in harmony with the
class-idea. The industrial union, on the other hand, widens the
mental horizon of the working man and his range of solidarity with
his fellow workers and thus serves better to strengthen his class
consciousness.[22]

From Marx the syndicalist movement takes over the doctrine
of the class struggle and gives it central, if not exclusive, importance. The important thing becomes the class conflict itself
rather than the end toward which in Marxian thought that
conflict leads.

The syndicalist advocates "direct action" by which he means
constant and unremitting conflict with the employers, such
action to take the form of the strike, sabotage, the union label,
and the boycott of goods produced by non-union labor.

The strike brings the workingmen face to face with the employers
in a clash of interests. A strike clears up, as if by a flash of lightning,
the deep antagonism which exists between those who employ and
those who work for employers. It further deepens the chasm between
them, consolidating the employers on the one hand, and the workingmen on the other, over against one another. It is a revolutionary
fact of great value.[23]

Sabotage may range from the deliberate destruction of machinery to loafing on the job, it consists of slowing up and
obstructing production. The label and the boycott emphasize
the importance of labor as consumers.

Like the Marxists, the syndicalists regard the State as an instrument of class coercion and propose to overthrow it completely. It is impossible, therefore, to work within the framework of the state, to collaborate with political parties, to bargain or compromise. Labor should have no country. "Ties of tradition, of a common intellectual and moral heritage do not exist for him." [24] The only sentiment worthy of labor is that of class solidarity. Syndicalism has been defined by the syndicalists as a trade union reading of the Marxian economic doctrine and the class war. They claim that it is the only true labor movement and that Marxian socialism is not. They oppose collective ownership of the means of production as much as they oppose private ownership of the means of production and contemplate the establishment of producers' co-operatives operating as independent political units.

There are many varieties of syndicalism, some less violent than others. Probably there is no "typical" syndicalist but within the syndicalist movement the most prominent intellectually has been Georges Sorel. He is also the most extreme in his views. Probably the central doctrine of his teaching is the "myth of the general strike." By a "myth" Sorel means "a body of images capable of evoking sentiment instinctively." It is not by reason but by myths that human behavior is largely determined. Myths are neither true nor false for they "are not descriptions of things, but expressions of a determination to act." For this reason, "myths are secure from all refutation." Christians have their "myth" in the vision of the Kingdom of God, liberals have their "myth" in the vision of a society embodying "liberty, fraternity, and equality"—now labor needs its own myth and the best myth for labor, according to Sorel, is the myth of the *general strike*, the vision of the catastrophic end of capitalism in a paralysis of production. Whether this actually takes place is not as important as the *belief* that it will take place. What happens afterward is not as important as what labor believes will happen. Sorel distinguishes between "myths" and "utopias":

. . . myths are not descriptions of things, but expressions of determination to act. A Utopia is, on the contrary, an intellectual product; it is the work of theorists who, after observing and discussing the known facts, seek to establish a model to which they can compare existing society in order to estimate the amount of good and evil it contains . . . the effect of Utopias has always been to direct men's minds towards reforms which can be brought about by patching up the existing system. . . . A myth cannot be refuted, since it is, at bottom, identical with the convictions of a group . . . and it is, in consequence, unanalysable into parts which could be placed on the plane of historical descriptions. A Utopia, on the contrary, can be discussed like any other social constitution; the spontaneous movements it presupposes can be compared with the movements actually observed in the course of history. . . .

For a long time Socialism was scarcely anything but a Utopia; the Marxists were right in claiming for their master the honour of bringing about a change in this state of things; Socialism has now become the preparation of the masses employed in great industries for the suppression of the State and property; and it is no longer necessary, therefore, to discuss how men must organize themselves in order to enjoy future happiness; everything is reduced to the *revolutionary apprenticeship* of the proletariat. . . .

Today the confidence of the Socialists is greater than ever since the myth of the general strike dominates all the truly working-class movement. No failure proves anything against Socialism since the latter has become the work of preparation (for revolution); if they are checked, it merely proves that the apprenticeship has been insufficient; they must set to work again with more courage, persistence, and confidence than before. . . .[25]

Sorel has nothing but contempt for the Parliamentary Socialists who have abandoned the idea of insurrection. They shrink from violence because they think it is a relic of barbarism and because they are "cowards." They seek to woo the middle class when they should be repudiating them.

To repay with black *ingratitude* the *benevolence* of those who would protect the workers, to meet with insults the homilies of the defenders of human fraternity, and to reply by blows to the advances of the propagators of social peace—all that is assuredly not in conformity with the rules of the fashionable Socialism . . . but it is a very practical way of indicating to the middle class that they must mind their own business and only that.

I believe also that it may be useful to thrash the orators of democcracy and the representatives of the Government, for in this way you insure that none shall retain any illusions about the character of acts of violence. But these acts can have historical value only if they are the *clear and brutal expression of the class war:* the middle classes must not be allowed to imagine that, aided by cleverness, social science, or high-flown sentiments, they might find a better welcome at the hands of the proletariat. . . .

Proletarian violence not only makes the future revolution certain, but it seems also to be the only means by which the European nations—at present stupified by humanitarianism—can recover their former energy . . . if properly conducted it will suppress the Parliamentary Socialists, who will no longer be able to pose as the leaders of the working classes and the guardians of order.[26]

By violence only, can the re-division of society into classes be accomplished and the class war intensified. Acts of proletarian violence should resemble acts of war, carried on without hatred and revenge, but with resolute and heroic determination to vanquish the enemy.

The social revolution is an extension of that war in which each great strike is an episode; this is the reason why Syndicalists speak of that revolution in the language of strikes; for them Socialism is reduced to the conception, the expectation of, and the preparation for the general strike, which, like the Napoleonic battle, is to completely annihilate a condemned regime. . . .

It would serve no purpose to explain to the poor that they ought not to feel sentiments of jealousy and vengeance against their masters; these feelings are too powerful to be suppressed by exhortations. . . . Social war, by making an appeal to the honour which develops so naturally in all organized armies, can eliminate those evil feelings against which morality would remain powerless. If this were the only reason we had for attributing a high civilizing value to revolutionary Syndicalism, this reason alone would, it seems to me, be decisive in favour of the apologists for violence.[27]

The sentiment of "honor" replaces in revolutionary Syndicalism the middle-class sentiment of justice. Through this sentiment of "honor," violence is transformed from something hateful and cruel into something noble and sublime. Labor needs to learn not how to love his employer but how to destroy him. Violence enlightened by the idea of the general strike, Sorel insists, is the only salvation of the modern world. The individual worker must not expect an immediate or individual reward for his services as a "hero" of labor but must be willing to sacrifice himself for the greater glory of labor.

There would never have been great acts of heroism in war if each soldier, while acting as a hero, yet at the same time claimed to receive a reward appropriate to his deserts. When a column is sent to an assault the men at the head know that they are sent to their death and that the glory of victory will be for those passing over their dead bodies to enter the enemy's position. However, they do not reflect on this injustice, but march forward.[28]

With syndicalism Marxian socialism is emptied of all specific content. The violence of revolutionary action becomes an end in itself and whatever justification for revolutionary action inhered in Marxian socialism is dissipated by the repudiation of any specific program for social reform. The kinship between Syndicalism and Fascism is a close one and it is no accident that Mussolini was an avid reader of the works of Sorel.

## Fabian Socialism

MARXIAN socialism found expression in England in the formation in 1881 of the Social Democratic Federation. Sympathetically disposed toward this Federation but independent of it there was formed in 1883 the Fabian Society (after Fabius who fought Hannibal). It included among its membership such men as George Bernard Shaw, Sidney Webb, Graham Wallas, H. G. Wells, J. Ramsay MacDonald, Keir Hardie, G. D. H. Cole and many others who have since become prominent in British life. In 1887 the Society drafted the following statement of principles:

The Fabian Society consists of socialists.

It therefore aims at the reorganization of society by the emancipation of land and industrial capital from individual and class ownership, and the vesting of them in the community for the general benefit. . . .

The Society accordingly works for the extinction of private property in land and of the consequent individual appropriation in the form of rent, of the price paid for permission to use the earth, as well as for the advantages of superior soils and sites.

The Society, further, works for the transfer to the community of the administration of such industrial capital as can be conveniently managed socially. . . .

If these measures be carried out, without compensation (though not without such relief to expropriated individuals as may seem fit to the community), rent and interest will be added to the reward of labor, the idle class now living on the labor of others will necessarily disappear, and practical equality of opportunity will be maintained by the spontaneous action of economic forces with much less interference with personal liberty than the present system entails.

For the attainment of these ends the Fabian Society looks to the spread of socialist opinions, and the social and political changes consequent thereon. . . . It seeks to achieve these ends by the general dissemination of knowledge as to the relation between the individual and society in its economic, ethical and political aspects.[29]

The Society produced numerous pamphlets and essays that had a widespread influence not only in Great Britain but in other countries as well. Perhaps the most important publication of the Society was the *Fabian Essays* edited by G. B. Shaw and delivered as lectures in London in 1888. According to Sidney Webb's essay on "The Historic Basis of Socialism" "No philosopher now looks for anything but the gradual evolution of the new order from the old, without breach of continuity or abrupt change of the entire social tissue at any point during the process." [30] He envisaged the emergence of a socialist society, in Great Britain particularly, as the result of democratic, gradual, peaceful and constitutional means. In his essay on "The Economic Basis of Socialism" George Bernard Shaw proclaimed the independence of the society from the "obsolete" economic theories of Karl Marx but declared that "The modern form of private property is simply a legal claim to take a share of the produce of the national industry year by year without working for it. . . . Socialism involves the discontinuance of the payment of these incomes, and addition of the wealth so saved to incomes derived from labor." [31] In an essay on "The Moral Basis of Socialism" Sidney Olivier declared that "Socialism is merely individualism rationalized, organized, clothed, and in its right mind." [32] Competition and capitalism, he declared, are immoral and dishonest. Socialism will improve the morality of society since "Nothing so well trains the individual to identify his life with the life of society as the identification of the materials of his material sustenance with those of his fellows, in short, as industrial co-operation . . . the completion of the co-operative form towards which the transition stage of individualist capitalism is hurrying us, will render a conformity with social ethics a universal condition of tolerable existence for the individual." [33] When society has satisfied man's primary economic needs "his advance in the refinements of social morality . . . is solely and entirely a matter of education." [34]

Discussing the non-profit incentives in a future socialist society Annie Besant declared that "The desire to excel, the joy in creative work, the longing to improve, the eagerness to win social approval, the instinct of benevolence; all these will start into full life, and will serve at once as the stimulus to labor and the reward of excellence." [35] If an individual worker nevertheless does shirk his work "he will be warned, and, if he prove incorrigibly idle, discharged from the communal employ." [36] In a concluding chapter on "The Outlook" for socialism Hubert Bland declared that

Inquiry proves that socialism is built upon a triple rock, historical, ethical, and economic. . . . By the light of the socialist ideal he sees the evil—yet sees it pass. Then and now he begins to live in the cleaner, braver, holier life of the future; and he marches forward, steeled and stimulated, with resolute step, with steadfast eye, with equal pulse.[37]

The Fabian Society continues in existence today with G. D. H. Cole as its president and in 1942 Cole defined the present-day role of the Society in these words:

We believe that there is need, somewhere in the socialist movement for a body which is entirely free to think out and to give publicity to new ideas, even where they run counter to socialist orthodoxies inherited from the past. Socialism . . . is a set of prin-

ciples that need continual re-interpretation in the light of changing
needs and conditions. . . . [The Fabian Society is] organized for
thought and discussion and not for electoral action. . . .[38]

## Guild Socialism

A LESS violent version of French syndicalism found expression
in Great Britain in the early part of the twentieth century in a
movement known as Guild Socialism. Many individuals contributed to the theoretical foundations of the movement which
drew some of its inspiration from the nineteenth-century writings of Ruskin, Carlyle, and Morris but its most effective
popularizer was G. D. H. Cole. As an organized movement it
might be said to have begun with the formation of the Guilds
Restoration Movement in 1906 and the National Guilds
League in 1915. Cole had tried unsuccessfully to interest the
Fabian Society in Guild Socialism and its refusal to commit
itself necessitated the formation of another group. The object of the National Guilds League was declared to be "the
abolition of the wage system, and the establishment of self-
government in industry through a system of national guilds
working in conjunction with the state."[39]

G. D. H. Cole explains that the idea of guild socialism was
borrowed in part from the medieval guild.

In the Middle Ages there were industrial sinners, but they were
conscious of sin; for commercial morality and communal morality
were the same. Today, commercial morality had made a code of its
own, and most of its clauses are flat denials of the principles of
communal morality. In the Middle Ages, the motives to which the
industrial system made its appeal were motives of free communal
service: today, they are motives of greed and fear.

Clearly, we cannot seek to restore the mediaeval . . . spirit in
industry by restoring the material conditions of the Middle Ages.
We cannot go back to "town economy," a general regime of handicraft and master-craftsmanship, tiny-scale production. . . . If the
mediaeval system has lessons for us, they are not parrot-lessons of
slavish imitation, but lessons of the spirit, by which we may learn
to build up, on the basis of large-scale production and the world

market, a system of industrial organization that appeals to the finest human motives and is capable of developing the tradition of free communal service. I fully believe that, when we have established these free conditions, there will come, from producer and consumer alike, a widespread demand for goods of finer quality than the shoddy which we turn out in such quantity today, and that this will bring about a new standard of craftsmanship and a return, over a considerable sphere, to small-scale production. But this, if it comes, will come only as the deliberate choice of free men in a free Society. Our present problem is, taking the conditions of production substantially as we find them, to reintroduce into industry the communal spirit, by refashioning industrialism in such a way as to set the communal motives free to operate.[40]

The guild is defined as "a self-governing association of mutually dependent people organized for a responsible discharge of a particular function of society."[41] Each guild is to include all those employed in a given industry, trade, or profession, managers as well as workers, and each is to have a monopoly of the particular activity it includes. The managers would be elected by the members of the guild but only those with prescribed qualifications would be eligible for election to positions requiring technical knowledge and skill. According to Cole:

A Guild factory, then, would be a natural center of self-government, no longer, like the factories of today, a mere prison of boredom and useless toil, but a center of free service and associative enterprise. . . .

In this factory there would doubtless be workshop committees, meetings, debates, voting, and all the phenomena of democratic organization; but, though these are essential, they are not so much of the quintessence of the new thing as the co-operative spirit which they exist to safeguard. Given free choice of leaders and free criticism of them when chosen, a good deal of the mere machinery of democracy might remain normally in the background.[42]

There would be not only industrial guilds but consumers' guilds, Civic Guilds, as well as guilds for the various arts and professions. These would all be organized locally, regionally and nationally.

In place of the state there would be substituted a "commune" organized locally, regionally, and nationally. According to Cole the communes would deal with

(1) financial problems, especially the allocation of national resources, provision of capital, and, to a certain extent, regulation of incomes and prices:
(2) differences arising between functional bodies on questions of policy;
(3) constitutional questions of demarcation between functional bodies;
(4) questions not falling within the sphere of any functional authority, including general questions of external relations;
(5) coercive functions.[43]

The National Commune would consist of representatives of the national guilds, agricultural, industrial, and civic; of the national councils (economic and civic) and of the regional communes.

Its general structure would thus be essentially the same as that of the smaller Communes which, equally with the national functional bodies, it would exist to coordinate. It would be a much less imposing body as the central organ of Society than the Great Leviathan of today, with its huge machinery of coercion and bureaucratic government. But it would be none the worse for that; for where the spirit of community is most at home, there is the machinery of central government likely to be least in evidence.[44]

In this and subsequent writings, however, Cole insisted that he did not

profess to be able to forecast with any confidence precisely how a planned socialist economy would decide to organize the machinery of production, and both the few words I have said here and the many detailed proposals which I have given elsewhere are intended rather to illustrate principles than to lay down dogmatically how they can best be applied.[45]

In the most recent pronouncement of his views he declared:

At one time I strongly advocated that socialized industries should be managed by Guilds representing the various groups of persons engaged in them—managers, technicians and manual and administrative workers—under the general policy control of the State. I did not suggest that such Guilds should control prices or production policy or their members' pay; for such things clearly raise general issues which must be settled by representatives of the entire community. I drew a distinction between policy, which includes such matters, and the actual management and technical control of industrial processes, which I believed should be in the hands of the workers. . . . I still hold this view, but not that it can be immediately applied.[46]

Guild socialism was and remains a kind of anemic version of French syndicalism.[47]

## The British Labor Party

ALTHOUGH Karl Marx lived and wrote in London, his ideas had very little currency in Great Britain during his lifetime and it was not until 1881 that a Social Democratic Federation organized by Henry Hyndman, William Morris, Eleanor Marx (Karl's daughter) and others appeared on the scene to champion Marxian socialism. The Fabian Society made its appearance in 1883. In 1889 a Scottish coal miner, Keir Hardie, founded the Scottish Labor Party and in 1892 was the first labor candidate to be elected to the British House of Commons. The following year, along with others, he founded the Independent Labor Party. Its program was similar to that of the Social Democratic Federation but it was much more sympathetic to the trade union movement. One of the early members of this party was J. Ramsay MacDonald who played a prominent role in enlisting the trade union movement in political action and who was destined to head the first Labor Party government in 1924.

In 1899 the British Trade Union Congress passed a resolution instructing the Parliamentary Committee of the Trade Union Congress to cooperate with all socialist, trade union, and other working-class organizations "to devise ways and means for the securing of an increased number of labor members to the next Parliament." Representatives of the Independent Labor Party, the Social Democratic Federation, and the Fabian Society met with the Parliamentary Committee and as a result of their efforts there was formed the Labor Representation Committee. In 1906 the name of this commit-

tee was changed to the British Labor Party. The British Labor
Party was formed, and remains today, primarily as a federation of labor groups rather than as a party of individuals.
Membership in the party is generally incidental to membership in a trade union or other labor group.[48] Before the election
of 1945 the Labor Party had been in power twice, once in 1924
and again from 1929–1931. Both times it was handicapped by
the fact that it had agreed to take over the government although it lacked a majority of the House of Commons and had
to depend upon the Liberal Party for support. In the postwar
election of 1945 Labor polled the largest vote in its history and
secured 393 seats out of a total of 640. For the first time Labor
took over the government with an overwhelming majority
and has since been endeavoring to put into practice many of
the ideas for which it has fought throughout recent decades.

According to the Constitution of the British Labor Party its
aim is:

> To secure for the workers by hand or by brain the full fruits of
> their industry and the most equitable distribution thereof that may
> be possible, upon the basis of the common ownership of the means
> of production, distribution, and exchange, and the best obtainable
> system of popular administration and control of each industry and
> service. Generally to promote the political, social, and economic
> emancipation of the people, and more particularly of those who
> depend directly upon their own exertions by hand or by brain for
> the means of life . . . to cooperate with the Labor and Socialist
> organizations in other countries and to assist in organizing a Fed-
> eration of Nations for the maintenance of freedom and peace. . . .[49]

In a Declaration of Policy adopted by the Labor Party Conference at Bournemouth in 1940 it was stated:

> The Labour Party is a Socialist Party; therefore it conceives of
> reconstruction in Socialist terms. But its Socialism is built upon . . .
> a determination to press for necessary social changes upon the basis
> of Democracy and Justice. We reject all demands for Dictatorship,
> whether from the Left or from the Right. We take our stand upon
> that faith in reason which looks to the declared will of the people as
> the only valid source of power. So long as that will is nationally
> respected, we are confident that the historic forms of Parliamentary

Democracy provide a highroad along which the nation can pass peacefully from an acquisitive to a Socialist society.[50]

In April, 1945, another Declaration of Policy prepared by the National Executive Committee for the forthcoming election and later approved by the annual Conference appeared. Specifically it advocated the following program: public ownership of the Bank of England; the establishment of a "National Investment Board" to "determine social priorities and promote better timing in private investment"; the building of new factories by the government when needed; public ownership of the fuel and power industries, of inland transport and of the iron and steel industry (these industries to be "taken over on a basis of fair compensation"); public supervision of monopolies and cartels; subsidization of the export trade; price control; if landlords "cannot or will not provide proper facilities for . . . tenant farmers, the State should take over his land at a fair valuation"; "a full program of land planning and drastic action to ensure an efficient building industry": greater opportunities for education and recreation; extension of health insurance and of social insurance; the "consolidation in peace" of the "great war-time association of the British Commonwealth with the U. S. A. and the U. S. S. R."; "The advancement of India to responsible self-government, and the planned progress of our colonial dependencies."

The British Labor Party seeks to steer a middle course between the dictatorial, totalitarian collectivism of the Soviet Union and the individualistic, competitive system of capitalistic free enterprise typical of the nineteenth century. It seeks to combine the economic principles of a socialist economy with the political principles of a parliamentary democracy. It likes to think of the program which it is now actively engaged in putting into practice as an experiment in "democratic socialism." And that experiment is being watched with considerable interest throughout the world for its success or failure would have a great influence upon the course of socialism in other countries.

Spokesmen for the British Labor Party frequently talk about "revolution by consent" and it is upon this that their claim to democracy is based. Socialism, they say, can be obtained by the consent of the people and it is the consent of the people that makes it democratic. Thus the late Harold J. Laski, a leading intellectual leader in Labor Party circles and a recent chairman of the Party declared:

> The Labour Party will seek to make a revolution by consent. It will try to build the socialist commonwealth for the creation of which it has a decisive mandate by the processes of constitutional democracy.[51]

But the question remains: does adherence to democratic principles mean simply that social changes should be effected in accordance with the consent of the people? Is the consent of the people alone a sufficient safeguard against tyranny? Do the people retain the right to reject socialism once they have consented to its establishment?

That the issue between "liberalism" and "totalitarianism" remains a live issue within the ranks of the British Labor Party and that some realize that "liberalism" may have to be sacrificed or, at least, modified to accommodate socialism is made apparent in a book published by G. D. H. Cole in 1948 in which he said:

> . . . even in a Socialist society, "after the revolution," there will be, an issue to be settled between totalitarians and liberals.
>
> I, like most British Socialists, am a "liberal." But I think we who take this view have to be on our guard against letting the liberalism of our ideals stultify our practice. We have learnt during the past few years that, on the international plane, "liberalism" . . . is a creed for which we may be required to wage total war, doing a host of things that we utterly dislike doing because we must either do them or suffer "liberal" values to go down in defeat. The same thing is true, I think, subject to the necessary modifications, in our internal affairs. We cannot afford to let the anti-democratic forces win by refusing to counter them by means which are distasteful to us. In the name of freedom, it was necessary to suppress blackshirt armies and to intern Sir Oswald Mosley. And, in the name of freedom and democracy, it is necessary for us to get Socialism, even if we have to take quite a number of high-handed steps in order to get it.[52]

That the economic end tends to loom larger in the minds of some British Socialist leaders than the political means is illustrated in a discussion of the nature of parliamentary democracy by Cole in his *Guide to Modern Politics:*

In the course of the nineteenth century there grew up in men's minds what was almost an identification of two very different things —parliamentarism and democracy. . . . "Parliamentarism = representative government = democracy" epitomises in a phrase the predominant creed of the Liberalism of the last century. But in fact no two of these things can be identified. Parliaments are not necessarily democratic nor are they always institutions of government. Representative government need not be either parliamentary or democratic. . . . Democracy need not take a parliamentary form or even base itself upon representative institutions in the ordinary sense of that term. In the nineteenth century the horizon of politics seemed to have been narrowed, leaving only parliamentarism above it. But today the facile identification of the three things is no longer possible. . . . It may turn out that the Soviet or something like it, is the necessary form of political organisation for the institution of a new social system. And it may be that out of the Soviet system through transformations and adaptations that it is impossible yet to foresee, mankind will develop new types of political organisation going far beyond parliamentarism towards the achievement of real democracy.

For democracy, if it is ever to become real, demands a far more flexible form of organisation than the parliamentary system affords.[53]

Harold J. Laski, whose orientation in recent years was more Marxian than that of many other British socialist leaders, has declared:

We have come to the boundaries of the final dividing line between liberalism and socialism. We are choosing between institutions which assume that freedom must be won by the few and institutions which assume that they must be planned by the many. Either we must have power in the hands of men who use scarcity as the means of compulsion, or we must give it to men who find abundance is the instrument of freedom. There is no middle way. . . . We must plan our civilization or we must perish.[54]

Increasingly in Laski's writings there was a tendency to equate "planned production" with democracy and throughout recent years there has been a growing tendency in his writings to praise the Communist system in Russia with complete indifference to its political tyranny.[55] In *The State in Theory and Practice* (1935) Laski defined the state in these terms:

> . . . the essence of the state is its power to employ coercion in order to enforce the will of that group or groups which control the government, for it is by the government that the authority of the state is brought into operation. The will of the government is, in its turn, finally determined by the character of the class-relations in society. . . .
>
> The state, we argue, is not above classes. It does not transcend particular interests and lead to the expression of the total good of society. It is not a way of moving towards the fulfillment of the desires of its citizens. It does not seek to realize the rights they must claim in order to maintain the full dignity of their capacity as moral beings. It does not maintain law and order simply as the atmosphere vital to the maximum satisfaction of demand. It does not legitimate the force it employs by devoting that force to the service of a community regarded as a body of men and women with an equal claim to what of common good imperfect human beings may hope to achieve.
>
> What, then, on this view, is the state? It is supreme coercive power used to protect the consequences inherent in the postulate of any given society. That power is exercised by the government in the name of the state since, of course, the latter can act only through persons.[56]

And he adds that "if the postulates of the state are capitalist, it must logically follow that the state will protect the consequences that a capitalist system requires"—it also logically follows from his analysis that if the postulates of the state are socialistic, that the state will protect the consequences of such a system. If the essence of the state is "supreme coercive power to protect the consequences inherent in the postulate of any given society" then that remains the essence of the state under a socialistic system as well as under a capitalistic one. And Laski, in 1935 at least, was less optimistic about the ability of a socialist government to persuade the capitalists to relinquish their "postulates" than are some of his former colleagues in the British Labor Party today.

The inability of capitalists to accept postulates different from their own is born of the situation in which they find themselves. . . .

We have got, somehow, to make up our minds, to the fact that the debate upon the rights of property has always, in history, aroused passions more profound than those involved in the analysis of any other theme. It is wholly natural that they should, since the relations which they give rise determine all the major contours of our social life. . . .

But the transformation, it is said, has the assurance of numbers on its side. The owners of property are few; the proletariat are many. As the latter grow to a consciousness of their power, by the nature of the case they must dominate the situation. In Great Britain, for example, they may vote themselves, when they will, into political authority. They can then command exactly the same instruments— in last resort, the armed forces of the state—upon which the domination of the possessing-class depends. . . .

I have already discussed, to some extent, the assumptions implied in this view. It is, I think, contradicted by a number of factors upon which too much stress can hardly be laid. It is important, in the first place, that there is too little assurance that numbers, even if they are persuaded, will be allowed to have their way. . . .

But even if a socialist government, which was determined on drastic change, were enthroned in office, its difficulties would only have commenced. . . . If it goes slowly, it will suffer from all the difficulties which confront any government which tries, upon the basis of capitalist postulates, to effect their piece-meal transformation. It tends to irritate its opponents by undermining confidence; and it fails to attract its supporters by inability to offer them the exhilarating spectacle of conviction turned into deed. If it proceeds rapidly—and the case for rapid action is overwhelmingly strong— it is likely to meet with sabotage and resistance. . . .

The conclusion seems clear that the logic of a revolution excludes the possibility of compromise, if it is to be a successful revolution. The state-power is not the kind of authority that can dwell in the twilight world of forms.[57]

Laski, it seems to me, points to the real problem when he says that "the logic of revolution excludes the possibility of compromise." The defeat of the Labor Party in a general election might signify to large numbers of the Party the defeat of "democratic socialism" in which case the counsels of Laski might be more highly regarded than they are today by the leaders of that Party.

The success of socialism in Great Britain will depend not

only upon the ability of the Labor Government successfully to meet the serious economic problems which it has inherited from the war years but even more upon its ability to inspire moral support for its objectives. As a British socialist, Victor Gollancz, has said: "There is little merit in socialism as a matter of pure economics. Nationalisation and all the rest of it is so much mere machinery, though essential machinery; the aim is, or should be, the enhancement of personality. A technically socialist state, in the economic sense, can be as illiberal, as materialistic, as inhumane as a capitalist one: indeed, it can be more so. In other words, socialism is valuable only in so far as it serves western values." [58] Inspired by respect for human personality, imbued with a consciousness of spiritual reality, intent upon preserving and extending individual freedom, British socialism may, indeed, be able to overcome many of the evils of a capitalistic system "which consecrates self-interest and greed over a large area of daily life," but if its leadership is taken over by men who value economic programs above human personality, who conceive of "the essence of the state" as "its power to employ coercion in order to enforce the will of that group or groups which control government" then it is certain to end in slavery and disaster.

## Anarchism

ANARCHISM has a long intellectual lineage extending to the earliest beginnings of Western political thought but it acquired a special point of view in the nineteenth century that puts many anarchists in the camp of the Socialists. F. W. Coker defines anarchism as "the doctrine that political authority, in any of its forms, is unnecessary and undesirable" and he adds, that "in recent anarchism, theoretical opposition to the state has usually been associated with opposition to the institution of private property and also with hostility to organized religious authority." [59]

One of the earliest expressions of anarchist thought in modern times was William Godwin's *Enquiry Concerning Political Justice and Its Influence on General Virtue and Happiness* (1793).

Godwin started from some of the presuppositions underlying liberalism: (1) that the mind is devoid of any innate principles or instincts, (2) that man is essentially good and rational, (3) that man, if not perfect, is perfectible in time and reached the logical conclusion, that liberalism refused to reach, that institutions are the greatest obstacle to justice. His arguments are based, as he himself declared, upon these presuppositions: (1) "that the moral characters of men are the result of their perceptions": (2) "that of all the modes of operating upon mind government is the most considerable"; (3) "that the good and ill effects of political institutions are not less conspicuous in detail than in principle"; and (4) that "perfectibility is one of the most unequivocal characteristics of the human species, so that the political as well as the intellectual state of man may be presumed to be in a course of progressive improvement." Moreover, "we bring into the world with us no innate principles: consequently, we are neither virtuous nor vicious as we first come into existence. . . . The moral qualities of men are the product of the impressions made upon them, and . . . there is no instance of an original propensity to evil." [60] Godwin quotes Locke in support of these contentions and says that his arguments are only an abstract from the arguments employed by Locke in his *Essay on Human Understanding*, by Hartley in his *Observations of Man* and by Rousseau in his *Émile*. Through the "uncontrolled exercise of private judgment and the rigid conformity of every man to the dictates of his conscience" it would be possible, Godwin declares, to produce a virtuous disposition that would render human institutions unnecessary.[61] That it is a relatively simple matter both to know and to follow the dictates of conscience he believes.

> Justice . . . is coincident with utility. I am myself a part of the great whole, and my happiness is a part of that complex view of things by which justice is regulated. The hope of reward therefore and the fear of punishment, confined within certain strict limits, are motives that ought to have influence with my mind.

There are two descriptions of tendency that may belong to any action, the tendency which it possesses by the necessary and universal laws of existence, and the tendency which results from the positive (or arbitrary) interference of some intelligent being. The nature of happiness and misery, pleasure and pain is independent of all positive institution; that is, it is immutably true that whatever tends to procure a balance of the latter is to be rejected. In like manner the promulgation of virtue, truth and political justice must always be right. There is perhaps no action of a rational being that has not some tendency to promote these objects, and consequently that has not a moral character founded in the abstract nature of things.

The tendency of positive institution is of two sorts, to furnish me with an additional motive to the practice of virtue or right, and to inform my understanding as to what actions are right and what actions are wrong. Much cannot be said in commendation of either of these tendencies.[62]

Morality requires that we should prefer actions because of their "intrinsic excellence" and that "we should be attentive only to the tendency which belongs to any action by the necessary and universal laws of existence"; [63] hence, when human institutions endeavor to "furnish . . . an additional motive to the practice of virtue" they are, in reality, perverting virtue. Similarly, "every proposition has an intrinsic evidence of its own. Every consequence has premises from which it flows; and upon them, and not upon anything else, its validity depends." [64] When human institutions endeavor to back up certain propositions by sanctions they are no longer relying upon the "intrinsic evidence" of the truthfulness of the proposition, the only basis upon which its truthfulness can be accepted. Punishment, in short, cannot make a man better nor can it convince him of error.

There can be no doubt that the proper way of conveying to my understanding a truth of which I am ignorant, or of impressing upon me a firmer persuasion of a truth with which I am acquainted, is by an appeal to my reason. Even an angry expostulation with me upon my conduct will but excite similar passions in me, and cloud instead of illuminate my understanding. There is certainly a way of expressing truth with such benevolence as to command attention, and such evidence as to enforce conviction in all cases whatever.[65]

If we believe that all men are rational, that they are capable of "pure" dispassionate reasoning, and that all truth is accessible to human reason, I do not see how we can refuse to be convinced by his arguments. Only if we believe that reason is fallible, that the particular reason of particular individuals is apt to be perverted by passionate self-interest, and that the whole truth is not accessible to human reason alone can we answer him. If ignorance alone is the root of evil, as Godwin believes, then surely argument and persuasion are the only appropriate means of combatting that evil and coercion in any form is not only undesirable but irrelevant. Coercion is justified only if we can conceive of situations in which men are wilfully wrong; restraint through the medium of social institutions is justified only if we believe that man is by nature so predisposed to evil that he must often be restrained not only for his own good but for the good of others. Godwin, Sir Leslie Stephen declared, "would expunge every vestige of tradition from the tablet of the human mind. He would raze to the ground the whole structure of political and religious belief, and substitute a new order of things in which the sole binding force should be derived from pure abstract reasoning. Godwin shared these views with a whole school, but no other English writer traces them back so thoroughly to first principles." [66] Liberalism contains in its presuppositions all the conclusions drawn by Godwin but few liberals were willing to draw the inferences which he drew. The proclamation of the autonomy of human reason, the declaration of the independence of reason from revelation, the denial of the existence of any innate principles in human nature, the equation of evil with ignorance or intellectual error, necessarily lead to the repudiation of all authority if only one is willing to draw the inferences which flow logically from the premises. In that sense Godwin could claim to be a better, or, at least, a more consistent, liberal than Locke.

There are many other examples of anarchist thought in the nineteenth century but of these two stand out prominently, Michael Bakunin (1814–1876) and Peter Kropotkin (1842–1921).

Peter Kropotkin was born in Moscow, Russia, in 1842, the son of Prince Alexei Kropotkin. He entered upon a military career at the age of fifteen but left the army in 1876 when he entered the university at St. Petersburg and became an official of the Russian Geographical Society. It was there that he joined revolutionary circles and in 1872 became a member of the International Workingmen's Association. Shortly thereafter, he became an anarchist and was imprisoned several times in different countries. He settled in England in 1886 and it was there that he did most of his literary work. He returned to Russia in June, 1917, but took no active part in the revolution. He died there in 1921.

Kropotkin endeavored to give anarchism a "scientific" basis by appealing to the "laws of natural evolution." In a book entitled *Mutual Aid*, he described the usual doctrine of evolution (as a struggle for existence with survival of the strongest) as a caricature of reality. Organic evolution, he argued, is not essentially or primarily characterized by conflict and competition but by cooperation and "mutual aid." Weaker species do not necessarily die out but perpetuate themselves by social combination, by the development of social instincts and mutual aid. This tendency plays a far more important role in organic evolution than competition, for the species that lack social life and that are dependent for survival solely upon physical superiority, do not survive as long as do those which develop social instincts and combinations. This principle of mutual aid manifests itself in human society in the principle that one should do to others as he would that others should do to him. Thus the Golden Rule is discovered to be a primary factor and law of organic evolution. Left alone to work out his destiny in accordance with the principles of evolution, man would eventually attain a perfect, harmonious society.

He is impeded in the attainment of that goal by the state, the institution of private property, and by religious institutions. All of these serve only to put obstacles in the way of that natural capacity for sympathy and mutual aid with which men are born. The only cooperation, in any case, that can be called real cooperation is that which is uncoerced.

The State, he argued, has neither natural nor historical justification because it is founded upon the false assumption that men are by nature unsocial and competitive. The State with its monopoly of coercive authority and its propensity to enact laws is a modern phenomenon. Before the modern State and legislation came into existence men lived under the rules of custom which were beneficial to them since they reflected their nature but, with the emergence of the State, law has less and less to do with custom and has become simply an instrument whereby the property owners sustain their power. Rather than defending the rights of individuals as it claims to do, the State exploits them. All the coercive activities of the State are more harmful than they are helpful. Prisons, for example, he argued, breed more crime than they prevent. Men voluntarily united in their own defense can better protect themselves than they can be protected by standing armies. In contests between professional armies and popular militia it is the latter who always win. It does not matter what form of government a state takes, it is always true that government is an enemy of real freedom.

Individual appropriation is neither just nor serviceable. All belongs to all. All things are for all men, since all men have need of them, since all men have worked in the measure of their strength to produce them, and since it is not possible to evaluate every one's part in the production of the world's wealth. . . .

If the man and the woman bear their fair share of work, they have a right to their fair share of all that is produced by all, and that share is enough to secure them well-being. No more of such vague formulas as "The right to work," or "To each the whole result of his labor." What we proclaim is THE RIGHT TO WELL-BEING: WELL-BEING FOR ALL! [67]

Kropotkin envisages a future society which will establish "Communism without government."

. . . if we observe the present development of civilized nations, we see, most unmistakably, a movement ever more and more marked tending to limit the sphere of action of the Government, and to allow more and more liberty to the individual. This evolution is going on before our eyes. . . . Like all evolutions, it only waits a revolution to overthrow the old obstacles which block the way, that it may find free scope in a regenerated society.

After having striven long in vain to solve the insoluble problem—the problem of constructing a government "which will constrain the individual to obedience without itself ceasing to be the servant of society," men at last attempt to free themselves from every form of government and to satisfy their need for organization by free contacts between individuals and groups pursuing the same aim. The independence of each small territorial unit becomes a pressing need; mutual agreement replaces law in order to regulate individual interests in view of a common object. . . .

Things are arranged more easily and more satisfactorily without the intervention of the State.[68]

The trend toward anarchy is inevitable, hence the anarchist is not properly regarded as an advocate but as a scientist, he "merely points out in which direction evolution goes. . . . It is no longer a matter of faith; it is a matter for scientific discussion." [69]

How would Kropotkin deal with criminals in an anarchistic society? According to him there would be no criminals in such a society because there would be no incentives to crime. "The more we study the question," of crime, he wrote, "the more we are brought to the conclusion that society itself is responsible for the anti-social deeds perpetrated in its midst, and that no punishment, no prisons, no hangmen can diminish the numbers of such deeds; nothing short of a reorganization of society itself." The overwhelming majority of crimes, he thinks, have their origin in the inequitable distribution of wealth, cure that and you will eliminate most crimes. For the other types of crime, which he does not think will be numerous, science will eventually find a remedy. In anarchistic society religion will be replaced by a "natural" morality for "a morality which has become instinctive" is the only "true morality, the only morality which endures while religions and systems of philosophy pass away." [70]

Bakunin was born in Russia in 1814 of an aristocratic family. His father was a retired diplomat. At first, Bakunin embarked upon a military career but abandoned it in 1834 in order to study philosophy. He went to Germany, to Switzerland, finally to Paris where he met Marx and Engels. Expelled from France he went to Belgium and in 1848 was back again in Germany. In May, 1849, he was one of the leaders in an insurrection in the city of Dresden, as a result of which activity, he was imprisoned and condemned to death. He was handed over to the

Austrian government, however, who wanted him for leading an insurrection among the Czechs in 1848. Again he was condemned to death. The sentence was commuted to life imprisonment but he was turned over to the Russian government which had already tried him *in absentia* for radical activities. He was exiled to Siberia in 1855, from which region he managed to escape six years later. Traveling by way of Japan and the United States he went to England. He died in Switzerland in 1876. For a few years he was associated with the International Workingmen's Association founded by Marx but in 1872 he and his followers were expelled.

For Bakunin the two chief obstacles to human freedom are belief in God and the State. He repudiates the State because, like the Marxians, he sees it as being an instrument of class coercion for the exploitation of the working class, and because it demoralizes governors as well as governed by ruling with compulsion rather than with persuasion. Like Godwin, he argued that true morality consists of behavior in accordance with private judgment and governance by the State is incompatible with the exercise of private judgment. The State's judgment overrides, of necessity, the judgment of individuals. Action in accordance with the dictates of the State is not moral action but compelled action. For, according to Bakunin, "Liberty, morality, and the human dignity of man consist precisely in this that he does good, not because it is commanded, but because he conceives it, wills it, loves it." [71] The State is not identical with society but represents "only an historical form of it, as brutal as it is abstract." The State is "born of the marriage of violence, war and conquest with the gods created by the theological fantasy of nations." It is the embodiment of "brutal force and triumphant inequality" and religion serves only to lend it "divine sanction." [72] It is the institution of private property that calls the State into existence and it is religion that sanctifies both private property and the State. Man is truly free only when he obeys the laws of nature voluntarily not when he is compelled to do so by any authority, human or divine, collective or individual. Bakunin is as much opposed to democratic government as he is to autocracy for democratic government is always a sham. In the last analysis democracy is an oligarchy controlled by the propertied class. Hence, he is opposed "to all legislation, all authority, and all influence, privilege, patented, official and legal, even when it has proceeded from universal suffrage," because he is "convinced that it must always turn to the profit of a dominating and exploiting minority against the interest of the immense majority enslaved." [73] He is in favor of substituting, then, for the present system a "society" that is anarchistic, collectivistic, and atheistic.

Bakunin was opposed to Communism. In a speech delivered in 1868 he said:

> I am not a Communist because Communism unites all the forces of society in the state and becomes absorbed in it; because it inevitably leads to the concentration of all property in the hands of the state, while I seek the abolition of the state—the complete elimination of the principle of authority and governmental guardianship, which under the pretense of making men moral . . . has up to now always enslaved, oppressed, exploited, and ruined them.

Of Marx he once said: "He called me a sentimental idealist and he was right; I called him a vain man, perfidious and crafty, and I also was right." Bakunin feared the cult of science as much as he feared the religion of Christianity, he could see little advantage in substituting a "priesthood" of scientists for the priesthood of the Church. Communism, he thought, was essentially a religion and to be disowned and distrusted as he disowned and distrusted all religion.

> *Of all despotisms that of the doctrinaires or inspired religionists is the worst.* They are so jealous of the glory of their God and of the triumph of their idea that they have no heart left for the liberty or the dignity or even the suffering of living men, of real men. . . . The government of science and of men of science, even be they positivists, disciples of Auguste Comte, or, a few, disciples of the *doctrinaire* school of German Communism, cannot fail to be impotent, ridiculous, inhuman, cruel, oppressive, exploiting, maleficent. We may say of men of science, *as such*, what I have said of theologians and metaphysicians; they have neither sense nor heart for individual and living beings. [74]

Contrasting Bakunin's thought with that of Marx, Professor Erich Voegelin points out that:

The materialistic conception of history contains for Bakunin a relative truth in so far as he too assumes that the social world, and the specifically human manifestation of the spirit, rest on the animal basis of man, and the animal basis in its turn on matter. But it can be the culmination of matter only because matter is not inorganic but contains spirit. The rise of matter to humanity means the release from matter of the independent principles of thought and revolt. The negation of mere animalism, the blossoming out of matter into the revolt of the soul, is the new independent factor forming history. The opposition between the principles of the free, independent soul in revolt and of the determination of thought through the economic situation, as well as the ensuing opposition between the two revolutionary tactics, has remained the issue between Bakuninists and Marxists to this day: on the one side, the faith in personality and the ability of free men to produce order out of revolutionary likemindedness without authoritarian leadership, on the other side the belief in the necessary march of history that progresses through the action of not-too-revolutionary souls under the authoritarian leadership of the executors of the historical will.[75]

In the *Confession* which Bakunin wrote at the invitation of the Tsar when in the Russian prison he said, speaking of his revolutionary activity:

I had only one confederate: Faith! I told myself that faith moves mountains, overcomes obstacles, defeats the invincible, and makes possible the impossible; faith alone is one half of victory, one half of success; complemented by powerful will it creates circumstances, makes men ripe, collects and unites them. . . . In one word: I wanted to believe, I wanted others to believe.[76]

Commenting upon this statement, Voegelin says:

This is perhaps the most perfect description ever given of the magic of evil, of creating a reality out of nothing. It is the opposition of the demonic faith under will to the Christian will under faith. This "faith under will" manifests itself later in Bakunin in the prodigious invention of non-existing revolutionary societies and the injection of such figments of imagination into reality with quite tangible results. . . . It is the first appearance of the black magic of the isolated will which later recurs in Nietzsche's "magic of the extreme," in Lenin's persistence through hopeless years until he grasped his kairos, and in Hitler's staying power and "Victory of Faith." [77]

## CHAPTER 14

# Socialism in the Soviet Union

A S A RESULT of the Revolution of November, 1917, there was established in Russia the Union of Soviet Socialist Republics and, for the first time, a state dedicated to the application, perpetuation and extension of the principles of Marxian socialism. Comprising about one-seventh of the land surface of the world and a population of over 190,000,000 people, or approximately one-tenth of the world population, the U. S. S. R. has gradually extended the orbit of its control and influence to include the larger part of Eastern Europe and of China. Although its dominion is less secure in some areas than in others the imperialistic ambitions of the U. S. S. R. give no appearance of abating, and the lust for world domination that destroyed Hitler and the Nazis in Germany appears to have infected the leaders of the Russian Kremlin. They appear, as Winston Churchill said in a recent address in the United States, to fear our friendship more than our hostility. To understand that fear we must examine not only the events which brought the Communists to power but the institutions, as well as the theories, upon which they have established that power. Does the present system reflect the real aspirations of the Russian people, or is that system a tyranny imposed upon the people by force and sustained by terror? If the latter, then we can understand why the Russian rulers and bureaucrats fear our friendship for the Russian people.

## The Revolution of 1917

FOR many centuries the Russian people lived under the autocratic rulership of the Russian Tsars and Tsarinas. Some were more enlightened than others but despite the sporadic attempts to introduce Western culture into Russia, the majority of the Russian people remained one of the most backward peoples culturally, politically and economically in all of Europe. The feudal system was introduced into Russia at the very time the last remnants of feudalism were dying out in Western Europe, and capitalism made its first appearance in Russia only shortly before the Revolution of 1917. It was not until 1861 that the Russian peasants were emancipated and not until 1905 that they were permitted to leave the village *mir* (where the land was more or less held in common and periodically distributed in dispersed strips) and to own their own property in one piece.

Russian history is punctuated by sporadic revolts among the peasants but it was not until 1905 that a political system resembling that of Western European democracies was established in Russia and even then the Tsar refused to abide by the spirit of the reform, nullifying it in action. The revolt had succeeded in persuading the Tsar to the establishment of a parliamentary assembly, the Imperial Duma, but it had very little actual power and was progressively weakened by the delimitation of the power it originally had and by the promulgation of electoral laws designed to prevent the democratic representation of the people.

The participation of Russia in World War I heightened the tension among the people, brought great suffering to soldiers and civilians alike, and focused attention upon the corruption and inefficiency of the government. Vigorous opposition to the government was expressed in the Duma by the liberal and socialist elements and the reply to their opposition was expulsion and arrest. Meetings of the Duma were then indefinitely postponed. With the army short of all supplies and the people facing starvation several thousand workers went on strike on February 27, 1917, in St. Petersburg. More and more workers joined the strikers and the cry for food and peace became more and more audible. Rioting was everywhere rampant. Soldiers on leave refused to return to the front and some of the Tsarist regiments joined the revolts which they had been sent to quell. On March 15, the Tsar abdicated at the request of the Duma and named his brother Grand Duke Michael as his successor.

Michael, however, refused to ascend the throne without a plebiscite from the people. The Duma then established a provisional government under the leadership of Prince Lvov. He was soon succeeded (in July, 1917) as premier by Alexander Kerensky, a Social Revolutionary. A non-Marxian socialist who was committed to liberal, agrarian reforms, Kerensky wanted to establish a liberal, constitutional government patterned after the parliamentary democracies of Western Europe. Reluctant to undertake any reforms without the explicit approval of the people he postponed the question of land reform and called for a meeting of a Constituent Assembly to draft a Constitution. He refused to repudiate the international obligations of the Tsarist government as some urged him to do and mistaking completely the mood of the Russian people urged the more vigorous prosecution of the war against Germany. His caution, if such it was, led some to suspect his motives and he was placed more and more in an ambiguous situation.

Meanwhile, Soviets (Councils) of Workers and Soldiers were set up in various towns and cities, controlled at first by the more moderate socialists. The leaders of the more radical, Marxian socialists, as a matter of fact, were not in Russia when the revolt broke out. It was not until April that Lenin returned to Russia from Switzerland with transportation provided by the German government and not until May that Trotsky returned. From April to November Lenin and Trotsky bent their efforts toward getting control of the local Soviets and guiding the All-Russian Congress of Soviets in opposition to the Provisional Government. The slogan they employed to win support for the Bolsheviki was "Peace, Land, and Bread." The Bolsheviki did not organize the revolt but rather rode the crest of the wave of discontent, promising the people what they said they wanted. The Bolsheviki numbered about 200,000 in 1917 and when they came to power in November, 1917, it was as a result of a *coup d'état* rather than as the consequence of overwhelming popular support for Marxian socialism. When the Constitutional Assembly called by Kerensky convened in January, 1918, the Bolsheviki were in the decided minority and it was immediately dissolved by them. With the rise to power of the Bolsheviki Russia was plunged into civil war, a war that lasted until about 1921.

The Bolsheviki represented one wing of the Russian Social Democratic Party which had been founded in 1898. At a London Congress of this Party in 1903 the Party had split into two groups: the Bolsheviki, led by Lenin, and the Mensheviki, led by Martov. (The Russian word for majority is *bolshinstvo*, for minority *menshinstvo* and the words Bolsheviki and Mensheviki were used to designate the members of the majority and minority groups. In reality, however, those who called themselves the majority (the Bolsheviki) were the less numerous of the two groups. They had split on the question of tactics.) The Mensheviki favored the admission to the Party of anyone who adhered to its program, supported it by material means, and furnished it assistance under the direction of one of its organizers. The Mensheviki favored participation in parliamentary government with other parties and argued that the problem of the revolution was essentially one of liquidating the monarchical regime. The Bolsheviki, on the other hand, favored a small, well-knit, highly disciplined Party of revolutionaries with membership carefully restricted to those who would obey the dictates of the executive committee of the Party without question. They anticipated coming to power only by violent revolution and urged the elimination in the transition period to socialism of all other political parties and the establishment of a dictatorship of the proletariat. The leader of this group was a man who probably had more to say about the course which the Revolution of 1917 followed than any other single individual, with the possible exception of Leon Trotsky, and that was Nicholai Lenin.[1]

## Lenin

LENIN (1870–1924) was born Vladimir Ilyitch Ulianov of middle-class parentage. His father was a government official in the town of Simbirsk. He attended the University of Kazan but was expelled for radical activities. He became a teacher of mathematics and physics and was raised to the rank of a noble-

man. Later he attended the University of St. Petersburg and
was admitted to the bar in 1892. He became an active organizer of radical working-class groups in the city of St.
Petersburg and in 1897 was exiled to Siberia. He left Russia in 1900 and
became co-editor of a revolutionary journal, the *Iskra* or Spark.
He returned to Russia during the revolution of 1905 but left
shortly thereafter and lived in Finland, Switzerland and France.
He spent a great deal of his time studying the works of Marx
and Engels and contributing himself to the theory of revolution. When World War I broke out he was interned in Austria
as an enemy alien but finally released. He went then to Switzerland where he stayed until April, 1917, when, with the
assistance of the German government, he returned to Russia.
With the establishment of the dictatorship in November, 1917,
he became the acknowledged leader of the Bolsheviki and
until he was stricken by illness in 1922 remained the most powerful single individual in Russia. He died on January 21, 1924.

Lenin was a rare combination of theorist and man of action.
He had a keen intellect and displayed considerable interest in
the theoretical aspects of Marxian socialism but his theoretical
interests were directed to the end goal of bringing about a
successful socialist revolution in Russia. Hence, questions of
revolutionary tactics and techniques loomed large in his thinking and writing. He was especially concerned with the period
of transition from capitalism to socialism and contributed
much in the way of theory on this subject that Marx and
Engels had neglected, or discussed ambiguously.

Although Lenin had nothing but contempt for those who
sought to "revise" Marxian doctrine it is significant that he
found it necessary himself to revise Marx in some important
particulars. First of all, he had to explain how a successful
socialist revolution could take place in a country that had not
yet experienced mature capitalism, since, according to Marx,
socialism could only come into existence as the result of the
contradictions inherent in a capitalistic economy. Lenin "explained" this possibility by saying that it was possible to experience capitalism "vicariously" and that is what Russia had
done. Moreover, Lenin realized that a successful revolution in
Russia could only take place with the support of the peasantry,

for the industrial proletariat in Russia in 1917 comprised but a small part of the population. But according to the *Communist Manifesto:* "The lower middle class, the small manufacturer, the shopkeeper, the artisan, *the peasant*, all these fight against the bourgeoisie, to save from extinction their existence as fractions of the middle class. They are, therefore, not revolutionary but conservative. Nay, more, *they are reactionary. . . .*" Moreover, Marx had contended that following a revolution the land should be immediately collectivized. Lenin, on the other hand, argued that the discontent of the peasantry could be successfully utilized to bring about a socialist revolution and, as a matter of tactic, encouraged the peasants to believe that following the revolution they would become individual land owners and for a time, following the Revolution, sustained them in that belief.

Lenin also differed from Marx in his attitude toward imperialism and national revolts. For the most part Marx favored imperialism since he believed that it would hasten the coming of socialism by extending capitalism to backward areas of the world and since socialism could only come into existence after capitalism had been established. Lenin, on the other hand, believed that national revolts should be encouraged whether socialist in character or not, since any allies against the capitalists were useful whether strictly proletarian or not. Uppermost in Lenin's mind was the desire to bring about a successful revolution in Russia, and if Marxian theory had to be sacrificed or modified to that end, then he was willing to sacrifice and modify it.

The most significant way, however, in which Lenin differed from Marx was in his interpretation of the role of the proletariat. According to Marx the proletariat would become increasingly class-conscious and militant as the contradictions in capitalism became more and more apparent and acute. According to Lenin the proletariat, if left alone, would develop only a "trade union mentality." In a book entitled *What Is To Be Done?* (1902) Lenin declared:

The history of all countries shows that the working class, exclusively by its own effort, is able to develop only trade-union consciousness, i.e., it may itself realize the necessity for combining in unions, to fight against employers, and to strive to compel the government to pass necessary labor legislation, etc. *The theory of Socialism*, however, *grew out of* the philosophic, historical, and economic *theories that were elaborated by the educated representatives of the propertied classes, the intellectuals.* The founders of modern scientific Socialism, Marx and Engels, themselves belonged to the bourgeois intelligentsia. Similarly, in Russia, the theoretical doctrines of Social-Democracy arose quite independently of the spontaneous growth of the labor movement; it arose as a natural and inevitable outcome of the development of ideas among the revolutionary Socialist intelligentsia.[2]

The working class, Lenin says specifically, is unable to develop a socialist consciousness of the irreconcilable nature of the class struggle unless it is *impregnated* with this consciousness "from the outside." This would appear to be a direct refutation of the Marxian thesis and so it appeared to a contemporary of Lenin's, Plekhanov, whose writings Lenin had previously described as "the best in the whole international literature of Marxism." "The disputed question," Plekhanov wrote, consists in this:

Does there exist an economic necessity which calls forth in the proletariat a demand for socialism, makes it instinctively socialistic, and impels it—even if left to its own resources—on the road to social revolution, notwithstanding the stubborn and continual effort of the bourgeoisie to subject it to its own ideological influence? Lenin denies this, in face of the clearly expressed opinions of all the theorists of scientific socialism. And in that consists his enormous mistake, his theoretical fall into sin.[3]

Mistake or not, it was Lenin's belief that the proletariat had to be impregnated with the socialist consciousness, organized and led into revolution and the instrument for this purpose was the Communist Party (the name Lenin urged the Bolsheviki to take in place of Social Democracy). Lenin described the Party as the "revolutionary vanguard" of the proletariat, an organization consisting "chiefly of persons engaged in revolutionary activities as a profession."[4] Where Marx and Engels had been vague about the nature of the "dictatorship of the proletariat" Lenin is more specific, the dictatorship of the proletariat is conceived by him as the dictatorship of the

Communist Party *for* the proletariat and in the name of the proletariat. Thus in *The State and Revolution* (1917) he wrote:

> The doctrine of the class-war . . . leads inevitably to the recognition of the *Political supremacy* of the proletariat, of its dictatorship, i.e., of an authority shared with none else and relying directly upon the armed force of the masses. The overthrow of the capitalist class is feasible only by the transformation of the proletariat into the *ruling class*, able to crush the inevitable and desperate resistance of the bourgeoisie, and to organize, for the new settlement of economic order, *all* the toiling and exploited masses.
>
> The proletariat needs the State, the centralized organization of force and violence, both for the purpose of crushing the resistance of the exploiters and for the purpose of guiding the great mass of the population—the peasantry, the lower middle-class, the semi-proletariat—in the work of economic Socialist reconstruction.
>
> By educating a workers' party, Marxism educates also the advance-guard, of the proletariat, capable of assuming power and of leading the whole community to Socialism, fit to direct and organize the new order, to be the teacher, guide, leader of all the toiling and exploited in the task of building up their common life without capitalists and against capitalists.[5]

Between the period of capitalism and the period of communism there lies a long period of transition, a "period of revolutionary transformation," and during this period "the State can only be the revolutionary dictatorship of the proletariat." [6] Lenin quotes a letter from Engels to Bebel in which Engels said that "the proletariat needs the State, not in the interests of liberty, but for the purpose of crushing its opponents" and continues:

> Only in Communist Society, when the resistance of the capitalists has finally broken down, when the capitalists have disappeared, when there are no longer any classes (that is, when there is no difference between the members of society in respect to their social means of production), *only then* "does the State disappear *and one can speak of freedom.* . . ." Only then will democracy itself begin to wither away in virtue of the simple fact that, freed from capitalist slavery, from the innumerable horrors, savagery, absurdities, and infamies of capitalist exploitation, people will gradually *become accustomed* to the observation of the elementary rules of social life, known

for centuries, repeated for thousands of years in all sermons. They
will become accustomed to their observance without force, without
constraint, without subjection, without the special apparatus for
compulsion which is called the State. . . .

We know that the fundamental social cause of excesses which
violate the rules of social life is the exploitation of the masses, their
want and their poverty. With the removal of this chief cause, excesses will inevitably begin to "wither away." We do not know how
quickly and in what stages, but we know that they will be withering
away. With their withering away, the State also will wither away.[7]

But "during the *transition* from Capitalism to Communism,
suppression is *still* necessary; but in this case it is the suppression of the minority of exploiters by the majority of exploited." [8] It will not be possible, Lenin says, during this
transition period to provide goods in accordance with individual needs nor to "produce justice and equality."

The first phase of Communism . . . still cannot produce justice
and equality; differences, and unjust differences, in wealth will still
exist, but the *exploitation* of one man by many, will have become
impossible, because it will be impossible to seize as private property
the *means of production*, the factories, machines, land, and so on. . . .
*It is not capable* of destroying at once the further injustice which is
constituted by the distribution of the articles of consumption according to "work performed" (and not according to need). . . .

This is a "defect," says Marx, but is unavoidable during the first
phase of Communism; for, if we are not to land in Utopia, we cannot
imagine that, having overthrown Capitalism, people will at once
learn to work for society *without any regulations by law;* indeed, the
abolition of Capitalism does not *immediately* lay the economic foundations for such a change.

And there is no other standard yet than that of "bourgeois law."
To this extent, therefore, a form of State is still necessary, which,
whilst maintaining the public ownership of the means of production,
preserves the equality of labor and equality in the distribution of the
products. . . . The State is not yet dead altogether, since there still
remains the protection of "bourgeois law," which sanctifies actual
inequality. . . .

The State will be able to wither away completely when Society
has realized the formula: "From each according to his ability; to
each according to his needs"; that is, when people have become ac-

customed to observe the fundamental principles of social life, and their labor is so productive, that they will voluntarily work *according to their abilities.*[9]

Let us turn, however, for a moment from the theory to the practice.

## War Communism and the New Economic Policy [10]

THE period from 1917 to 1921 is recorded in Soviet history as the period of War Communism. Upon coming to power the Bolsheviki sought immediately to put into practice most of the principles of a Communistic society. Private ownership in land was abolished, and all banks, industrial enterprises, handicraft industries and commercial establishments were nationalized. The railway and post-office were already owned and managed by the State. In the cities the government took possession of all public buildings, theaters and large dwelling places. By 1920 all private capital had been confiscated and laws had been enacted forbidding the exchange of products for money. All private trade, as a matter of fact, was forbidden. Foreign trade was declared to be a state monopoly. In the cities everything was rationed including housing, fuel, transportation, newspapers, and entertainment. The workers received ration cards entitling them to goods in proportion to the amount of labor with which they were credited, the more important and skilled workers receiving higher rations than others. To enforce these measures as Extraordinary Commission to Combat Counter-Revolution, Sabotage, and Speculation (known as the *Cheka*) was established and under its direction a veritable reign of terror broke out.

The government encountered most difficulty with the peasants. The abolition of private ownership in land did not appeal to peasants who had been encouraged in the early days of the Revolution to take land from large landholders in the belief that they could keep for themselves what they had thus acquired. Moreover, the collection, requisition, and distribution of agricultural products had been declared to be a State monopoly and the peasants could see no advantage in raising products that were being taken away from them with nothing in return but the promise of manufactured goods at some distant date in the future. Thus, they began to hide and hoard their surpluses and when this was countered by terroristic tactics they simply refused to plant as much as they had formerly. The result was famine.

Lenin then decided that the changes inaugurated had been too drastic. It was better he thought, "to recoil in order to leap forward" and in 1921 he announced the establishment of a New Economic Policy, a policy that re-introduced many features of the capitalistic economy. It is sometimes said that the Civil War was as much responsible for the failure of War Communism as the famine created by the revolt of the peasants and, undoubtedly, it added greatly to the difficulties under which the government labored, but Lenin attributed the difficulty primarily to the fact that Russia was still a "petty-peasant country." In a speech which he delivered on October 14, 1921, in commemoration of the fourth anniversary of the October Revolution, he declared:

. . . how could one expect a task so new to the world to be begun without failures and without mistakes? But we have begun it. We are continuing it. By our "New Economic Policy" we are just now engaged in correcting a number of our mistakes. We are learning how to continue the building of a socialist edifice in a petty-peasant country without committing such mistakes. . . .

We calculated—or perhaps it would be truer to say that we presumed without sufficient calculation—to organize the state production and the state distribution of products on communist lines in a petty-peasant country by direct orders of the proletarian state. Experience has demonstrated our mistake. A number of transitional stages proved necessary: state capitalism and socialism, so as to prepare, by many years of work, for the transition to communism. Not directly relying on enthusiasm but . . . on the basis of personal interest, personal benefit, and business principles, you must set to work in this petty-peasant country to build solid little bridges leading to socialism by way of state capitalism. Otherwise you will never get to communism. . . . That is what experience has taught us. . . .

And we, who during these three or four years have learnt to make abrupt changes of front . . . have begun, zealously . . . to make a new change of front, the "New Economic Policy." The proletarian state must become a cautious, assiduous and shrewd "business man," a punctilious *wholesale merchant*—otherwise it will never succeed in putting this petty-peasant country economically on its feet. . . . A wholesale merchant would appear to be an economic type as remote from communism as heaven is from the earth. But that is one of the contradictions which in actual conditions of life lead from a petty-peasant economy, by way of state capitalism, to socialism. . . .

No matter what the cost . . . despite disaster, famine and disruption, we shall not lose heart, and shall carry our cause to a triumphant conclusion.[11]

Under the New Economic Policy individual initiative and personal profits were re-introduced within limits. Large-scale industry and foreign trade remained state monopolies as did all banking, transportation and publishing. But some private control of the means of production was permitted with the possibility of realizing profits from such control. In fact a state bank was established in 1921 that extended credit to individuals for this specific purpose. Private trade for profit was re-introduced along with the return of money as a legal means of exchange. The employment of labor by individuals was permitted within limits. The peasants were allowed to own land and confiscation of their products was discontinued, a fixed tax in kind (*prodnalog*) being substituted for governmental collection and requisition. The peasant could dispose of any surplus products by private trade. It was further permitted to rent land and to hire farm labor.

Under the stimulus of the New Economic Policy the Russian economy began to revive, although in 1923 a severe crisis threatened the economy once again, when the gap between the prices of agricultural products and those of manufactured goods became disproportionately great. In 1924 the government began to impose heavy taxes and other restrictions upon the Nepmen, as they were called, and private trade and manufacturing began to decline.

## The Death of Lenin and the Rise of Stalin

THE death of Lenin in 1924 precipitated a political crisis in Soviet affairs. One faction of the Party, led by Trotsky, and another faction, led by Stalin, sought to gain control of the Party and government. The struggle between the two men was partly personal, partly ideological and tactical. Each was ambitious for power but apart from that they had conflicting ideas on the immediate tactics to be pursued both in the Soviet Union and throughout the world. Trotsky believed that the peasants should be immediately collectivized while Stalin, at least in 1926, believed that they should be granted further concessions. Trotsky believed that the Third International with its headquarters in Moscow should be the spearhead of world-wide revolution and that every opportunity to bring about a Communist revolution in other countries should be immediately utilized. Stalin, at least in 1924–1926, believed that greater effort should be made to build socialism in Russia before embarking upon world revolution. Aided by Zinoviev and Kamenev (both of whom were later to be liquidated in the purges of the 1930's) Stalin succeeded in winning the support of the Communist party for his views and in December, 1927, Trotsky was expelled from the Party and sent into exile. In his struggle with Trotsky for control of the Party Stalin had the advantage of being Secretary-General of the Party, a position he had held since the early twenties. Since all orders were transmitted through his office the rank and file members of the Party were accustomed to his leadership. So powerful did that office become in the years following 1924 that Stalin was able to rule the country without holding any official government position and it was not until 1941 that he accepted such a position, one which he has since relinquished.[12]

## The Five Year Plans

THE period since 1928 is spoken of by Soviet historians as the period of the "resumption of the socialist offensive" and it has been a period of successive "five-year plans." The first Five Year Plan was formally adopted on October 1, 1928. The emphasis was upon the rapid industrialization of the economy and the production of capital goods. It was planned to increase the production in heavy industry, for example, by 231 per cent. The results in the field of industry were as spectacular as the plan and were especially successful in the rapid development of the electrical industry. The Plan also contemplated, despite Stalin's controversy with Trotsky, the rapid collectivization of farms and by March 1, 1930, 55 per cent of the peasant farms had been collectivized. Not, however, without great cost in human lives, for the peasants resisted the collectivization and had to be terrorized into submission. No one knows how many peasants were killed but conservative estimates place the number at well over a million. So drastic were the means employed to bring about this collectivization that Stalin felt impelled to issue an order in March, 1930, warning against "dizziness from success" and calling a halt, temporarily, to enforced collectivization. During this period, large quantities of livestock and agricultural products were destroyed and the country was faced again with a famine. According to one student of this period, "between the harvests of 1932 and 1933 it is estimated that perhaps nine million people died of hunger or its sequels." [13] Officially it was denied that a famine existed and no mention of it appeared in the Soviet Press.

The Second Five Year Plan (1933–1937) placed greater emphasis upon the production of consumers' goods. And according to its authors it was designed "to liquidate completely all exploiting classes, to destroy forever the causes which breed the exploitation of man by man and the division of society into exploiters and exploited, i.e., to liquidate private ownership of the means of production." [14] But although the plan promised a larger quantity of consumers' goods the emphasis in practice was upon the building up of heavy industry and considerable attention was given to the development of electric power and the production of automobiles, tractors, and airplanes.

The Third Five Year Plan (1938–1942) was officially proclaimed "to complete the construction of a classless socialist society and to accomplish the gradual transition from socialism to communism." Because of the international situation, considerable emphasis in fact was given to the production of weapons for war and with the outbreak of war between Russia and Finland, between Russia and Poland and later between Russia and Germany still greater emphasis was placed upon the production of military weapons. During World War II many industrial centers were established in the Urals and in Asiatic Russia.

Accurate figures on the growth of industrial production in Russia are difficult to obtain for the government figures, most experts believe, are designed more for propaganda purposes than as an actual reflection of true conditions. Nevertheless, no one denies that prodigious strides in the realm of industrial production have been made and it is commonly stated on the basis of Soviet statistics that during the period from 1913 to 1940 industrial production increased eight and a half times and that consumers' goods increased during the period 1928–1940 by something over four times. In 1940, however, approximately sixty-one per cent of the total industrial production was devoted to the production of producers' goods.[15] How much of this increase would have taken place under a different government no one can say with certainty, but that some increase in industrial production might have been expected "normally" no one denies.[16]

While on a comparative basis, the rate of industrial growth in the Soviet Union under the Five Year Plans has been greater than that in other industrial countries, the cost of production has been much higher and the quality of goods produced has been much lower. According to a Soviet source as recorded in a report by Voznesensky in 1941: "Tens of thousands of tons of metal are rejected on account of poor workmanship in the steel and metal-working plants." [17] At the time the Third Five Year Plan was submitted, Molotov declared: "we still suffer from much mismanagement, wasteful expenditures, abominably great waste of raw materials, and squander much fuel and electric energy; keep our plant equipment idle for shamefully long periods, all of which means that there is no real effort to reduce costs of production and construction." [18] Yugow declares that the cost of production of manufactured goods is 30–50% higher in Russia than in other European countries and their selling price 100–200% higher.[19] The cost of this increased production has not only been high in economic terms but also in terms of human suffering and misery. It has been made possible only by the slaughter and imprisonment of millions and by the enforcement of the most rigid and severe regulations under the surveillance of a vast network of secret police.

The prodigious increase in industrial production has not, moreover, resulted in an equally proportionate increase in the standard of living of the average worker. Using some figures published in an official Soviet periodical (*Planovoie Khoziaistvo*) concerning the food consumption of an average family of textile workers in St. Petersburg in 1913 together with official Soviet statistics since 1913, one writer arrived at the following figures: [20]

|  |  | 1913 | 1929 | 1937 |
|---|---|---|---|---|
| Cost of one week's food | Roubles | 3.40 | 5.90 | 49.60 |
| Index of food prices | Per cent | 100 | 172 | 1449 |
| Average money wages | Roubles | 25 | 66 | 245 |
| Index of real wages | Per cent | 100 | 154 | 68 |

According to these figures, which are in substantial agreement with similar studies that have been made by other individuals, the standard of living was 54% higher in 1929 than in 1913 but 32% lower in 1937 than in 1913.

Differentiation in real income and wages is as large, if not larger, in the Soviet Union, moreover, as in certain capitalistic countries. In the Red Army, for example, the pay of a private soldier is 10 roubles per month, of a lieutenant 1000 roubles per month and of a colonel 2,400 roubles per month. The ratio of a private's to a lieutenant's pay in the British Army is approximately 1 to 4; in the United States Army 1 to 3; and in the Soviet army 1 to 100.[21] Explaining this disproportion in army pay a Communist periodical "Russia Today" declares:

Another item on which there has been a great deal of misunderstanding concerns army remuneration, the fact that whereas a private soldier gets a mere pittance, Red army officers receive relatively high pay. . . .

Obviously Soviet millionaires are not going to develop on the pay of a ranker, but equally obviously *this is no question of class differentiation but one of sound socialist policy, in line with the general wages policy of the U. S. S. R.*

Every male citizen is liable to military service in the U. S. S. R.; for a limited period of time he gives his services to the state receiving in return a pocket-money allowance. At the end of that time he returns to civil life, usually better equipped for his vocation than when he was called up. Although his remuneration in the army has been tiny, he has had so many free services—postage, travel, cleaning materials, entertainment, smokes, etc.—that he has been at least as well off as soldiers of other countries.[22]

Arthur Koestler reports on the differentiation of pay among mine workers by quoting from a Soviet newspaper:

. . . according to the Moscow paper *Trud* (20/1/1936) sixty employees of a Donetz mine earned monthly wages of 1000–2,500 roubles per head; seventy-five employees earned 800–1,000 roubles per head; four hundred earned 500–800 roubles per head and the remaining thousand *averaged* 125 roubles. The top wages in this average mine were about thirty times higher than the minimum wages. But the director of a mine of 1,500 employees belongs only to the medium stratum of the technocracy; the salaries of directors, chief engineers and administrators in the top stratum are up to 100 times higher than the average wage and up to 300 times higher than the minimum wage. In 1943 the appearance of the first "proletarian millionaires," enthusiastically welcomed by the Soviet press, completed the development.[23]

It is not uncommon for writers and artists in the Soviet Union to receive as much as 80,000 roubles per year and together with engineers and bureaucrats they are among the highest paid. The question is not whether they deserve this higher pay but whether such contrasts in income are compatible with the professed aims of socialism and whether such contrasts in standards of living are compatible with a "classless society." [24] It is now possible to invest excess income in the Soviet Union in government bonds yielding 7% interest or to put it in a Savings Bank paying 8% interest.[25] All deposits in Savings Banks are exempt both from income and inheritance taxes. That the Soviet Union under the dictatorship of Stalin has abandoned any notion of economic equality was made explicit in a speech which Stalin delivered in 1934 before the Seventeenth Congress of the Communist Party of the Soviet Union in which he stated:

. . . equality in the sphere of requirements and personal life is a piece of reactionary petty-bourgeois stupidity worthy of a primitive sect of ascetics, but not of a Socialist society organized on Marxian lines, because we cannot demand that all people should have the same requirements and tastes, and that all people shall live their individual lives in the same way. . . .

By equality Marxism means, not equality in personal require- ments and personal life, but the abolition of classes, i.e., (a) the equal emancipation of all toilers from exploitation after the capi- talists have been overthrown and expropriated; (b) the equal aboli- tion for all of private property in the means of production after they have been transformed into the property of the whole of society; (c) the equal duty of all to work according to their ability and the equal right of all toilers to receive according to the amount of work they have done (*socialist* society); (d) the equal duty of all to work according to their ability and the equal right of all toilers to receive according to their requirements (*communist* society). And Marxism starts out with the assumption that people's tastes and *requirements are not, and cannot be equal in quality or in quantity, either in the period of social- ism or in the period of communism.* . . . It is time it was understood that Marxism is opposed to leveling.[26]

The differentiation in pay that is a characteristic feature of the Soviet economy prevails also in agriculture. On collective farms the produce is not distributed equally but according to "working days" and the "working day" is defined not in terms of hours but in terms of skill or responsibility. In the 1930's the ordinary farm worker was credited with half a "working day" as compared with the driver of a tractor who was credited with five "working days." The administrative personnel of a collective farm were credited with five to ten "working days" for each half "working day" credited to the ordinary laborer. Those among the Russian Communist Party who protested against the unsocialist character of this dif- ferentiation were described by Stalin, in the speech from which we quoted above, as "Left deviationists" and as "Leftist blockheads" and Stalin declared that "if these 'Leftist' views were to triumph in the Party, the Party would cease to be Marxian." [27] Needless to say, those who held such views and persisted in them were tried for treason and imprisoned or killed.

Not only is the average standard of living low and the differences in standard of living as great, if not greater, in the Soviet Union as in capitalistic countries but the restrictions imposed upon labor are more severe than those which Soviet propaganda agencies claim to be characteristic of capitalistic economies. There are no independent trade unions in the Soviet Union, no system of collective bargaining and no strikes. According to a law of November 15, 1932, a worker who is absent from work without excuse is subject to dismissal and unexcused lateness is subject to criminal prosecution. A decree of June 28, 1940, forbids workers to change their employment without permission on pain of six months "correctional labor" and a cut of 25% in their wages. A law of October 2, 1940, established industrial conscription for youths between the ages of 14 and 17 and a decree issued during the same month empowered the government to transfer workers and their families from one part of the country to another as required by economic conditions.[28] After the outbreak of war, the restrictions became even more severe and since December, 1941, "all branches of Soviet industry and transport directly or indirectly connected with the war were placed under martial law; absenteeism, idling and carelessness became capital offences." [29] Throughout the Soviet Union there are numerous "corrective labor" camps where millions, no one knows exactly how many, are condemned to forced labor under the most primitive conditions of life.[30] In February, 1949, the Economic and Social Council of the United Nations, acting on a petition submitted by the American Federation of Labor, voted to ask the International Labor Organization to investigate the existence of forced labor in the U. S. S. R. Although the Soviet Union officially denied the existence of such camps, it strongly opposed the investigation. The eye-witness accounts, however, are too numerous to be ignored or brushed aside as fabrications.[31]

The existence of these conditions reveals a wide discrepancy between Soviet propaganda and Soviet reality. A similar, although less stark discrepancy, exists in the field of Soviet taxation. In 1918 Lenin declared that, "Indirect taxes are taxes on the poor. Social democracies demand the abolition of indirect taxes and the institution of a progressive tax on incomes and inheritance." [32] Contemporary writers in the Soviet Union declare that "the Soviet system of taxation knows not regressive taxes which are contradictory to the social and economic politics of the Soviet government." [33] The facts, however, belie this statement. For the government's primary source of revenue in the Soviet Union is what is called the "turnover tax," in reality a sales-tax of gigantic proportions. The turnover-tax is imposed on the producing or wholesale selling organization and is passed on to the consumer in the form of higher prices so that one-half to two-thirds of the amount which the population spends on retail purchases in state and cooperative outlets goes to pay for the turnover tax. Levied on articles of consumption the tax ranges from 50 to 90% of the cost of the article. In 1943, for example, the turnover tax on toilet soap was 78% of the retail price. Cheese had a tax of 54% in 1940. In 1936 a kilogram of sugar cost 420 kopecks, of which 357 kopecks represented the turnover tax. The importance of the tax as a source of revenue was clearly revealed in the 1949 budget in which turnover tax receipts were estimated at 262 billion roubles, or approximately three-fifths of the total planned revenue of 446 billion roubles. Because the tax applies to articles of consumption it falls most heavily on those least able to pay. For those deriving their income from state and cooperative enterprises there is a mildly graduated income tax applicable to incomes up to 12,000 roubles a year. Above this amount there is a surtax of 13% which is not graduated further. The progression stops at a level which is less than double that earned by the average Soviet worker. Those with incomes of 70,000 to 80,000 roubles per year are thus given a great advantage over the average citizen. According to the planned 1949 budget for the U. S. S. R., the total tax collections (including state loans) will take the equivalent of nearly 2,300 roubles per year for every person in the Soviet Union, which must mean about twice this amount for every working member of the population. Compared with the estimated average annual earnings of the individual worker at between 6,300 and 6,900 roubles, and a smaller figure for agricultural workers, the per capita tax is, to say the least, impressive.

## Political Institutions [34]

THE discrepancy between the Soviet myth and the Soviet reality apparent in the economic field is equally apparent in the political realm. According to the most recent (1936) Constitution, the U. S. S. R. is a democratic republic governed by a bicameral legislature and a plural executive composed of two separate bodies: the Council of People's Commissars and the Presidium. The Supreme Soviet, or "parliament," is composed of the Soviet of the Union and the Soviet of Nationalities to which delegates are "elected" by the people.

The first elections to the Supreme Soviet under the new Constitution were held in 1937. In that election, and in all subsequent elections, only one candidate was submitted to the voters in each electoral district although several were nominated. Before the actual election, the nominees in each district withdrew their names in favor of one nominee approved by the Communist Party. In practice, the Supreme Soviet assembles periodically to listen to speeches by high government and Party officials. There is no debate and all laws, submitted by higher bodies, are approved unanimously. Official spokesmen for the Soviet Union and their apologists declare that this is not evidence of dictatorship but of the high degree of unanimity which characterizes a "Socialist State of workers and peasants."

Actual political power in the Soviet Union is lodged in the Communist Party hierarchy and more particularly in the Politburo which is the highest governing body in the Party and is composed of about a dozen prominent Communist Party leaders. According to a principle known as "democratic centralism" each subordinate unit of the Party is bound by the decisions of the next higher unit. Freedom of discussion is permissible only so long as the subject under discussion has not been made the subject of a decision by a higher unit of the Party. This principle is superior to the ordinary principle of democratic discussion and procedure, Soviet spokesmen declare, because it ensures action and the end of debate once a decision has been reached. In practice, it means that any decision reached by the Politburo is binding on all the members of the Party and that such decisions are not subject to debate or discussion. Although nominally chosen by the Central Executive Committee of the Party, the members of the Politburo who prepare the agenda for the meetings of the Executive Committee and make nominations, are actually self-perpetuating. Since there is only one lawful party in the Soviet Union and since the overwhelming majority of the members of the government are members of the Party (both the Presidium and the Council of People's Commissars are composed entirely of Party members) it is easy to understand how the Party controls the government. There is, in addition, of course, the fact that the Party controls the army, police, and secret police. In every government agency, factory, Red Army unit, university, school, collective farm, town, and village there is a Communist Party "cell" whose function it is, among other things, to keep an eye on the activities of the organization to which it is attached and to report any grumbling, inefficiency, or deviations from Party orders. A vast network of secret police watches in turn over the same activities and the activities of Party members and a Party Control Commission "purges" the Party periodically of "undesirable" members. In March, 1939, the Party had some 1,588,000 members. In addition to regular Party members there are a number of youth groups from which Party members are later recruited: The Young Octobrists (8–11), the Young Pioneers (10–16), and the Komsomol (15–30) whose membership in 1939 totaled around 12 million. It is not easy to become a member of the Party. The potential member must be recommended by at least three Party members and the possibility of being "purged" as the result of what might turn out to be a "poor" recommendation is a powerful deterrent. The candidate, once accepted for membership, must serve a one-year probationary period. He must prove that he has no "ulterior motives" in joining the Party, that he is well grounded in Marxist ideology and willing to continue its study, that he is devoid of all traces of "bourgeois mentality," that he is neither "addicted to drink or to religion" and that he is willing to obey the directives of his Party superiors.

The Party tolerates no factions or factional disputes. According to the rules of the Communist Party of the Soviet Union as adopted at the 18th Congress in March, 1939:

> The Party exercises the leadership of the working class, the peasantry, the intelligentsia, of the entire Soviet people, in the struggle for the consolidation of the dictatorship of the proletariat, for the consolidation and development of the socialist system, for the victory of communism.
>
> The Party is the nucleus of all organizations of the working people, both public and state. . . .
>
> The Party is a united militant organization bound together by a conscious discipline which is equally binding on all its members. The Party is strong because of its solidarity, unity of will and unity of action, which are incompatible with any deviation from its program and rules, with any violation of Party discipline, with factional groupings, or with double-dealing. The Party purges its ranks of persons who violate its program, rules or discipline. . . .
>
> A Party member is one who accepts the program of the Party, works in one of its organizations, submits to its decisions and pays membership dues.[35]

The Party demands absolute obedience to the higher organs of the Party and ultimately to the Politburo and to Stalin as the most powerful member. This was made dramatically clear in the great "purges" which took place in the 1930's. No one knows how many rank and file members of the Party were "purged" (a euphemism frequently for murder) but the list of the more prominent members of the Party who were purged is impressive, both in terms of quantity and in terms of service to the Party. W. H. Chamberlin has said that the purge list reads like a Communist *Who's Who* of the 1920's. "If one can imagine a proscription list drawn up, in a moment of impotent rage, by some surviving Russian aristocrat, kulak or conservative intellectual who hated the Revolution and everything for which it stood, this proscription list would have coincided very closely with the victims of Stalin's purge." [36]

At Lenin's death in 1924, the Politburo consisted of: Stalin, Trotsky, Zinoviev, Kamenev, Rykov, Bukharin and Tomsky. Trotsky was exiled in 1927 and was murdered, it is thought by agents of the Soviet Union, in Mexico in 1940. Zinoviev and Kamenev were accused of "Left deviation" and shot in 1936. Rykov and Bukharin were accused of "Right deviation" and shot in 1938. It was officially reported that Tomsky committed suicide. Of all the members of the Politburo in 1924 only Stalin remains and it is his claim that he alone has remained "faithful" to the principles of the Revolution of 1917. On the rank and file members of the Party, Arthur Koestler reports the following statistics:

The 17th Congress of the All-Soviet Bolshevik Party was held in January-February, 1934, before all the purges.

The 18th Party Congress was held in March, 1939, just after the purges.

At the 17th Congress 22.6% of the delegates had been party members since before 1917, that is, since before the Revolution.

At the 18th Congress the corresponding figure was 2.4%. In other words only one-tenth of them had survived the Party purge.

At the 17th Congress 17.7% had been Party members since 1917. . . . At the 18th Congress the corresponding figure was 2.6%.

In round figures at the 17th Congress 40% of the delegates dated their membership from before the Civil War; at the 18th Congress only 5%.[37]

The diplomatic corps was "purged" of two Vice-Commissars for Foreign Affairs and at least a score of former ambassadors and ministers. In 1937, seven prominent Red Army generals were shot including Marshal Tukhachevsky who had been one of the most brilliant field commanders in the Civil War and who had been described in official Soviet circles in the early 1930's as the man chiefly responsible for building up the Red Army. A large number of admirals also were "purged." Many of the prominent historians, the head of the Gosplan during the First and Second Five Year Plans, a leading au-

thority on Soviet legal theory, two chiefs of the secret police
(Yagoda and Yezhov) and the state prosecutor in many of the
"purge" trials, Krylenko, all eventually were killed. Several
prominent members of the Communist International who had
sought refuge in Russia were also imprisoned or killed: including the Hungarian Communist leader Bela Kun, the
German, Heinz Neumann, and the Polish Communist
Dombal.

The majority of those "liquidated" never came to public
trial but three public "trials" were held in 1936, 1937, and
1938. At these trials the accused offered no defense whatsoever, all pleaded guilty and signed detailed confessions ac-
cusing themselves of treason and sabotage.[38] Apart from these
confessions there was no evidence presented to the court and
no witnesses called to testify against them. Rather than supporting the government's claim that these men were guilty
the odd behavior of the accused clamors for explanation. The
official thesis of the government is that they were all engaged
in a widespread plot organized by Trotsky to overthrow the
government.[39] In view of the high positions held by these men
and the wide ramifications of the so-called "conspiracy" the
wonder is that it did not succeed.

Before the purges took place it was required by the rules of
the Party that all members should "master the principles of
Marxism-Leninism." Since the purges the Central Executive
Committee has decided that Party members need not demonstrate mastery of Marxism but simply "acceptance." And at
the 18th Congress Stalin castigated "the infatuation for the
system of propaganda through study circles" and said that
the Central Committee "considered the method of individual
study of the principles of Marxism-Leninism by Party members to be more expedient." In place of study groups, he announced that the Party would center its attention "on
propaganda through the press and on the organization of a
system of propaganda by lectures." [40] Apparently, it was believed that the group study of Marxism was one of the factors
responsible for "deviations" from the Party line.

The Party leaders claimed in 1939 to have liquidated all
capitalistic and exploiting elements and to have achieved

socialism. According to a resolution adopted at the 18th Congress:

> The victory of socialism in the U. S. S. R. has ensured the dominance of the socialist economic system. The class composition of the population of the U. S. S. R. has changed in conformity with the profound changes in the economic sphere. All exploiting elements—capitalists, merchants, kulaks and profiteers—have been eliminated in the period of socialist construction. . . .
>
> The working class has radically changed. It has been transformed into an entirely new class, a class emancipated from exploitation; it has abolished the capitalist economic system and has established the socialist ownership of the means of production.
>
> The peasantry has radically changed. It has been transformed into an entirely new peasantry, a peasantry emancipated from all exploitation. In its overwhelming majority, it consists of collective farm peasants, who base their work and wealth not on private farming, individual labor and backward technique, but on collective property, collective labor and modern technique.
>
> The intelligentsia has changed, having for the most part become an entirely new intelligentsia, bound by all its fibres with the working class and the peasantry. The Soviet intelligentsia consists of yesterday's workers and peasants, and sons of workers and peasants, who have been promoted to commanding posts. The Soviet intelligentsia does not serve capitalism, as the old intelligentsia did, but socialism, and is an equal member of socialist society.[41]

Now, if the capitalist and exploiting elements have been completely eliminated and if the class structure of Soviet society has been profoundly altered, why is it still necessary to maintain the dictatorship of the proletariat? Why does coercion increase instead of diminish? Why does the State not begin to show signs of "withering away" as Marx and Lenin predicted that it would with the end of capitalist exploitation? These questions, apparently, have been asked in the Soviet Union and asked frequently and insistently enough to provoke an "answer" from Stalin himself. He discussed this "problem" at the 18th Congress in these words:

> Another of the defects of our propagandist and ideological work is the absence of full clarity among our comrades on certain theoretical questions of vital practical importance. . . . I refer to the question

of the state in general, and of our socialist state in particular, and to the question of our Soviet intelligentsia.

It is sometimes asked: "We have abolished the exploiting classes; there are no longer any hostile classes in the country; there is nobody to suppress; hence there is no more need for the state; it must die away.—Why then do we not help our socialist state to die away? Why do we not strive to put an end to it? Is it not time to throw out all this rubbish of a state?"

Or further: "The exploiting classes have already been abolished in our country; socialism has been built in the main; we are advancing towards communism. Now, the Marxist doctrine of the state says that there is to be no state under communism.—Why then do we not help our socialist state to die away? Is it not time we relegated the state to the museum of antiquities?"

These questions show that those who ask them have conscientiously memorized certain propositions contained in the doctrine of Marx and Engels about the state. But they also show that these comrades have failed to understand the essential meaning of this doctrine; that they have failed to realize in what historical conditions the various propositions of this doctrine were elaborated; and, what is more, that they do not understand present-day international conditions, have overlooked the capitalist encirclement and the dangers it entails for the socialist country. These questions not only betray an underestimation of the capitalist encirclement, but also an underestimation of the role and significance of the bourgeois states and their organs, which send spies, assassins and wreckers in to our country and are waiting for a favorable opportunity to attack it by armed force. They likewise betray an underestimation of the role and significance of our socialist state and of its military, punitive, and intelligence organs, which are essential for the defense of the socialist land from foreign attack.[42]

The phrase "capitalist encirclement" is one which now frequently occurs in Soviet writings and is the principal justification for the continuation of the dictatorship. Some persons are of the opinion that the Russian government is "obsessed" with an irrational fear of attack and that relations with the Soviet Union can be improved only by overcoming this irrational fear. The quotation above indicates, I believe, that it is not an irrational fear or an obsession but a very rational and calculated strategy to maintain the present Party leaders in power. Unable to explain the continuation of the dictatorship in any other terms and desirous of maintaining that dictatorship, the leaders have no alternative to abdication but the spreading of fear of attack. It is possible that large numbers of the Russian people may be "obsessed" with this fear of attack but it is highly doubtful if the leaders themselves are so "obsessed." Their motives for "believing" in "capitalist encirclement" are crystal clear.

In the speech in which Stalin explained why the dictatorship of the proletariat could not "wither away" he went on to say that Marxism, in any case, is not a fixed body of doctrine but only a set of general principles which have to be interpreted and applied differently in particular situations and at particular times.

We have no right to expect of the classical Marxist writers, separated as they were from our day by a period of forty-five or fifty-five years, that they should have foreseen each and every zigzag of history in the distant future in every separate country. It would be ridiculous to expect that the classical Marxist writers should have elaborated for our benefit ready-made solutions for each and every theoretical problem that might arise in any particular country fifty or one hundred years afterwards, so that we, the descendants of the classical Marxist writers, might calmly doze at the fireside and munch ready-made solutions.[43]

Under Stalin, Marxian socialism has been emptied more and more of any specific content. Increasingly, socialism in the Soviet Union is simply what Stalin says it is. It is impossible to criticize the course of political or economic developments in the Soviet Union on the grounds that such developments violate the principles of Marxian socialism since in the last analysis it is Stalin who decides what the "correct" interpretation of Marxian doctrine is. To dispute his interpretation is to court death and to be guilty of heresy. The chain of Marxian logic is now complete:

(according to Marx) justice and truth = the will of the proletariat

(according to Lenin) will of the proletariat = will of the Communist Party

$$\text{(according to Stalin) will of the Communist Party} = \text{will of Stalin}$$
$$\text{Justice and truth} = \text{will of Stalin}$$

A doctrine that begins by defining justice and truth in terms of will cannot help but find practical expression in tyranny. In this sense the Stalinist tyranny is not a perversion of Marxism but its logical fulfillment. Speaking editorially of the 18th Congress the newspaper *Pravda* was quick to catch the logic of that meeting: "Stalin," the newspaper declared, "is the symbol of victorious socialism. . . . Stalin is the personification of the moral and political unity of the Soviet people." Stalin is the infallible interpreter of Marxian doctrine, what Stalin wants and orders *is* socialism. More and more Stalin has been extravagantly praised in a Führer cult that resembles that which was cultivated in Germany under Hitler. He is hardly ever mentioned without the appellation "Great." According to a literary journal in the Soviet Union (*Znamia*, No. 10) "The most characteristic feature of Soviet poetry is its main topic—the person of The Chief. Whoever omits this subject cannot understand the real essence of our art. For a contemporary artist the conception of The Chief is the ideal incarnation of the philosophical conception of the people." Two examples will illustrate the new "essence" of Soviet art. Speaking of Stalin, Djamboul Djabaev, one of the leading poets in the Soviet Union, declares:

> I would have compared him to a white mountain—but
> the mountain has a summit.
> I would have compared him to the depths of the sea—but
> the sea has a bottom.
> I would have compared him to the shining moon—but
> the moon shines at midnight, not at noon.
> I would have compared him to the brilliant sun, but
> the sun radiates at noon, not at midnight.

And of this poem the Soviet critic, Selvinski, has said: "In spite of its hyperbole it is the most accurate picture of Stalin, as Djamboul has what all of us lack—Stalin's sweetness." [44] Another poem published in *Pravda* reads:

O great Stalin, O leader of the peoples,
Thou who broughtest man to birth,
Thou who purifiest the earth,
Thou who restoreth the centuries,
Thou who makest bloom the Spring,
Thou who makest vibrate the musical chords.

. . . . . . . .

Thou, splendor of my Spring, O Thou
Sun reflected of millions of hearts.[45]

# The Third International and Russian Nationalism

THE Third (Communist) International was founded in March, 1919, under the aegis of the Communist Party of the Soviet Union.[46] It included all the Communist parties throughout the world. A draft program was adopted in final form at the Sixth Congress in 1928 and, in a sense, is the Communist Manifesto of 1848 brought up to date. It predicts the coming of an "international proletarian revolution logically" emerging "out of the conditions of development of capitalism generally, and out of its imperialistic phase in particular." The program states that "The ultimate aim of the Communist International is to replace world capitalist economy by a world system of Communism" and more particularly to remake world society "into a World Union of Soviet Socialist Republics uniting the whole of mankind under the hegemony of the international proletariat organized as a State." The Soviet Union "being the land of the dictatorship of the proletariat and of socialist construction . . . inevitably becomes the base of the world movement of all oppressed classes, the center of international revolution, the greatest factor in world history." On the matter of tactics the program of the Third International declares:

The successful struggle of the Communist International for the dictatorship of the proletariat pre-supposes the existence in every country of a compact Communist Party, hardened in the struggle, disciplined, centralised, and closely linked up with the masses. . . .

It is a revolutionary organization, bound by an iron discipline and strict revolutionary rules of democratic centralism. . . .

In order that it may fulfill its historic mission . . . the Communist Party must first of all set itself to accomplish the following fundamental strategic aims:

Extend its influence over the majority of the members of its own class. . . . To achieve this the Communist Party must secure predominant influence in the broad mass proletarian organizations (Soviets, trade unions, factory councils, co-operative societies, sport organizations, cultural organizations, etc.). It is particularly important . . . to capture the trade unions. To work in reactionary trade unions and skilfully to capture them. . . .

In determining its line of tactics, each Communist Party must take into account the concrete internal and external situation . . . the degree of stability and strength of the bourgeoisie, the degree of preparedness of the proletariat . . . etc. The Party determines slogans and methods of struggle in accordance with these circumstances. . . .

When the revolutionary tide is rising, when the ruling classes are disorganized, the masses are in a state of revolutionary ferment . . . the Party of the proletariat is confronted with the task of leading the masses to a direct attack upon the bourgeois State. This it does by carrying on propaganda . . . and by organizing mass action. This mass action includes: strikes; a combination of strikes and armed demonstrations and finally, the general strike conjointly with armed insurrection against the State power of the bourgeoisie. The latter form of struggle which is the supreme form, must be conducted according to the rules of war; it pre-supposes a plan of campaign, offensive fighting operations and unbounded devotion and heroism on the part of the proletariat. An absolutely essential condition precedent for this form of action is the organization of the masses into militant units . . . and intensified revolutionary work in the army and the navy. . . .

Despite the bloody terror of the bourgeoisie, the Communists fight with courage and devotion on all sectors of the international class front, in the firm conviction that the victory of the proletariat is inevitable and cannot be averted.[47]

During World War II, the dissolution of the Third International was announced from Moscow (1943) but shortly after the War, in 1947, it was revived in the form of the Cominform. There is no good reason to doubt that the program of the Cominform is identical with that of the Third International.

In the early days of Bolshevik power, the concept of Communist world rule was not associated with Russian hegemony and during that period Lenin declared: "The idea that the Russian proletariat is a chosen revolutionary proletariat among the workers of the world is absolutely alien to us." [48] But with Lenin's death and the subsequent seizure of Communist control by Stalin the nationalistic visions and aspirations that inflamed Russia under the Tsars were revived. In Lenin's time the Tsars were portrayed as ruthless imperialists who waged war against the oppressed peoples of the world. Today the Kremlin's policy is to depict the Tsars as liberators of the Russian people. In 1939 Glinka's opera "Life for the Tsar" was presented for the first time since the Revolution. It was performed in Moscow with Stalin in attendance. The story of the opera concerns the revolt of the Muscovites against the Poles in 1613 and glorifies the revolt as a war for independence. One change was made in the final chorus: where Glinka had intended the chorus to chant "Glory, glory to the Tsar" the chorus now sings "Glory, glory to the Fatherland." The textbooks in Russian history have been rewritten and whereas Minin, the leader of the 1613 revolt against the Poles, was depicted, as late as 1930, as a reactionary leader of the bourgeoisie, he is now described as a national hero.

High school students in Soviet schools use a textbook on Russian history edited by Professor A. M. Pankratova. A comparison of the 1940, 1945 and 1946 editions reveals a number of striking changes in content and interpretation. In the 1940 edition, the Russo-Japanese War of 1904–05 was described as an imperialist struggle over China, with Russia seeking to control Korea and Manchuria and "brazenly plundering the Chinese people." The 1945 edition tones down the references to Tsarist imperialism and emphasizes instead the heroism displayed by the Russian army and navy. In the 1940 edition, Trotsky was described as supporting the war; but in the 1945 edition Trotsky is not mentioned at all.

The military efforts of the Western Allies in World War II are differently evaluated in different editions. The 1945 edition of Pankratova's book praises the war effort of the Western Allies and cites Stalin's description of the Allied landing in

Normandy as a "brilliant success." "The history of war knows no other enterprise like it for breadth of purpose, grandiose scale and masterful execution." These remarks of Stalin are deleted from the 1946 edition and the only Western military operation mentioned is described in this brief phrase—"on the sixth of June, 1944, Allied forces accomplished a landing in Northern France."

The dissolution of the Comintern was described in some detail in the 1945 edition. No mention of the dissolution of the Comintern occurs in the 1946 edition.

The 1948 edition of a one-volume Soviet encyclopedia, the *Kratkaya*, reveals similar political editing. The changes in the description of the Russo-Japanese War parallel those made in Pankratova's book. The term "Russian Army" is substituted for the term "Tsarist Army" which appeared in the 1943 edition although the defeat is still ascribed to the "Tsarist government." A dramatic change occurred on the question of who sought peace in the war of 1904–05:

| *1943 edition* | *1948 edition* |
|---|---|
| The war in fact hastened the development of the Revolution of 1905–07 in Russia. In order to be able to deal with the revolution, Tsarism hastened to conclude peace with Japan on August 23 (Sept. 5) 1905. | Japan was rendered so exhausted by war that after the battle of Tsushima she was forced to present a peace proposal. |

Examples of such changes could be multiplied indefinitely but enough has been said to indicate that the interpretation of history follows the Party line and the Party line at present is ardently chauvinistic and Pan-Slavic. The Communist press, radio, literature, school texts, and even music continuously play variations on one theme: Russia is the "standard-bearer of the new epoch in human history." One example from the Soviet magazine *Bolshevik:*

Soviet patriotism and national pride are based on the realization of the world-historic significance of the successes of socialism and of the leading part of this country and her people in the world history of mankind. The feeling of Soviet national pride is based on the understanding of the great and unequalled superiority of Soviet culture, ideology, science, and morals.[49]

The Russian army is organized more and more like the Tsarist armies of old. Segregation of officers and privates, discouraged in the early days of the Soviet Union, is now encouraged. The Order of Lenin and the Order of the Red Banner were replaced by the Orders of Suvarov, Kutuzov and Alexander Nevsky on July 29, 1942. A decree of January 6, 1943, re-established the epaulettes worn by the officers of the Tsarist Army. The army oath has been changed. Where formerly Soviet recruits swore to fight for the emancipation of the proletariat throughout the world, since 1939 they swear "to serve to my last breath my Fatherland and Government." On March 15, 1944, the "Internationale" was abolished as the national anthem and replaced by a new anthem praising "Russia the Great" and omitting any reference to internationalism.

The intent of this Soviet chauvinism, comprising a blend of nationalism, imperialism and militarism is not difficult to discover. It is fabricated not only to glorify "the new Soviet man" in the "new Soviet society" but also to distract attention from the weaknesses and deficiencies of the Communist regime. So insecure does the Kremlin feel in its power that it refuses to allow free entrance to and exit from Russia and seeks to prevent the Russian people from learning how the people in Western democracies live. In place of socialism the leaders of the Kremlin have substituted Pan-Slavic imperialism and as an end goal, world dominion in the form of a "World Union of Soviet Socialist Republics" under the domination of Soviet Russia. Through Machiavellian diplomacy, ruthless use of power against weaker peoples, and the manipulation of Communist Parties in other countries the Soviet Union has already annexed some 280,000 square miles of territory since 1939. In addition to the absorption into the Soviet Union proper of Latvia, Lithuania, and Estonia, the Soviet Union has annexed territory from Poland, Rumania, Germany, Czechoslovakia, China and Japan. It has expanded its power further by the imposition of Soviet controlled regimes on the peoples of Poland, Hungary, Rumania, Bulgaria, Albania and Czechoslovakia.[50] And today the largest part of China is under Communist domination. Only in Jugoslavia has a Communist Party in power resisted Soviet control. So that in practice the extension of power by the Communist Party means an extension in power for the Soviet Union.

# The Revolution of Nihilism

## CHAPTER 15

# The Revolt Against Reason

THE declaration of the independence of reason from revelation, the proclamation of the autonomy of human reason at the time of the Renaissance, bears fruit in the twentieth
century in the repudiation of reason and the glorification of
instinct or will. The revolt against reason was a long time in
the making; the seeds of the revolt were sown by the Nominalists in the thirteenth century, cultivated by Descartes and
embodied in the empirical theory of knowledge in the seventeenth. But the Christian conscience lingered long after the
repudiation of Christian theology and the divorce of reason
from faith and for a time it was believed that the subjective
reason of the individual yielded many of the same truths that
earlier centuries recognized as the revelation of God in Christ.
Philosophy appeared able to prove by "natural" reason what
theology derived from revelation. Man stood no longer in
need of enlightenment by grace, for truth and salvation were
now thought to be attainable by the unaided powers of natural
reason and the "good will" of natural man. This optimistic
view of man reached its climax in the eighteenth century and
persisted throughout the nineteenth when progress was
thought to be a "natural law" of the universe.

But as the empirical theory of knowledge was pressed to its
ultimate conclusion, philosophy, to the extent that it premised
its speculation upon that theory, was forced to yield more and
more ground to the natural sciences or to the new social
sciences that purported to apply the methods of the natural
sciences to the observation and explanation of social phenomena. The valiant attempt of the idealists to salvage meta-

physics from the critical onslaught of Hume only succeeded in creating an impassable gulf between being and reality, thought and action. Henceforth, most philosophers were pre-occupied with problems of epistemology and could no longer tell us much, if anything, about the nature of reality since they had not yet decided if we can know anything, or, indeed, what "knowing" anything really means. Wandering in the morass of epistemological speculation the philosopher yielded his place to the scientist and in default of genuine metaphysical speculation the scientist was given free range to exercise his imagination as he would.

Borrowing from the prestige of the natural sciences and claiming to be one of them, a new science of society, sociology, attempted to provide the synthesis of knowledge that had earlier been supplied by metaphysics. Comte and his followers believed that they could discover "laws" of social order precisely analogous to those which governed the physical order. This belief was premised necessarily upon the supposition that man belongs wholly and completely to the natural order. As the immanent conception of order was widened to include human nature and to exclude any conception of transcendent reality, the conception of man as a rational animal created in the image and likeness of God faded more and more from the consciousness of the Western world.

Man is best described as a rational animal; deprive man of reason, and what is left is not man, but animal. This looks like a very commonplace statement, yet Western culture is dying wherever it has been forgotten; for the rational nature of man is the only conceivable foundation for a rational system of ethics. Morality is essentially normality; for a rational being to act and to behave either without reason or contrary to its dictates is to act and behave, not exactly as a beast, but as a beastly man, which is worse. For it is proper that a beast should act as a beast, that is, according to its own nature; but it is totally unfitting for a man to act as a beast, because that means the complete oblivion of his own nature, and hence his final destruction.[1]

The attempt to reduce human life to a mathematical equation, a purely biological fact, or a physical apparatus, could only end in the repudiation of human personality and dignity.

Contempt for human personality finds its practical expression in the tyranny of the totalitarian dictatorships of the twentieth century.

Far from making up for the loss of philosophy, the discovery of the scientific substitutes for it leaves man alone with nature such as it is, and obliges him to surrender to natural necessity. Philosophy is the only rational knowledge by which both science and nature can be judged. By reducing philosophy to pure science, man has not only abdicated his right to judge nature and to rule it; but he has also turned himself into a particular aspect of nature, subjected, like all the rest, to the necessary law which regulates its development. A world where accomplished facts are unto themselves their own justification is ripe for the most reckless social adventures. Its dictators can wantonly play havoc with human institutions and human lives, for dictatorships are facts and they also are unto themselves their own justification.[2]

The twentieth century purports to have discovered that man is not a rational animal and is prepared, moreover, to demonstrate the truthfulness of this proposition by rational argument. Man is a creature of instinct and impulse driven this way and that by irrational forces over which he has little or no control, his "rationality" no more than the slightly more complex capacity of the chimpanzee to retrieve a banana fallen from his cage or of a rat to find his way out of a maze constructed by men to observe the process of learning by trial and error. Reason has an instrumental function only. It can tell us how to do what we want to do but not why or whether. It can supply us with "good reasons" for bad motives but is powerless to resist these motives or to prefer one to another. Cut loose from its moorings in faith, reason drifts with the currents of fashion unable to distinguish the real from the unreal, the true from the false, the good from the bad.

## Psychology

THESE conclusions have been fostered in part by a new "science" of human nature, psychology, which emerged during the latter half of the nineteenth century.[3] Prominent among its founders were the American, William James (1842–1910) and the German, Wilhelm Wundt (1832–1920). First conceived as a science of mind or consciousness, psychology later was conceived more and more as a science of behavior. According to a contemporary psychologist, Professor R. S. Woodworth, "A broadly defined functional psychology starts with the question 'What man *does*' and proceeds to the questions 'How?' and 'Why?' " [4] It attempts to answer these questions by adhering to the concepts and methods of the natural sciences and by employing, depending upon the particular school of psychology, experimental and introspective methods. According to John B. Watson, the founder of one of the more prominent schools of contemporary psychology (behaviorism): "Psychology . . . is a purely objective experimental branch of natural science. Its theoretical goal is the prediction and control of behavior." [5] Relying heavily upon the observation of animal behavior as a clue to the behavior of human beings, Behaviorism lays considerable emphasis upon the description and explanation of behavior in terms of stimulus and response. With the emergence of behaviorism, according to one psychologist, man was "placed in the phylogenetic and evolutionary series . . . and as a consequence psychology was freed from the idea that human beings constitute a unique and special case in the order of nature." [6] But there are many conflicting schools of thought among psychologists and very little agreement. After examining seven contemporary schools of psychology a professor of psychology declares:

System after system announces its principles, each imposes its order on the facts that arrest its attention, and each puts its case with a degree of plausibility. The difficulty is that they all do so and that they are all more or less at odds with each other. It is significant, too, that the more definitely a system draws the line of its pattern, the more rigidly it selects its facts; that the clearest and most consistent systems are those most given to denials and exclusions. Besides, no system, not even the most aggressive, can or does claim that it is as yet fully established by fact. And when it is remembered that the systems just considered are only a few of those current in psychology, the confusion grows and multiplies. Yet this is the situation after

more than half a century of effort: systems in plenty, but no one
interpretation of the facts of psychology to which all psychologists,
or even a majority, agree.[7]

But, the same author declares, "there is a notable agreement
among psychologists that the rational and cognitive sides of
human nature have been enormously overemphasized in the
past." [8]

There is also agreement among contemporary schools of
psychology, the same author writes, concerning the unim-
portance of a problem that loomed large in the minds of early
psychologists, namely, the problem of the relation between
mind and body.

There is a growing tendency to disregard the metaphysics of the
mind-body problem, a tendency which is one of the surest signs that
psychology is becoming a science. . . . From the empirical standpoint the mind-body relations are no more unintelligible, and no less
so, than the relations encountered in other sciences; and if they seem
to constitute a peculiarly significant problem, they do so because
personal concerns and emotional values have singled them out as a
special case. Eventually every natural science arrives at facts and
relations that it cannot explain. . . . And this does not mean that
science is pervaded with mystery. On the contrary, science gets on
with its work precisely because it accepts certain empirical facts and
relations as given and as constituting the practical limits of its inquiry, without pausing to ponder at length how they can possibly be
so.[9]

One of the first to define psychology as a science of human
behavior was William McDougall (1871–1938). He was also
one of the founders of social psychology. "His general assumption was that there must be a number of fundamental motives
which are natural and hereditary and that all other motives
must be derived from these primaries in the course of the
individual's experience." [10] In 1908, he published a list of
these primary motives which he first called instincts and later
called propensities. He revised the list several times and "by
1932 had a list of seventeen besides a number of minor ones
such as the breathing instinct, or desire to breathe when out
of breath, and similar desires to sneeze, cough, etc." [11] His
original list of instincts included:

1. To desire food periodically (hunger)
2. To reject certain substances (disgust)
3. To explore new places and things (curiosity)
4. To try to escape from danger (fear)
5. To fight when frustrated (anger)
6. To have sex desire (mating propensity)
7. To care tenderly for the young (mothering propensity)
8. To seek company (gregarious propensity)
9. To seek to dominate (self-assertive propensity)
10. To accept obvious inferiority (submissive propensity)
11. To make things (constructive propensity)
12. To collect things (acquisitive tendency) [12]

In his *Introduction to Social Psychology* McDougall declared that:

Directly or indirectly the instincts are the prime movers of all human activity . . . determine the ends of all activities and supply the driving power . . . and all the complex intellectual apparatus of the most highly developed mind is . . . but the instrument by which these impulses seek their satisfaction.[13]

Man is not motivated by any logical or rational principles nor by any rationally calculated desire for a preponderance of pleasure over pain. He is primarily a creature of instinct "whose principal springs of activity are essentially similar to those of the higher animals." [14] Nature has arranged it, however, so that "in general the behavior so occasioned is a kind to promote the welfare of the individual animal or of the community to which he belongs, or to secure the perpetuation of the species." [15]

The individual is motivated, however, not only by these primary instincts or propensities but by the influence exerted by the social environment. "Each man is an individual only in an incomplete sense; he is but a unit in a vast system of vital and spiritual forces which are expressing themselves in the form of human societies and working towards ends which no man can foresee." [16] It is the group to which an individual belongs that largely conditions how he shall think and how he shall act. As a product of long evolution "Society has ideals and aims and traditions loftier than any principles of conduct the individual can form for himself unaided, and only by the further evolution of organized society can man be raised to higher levels." [17] The individual apart from society yields to "non-moral and purely egoistic tendencies" but under the restraint imposed by social living "man's conduct" is raised "above the plane of pure egotism" and he is led "to think and care and work for others as well as himself." [18] In McDougall's theory "the group mind" takes the place of conscience. How it is possible for society to have a "mind" is by no means clear but that it has one McDougall is insistent. It is superior, moreover, both in intelligence and in morality to the individual mind.

The collective actions of the well organized group become truly volitional actions expressive of a degree of intelligence and morality much higher than that of the average member of the group, and even, by reason of exultation of emotion and organized co-operation in deliberation, above that of its highest members. [19]

A society has not only a mind, but a life and destiny apart from that of the individuals who happen to compose it at any given time.

Probably the dominant school of psychology today, and certainly the one most popularly known, is that of the psychoanalysts founded by Sigmund Freud (1856–1939) of whom McDougall wrote that he had "done more for the advancement of our understanding of human nature than any other man since Aristotle." [20] An outgrowth of medical practice rather than of academic psychology, psychoanalysis nevertheless propounds a theory of human nature and behavior that has seriously challenged the older schools of academic psychology and exerts a profound influence on contemporary thought generally. It has given rise to an influential school of psychiatry that is the subject of considerable controversy both in and out of the medical profession. And in the writings of neo-Freudians like Erich Fromm and Karen Horney it has been given an application to social problems that challenges the older forms of social psychology.

Probably the most significant aspect of Freud's psychology is his emphasis upon the reality and importance of unconscious mental processes. Every human action, thought, and emotion is motivated and when there is no conscious motive there is always an unconscious motive that can be unearthed by psychoanalytic methods of analysis. Nothing happens by chance and even such apparently innocent "chance" happenings as slips of the tongue are determined by the unconscious. The apparently aimless and nonsensical character of dreams Freud believed to be rich in meaning.

The psychic life of the individual is characterized by more or less constant tension or conflict between conscious and unconscious motivation. The conscious self or "ego" is at war with the unconscious self or "libido." In his early theory Freud described the ego motives as those associated with self-preservation (such as hunger, fear of danger, self-assertion) and conceived of the "libido" as the pleasure-seeking or sex motive.

The unconscious motives do not lie dormant. From time to time, at least, they become urgent and seek to emerge into conscious behavior. But they are not pretty, pleasant motives. When they threaten to emerge they awaken anxiety, shame, and a guilty feeling in the conscious self, which therefore resists and tries to hold them down. . . . The unconscious motive presses up and outward, and the conscious self exerts a contrary force, pressing down and inward. In sleep the conscious self relaxes its vigilance and allows the unconscious motives to emerge to a certain extent, provided they disguise themselves in the symbolism of the manifest dream.[21]

It is the repression of certain kinds of unconscious motives that leads to neuroses. Freud believed that most repressions that later give rise to neurotic behavior in adults take place in childhood. It was his original conclusion, also, that sexual life begins not at puberty but in infancy. All forms of love and pleasure-seeking he defined as sexual. He distinguished three stages in sexual development and sought to explain particular types of personality or behavior in terms of this development. When such development is arrested at one particular stage, one kind of personality results, etc. Freud placed a great deal of emphasis upon the attachment of a boy for his mother and of a girl for her father as a key to the explanation of behavior patterns in later life.

In his later writings Freud conceived of the instincts of self-preservation and reproduction as but two aspects of one instinct for life and opposed to this, another basic or primal instinct, the drive toward death.

Just as the libido is generated within the organism but attaches itself to external objects, so also with the death instinct. It manifests itself for the most part not as a desire to die but as a desire to kill. Turned outward it is the urge to destroy, injure, conquer. It is the hostility motive, the aggressive tendency. . . . Finding something outside to destroy, it does not need to destroy the self. But when frustrated in an external aggression it is likely to turn back upon the self as a suicidal tendency. . . . It is not limited to homicide and suicide but covers the milder forms of aggressiveness, whether directed toward the self or toward external objects. . . .

In his earlier thinking on social psychology Freud emphasized the conflict between the sexual demands of the individual and the restrictions made necessary by social life. In his later works he laid at least equal emphasis on the natural hostility of man to man as the great obstacle to civilization. The individual's demand for justice and fair play arises from jealousy. Each child in a family wants to be the favorite but finally backs down to the extent of saying "If I cannot be the favorite, neither shall you. We will all be equals." Eros tends to bind men together in families, clans, and ever larger groups, always with love and justice within the group but with hostility and aggression for outsiders. Civilization develops through the conflict and fusion of these major drives.[22]

In his later writings Freud also modified his earlier theory of the unconscious. To the unconscious he gave the name "id" and divided the "ego" into the "ego" and the "superego."

The id consists primarily of drives, inherited instincts, or urges. These are not quiescent but continually strive outward toward satisfaction in behavior. But the id has no direct access to the environment; it has no sense organs or muscles. It is unorganized, unstructured, like a boiling cauldron of mixed desires, libido, and destructiveness seeking an outlet. The only outlet is through the ego, which at first is little developed and offers little resistance to the surging of the id. But the ego . . . gets to know the dangers of the environment and the necessity of restraining the id. . . . But when it "represses" a desire of the id, this repressed desire and its associated objects and experiences are driven down and added to the id, so making it even more troublesome than before. . . .

The ego is split into two: the doer or executive which remains the ego proper, and the watcher and moral critic which is the superego.

The superego corresponds to what we ordinarily call conscience, so far as conscience means a blind feeling of right and wrong rather than a knowledge of what is good for us and socially valuable. The superego . . . cannot explain its commands because the source of its authority is buried in the unconscious.[23]

There is a sense in which psychoanalysis and Christianity superficially resemble one another, in the sense that both recognize the importance of guilt and the need for removing it. The psychoanalyst, however, believes that guilt is an undesirable and irrational feeling and proposes to eradicate it by making the individual conscious of the unconscious repressions that give rise to it. The psychoanalyst believes that if the individual can be brought to recognize the cause of his feeling of guilt he will no longer feel guilty. The Christian believes that guilt (in a normal individual) has a rational basis and, to the extent that it is a rational recognition of failure to fulfill the moral law and will of God, that it is a desirable feeling, since only out of such rational recognition of failure can there be improvement. It is not a pathological symptom, the Christian believes, to feel guilty when one ought to feel guilty. The Christian would agree with the psychoanalyst that it *is* pathological to feel guilty when there is no rational reason to feel guilty but unlike the psychoanalyst he does not regard *all* feelings of guilt as irrational. Moreover, the Christian does not believe that the recognition of the cause of the feeling of guilt will, if a rational cause, relieve the individual of guilty feelings. The Christian recognizes the therapeutic value of catharsis, which he calls confession, but he also recognizes the need for *forgiveness* which the psychoanalyst ignores. The Christian, moreover, believes that through penitence the individual receives *power* from God to lead a more perfect life. The Freudian believes that under the guidance of a psychiatrist the individual will discover resources within himself to achieve an "integrated" life. The Christian regards man as a theonomous being, the Freudian as an autonomous one. The Christian believes that man finds his happiness in submission to the will of God through love; the Freudian believes that any submission to "authority" is dangerous and undesirable except, perhaps, the authority of the analyst. Both Christians and Freudians recognize that life is frustrating but the Christian explains this frustration as being rooted in the sinful nature of man himself; the Freudian denies that man is by nature sinful and conceives of his frustration as arising from the repressions of early childhood.[24]

Applications of Freudian psychology to social phenomena have been made and are being made by many individuals. Perhaps the most significant contributions in recent years have been made by Karen Horney, Erich Fromm, and J. C. Flugel.[25] An American political scientist, Harold D. Lasswell, has sought to apply Freudian psychology to the study of politics in a book entitled *Psychopathology and Politics* (1930). The psychoanalysis of political leaders, he believes, reveals significant knowledge about politics. Knowledge, for example, of the sexual experiences of political leaders as children will reveal in his opinion why some are radicals and others conservatives, why some are agitators and others administrators. A sample of his thinking follows:

Agitators as a class are strongly narcissistic types. Narcissism is encouraged by obstacles in the early love relationships, or by over-indulgence and admiration in the family circle. Libido which is blocked in moving outward towards objects settles back upon the self. Sexual objects like the self are preferred, and a strong homosexual component is thus characteristic. Among the agitators this yearning for emotional response of the homosexual kind is displaced upon generalized objects, and high value is placed on arousing emotional responses from the community at large. The tremendous urge for expression in written or spoken language is a roundabout method of gratifying these underlying emotional drives.[26]

It is Lasswell's opinion, moreover, that "the significance of political opinions is not to be grasped apart from the private motives which they symbolize." Since "political movements derive their vitality from the displacement of private affects upon public objects" and since "primitive psychological structures . . . in more or less disguised form . . . control"

individual "thought and effort" we can discover significant
knowledge about political beliefs and behavior through the
use of psychoanalysis. As this "fact" becomes increasingly
accepted the social psychiatrist will replace the social philosopher and the politics of the future will be more "preventive"
in character. Political problems will be solved in the future
less and less by discussion and more and more by psychoanalytical therapy.

The time has come to abandon the assumption that the problem
of politics is the problem of promoting discussion among all the interests concerned in a given problem. Discussion frequently com-
plicates social difficulties, for the discussion by far-flung interests
arouses a psychology of conflict which produces obstructive, fictitious, and irrelevant values. The problem of politics is less to solve
conflicts than to prevent them; less to serve as a safety valve for social
protest than to apply social energy to the abolition of recurrent
sources of strain in society.

This redefinition of the problem of politics may be called the idea
of preventive politics. . . .

Our thinking has too long been misled by the threadbare terminology of democracy versus dictatorship, of democracy versus aristocracy. Our problem is to be ruled by the truth about the conditions
of harmonious human relations, and the discovery of the truth is an
object of specialized research; it is no monopoly of people as people,
or of ruler as ruler.[27]

"The truth about the conditions of harmonious human relations," of course, is that yielded by psychoanalytical methods
and those who conduct such "research" and apply their findings (the social scientists like Lasswell) will be the rulers of
society. "The preventive politics of the future will be intimately allied to general medicine, psychopathology, physiological psychology, and related disciplines."[28] Political conflict is conceived by this school of thought as being essentially
pathological in character and requiring the services of psychiatry to resolve it.

## Irrationality in Social Theory

WE HAVE already discussed in an earlier chapter the political
theory of Georges Sorel in which violence was exalted over

reason as the salvation of the proletariat. There were a number of other social theorists in France and in Italy who emphasized the irrational character of social action although their conclusions generally were less extreme than those of Sorel. The most notable, probably, were Tarde, Durkheim, Le Bon, and Pareto. Their theories have exerted a wide influence not only in their own countries but throughout the world.

Social phenomena, according to Gabriel Tarde (1843–1904), are the product of the interaction of individual minds. This mental interaction takes three principal forms: repetition or imitation, opposition, and adaptation or invention. These correspond to the basic or innate tendencies of individual human behavior. Individual thought and action is not the product of individual reason but of this mental interaction between individuals. Thought and action is largely guided and determined by imitation of the thoughts and actions of others. When two different kinds of imitative thought and action meet we have opposition. This opposition may result in the mutual annihilation of both kinds, the absorption of the weaker by the stronger, or in a mutual adaptation. A new invention or adaptation begins a new wave of imitation and thus the social process continues indefinitely. Tarde rejected, however, any conception of a group mind or collective "soul." [29]

According to Emile Durkheim (1858–1917) the individual mind is but a reflection of the group mind, all logical categories, abstract concepts, religious ideas, and moral values are the product of social interaction. He posits the existence of a "collective consciousness" that differs specifically from individual consciousness. This collective consciousness has ideas of its own, or "collective representations," which are transmitted to the individual consciousness in the form of moral, religious, juridical and legal rules. Moreover, they possess an inherent power of coercion which the individual is unable to resist. He reaches the conclusion that society is not an illogical or incoherent being but, on the contrary, the embodiment of the highest form of mental life.

Society is not at all the illogical or a-logical, incoherent and fantastic being which it has too often been considered. Quite on the contrary, the collective consciousness is the highest form of the psychic life, since it is the consciousness of consciousness. Being placed *outside of* and *above* individual and local contingencies, it sees things only in their permanent and essential aspects, which it crystallizes into communicable ideas. . . . Society sees farther and better, than individuals.[30]

It is from society that we derive such notions as time and space. Speaking of the social origin of "time" Durkheim wrote:

> Try to represent what the notion of time would be without the processes by which we divide and measure it. . . . This is something nearly unthinkable! Now what is the origin of this differentiation? It is not so much our personal experience because it is not *my time* that is thus arranged; it is time in general. . . . That alone is enough to give us a hint that such an arrangement ought to be collective. The division into days, weeks, months, years, etc., corresponds to the periodical recurrence of rites, feasts, and public ceremonies. A calendar expresses the rhythm of the collective activities, while at the same time its function is to assure their regularity.[31]

A nominalist, Durkheim mistakes the name for reality, the calendar for time. That the names by which we designate divisions of time are socially determined may be granted but that society itself determines what time *is,* is nonsense. There has to be some reality to be designated and divided and such designations cannot be completely arbitrary if they are to have any correspondence to reality and be socially acceptable because they do. In similar fashion, Durkheim endeavors to prove that space, too, is a socially imposed category.

Religious phenomena, likewise, are "explained" in terms of society. God is nothing but society personified, the particular religious conceptions of any given religion, the reflection of the characteristics of a particular society. Religion's *raison d'être* consists in the creation and maintenance of social solidarity.

> Religious representations are collective representations which express collective realities; the rites are a manner of acting which take rise in the midst of the assembled groups and which are destined to excite, maintain, or recreate certain mental states in these groups. . . . The religious life is the concentrated expression of the whole collective life. . . . The idea of society is the soul of religion. Religious forces are therefore human forces, moral forces. . . .[32]

Gustave Le Bon (1841–1931) agreed with Durkheim in believing in the existence of a group mind but, unlike Durkheim, believed that the collective consciousness of men in the mass was inferior in intelligence and morality to that of the individual mind. The isolated individual occasionally demonstrates an ability to think and act rationally but in association with other individuals, in a group or crowd, he is dominated by irrational considerations. "The psychological crowd is a provisional being formed of heterogeneous elements, which for a moment are combined, exactly as the cells which constitute a living body form by their reunion a new being, which displays characteristics very different from those possessed by each of the cells singly." [33] In a crowd, Le Bon argued, the individual is anonymous and, as a consequence, is more likely to yield to instincts which under isolated conditions he would restrain. The crowd fills him with a sense of invincible power. His sense of responsibility disappears. As a member of a crowd the individual is more predisposed to suggestion and to contagious sentiments; he is like one hypnotized, the unconscious personality predominating over the conscious personality.

A crowd is at the mercy of all external exciting causes, and reflects their incessant variations. It is the slave of the impulses which it receives . . . the isolated individual possesses the capacity of dominating his reflex actions . . . a crowd is devoid of this capacity.

The varying impulses which crowds obey may be, according to their exciting causes, generous or cruel, heroic or cowardly, but they will always be so imperious that the interest of the individual, even the interest of self-preservation, will not dominate them. . . .

A crowd may easily enact the part of an executioner, but not less easily that of a martyr. It is crowds that have furnished the torrents of blood requisite for the triumph of every belief. [34]

Crowds are impulsive, irritable, highly suggestible, and credulous. Crowds are incapable of reasoning, of distinguishing truth from error or of forming a precise judgment on any matter. They can tolerate neither discussion nor contradiction.

Le Bon enlarges the concept of crowd to include not only those associations of individuals that are commonly called "crowds" but to include juries, sects, classes, electorates, and parliamentary assemblies.

Electoral crowds—that is to say, collectivities invested with the power of electing holders of certain functions—constitute hetero-geneous crowds, but as their action is confined to a single clearly determined matter, namely, the choosing between different candi-dates, they present only a few of the characteristics previously de-scribed . . . they display in particular but slight aptitude for rea-soning, the absence of the critical spirit, irritability, credulity and simplicity. In their decision, moreover, is to be traced the influence of the leaders of crowds and the part played by the factors we have enumerated: affirmation, repetition, prestige, and contagion.[35]

It makes no difference whether the suffrage be restricted or not for "a vote recorded by forty academicians is no better than that of forty water-carriers." Because an individual is learned it does not mean that he has any special knowledge of, or ability to decide, social questions. "With regard to social problems, owing to the number of unknown quantities they offer, men are substantially, equally ignorant." [36]

In parliamentary assemblies we find many of the char-acteristics of heterogeneous crowds: intellectual simplicity, irritability, suggestibility, exaggerated sentiments, and the preponderate influence of a few leaders. But such assemblies only constitute crowds at certain moments so that they are able to turn out some excellent technical laws especially when the law is framed by a technical expert and all the assembly has to do is to vote its approval.

The best we can hope for is rule by a rational minority.

## *Vilfredo Pareto* (1848–1923)

OF ALL the more recent social theorists probably Pareto is the most important. An economist who later became a soci-ologist his principal work is the two volume *Trattato di sociologia generale* (1915–1916) which has been translated into English under the title *The Mind and Society*. Like the other social theorists whom we have been discussing Pareto con-

ceived of his work as a scientific description of social reality
and disavowed any predilection for one system over another.
He claims that his sociology rests upon no *a priori* principles
and that it is simply a description of social facts and their
observed uniformities. It differs from sociological theories in
the past, he thinks, in that it is free of all moral evaluations,
metaphysical speculation, and "non-logico-experimental"
elements.

He discarded the categories of "cause" and "effect" which
he thought gave a one-sided and hence over-simplified and
superficial view of social change, in favor of the terms "variable" and "function." Society is composed of many variable
elements which react upon one another and it is impossible to
select one and call it the "cause" and another and call it the
"effect." The relationship between politics, economics, religion, ethics, learning, etc., is a functional not a causal relationship. In addition, he suggested that sociologists should
confine their attention to those constant and uniform elements of a social system that could be measured quantitatively.

For Pareto, society is neither an organism nor a mechanism
but simply a "social system" in which the disruptive forces
are held in check by the integrating forces. Social systems may
take many and various forms. The form of a society is determined by all the elements which influence it. These elements are of three general kinds: (1) soil, climate, flora,
fauna, geological conditions and other physical features;
(2) other elements exterior to the given society at a given
time; such as other societies which are exterior to a given
society spatially, and societies antecedent to the given society
in time; (3) the inner elements of a social system; such as
race, the character of the residues and feelings, interests,
ideologies and other qualities of the human molecules which
compose the given society.[37] If we could know all these elements quantitatively, their effects, combinations and correlations, we would have a complete explanation of society.

Pareto draws a sharp distinction between thought and
action, between theory and practice. Reason has a technical
efficacy only. It can tell us how to do what we want to do but

it cannot tell us anything about the desirability or intrinsic goodness of our wants. As a consequence, most human conduct is motivated by non-logical factors. In science, reason reigns supreme, but science however important it may be in yielding knowledge is of little or no use as a guide to action.

> For purposes of knowing, logico-experimental science is the only thing of any value; for purposes of doing, it is of much greater importance to follow the lead of sentiments. . . . Practice is the better the more practical it is and theory the better the more theoretical it is. Altogether wretched, in general, are "theoretical practices" and "practical theories."[38]

Aristotle, Pareto says, declares that we should seek to determine the best state but in order to do that we would have to determine the best life and that is impossible. Aristotle, he says, merely found the solution to the problem that best accorded with his own sentiments and that is all anyone does or can do.

The greater part of Pareto's treatise on sociology is devoted to a classification and description of the non-logical factors that motivate men. He believes that he has discovered a fairly small number of more or less constant drives that are the same in every society at every period of history. These drives he calls "residues." They are not the same as instincts nor are they exactly sentiments but "the residues are the manifestation of instincts and sentiments as the elevation of mercury in a thermometer is the manifestation of a rise in the temperature." [39] There are six principal types of residues: (1) *Residues of Combinations:* the tendency characteristic of human beings to combine or manipulate things and thoughts; (2) *Residues of the Persistence of Aggregates:* the drives which lead to the worship, defense, and protection of established combinations; (3) *Residues (or Needs) of the Manifestation of Sentiments Through External Acts:* the need people feel to "do something." The need which expresses itself in political agitation, making speeches, campaigning for votes, advocating reforms; (4) *Residues Connected with Sociability:* the drives which lead the individual to conform to the group and to enforce conformity on others, the drives associated with pity and cruelty; (5) *Residues of the Integrity of Personality:* the drives which lead men to guard their personal integrity, the drive for equality; and (6) *Sexual Residues:* the biological sex urge manifested in some verbal form.[40] All six residues are present in all individuals but their distribution varies with individuals and groups. The preponderance of one kind of residue produces one type of society, the preponderance of another kind, another type.

When these residues manifest themselves verbally the result is, what Pareto calls, a *derivation.* He means to imply by the use of that word what Sorel implied by the use of the word "myth," what Freud called "rationalization" and what Marxians call "ideology." According to Pareto:

Concrete theories in social connections are made up of residues and derivations. The residues are manifestations of sentiments. The derivations comprise logical reasonings, unsound reasonings, and manifestations of sentiments used for purposes of derivation: they are manifestations of the human being's hunger for thinking. If that hunger were satisfied by logico-experimental (i.e. empirical-scientific) reasonings only, there would be no derivations; instead of them we should get logico-experimental theories. But the human hunger for thinking is satisfied in any number of ways; by pseudo-experimental reasonings, by words that stir the sentiments, by fatuous, inconclusive "talk." So derivations come into being.[41]

Practically all political philosophies, theologies, systems of ethics, and doctrines are regarded by Pareto as derivations. Only scientific theories, in his opinion, are rational. A derivation is accepted not because it is true or false but because it corresponds to our residues. Only science yields truth. Theories of progress, democracy, justice, socialism, nationalism, internationalism are all non-logical derivations. A belief in "natural rights," in "justice," or in "law" is a kind of superstition or prejudice. None of them are "scientific" concepts. As a consequence, derivations are not very important in determining social change, the residues are much more important and influential. Says Pareto:

Theologians, metaphysicists, philosophers, theorists of politics, law, and ethics, do not ordinarily accept the order indicated. They are inclined to assign first place to derivations. What we call residues

are in their eyes axioms or dogmas, and the purpose is just the conclusion of a logical reasoning. But since they are not as a rule in any
agreement on the derivation, they argue about it till they are blue in
the face and think that they can change social conditions by proving
a derivation fallacious. That is all an illusion on their part. They fail
to realize that their hagglings never reach the majority of men, who
could not make head nor tail to them anyhow, and who in fact disregard them save as articles of faith to which they assent in deference
to certain residues.[42]

According to Pareto there are two principal social types of
individuals: the speculators or "foxes," and the *rentiers* or
"lions." The first are strong in the residues of combination,
the second in the residues of the persistence of aggregates.
The "foxes" live by their wits and rely on fraud, deceit, and
cleverness. They are adventurous, like change and novelty,
and in economic affairs are likely to engage in speculation
and all kinds of promotion schemes. The "lions" are the conservative type, patriotic, loyal to tradition, tied to family,
nation and Church. They value "character" over cleverness
and talk much of "duty." In economic matters they are
thrifty and cautious. They rely more upon force than upon
intelligence.

Every society no matter what its form or name is divided
into two strata: the élite and the non-élite, the upper and lower
classes, the successful and the unsuccessful. The élite is further
subdivided into the governing and the non-governing élite.
And within the governing élite there is still a smaller group,
class, or committee which in effect exercises control. This is
true whether the government be called a democracy, an
aristocracy, a monarchy, or a dictatorship. In reality there
are only two kinds of government: (1) those which rely chiefly
on physical force and on religious or similar sentiments, and
(2) those which rely chiefly on intelligence and cunning.[43]
Whether universal suffrage is practiced or not, it is always an
oligarchy that rules.

Who is this new god called Universal Suffrage? He is no more
exactly definable, no less shrouded in mystery, no less beyond the
pale of reality, than the hosts of other divinities; nor are there fewer
and less patent contradictions in his theology than in theirs. Wor-

shippers of Universal Suffrage are not led by their god. It is they who lead him—and by the nose, determining the forms in which he must manifest himself. Oftentimes proclaiming the sanctity of "majority rule," they resist "majority rule" by obstructionist tactics, even though they form but small minorities, and burning incense to the Goddess Reason, they in no wise disdain, in certain cases, alliances with Chicanery, Fraud, and Corruption.[44]

In every society, Pareto declares, there is an almost constant "circulation of the élite." In every society there is a constant shifting of individuals from the lower to the upper classes and every élite is doomed eventually to disappear. "History is the graveyard of aristocracies." [45] The structure and composition of every élite is constantly changing not simply in the sense that members of the élite die and are replaced by other individuals but in the sense that there are more or less constant changes in the types of individuals who compose the élite. A free circulation of the élite in which those of ability "naturally" rise to the top would be desirable but is never found in reality. So long as a governing élite is willing to assimilate or to destroy individuals seeking entrance into the élite the society will be relatively stable but if it refuses to accept new members and is too corroded by the "poison" of humanitarianism to use force to destroy them then revolution is likely. As the "foxes" become numerous in the élite the probability of their being ousted by the "lions" becomes greater. On the basis of this analysis Pareto predicted the downfall of the governing élites of the Western democracies, which he identified with the speculators or "foxes." Pareto is insistent that the art of governing depends upon deceit and violence:

The art of governing lies in finding ways to take advantage of . . . sentiments, not in wasting one's energies in futile efforts to destroy them. . . . The person who is able to free himself from the blind dominion of his own sentiments is capable of utilizing the sentiments of other people for his own ends. . . .[46]

The use of force is indispensable to society; and when the higher classes are averse to the use of force, which ordinarily happens because the majority of those classes come to rely wholly on their skill at chicanery, and the minority shrink from energetic acts now through stupidity, now through cowardice, it becomes necessary, if society is to subsist and prosper, that that governing class be replaced by another which is willing and able to use force. Roman society was saved from ruin by the legions of Caesar and Octavius.[47]

Under the guise of purely scientific research Pareto has rewritten Machiavelli's *Prince* and brought it "up to date." As an American philosopher, Professor Melvin Rader, declares:

The advantage of Pareto's book is that it not only suggests ruthless tactics, but offers a clever defense against the pangs of conscience. It enlists the prestige of science in support of the will-to-power. As an apostle of the "logico-experimental method," Pareto bedecks his pages with algebraic signs and graphs, most of which are employed to excellent purpose. He "proves" his view that values are purely sentimental by marshaling a large amount of "inductive evidence." He thus appears to be a resolute defender of science, intent upon keeping "theory" uncontaminated by "practice" and "sentiment."

Since he adopts the role of a scientific purist, the casual reader is apt to misunderstand the import of his argument. His treatise in effect is an attack upon the life of reason, and this is true despite his apparent attachment to strict scientific method. As a matter of fact, he so unduly restricts the field of science that a great portion of existence is turned over to violence and passion.[48]

A disillusioned liberal, Pareto's work is premised upon cynicism and a frank contempt for human personality. It is a curious twentieth-century phenomenon that so many intellectuals should be so actively engaged in the task of persuading other intellectuals *by reason* that men are essentially irrational. That rational justification for such a view of man should be thought either necessary or possible is itself refutation of the conclusion these intellectuals seek by rational argument to persuade others to accept. That they should concede, moreover, that men do, in fact, feel some necessity for providing "good" reasons for "real" ones, for "rationalizing" their behavior, says a great deal more about the rationality and ethical sensibilities of men than they intend to concede. Why, indeed, should individuals feel any necessity whatsoever for "rationalizing" their behavior, for providing "good" reasons for "real" ones, if they are essentially irrational, a-moral, and controlled by forces completely outside themselves? How is it *possible* for them to do so? Is the "scientist," moreover, exempt from the irrational forces that determine the thought and conduct of other individuals? And on what grounds? If he is not, of what value is his science? If Pareto, for example, is correct in his view of the irrational forces which determine human thought and action is not *his* social theory but another example of a derivation or an ideology? On what grounds is his theory exempted from the designation which he applies to other people's theories? If there are no objective values and no truth, moreover, how is it possible for *anyone* to claim that his theory is true or valuable?

In a recent book C. S. Lewis has discussed this problem with characteristic skill. "We may state it as a rule," he said, "that no thought is valid if it can be fully explained as the result of irrational causes." [49] It is a rule, he says, which we apply every day of our lives. If a sober man tells us that his house is full of snakes we may go with him to look for them; if we suspect him, however, of suffering from *delirium tremens* we do not even bother to look for them. In any situation in which we even *suspect* an irrational cause we do not pay much attention to the opinions or beliefs of the person holding them. On the other hand, if we think that a belief or opinion is false we generally look for some irrational cause to explain it.

Now it would clearly be preposterous to apply this rule to each particular thought as we come to it and yet not to apply it to all thoughts taken collectively, that is, to human reason as a whole. Each particular thought is valueless if it is the result of irrational causes. Obviously, then, the whole process of human thought, what we call Reason, is equally valueless if it is the result of irrational causes. Hence every theory of the universe which makes the human mind a result of irrational causes is inadmissible, for it would be a proof that there are no such things as proofs. Which is nonsense.

But Naturalism, as commonly held, is precisely a theory of this sort. The mind, like every other particular thing or event, is supposed to be simply the product of the Total System. It is supposed to be that and nothing more, to have no power whatever of "going on of its own accord." And the Total System is not supposed to be rational. All thoughts whatever are therefore the results of irrational causes, and nothing more than that. The finest piece of scientific reasoning is caused in just the same irrational way as the thoughts a man has because a bit of bone is pressing on his brain. If we continue to apply our Rule, both are equally valueless. And if we stop applying our Rule we are no better off. For then the Naturalist will have to admit that thoughts produced by lunacy or alcohol or by the mere wish to disbelieve in Naturalism are just as valid as his own thoughts. What is sauce for the goose is sauce for the gander. The Naturalist cannot condemn other people's thoughts because they have irrational causes and continue to believe his own which have (if Naturalism is true) equally irrational causes.[50]

## Irrationality in Philosophy

IDEAS are nothing but arbitrary and convenient fictions, truth is that which it is useful to the individual to believe, the test of the truthfulness of an idea is not its logical consistency nor its correspondence to reality but an idea is true if it "works" —so Pragmatism declares. The founders of this philosophy were the Americans C. S. Pierce (1840–1914) and William James (1842–1910) and it has since been perpetuated by Professor John Dewey in the United States and by Dr. F. C. S. Schiller in Great Britain. In Germany it found expression in the writings of Hans Vaihinger (1852–1933). Pragmatism is not so much a philosophy as it is an attitude about philosophy. Starting from a premise given wide currency by psychology: that people hold beliefs to be true which are emotionally satisfying, Pragmatism proceeds to derive from it a very different conclusion: that a true belief is one which is emotionally satisfying or one that "works."

Philosophy, William James tells us, is largely a matter of individual temperament, "the history of philosophy" being largely "a clash of temperaments." A philosopher's conception of the universe is nothing more than that which suits his temperament. "Plato, Locke, Hegel, Spencer, are such temperamental thinkers." [51] Philosophers can be broadly classified into two types: the "tender-minded" and the "tough-minded." The first type is rationalistic, idealistic, optimistic, religious, dogmatic; the second type is empiricist, sensationalist, materialistic, pessimistic, irreligious, fatalistic, skeptical.

Pragmatism is not a system of ideas, "it is a method only."

If you follow that method you will not ask is this philosophy or theory true, is it logically consistent, does it accord with reality, but rather you will ask: what practical difference does it make to me if it be true? [52] You will ask: what is the "cash-value" of this idea? "*Theories thus become instruments, not answers to enigmas, in which we can rest. . . .* It agrees with nominalism . . . in always appealing to particulars; with utilitarianism in emphasizing practical aspects; with positivism in its disdain for verbal solutions, useless questions, and metaphysical abstractions." [53] It is arrayed "against rationalism as a pretension and a method . . . it stands for no particular results. It has no dogmas, and no doctrines save its method." [54] As an attitude it looks away from first principles and categories and looks toward "fruits, consequences, facts." William James advises us to "give up logic, fairly, squarely and irrevocably" and to substitute "reality, life, experience, concreteness, immediacy." He advises us to give up the old doctrine that based truth on logical consistency and to recognize that an idea is true if it "works." For "ideas become true just in so far as they help us to get into satisfactory relation with other parts of our experience." [55]

Let us see how William James defines truth.

"*The true*" to put it very briefly, *is only the expedient in the way of our thinking, just as "the right" is only the expedient in the way of our behaving*. Expedient in almost any fashion; and expedient in the long run and on the whole of course; for what meets expediently all the experience in sight won't necessarily meet all farther experiences equally satisfactorily. . . .

We have to live today by what truth we can get today, and be ready tomorrow to call it falsehood.[56]

Our obligation to seek truth is part of our general obligation to do what pays. The payment true ideas bring are the sole why of our duty to follow them. Identical whys exist in the case of wealth and health.[57]

The truth of an idea is not a stagnant property inherent in it. Truth *happens* to an idea. It *becomes* true, is *made* true by events. Its verity *is* in fact an event, a process: the process namely of its verifying itself, its veri-*fication*. Its validity is the process of its valid-*ation*.[58]

Truth is not something to be discovered but something to be *made*. Truth is not something absolute and constant, but something relative and ever-changing. Truth is whatever "works" here and now. But who is to decide what "works" means? You or me or someone else? The pragmatist uses the word "works" as though it were self-evident in meaning and does not appear to be seriously perturbed by the problem as to who is to decide whether or not an idea or theory is "workable." But it is of a considerable practical importance whether a William James is to decide what is "workable" or whether a Hitler is to decide since Pragmatism itself provides us with no standard or principles with which to choose between William James's conception of expediency "in the long run and on the whole of course" and Hitler's. If truth, moreover, is in a constant process of being made and un-made and there is no assurance whatever that what we regard as true today may not be false tomorrow then there is no standard with which to measure the truthfulness of anything—truth is just whatever happens to be regarded as true at a particular moment and by particular individuals.

Associated with James's conception of truth is his idea of the "will to believe." In an essay by that title he defended the thesis that "Our passional nature not only lawfully may, but must, decide an option between propositions, whenever it is a genuine option that cannot by its nature be decided on intellectual grounds." [59] When he used the phrase "on intellectual grounds" he meant "on scientific grounds"—thus, when a proposition is such that it cannot be validated by science we not only may but must follow the lead of our passions. To refuse to decide is nevertheless a decision. In this essay James was anxious to "rescue" religion from the onslaught of skepticism but whether he did religion a service is open to serious doubt. Moral and religious questions, he argued, are of such a vital nature that their "solution cannot wait for sensible proof" and on such questions we must consult our "hearts" rather than our heads.[60] In such matters we must be "willing to believe"—"we have the right to believe at our own risk *any* hypothesis that is live enough to tempt our will." [61] This is a dangerous doctrine. For it is a doctrine that may be used to justify believing in *anything*. We may be "tempted by our will" to believe in all kinds of irrational fantasies and it is just as likely, if we followed William James's advice, that many would be tempted to believe in Hitler, Stalin, the myth of racial superiority, as in God, or good moral behavior. If reason is powerless to guide our will or to substantiate the validity of the path taken by our will then no standard remains by means of which to judge the validity of our beliefs. It is one thing to make our will subservient to our faith (the orthodox Christian doctrine) and quite another thing to make our faith subservient to our will (the pragmatist doctrine).

Although Pragmatism disclaims all axiomatic thinking it starts, of necessity, from certain axioms concerning the nature of man and the universe and especially from the ancient Protagorean axiom that "Man is the measure of all things." From this axiom it arrives at the highly original conclusion that truth and reality are in the constant process of being *made* by the will of man. It "subjects truth to the domination of the human mind, and insists that in the long run that alone is true which it suits human beings to think true" and thus ministers "to human complacency by assuring human beings that right and wrong, beauty and ugliness, reality and unreality, are not external facts, features of the universe to which human beings must in the long run subject themselves, but are the products of human consciousness and, therefore, amenable to human desires." [62] "Wishful thinking" is thus erected into a philosophy of life. And that helps to account for its widespread popularity for all of us are tempted to believe, however absurd we may know it to be in our more rational moments, that "wishing will make it so."

In essence the philosophy of John Dewey (1859–) is very similar to that of William James. Under the influence of Darwin and of evolutionary thought generally John Dewey has sought to erect a philosophy, if not a religion, upon the foundations of biological evolution and the methods of natural science. He discards the conception of truth for a conception he calls "warranted assertability" and for the traditional search for truth he would substitute "inquiry" by the methods and with the concepts of natural science. Truth is what indi-

viduals who carry on such "inquiry" agree upon. Thinking
is more important than thought, the search for truth more
important than its discovery. The search for first causes and
ultimate goals is abandoned. "Philosophy forswears inquiry
after absolute origins and absolute finalities in order to explore specific values and the specific conditions that generate
them." [63] Truth "evolves"—it is a product of the evolutionary
process and the process is the only lasting truth. To understand the process is the task of philosophy as the handmaiden
of science. (But why one should devote his energies to the
search after truth if its discovery is dangerous or impossible
is by no means clear.)

For Dewey the purpose of life is mastery over the environment, with Bacon and with Faust, he is captivated by the
thought that "Knowledge is power." With the great advances
made by the natural sciences in their "control" of nature
Dewey foresees man finally coming into his own as the master
of his destiny. Intelligent planning is all that is required. True
beliefs are those which foster such mastery, for, like William
James, he believed that it is the effect of an idea that determines its validity. Like the psychologists who fostered the
conception of a "group mind" Dewey argues that "Anything
which may properly be called mind or intelligence is not an
original possession, but is a consequence of the manifestation
of instincts under the conditions supplied by associated life
in the family, the school, the market-place and forum." [64]
Human nature is not a reflection of the image of God but of
society.

The failure of classical liberalism, Dewey believes, was "its
failure to recognize what the true and final source of change
has been, and now is, the corporate intelligence embodied in
science." [65] The problem of the reconciliation of freedom and
authority, Dewey thinks, will be solved, if it can be solved at
all, only by accepting the authority of science.

Neither the past nor the present afford . . . any ground for expecting that the adjustment of authority and freedom, stability and
change, will be achieved by following the old paths. . . . The issue
in my judgment, can be narrowed down to this question: Are there

resources that have not as yet been tried out in the large field of human relations, resources that are available and that carry with them the potential promise of successful application? . . .

The resource that has not yet been tried on any large scale, in the broad field of human, social relationships is the utilization of organized intelligence, the manifold benefits and values of which we have substantial and reliable evidence in the narrower field of science.[66]

This is the gospel of social salvation by science—if only we will allow our lives to be controlled by the latest findings of science, our beliefs to be tested in the scientific laboratory, and submit to the authority and government of trained specialists then we may hope, if not for the millennium, then for social utopia.

Commenting upon Dewey's philosophy, the English philosopher, Bertrand Russell, declares:

His philosophy is a power philosophy, though not, like Nietzsche's, a philosophy of individual power; it is the power of the community that is felt to be valuable. It is this element of social power that seems to me to make the philosophy of instrumentalism attractive to those who are more impressed by our new control over natural forces than by the limitations to which that control is still subject. . . .

Modern technique, while not altogether favorable to the lordly individual of the Renaissance, has revived the sense of the collective power of human communities. Man, formerly too humble, begins to think of himself as almost a God. The Italian pragmatist Papini urges us to substitute the "Imitation of God" for the "Imitation of Christ."

In all this I feel a grave danger, the danger of what might be called cosmic impiety. The concept of "truth" as something dependent upon facts largely outside human control has been one of the ways in which philosophy hitherto has inculcated the necessary element of humility. When this check upon pride is removed, a further step is taken on the road towards a certain kind of madness—the intoxication of power—the intoxication of power . . . to which modern men, whether philosophers or not, are prone. I am persuaded that this intoxication is the greatest danger of our time, and that any philosophy which, however unintentionally, contributes to it is increasing the danger of vast social disaster.[67]

## The Will to Power

THE revolt against reason finds, perhaps, its most dramatic and vivid expression in the writings of the German philosopher, Friedrich Wilhelm Nietzsche (1844–1900). Of all those who participated in the rejection of reason as a guide to life Nietzsche was more acutely aware of what he was doing and why. He was under no illusion that science could do what religion, in his opinion, had failed to do and, more consistently than most of those who rejected reason, he refused to worship at the altar of science when he could no longer worship at the altar of God. In Nietzsche the tortured soul of modern man is laid bare for all to see, in him all the conflicts of modern thought find a focal point, in him are embodied all the anxieties that the separation of reason from faith has engendered. He *is* modern man—modern in his rejection of God, in his consequent rejection of reason, in his anxiety, in his passionate avowal of salvation by power, and in his self-destruction through madness. Nietzsche is all the neuroses of the twentieth century rolled into one.

Nietzsche utters the terrible words which countless other men of his times have felt but been reluctant to say: "God is dead." How can we continue to live in a universe without God? That is the question which engages Nietzsche's attention but it is much more than an intellectual problem, it is both a personal and a social catastrophe, it is the death knell of civilization. Nietzsche understands the implications of the loss of faith better than any of his contemporaries. They live, he says, in smug complacency, paying lip service to Christian morality, while all the time their lives belie their beliefs and their civilization totters upon the brink of the abyss. He wants to shock them out of their complacency and his voice takes on the strident notes of hysteria as he strives to make himself heard above the din of optimistic babbling about the inevitability of progress and of salvation through science. His words fall upon more sympathetic ears today than they did when he first wrote them for there are few left today who can confidently proclaim their conviction in the inevitability of progress or who are prepared to deny the reality of evil and the sense of tragedy.

One theme runs continuously throughout his works: modern civilization is decadent. Modern civilization pays lip service to the Christianity upon which it was founded but repudiates it in its life. It clings, at least verbally, to Christian morality at the very moment when it has repudiated Christ, it seeks to keep Christian morality while it rejects the Christian religion. This is not only inconsistent, it is impossible. The first reaction to the repudiation of God has been one of relief but our culture is destined, he believed, to experience as a consequence of this repudiation "rupture, destruction, downfall, revolution" and a "stupendous logic of terror." [68] Nietzsche proposes to lead men through this crisis not by taking them back to the God they have repudiated (for "God is dead") but to redemption through the "will to power."

The decadence of modern civilization is manifested in numerous ways: in the excess of self-righteousness, the refusal to face the fact of evil, the condemnation of the worker to "anonymous slavery," the search for money as an end in itself, the fawning sycophancy of democratic politicians, the idolatry of the state, the conception of man as "a meaningless accident in a cosmic mechanism, the pawn of environmental forces," the "preponderance of scholarship over creativeness," the cultivation of mediocrity in all fields of endeavor, in the realm of art the "bizarre combinations of charlatanism and virtuosity, brutality and over-refinement, stimulants and opiates," the cult of the ugly, the morbid, the exotic—in short, the "pestilence of hypocrisy and self-deceit." [69]

We may quarrel with the details of Nietzsche's indictment but in broad outline we are forced to say, if we are honest, that his indictment strikes home. There is enough truth in it to make us feel, at the very least, uncomfortable in his presence. We may agree with the writer who said that "Nietzsche is a good tonic, but a bad food." [70] It is in the manner in which Nietzsche proposes to "redeem" mankind that the perversion of his analysis is revealed. You cannot give up God, he tells us over and over again, without giving up the moral system that is sustained by faith in God. Have the courage of your convictions—you believe that "God is dead," then act as though you believed it. Christian morality is fit only for slaves, it exalts weakness, engenders compassion, encourages submission, condemns pride. It is a morality for the masses. The New Morality is for the few, those Supermen of the future who must learn to be self-reliant, hard, and cruel if they are not to perish with the mass and to be engulfed by mediocrity. Life is tragic, hard and cruel but it is its own reward for those with strength and courage enough to do battle with it. Only the few can hope to win, to become "new creatures," to be the Supermen, but in their "creation" lies the meaning of life itself.

*I teach you the Superman.* Man is something that is to be surpassed. What have ye done to surpass man?

All beings hitherto have created something beyond themselves: and ye want to be the ebb of that great tide, and would rather go back to the beast than surpass man?

What is the ape to man? A laughing-stock, a thing of shame. And just the same shall man be to the Superman: a laughing-stock, a thing of shame. . . .

Lo, I teach you the Superman! The Superman is the meaning of the earth. Let your will say: The Superman *shall be* the meaning of the earth! [71]

If God is dead there is no alternative but for men "to become Gods."

Do ye know what "the universe" is to my mind? Shall I show it to you in my mirror? This universe is a monster of energy, without beginning or end; a fixed and brazen quantity of energy which grows neither bigger nor smaller, which does not consume itself, but only alters its face . . . surrounded by nonentity as by a frontier. . . . It is . . . energy everywhere, the play of forces and force-waves, at the same time one and many, agglomerating here and diminishing there, a sea of forces storming and raging in itself, for ever changing, for ever rolling back over incalculable ages to recurrence . . . producing the most complicated things out of the most simple structures . . . a becoming which knows not satiety, or disgust, or weariness: this, my Dionysian world of eternal self-creation, of eternal self-destruction, this mysterious world of twofold voluptuousness; this my "Beyond Good and Evil," without aim, unless there is an aim in the bliss of the circle; without will, unless a ring must by nature keep good-will to itself—would you have a name for my world? A *solution* of all your riddles? Do ye also want a light, ye most concealed, strongest, and most undaunted men of the blackest midnight? This world is the *Will to Power*—and nothing else! And even ye yourselves are this will to power—and nothing besides! [72]

Not matter, not ideas, but the will to power is the essential reality, that which includes both spirit and matter. The world is not an organism nor a machine but a chaos, without beginning or end, meaning or purpose. It is a process of Eternal Recurrence. Only one thing can redeem life in this world from futility and that is *courage*. If life is to be something more than "a tale told by an idiot, full of sound and fury, signifying nothing," it must be embraced in all its misery and tragedy with a passionate defiance or courage that "strikes even death dead." Of all the traditional virtues only one, courage, survives in Nietzsche's philosophy and upon that one virtue he seeks to erect an entire philosophy of "life." Like Machiavelli's man of *virtù*, Nietzsche's Superman is the man who wrestles with Fate, who learns to love Fate, to stake his life against Chance. In pitting his will against Fate he redeems life from futility and meaninglessness. "To redeem what is past, and to transform 'It was' into 'Thus would I have it!'—that only do I call redemption." [73] Only when the individual learns to say and believe: "I myself am fate and condition existence from all eternity" [74] can he learn to live beyond good and evil. Then he will learn to accept suffering and pain as a part of life, nay, he will welcome them as a source of joy. Thus will he learn not only how to live but how to "die at the right time" [75] for thus will Fate be finally vanquished when man has learned to die by his own hand and at the time of his own choosing.

Nietzsche agrees with Christianity in saying that man can be saved only by becoming a "new creature" but the new creature envisaged by Nietzsche is the exact opposite of Christ. The "new creature" envisaged by Nietzsche is a man motivated by "voluptuousness, passion for power, and selfishness," [76] he is devoid of all sympathy for his fellow men, cunning, treacherous, cruel. Indeed, Nietzsche once described himself as the Anti-Christ. As Nietzsche looks back over history he singles out as examples of the truly great men Caesar, Napoleon, and Cesare Borgia. Lincoln is an example of decadent weakness. Bertrand Russell declares that "Nietzsche's philosophy in a nutshell" [77] is summed up in the utterance of King Lear, on the verge of madness

> I will do such things—
> What they are yet I know not—but they shall be
> The terror of the earth.

The writings of Nietzsche are filled with praise of the warrior. None is more explicit than the following:

You I advise not to work, but to fight. You I advise not to peace, but to victory. Let your work be a fight, let your peace be a victory. . . .

Ye say it is the good cause which halloweth even war? I say unto you: it is the good war which halloweth every cause.

War and courage have done more great things than charity. Not your sympathy but your bravery hath hitherto saved the victims. [78]

Is Nietzsche in such passages glorifying war? Does he mean war in a literal sense or is he speaking of the warfare of ideas? Commenting on this J. N. Figgis declares:

Some defenders of Nietzsche have argued that in no real sense does he desire a tyranny of masters . . . that his words about war refer only to the warfare of ideas. . . . That may be true. It is irrelevant to the consideration of the meaning of his substitute for the good tidings preached to the poor. Nietzsche's moral system is the apotheosis of pride. His own feeling that he was of a different rank to other men. . . . However much Nietzsche's wildness be trimmed, his effect would be to endow the "superior person," out of whose loins the superman shall come, with a sense of cold aloofness from the rest of mankind, and to destroy all sense of duty towards them. Nietzsche admits this.

Nietzsche's gentle and delicate nature is often pleaded in extenuation. The truth remains that his doctrine is, what it professes to be, a philosophy of force and nothing but force, that it is certain to stimulate that pride from which tyranny comes in its disciples, and that it ministers to the worst prejudices of cultivated men, that other people are of no account. [79]

Nietzsche predicted and welcomed the coming of the "new barbarians" the "cynics, experimentalists and conquerors" who would unite in their persons intellectual superiority and physical prowess.

I point to something new: certainly for such a democratic community there is a danger of barbarians; but these are sought only down below. There are also other kinds of barbarians who come from the heights: a kind of conquering and ruling natures, which are in search of material that they can mold. Prometheus was a barbarian of this stamp.

*Principal standpoint:* one should not suppose the mission of a higher species to be the *leading* of inferior men (as Comte does, for instance); but the inferior should be regarded as the foundation upon which a higher species may live their higher life—upon which alone they *can stand.* . . .

Man is a combination of the beast and the superbeast; higher man a combination of the monster and the superman; these opposites belong to each other. With every degree of a man's growth towards greatness and loftiness he also grows downward into the depths and into the terrible; we should not desire the one without the other; or better still, the more fundamentally we desire the one, the more completely we shall achieve the other.[80]

The mass of humanity is a tool to be exploited by the Superman. Power is its own truth and its own justification. The real danger in Nietzsche's philosophy is the appeal which it has to people who fancy themselves superior to other people. He seems to be talking to them especially and to be saying—for you all things are permitted. Intellectuals, artists, talented people generally, are more susceptible to this kind of appeal than others for they already have a tendency to despise other people. Nietzsche encourages this tendency and gives it the semblance of a justification. Nietzsche encourages "the individual with gifts to set himself against all authority" [81] and tradition, to believe that he has the right to make his own standards and his own rules. The problem of the nature and source of authority is one of the great problems of our times. "Nietzsche's answer is that in the rare person: 'Authority is what I command.' " [82]

Although Nietzsche stands unalterably opposed to the

Christian religion and morality there is a sense in which he has unintentionally done Christianity a service. He rightly castigated, it seems to me, a Christianity that had converted orthodox Christianity into a sentimental humanitarianism, a Christianity that had lost sight of the Cross and of the truth that we can find life only through suffering and the sacrifice of our own lives. For the Gospel of Christ without the Cross Nietzsche sought to substitute a Gospel of the Cross without Christ. But that could never succeed for without Christ the Cross becomes but a torture-rack and the end of suffering, not life, but death. Nevertheless, as J. N. Figgis declares:

Nietzsche knew the tragedy of things. He never thought that evil was only an appearance, nor was suffering to him merely the creases in the eternal smile of the Absolute. No facile optimism, whether of Hegel or of Rousseau, no blind faith in the idol of automatic progress, no romantic idealization of nineteenth-century enlightenment marred the clearness of his vision. He knew that life is tragic, and that man needs redemption. He knew, too, that the cost of any redemption that is worth having must be terrific. The price for the world's ransom must be paid in blood. The world would not be worth redeeming could it be paid in any lower coinage. In this sense Nietzsche is at one with all that is best in Christianity. . . . Modern civilization is the apotheosis of vulgarity—or was. In its gaudy and clamorous prosperity, with every shop-window shouting, men have mistaken all their values and mixed the colors of the world. In religion an idol has been made of easy amiability, and for the enthralling spectacle of God as Father men have substituted a pretty picture of the eternal grandmother. The "splendor of God" has become a tawdry oleograph, and a milk-and-water sentimentalism has usurped the once austere name of Christian piety. The reaction against Puritanism had led to a religion of weak good nature and the refusal of all austerity. It was against this that Nietzsche tilted when he denounced the shallowness of free-thinking optimists. He was right. This, at least, we in our generation may learn. . . . This does not make faith easy. It makes it strong. Deafened by the thunder of the guns and dazed by the spectacle of a world in ruins, many a man and woman have lost all faith in a God who is Love. Those who keep their faith keep it with a difference. . . . Love is known for what it is, no sentimental wish for another's pleasure, which will be changed by a show of tears, but a resolute will for his true good—ready to purchase that good at any cost in pain, not only to himself but also to the loved one . . . one great quality will come back to all religion that is real—the awe of God. Men have dreamed that they could love God yet cease altogether to fear Him. They have found that to love God without a holy fear is not possible. In the long run Love goes too, and self reigns alone.[83]

Nietzsche could see the tragedy and frustration of life which only recent events have brought home to many of us, he pricked the bubble of that facile optimism based upon a belief in automatic progress through the "grace" of Nature and the knowledge of Science, but he could not name the evil nor explain it.

## CHAPTER 16

# *Nationalism*

NATIONALISM has been called the religion of the nineteenth and twentieth centuries. The outright rejection of Christianity by many individuals and its secularization by others, created a religious void that many have sought to fill with nationalism. As an object of passion the nation, increasingly, has been substituted for God and the adoration and worship formerly thought only worthy of God has increasingly been turned in the direction of the nation-state.

The modern nation-state, as we saw in an earlier chapter, was a product of the Renaissance and the Reformation but it was not until the middle of the eighteenth century that nationalism as we commonly think of it today emerged in clear form. The great landmark of modern nationalism was the French Revolution. Nationalism and liberalism developed concomitantly—"fraternity" no less than "liberty" and "equality" was an integral part of the liberal platform and the principle of the "self-determination of peoples" was no more than a logical extension of the liberal doctrine of popular sovereignty.

Nationalism is a compound of many factors some of which have their roots in human nature and many of which have a long history. Yet nationalism, as we understand it today, is nevertheless a modern phenomenon. To discover exactly what it is is a difficult undertaking and to define it in succinct phrases is even more difficult. In one sense nationalism is but an extension to the group to which one belongs of the pride that is inherent in fallen man. In that sense nationalism is but a form of collective egotism. In a negative sense it is a manifestation of that fear of the stranger which has its roots deep in human nature. In a more positive sense it is born of that love of the familiar land and people which is often regarded as the core of patriotism. But fear of the strange and love of the familiar cannot completely explain the phenomenon of modern nationalism for they are as old as human nature and nationalism is comparatively new. A prominent scholar and student of the problem, Professor Carlton J. H. Hayes, declares that it is much easier to define "nationality" than it is to define nationalism. "In general," he states,

"nationality" is far less ambiguous than "nation" and is most commonly and can be most properly used to designate a group of people who speak either the same language or closely related dialects, who cherish common historical traditions, and who constitute or think they constitute a distinct cultural society.[1]

There may be cultural nationality without political nationality although "the tendency has been pronounced in modern times for every self-conscious nationality to aspire to political unity and independence."[2] Professor Hans Kohn, another prominent student of nationalism, speaks of nationalism as "a state of mind . . . striving to correspond to a political fact."[3] Like Hayes he regards nationalism as a cultural phenomenon and declares that "Nationality is an historical and political concept."[4]

Hayes points out that the word "nationalism" has been used in many different ways and that it is frequently used to describe the historical process in terms of which actual nation-states have come into being but he points out that it is commonly used

to denote a condition of mind among members of a nationality, perhaps already possessed of a national state, a condition of mind in which loyalty to the ideal or to the fact of one's national state is superior to all other loyalties and of which pride in one's nationality and belief in its intrinsic excellence and its "mission" are integral parts.[5]

Its modernity consists not in its patriotism, which is an old phenomenon, but in the fusion of patriotism with nationality

and *the subordination of all other loyalties to this one loyalty.* In
this demand for absolute and unconditional loyalty modern
nationalism also reveals its religious character and the passion
with which men have devoted themselves to nationalistic
enterprises and to the furtherance of nationalistic causes
further attests to its character as a substitute for loyalty to
God. In its earliest modern forms, however, this aspect of
nationalism was not as apparent as it later came to be and so
long as nationalism was allied to liberalism, in its classical or
integral form, it had a humanistic content that overshadowed
its anti-humanistic potentialities. In other words, it appeared
at first to be and was, in fact, an ally of democratic constitutionalism and of the liberal movement for the political recognition of the rights of man but as liberalism became formalized
and the emphasis was placed more and more upon liberal
forms to the exclusion of liberal content, the anti-human
potentialities of nationalism came more and more to the fore-
ground.

## The Rise of Nationalism

NATIONALISM was preceded by the emergence of national consciousness and the differentiation of nationalities which took
place between the fifteenth and the eighteenth centuries. Professor Hayes attributes the emergence of this national consciousness to several factors "(1) linguistic and literary,
(2) political, (3) commercial and economic, (4) ecclesiastical,
religious, and cultural." [6]
Through the Middle Ages the principal literary languages
were Latin and Greek which in themselves exerted considerable influence in transcending differences among nationalities
and fostering the idea of a universal society. With the appearance of literary masterpieces in the language of the mass
of the people, such as Dante's works in Italian and Chaucer's
works in English in the fourteenth century, the vernacular
language began successfully to compete with Latin and Greek
as a medium of communication. The translation of the Bible
into the vernacular by Luther and the invention of printing

both encouraged the substitution of vernacular languages for Greek and Latin among educated people. And with the writings of Shakespeare the existence of a peculiarly national literature might be said to have been firmly established.

A national consciousness was fostered also by the acceptance of the Bodinian conception of sovereignty and the rise of sovereign states. Despite the inter-dynastic relationships that existed among the ruling families of Europe:

Monarchy played a leading role in exalting national consciousness and national sentiment. The monarch was the symbol of national unity and independence, and in him resided national sovereignty. . . . It was about the institution of monarchy that national traditions grew up, and it was under the patronage of individual monarchs that much national literature was produced. In the seventeenth century, it is true, England denied or narrowed the sovereign rights of her monarch, but the elaboration of constitutional government did not lessen the national patriotism of Englishmen. It merely transformed the object of patriotism . . . into loyalty to the national state.[7]

With the rise of national states the nation increasingly became the center of economic life replacing the older commercial cities (like Venice, Genoa, Hamburg, etc.) as centers of financial and commercial power. The theory of mercantilism and colonial expansion and trade did much to strengthen this tendency.

The division of Christendom into West and East gave rise at an early date to Armenian, Coptic, Greek and Russian churches "each employing its own national language and either contributing to the unity and distinctiveness of a national state in victory and success, as was the case with Russia, or, as exemplified by the Armenian and Coptic churches, cementing and preserving a nationality in defeat and subjection."[8] For many centuries Western Europe remained united under the Roman Catholic Church but the Protestant Reformation and the principle adopted at Augsburg that each people should take the religion of the ruler did much to foster the emergence of a national consciousness. National appeals were made, however, not only by the Protestants but by the Catholics as well.

One cannot adequately understand why religious reformers secured the numerous and widespread popular following which they did secure unless one reads the national appeals which Luther addressed to Germans, Calvin to Frenchmen, and Knox to Scotsmen. Nor can one fully appreciate how the pope managed to retain a hold upon large numbers of Christians, except as one studies the increased favors which he accorded to national sovereigns, notably to those of Spain, Portugal, and France, and the national appeals which were made in his name.[9]

Ever since the sixteenth century the divisions among Christians have been strongly flavored not only by religious differences but by nationalist sentiments.

In Protestant countries Catholics were long suspected of being unpatriotic because they did not prize the religious customs and traditions of the majority of their fellow countrymen. This was one of the reasons undoubtedly why Catholics suffered persecution at the hands of Protestants, and a similar reason may be assigned for the persecution of Protestants by Catholics. Catholicism was as much a symbol of national patriotism in Spain and France as was Protestantism in England and Scotland. The retention of the Catholic faith by the Irish at the very time when the English became Protestant, served to continue and emphasize between these nationalities differences which the diffusion of the English language and the decline of Gaelic had promised to bridge. The more rigorously the English monarchs attempt to Anglicise the Irish . . . the more stubbornly the Irish clung to Catholicism as a sign of their continuing existence as a distinct nationality.[10]

National consciousness was also fostered by the doctrine of popular sovereignty and its corollary the right of national self-determination and by the transformation of individuals from subjects into citizens. Political democracy has fostered the growth of national consciousness, according to Hayes, by invariably creating "a demand for state-directed systems of popular elementary education, for state-controlled systems of universal military training, and for the multiplication of public journals and newspapers."[11] The English Revolution of the seventeenth century and the American and French Revolutions of the eighteenth gave practical expression to the theory of popular sovereignty and "the 'people' whoever they might be in theory, turned out in practice to be a nationality." [12] The American and French Revolutions created the first national symbols—the national flag, the national anthem, national holidays and gave birth to the first citizen armies.

But let us examine a few of the forms which nationalism took in theory.

## *Humanitarian Nationalism*

A CULTURAL and humanitarian nationalism found systematic expression in the writings of the German scholar Johann Herder (1744–1803) especially in his *Ideen zur Philosophie der Geschichte der Menschheit* (1784) translated into English as *Outlines of the History of Man.* Mankind is divided by Nature and by Reason into separate nationalities and it is through the cultivation of the particular genius of the nationality that both the individual and humanity as a whole make progress toward perfection. Anticipating the nineteenth-century doctrine of evolution, Herder emphasized the creative process of nature and of history and the principle of organic growth. Each national organism has its own peculiar individuality, a gift of Nature, and it is the duty of individuals who are a part of this organism to cultivate that peculiar genius which differentiates one organism from another, to strive toward perfection. Nationalities are distinguished from one another by virtue of different geographic and climatic factors, by peculiar historical traditions, by the possession of their own language, literature, systems of education, customs and in a well-developed nationality by the possession of a "national soul" or national "character." The creative spirit of a nation finds its most sublime expression in its literature and especially in its folk-songs and folk poetry. The nation singing is the nation baring its soul.

Herder did not preach, however, the superiority of one nation over another, and his nationalism was unpolitical. He regarded nationality as being both reasonable and natural but "regarded the state as something artificial and accidental." [13]

Each nationality was to him a living organism . . . something sacred which should not be destroyed but cultivated. Every man, so he taught, could fulfill his human destiny only within and through his nationality. This was true of all nationalities: all were equally sacred, the seemingly advanced ones and those called "primitive," through them all, in different ways, the destiny of mankind fulfilled itself. A nationality lived above all in its civilization; its main instrument was its language . . . each man could be himself only by thinking and creating in his own national language. With the respect for all other nationalities went the respect for their languages. Herder was the first for whom the rights of nationality and language took precedence before the rights of the state.[14]

"The human race," Herder wrote, "is one whole; we work and suffer, sow and harvest, each for all." [15] The happiness of one nation cannot be forced upon another, each must seek and find its own happiness in its own way. But one nation can learn from another.

Manifestly Nature wishes that just as one man and one generation has to learn from and with others, one people should learn incessantly with and from other peoples, until all have understood the difficult lesson that no people is specially chosen by God, but that truth must be sought, and the garden of the common good cultivated, by all. All nations, each where it is, should weave their part of the great veil of Minerva, without harming one another, and without sowing discord by their pride.[16]

Above all nations stands the ideal of Humanity as a goal and guiding principle, a potentiality to be developed and cultivated. By becoming more human (by becoming better men) nations realize their true destiny.

In the ancient Hebrew nation Herder found a model for all other nationalities to follow:

For it is what all men have desired, what all wise leaders have tried to accomplish, and what Moses alone so early had the heart to realize; namely, that law and not a lawgiver should rule, that a free nation should freely accept and willingly obey the invisible rational and benevolent power which governs us but does not fetter and chain us. This was Moses' idea: could there be a purer or a higher one? [17]

Among the Hebrew people we find, he declares, a fellowship and oneness that is exemplary.

One finds himself in a community in which one stands for all, all for one. The whole people shoulders the burden of the Commandments, its blessings and curses. Songs of gratitude rise from all, even for the most insignificant individual happenings, because the individual is part of the whole people. Thus in the prophetic punishments each Israelite carries the guilt of the rest; yet he also shares in the consolations of the rest; common desires and a common vision raise the heart, both in joy and in sorrow.[18]

The greatness of Hebrew nationalism lay in its ethical aspirations and spiritual unity. Because its basis was not a desire for power nor worldly glory, it was a genuine and exemplary form of nationalism.

Herder was vehemently opposed to imperialism and wars of conquest for rather than furthering the cultivation of nationality they trampled upon it and denied it. It is an irrational despotism that seeks to bring peoples of different nationality under one rule.

The most natural state is *one* nationality with one national character. This it retains for ages, and this is most naturally formed when it is the object of its native princes; for a nationality is as much a plant of nature as a family, only with more branches. Nothing therefore appears so indirectly opposite to the end of government as the unnatural enlargement of states, the wild mixings of all kinds of people and nationalities under one scepter. The human scepter is far too weak and slender for such incongruous parts to be engrafted upon it. Glued together indeed they may be into a fragile machine, termed a machine of state, but it will be destitute of inner life and mutual sympathy of the parts . . . history sufficiently shows that these instruments of human pride are formed of clay, and, like all other clay, will crumble to pieces or dissolve.[19]

Through an international law founded on the principles of Christianity, nations must learn to respect one another's rights and to give up their brutality toward one another.

Does Christianity teach anything else than pure humanity? It must found thereon its international law. Nobody should be confused by grievous mistakes and contradictions which he has experienced:

reason and equity surely continue their march. It is evident that what one nation demands or desires from another it must be willing to reciprocate. Brutal outrages, perfidy, and insolent arrogance of one nation against another, arouse the indignation of all nations. This international law is engraved in the hearts of every human being.[20]

As a liberal, Herder had a profoundly optimistic faith in the rationality and natural goodness of human beings. As a liberal, moreover, he opposed every form of despotism and declared that "Under the yoke of despotism even the noblest people in a short time will lose its nobility: its highest talents will be abused for falsehood and fraud, for crawling and servility and luxury; no wonder then that it finally gets accustomed to its yoke and even kisses it." [21] As a liberal and a nationalist Herder welcomed the French Revolution and saw in it the fruition of "enlightenment."

Similar ideas found expression in the writings of another German philosopher, Johann Fichte (1762–1814). Fichte's ideas underwent a considerable change during his lifetime. In his youth he was strongly attached to the principles of liberal individualism but as he grew older he became more and more ready to accept a considerable degree of state control and collectivism. But it is not correct, I believe, to say that Fichte glorified the nation-state above all other loyalties, as some interpreters of his writings insist, for as late as 1808 he wrote: "the State, merely as the government of human life in its progress along the ordinary peaceful path, is not something which is primary and which exists for its own sake, but is merely the means to the higher purpose of the eternal, regular, and continuous development of what is purely human in this nation." [22] Throughout his writings he insisted upon service to humanity as the highest goal of life. No individual, he declared, can exist, think, and act for himself alone.

Rational life consists in each person forgetting himself in the species, tying his own life up with the life of the whole, and sacrificing himself for the sake of the whole. Irrational life, on the other hand, consists in each person thinking only of himself, loving only himself, and in relation to himself, and spending his entire existence seeking his own personal welfare.[23]

Like Herder he believed that the individual best serves mankind through service to the nation and the cultivation of the particular genius of the nation. Like Herder he believed that wherever a separate language is found, a separate nation exists.

. . . the first, original, and truly natural boundaries of States are beyond doubt their internal boundaries. Those who speak the same language are joined to each other by a multitude of invisible bonds by nature herself, long before any human art begins; they understand each other and have the power of continuing to make themselves understood more and more clearly; they belong together and are by nature one and an inseparable whole. . . . From this internal boundary, which is drawn by the spiritual nature of man himself, the marking of the external boundary by dwelling-place results as a consequence; and in the natural view of things it is not because men dwell together between certain mountains and rivers that they are a people, but, on the contrary, men dwell together—and, if their luck has so arranged it, are protected by rivers and mountains—because they were a people already by a law of nature which is much higher.[24]

Fichte wrote his *Addresses to the German Nation* (1808) after the Napoleonic conquest of Prussia and they were designed to arouse the German people (there was as yet no national German state) to the necessity for unity in the face of foreign invasion. They were couched, as a consequence, in highly chauvinistic language, the language national patriots of all countries have used when they have sought to engender resistance to foreign rule. To such language, at least in part, must be attributed the Prussian contribution to the final defeat of Napoleonic tyranny.[25] It was out of such appeals to unity that a German national state finally emerged during the latter half of the nineteenth century. In Fichte, cultural nationalism became politically conscious and active.

In a work entitled *The Closed Commercial State* (1800) Fichte also argued in behalf of economic nationalism.[26] Unless a nation became economically self-sufficient, he argued, it could not long survive as a political entity. International free trade, Fichte believed, led to imperialism and war, rather than promoting unity among nations it sowed the seeds of discord and rivalry. Let each state strive for economic self-sufficiency

568 _Main Currents in Modern Political Thought_

and one of the basic causes of war will be removed. He opposed international free trade also on the ground that it would lower the standard of living to the level of that people with the lowest standard of living. Foreign trade should be reduced to an absolute minimum and the conduct of foreign trade be made a state monopoly. He favored the abolition of the gold standard as a measure of value of national currencies.

Rejecting the economic liberalism which he espoused as a young man, Fichte further argued in behalf of a kind of socialism. Property rights are not absolute but conditional, a man has a right to his property only so long as he uses it in a way that is deemed beneficial to society by the state. Property ownership includes not only rights but obligations. No one has an absolute right to do with his property as he pleases. All property is subject to control by the state and ultimately to confiscation. The right to work, the right to make a living, is an even more basic right than the right to own property. It is one of the principal functions of the state to guarantee this right. In order to do this the state must control the economy in minute detail. He does not favor state ownership of the means of production but he does favor a very rigid regulation of economic activity and organization. He suggested many types of regulation similar to those which were established in the United States under the New Deal and went further in many of his recommendations. He suggested, for example, the regulation of agricultural production through a system of quotas and penalities and argued in behalf of something like Henry Wallace's "ever-normal granary." He also argued for a similar regulation of the production of manufactured goods. He favored price control by the state as well as state control of all credit agencies.

A precursor of modern collectivism, Fichte has often been called the intellectual godfather of the National Socialist regime in Germany. To the extent that any movement toward collectivism is a movement toward something like National Socialism, then Fichte is certainly a spiritual harbinger of Nazism, but it should be pointed out, in fairness to Fichte, that in his basic philosophy he was opposed to most things the Nazis stood for. He had a sincere attachment to human values, although he argued in behalf of the cultural pre-eminence of the German people he did not argue for their racial pre-eminence or superiority, he did not glorify the state as an end in itself but thought of it as a means to the attainment of human values. To the extent, however, that he did exalt the nation as the most perfect embodiment of the human values of a particular people he did contribute to that cult of nationalism which has been the bane of political life in the nineteenth and twentieth centuries.

Another representative of liberal, humanitarian nationalism and the most important intellectual leader in the rise of the Italian national state was Guiseppe Mazzini (1805–1872). The founder of the movement known as Young Italy (which later expanded into a movement known as Young Europe), Mazzini not only stirred the passions of the Italian people on behalf of national unity and independence from foreign rule but stimulated similar nationalistic movements throughout Europe. Like Herder and Fichte, Mazzini declared that every people has its special mission and that mission constitutes its nationality. This special mission is only a particular fulfillment of the general mission of humanity.

Humanity is the association of Nationalities, the alliance of the peoples in order to work out their missions in peace and love; the organization of free and equal peoples that shall advance without hindrance or impediment—each supporting and profiting by the other's aid—towards the progressive development of one line of the thought of God, the line inscribed by Him upon the cradle, the past life, the national idiom, and the physiognomy of each. . . . The Pact of Humanity cannot be signed by individuals, but only by free and equal peoples, possessing a name, a banner, and the consciousness of a distinct individual existence.[27]

The period concluded by the French Revolution, according to Mazzini, emphasized the individual and his natural rights, the "new epoch" will emphasize "collective humanity" and "the duty of association." The period culminating in the French Revolution had emphasized liberty as an end in itself but liberty, Mazzini constantly points out, is in itself "a negation; it does not constitute anything. It destroys and does not found; it merely leaves the ground in a condition to receive foundations. . . . Liberty constitutes for us that stage which enables us to proceed to something organic; and this something is Equality, the element of the People, the element which alone can make us triumph." [28] Liberty, he argues, is not the negation of authority but only "the negation of every authority that fails to represent the Collective Aim of the Nation." [29] Liberty is not so much concerned with the enjoyment of rights as it is with the performance of duties and the whole duty of man is the discovery and fulfillment of the Law of Progress through labor and voluntary self-sacrifice. Partial revelations of the Word of God have been given by all the founders of the various religions of Humanity in the past and each has revealed some part of the Law of Progress but the revelation of the Word of God is continuous and all previous revelations are false to the extent that they claim to be complete and final. Religions die, but religion, i.e., the continuous, progressive aspiration of man toward God, is eternal. A new epoch is dawning, Mazzini believed, when the People will replace the Church as the interpreter of God's word and will.

A third Rome, a Rome of the People, is destined to take the place of the Rome of the Caesars and the Rome of the Popes. In impassioned words addressed to the youth of Italy at the conclusion of the Franco-Italian war in 1859, Mazzini orated:

Come with me: follow me where begins the vast Campagna which, thirteen centuries ago, was the meeting-place of the races of humanity, that I may recall to you where beats the heart of Italy . . .

Pause and gaze southwards towards the Mediterranean, far as the eye can reach; in the midst of the immense expanse before you, like a Pharos in mid-ocean, rises an isolated point, a sign of distant grandeur. Kneel down in worship—there throbs the heart of Italy; there in eternal solemnity, lies ROME!

The isolated point is the capital of the Christian world, and, but a few paces distant, stands the capital of the Pagan world. And these two worlds lie there awaiting a third world; vaster and more sublime than they, in course of elaboration amid their potent ruins. It is the Trinity of that history whose Word is in Rome.

And tyrants and false prophets may delay, but none can prevent the incarnation of the Word. For while many cities have perished on earth, and many will yet perish in their turn, Rome is, by the decree of Providence, divined by the peoples, the ETERNAL CITY; because to her has been entrusted the mission of diffusing over the world the word of unity. And the life of Rome reproduces itself ever amplified and extended . . .

And when the Pact of the new faith shall be displayed upon the pantheon of humanity which the nations will one day build up,—between the Capitol and Vatican, and dominating both—the long distance between heaven and earth, soul and body, matter and spirit, reason and faith, will cease into harmony of life.

And all these things will be when you have learned that the life of a people is religion—when, asking counsel only of conscience, and of tradition, not of the sophists, but of your own nation and other nations of humanity,—you shall constitute yourselves priests, not of Rights but of Duty. . . . These things shall be when you remember the prophetic cry which re-awakened Rome sent forth to Italy ten years since and inscribe upon your banner and upon your hearts:

*We own but one Master in heaven—God; and but one interpreter of His law on earth—the People.*[30]

Like Hegel, Mazzini believed that the nation-state was the medium and agency through which history manifested itself in its progressive development toward greater human freedom. Through association in nations individuals are able to fulfill their destiny in a way that would be impossible for them as isolated individuals. Over and above individuals, comprising them in their totality, is Humanity and humanity manifests itself most clearly in nationalities.

Humanity is a great army moving to the conquest of unknown lands. . . . The Peoples (or Nations) are the different corps and divisions of that army. Each has a post entrusted to it, each a special mission to perform, and the common victory depends on the exactness with which the different operations are carried out.[31]

Mazzini emphasized not rights but duties. There are no such things as "natural" rights, there are only natural "duties." A man has an obligation to himself, to his family, to his community and whatever rights he may be said to have, are an outgrowth and reflection of these obligations. An idealist in philosophy Mazzini insisted that true freedom consists in doing what we ought to do, so that in fulfilling these obligations we attain to the only real freedom there is. We discover our "duty" not only by consulting our own individual consciences but by submitting to the conscience of the community and ultimately to the conscience of Humanity.

The conscience of the individual speaks in accordance with his education, his tendencies, his habits, his passions . . . the voice of the individual conscience is not enough in all conditions of things and without any other guide to reveal the law to us. . . . Your individual intellect will not be enough to teach you the law of God. . . . God has placed beside you a being whose life is continuous, whose faculties are the sum of the individual faculties which have been exercised for perhaps four hundred centuries, a being which amid the errors and faults of individuals ever advances in wisdom and morality, a being in whose development God has written and writes in every epoch a line of his law. This being is Humanity.[32]

The highest obligation a man has is to serve Humanity, for only by truly serving humanity can he truly serve himself and his country. Only by forming national states can nationalities serve Humanity but over and above loyalty to the nation Mazzini places loyalty to Humanity. "You are men," he wrote, "before you are citizens or fathers."

Ask yourselves whenever you do an action in the sphere of your Country or your family, *if what I am doing were done by all and for all, would it advantage or injure Humanity?* and if your conscience answers, *It would injure Humanity,* desist; desist, even if it seem to you that an immediate advantage for your Country or your family would ensue from your action. Be apostles of this faith, apostles of the brotherhood of nations, and of the unity of the human race—a principle admitted today in theory, but denied in practice.[33]

Although Mazzini favored wars of liberation that would result in the achievement of unity and independence for nationalities, he looked forward, after the restoration of the map of Europe to its "natural" national boundaries, to a world dedicated to universal and perpetual peace and united in a League of Nations. But the vision of a world of sovereign, democratic states living in perpetual peace was destined to be shattered. As Professor Morgenthau points out:

The victories in the liberal wars, far from fulfilling the liberal hopes, even brought about the very evils which they were supposed to destroy. Far from being the "last wars," they were only the forerunners and pioneers of wars more destructive and extensive than any the liberal epoch had witnessed. National unification and democratic liberation, instead of doing away with the only remaining causes of war, intensified international antagonisms and made the broad masses of peoples active participants in them. The unified nations, instead of being deprived of an incentive for war, now had the cohesion and emotional impetus necessary for policies of conquest, colonial and otherwise. International disputes, which formerly had been largely rivalries of princes . . . now became controversies between nations, where the interests of the peoples themselves appeared to be at stake and in which the peoples themselves had the opportunity to play a determining part. The triumph of nationalism and democracy, brought about by the liberal wars, therefore strengthened immensely the sovereignty of the state and with it the anarchical tendencies in international society. The particularism of democratic nationalism was thus bound to be the foremost obstacle to the realization of those devices, such as free trade, international law, international organization, by which liberalism endeavored to secure international peace. In a tragic contradiction . . . liberalism in the international field was to be destroyed by the very forces it had, if not created, at least helped to dominate the Western world.[34]

## National Expansion

WITH the substitution in the latter half of the nineteenth century of an immanent conception of order for the earlier transcendental conception, the theoretical justification of nationalism tended to shift from a moral and spiritual basis to a "scientific" and biological one. Nationalism was discovered by some writers to have a biological basis and imperialism was discovered to be but a working out of the evolutionary principle of the struggle for existence and the survival of the fittest. With this change in the intellectual climate of opinion a "scientific" justification could be given to imperialism. Since it involved strife between nations it could by analogy be compared to the competition between species for survival. Military victory could be interpreted as a "natural" judgment on the fitness of a nation to survive. For some writers

It was "natural" and, to some, it was essential to human progress, for strong nations to struggle for aggrandizement, and for the superior "races" to prevail. Given this biologic urge on the part of healthy "races," and the presence of accessible "backward races," and the logic of imperialism is inescapable. It needs, indeed, no further defense or explanation. It is independent of time and place, and, finally, whether one regards imperialism as brutal or beneficent, it is no more a question of man's choice than is an earthquake. From this point of view . . . imperialism can be regarded as entirely consistent with the theory of subjugation and annexation of weaker nationalities and backward peoples by states claiming statehood on the basis of nationality.[35]

For the Austrian-Polish sociologist Ludwig Gumplowicz (1838–1909) the "most natural tendency" of states "is incessant increase of power and territory."[36] National expansion is an expression of the very being of a state, it is an inevitable tendency that rulers and people are powerless to resist. "So necessary and so strong is the tendency to foreign conquest that no state can escape it what ever may be the feeling of the ruler at the time."[37] States, whatever their size, will attempt to expand in territory and power and they will cease to do so only when they cease to exist. For Gumplowicz this is a "social law" as rigid as any law of nature.

Among English writers who rose to the defense of British imperialism none was more important and influential than the historian, J. R. Seeley (1834–1895). "We seem, as it were," he wrote, "to have conquered and peopled half the world in a fit of absence of mind."[38] And he urged his fellow-country men to become conscious of their "destiny" to undertake their imperial responsibilities with deliberation. Although he did not defend the more extreme versions of British imperialism he spoke of the "natural causes" which had led to the British conquest of Canada and Australia. He used the word "destiny" to describe the British imperialistic "mission" much in the same way that the phrase "manifest destiny" was used in the United States during the nineteenth century to justify Westward expansion and by some to cover even more ambitious territorial aspirations. A more extreme defense of British imperialism was provided by the English historian,

J. A. Cramb (1862–1913).[39] For Cramb, the British were a race "dowered with the genius for empire" and such a race, he argued, "is compelled to dare all, to suffer all, to sacrifice all for the fulfillment of its fate-appointed task." [40] The British must go forward with their imperialistic ventures or die as a race.

In political life, in the life-history of states, as in religions, as in intellectual and social history, change or growth, or what we now name Evolution, are perpetual, continuous, unresting. The empire which has ceased to advance has begun to recede. Motion is the law of its being, if not towards a fuller life, motion toward death. Thus in a race dowered with the genius for empire, as Rome was, as Britain is, Imperialism is the supreme, the crowning form, which in this process of evolution it attains. The civic, the feudal, or the oligarchic State passes into the national, the national into the imperial, by slow or swift gradations, but irresistibly, as by a fixed law of nature.[41]

Similar defenses of imperialism appeared about the same time in the United States. According to an American political scientist, J. W. Burgess (1844–1931) Providence has entrusted the Teutonic nations with "the mission of conducting the political civilization of the world." [42] The backward peoples of the world must be taught by conquest and the rulership of the Teutonic nations how to live. An American sociologist, Franklin H. Giddings (1855–1931) declared that "the combination of small states into large political aggregates must continue until all the semi-civilized, barbarian and savage communities of the world are brought under the protection of the larger civilized nations." [43] He described the Spanish-American War of 1898 as being "as inevitable as any event of nature" and declared that at that particular "stage in the development of the United States, territorial expansion" was "as certain as the advent of spring after winter." [44] Imperialism and war found an ardent champion in the German writer Heinrich von Treitschke (1834–1896). As a younger man, Treitschke defended a liberal nationalism of the Mazzini variety but as he grew older the liberal content in his philosophy was submerged as he came to hold the view that "the State is primarily power." [45] More and more he came to believe that the state, rather than being a means to an end, was a self-sufficient end in itself. The State, he declared, "must seek its own goal within itself" and "no individual has the right to regard the State as a servant of his own aims, but is bound by moral duty and physical necessity to subordinate himself to it." [46] The State as a moral community dedicated to the improvement of the human race embodies interests superior to those of any particular individuals. Nor can we specify any limits to the activities of the state for "theoretically no limit can be set to the functions of the State. . . . History shows us how the sphere of the State's activity increases with the growth of culture. . . . Experience teaches that the State is better fitted than any other corporate body to take charge of the well-being and civilizing of the people." [47]

War is "the form of litigation by which States make their claims valid" and a drastic though beneficial "remedy for an ailing nation." [48]

We have learned to perceive the moral majesty of war through the very processes which to the superficial observer seem brutal and inhuman. The greatness of war is just what at first sight seems to be its horror—that for the sake of their country men will overcome the natural feelings of humanity, that they will slaughter their fellowmen who have done them no injury, nay, whom they perhaps respect as chivalrous foes. Man will not only sacrifice his life, but the natural and justified instincts of his soul; his very self he must offer up for the sake of patriotism; here we have the sublimity of war. . . . He who knows history knows also that to banish war from the world would be to mutilate human nature. [49]

War is a test whereby the weak and cowardly are recognized and "perish justly." [50] War must be waged "in the most effective manner possible" and "for this reason the blow must be aimed at the enemy's heart, and the use of the most formidable weapons is absolutely justifiable." [51] International law has its basis solely in "a mutual recognition of personal advantage" [52] and beyond that it neither exists nor is binding. Small states have a duty to grow larger for such growth "is a sign of the moral stamina of a people." [53] It is essential to the pride of a state and to the belief in its own future that it should seek to grow in size. But:

The idea of one universal empire is odious—the ideal of a State co-extensive with humanity is no ideal at all. . . . All nations like all individuals have their limitations, but it is exactly in the abundance of these limited qualities that the genius of humanity is exhibited. . . . The grandeur of history lies in the perpetual conflict of nations, and it is simply foolish to desire the suppression of their rivalry.[54]

Treitschke urged Germany to embark upon the imperialistic ventures that had made England such a great country. If Germany was to achieve the status of a first-rate power among the nations of the Western world she would have to acquire overseas territory. This was the brunt of his argument.

Increasingly the nationalism that had first been justified as a means of realizing and extending the liberal principles of the French Revolution was conceived as an end in itself.

## Integral Nationalism

LIBERAL, humanitarian nationalism, of which Woodrow Wilson was one of the last great exponents, has increasingly been replaced in the twentieth century by a new form of nationalism which has misleadingly been called "integral nationalism." It was a Frenchman, Charles Maurras, who first used this designation to describe the new form which nationalism took and he defined it as "the exclusive pursuit of national policies, the absolute maintenance of national integrity, and the steady increase of national power."[55] The nation is conceived less and less as a means to an end—the perfection of humanity in its diversity—and more and more as an end in itself. It repudiates the internationalism that characterized liberal, humanitarian nationalism and tends to exalt both militarism and imperialism. Domestically, it repudiates the democratic constitutionalism that was the ally of liberal nationalism and tends to champion political autocracy if not tyranny. It is reactionary in its social philosophy and specifically repudiates the liberalism of which it was an outgrowth. It demands absolute loyalty to the nation and exalts national interests above those of the individual and even of humanity.

One of the earlier advocates of "integral nationalism" was the Frenchman, Maurice Barrès (1862–1923). According to Professor Hayes, "Barrès's ideal for the government of France was a Caesarian republic, a national dictatorship, which, while fostering considerable regionalism, should unite the whole country in pursuit of military glory." [56] Barrès believed that French nationalism could most effectively be promoted by encouraging regionalism, purifying the French language by purging it of foreign words and borrowing from local dialects, and by encouraging the veneration of French military heroes like Napoleon. And, although personally a religious skeptic, he believed that French nationalism could further be promoted by the veneration of the Roman Catholic Church as the "traditional" Church of France. "It is not necessary," he declared, "to possess a perfect faith in order to have the pleasure of venerating the supreme image of that faith." [57] Hatred of Germany strongly motivated Barrès and he spoke frequently of the "noble instinct of revenge." Basically, Professor Hayes declares, Barrès's

doctrine was deliberately irrational. It was founded on emotional exaltation and was to be realized through spiritual intoxication. Nationalists should frankly recognize, he said, that facts very often contradict principles, so that principles have to be adapted to facts. Nationalists should cast logic aside and all barren intellectualism. They should judge everything in relationship to the nation as it is. Above all, they should be guided by sentiment and should be driven by national feeling as by a tempest. [58]

According to Barrès, a man thinks those thoughts which he must think as the member of a particular race or nationality. Blood and soil are the twin foundations of nationalism and the determining elements of life, both individual and social.

These ideas were perpetuated and extended by another Frenchman, Charles Maurras (1858–) the organizer of the *Action Française* (1898). This organization, together with a youth organization known as the *Camelots du Roi*, did much to spread the doctrine of "integral nationalism" throughout France, making its appeal to the reactionary, conservative, and royalist groups. A daily newspaper was one of the chief organs for the propagation of the faith. "A true nationalist," Maurras defined as one who "places his country above everything; he therefore conceives, treats, and resolves all pending questions in their relation to the national interest." [59] Like Barrès he argued for a veneration of the dead as "the most active of the living" and declared that it is from the dead that the living derive the only initiative they can know. Not only did he cultivate the cult of "blood" but, like Barrès, sought to encourage what he himself called "the cult of the sacred soil." [60]

Nationalism could be most effectively nourished, he believed, by the classical spirit of Greece and Rome, institutional Catholicism, and monarchy. But, like Barrès, Maurras was a skeptic in religion, if not a pagan, and his veneration of the Catholic Church as an institution had nothing to do with the acceptance of Christianity as a faith. He specifically rejected what he called "Hebrew Christianity."

The Hebrew Christ comes into the world, redeems the slaves, dethrones the strong, and places the first lower than the last in order that His glory may be sung through life eternal. . . . Almost three hundred and seventy-three Olympiads have passed since the Hebrew cried on his cross: "It is finished." Yes, it was finished; since that moment the slave has had governments after his own heart. [61]

His veneration of the Catholic Church was purely utilitarian and in 1926 Pope Pius XI condemned the doctrines and writings of Maurras and forbade Catholics to support the *Action Française*. Summarizing his influence, Professor Hayes declares that:

Throughout the writings of Charles Maurras and throughout the journalism which he has sponsored, his integral nationalism appears as a breeder of hatreds. He tirelessly preaches hatred of "alien" influences within France: Jewish, Protestant, masonic, liberal, republican, communist, and latterly, papal. He ceaselessly directs tirades against foreigners: Germans, Englishmen, Americans, Bolshevist Russians. Always he upholds a hundred-per-cent French nationalism, which is at once suspicious and forceful. . . . There is scarcely conceivable an excess of nationalism beyond the integral variety of Maurras, the doctrinaire and the demagogue. [62]

In the person of Mussolini and the movement of Italian Fascism, "integral" nationalism found practical embodiment —to be imitated and extended in even more ruthless fashion a decade later by Hitler and the Nazis in Germany. The same intellectual forces that transformed the liberal nationalism of the French Revolution into the "integral" nationalism of Barrès and Maurras in France, transformed the liberal nationalism of Mazzini in Italy. Through the writings and activities of men like Benedetto Croce, Giovanni Gentile, Vincenzo Gioberti, Gabriele d'Annunzio and Enrico Corradini nationalism was gradually divorced from liberalism and transformed into a cult of "sacred Egoism." [63] According to Mussolini:

> The foundation of Fascism is the conception of the State, its character, its duty, and its aim. Fascism conceives of the State as an absolute, in comparison with which all individuals or groups are relative, only to be conceived of in their relation to the State. . . .
>
> For us Fascists, the State is not merely a guardian, preoccupied solely with the duty of assuring the personal safety of the citizens; nor is it an organization with purely material aims. . . . Nor is it a purely political creation. . . . The State, as conceived of and as created by Fascism, is a spiritual and moral fact in itself. . . . That State is the guarantor of security both internal and external, but it is also the custodian and transmitter of the spirit of the people, as it has grown up through the centuries in language, in customs, and in faith. . . . It is the State which educates its citizens in civic virtue, gives them a consciousness of their mission and welds them into unity. . . . It leads men from primitive tribal life to that highest expression of human power which is Empire: it links up through the centuries the names of those of its members who have died for its existence and in obedience to its laws, it holds up the memory of the leaders who have increased its territory. . . .
>
> The Fascist State is an embodied will to power and government: the Roman tradition is here an ideal of force in action. . . . For Fascism, the growth of empire, that is to say the expansion of the nation, is an essential manifestation of vitality, and its opposite a sign of decadence. . . . But empire demands discipline, the coordination of all forces and a deeply felt sense of duty and sacrifice: this fact explains many aspects of the practical working of the regime . . . and the necessarily severe measures which must be taken against those who would oppose this spontaneous and inevitable

movement of Italy in the twentieth century. . . . If every age has its own characteristic doctrine, there are a thousand signs which point to Fascism as the characteristic doctrine of our time.[64]

In Fascism, nationalism becomes completely degenerate and nihilistic. War is exalted as a good end in itself and the character of war itself changes. In the twentieth century war has become totalitarian, the former distinction between combatants and noncombattants progressively obliterated, and the goal of war not the defeat but the annihilation of the loser. The war front tends to become co-extensive with the nation and the life of the nation itself is at stake. Wars formerly were concluded by peace treaties, which, although often drastic in their provisions, rarely contemplated the annihilation of the defeated nation. Today the annihilation of a nation is more common than its rehabilitation, especially when the victor is a totalitarian dictatorship. The idea of a community of sovereign nation states is gradually giving way to the idea of a national hegemony extending throughout the world and the substitution of one nation-state for all. Nationalism thus appears to be developing into the very anti-thesis of nationalism while retaining the slogans of nationalism. It is a "nationalism" that theoretically can tolerate no nationalism but that of one nation.

## The Doctrine of Racial Superiority

CLOSELY associated with the so-called "integral" nationalism of the twentieth century has been the doctrine of racial superiority. The classic pronouncement of this doctrine was made in 1855 by a Frenchman, Count Arthur de Gobineau (1816–1882), in a widely influential book entitled an *Essay on the Inequality of Human Races*. A ponderous work in four volumes it endeavored to prove that the key to the understanding of history lies in the differences in quality and aptitude among the human races. That mankind consists of separate races distinguished by special physical, emotional and spiritual characteristics Gobineau posited as an axiom. There are not only obvious physical differences between such people as the Negroes, the European whites, and the Chinese and other oriental peoples but, the Count de Gobineau argued, less visible but no less basic differences between the spiritual and intellectual capacities of these three principal types of people. Dividing mankind into three principal races—the White, Yellow and Black—Gobineau ascribes marked superiority to the White or Aryan race. (The word Aryan is not a biological concept but a term borrowed indiscriminately from philology in which field it was originally used to describe a group of related Indo-European languages. It has been used by racialists as a term synonymous with white, or more often as a term describing some particular portion of white skinned people and frequently simply to mean "non-Jewish." As a consequence, it has little or no meaning in an objective sense except perhaps negatively.) In the dedication of his *Essay* to George V of Hanover, the Count de Gobineau declared:

Gobineau

> Gradually I have become convinced that race overshadows all other problems in history, that it holds the key to them all. . . . I convinced myself at last that everything great, noble and fruitful in the works of man on this earth, in science, art and civilization—belongs to one family alone, the different branches of which have reigned in all the civilized countries of the universe.[65]

Although he believed that no race at the present time was entirely "pure" and that a slight admixture of races was desirable he nevertheless contended that "Peoples degenerate only in consequence of the various admixtures of blood which they undergo" and that "their degeneration corresponds exactly to the quantity and quality of the new blood." [66] While the black race possesses artistic capacities, only the Aryan race demonstrates perseverance, instinct for order, love of liberty, honor, and political genius. The Aryan race is by nature a race of rulers.

Since no nation is composed of a "pure" race he argued that it is only the racially *élite* within nations that are the true Aryans. Thus he was not pro-French, or pro-German, or pro-English but pro-aristocracy. He argued not in behalf of national superiority but in behalf of the superiority of a racial aristocracy. The purest Aryan blood, he thought, was to be found among the Anglo-Saxons in England and the United States. But even here racial admixture was threatening that supremacy. Convinced that the human race was destined to ultimate extinction the Count de Gobineau sought at the same time to find a new natural aristocracy that could take the place of the old aristocracy and he believed that he had found this new aristocracy in a racial *élite*.

Instead of princes, he proposed "a race of princes," the Aryans. . . . Thanks to race, an *élite* would be formed whose members could lay claim to the old prerogatives of feudal families, and this only by asserting that they felt like noblemen; the acceptance of the race ideology as such would become conclusive proof that an individual was "well-bred. . . ." From an identical political event, therefore, the decline of the nobility, the Count drew two contradictory consequences—the decay of the human race and the formation of a new natural aristocracy. But he did not live to see the practical application of his teachings which overcame all inherent contradictions, when the new race-aristocracy actually started out to effect the inevitable decay of mankind in a supreme effort to destroy it.[67]

Although Gobineau's theories were anti-German rather than pro-German they met with considerable success in Germany during the latter half of the nineteenth century when a Gobineau association was founded in 1894. Under the aegis of Houston Stewart Chamberlain, however, the theories were given an interpretation to the advantage of the Germans that made them especially appealing. It is a curious fact that the man most influential in arousing and propagating doctrines of Germanic racial superiority should have been not a German but an Englishman by birth. As a young man Houston Stewart Chamberlain went permanently to Germany to live, became a German subject, married the daughter of the composer Richard Wagner and began to write books arguing in behalf of the racial superiority of the Germans. (His brother curiously enough embarked upon a similar life in Japan.) His most important and influential work was entitled *Die Grundlagen des Neunzehnten Jahrhunderts* (1899) which was later translated into English as *The Foundations of the Nineteenth Century*.

Chamberlain abandoned the word Aryan as a description

of the superior race in favor of the word Teuton which he used in the same broad and ambiguous sense in which Gobineau had used the word Aryan. He claimed as Teutons not only all the great Germans but Louix XIV, Dante, Michelangelo, Marco Polo and even argued that Jesus Christ was probably of "Aryan" rather than of Jewish descent. He also argued that St. Paul possessed characteristics that could not be explained if his origin was entirely Jewish and suggested that in all probability he must have had a Greek mother. He regretted that "the personality, the life, the message" of Jesus Christ "were . . . chained to the fundamental ideas of Judaism" [68] and declared that it was not until the Reformation that Christianity was purged of these "contaminating" Jewish influences under the leadership of Teuton reformers.

His glorification of the Teutons had as its counterpart the castigation of the Jews. "The presence of an indefinite number of Jews," he wrote, "is so pernicious to the welfare of a European state that we dare not be influenced by general humane principles." [69] Jews are by nature egotistical, he declared, materialistic, and coldly rationalistic. They cannot be distinguished by physical characteristics and "one can very soon become a Jew, often it needs only to have frequent intercourse with Jews, to read Jewish newspapers, to accustom one's self to Jewish philosophy, literature and art." [70] The intermarriage of Jews and Aryans he condemned as a pollution of the Teuton race and the breeding of "a herd of pseudo-Hebraic mestizos, a people beyond all doubt degenerate, physically, mentally and morally." [71] Whenever Jews are admitted to power they abuse it and their political and social influence, he argued, is generally pernicious.

But the Teuton, on the contrary,

is the soul of our culture. . . . If we look around we see that the importance of each nation as a living power today is dependent upon the proportion of genuinely Teutonic blood in its population. . . . [72]

Only countries in which those of Teuton stock predominate, he declared, are civilized. In such countries as Italy, Spain, and France the contributions to civilization were made by descendants of Teuton conquerors. "All the famous Italian nobility," he wrote, "are of Teuton descent and the evidence will undoubtedly show that the artistic and intellectual ability of this people was of Teuton origin." His conclusion is that "Physically as well as mentally the Teutons surpass all other human beings; therefore, rightfully, they are the overlords of the world" [73] and that, as the home of the "purest" representatives of this race, "Germany . . . within two centuries may get to the point where it will govern the whole earth. . . ." [74]

The writings of Chamberlain, like those of Gobineau, are full of contradictions. Both use the word race in a very loose and ambiguous sense and confuse linguistic and racial groups. Chamberlain, on the one hand, argues that differences in character and ability have their origin in racial differences and, on the other hand, that races cannot be clearly distinguished on the basis of physical characteristics alone. Teutons he declares may be blonde-haired or black-haired, long headed and round headed—in the last analysis, he insists, we distinguish members of the Teutonic race by their "spiritual" affinity. As one writer says, Chamberlain "rejects all established criteria of racial discrimination in favor of spiritual clairvoyance and spiritistic divination. And yet he ends in the exalted and emotional rhapsodies of the race worshipper." [75] A distinguished anthropologist, Franz Boas, has stated that:

It is a fiction to speak of a German race. We should rather ask what types of physical build are represented among the Germans. Here we encounter a complete lack of unity. Blondes with long heads in the North, darker people with short heads in the South; broad faces here, narrow faces there; noses turned up and aquiline, the general build tall and short, broad and slight. There is no "German race"; there are only local types which are very different one from another . . . so that representatives of all these types may be found in any part of Germany and of the neighboring countries.[76]

Despite the fact that Chamberlain's theories rested upon very nebulous grounds they found many adherents in Germany and were given a pseudo-scientific undergirding by a group of German anthropologists headed by Hans Günther in the twentieth century. Like the orthodox anthropologists, Günther believed that physical characteristics were measurable and that such measurements would reveal racial dif-

ferences but unlike them and in agreement with Chamberlain
he believed that different physical or racial types embodied
different emotional, intellectual, and spiritual aptitudes and
qualities. He conceived of Europeans as being composed of
five different races: the Nordic, the Alpine, the Mediterranean,
the East Baltic, and the Dinaric, each differing markedly
from the other in physical characteristics.[77] Of these "races"
Günther concluded that the Nordic "race" was the most superior.

We may take judgment, truthfulness, and energy to be the qualities
which are always found marking out the Nordic man. . . . He feels
a strong urge towards truth and justice. . . . He is distinguished by
a highly developed sense of reality, which in combination with an
energy that may rise to boldness urges him on to far-reaching undertakings. . . . The sense for reality, the energy, self-reliance and
boldness of the Nordic race are one reason why all the more important statesmen in European history would seem to be predominantly
Nordic. . . .[78]

Other European races are greatly inferior to the Nordic race
and the Alpine race, for example, is sullen, mistrustful, and
slow.

The Alpine man and his family make up a close, busy, selfish
group. All individuality is foreign to him; in political life, too, he
inclines to broad mass organization. He is far removed from any
warlike inclination as also from any wish to govern or to lead. . . .
The Alpine woman is even more given than the man to plodding
industry and soulless toil. . . . Fraud, blackmail and threats would
appear to be more frequent in the predominantly Alpine parts of
Germany.[79]

The ideas of Günther found fertile soil in the Nazi movement
and Günther himself served as a kind of official anthropologist
for the National Socialist government. It was Günther's task
to explain, for example, after the alliance of Germany with
Japan that the Japanese originally had Nordic ancestors.

## Racism in the United States

THE virulent doctrine of racial superiority has not been confined, as we have seen, alone to Germany although it has

found its most ruthless and brutal application in that country. It has appeared in the United States in a milder but no less potentially dangerous form. During the slavery controversy in the nineteenth century, and, as a matter of fact, ever since there have been numerous writers who have argued that the Negroes are "naturally" inferior to the whites and for many Americans this is an axiomatic truth that is not even open to argument. Not only is there a considerable body of literature attesting to the truthfulness of this proposition but throughout the United States, and especially in the South, political, social and economic institutions are established upon that premise. The discrepancy between the American profession of faith in human equality and the actual situation as it affects the Negro population is one that has struck the foreign observer with particular force [80] and is one that has increasingly troubled the conscience of the American himself.

The doctrine of racial superiority has found expression in America, however, not only in the doctrine of "White superiority and supremacy" but also in the belief that a particular portion of the white race, called Anglo-Saxon, Teuton, or Nordic, is superior to other portions of the white race. In the latter part of the nineteenth century a considerable body of American literature emphasized the superiority of Germanic peoples and institutions. Thus, for example, Professor J. W. Burgess classified the great races of the world as "the Greek, the Latin, the Celt, the Teuton and the Slav" and concluded that "the Teuton really dominates the world by his superior political genius." [81] According to Burgess:

Indifference on the part of Teutonic states to the political civilization of the rest of the world is . . . not only mistaken policy but disregard of duty. In the study of general political science we must be able to find a standpoint from which the harmony of duty and policy may appear. History and ethnology offer us this elevated ground, and they teach us that the Teutonic nations are the political nations of the modern era; that, in the economy of history, the duty has fallen to them of organizing the world politically; and that if true to their mission, they must follow the line of this duty as one of their chief practical policies.[82]

Other historians and political scientists of the same period emphasized the superiority of Anglo-Saxon or Teutonic peoples and attributed the best in American culture and political life to the predominance of these types of people in the population. One of the most extreme versions of this doctrine appeared in Madison Grant's *The Passing of the Great Race* (1916). In a manner similar to that of Gobineau and Chamberlain, Grant declares that race manifests itself not only in immutable physical characteristics but in "psychical predispositions and impulses." [83] Of all the races the Nordic is "the white man par excellence" and "all over the world" they are "a race of soldiers, sailors, adventurers and explorers; and above all of rulers, organizers and aristocrats." [84] Like Chamberlain he argues that all the leading figures of European history and culture were Nordic or of Nordic descent including men very different in physical appearance. The health of a nation can be measured in terms of the proportion of those of Nordic ancestry to those of non-Nordic origin. A nation declines as the result of the mixture of races. Until the Civil War, Grant declared, the white population of the United States was "not only purely Nordic but also purely Teutonic," but since the Civil War larger and larger numbers have emigrated to the United States from non-Nordic countries. [85] The predominance of these people of inferior racial stock signalizes "the passing of the great [Nordic] race" and as a result Grant predicts the decline of the United States as a great power.

Madison Grant's theory of racial superiority was not an isolated phenomenon in the United States but found expression in the writings of many other individuals. [86] It has found practical embodiment in "native Americanism," in fear of the alien immigrant, and in the adoption by the government of more and more restrictive legislation in the field of immigration. Partially as the result of this kind of thinking the United States Congress adopted a "quota" system of immigration in 1921 (modified in 1929) whereby, in addition to the restrictions imposed upon "undesirable" individuals, there were added restrictions in terms of the national origins of the people emigrating to the United States. The legislation was frankly designed not only to limit the quantity of immigration but to give preference to those racial stocks deemed to be superior in quality to others and to preserve the "balance" of nationalities within the United States as it stood at the census of 1890. Under the tension of World War II the United States Supreme Court succumbed to racial prejudice when it approved as constitutional the mass evacuation from the West coast of United States citizens of Japanese ancestry without requiring any test of individual loyalty.[87]

## Conclusion

A PROMINENT contemporary historian, Arnold J. Toynbee, declares that the attempt to explain differences in human behavior and culture in terms of race is "either an ineptitude or a fraud." [88] The correlation, if any exists, between psychic qualities and physical characteristics has never been conclusively demonstrated and there is no evidence at all even for the existence of what has been variously called Nordic, Teuton or Aryan man. Such a "race" is a figment of the imagination, obviously flattering to those who regard themselves as belonging to it, but having no demonstrable, objective existence. It is sometimes assumed that racial prejudice has its roots in ignorance and that it can be eradicated by education but this is gravely to underestimate the spiritual depths out of which it grows. Men cling to their racial prejudices in the face of all objective and rational argument to the contrary with a passionate obstinacy that demonstrates that its roots go deeper into human nature than we frequently realize. Reinhold Niebuhr has explained this very well when he says:

Racial prejudice is indeed a form of irrationality; but it is not as capricious as modern universalists assume. Racial prejudice, the contempt of the other group, is an inevitable concomitant of racial pride; and racial pride is an inevitable concomitant of the ethnic will to live. Wherever life becomes collectively integrated it generates a collective, as well as an individual, survival impulse. But, as previously observed in dealing with individual life, human life is never content with mere physical survival. There are spiritual elements in every human survival impulse; and the corruption of these elements is pride and the will-to-power. This corruption is deeper and more universal than is understood in our liberal culture. . . .

Even while American liberalism anticipated a frictionless harmony of ethnic groups and their eventual assimilation in one racial unity, public pressure prompted legislation which gave preference to north-European groups in our policy of immigration, thereby proving that our real convictions, in distinction from our pretensions, were that the American amalgam should not contain too high a proportion of Latin or Slav ingredients.[89]

The root of racial prejudice is pride and only the cultivation of humility can cure it. Only the recognition of the "fatherhood of God" can sustain "the brotherhood of man."

Nationalism, now frequently allied with racialism, is probably the religion most common to the great majority of mankind today. Many nominal Christians have succumbed to it and even many churches have tended to identify Christianity with the political, cultural, and social institutions of the particular country in which they find themselves. It is not uncommon in the United States, for example, for "Americanism" to be identified with Protestantism and it is doubtful whether the loyalty professed in such instances is to Christ or to the nation. As a religion, Professor Hayes declares

Nationalism . . . inculcates neither charity nor justice; it is proud, not humble; and it signally fails to universalize human aims. It repudiates the revolutionary message of St. Paul and proclaims anew the primitive doctrine that there shall be Jew and Greek, only that now there shall be Jew and Greek more quintessentially than ever. Nationalism's kingdom is frankly of this world, and its attainment invokes tribal selfishness and vain glory, a particularly ignorant and tyrannical intolerance,—and war.[90]

Nationalism is nourished not on love but on hate, it inculcates not trust but fear, and in its fearful insecurity it is driven inexorably to more and more extravagant claims and enterprises. Nationalism has found its most brutal and ruthless embodiment in Italian Fascism and German National Socialism but it lives on today in Communist Russia and in democratic America.

## CHAPTER 17

# Fascism and National Socialism

THE military power of Italy and of Germany has been destroyed, the Italian Fascist and the German National Socialist regimes are buried in ruins, but it would be foolish to suppose that the crisis which gave rise to those regimes has passed or that the spirit which informed them has, like their respective leaders, died. It is not necessary to recall here in detail the events which brought about the establishment by a *coup d'état* of the Fascist regime in Italy in 1922 or the establishment with the approval of the German Reichstag of the Nazi regime in Germany eleven years later. There were marked differences between the two movements but the similarities were more pronounced than the differences and, for the sake of brevity, we shall speak of both movements as Fascist.

What is Fascism? The answer to that question is important for it is only by understanding the disease that we can hope to cure it. If our diagnosis is incorrect we may be led to apply therapy that is not only useless but harmful. Much of our confusion in this postwar period stems, I believe, from an inadequate or erroneous conception of the nature of the crisis through which we are passing and of which Fascism is but a particularly virulent manifestation. There is little agreement among scholars or anyone else as to what Fascism exactly was or is and many different interpretations have been suggested. Let us examine some of the more important and popular explanations. In order to simplify our task, however, we shall confine our attention to the various theories that have been advanced to explain the National Socialist movement in Germany.

591

## The Marxist Interpretation

ONE of the most widely held theories, especially in the early days of the Nazi regime, was that propounded by the Marxists and those who held to the economic interpretation of history. According to this theory National Socialism was the last bulwark of capitalism, a conspiracy of capitalists bent upon the preservation of capitalistic property and the system of profits.[1] If Marx was to be vindicated as a prophet, and if the system was not socialistic then it *had* to be capitalistic. The evidence adduced in support of this theory was that many capitalists had subscribed heavily to the Nazi movement, that some were closely allied to Hitler and remained so after he came to power, that Hitler nowhere repudiated the concept of private property, that he denounced Communism in the harshest terms promising to deliver Germany from such a regime, and that upon coming to power he enacted repressive labor legislation and left the capitalists in control of their property. If this diagnosis is correct the cure is the establishment of socialism.

There are elements of truth in this theory but it is not the whole truth nor the principal truth. That many capitalists supported Hitler financially and otherwise with the intention of preserving their own property from the Communist expropriation which they feared, is true enough but what they wanted and what they received are two different things. Once in power, Hitler not only proved to be capable of acting independently of the capitalists, he often did so. Capitalists, since they had the money, supported many political parties and do so now, but they do not always act from purely selfish motives and do not always get what they think they will when they do. The successful campaign of Franklin D. Roosevelt in the 1933 United States presidential election was supported by many capitalists, but it does not and did not follow that upon coming to office he bowed to the dictates of his capitalist supporters. When Fritz Thyssen, one of the financial supporters of Hitler in the days before he came to power, complained after Hitler came to power of some of the Nazi policies, his property was expropriated by the Nazi government and he was sent into exile. Those capitalists who were willing, after Hitler came to power, to do his bidding were tolerated and left generally unmolested but those who balked at his orders soon found themselves without property and in prison or exile. There is no doubt that many capitalists *thought* that Hitler could be managed, that he would be a mere puppet in their hands, but events proved otherwise. It was to Hitler's advantage in the days before he came to power to encourage that belief, and he did.

But he also promised in true demagogic style, all things to all men, adapting his promises to his audience. When he spoke to laboring groups he emphasized the socialistic features of his "program," and there were some; when he spoke to capitalistic groups he emphasized his horror of Communism and his intention of combatting it in every form. He made his appeal to the malcontents of every party and class and was never disturbed by the fact that his promises were often contradictory. Unlike the Communists, it is true, he had no program for abolishing private property but after coming to power it became clear that while he intended to leave the title to property in the hands of individuals he had every intention of appropriating the rights generally associated with private property in the name of the State. The Marxian interpretation of Fascism ignores the steps that were taken progressively to *destroy* capitalism in Germany after Hitler's rise to power. These steps have been admirably documented and summarized in an article by Frieda Wunderlich.[2] Not only was labor shackled by repressive legislation but capital, too, was made to do the bidding of a state that was intent from the very beginning upon war. Through the rigid control of foreign trade and raw materials, control of investments, complete regulation of agricultural production and distribution, price fixing and the regulation of wages and interest, control of profits and the complete mobilization and control of the economy as if for war—the Nazis made it abundantly clear that political and military considerations were to be given predominance over economic considerations. Under the Nazi government the economy was gradually transformed into an economy that was neither capitalistic nor socialistic although it used some socialistic *forms* for the attainment of its political and military aims. Frieda Wunderlich summarizes some of the changes that took place in the structure of the economy by pointing to the

(1) displacement of the market price system by a planned political price system,
(2) gradual displacement of individual decision and initiative by state regulation,
(3) displacement of the yardstick of profitability by other criteria,
(4) restriction of private profits,
(5) abandonment of national wealth and of the individual standard of living as ethical aims,
(6) alteration of the conception of ownership.[3]

Industrialists progressively became "nothing more than paid managers in their own enterprises." The institution of private property survived in form only. The Nazis did not hesitate to resort to outright expropriation when such was expedient and in the case of property owned by the Jews this was done without legal warrant of any kind. Large portions of agricultural land were entailed and could not be sold, mortgaged or divided. Moreover, the owner of a farm could lose his property whenever, in the opinion of the Nazi party and government, he was considered unfit for such ownership. An Exchange Law of December, 1936, empowered the government to administer the property of any citizen suspected of intending to emigrate from Germany. The Nazi government found many devices short of expropriation by means of which so-called private property could be controlled—the infiltration of Nazi party members into the membership of the governing boards of large corporations was one device frequently employed. Frieda Wunderlich concludes her analysis of the transformation of the German economy in these words:

In spite of the support National Socialism received from the middle classes before it came into power, its defense economy has worked contrary to the interests of the small entrepreneurs, many of whom have lost their independence. Large concerns, favored in the allotment of raw materials and foreign exchange, have expanded at the expense of the smaller plants. The economic policy of National Socialism tends to concentrate business in a few mammoth concerns.

The sphere of private business, however, is constantly restricted in favor of state business. With the ideological transformation of the concept of property and increasing state interference, National Socialism strengthens tendencies to state socialism which were already inherent in the Democracy. Totalitarianism carries these tendencies to the extreme, toward the abolition of private initiative.

National Socialism is based on an ideological socialist foundation. In limiting profits and wealth, in abolishing privileges, it achieves greater equality than the socially minded democratic government was able to achieve. But while Socialism in pre-Nazi Germany was demanded in the name of freedom, National Socialism uses socialistic institutions for the sake of the totalitarian state which suppresses freedom. It thereby reveals, just as does Russian Bolshevism, that Socialism as an institution carries no value in itself. Such value as it may have, derives solely from the ethical idea with which it is connected. If used for war, it loses its character as mankind's redemption, drawn from Christianity and from idealistic philosophy; the equality it achieves is the equality of slavery.[4]

The Nazi economy was, perhaps, most accurately described, as the Nazis themselves described it, as a *Wehrwirtschaft*—a war economy. But it was a war economy instituted in a time presumably of peace and as a *permanent* form of the economy. Military considerations from the very beginning of the regime overshadowed economic considerations. The Nazis, it is true, had no objection to the profit system as such but when there was any conflict between what was militarily expedient and what was profitable, the latter consideration always gave way to the former.

Much has been made of the fact that the Nazi regime was established in a period of severe economic crisis. But the relationship between that crisis and the establishment of Nazism is not a simple one of cause and effect. The economic crisis of the early 1930's was world-wide and even more severe in some countries, like the United States, than it was in Germany. Not every country whose economy was severely strained by that crisis succumbed to Fascism. People may react to an economic crisis in many different ways, the mere existence of such a crisis does not in itself pre-determine the way in which people will react to it. That the economic crisis accelerated and deepened the feeling of despair with which the German people were already infected is very true, but that it alone caused that feeling of despair is not true. For the roots of despair are spiritual and intellectual not material. The economic crisis might have been accepted as a challenge to creative activity rather than as a goad to desperate and irrational action—for an explanation of the way in which the German people reacted to it we must go behind the economic crisis to the mental and spiritual state out of which the action of despair grew.

## A Personal Dictatorship?

THE Nazi regime was sometimes described in the early days of the regime, as a personal dictatorship and it was thought that if Hitler could be eliminated the regime would collapse. The Hitlerian dictatorship was likened to the Napoleonic regime and to similar dictatorships throughout history. This explanation, as we soon came to realize, was a gross oversimplification of reality. It ignored the fact that despite the personal magnetism and daemonic energy of Hitler the Nazi movement rested upon a broad popular base. We refused for a long time to recognize the popularity of the movement since, consciously or sub-consciously, we suspected that if true it would challenge one of our most cherished illusions, namely, that a government founded upon the consent of the governed could never be inhuman, illiberal, or dictatorial. The optimistic conception of human nature upon which this illusion was based would be severely challenged if we had to admit that large numbers of people could willingly condone the brutal things which the Nazi regime did. But the facts we soon came to realize were otherwise. In the last free election (March 5, 1933) the Nazis polled slightly less than a majority of the popular votes cast, but if we count the votes given to the Nationalists, a party closely allied to the Nazis, they polled a majority and with the support of the Nationalists, the Nazis controlled a majority of the seats in the Reichstag. An Enabling Act passed by this Reichstag legally conferred dictatorial powers upon the Nazi controlled government. With the assistance of the Catholic Center party the Enabling Act was passed by the constitutionally required two-thirds majority although the Communists were excluded from the Reichstag and the Social Democrats voted against it. The vote was 444 in favor of the Act as opposed to 94 votes against it. Technically the Nazi regime was legally voted into power which vividly illustrates that legal barriers, contrary to the nineteenth-century liberal belief, are no bulwark against tyranny. Why did the Catholic Center party—a party devoted to liberal doctrines—help the Nazis to secure the two-thirds vote necessary for amending the Constitution? Professor Arnold Brecht declares:

One has tried to find the explanation for this baffling action— outstanding in the long series of abortive attempts at a policy of appeasement—in personal frailty or treason, in backstage bargaining or bribery. Never would the entire party, never a man like Brüning, have cast their votes on such grounds, even if a number of members had. The true explanation is contained in the party's conception of the alternative. They believed . . . that if they refused to vote for the measure the revolution would go ahead on illegal roads, starting with an orgy of cruelty and bloodshed. Their consent, so they hoped, might avoid such disaster.[5]

Here we have, it seems to me, an excellent illustration of how a decadent liberalism helped to pave the way for totalitarian dictatorship. So much faith had the liberals in legality that they could not conceive of "an orgy of cruelty and bloodshed" being instituted by legal means; if only Hitler were given legal powers the legality of such powers would, they believed, restrain him from using them in a cruel and inhuman fashion. Some of them lived to see this illusion shattered but it was a fatal illusion that infects the minds of many liberals in other countries even today. When the conception of legality is divorced from justice, as it is in decadent liberalism, legality constitutes no barrier to tyranny whatsoever.

Whether we can accurately say that the Nazi regime rested upon the consent of the majority of the German people or not, it is clear that it rested upon the consent of a very large portion of the population, that it was a mass movement and not simply a small conspiracy of a few individuals. This fact should should make us wary of believing, as we have in the past, that a regime founded upon the freely given consent of the people is necessarily a good or democratic regime and that such a principle *in itself* is the only requirement of good government.

Not only did the theory of a "personal dictatorship" obscure the mass support which Fascism had, but it also obscured the *totalitarian* character of the dictatorship. The dictatorship was not confined, as many dictatorships in the past have been, to the realm of the political, but every conceivable aspect of individual life was subjected to political control or supervision, from the propagation of children to the writing of poetry. It is this totalitarian character of modern dictatorships which so sharply distinguishes them from dictatorships in the past.

The comparison of Hitler and Mussolini with figures like Napoleon, moreover, ignores the extent to which Hitler and Mussolini were not only outside the traditions of Western civilization but the passionate ferocity with which they endeavored to destroy those traditions and the institutions connected with them. For all his ruthlessness Napoleon still adhered to many of the traditions of Western civilization and in the Napoleonic Code actually sought to preserve and perpetuate some of them. Hitler ranged himself and his movement against every idea and institution traditionally associated with Western civilization and he was bent upon no less a venture than the destruction of that civilization by every weapon at his command. However odious we may regard the comparison of Hitler with Napoleon such a comparison underestimates the daemonic nature of the Fascist regimes. No dictatorial regime in the history of the Western world has engaged in the perverted brutality or the thorough-going destruction of Western institutions that is characteristic of Fascism.

That is why the early attempts to ridicule Hitler and Mussolini out of existence (as, for example, in Charlie Chaplin's "The Dictator") now appear so incongruous with the reality.

We have come through tragic experience to learn that Hitler and Mussolini were no laughing matter, that they could not be brushed aside with a contemptuous smile or defeated by irony. However ridiculous and irrational they may personally have been, they and their followers believed in their god-like infallibility and "mission" with a passion that was impervious to reason. Again we have been taught by bitter experience a lesson—the most absurd and irrational myths may be seized upon by a desperate people as the truth. Human nature is not so constituted that it automatically rejects the absurd nor is its rationality so instinctive that it cannot be led astray by passionate devotion to unworthy objects.

## A German Menace?

ANOTHER interpretation of National Socialism that gained in acceptance during and after the war with Germany attributed the rise of National Socialism in Germany to characteristics inherent in the German people or in German culture or history. The German people, so this theory goes, have always been predisposed to the acceptance of authoritarian, dictatorial governments. They have never experienced or wanted to experience genuine democratic government. They never had any genuine liberal revolution and they have always been militaristic in spirit and institutions. They are by nature, others add, a brutal people who have been insensitive to human values in every sense except a sentimental one.[6] If this diagnosis is correct the therapy, if therapy is possible, would be the re-education or rehabilitation of the German people in terms of the ideas and institutions associated with Western democracies. In the meantime, Germany must be "kept down," her economy must be controlled in such a way as to prevent the production of weapons for war, her military forces disbanded, and her political institutions closely supervised. A more effective cure, presumably, would be the extermination of the German people but this is not seriously proposed by those who hold this theory.

This theory suffers, it seems to me, from the same fallacies as anti-Semitism and is a kind of anti-Semitism in reverse. "I do not know how," Burke has said, "to indict a whole people." The German people consist of individual human beings who like individual human beings everywhere have good and bad qualities. Like any group of people they are more like other human beings than they are different. Inherently they are no better or worse than any other people. To say that the German people are inherently and incorrigibly bad is to talk nonsense, just as it is nonsense to say that all Jewish people have undesirable personality traits, that all Oriental peoples are untrustworthy or that all Americans are by nature friendly and generous. It is clearly flattering and self-gratifying to ascribe all good qualities to one's self and all bad qualities to some other group of people but we can do so only by doing violence to the facts. Self-righteousness is a common human failing but it is a dangerous fallacy upon which to establish a public policy with regard to other people. It breeds, as a matter of fact, the very evil it seeks to cure.

We can explain the rise of National Socialism in Germany solely in terms of German history or culture only by ignoring those elements in German history and culture which were opposed to everything the Nazi movement represented. Germany, it is true, had a long history of authoritarian government but it never had a dictatorship remotely resembling that of the Nazis. Hitler differed from Bismarck and Frederick the Great not only in degree but in kind. The German people and German institutions, it should be remembered, were the first victims of Hitler's brutally destructive regime, rather than preserving and perpetuating the German political tradition he perverted and sought to destroy it. Although Germany was long ruled by a monarchy it was a constitutional monarchy with many of the liberal features which characterize parliamentary democracy in other countries. It was more autocratic than many other governments but it was informed by the spirit of the *Rechtsstaat* and in local government the spirit of democracy was especially strong.[7] To equate Hitlerism, moreover, with authoritarianism or autocratic government is gravely to underestimate the nature of National Socialism and the daemonic fury with which it sought to

destroy every vestige of Western civilization. Despite the unsuccessful German liberal revolution of 1848 it is not accurate
to say that Germany never experienced liberalism in thought
or practice. For through the reforms and writings of men like
the Baron von Stein, Wilhelm von Humboldt, Goethe,
Schiller, Kant, Dahlmann, Mohl and many others liberalism
as a social philosophy and way of life found practical expression in Germany as elsewhere. Only a distorted interpretation of German history can ignore this tradition and to dismiss
it as "untypical" is to do violence to the facts. That Germany
never experienced the degree of liberalism that Great Britain
did, is certainly true, that she never experienced liberalism at
all, is untrue. Under the Weimar Republic which was established in 1918 Germany adopted a constitution which was at
least as democratic, if not more so, than those in effect in
other Western democracies. The assertion that German culture is inherently barbaric and anti-humanistic ignores the
important cultural contributions which Germany has made
to the Western world, it ignores the work of Goethe, Schiller,
Bach, Beethoven, Brahms and many others of similar stature.
To put Hitler in this tradition is to attribute a dignity to his
regime to which it has no legitimate claim. Hitler was unalterably opposed to that tradition and sought to exterminate
it not only in Germany but throughout the world.

Much is said about the kinship between Hitlerism and
Prussian militarism but, again, this identification can only be
made by doing violence to the facts. It is no defense of Prussian militarism to recognize the fact that Hitler was an Austrian not a Prussian; that he never had any intimate connection with the Prussian aristocracy or military corps before
coming to power; that upon coming to power he dismissed or
demoted many of the Prussian leaders of the German armed
forces; that he often acted contrary to the advice of the German General Staff; and that the July 20th (1944) revolt
against his regime was led by many members of the Prussian
aristocracy and military corps.[8] That some of the Prussian
aristocrats in the days before Hitler came to power, like some
of the German industrialists, supported the Hitler movement
in the belief that Hitler could be "managed" in their own

interests, is undoubtedly true, but Hitler proved himself as capable of acting independently of their control as he had in the case of the industrialists. It is also true that many Prussian aristocrats opposed Hitler from the very beginning. That Hitlerism was something much more dangerous than a revival of Prussian militarism this identification of the two obscures.

The theory that identifies National Socialism with the spirit of the German people or regards it as a manifestation of tendencies peculiar to German history ignores the fact that the phenomenon of Fascism first appeared eleven years before National Socialism in a country devoid not only of the Prussian military tradition but of any military tradition. It ignores the Fascist mentality that has grown up in countries like Spain and Argentina, it ignores the similarities that exist between Fascism and Stalinism, and it ignores the Fascist movements that have appeared in countries like Great Britain and the United States. The theory that identifies Fascism as a peculiarly German phenomenon underestimates the universality of the Fascist spirit and the danger still lurking in the world today. Were Fascism but a peculiarly German phenomenon we could rest content with the military destruction of the German armed forces but if Fascism was and is a manifestation of a crisis peculiar not alone to Germany but to the Western world then we cannot relax our vigilance nor rest content with keeping Germany "down."

## The Fascist Ideology

WHEN we turn to the writings of the Fascists or to their "programs" for an explanation of what precisely Fascism is we are not materially assisted for their writings and "programs" are couched mostly in negative terms and are full of contradictions and inconsistencies. Nevertheless, we are given some clues to the real explanation which are helpful.

In Benito Mussolini's article on *The Political and Social Doctrine of Fascism* he tells us explicitly what Fascism is *not*—it is not liberalism, socialism or democracy. "After Socialism, Fascism combats the whole complex system of democratic ideology, and repudiates it, whether in its theoretical premises or in its practical application." It has nothing in common, he declares, either with monarchy or with republicanism as those institutions have previously existed in Western civilization. Both in the political field and in the realm of economics, he says, "Fascism has taken up an attitude of complete opposition to the doctrines of liberalism." It repudiates the concept both of individual liberty and of equality. It is not to be equated with traditional reactionary political movements— "the Fascist negation of Socialism, Democracy, and Liberalism must not be taken to mean that Fascism desires to lead the world back to the state of affairs before 1789. . . . Fascism has not chosen De Maistre for its high priest." But if it is none of these things what is it? On that point Mussolini tells us little more than that Fascism is "an embodied will to power," that it conceives of the State as having absolute authority over the individual, that the individual exists for the sake of the State rather than the State for the sake of the individual, that the State is conceived as "a spiritual and moral fact in itself." As a matter of fact, he states, Fascism has no specific program or doctrine.

Fascism was not the nursling of a doctrine worked out beforehand with detailed elaboration; it was born of the need for action and it was itself from the beginning practical rather than theoretical; it was not merely another political party but, even in the first two years, in opposition to all political parties as such . . . if one were to re-read, in the now dusty columns of that date, the report of the meeting in which the *Fasci Italiana di combattimento* were constituted, one would find there no ordered expression of doctrine, but a series of aphorisms, anticipations, and aspirations. . . .

The years which preceded the march to Rome were years of great difficulty, during which the necessity for action did not permit of research, or any complete elaboration of doctrine. There was much discussion, but what was more important and more sacred—men died. They knew how to die. Doctrine, beautifully defined and carefully elucidated, with headlines and paragraphs, might be lacking; but there was to take its place something more decisive—Faith.[9]

Fascism, he says in effect, is nothing but an unrationally motivated will to power, the manifestation in practice of the twentieth-century revolt against reason. This aspect of Fascism was also vividly described by one of the leaders of the British Union of Fascists in 1934 when he said:

Fascism is real insurrection—an insurrection of *feeling*—a mutiny of *men* against the conditions of the modern world. It is completely characteristic of this aspect of Fascism in its early stages, both in Italy and in Germany, that the movement should have grown to full strength without either logical theory behind it or cut-and-dried program in front of it. The men who built Fascism in Italy and Germany—who are the "common men," the "men in the street," leave theories to the intellectuals and programs to the democrats who have betrayed them with programs for a century. The Fascist . . . acts, in fact, instinctively, and not theoretically.[10]

The Fascist rejects the conception of any absolute, universal, and eternal truth and as a consequence believes that all values, all judgments of right and wrong, are relative. As an American exponent of Fascism, Lawrence Dennis put it very succinctly: "The Fascist scheme of things is an expression of human will which creates its own truths and values from day to day to suit its changing purposes." [11] Truth is whatever the dictator declares it to be, right is whatever he wills. In the words of a Nazi spokesman, W. Stapel:

According to the National Socialist principle, what guarantees the maximum formation of state-power is Right. The feeling of Right is brought in relation to the State, not to the individual. Therefore nothing is "safe" from State interference. . . . Right is not a matter of agreement: it is determined by the Führer. It is based not on contract but on command. . . . We have no longer any competition between ideas: only ideas that are made good, and ideas that are expunged.[12]

Following the lead given by Sorel, the Fascist seeks to substitute "myth" for truth, the important consideration is not whether an idea is true or not but whether it can be made to appear true to the mass of the people. Truth itself is thus subjected to politics and propaganda replaces education. According to Mussolini, Italian Fascism was based upon the "myth" of the nation:

We have created our myth. The myth is a faith, it is a passion. It is not necessary that it shall be a reality. It is a reality by the fact that it is a goad, a faith, that it is courage. Our myth is the Nation, our myth is the greatness of the Nation! And to this myth, to this grandeur, that we wish to translate into a complete reality, we subordinate all the rest.[13]

Taking a cue from Pragmatism, the Fascist believed that he could create a new reality simply by emotionally affirming its existence. Believing that the reality of an idea depends upon the emotional intensity with which it is affirmed, the Fascist believed that he could create a reality of his own choosing simply by "willing to believe." Whereas Italian Fascism sought to create a new political "order" upon the base of the "myth" of the nation, German National Socialism resorted to the "myth" of race. According to Alfred Rosenberg, the chief "intellectual" spokesman for the Nazi movement:

Today a new faith is awakening: the myth of blood, the belief that it is by the blood that the divine mission of man is to be defended; the belief, based on the clearest knowledge, that Nordic blood represents that mystery which has overcome and replaced the ancient sacraments.[14]

The life of a race and of a people is not a philosophical creation which develops logically . . . it is rather the formation of a mystical synthesis, a manifestation of the soul, which cannot be explained by the logic of reason nor by causal analysis.[15]

This myth of Aryan or Nordic superiority was accompanied by the depiction of the Jew as the very incarnation of evil, the cause of all political, social and economic troubles, the manipulator of international capitalism and, at the same time, the leader of international Communism.[16] The attack upon the Jew did not stop as we know with verbal assaults upon his person and integrity but millions of Jews were exiled and slaughtered, tortured and burned, as living sacrifices to perverted passion. Although the Jews were the most numerous victims of Nazi brutality, Protestants and Catholics, too, were also persecuted and killed when they sought to remain faithful to their beliefs, as was anyone who opposed the will of Hitler or the Nazi Party. Brutality and violence of a kind unprecedented in modern history characterized both the Italian Fascist and the German Nazi movements. "Who can deny," an Italian Fascist asked, "that a strong man breathes much more freely, eats much better and sleeps more soundly after having slapped and knocked down an enemy?

Who can deny that the word man and the word fighter are synonymous? Hence we conclude that when we speak of war it is the better part of our blood, the futurist part, that speaks in us. . . .

Violence has today become the best condition of real health for a people. Order, pacifism, moderation, the diplomatic and reformist spirit, are they not perhaps arterio-sclerosis, old age and death? . . . For to the present aesthetics of filthy lucre we oppose—and let it come, let it come—an aesthetics of violence and blood! [17]

### According to Hitler:

War is eternal, war is universal. There is no beginning and there is no peace. War is life. Any struggle is war. War is the origin of all things. Let us go back to primitive life, the life of the savages. What is war but cunning, deception, delusion, attack and enterprise? People have killed only when they could not achieve their aim in other ways. Merchants, robbers, warriors—at one time, all these were one. There is a broadened strategy, a war with intellectual weapons. [18]

Throughout the Fascist literature violence and war are described as "the most simple affirmation of life," "the climax of human achievement," and as "a purifying bath of steel."

The Fascist ideology extolled the leaders of these movements in the most extravagant fashion. They were depicted as the "saviors" who would "redeem" the nation or the race from their misery and in no uncertain terms they were identified with God himself. According to the Reich Minister for Church Affairs under the Nazi regime: "There has arisen a new authority as to what Christ and Christianity really are—Adolf Hitler. Adolf Hitler . . . is the true Holy Ghost." According to Dr. Engelke, one of the leaders of the so-called German Christian movement, "God has manifested Himself not in Jesus Christ but in Adolf Hitler." [19] According to Göring:

Everyone who knows the close inner bond between Hitler and his men will understand that for us followers it is axiomatic that the

Leader must possess any quality attributed to him in its highest perfection. Just as the Roman Catholic considers the Pope infallible in all matters concerning religion and morals, so do we National Socialists believe with the same inner conviction that for us the Leader is in all political and other matters concerning the national and social interests of the people simply infallible.[20]

But we search the Fascist literature and "programs" in vain for any consistent statement of Fascist "philosophy" for the simple reason that there is none. As Hans Morgenthau has pointed out:

If a political philosophy is a coherent system of thought intent upon justifying before ethics and reason a certain political program and certain political institutions, Naziism has not developed a political philosophy. What passes as the political philosophy of Naziism is a conglomeration of fragments of ideas, often inconsistent with each other, always vague and capable of contradictory interpretations, and hence adaptable to the exigencies of changing political conditions.[21]

When Hitler and Mussolini were appealing for the support of the people they did not present detailed and specific programs for the reform of political, social and economic institutions, they disdained to enter into anything resembling rational discussion of their aims, they did not debate the issues of the day—they appealed, in short, not to the reason of their potential supporters but to their passions. In effect they said: "Liberalism, socialism, democracy are bankrupt. The worst defect of democratic, parliamentary institutions is that so much time is lost in fruitless debate and argument. Action is more important than theory, what we need is not deliberation but action. We promise you action. Do not ask us to be more specific than that. We cannot ourselves tell you specifically what action we will take, we can tell you only that it will not resemble the action associated with liberalism, socialism or democracy. We ask but one thing: that you put absolute trust and confidence in us and we will never let you down. We do not necessarily promise abundance and security but we promise you something even more valuable—a mission in life, a mission to which you may be asked to sacrifice your very life, but a mission that will restore meaning and purpose to life by giving you something to do, something to which you may devote your entire energy and resources." What this "something" was, was never more specifically described than the "nation" in the case of Italy, or the "race" in the case of Germany. "Take up your yoke and follow me" was the ever constant refrain but where the people were being led or for what purpose was never made clear.

Although it seems to me that he is wrong in some details, Hermann Rauschning has aptly described the Fascist movement when he called it "the revolution of nihilism." [22] It is, he states, a revolution without a doctrine, "dynamics *in vacuo*," action for the sake of action alone, power sought for its own sake. It uses ideas, of course, but the ideas are means, not guiding principles and whatever "doctrines" are espoused are "deliberately and carefully manufactured" [23] for the particular time and occasion. There are no doctrines that cannot be changed or discarded as expediency demands. Nationalistic in appearance it is not confined to nationalistic aspirations, these are but the "window-dressing." For a long time we sought to deal with the German Nazi government on that basis and it was the basis for the hope of Prime Minister Neville Chamberlain that war with Germany could be averted by yielding to Germany's nationalistic aspirations. Hitler encouraged that belief by declaring that if Germany were given the Sudetenland he would have no more territorial ambitions in Europe. It soon became clear that Hitler had no intention of being confined by nationalistic aspirations and that his regime was "totally despotic and totally destructive" even of nationalistic conceptions and achievements. [24] Rauschning further describes the Nazi regime as a "permanent revolution" [25] by which he means that unlike former revolutions it sought to keep the nation in a continuous revolutionary turmoil. Since it had no aspirations that could be satisfied, no program that could be realized, it had no choice but to keep the nation in a constant state of crisis and when no real crisis existed it had to manufacture one.

What is the actual revolutionary goal of National Socialist dynamism, whether disguised by the make-believe philosophy of the moment or by its immediate objectives? How do the present élite themselves envisage the victory of their movement? We may accept Hitler's reply: it is the victory of the revolutionary new order. But what is this new order? It is simply action, whether conceived as a German social and economic revolution or as a world revolution or, finally, as the "eternal war" which many men in high places in the movement consider to be the future condition of human society.

That war, however, is not the father but the destroyer of all things, the destroyer of all order and all the things of the mind. There is nothing that this destruction would spare. And nothing will be taken over from the old order into the new, neither army nor church, neither the institutions of property nor the elements of culture. . . .

Whatever it cannot dominate it must destroy, whatever it cannot absorb and master must go. Such is the truly barbaric maxim of National Socialism. It is the process of an enemy occupation of all the vital elements in the nation, ending in their destruction.[26]

We can vividly see today the goal of National Socialist revolutionary activity in what Germany has become—a nation literally buried in ruins. Hitler once boasted that he would not die without taking the German nation with him to his death —it is the one boast he has made good.

The totalitarian Fascist regime, Peter Drucker declares, sought to substitute organization for order. Unable to produce a genuine orderly existence in the political, social or economic sphere it sought to create the illusion of order through elaborate and complex organization. But this could not in the last analysis satisfy the people's hunger for real order. How can we explain, then, their acceptance of it for so long? Peter Drucker, in a suggestive analysis, declares:

The masses must have something. They cannot endure the vacuum. Though they are deeply dissatisfied with what totalitarianism has to offer, they cannot get anything else. Therefore totalitarianism must be the valid answer. The less satisfied they are with what it gives, the more must they try to persuade themselves that it is enough. . . .

This creates the continuous tension under which the masses in the totalitarian countries live. They are deeply unhappy, deeply disappointed, deeply disillusioned. But they must force themselves with all their power to believe in totalitarianism just because they are disillusioned and dissatisfied. What is left to them when they give up the only thing they have? They are like drug addicts who have to take increasing doses of the poison, knowing that it is a poison, but unable to give it up because they must find oblivion and the happiness of dream. That explains the hysteria which grips the masses in every totalitarian meeting, parade, or pageant. . . .

The intellectual tension of this constant self-persuasion to believe against belief, to trust against evidence, and to cheer spontaneously after careful rehearsal is so great that no amount of self-doping could keep it from snapping. An entity must be found in which the contradiction resolves itself. . . . No man and no organization can resolve the contradiction between the need for an order and the impossibility of producing one, between the disillusionment over totalitarianism and the need to believe in it. And since the totalitarians have no God, they must invent a Demon, a superman and magician in whom the contradictory becomes one. To be this demon in whom wrong is right, false true, illusion reality, and emptiness substance is the function of the "leader." [27]

## The Action of Despair

IF THE phenomenon of Fascism cannot adequately be explained as a conspiracy of capitalists or of militarists, if it is something more than a personal dictatorship, if it is not a peculiarly German phenomenon or a product solely of German history and culture—what is it? It is the political manifestation, I believe, of a crisis peculiar not alone to Germany or to Italy but to Western civilization. So far it has expressed itself in its most virulent and brutal form in Germany but it is something that can happen anywhere and the forces which produced it in Italy and in Germany are present everywhere throughout the Western world.

It is the political manifestation of spiritual, intellectual, social, and political anarchy. For despite its ostensible appearance of order its totalitarian tyranny is a confession of disorder. The totalitarian dictatorship is the embodiment not, as some insist, of authority but of naked power—it repudiates reason, justice, God, and comes into existence only as a consequence of the prior repudiation of reason, justice and God by the mass of the people. It is an effort to fill the void left by the repudiation of reason and of God by a will that is unguided by reason, unrestrained by considerations of justice, and unmindful of the commandments of God. It is not government in the true sense of that word, but a perverted attempt to employ the techniques of government when government fails. The total character of the dictatorship is necessitated by the *lack* of any common authority. Compulsion replaces consent in every sphere of life because there is no common agreement obliging consent in any sphere. It is a common mistake to equate totalitarianism with authoritarianism but this mistake arises from mistaking the appearance of order for genuine order and from failure to understand the meaning of authority. Authority means the right to enforce obedience, it means the rightful use of power. No rational justification of the use of power is made by the Fascist for he denies that either God or reason has any claim upon him—his "will to power" is its own "justification," its own *raison d'être*. The Fascist denies that there is any objective reality to which he must submit—for truth and reality are simply what he declares them to be, what he "wills to believe," nothing more and nothing less.[28] Unrestrained by principles of any kind Fascism is a reflection not of authority but of anarchy. Ostensibly and organizationally it appears to be authoritarian but no authority exists to which any appeal can be taken or in terms of which the actions of the dictatorship may be judged. The will of the "leader" is the final court of appeal and that will is a purely arbitrary one. It is useless to appeal to the "leader's" reason or sense of justice for the leader denies that he must justify his will in terms of reason or justice. It is enough that he has commanded an action—the rightfulness of his command is not subject to debate or question. This is not authoritarianism but tyranny. The most absolute monarchs who claimed to rule by divine right provided in that formula a measure by means of which their actions might be tested and evaluated—at least in theory if not always in practice—but the modern totalitarian dictatorship does not provide even this theoretical means of judgment. If the absolute monarchs claimed to be chosen by God to rule at least they did not claim, as the modern tyrants do, to be God Himself. A ruler who claims to be chosen by God at least leaves the way open for judgment concerning the fulfillment of his duty in terms of God's commandments but a ruler who insists that he *is* God removes his actions from any judgment whatsoever. He is responsible not even to God for his actions which those who claimed to rule by divine right at the very least conceded.

At the very base of Fascism lies despair. Through the many intellectual forces we have examined in previous chapters we have seen how faith in reason was gradually undermined, how men everywhere came to believe that there is no such thing as absolute, universal, eternal truth, how they came to believe that all value judgments are subjective and relative and how they finally reached the conclusion that man is essentially an irrational creature impelled this way and that by forces over which he has little or no control. Having lost their faith in God, men were not long in losing their faith in reason. Not only was Fascism nourished by intellectual anarchy and the loss of faith in reason but also by political and economic conditions that seemed to bear out the despair engendered by the loss of that faith. Rightly or wrongly the Italian and German despaired of finding solutions to their political and economic problems through the medium of liberal political and capitalistic economic institutions. The formalization of liberal concepts emptied liberalism of any specific content. How was it possible for prominent German intellectuals, jurists, lawyers, professors and civil servants who before 1933 were professed liberals, to accept, and many of them even to acclaim, a despotism that repudiated in word and deed the fundamental postulates of liberalism? It was possible because the "liberalism" they espoused was more closely akin to the nihilism of the National Socialists than to the doctrine whose concepts they repeated but whose substance they repudiated. They were forced by their own logic to accept the tyranny that was forged in the crucible of intellectual and political anarchy. Reason was denied the function either of understanding the world or of ordering it. Tyranny alone could restore a semblance of order and meaning. And these professed liberals had neither the standards nor the will to declare this despotism wrong. As positivists they could accept it only as a fact—a positive fact. There was, as a matter of fact, no great liberal uprising against the Nazis, because the "liberals" saw nothing to fight about. They had no ideas, no values, for which to fight; they had no doctrine, no way of life, to defend. Having denied conscience a valid role in the scheme of things, having denied the possibility of submitting opinions to a forum of reason and conscience for judgment, these professed liberals had no alternative but to accept the arena of force as the final arbiter of "right" and "truth." Having placed the law beyond good and evil, the "liberal" jurists lost by that act the capacity for condemnation. The appeal could only be made, as they themselves had taught, to superior force. The liberal positivistic conception of law—that law is the product of will and the embodiment of power—was a conception entirely congenial to tyranny.[29] It was the liberals, long before Mussolini and Hitler, who taught that might makes right and it was the positivistic liberals with their denial of the inalienable rights of man who prepared the way, albeit unwittingly, for Lidice and Dachau.

Aurel Kolnai points out that there are definite correlations between degenerate liberalism and Nazism:

In its cult of "relativism," "tolerance" and "indifferentism," in its explanation of social phenomena by "psychology," or by a succession of different "modes of general outlook" or world attitudes of mind, the Liberal Spirit has definitely over-reached itself.

Here is a mood of meek generosity and arbitrary irresponsibility, which throws the doors wide open to the wildest subjectivism on the one hand and arbitrary despotism on the other; subjectivism in those who delight in the pose of comfortable inertia and aesthetic passivity; despotism in those who are unwilling or unable to accept that pose.

Mincing criticism ends in shameless irrationalism; overrefined scientific skepticism in brutal pragmatism; distrust of mind, in a return to fetishistic tribalism; "breadth of mind" in the cowardly acceptance of tyranny and class or national exclusiveness.

Another aspect of self-destruction of Liberal idealism is the glorification of urges and instincts, of complexes and natural desires which attributes overwhelming power to sensual lust and unconscious impulse.[30]

Face to face with Fascism the degenerate liberal could not literally find words with which to condemn it. How, indeed, could he condemn the regime as unjust when he had purged the word justice from his vocabulary? The German liberals were not alone in finding it difficult to find words to condemn Nazism for liberals throughout the world were rather slow to find the words themselves. It is sometimes said when the July 20th revolt is mentioned that the German people were rather slow to awaken to the danger of Hitler but it should be noted that people throughout the world were rather slow to awaken to the danger themselves and that only Pearl Harbor could arouse the United States from its complacency when the Blood Purges and pogroms of 1934 could not.[31] France succumbed to the armed might of the Nazis in little less than a month, not simply because of the military superiority of the forces arrayed against her but because at first she had no spirit for the fight. For a long time we watched Great Britain fight alone convinced that the struggle between her and the forces of Fascism were no vital concern of ours. We awakened to the vitality of our interests only when we were ourselves attacked. Thus we demonstrated that we were victims of the same myopia that we attributed as a peculiarity to the German people. In 1933, there appeared a book entitled the *Brown Book of the Hitler Terror* (New York, 1933) which attempted to expose many of the brutalities characteristic of the Nazi movement and dictatorship. Like similar accounts which were published at that time the American public greeted it with apathy and in a review of the book written by Mr. James W. Gerard, a former United States Ambassador to Germany, for *The New York Times* of October 15, 1933, it was stated: "Hitler is doing much for Germany, his unification of the Germans, his destruction of communism, his training of the young, his creation of a Spartan state, animated by patriotism, his curbing of parliamentary government, so unsuited to the German character, his protection of the rights of private property, are all good." Mr. Gerard in the same review brushed aside the accounts of brutality with the remark that "No man who attains to great prominence escapes the suspicion of some form of immorality." [32] Mr. Gerard was not alone in thinking as he did in 1933 but it is a fact of some importance that the indignation which the American public felt in 1945 with the "revelations" of brutality at Buchenwald and Dachau it did not feel at all in 1933 when the same brutality was equally evident to those who cared to see it. If a large number of Germans closed their eyes to the evidence of brutality in the early days of the Nazi regime so did the overwhelming majority of Americans. It was in 1935 that Winston Churchill praised Hitler "for the courage, the perseverance, and the vital force which enabled him to challenge, defy, conciliate, or overcome all the authorities or resistances which barred his path." [33] And three years later he said: "I have always said that if Great Britain were defeated I hoped we should find a Hitler to lead us back to our rightful position among the nations," but, he added, "I am sorry . . . that he has not been mellowed by the great success that has attended him." [34] Hans Rothfels suggests that "whoever throws the stone in a self-righteous mood of moral superiority should carefully consult his own conscience or try to find an adequate testing ground. It is easy and may often be pharisaic to pass judgment without having been exposed to anything like the German experience after 1933, or without realizing that one might have likewise failed, perhaps, in smaller matters, as miserably as many Germans did." [35]

In one of the best philosophical analyses of the rise of National Socialism in Germany, Professor Helmut Kuhn points out that the rise of the Nazis to power was paved by intellectuals decades before. He describes the Nazi movement as a "flight from freedom into forgetfulness."

National Socialism is interpreted as an act of oblivion: succumbing to despair, a nation discarded the remembrance of freedom as an essential of human nature. The act of forgetfulness may also be described as a perverted recollection. Totalitarianism actively remembers man's passionate nature—his innate yearning for an absolute gratification—but it substitutes a finite reality, state and race, for the transcendent goal. Thus it divinizes worldly power, perverts faith into fanaticism, and releases the demonic vitality of corporate life. [36]

Freedom unites the will of man with his reason, it consists "in our ability to choose in accordance with our insight into the choice-worthiness or goodness of alternatives." It requires both knowledge of the good and the will to choose the good. The denial of either is a denial of freedom and the denial of freedom is the rejection of that moral agency in man which characterizes his humanity. Long before Hitler appeared on the scene intellectuals were bent upon the task of destroying or denying one or other of these aspects of freedom—one school of thought attacking the choice, the other its rationality.

Freedom is rational choice. The flight from freedom into forgetfulness presented itself, within the rarefied atmosphere of abstract thought, as a dialectic through which Reason was divorced from Choice. The Historicist, fastening on understanding to the exclusion of choice, reduced the mind to an impotent spectator. The Existentialist, exalting choice at the expense of reason, entrusted the self with a blind power of decision, thus reducing it to an irresponsible agent. After whittling away freedom from both ends, the two found themselves united in the task of consecrating the unfreedom of the totalitarian state. A pre-established harmony obtained between their joint teaching on the one hand and the behavior which the Third Reich expected from its citizens on the other. The required attitude combined the passivity of the spectator with the blind spontaneity of the unreasoning agent.[37]

Under the influence of liberalism we had come to believe that love of freedom is something innate in human nature. Before the rise of Fascism we would not believe that a people could willingly give up their freedom. Yet this is exactly what the Italian and German people in their desperation did and it is what any people in equally desperate circumstances may be tempted to do. They despaired of freedom. They despaired of freedom because they had repudiated the only source which can sustain it—belief in God and the rationality of his will. "Driven out by the analytic pitchfork" passion returns "professing scorn for reason. Fascism is the revenge of Passion frustrated and degraded." [38]

Fascism is a kind of substitute religion. Man's passionate nature cannot and will not be denied. Fascism seeks to fill the void left by the repudiation of Christianity. Impelled by passion, suspended between absolute hope and absolute despair, men will make a pact with the devil if they cannot worship God. Men feel the necessity of giving themselves up absolutely to something greater than themselves. Unable or unwilling to give themselves up in love and with hope to God, the German people gave themselves up in despair and with hatred to Hitler.[39]

# The Crisis of Our Times

## CHAPTER 18

# The Crisis of Our Times

IT REQUIRES no great seer or prophet to discern today the signs of decadence that are everywhere manifest. Only the most stubborn and obtuse would venture optimistic predictions for the future of the world and its civilization. The complacent optimism of the last century has given way to a deep-rooted despair and men everywhere are gripped by fear and insecurity. Anxiety gnaws at their vitals. Everywhere men tremble, whether they are yet conscious of the cause of their fears, before the judgment of God.

The sickness of the modern world is the sickness of moral confusion, intellectual anarchy, and spiritual despair. The revolution of nihilism, born of this confusion and despair, is peculiar not alone to any one country or people but in varying degrees is taking place everywhere. With almost frantic zeal we search for the political or economic panacea that will save us and the world from disaster, not seeing, apparently, that the disaster is already upon us and that for the cure we must examine the state of our own souls. The political and economic crises from which the world suffers are not causes but symptoms of a crisis that is even more profound—a spiritual crisis within the soul of man. Having alienated himself from God, having discredited the reason with which he was endowed by God, unable or unwilling to identify the evil with which the world of man is infected—modern man oscillates between extravagant optimism and hopeless despair. As his optimism is shattered more and more by the force of events he sinks lower and lower into the slough of despondency. In his despondency he is tempted to strike out against the enemy he cannot identify, whose name he does not know, in desperate action. In his anxiety to escape from utter futility and meaningless existence he is tempted to give up his most priceless heritage— his freedom—to any man who even promises deliverance from insecurity. He is tempted to put his faith in the most absurd doctrine, to submit his will to the most brutal dictator, if only in such a way he can find that for which he longs with all the passion of his being—a meaningful existence, a life worth living, a life worth dying to preserve.

Modern man's great lack is lack of conviction, particularly the conviction that good and evil are real. Mistaking indifference for tolerance he refuses to become convinced of anything for fear that his convictions may lead him to be intolerant. In a book that is both delightfully witty and profound, G. K. Chesterton has explained it in this way:

. . . what we suffer from today is humility in the wrong place. Modesty has moved from the organ of ambition. Modesty has settled upon the organ of conviction; where it was never meant to be. A man was meant to be doubtful about himself, but undoubting about the truth; this has been exactly reversed. Nowadays the part of a man that a man does assert is exactly the part he ought not to assert— himself. The part he doubts is exactly the part he ought not to doubt —the Divine Reason. Huxley preached a humility content to learn from Nature. But the new sceptic is so humble that he doubts if he can learn. . . . The old humility made a man doubtful about his efforts, which might make him work harder. But the new humility makes a man doubtful about his aims, which will make him stop working altogether. . . . We are on the road to producing a race of men too modest to believe in the multiplication table. We are in danger of seeing philosophers who doubt the law of gravity as being a mere fancy of their own. Scoffers of old times were too proud to be convinced; but these are too humble to be convinced. The meek do inherit the earth; but the modern sceptics are too meek even to claim their inheritance.[1]

Genuine humility is a virtue but indifference disguised as humility is a corrosive poison. Despair disguised as humility and indifference parading as tolerance are manifestations of the sickness of the modern world. Good and evil, truth and falsehood, have no positive dimensions.

Lulled into complacent self-satisfaction by the liberal positivistic doctrine of the nineteenth century modern man
became a blind devotee of the Goddess Progress who, he
believed, bestowed her blessings upon man in the form of increased knowledge and control over nature through an automatic and impersonal process, in which man, at best, was but
a passive tool of Nature or of History. Where formerly men
looked to God for the salvation of their souls, they now looked
to science and technology for the gratification of their desires.
Paradise on earth was substituted for eternal spiritual salvation as an aspiration worthy of men's efforts. The method for
bringing about this paradise, moreover, had been found to lie
within the power of man: paradise on earth waited only upon
the proper execution of a plan to be discovered in the truths
and with the methods of the natural sciences. It required no
sacrifice on the part of man, no change in his behavior, no
moderation of his appetites—it required simply the application of intelligence, directed by science, to social problems.
Progress was conceived as automatic, irreversible, and inevitable. Time alone would heal all wounds, cure all evil and
solve all problems. In his search for bodily well being and
comfort, in his search for economic security and political
utopia, modern man appears not simply to have lost his soul
but to have forgotten that he has a soul to lose. Everyday in
every way, until very recently at least, modern man believed,
the world is getting better and better. Through increased
knowledge of and control over nature, through education and
technology, man through science would overcome all the evil
with which the world is infected and live in perpetual peace
and harmony with his neighbor. This, at least, was his fervent
hope and his faith.

The optimism that characterized the nineteenth century
has given way in the twentieth to a deep-rooted despair. The
very Science upon which the nineteenth century pinned its
hopes for the realization of Utopia has led many individuals
in the twentieth century to the brink of meaninglessness. Man
is but a chance product of the earth, his aspirations and his
ideals products of vain imagination—only a kind of desperate
bravado serves to keep him afloat in a sea of meaningless

existence. This is vividly illustrated in a passage written by
Bertrand Russell, an eminent British philosopher, shortly
after the turn of the century:

Such, in outline, but even more purposeless, more void of meaning, is the world which Science presents for our belief. Amid such a
world, if anywhere, our ideals henceforward must find a home. That
man is the product of causes which had no prevision of the end they
were achieving; that his origin, his growth, his hopes and fears, his
loves and his beliefs, are but the outcome of accidental collocations
of atoms; that no fire, no heroism, no intensity of thought and feeling, can preserve an individual life beyond the grave; that all the
labours of the ages, all the devotion, all the inspiration, all the noon-
day brightness of human genius, are destined to extinction in the
vast death of the solar system, and that the whole temple of Man's
achievement must inevitably be buried beneath the debris of a universe in ruins—all these things, if not quite beyond dispute, are yet
so nearly certain, that no philosophy which rejects them can hope to
stand. Only within the scaffolding of these truths, only on the firm
foundation of unyielding despair, can the soul's habitation henceforth be safely built. . . . .
Brief and powerless is Man's life; on him and all his race the slow,
sure doom falls pitiless and dark. Blind to good and evil, reckless of
destruction, omnipotent matter rolls on its relentless way; for Man,
condemned today to lose his dearest, tomorrow himself to pass through
the gate of darkness, it remains only to cherish, ere yet the blow falls,
the lofty thoughts that ennoble his little day; disdaining the coward
terrors of the slave of Fate, to worship at the shrine that his own
hands have built; undismayed by the empire of chance, to preserve
a mind free from the wanton tyranny that rules his outward life;
proudly defiant of the irresistible forces that tolerate, for a moment,
his knowledge and his condemnation, to sustain alone, a weary but
unyielding Atlas, the world that his own ideals have fashioned despite the trampling march of unconscious power.[2]

Most men today no longer believe that progress is automatic,
irreversible, and inevitable though many still cling, if with
much less assurance than formerly, to a belief in education,
science and technology as the way out of our difficulties. With
the invention of the atom bomb modern man realizes that the
blessings of science are not unmixed, that science can be used
for evil purposes as well as good and that science itself is silent

on the question as to what purposes its knowledge should be put. Man's technical knowledge and capacity has outstripped his moral capacity. Evil has manifested itself so unmistakably in the twentieth century that modern man finds it increasingly difficult to deny its reality, even if he still has considerable difficulty calling it by name.

The liberals of the last century ascribed evil to men's ignorance and to their faulty political institutions. Evil was to be overcome by education and political reform. Equating evil with intellectual error the liberals were led, as Lewis Mumford points out, "to the flattering conclusion that the intelligent cannot sin and that the mentally adult can do no evil." The inability or unwillingness of the liberal to recognize the reality of evil lulled him into a false sense of security.

Good and evil are real, as virtue and sin are real. Evil is not just a mental aberration which only pathological characters are the victims of; and sin is not just a symptom of mental immaturity, as the pragmatic liberal would have it. Both these optimistic interpretations of sin and evil lead always to the flattering conclusion that the intelligent cannot sin and that the mentally adult can do no evil. These conclusions are plainly gratifying to those who fancy themselves intelligent and mature, because it leads them to a super-Calvinistic state of grace, in which all things are possible, and whatever one does is blessed.

At that point, the pragmatic liberal and the fascist—coming from opposite poles—meet face to face.[3]

While the liberals denied the reality of evil and ascribed the appearance of evil in the world to faulty political institutions and lack of "enlightenment," the Marxians explained the appearance of evil in the world to the prevailing capitalistic mode of production, to the institution of private property and to the class conflict engendered by that institution. Evil would disappear, they predicted, inevitably and automatically, with the establishment of a classless society through the medium of revolution and the dictatorship of the proletariat. With the distribution of material goods in accordance with men's needs, men would no longer be frustrated in their search for material satisfaction and all evil would disappear.

However profoundly liberalism may differ from Marxism in details and in conclusions both start from the assumption that human nature is essentially good and ascribe whatever evil there is in the world to bad or faulty institutions. But why these institutions, political and economic, should be so bad, and so much in need of reform, if men are essentially good is a question to which neither has a very satisfactory answer. Or why men should believe that they will be able to do in the future what they have never succeeded in doing in the past, namely, to establish a perfect political and economic system, is never explained.

In recent years one of America's most astute thinkers, Reinhold Niebuhr, has recalled to our consciousness a fact which both liberalism and Marxism have ignored with almost fatal consequences to our civilization. Evil, he points out, is something real and the name for it is sin. Its locus is not in institutions, which are but a reflection of human purposes, but in human nature itself. Professor Niebuhr declares:

The utopian illusions and sentimental aberrations of modern liberal culture are really all derived from the basic error of negating the fact of original sin. This error . . . continually betrays modern man to equate the goodness of men with the virtue of their various schemes for social justice and international peace. When these schemes fail of realization or are realized only after tragic conflicts, modern men either turn from utopianism to disillusionment and despair, or they seek to place the onus of their failure upon some particular social group, or upon some particular form of economic and social organization.

Obviously there are varying degrees of sin and guilt and some men and nations are more guilty than others of "disobedience to the heavenly vision." Also there are specific evils in history, arising from specific maladjustments in social and political organization. But these evils can be dealt with most adequately, if men do not give themselves to the illusion that some particular organization of society might be found in which men would no longer stand in contradiction to the law of their own being. Furthermore, particular virulent forms and types of sin in particular men and nations can be checked most successfully if it is recognized that these types are but aggravations of a general human situation.

Both modern liberalism and modern Marxism are always facing

the alternatives of moral futility or moral fanaticism. Liberalism in its pure form usually succumbs to the peril of futility. It will not act against evil until it is able to find a vantage point of guiltlessness from which to operate. This means that it cannot act at all. Sometimes it imagines that this inaction is the guiltlessness for which it has been seeking. A minority of liberals and most of the Marxists solve the problem by assuming that they have found a position of guiltlessness in action. Thereby they are betrayed into the error of fanaticism. The whole history of modern culture, particularly in its more recent efforts to defend itself against inferior and more demonic cultures, is a pathetic revelation of the weakness and confusion which result from these illusions about the character of man.[4]

The crisis of our times stems from this inability or unwillingness to recognize the evil in the world for what it is, the sin of man. What describes more accurately the evil that is rampant in the world today if it be not the perversion of men's wills? What describes more realistically the evils we must seek to overcome by God's grace if not pride, self-righteousness, greed, envy, hatred, and sloth? What has for centuries brought men to catastrophe if it has not been their attempt to create a god in their own image rather than seeking to make their own image more like that of God? What is the root of all evil if it is not that man seeks to make himself God? "For the wrath of God," St. Paul declares, "is revealed from Heaven against all ungodliness and unrighteousness of men, who hold the truth in unrighteousness . . . because that when they knew God, they glorified him not as God, neither were thankful; but became vain in their imaginations, and their foolish heart was darkened. Professing themselves to be wise, they became fools, and changed the glory of the incorruptible God into an image made like to corruptible man, and to birds, and to four-footed beasts, and creeping things." [5]

But if modern man has lost sight of the sinfulness of man he has also lost sight, in his despair, of the image of God in man; and man has become progressively dehumanized. The inhumanity of man to man has manifested itself in varying degrees throughout the ages man has lived but not until modern times has man's inhumanity to man been pursued as a matter of principle. As Nicholas Berdyaev sees it:

We are entering an unhuman world, a world of inhumanness, inhuman not merely in fact, but in principle as well. Inhumanity has begun to be presented as something noble, surrounded with an aureole of heroism. Over against man there rises a class or a race, a deified collective or state. . . . No longer is every man held to be a man, a value, the image and likeness of God. . . . The old bestialism, naive, barbarian, instinctive, was not self-conscious; it was pre-conscious. But modern bestialism is conscious, deliberate, the product of reflection and civilization, self-justified. . . .

There may have been a time when the image of man, his truly human nature, was not yet revealed—man was in a sort of potential state. This was the case with the past. But now we face something quite different. The image of man has been shaken and has begun to disintegrate after it was revealed. This is going on in all spheres. Dehumanization has penetrated into all phases of human creativity. In making himself God, man has unmanned himself. . . . The new world which is taking form is moved by other values than the value of man or of human personality, or the value of truth: it is moved by such values as power, technics, race-purity, nationality, the state, the collective. The will to justice is overcome by the will to power. The dialectic of this process is very delicate. Man desires power, power for himself, but this leads him to put power above self, above man; it leads him to readiness to sacrifice his own humanity for the sake of power. Power is objectified and drawn away from human existence. Such values as those of technics, the state, the race or the class bestialize man: for the sake of these sorts of power, any desired treatment of the individual is permitted.[6]

This dehumanization of man is made manifest in all spheres of life. In the factory it is not the individual personality that is the important factor in production but the machine and if the machine is to operate with the maximum efficiency for which it is designed, the individual man must become more and more like a cog in the machine, an adjunct to it. The individual may falter, the machine cannot and the individual who cannot keep up with the pace of the machine must give way to one who can. For the producer of goods man is primarily a consumer. If his appetite lags it must be stimulated artificially, he must be stimulated to buy if for no other reason than envy of others who buy. It is not a question of how much or what kind is good for him as a human being but how much he must buy if the producers are to go on producing. Capitalism, Professor Tillich declares, aims "to provide the greatest possible number of men with the greatest possible amount of economic goods" and "seeks to arouse and to satisfy ever-increasing demands without raising the question as to the meaning of the process which claims the service of all the spiritual and physical human abilities." [7] Few question *why* men should have more and more goods or whether it is good or necessary for them to have as many as they do. Material comfort and the accumulation of wealth are considered to be self-sufficient ends. From an aspect and means of life, economic activity has increasingly become, an end in itself, an end to which the spiritual nature of man is subordinated if not obliterated.

The dehumanization of man in modern art is so obvious as hardly to require mention. The artist today who paints an individual in such a way that he clearly resembles a human being is regarded not only as out-moded but as lacking in "artistic" talent. The more abstract the art, the more morbid its subject matter, the further it is removed from human values, the "better" it is thought to be as "art" by many moderns. And what is true of art is true also of modern literature.

If we consider two of the most prominent French novelists, Proust and André Gide, we cannot fail to remark that in their works man is decomposed, that a whole image no longer exists, that there are only elements of sensation and intellectual or rational states. . . . These novels no longer contain a wealth of human types, . . . but only fragments and elements of that being which once was called man. The modern psychological novel, talented and refined, is concerned with the analysis of the subconscious, is plunged into the uncertain world of sensations. . . . The creative gift of transfiguration is disappearing from art. . . .
In the works of Lawrence, man as an integral being is lost in the mystical elements of sex; man becomes a function of sex, instead of sex being a function of man. This is not pornography, it is a reflection of the same dehumanizing process now going on in the world, expressed with great artistic talent.[8]

The outstanding characteristic of modern culture is its fragmentarianism and discontinuity. It is a chaos not an order. No single thread binds it together.[9] Man as an integral being, physical and spiritual, rational and passionate, has been analyzed out of existence—some one part of his nature is taken as his essential characteristic. Man as such has been dissolved into one of his component parts.

An English writer and publisher, Victor Gollancz, believes that we are experiencing something quite new in the history of Western civilization, not simply the rejection of the values traditionally associated with that civilization but something even more ominous—the complete reversal of those values and the glorification of their opposites.[10] This reversal of the values traditionally associated with Western civilization finds its most characteristic expression in the twentieth century in contempt for human personality, in the denial of "the *essential* spiritual equality of all human beings." [11] Having lost sight of the fact that God created all men in His image, that God is the Father of all men and that consequently all men are brothers, the modern world has no basis for believing that men *are* equal. Where individuals still cling to the belief in individual equality it is often without any an understanding of the basis for that belief and consequently without any rational means of defending it.

> Respect for personality, our value of values, is today everywhere threatened. In thought, in speech, in act it suffers hourly dishonor. I must repeat that this, and not the atom bomb, is the major threat to our civilization.
>
> It is in fascism, of course, that contempt for personality reaches its final expression; for it passes beyond contempt, and becomes hatred. . . .
>
> Hitler is dead and Germany is in ruins. But has the horror passed? I do not think so. Nazism was not an isolated phenomenon; it was merely the final expression, so far, of tendencies which had for a long time been growing stronger. Those tendencies are still at work; some of them are more widespread than ever; and even here in England there are disquieting signs that respect for personality, which we have guarded, and in spite of everything still guard, more devotedly perhaps than other people, is growing weaker.[12]

Victor Gollancz sees this contempt for human personality exemplified not only in the growth and extension of the tyrannical power of the Soviet Union but by the policy pursued by Great Britain (and we might add the United States and France) toward defeated Germany. Pity, mercy, and humility, he points out, are the counterpart of respect for human personality and individual equality—yet almost everywhere pity, mercy, and humility are regarded not as virtues but as weaknesses, if not, indeed, as vices.

If pity and mercy are inseparable from the Christianity or liberal humanism in which we profess to believe, so no less is some degree of personal and national humility, some attempt at least to modify the complacent self-righteousness that comes so easily to almost every one of us. In our relations with the Germans have we made the slightest attempt, either during the war or since, to modify this self-righteousness? Have we not rather, nearly all of us, enjoyed it and luxuriated in it to the full? I could deal, if I had the space, with the outcry that deafened us at the time of the Buchenwald "revelations," which were no revelations at all to those who had been trying ever since 1933 to rouse a lazy and sceptical public and to speak for men and women who, shut away from the world and without voices of their own, were suffering unspeakable torments in those camps of iniquity. Now at last we knew, people said, that the whole German nation was guilty: if not, why didn't they protest against these outrages and revolt against Hitler, no matter what the cost? It did not occur to them to ask what they would have done in similar circumstances: they did not pause to wonder whether, when the cost of which they talked so glibly would have been death or torture not for themselves alone but for their children also, they would have been, without any possibility of doubt, sufficiently heroic to run the risk of it. They did not ask themselves why, so long as we were still at peace, Buchenwald had been no concern of theirs, even though to raise their voices in protest would have meant not death or torture or even the risk of imprisonment, but the loss of a few seconds of time and the expenditure of some negligible fraction of energy. Instead of asking themselves things like that, they preferred to luxuriate in the sense of their own immense superiority. [13]

The same self-righteousness is revealed in the way we speak of the task which now confronts us in defeated Germany—the Germans, we say, must be "re-educated." Re-education in the true meaning of that word is, indeed, what the Germans need but when we use the word we do not use it with humility and with the understanding that in many things we need re-education ourselves but we use it frequently to mean that the Germans must be taught *our* way of doing things, to revere *our* statesmen, to imitate *our* political and cultural institutions, to learn from *our* history—in short, we seem to mean that all would be well if only the Germans could be made over in our image. As Victor Gollancz declares: In effect we are saying: "We, being without sin, will graciously teach you, very gradually we are afraid, to become a decent people—in fact, to become in the end perhaps almost as good as ourselves." What we should be saying, he declares, is something like this:

We have all sinned, and no one of us can cast stones. We in Britain have had a fortunate history, which has enabled us to win a large measure of freedom and democracy. Your history, on the other hand, has been unfortunate: when you have tried to advance to freedom and democracy circumstances have thwarted you, and the thwarting has weakened you in independence and civic courage—which is not to deny that there has been a magnificent minority that has stood firm against fearful odds. Finally, very evil men, God forgive them, have got control of you, and have committed in your name, and have led some of you to commit, unspeakable wickedness. You are now stricken to the dust, and we feel for you as members of our common human brotherhood. We hold out a helping hand; accept it, please, and take from our history and our way of life anything that may seem good and useful to you.[14]

In the last analysis, it will be the deeds not the words of democracy that will make a lasting impression for "there is really only one way to re-educate people, and that is by force of example." The choice the Western world faces, Mr. Gollancz believes, is not essentially between rival economic or political systems (though some are better than others) but between the re-affirmation of the values traditionally associated with Western civilization and their negation.[15] The crisis we are experiencing is not essentially a political or economic one, but a moral and spiritual one.

## Existentialism

THE crisis of our times finds dramatic intellectual expression in the emergence of a new philosophy called existentialism.

Although it had its roots in the nineteenth century it was not until it became the dominant philosophy in postwar France through the influence of men like Jean-Paul Sartre, Albert Camus, Gabriel Marcel and others that it attracted world-wide attention. But even before the war it exerted considerable influence in Germany through the writings of the German philosophers Heidegger and Jaspers. It was reflected in Great Britain in the poetry of men like W. H. Auden. In the United States it has found, perhaps, most prominent expression in the writings of the Protestant theologian, Reinhold Niebuhr, and was anticipated in the drama of men like Eugene O'Neill and Maxwell Anderson, and in the American philosophy of pragmatism. There are some who are inclined to dismiss existentialism as an intellectual fad of but ephemeral significance but others see in it the revival, if only negatively, of the great philosophical tradition which has lain buried for decades under the weight of Science. If it succeeds in nothing else but the revival of genuine philosophical discussion of the great and perennial problems of human existence, it will render a greater service to Western civilization than it knows or intends.

What is Existentialism? Professor Helmut Kuhn, in a recent analysis, describes it as the "encounter with nothingness."

In living our lives we think and will something. This something thought and willed is infinitely complex and rich, and as a rule we do not wonder in what precisely it consists. We prepare for and we practice a profession; we fall in love and we get married; we buy a car and build a house to live in; we hope that a world government will succeed in imposing peace, and we vote for the candidate most likely to promote this end. And in our eagerness to achieve the manifold purposes which grow upon us out of the moving pattern of our lives, we surrender ourselves without being aware of this abandon. Those multiple interests do not confront us—rather, we live in them. We are our interests. . . . Life is attention to objectives upon which we are bent in the almost literal sense of this word, and each one of these objectives is concrete, exacting, and obtrusive even while it fails to be absorbing. Life, in one word, is pursuit.

Life is pursuit—until it is forced to a standstill. Existentialist philosophy undertakes so to arrest us. . . . Generally in life we are stopped by an obstacle. Some objective proves unattainable. Then we fret and chafe, subsiding finally in bitterness, or, the more frequent course of events, we find consolation in objectives more easily reached. We circumvent the obstacle and continue in pursuit. The Existentialist does not add a new, more formidable obstacle in order to arrest us effectively. Instead of throwing into our path something that might serve as a barrier, he arrests us with—nothing. You are free, he tells us; nothing constrains what all the combined powers of nature and man are unable to achieve—since nothing forces upon our reluctant ego the unnatural pause, we may well raise it to the status of a quasi essence and speak of nothingness. The halt imposed by Existentialism is an Encounter with Nothingness.[16]

Existentialism endeavors to shock us out of our complacency by pointing out that the rock upon which we thought we stood is, in reality, quicksand. It points out that what we thought was truth is only conjecture or at best probable opinion. It points out that all our imagined absolutes are only relatives.

What do you will with unwavering devotion, so that everything else is willed and loved only for the sake of this first objective and greatest good? Again the reply will be a string of negations: not the promotion of what belongs in the field of my professional duties; not wife, children, and friends; not wealth, learning, or power; not higher living standards for all men; not . . . and in so passing from negation to negation I, as Existentialist, obliterate this rich and complex world in which we sometimes so comfortably live—the world which our thinking and willing builds up for us. As this world, deprived of ultimate meaning and cohesion, crumbles, there rears itself behind it, more real than Being, the origin of all negations, Nothingness. This is the true arrest, the total paralysis. . . .

The Existentialist claims to initiate us, through acquaintance with Nothingness, into the maturity of disillusionment.[17]

In pointing to the "reality" of Nothingness, Existentialism but confirms what our complacency has long hid from view but what events of recent decades have forced us to recognize. But Existentialism not only takes cognizance of the despair into which modern man has plunged himself but encourages him in that despair in the hope that he may overcome that despair by making the most of it, by realizing that his freedom is such that he can think and will anything he chooses. But the freedom envisaged by Existentialism is not a freedom bound by law, dedicated to the truth, and inspired by love, but a freedom impelled by nothing but despair and submissive to nothing but the subjective truth of the moment.

Modern existentialism had its origins in the writings of a recently discovered Danish theologian, Soren Kierkegaard (1813–1855) who has been described by Reinhold Niebuhr as "the profoundest interpreter of the psychology of the religious life since St. Augustine." [18] It is not, however, as an interpreter of religious psychology that we shall be concerned with him here but as the founder of a movement of thought that finds its most characteristic expression today in the writings of non-Christians and atheists. Rebelling against the abstract complexity of metaphysical speculation, especially as exemplified by Hegel, and what he thought was its futility, Kierkegaard set himself the task of finding out "where the misunderstanding lies between speculation and Christianity" and of answering the question: "How far does the Truth admit of being learned?" [19] As a Christian, Kierkegaard was particularly concerned with shocking Christians out of their complacency, with pointing to the truth which seemed to him obliterated by Christian speculation and institutions, that a Christian is not one who gives intellectual assent to an hypothesis but one who lives a Christian life, one who lives as though he truly believed that God is his judge and Christ his Savior. Christianity in the nineteenth century had become weak and flabby, sentimental and complacent, intellectually over-refined and more concerned, it seemed to him, with theological concepts than with Christian living. After leading us along a long and tortuous path he reaches the conclusion that Christianity has nothing to do with metaphysical speculation and that truth is something one subjectively experiences rather than objectively learns. It is not the objective content of the truth which is most significant but the way in which the truth is held. Thus Kierkegaard wrote:

If one goes up to the house of the true God, with the true conception of God in his knowledge, and prays, but prays in a false spirit; and one who lives in an idolatrous community prays with the entire passion of the infinite, although his eyes rest upon the image of an idol: Where is there most truth? The one prays in truth to God, though he worships an idol; the other prays falsely to the true God and hence worships in fact an idol.[20]

It is not "what" one worships or thinks that is important but "how" one worships and thinks. Truth is subjectivity. It is the passionate intensity with which one embraces the truth that is the important thing and the real test of one's belief is the willing submission to it in action. But, as Professor Kuhn points out,

> If everything depends on how a truth is held, with what passionate zeal, while the reference to an object is of little or no account, strange consequences result. We have heard people praised for their sincerity and passionate devotion to National Socialism or Communism. Are they right because they are sincere? Is their faith true because they cling to it with fanatical zeal? Or is not rather their passionate devotion indicative of the degree to which their minds are enmeshed in error? [21]

The belief in Christ as the Savior of mankind, as the incarnation of God, cannot be sustained, Kierkegaard believed, on rational grounds. It is an ultimate decision which rests on purely arbitrary grounds. We are faced in life with a Great Choice, the acceptance of God or the rejection of God—it is the most vital choice we shall ever be called upon to make, for from it flow all our other choices and in choosing God or rejecting Him we choose our ultimate destiny—but in making that choice, reason is of no assistance. If not reason, what is it, then, that impels men to choose God? And Kierkegaard answers: despair. We can truly turn to God only when we have plumbed the depths of despair, only then are we prepared to make the "leap," to embrace an "absurdity" (the incarnation of God in Christ) which, if it does not lessen our tension, at least gives it meaning. We accept God, he says, because we despair of everything else. It is impossible to believe in God, it is impossible not to believe in God—only in despair when all hope has vanished and all reason faded can the paradox be resolved, when, in desperation, we choose God. As a Christian, Kierkegaard was certain that the choice in desperation could only be for God but, except for a faith which he denies can have a rational basis, it is by no means self-evident that desperation will drive men into the arms of Christ. It may drive them, as it drove many Germans, into the arms of Hitler. We meet in despair not only Something but Nothing, not only Christ but the devil, and the outcome of that encounter is by no means predetermined. That truth is won by suffering we may acknowledge, but if that suffering is to be meaningful, if we are to discover a goal beyond that suffering, we shall require the reason which Kierkegaard bids us leave at the edge of the abyss. A "leap in the dark" may land us anywhere and we shall not necessarily escape the despair which Kierkegaard declares impels us to make that leap unless we have some idea as to the direction in which to make the plunge. If we value our lives not choice alone but the right choice must be made and we can know if it is right only if we have some idea, however obscured it may be by our fallible reason, of what that rightness consists in. It requires some knowledge of the good, however elementary or however fragmentary to recognize God when we encounter Him. Otherwise we may mistake the "wiles of the devil" for the ways of God.

Modern existentialism, for the most part, rejects Kierkegaard's Christianity but clings to his conception of truth as subjectivity. No observation or analysis of the world can reveal the truth, truth is revealed only in the subjective experience of living. My truth is the way I live, your truth is the way you live—beyond these subjective experiences there is no truth common to us both. In fact beyond this there is Nothing. The concrete, specific individual living in the present moment is the only reality there is.

This concrete individual, rather than living in the world, is his "world.". . . "World" in this subjective sense is neither meaningless nor meaningful but it has just as much meaning as the individual succeeds in conferring upon it. "The world is human," Sartre writes; in fact, so human that it ceases to be *the* world. It is an archaic world, or a Renaissance world, or an American world, or, in a final advance to undiluted particularity and concreteness, Alexander's world, my world, someone's world. In the absence of the world, worlds multiply. Heraclitus remarked scornfully that men behaved as though they lived each in his separate world. And they so live because they must, the Existentialist retorts.[22]

With the German historian, Oswald Spengler, the modern existentialist agrees that:

Life has no "aim." Mankind has no "aim.". . . Life is the beginning and the end . . . life has no system, no programme, no reason; it exists for itself and by itself . . . it cannot be dissected according to good or bad, right or wrong, useful and desirable.[23]

The only meaning that life has is the meaning which a particular individual gives to his own particular life. No principles of right and wrong, truth and falsehood, exist independently of individuals nor prior to their choices. Values come into being only when an individual wills to live by them and only then for those particular individuals who will them into existence and so long as they cling to them. The Existentialist declares that freedom is the supreme good, the ultimate reality —freedom being understood as the possibility of willing anything.

To be free in knowledge about one's freedom means to be confronted with the nothingness of sheer possibilities. For if everything is possible, nothing is determined. Somewhat poetically the Existentialists speak of an abyss of freedom and they describe the attitude of one placed at the brink of this abyss as anguish. . . . Man is not only free—he is his freedom. If, then, anguish is the awareness of freedom, it is equally correct to assert with Sartre that man is anguish. Anguish as the Existentialists understand it differs from fear in the same way in which absolute despair differs from relative despair. In fear we shrink from anticipated evil, and so there is always an object of fear, a definable danger such as being hit by a car in crossing the street, social disgrace as the consequence of violating a rule of good behavior, or eternal damnation as the wages of sin. But as we look for an object of anguish, we find—Nothing.[24]

The "anguished awareness of freedom" is the hallmark of existentialism. In Sartre's words: "Man is condemned to be free," i.e., whatever order or meaning life is to have the individual himself must give it, unguided, undirected, and unassisted. The individual has the dreadful task imposed upon him of making something out of nothing. He must screw up his courage, "leap" in the dark, "engage" himself in action, for only by absolute and whole-hearted devotion, only by total commitment, can he hope to rescue his life from futility and meaninglessness. But where should he leap? To what should he devote himself? What is worthy of the sacrifice of himself? To these questions the Existentialist has no answer.

But, nevertheless, Existentialism recognizes a truth which liberalism obscured, namely, that man is a passionate being, that the liberal ideal of "dispassionate reason" is an illusion, that man is not primarily, as Descartes believed, a "thinking thing." Yet Existentialism refuses to acknowledge that passion has a proper object of devotion and hence has no way of distinguishing between good passion and evil passion. Under the spell of liberalism and the nineteenth century gospel of progress we had begun to think of man as a gentle animal who through education and the advances of science, was becoming gentler every day. Intolerance, tyranny and war were things of the past or rapidly becoming extinct. "Religion with its appeal to an ultimate hope and an ultimate fear" could be dispensed with for it only served to keep alive the "intemperance of aspiration."

In attacking this secularist credo, the Existentialist rightly affirms that passion is of the essence of man. The champions of the "gentle animal" purge away the humanity of man along with his fierceness. That same passionate intensity which as insane fury drives nation against nation in internecine warfare is also responsible for all the great things man has ever achieved—his discoveries and peaceful conquests; his works of technical skill, fine art, and statecraft; his acts finally of devotion, self-sacrifice, and saintliness. Not by stifling the deep urge of man can he become civilized but only by releasing that passionate devotion which is creative of order rather than antagonistic to it. . . .

Once more the great and timely truth which the Existentialist proclaims is marred by an oversight. The concept of passion defined in terms of absolute intensity and detached from an object deprives him of the possibility of distinguishing between good passion and evil passion, between the divine and the demonic. . . .

Love is passion that has come into its own, and the proper object of love, God, as the First Love, the *summum amabile*, is also the regulating and guiding principle of theoretical life—the assurance that the intellectual quest leads to something worth knowing. . . .[25]

That what a man thinks and does will be determined ultimately by what he loves and hates is a truth requisite to the proper understanding of man and his behavior, but the Existentialist notion that passion is "unattached" and has no proper object of devotion is a dangerous doctrine. A passion that is attached to "nothing" is a passion that may be attached to "anything."

There is a similarity between the Existentialist conception of crisis and the Christian idea.

Christian is the idea of crisis itself and of rebirth, of a dread passage through despair and consciousness of guilt; Christian the emphasis placed on the supreme hour of death, on the individual on whose free decision weal and woe depend and who is yet finite, not spirit encased in a body but body-spirit, interpenetration and fusion of the physical and psychical. But each of these features is so twisted within the Existentialist pattern of thought that a terrifying yet meaningful distortion results. The Encounter initiating crisis is not an encounter with God who discovers our Nothingness but with Nothingness as the vacuum left by the nonexistent God as in Sartre, or the absent God as in Heidegger. Rebirth does not issue in the new childhood of faith but in the hardened masculinity of the superman. The consciousness of guilt is not consciousness of sin, that is, of failure to be like unto God, but the separateness of existence itself is viewed as guilt. Freedom is not rational choice guided by pre-existing norms and impeded by both the infirmity of will and the dimness of vision but, for the Existentialist, it is the creation of norms out of nothing. For the Christian, death is a dual reality—for each one the *hora suprema* in the sense of a last chance and a last peril, the moment in which a whole lifetime may be confirmed or annulled. . . . From this disparity the fundamental disagreement about life results: life is not life temporal in which life eternal germinates, but it is temporality through and through, the Existentialist affirms. With a concordant voice Hellenic philosophy and Christian faith exhort us "to think the deathless." "Think death!" comes the Existentialist's rejoinder.[26]

Negatively, however, Existentialism suggests a way out of the intellectual and spiritual crisis of our times for in "the Nothingness which Existentialism encounters" in the depths of despair, there "is the shadow of the repudiated God."[27] In the recovery of Being lies the way to the recovery of intellectual

health, in the recovery of metaphysics we may escape from the
factual inanity and sterile futility of positivism, in the contemplation of the transcendent and eternal we may discover meaning in the immanent and temporal. Only in terms of that
which is absolute, universal, and eternal can we understand
and create order out of that which is relative, particular, and
temporal. But if this intellectual recovery of metaphysics is to
be fruitful and healing it must be accompanied by spiritual
regeneration and a recovery of faith. In Christ we find the perfect embodiment of that which is absolute, universal, and
eternal in that which is relative, particular, and temporal; in
Christ, we find the object to which we can attach both our
passion and our reason without destroying either; in the Christian faith we have a faith in which passion sustains our reason
and reason sustains our passion. Our present crisis stems from
the declaration during the Renaissance, if not before, of the
autonomy of human reason, in the separation of reason from
faith, and that declaration of autonomy has borne fruit in the
twentieth century in the denial of autonomy and the rise of
totalitarian dictatorship. The bifurcation of the universe into
matter and mind, body and soul, object and subject, has had
almost fatal consequences for our civilization. The attempts
to resolve this bifurcation by declaring that all is matter (materialism) or that all is mind (idealism) have failed because
they have been half-truths at best. In the Christian conception
of the soul in which mind is enclosed in matter and matter is
informed by mind, in which temporality comes in contact
with eternity, are the two notions most perfectly resolved. For
Christianity, despite some popular misconceptions, is not idealism. The God of Christianity is not some idea of God but God
made Flesh. Christianity denies neither the reality of mind
nor of matter, of body or of spirit, it holds out to men the hope
not only of spiritual salvation but of bodily redemption. It
promises not only to save our souls but to clothe our bodies in
a flesh that shall be incorruptible. It promises us, not like
some religions, dissolution into the Absolute but personal survival. That which the world calls death, the Christian recognizes as a potential passage to life eternal. But unlike the secular philosophies which have dominated our thinking during

the eighteenth and nineteenth centuries it does not conceive of the attainment of paradise as something easy, inevitable, or automatic—for the passage to paradise is through suffering, self-sacrifice, and ultimately death. Heaven, it proclaims, will be won not by way of revolution, education, or technological advances but by way of the Cross. Only from ultimate defeat can there emerge ultimate victory but a victory that redeems those defeats by making them meaningful.

Christianity believes both in the rationality of the universe and of man because it believes that the universe is the creation and man the creature of a God who is the perfect embodiment of Reason. It believes in the essential goodness of the universe because it believes that God is the perfect embodiment of Love. It ascribes the evil in the world not to God but to man, who, in rebellion against God, seeks to defy His will. The recovery of reason and of goodness hence lies in the surrendering of one's will to God's will through repentance and the humble recognition that we are not self-sufficient and independent beings but dependent creatures of God. Christianity teaches us that:

Reason embodied in human society as rational order is justice. . . . At the same time, Christian wisdom is not blind to the fallibility of men in applying the principle of justice to the complex facts of life nor does it minimize the inevitable distortions of vision caused by will to power, fear, and vindictiveness. But it teaches us to approach the grave problems of political order and peace with a broken and a contrite heart, not with a broken and discredited intellect. It bids us to seek justice and righteousness with a passion greater even than our fear of sin, and to be aglow with a love of truth greater than our fear of error. Our generation is called upon to build a new house for mankind to dwell in peacefully. This is no work for half-hearted workmen. The true builder gives his all and wastes away in the service so that once, when he lays aside his tools, both trowel and sword, he may say of himself: "The zeal of thine house hath eaten me up." [28]

## The Meaning of History [29]

THE crisis of our times has focused men's attention once again on the great and perennial problem of the meaning of history.

In the optimistic climate of opinion that prevailed in the nineteenth century we were too complacent to be concerned with history as a problem—history was progress we proclaimed and let it go at that. But events in the twentieth century have given the lie to that facile generalization and we have been forced once again to ask—what is the meaning of history? More particularly we want to know: what are the prospects for Western civilization?

Early in the twentieth century a German historian, Oswald Spengler, attracted world-wide attention with the answer that Western civilization is inevitably doomed to destruction. In *The Decline of the West* (1917–22) he argued that every culture is an organism and that, like all organisms, every culture is destined to ripen into maturity, sink into senility, wither and die. Applying the methods of comparative morphology to the study of history he started from the premise that morphologically the history of any culture is the exact equivalent of the history of the individual man, of the animal, of the tree or the flower. Just as the individual man begins in infancy, reaches adolescence, achieves maturity, lapses into senility and finally dies, so all cultures are destined to pass through the same cycle. It is an inevitable, pre-determined cycle and there is no escaping it. At the very best we may stave off for a short time the ultimate death of a civilization but we cannot hope indefinitely to preserve that which is predestined to perish.[30]

Recently another historian, an Englishman, Arnold J. Toynbee, has suggested another interpretation of the meaning of history. His work is not yet complete although he has published six volumes of a work entitled *A Study of History* (1933–1939) in which he covers much of the same ground covered earlier by Spengler.[31] His scholarship is generally recognized as being sounder than that of Spengler and his sense of values much more profound. His work is devoted to a study of the genesis, growth, break-downs, interactions and prospects of twenty-one civilizations. He rejects at the outset, however, any notion that civilizations are organisms in any literal sense of the word and he denies that the course of any civilization is pre-determined. As a historian he notes trends but he denies that any trends are inevitable. His interpretation of history is neither optimistic nor pessimistic. Unlike Spengler who believed that each culture was a separate and disparate whole, Toynbee believes that all civilizations are but varied manifestations of an underlying unity, interacting, conflicting, and coöperating with each other. Spengler argued that all cultures are structurally alike, Toynbee argues for their "philosophical contemporaneity." [32]

In explaining the emergence of civilizations historians and others have generally relied upon race and environment as the key to the understanding of their genesis.

Both the race theory and the environment theory try to account for the observed diversity in the psychical (intellectual and spiritual) behaviour and performance of different fractions of mankind by supposing that this psychical diversity is fixedly and permanently correlated, in the relation of effect to cause, with certain elements of observed diversity in the non-psychical domain of nature. [33]

One seeks to correlate character with physique, the other to correlate character with climatic or geographical conditions but this Toynbee declares is "preposterous." But if the geneses of civilizations cannot be explained in terms of biology or geography then "they must be the result of some kind of interaction between them. In other words, the factor which we are seeking to identify is something not simple but multiple, not an entity but a relation." [34] And Toynbee believes that the geneses of civilizations can best be understood in terms of the conception of Challenge-and-Response.

We shall no longer be on the look-out for some simple cause of the geneses of civilizations which can be demonstrated always and everywhere to produce an identical effect. We shall no longer be surprised if, in the production of civilizations, the same race or the same environment appears to be fruitful in one instance and sterile in another. . . . We shall be prepared now to recognize that, even if we were exactly acquainted with all the racial, environmental, and other data that are capable of being formulated scientifically, we should not be able to predict the outcome of the interaction between the forces which these data represent. . . .

There is one thing which must remain an unknown quantity. . . . This unknown quantity is the reaction of the actors to the ordeal when it actually comes. These psychological momenta, which are inherently impossible to weigh and measure and therefore to estimate scientifically in advance, are the very forces which actually decide the issue when the encounter takes place.[35]

Civilizations have come into existence as responses on the part of individuals to challenges. These challenges have taken many forms, both of a physical and of a social nature—a harsh climate, slavery, prolonged and chronic warfare. The popular assumption is that civilizations emerge when environmental conditions are conducive to an easy life but Toynbee believes that history illustrates the opposite, namely, that adversity is a greater challenge to creativeness than ease. But some challenges have proved too great for men to respond effectively to them. "The most stimulating challenge is to be found in a mean between a deficiency of severity and an excess of it," [36] for "a deficient challenge may fail to stimulate the challenged party at all, while an excessive challenge may break his spirit." [37] The history of civilizations is marked by a rhythmical pattern in which the civilization is carried from challenge to response to further challenge and a new response. If the responses are adequate to the challenges the civilization grows and develops, if they are inadequate the civilization declines and dies.

In his view of society Toynbee rejects both the notion that society is nothing but "an aggregate of atomic individuals" and that "society is a perfect and intelligible whole" in which the individual is simply a part.[38] Rather, he insists, and correctly it seems to me, that

society is . . . a system of relationships between human beings who are not only individuals but are also social animals in the sense that they could not exist at all without being in this relationship to one another. A society, we may say, is a product of the relations between individuals, and these relations of theirs arise from the coincidence of their individual fields of action. This coincidence combines the individual fields into a common ground, and this common ground is what we call a society.[39]

It follows from this conception of society that there can be no social action apart from individual action. Society is not an entity with a mind and will of its own but a field of action and mutual relationships and, if this conception of society is correct, the *origin* of all action is action by individuals. The character of any given society will depend upon the character of the thought and actions of the individuals composing it. This would seem a self-evident truth were it not for the fact that many persons today are under the illusion that society somehow operates independently of the thoughts and actions of the individuals who compose it.

All acts of social creation are the work either of individual creators or, at most, creative minorities; and at each successive advance the great majority of the members of the society are left behind. If we glance at the great religious organizations extant in the world today, Christian, Islamic, and Hindu, we shall find that the great bulk of their nominal adherents, however exalted the creeds to which they profess lip-service, still live in a mental atmosphere which, so far as religion is concerned, is not far removed from a simple paganism. It is the same with the recent achievements of our material civilization. Our Western scientific knowledge and our technique for turning it to account is perilously esoteric.[40]

A growing, dynamic, and healthy civilization is one in which there are a number of creative individual personalities who are able to break through the inertia of the mass and inspire creative action. But unless the mass of individuals are disposed to follow their lead their individual victory in breaking through "the cake of custom" will end in social defeat. How can the mass be disposed to follow the leadership of the creative minority? Toynbee answers: by inspiration and imitation.

The direct kindling of creative energy from soul to soul is no doubt the ideal way, but to rely upon it exclusively is a counsel of perfection. The problem of bringing the uncreative rank and file into line with the creative pioneers cannot be solved in practice, on the social scale, without bringing into play the faculty of sheer mimesis—one of the less exalted faculties of human nature, which has more in it of drill than of inspiration.[41]

Social growth like individual growth occurs when the response to a challenge is not only adequate to the challenge but prepares the respondent for new challenges. Just as individuals have found it necessary to withdraw temporarily from the world in contemplation in order to find the resources with which they might return to the world to overcome the obstacles which confront them there, so societies undergo the same process of withdrawal and return. Disillusionment and despair may plunge individuals and societies into depths from which they can never climb again but they may be the occasion for a temporary withdrawal and contemplation that may end in transfiguration and the renewal of life.

Every civilization, Toynbee observes, has had its Time of Troubles. Some societies have been crushed in such times, others have tapped spiritual resources sufficient to meet the challenge and in the very act of struggle have achieved a renaissance, others going down to defeat have given birth to new and vigorous civilizations. Civilizations, Toynbee declares, are not murdered, they commit suicide. The English poet, Meredith, he says "divined with sure intuition" the cause of breakdowns in civilization when he wrote:

> In tragic life, God wot,
> No villain need be! Passions spin the plot:
> We are betrayed by what is false within.[42]

It is not the Challenges from without that lead to breakdowns and disintegration but the inadequacy of the Responses from within. It is not the external obstacles which constitute the most formidable barrier but the internal. Unless we can resolve the internal discord that threatens our existence we cannot successfully impose order on the outside. "Whence come wars and whence come fightings among you? come they not hence, even of your pleasures that war in your members?" (Jas. 4:1). We are easily betrayed into the idolization of an ephemeral self, an ephemeral institution, or an ephemeral technique, and, with such idolization of that which is temporal, relative and particular we lose our capacity for creativity.

At the time of the breakdown of civilization there are three classes: the Dominant Minority, the Internal Proletariat and the External Proletariat. The Dominant Minority comes into being when the creative minority that existed at the birth of a civilization fails to work out an effective response to a given challenge, fails as a consequence to evoke mimesis from the mass of the people by persuasion and attempts to hold by force a position of leadership and privilege which it no longer merits. They endeavor to make up for their spiritual weakness by physical strength. Toynbee conceives of the proletariat as "an element or group in a community which has no 'stake' in that community beyond the fact of its physical existence." [43] It is *in* but not *of* the society. Or, as Toynbee says in another place, "The true hallmark of the proletarian is neither poverty nor humble birth but a consciousness—and the resentment which this consciousness inspires—of being disinherited from his ancestral place in Society and being unwanted in a community which is his rightful home; and this subjective proletarianism is not incompatible with the possession of material assets." [44] He conceives of the proletariat as being of two kinds: the internal and the external. The Internal Proletariat consists of those persons who were once a part of the civilization but are now compelled to submit to the Dominant Minority by force or threat of force. As examples of such a proletariat, Toynbee mentions the unemployed in capitalistic countries, the share-croppers in the American South and Middle West, the Europeans who for several years were under Nazi domination. The External Proletariat is composed of persons, forcibly in most instances, brought from alien civilizations to live in another civilization. Examples of such a proletariat are the barbarians living on the fringes of the Roman Empire, the Negroes in the United States, and the American Indians. With the progressive disintegration of civilization and the further estrangement of the proletariat from the dominant minority, that minority seeks to maintain its position by resorting more and more to violence. The proletariat, especially the internal proletariat, is tempted to counter "injustice with resentment, fear with hate, and violence with violence" [45] but to the extent that they yield to this temptation they bring disaster upon themselves.

The schism in the body social, however, is only a reflection of the schism in the soul. "The schism in the body social . . . is a collective experience and therefore superficial. Its significance lies in its being the outward and visible sign of an inward and spiritual rift." [46] As an alternative to creativity in societies that are disintegrating individuals are tempted to adopt one of two attitudes: an attitude of abandon or an attitude of self-control. One is a passive, the other an active, reaction to a consciousness of moral defeat.

Both of them are attempts at self-expression. The passive attempt consists in an *abandon* in which the soul "lets itself go" in the belief that, by giving free rein to its own spontaneous appetites and aversions, it will be "living according to nature" and will automatically receive back from that mysterious goddess the precious gift of creativity which it has been conscious of losing. The active alternative is an effort at self-control in which the soul "takes itself in hand" and seeks to discipline its "natural passions" in the opposite belief that nature is the bane of creativity and not its source and that to "gain mastery over nature" is the only way of recovering the lost creative faculty.[47]

In the realm of feeling the passive response leads to a "sense of drift," the active response to "a sense of sin." To the man imbued with the "sense of drift," the Power which rules the world appears now as Chance, now as Necessity but the two notions are "merely different facets of one identical illusion."

For example, the disorderly motion of the rudderless ship, which stands in Plato's eyes for the chaos of a Universe abandoned by God, can be recognized by a mind endowed with the necessary knowledge of dynamics and physics, as a perfect illustration of the orderly behaviour of waves and currents in the media of wind and water. When the human soul adrift apprehends that the force baffling it is not simply a negation of the soul's own will but is a thing in itself, then the countenance of the invisible goddess changes from the subjective or negative aspect in which she is known as Necessity—but this without any corresponding change in the essential nature of the goddess or in the predicament of her victims.[48]

The "sense of drift" has the effect of an opiate since it encourages acquiescence in evil by assuring the individual that the evil lies in "circumstances beyond the victim's control." The "sense of sin," on the other hand, "has the effect of a stimulus because it tells the sinner that the evil is not external after all but is within him and is therefore subject to his will— if only he wills to carry out God's purpose and to render himself accessible to God's grace."[49]

Corresponding to these two ways of personal feeling are two ways of social feeling. The passive response Toynbee characterizes as "a sense of promiscuity." It manifests itself in every sphere of social life: in manners and customs, in language and literature, in the arts and in religion. It is marked by the progressive deterioration of style and form and the substitution of a standardized style. In customs and manners it is marked by vulgarity and the borrowing of customs and manner from the proletariat. It is the inversion of mimesis. In the sphere of religion it is manifested in "the syncretism or amalgamation of rites, cults and faiths." [50]

The active response to the loss of "style" is the adoption of "another style which partakes of what is universal and eternal." [51] It is the awakening of a consciousness of unity, of a law that is universal and irresistible and of a God who is unique and omnipotent. Frequently, however, civilizations that have made this response emphasize either the law at the expense of God or God at the expense of the law.

## Alternative Ways of Life

TOYNBEE declares that there are four typical kinds of responses that may be made to challenging circumstances, four ways of life that present themselves as possibilities to a society that is disintegrating. These are: Archaism, Futurism, Detachment, and Transfiguration. The first two are violent kinds of responses, the latter two are gentle types.

Both Archaism and Futurism seek to escape from the Time of Troubles by concentrating attention upon either the past (archaism) or the future (futurism). Both "are alternative attempts to substitute a mere transfer in the time-dimension for that transfer of the field of action from one spiritual plane to another which is characteristic of growth." Both are in pursuit of a Utopia which can be reached without any change in the spiritual life of the individual; "the soul proposes to perform what is required of it by making its move from the present disintegrating state of society to a goal which is simply the same society as it may once have been in the past or as it

may sometimes come to be in the future." [52] Just as archaism
is "a reversion from the mimesis of contemporary creative
personalities to a mimesis of the ancestors of the tribe" so
futurism is "a repudiation of the mimesis of anybody." [53] In
the literal sense of the word Utopia means Nowhere, and because archaism and futurism are in search of a Utopia that is
literally nowhere both are doomed to defeat as effective responses to challenging circumstances. For both seek to change
by violence that which can only be changed by spiritual transformation or rebirth. Since that is an impossibility both are
destined to end in a violence that is both self-defeating and
disastrous.

The gentle responses, Detachment and Transfiguration,
"differ from both futurism and archaism in substituting a
genuine change in spiritual clime, and not a mere transfer in
the time-dimension. The kingdoms that are their respective
goals are both of them 'otherworldly' in the sense that neither
of them is an imaginary past or future state of mundane existence. This common 'otherworldliness,' however, is their only
point of resemblance; in every other respect they present a
contrast to each other." [54] The goal of detachment is an asylum; it seeks to escape from the Time of Troubles by detachment from the world, by retreat into another world that is
more "real" than this world. It finds classic expression in
Stoicism and Epicureanism, in Buddhism and in the Hindu
conception of Nirvana. It is a withdrawal from the world
"according to plan rather than a pilgrimage inspired by
faith." [55] To escape from the world is the principal objective of
detachment, what one does after one has "escaped" is not of
primary importance. The individual seeking asylum by way
of detachment from the world and its Time of Troubles is
impelled not by "a pull of desire" but by "a push of aversion."
Nevertheless, it involves a spiritual discipline that is a more
realistic response to the Time of Troubles than either archaism
or futurism for it recognizes that the sickness of society cannot
be cured by "any less radical remedy than a change in the
spiritual clime or dimension." But withdrawal from the world
cannot solve the problems with which the world is beset unless
there is a return to the world. The response of Detachment is a

withdrawal only, it neither contemplates nor desires to return to the world. Hence as an effective response to the challenges with which a disintegrating society is faced, it is, like archaism and futurism, doomed to failure. Detachment represents a formidable intellectual and moral achievement but it achieves its "serenity" by giving up the good passions as well as the evil. Neither pity nor love can be allowed to disturb the calm won by way of detachment from the world. As the Stoic philosopher Seneca wrote:

> Pity is a mental illness induced by the spectacle of other people's miseries, or alternatively it may be defined as an infection of low spirits caught from other people's troubles when the patient believes that those troubles are undeserved. The sage does not succumb to such-like mental diseases.[56]

Such an attitude, Toynbee says, is "logically inevitable" if one pursues the way of detachment but it soon demonstrates itself to be "morally intolerable."

There is only one kind of response, he declares, that is an effective response to challenge and that is Transfiguration. Like the way of Detachment the way of Transfiguration is "otherworldly." It withdraws from this world and its Time of Troubles in contemplation of a more real world, the Kingdom of God, but it withdraws only to return transfigured in the image of the God with whom it seeks communion. It returns with renewed vitality to take up the tasks with which the world is confronted and with the assurance of the help of God in meeting the challenge. Many, Toynbee says, will scoff at this suggestion but it is well to remember that "God hath chosen the foolish things of this World to confound the wise; and God hath chosen the weak things of the World to confound the things which are mighty." [57] In Christ Crucified, he declares, we find the way of Transfiguration most perfectly exemplified. Popularly but erroneously Christianity is sometimes conceived as a form of escapism but unlike the way of detachment, which *is* a form of escapism, the way of Christ is a way through evil, pain and suffering to goodness and happiness. The Kingdom of God is attained not by way of contemplation alone but by way of the Cross, we withdraw to

commune with God only to return to do battle with the forces
of evil in the world and we meet inevitably what appears to be
ultimate defeat (death) but what can be passage to eternal life.
The Kingdom of God is not of this world but neither is it a
dream of the future but rather "a spiritual reality interpene-
trating the present." [58] The love which the way of detachment
suppresses along with the evil passions finds an active role in
Christianity, for it is the medium through which we recognize
God in Christ and are led by way of the Cross to the Kingdom
of God. Only through the transfiguration of human nature,
only through the recovery of the image of God in man, only
by spiritual transformation can the world be transformed.
Whether it will or not depends upon the grace of God and our
willingness to place ourselves in a position accessible to that
grace.

Western civilization is in its Time of Troubles. It is beset
on all sides by challenges which threaten to destroy it. It is the
kind of response which we make to those challenges, however,
rather than the challenges themselves, which will determine
the outcome.

## CHAPTER 19

# Christianity and the Social Order

IT HAS been suggested throughout these pages that the basic insights of the Christian faith provide the best insights we have into the nature of man and of the crisis in which we find ourselves. That crisis is the culmination of modern man's progressive attempt to deny the existence of a transcendent or spiritual reality and of his progressive failure to find meaning and salvation in some wholly immanent conception of reality. Modern man's worship of the Class, the Race, or the State has only further alienated him from reality, plunged him deeper into despair and impelled him further along the road to destruction and annihilation. Only through a return to faith in God, as God revealed Himself to man in Jesus Christ, can modern man and his society find redemption from the tyranny of evil.

But immediately it is suggested that spiritual health and sanity lies in a return to Christianity someone retorts that this suggestion, even if desirable, is an impossibility—for, he says, "you can't turn the clock back." It is an impossibility, of course, to go back in time and no suggestion is made here that we should attempt that impossibility. It is possible, fortunately, to retrace one's steps spiritually, to begin again in contrition from a new point, and that is the proposal which is made here. C. S. Lewis suggests that you can turn the clock back in this sense and that when the hands point to the wrong time it is a sensible thing to do. Sometimes the only way to go forward is to go backward and begin again. The most sensible way to go forward is to start from the right place and to follow the right path. If we have turned down the wrong path the common sense thing to do is to retrace our steps, to begin again, and to take this time the path which we by-passed on our original journey. C. S. Lewis says: "We all want progress. But progress means getting nearer to the place you want to be. And if you've taken a wrong turning, then to go forward does *not* get you any nearer. If you're on the wrong road, progress means doing an about-turn and walking back to the right road; and in that case the man who turns back soonest is the most progressive man. We've all seen this at our jobs, haven't we? When I have started a bit of work the wrong way, the sooner I admit this and go back and start over again, the faster I shall get on. There's nothing progressive about being pig-headed and refusing to admit a mistake. And I think if you look at the present state of the world, it's pretty plain that humanity has been making some big mistake. We're on the wrong road. And if that is so, we must go back. Going *back* is the quickest way on." [1]

I am not suggesting, as some may suppose, that we go back to the Middle Ages in any sense except a spiritual one. Even if we could, which we cannot, we should not make spiritual, intellectual, or social progress by blindly copying the social institutions or patterns of life of another age. Social institutions and patterns of life which are informed by the same spirit may, indeed, closely resemble one another but they will never be identical. A highly industrialized, urban society will require very different institutions from a society that is essentially agrarian but while the institutions of society may and must change the *spirit* and *principles* which inform them ought always to be the same. I am suggesting that we go back to the Middle Ages only in the sense that we go back in spirit to a society that, intellectually and spiritually, was God-centered rather than man-centered. We will not in this way eliminate our problems but we will have the spiritual and intellectual resources with which better to understand those problems and to grapple with them—not alone, but with the help of God.

If, as I believe, and the evidence of history seems to confirm, human nature is everywhere and at all times the same, then the problems encountered by human beings have been and will be, as long as man inhabits the earth, essentially the same in spirit, if not always in form. The *principles* in terms of which we search for proximate solutions to our problems ought, then, to be the same for all times and for all peoples. These principles are not modern, medieval, or ancient—they are either true or false. If the principles in terms of which men can find personal happiness and social justice were discovered in ancient or in medieval times, then those principles are just as valid for people today as they were at the time they were first formulated. The important thing is not when the principles were discovered but whether they are truly adequate to men's needs. Truth, in short, is timeless. We labor in the twentieth century, however, under the curious illusion that originality is more highly to be prized than truth. The highest praise we can pay to a work of art, a work of scholarship, or a theory is to say that it is "highly original." Confronted with a theory or an idea we are inclined to ask: is it modern? is it new? is it progressive? Rarely do we ask the most important question of all, namely, is it true? A man whose ideas are so "original" that they resemble those of no other human being, we generally regard as insane. The only genuine test of an idea or of a theory is not its modernity nor its originality but its truthfulness, i.e., its correspondence to reality. The principles that, in my opinion, most closely correspond to reality, the principles that ought to animate our personal and social lives, are those principles that were discovered and formulated by the Jewish prophets, the Greek philosophers, especially Plato and Aristotle, and the Christian religion as exemplified in the teachings of St. Augustine and St. Thomas Aquinas.[2]

If a principle or an idea is true it is true for all times and for all peoples; if it is not true for all times it is not true at any time. The contention, frequently encountered today, that truth is relative to particular times and to particular peoples is a denial of the conception of truth itself, for to speak of the relativity of truth is to speak a contradiction. Human conceptions of the truth may and do vary because men are not infallible or omniscient and their conception of the truth will always be somewhat perverted by their own self-interest and self-centeredness. But while we acknowledge the relativity, in this sense, of human judgments concerning the truth it does not and need not follow that truth itself is relative. As a matter of fact, it is only by positing a truth which is absolute, eternal, and universal that we can say that particular individual judgments concerning that truth are relative, partial, and particular. Our confusion on this subject arises from a failure to distinguish between the truth itself and the truth as manifested in the particular theories of particular individuals. Because individual conceptions of the truth have been and always will be relative, partial and particular it does not logically follow that all truth is relative but rather, that all individuals are fallible. The fallibility of individual judgments, moreover, does not mean that all individual judgments concerning the truth are equally valid for there are degrees of fallibility and degrees of truth. Some individual conceptions of the truth will be closer to the absolute truth than others although no single individual will ever know the whole and complete truth. There is no logical or necessary connection, as some mistakenly suppose, between a belief in absolute truth and a belief in personal infallibility. And it does not logically follow that because a person believes that he knows a portion of the truth which he shares with others that he believes that everyone should be coerced into the acceptance of that truth. That a conscientious devotion to truth and justice leads inevitably to dogmatic despotism or to an espousal of personal infallibility, seems to me, not only illogical but unnecessarily cynical. As a matter of fact, there is a much closer relationship in practice between the conception of "the relativity of truth" and the assertion of personal infallibility. For if all "truth" is relative then "my" truth is just as "true" as any one else's. If there is no absolute truth in terms of which "my truth" can be tested and judged there is no basis for contending that "my truth" represents a partial, imperfect, or fallible judgment. Unless we are conscious of our own intellectual and spiritual limitations, unless we are conscious of the way in which our passions betray our most virtuous motives and our best thought, we cannot approach the problem of truth and of justice with that humility and contrition that is the beginning of wisdom. The contention, which we encounter frequently today, that there is no truth at all because all individual judgments are fallible is a confession not of humility but of despair, not of contrition but of loss of faith.

It is my contention that the principles and doctrines of Christianity correspond to the reality of the situation in which we find ourselves, they explain better than any rival religion or philosophy both our individual and social experiences, and if grasped with faith hold out the best hope man has for individual and social redemption. Merging the insights of the ancient Hebrew prophets with those of the great Hellenic philosophers Christianity crowns that wisdom with the promise of redemption through self-sacrifice and suffering. Of all the so-called "higher religions" of the world, with which it shares many truths, Christianity is the most complete and perfect revelation we know of the nature of God and of God's will for man. This is not the place, however, to explain in detail the doctrines of Christianity nor to argue in behalf of their truthfulness but there are many books available to those who wish to pursue that question.[3]

It is impossible to survey here all of the Christian answers that have been given throughout the centuries or even in recent decades to the problem of the relationship of Christianity to the social order. Instead we shall examine briefly three types of answers which are more or less representative of Christian thought today. The agreement among Christians is greater than this analysis may indicate or than many of the critics of Christianity realize, but the division among them is, nevertheless, a real division and no less scandalous to Christians than to their detractors. Probably the three most important divisions of thought within Christianity today are represented by liberal Protestantism, Protestant Neo-Orthodoxy, and Roman Catholicism. Anglicanism might be mentioned as a fourth form of Christianity which seeks to steer a middle course between Protestantism, on the one hand, and Roman Catholicism on the other. In its Anglo-Catholic expression it is closer to Roman Catholicism but not identical with it.

## Liberal Protestantism

LIBERAL Protestantism is primarily an American movement that flourished in the United States between 1865 and 1930 and reached its climax in the early decades of the twentieth century.[4] In recent years it has been placed more and more on the defensive but still has many zealous adherents, if no longer among the more prominent Protestant theologians, then among many of the rank and file of Protestant churches and especially among those engaged in church-related social and political activities. It has had many exponents among Christian writers and theologians but none, perhaps, more able, representative, and influential than Walter Rauschenbusch. His first important work *Christianity and the Social Crisis* was published in 1907. It was followed by a work entitled *Christianizing the Social Order* (1912) and still later by *A Theology for the Social Gospel* (1917).

Liberal Protestantism emphasizes the importance of Christianity as an ethical system and insists that the gospel or "good news" brought to men by Jesus Christ was a new view of life which would lead to the creation of a new and perfect society upon earth. According to Rauschenbusch:

The higher spiritual insight of Jesus reverted to the earlier and nobler prophetic view that the future was to grow out of the present by divine help . . . Jesus had the scientific insight which comes to most men only by training, but to the elect few by divine gift. He grasped the substance of that law of organic development in nature and history which our own day at last has begun to elaborate systematically . . . his end was not the new soul, but the new society; not man, but Man.[5]

Jesus, according to this view, was primarily a great prophet and teacher and a noble example of humanity at its best. His life alone is sufficient inspiration to awaken in us both the desire and the capacity to emulate his achievements. Linking the nineteenth-century "scientific" evolutionary gospel of progress with the "social gospel" of the New Testament, liberal Protestantism affirms the inevitability of progress toward political and social utopia which it identifies as the Kingdom of God. This inevitable progress is conceived not only as "natural" but as "divine," impelled not only by the laws of Nature and of History but by the will of God.

It was the social conditions that followed in the wake of industrial capitalism that especially aroused Rauschenbusch's indignation and it seemed to him that the greatest service Christianity could render man was the awakening of a social conscience. It was not the individual who stood so much in need of redemption as it was society. Capitalism in all of its aspects represented to Rauschenbusch, all that was evil in the world. It was neither democratic, American, nor Christian. "Competition as a principle," he declared, "is a denial of fraternity" and monopoly an enemy of democracy.[6] "In business the autocratic principle is still in full possession, unshaken and unterrified, with its flag flying from every battlement. Business is the last entrenchment of autocracy, and wherever democracy is being beaten back, the sally is made from that citadel." [7] Capitalism, he declared, is motivated by calculated dishonesty and irresponsible selfishness. Its business practices involve the adulteration of products, the giving of short weight, and the advertisement of spurious claims. Profit is a form of tribute which the strong demand from the weak and private property is simply a form of exploitation. "A condition in which one-fourth of the race holds all the opportunities of livelihood in its arbitrary control, and the other three-fourths are without property, without access to the earth, and without an assured means of even working for a living, is neither American nor Christian. Property is a means of grace, and a good job is another." [8] The captains of industry and of commerce seemed to Rauschenbusch, if not the incarnation of evil, at least the most tangible enemies of mankind. "We can at least refrain from perpetuating and increasing the handicap of the feebler of such enormous inequalities of property as now we have. . . . They are the institutionalized denial of the fundamental truths of our religion, and Democracy is the archangel whom God has sent to set his blazing foot on these icebergs of human pride and melt them down." [9]

Rauschenbusch proposed to substitute for capitalism a just society that would be socialistic in character. He would begin with the nationalization of natural resources. He did not advocate revolution but believed that such a society could be ushered in, and would be established in time, by evolutionary, peaceful means. In substance his social philosophy was very similar to that of the revisionist socialists, like Bernstein, whom we considered in an earlier chapter. He looked to labor as "the most modern of all classes, the product of today, the creator of tomorrow, the banner bearer of destiny" to accomplish this task.[10] And this society would be the Kingdom of God of whose coming Christ had foretold. Only man's inadequate conception of this Kingdom has impeded its realization until now. Now that we know what the Kingdom foretold by Christ "really" is, that ideal will release sufficient moral energy to achieve it with the assistance both of nature and of history.

The Kingdom of God is Democracy and the "social gospel" is nothing more nor less than "the democratic spirit."

The social movement is the most important ethical and spiritual movement in the modern world, and the social gospel is the response of the Christian consciousness to it. Therefore it had to be. The social gospel registers the fact that for the first time in history the spirit of Christianity has had a chance to form a working partnership with real social and psychological science. It is the religious reaction on the historic advent of democracy. It seeks to put the democratic spirit, which the Church inherited from Jesus and the prophets, once more in control of the institutions and teachings of the Church.[11]

Science and technology provide the means and self-sacrificing love, inspired by the example of Jesus, the motive power for the achievement of this Kingdom.

This conception of the Kingdom of God as a utopia to be established on earth as the result of an evolutionary historical process required a modification, if not an outright rejection, of the orthodox, traditional doctrines of Christian theology. But, in any case, "The social gospel," Rauschenbusch wrote, "is not primarily interested in metaphysical questions" and, as a consequence, he reaches the conclusion that, in doctrinal matters, "safety lies in vagueness." [12] Thus it is difficult to say exactly what he did believe theologically. It is easier to say what he did not believe. He did not accept the orthodox conception of the divinity of Christ although he continued to speak of the divinity of Jesus's "inheritance" or "endowment." He speaks of Jesus as being primarily "a real personality who could set a great historical process in motion." [13]

God he conceives of, not as a transcendent Being, but as "immanent in humanity" and prefers this conception of God to the older, traditional conception because it is more "democratic."[14] In any case since "our consciousness of God" is simply "the spiritual counterpart of our social consciousness"[15] the attributes of God will be no more than those which we, in our social consciousness, ascribe to him. God, in short, does not exist independently of our social consciousness of his existence.

He rejects the doctrine of original sin partly because "The social gospel is above all things practical" and "it would have no motive to be interested in a doctrine which . . . concentrates attention on a past event which no effort of ours can influence."[16] The only evil worthy of our attention is the evil we can cure by our own efforts. Sin is essentially selfishness or unsocial thought and behavior and its cure consists in the stimulation of social awareness and a social conscience. Sin is lodged primarily in "social customs and institutions and is absorbed by the individual from his social group."[17] Hence, it is the reformation of social institutions that is the primary means of eradicating sinful behavior. Rauschenbusch rejects the idea of anything daemonic in the world as a superstition. Likewise, he rejects the orthodox conceptions of Heaven and Hell. Baptism is not a sacrament in the orthodox sense "but an act of dedication to a religious and social movement."[18]

In essence liberal Protestantism is closer to the deism of the Enlightenment than it is to orthodox Christianity. Rauschenbusch declares that "it was the blessed skepticism of the age of Enlightenment and the dawn of modern science which saved humanity from the furies of a theology which had gone wrong."[19] The Church, for Rauschenbusch, is primarily an institution for bringing "social forces to bear on evil" and it is characterized by "a collective will set on righteousness."[20] The social gospel is liberalism of the idealistic, nineteenth-century variety infused with religious fervor. Rauschenbusch summarizes his hope in these words:

Scatter through all classes and professions a large number of men and women whose eyes have had a vision of a true human society

and who have faith in it and courage to stand against anything that
contradicts it, and public opinion will have a new swiftness and
tenacity in judging on right and wrong. . . . It takes so long to
"work up public sentiment," and even then it stops boiling as fast
as a kettle of water taken off the fire. There are so many Christian
people and such feeble sentiment on public wrongs. It is not because
people are not good enough, but because their goodness has not
been directed and educated in this direction. The multiplication of
socially enlightened Christians will serve the body of society much
as a physical organism would be served if a complete and effective
system of ganglia should be distributed where few of them existed.
The social body needs moral innervation; and the spread of men
who combine religious faith, moral enthusiasm, and economic information, and apply the combined result to public morality, promises to create a moral sensitiveness never yet known.[21]

There has been, he thinks, "during the last hundred years" an
"unprecedented leap forward" in the intellectual life of man
and if individually we are not more gifted than our grand-
fathers, "collectively we have wrought out more epoch-making
discoveries and inventions in one century than the whole race
in the untold centuries that have gone before. If the twentieth
century could do for us in the control of social forces what the
nineteenth did for us in the control of natural forces, our
grandchildren would live in a society that would be justified
in regarding our present social life as semi-barbarous." [22] The
achievements of science and technology in enabling us to control the forces of nature point, he believes, to "the immense
latent perfectibility in human nature." [23]

For liberal Protestantism social and political issues are relatively simple and generally present themselves in terms of
easily discernible alternatives. For men like Walter Rauschenbusch and many others the principal problem confronting
mankind in the present age is economic in character and the
principal evil is the inequitable distribution of wealth and
property with its attendant poverty and exploitation. Capitalism is bad, socialism is good; capitalism is un-Christian, socialism is Christian. For other liberal Protestants the principal
issue confronting mankind today is the issue of war or peace.
War is bad, peace is good. The true Christian must be a

pacifist. Some link this pacifism with socialism, others believe that it is an end in itself.[24]

Many Christians, however, find it difficult intellectually and spiritually to accept the dichotomous division of social and political issues and programs into the easily discernible good and evil. Many Christians are impressed with the ambiguous character of many of the problems with which we are confronted socially and politically, they see good mixed with evil and evil mixed with good. They are impressed not only with the mixture of good and evil in social programs and systems but with the mixture of good and evil in individual thought and behavior and especially with the ambiguous character of their own individual motivations. They find it difficult, if not impossible, to attribute righteousness to one group of people, class, nation, political party, or social program and unrighteousness to other groups of people, classes, nations, political parties, or social programs. It was this sense of the ambiguity of all thoughts and undertakings that motivated, at least in part, a reaction to liberal Protestantism in the last two decades of the present century. That reaction is generally associated with a movement of thought known as Protestant Neo-Orthodoxy.

## Protestant Neo-Orthodoxy

PROTESTANT Neo-Orthodoxy is represented on the European continent by theologians like Karl Barth and Emil Brunner [25] and in the United States by Reinhold Niebuhr. There are significant differences of emphasis in the theologies of these three men but we shall confine our attention here to the thought of Niebuhr. Liberal Protestantism, like the secular liberalism with which it is associated, and, indeed, like almost all modern theories of man and of society, embodies a false optimism which must eventually, as a result of disillusionment, become despair because it is based upon a false and unrealistic conception of the nature of man and of history. Only by rediscovering the reality of the orthodox Christian conception of original sin can we adequately understand the nature of man and of history. Following the analysis of Kierkegaard, Reinhold Niebuhr describes man as "standing in the paradoxical situation of freedom and finiteness." This tension between freedom and necessity produces anxiety which is the psychological and "internal description of the state of temptation." [26] This anxiety is not itself sin but the precondition of it. Anxiety is the basis not only of sin but of human creativity.

It is not possible to make a simple separation between the creative and destructive elements in anxiety; and for that reason it is not possible to purge moral achievement of sin as easily as moralists imagine. The same action may reveal a creative effort to transcend natural limitations. And a sinful effort to give an unconditioned value to contingent and limited factors in human existence. . . .

The parent is anxious about his child and this anxiety reaches beyond the grave. Is the effort of the parent to provide for the future of the child creative or destructive? Obviously it is both. It is, on the one hand, an effort to achieve the perfection of love by transcending the limits of finiteness and anticipating the needs of the child beyond the death of the parent. On the other hand, as almost every last will and testament reveals . . . it reveals parental will-to-power reaching beyond the grave and seeking to defy death's annulment of parental authority.

The statesman is anxious about the order and security of the nation. But he cannot express this anxiety without an admixture of anxiety about his prestige as a ruler and without assuming unduly that only the kind of order and security which he establishes is adequate for the nation's health. The philosopher is anxious to arrive at the truth; but he is also anxious to prove that his particular truth is the truth. . . .

Anxiety about perfection and about insecurity are thus inexorably bound together in human actions and the errors which are made in the search for perfection are never due merely to the ignorance of not knowing the limits of conditioned values. They always exhibit some tendency of the agent to hide his own limits, which he knows only too well. Obviously the basic source of temptation is, therefore, not the inertia of "matter" or "nature" against the larger and more inclusive ends which reason envisages. It resides in the inclination of man, either to deny the contingent character of his existence (in pride and self-love) or to escape from his freedom (in sensuality). . . .

Anxiety, as a permanent concomitant of freedom, is thus both the source of creativity and a temptation to sin. . . . The ambition of man to be something is always partly prompted by the fear of meaninglessness which threatens him by reason of the contingent character of his existence. His creativity is therefore always corrupted by some effort to overcome contingency by raising precisely what is contingent to absolute and unlimited dimensions. This effort, though universal, cannot be regarded as normative. It is always destructive.[27]

Every thought and action of man, Reinhold Niebuhr contends, is involved in sin and every attempt at creative achievement will be marred inevitably by the corrupting influence of human pride. Sin is not primarily sensuality, as many Christians believe, but pride or self-love. "Every man," Bertrand Russell once observed, "would like to be God if it were possible; some few find it difficult to admit the impossibility." [28] Pride manifests itself in a variety of forms among different individuals and groups but basically and universally it is an expression of rebellion against God, an assertion of the self-sufficiency of man and a denial of his dependency and the contingent character of his life. There is a pride of power, of knowledge, and of virtue. The will-to-power is an attempt to escape from that insecurity of life which expresses itself psychologically in fear. All pride is a form of self-deception as we attempt by our displays of power, knowledge, or virtue not only to convince others of our own importance but to convince ourselves and to hide from ourselves the insecurity which we are reluctant to acknowledge.

The sinful self needs these deceptions because it cannot pursue its own determinate ends without paying tribute to the truth. This truth, which the self, even in its sin, never wholly obscures, is that the self, as finite and determinate, does not deserve unconditioned devotion. But though the deceptions are needed they are never wholly convincing because the self is the only ego fully privy to the dishonesties by which it has hidden its own interests behind a façade of general interest. . . .

If others will only accept what the self cannot quite accept, the self as deceiver is given an ally against the self as deceived. All efforts to impress our fellowmen, our vanity, our display of power, or of goodness must, therefore, be regarded as revelations of the fact that

sin increases the insecurity of the self by veiling its weaknesses with
veils which may be torn aside. . . . Thus sin compounds the insecurity of nature with a fresh insecurity of spirit.[29]

Sin is "original" in the sense that it is an inherited corruption
but, nevertheless, not a part of man's essential nature. According to Niebuhr:

Sin is natural for man in the sense that it is universal but not in
the sense that it is necessary. . . . Sin is to be regarded as neither
a necessity of man's nature nor yet as a pure caprice of his will. It
proceeds rather from a defect of the will, for which reason it is not
completely deliberate; but since it is the will in which the defect is
found, and the will presupposes freedom the defect cannot be attributed to a taint in man's nature.[30]

However paradoxical it is nevertheless true that sin is inevitable and that man is responsible for his sins because "it is
within and by his freedom that man sins." [31]
    Modern culture, Niebuhr declares, has seen only the crea-
tive possibilities of human freedom and it has ignored or neglected the destructive elements that are involved in every
expression of freedom. It has falsely believed that growth in
human freedom is inevitable and that freedom is identical
with virtue. Since "modern rationalism" starts from the assumption that "the evil in human nature is the consequence
of natural finiteness and physical impulses" it naturally inclines "to the conclusion that the development of rational
capacities is in itself, a process of gradual emancipation from
evil." [32]

The assumption of rationalists in the past centuries has been that
either education or the equalization of economic interests would
finally fashion the mind into a perfect instrument of universal and
absolute knowledge, and would ultimately destroy social friction by
eliminating the partial perspectives which prompt men to assess
social issues in conflicting terms. But this assumption fails to recognize that the most intelligent and disinterested person can never
escape his fate as a child of nature and finitude. The same intelligence
which provides universal rather than partial perspectives must inevitably also operate to give partial perspectives the authority of
the absolute. Thus even the most refined spiritual achievements of

humans can never result in an unqualified synthesis of human hopes and aspirations. At some point they will always accentuate social conflict by making men more stubborn in the defense of their interests, under the illusion that their interests represent universal values.[33]

In its most naive form, modern rationalism believes that in the applications of the "methods of Science" to the problems of political and social order it can finally and completely conquer the forces of evil in the world.

The identification of socialism or of pacifism with Christianity, such as we saw in the case of liberal Protestantism, is an example of how men are tempted to convert a partial and particular truth into a complete and absolute truth and to ignore the moral weaknesses in themselves in their condemnation of the unrighteousness of others. Says Niebuhr:

Modern technical society is desperately in need of the socialization of economic power in order that it may minimize the injustices which result inevitably from endowing the anarchic ego with unlimited power over other life. That the proponents of this necessary social change should confuse the issues by falsely claiming to be the instruments of a perfect society and of a universal culture is itself one of those manifestations of the fateful human tendency to confuse the immediate and the ultimate. Radical theories have no understanding for this perennial problem of the human spirit; but radical social strategy offers abundant proof of its universality.[34]

The Kingdom of God, Niebuhr declares, cannot be identified with any human institution or social program. And he believes that the Roman Catholics have erred in identifying it, even in part, with the Church as much as the liberal Protestants have erred in another direction in identifying it with a particular kind of social utopia. There is no possibility of achieving "a transcendent perfection within history." [35] It is a "perversion of Christian faith," he believes, to expect "the complete realization of the kingdom of perfect righteousness in history." [36] For so long as there is human freedom there will remain the possibility of evil. Christianity does not remove the tensions of history but only serves to make them meaningful.

. . . the New Testament faith is radically different from Old Testament messianism. That fact is signified by the rejection, by those who expect the Messiah, of a Messiah who died upon a Cross. This Messiah, whom the church accepts as the true Messiah, does not correct the moral disbalances of history. He does not establish the triumph of the righteous over the unrighteous. The perfect love which His life and death exemplify is defeated, rather than triumphant, in the actual course of history. Thus, according to the Christian belief, history remains morally ambiguous to the end. The perfect love of Christ is both the ultimate possibility of all historic virtues and a contradiction to them. Justice remains imperfect unless it culminates in this perfect love of self-giving. But every form of historic justice contains elements which place it in contradiction to such perfect love.

For the Christian faith the enigma of life is resolved by the confidence that this same love has more than a historical dimension. This love is the revelation of a divine mercy which overcomes the contradictions of human life. Suffering innocence, which reveals the problem of moral ambiguity of history, becomes in the Christian faith the answer to the problem at the point, when it is seen as a revelation of a divine suffering which bears and overcomes the sins of the world. . . .

The Christian faith promises indeterminate renewals of life in history. But on the other hand the total historical enterprise is not progressively emancipated from evil. . . . It gives life a final meaning without promising the annullment of history's moral obscurities. Above all it holds out the hope of redemption from evil, upon the basis of a human acceptance of human finiteness and a contrite recognition of the evil in which men are involved when they seek to deny their finitude.[37]

The Kingdom of God is not a simple historical possibility waiting only upon the willingness of men to "take Christ seriously," for its coming depends not upon men but upon God. History moves to its climax, to the day of Last Judgment, not by a gradual process of organic growth in which the world becomes progressively better but by a dialectical process in which, to the very Last Day, good is engaged in the struggle with evil and both Christ and the Anti-Christ are ultimately revealed. The Kingdom of God is not of this world, yet it is relevant to every problem of the world for it is in the light of the Kingdom of God which will be established on the Last Day that our actions here and now are to be judged. Moreover, it gives meaning to a suffering that otherwise would be unmitigated and meaningless tragedy.

Liberal Protestantism in its emphasis upon Christianity as an ethical system lost sight, according to Niebuhr, of the more important truths in Christianity. For liberal Protestants the "core" of Christianity is the law that we ought to love one another, this, they say, is the gospel or "good news." But it is much more difficult to love one another than liberal Protestantism generally acknowledges. For although "we know we ought to love our neighbor as ourself, there is 'a law in our members which wars against the law that is in our mind,' so that, in fact, we love ourselves more than our neighbor." The gospel, or good news, according to Niebuhr, is not the law that we ought to love one another but rather "that there is a resource of divine mercy which is able to overcome a contradiction within our own souls, which we cannot ourselves overcome." [38] Theologically this resource is spoken of as the grace of God in Christ. Apart from the recognition of the need of grace, the law of love very rapidly degenerates into sentimentality and false piety. The denial, moreover, "that man remains a tragic creature who needs the divine mercy as much at the end as at the beginning of his moral endeavors" is really a substitution of faith in man for faith in God and in such Christianity, Christ becomes simply the "symbol of their faith in man." [39] The law of love is a principle of criticism "upon all forms of justice" rather than a law which we can fulfill completely and absolutely even with the grace of God. [40] This does not mean that it is practically ineffective for as a principle of criticism, as a standard of judgment, it "is actually a resource of justice, for it prevents the pride, self-righteousness and vindictiveness of men from corrupting their efforts at justice." [41] Pacifism seizes upon one part of the Christian ethic and attempts to convert it into the complete and absolute ethic but it is able to do this only by ignoring the ethic of Jesus in its completeness and its own involvement in sin. It underestimates the tragedy of human history and overestimates the possibility of doing God's will even when we are certain what that will is. It is not enough to tell men that they ought to love one another. Most of us know that. The difficulty is in doing it.

In a recent book entitled *The Children of Light and the Children of Darkness*, Reinhold Niebuhr has turned his attention to an analysis of political liberalism and the problems of democracy. Long sustained by liberalism, democracy, Niebuhr believes, needs "a more realistic philosophical and religious basis, not only in order to anticipate and understand the perils to which it is exposed; but also to give it a more persuasive justification." [42] As the excessively optimistic liberal conceptions of human nature and of history are shown increasingly to be false by events, there is the danger that the democratic ideal may succumb to the same disillusionment. If democracy as a form of government is to survive the rejection of liberalism as a political and social philosophy it must be based upon a more realistic conception of man's nature and destiny. This conception is contained in Christianity. The Christian conception of man, unlike the liberal conception, neither overestimates men's motives nor underestimates their potentialities. It is neither optimistic nor pessimistic and avoids the pitfalls, therefore, both of fatuous optimism and hopeless despair. In a brief formula, Niebuhr suggests that it is "Man's capacity for justice" which "makes democracy possible; but man's inclination to injustice" which "makes democracy necessary." [43]

In his analysis of some of the major problems of modern democracy Niebuhr examines the proposals made by two different types of individuals, one group whom he designates as "the children of light" and the other, as "the children of darkness." The "children of light" are "those who believe that self-interest should be brought under the discipline of a higher law"; while "the children of darkness" are "the moral cynics, who know no law beyond their will and interest." [44] For brevity's sake we will speak of the moral idealists and the moral cynics. The moral idealists are generally virtuous but foolish, while the moral cynics are generally evil but wise. The moral idealists are usually foolish because they do not know or underestimate the power of self-interest and of evil in the world; while the moral cynics are usually wise in the ways of the world because they understand very well the power and universality of self-interest.

It must be understood that the children of light are foolish not merely because they underestimate the power of self-interest among the children of darkness. They underestimate the power among themselves. The democratic world came so close to disaster not merely because it never believed that Nazism possessed the demonic fury which it avowed. Civilization refused to recognize the power of class interest in its own communities. It also spoke glibly of an international conscience; but the children of darkness skilfully set nation against nation. They were thereby enabled to despoil one nation after another, without every civilized nation coming to the defence of each. Moral cynicism had a provisional advantage over moral sentimentality. Its advantage lay not merely in its own lack of moral scruple but also in its shrewd assessment of the power of self-interest, individual and national, among the children of light, despite their moral protestations.[45]

The deficiency of both liberalism and of Marxism reveals itself in their ignorance or underestimation of the spiritual dimension in human nature, in their inability to understand man's "transcendent freedom over both the natural and the historical process in which he is involved."[46] It is the transcendence of man's spirit over the physical, natural, and historical processes which distinguishes man from the beast, it accounts for his creative possibilities and also for his destructive tendencies. It is for this reason that human nature can never be completely comprehended or explained in physical, biological, or natural terms. The hunger and sex impulses which man shares with the animal, for example, are "never purely as biological in man as in the brute."[47] They have a spiritual dimension which does not exist in the animal world. Sex in man is bound up with love and when man endeavors to make the sexual act a purely biological experience it is only by an act of perversion that he is able to do so. Only man is capable of perverting his natural impulses, animals are not. The same thing is true of man's economic desires. They are never purely biological or "natural." They, too, have a spiritual dimension.

Economic desires are never merely the expression of the hunger or the survival impulse in human life. The desires for "power and glory" are subtly compounded with the more primeval impulse. The lion's desire for food is satisfied when his maw is crammed. Man's desire for food is more easily limited than other human desires; yet the hunger impulse is subject to the endless refinements and perversions of the gourmand. Shelter and raiment have much more extensible limits than food. Man's coat is never merely a cloak for his nakedness but the badge of his vocation, or the expression of an artistic impulse, or a method of attracting the other sex, or a proof of social position. Man's house is not merely his shelter but, even more than his raiment, the expression of his personality and the symbol of his power, position and prestige. The houses and raiment of the poor remain closer to the original "natural" requirement; but it is significant that the power to transmute them into something more spiritual and symbolic is invariably exploited.[48]

Both liberalism and Marxism underestimate the human passions and rest upon the mistaken belief that man's needs are limited and more or less easily satisfied.

They also erroneously assume that the meaning of human life can be realized completely within the historical process. They fail to recognize that it is man's transcendent freedom over the historical process that distinguishes man as a spiritual creature from the beast. History is necessarily ambiguous and frustrating and it is only from the perspective of eternity that these ambiguities and frustrations become meaningful. "The individual whose freedom over natural process makes history possible, and whose freedom over history creates indeterminate new possibilities in it, has a final pinnacle of freedom where he is able to ask questions about the meaning of life which call the meaning of the historical process itself into question." Recognizing that "his own life is not completely fulfilled by its organic relation to a social process" the individual is able to transcend the frustrations of history by comprehending with faith "some ultimate fulfillment beyond his life." [49]

In their conceptions of property, Niebuhr believes, the Marxists are nearer to the truth than the liberals, but both "share a common illusion" for "neither understands property as a form of power which can be used in either its individual or its social form as an instrument of particular interest against general interest. Liberalism makes this mistake in regard to private property and Marxism makes it in regard to socialized property." [50] The Marxist illusion springs from an unrealistic conception of human nature, from the belief that corruption was first introduced into history by the establishment of the institution of private property, and also from the belief that ownership of property is the only source of economic power. The problem of economic justice cannot be solved by any simple formula, the solution is neither the retention of private property nor the establishment of socialized property but what is required is the recognition that "all property is power" and the continuous search "within the framework of democratic procedure" for the best means of preventing that power from being abused. "For democracy," Niebuhr believes, "is a method of finding proximate solutions for insoluble problems." [51] Since Niebuhr rejects, however, any conception of absolute and universal justice it is difficult to understand what the solutions are to "approximate" or how we are to determine or evaluate the degree of "proximity" attained.

In a similar manner Niebuhr analyzes, with many acute insights, the problem of democratic toleration and the problem of establishing a world community. The moral idealists, he says, conceive of the problem of establishing a world community "in purely constitutional terms because they do not recognize or understand the vital social processes which underlie constitutional forms and of which these forms are only instruments and symbols." [52] The power of government alone cannot achieve the unity these idealists desire for they underestimate the importance of tradition, cultural and ethnic differences, and the force of "collective self-consciousness."

America has produced so many pure constitutionalists in international political theory partly because American history encourages the illusion that the nation was created purely by constitutional fiat and compact. This is an illusion because the constitution was the end and not the beginning of an historical process which began with a common conflict against an imperial overlord.[53]

Liberalism generally underestimates the organic nature of political life and the importance of historical tradition and growth. The transition from national governments to world government involves not simply a transition which is different in degree but a transition which is different in kind. Because the international community as it exists today lacks a common culture and tradition, because it has "few elements of inner cohesion" it must be held together primarily by power.[54] The moral cynics are wiser in this respect than the moral idealists for they understand that national pride "stands between the conviction of nations that they ought to abridge their sovereignty and their capacity to do what they ought by a clear act of renunciation." [55] Although the "balance of power" principle advocated by the moral cynics "is in fact a kind of managed anarchy" it "is not as iniquitous as idealists would have us believe" for even in "the most perfectly organized society" there must be some "equilibrium of power." [56] But the danger in relying upon power alone is that it may rapidly degenerate into tyranny. Initial unity must be achieved by power but if that power is not to become tyrannical some moral and constitutional checks must be placed upon it. If a world community is to be established it must take cognizance of the fact that while "order precedes justice in the strategy of government" yet "only an order which implicates justice can achieve a stable peace." [57] Niebuhr argues that the establishment of a world community must necessarily remain both "the final possibility and impossibility of human life . . . in actuality the perpetual problem as well as the constant fulfillment of human hopes." [58]

In endeavoring to find proximate solutions to the perennial problems of political and social order "the children of light" must borrow some of the wisdom of "the children of darkness" but they must be careful not to borrow too much. The Christian faith will help us to understand why no absolute and final solutions to our political and social problems can ever be found but it will also help us to avoid the pitfall of despair by "the revelation of a divine mercy which understands and resolves the perpetual contradictions in which history is involved. . . . The hope of Christian faith that the divine power which bears history can complete what even the highest human striving must leave incomplete, and can purify the corruptions which appear in even the purest human aspirations, is an indispensable prerequisite for diligent fulfillment of our historic tasks." [59]

## Protestant Unity

SINCE Protestants are divided into a number of different denominations with ecclesiastical forms of government peculiar to each and independent of one another there is no one organ which can speak for them collectively. With the establishment in 1908 of a Federal Council of the Churches of Christ in America, American Protestants have found a central organ which can speak for many of them on matters of social and political importance but it does not include all Protestant denominations and its pronouncements are not uniformly and universally regarded as authoritative or official among the Protestant groups which do belong to it. In August, 1948, a World Council of Churches was established at Amsterdam, Holland, composed of the representatives of some 140 churches. But while many of those who were active in the establishment of this Council hoped to find or achieve in this meeting *The* universal *Church*, the realities of the situation forced upon them the reluctant conclusion that, at least for the time being, they must be content with a loose confederation of churches.

At the meeting of the first assembly of the World Council of Churches many mutual problems were discussed including the nature of the Church and its relation to society. In its report on the Church and the disorder of society several points of conflict between Christianity and communism, on the one hand, and Christianity and capitalism, on the other, were noted. The points of conflict between Christianity and Marxian communism were enumerated as consisting of: (1) the communist promise of what amounts to a complete redemption of man in history; (2) the belief that a particular class by virtue of its role as the bearer of a new order is free from the sins and ambiguities that Christians believe to be characteristic of all human existence; (3) the materialistic and deterministic teachings, however they may be qualified, that are incompatible with belief in God and with the Christian view of man as a person, made in God's image and responsible to Him; (4) the ruthless methods of communists in dealing with their opponents; (5) the demand of the party on its members for an exclusive and unqualified loyalty which belongs only to God, and the coercive policies of communist dictatorship in controlling every aspect of life.[60] The churches were urged to resist the extension of any system that not only includes oppressive elements but fails to provide any means by which the victims of oppression might criticize or act to correct it. The nature of this resistance was not, however, specifically defined although the churches were urged to raise their voices in protest against terroristic tactics and the denial of fundamental human rights.

Points of conflict between Christianity and capitalism were also noted. It was observed that although capitalistic practices vary from country to country, nevertheless, capitalism universally (1) tends to subordinate what should be the primary task of any economy—the meeting of human needs—to the economic advantages of those who have most power over its institutions. (2) It tends to produce serious inequalities. (3) It has developed a practical form of materialism in western nations in spite of their Christian background, for it has placed the greatest emphasis upon success in making money. (4) It has also kept the people of capitalist countries subject to a kind of fate which has taken the form of such social catastrophes as mass unemployment.[61]

The World Council of Churches rejected both the ideologies of laissez-faire capitalism and of communism and denied that these represent the only alternatives available to men today. It is the duty of Christians, it declared, to seek new, creative solutions which will neither destroy justice nor freedom.

The churches themselves, the Council declared, can do much to overcome national, social and racial barriers by refusing to recognize these barriers within their own membership. This is especially clear in the case of racial distinction for it is here that the church itself has failed most lamentably and by its example tended to sanctify racial prejudice. If the church is to succeed in calling society away from prejudice based on race and color and from the practices of discrimination and segregation which are denials of justice and human dignity, it must take steps itself to eliminate these practices from the Christian community. All men are children of God and any theory or practice which denies this is incompatible with the teachings and practice of Christianity.[62]

The World Council observed that in some countries there exist Christian political parties but, in general, condemned the formation of such parties because they tend to confuse Christianity with the compromises inherent in politics. The church should not identify itself with any political party or act as though it were a political party. Nevertheless, in some situations individual Christians may find it desirable to organize themselves into a party for specific objectives so long as they do not claim that it is the only possible expression of Christian loyalty in the situation. Primarily, however, the social influence of the church must come from its spiritual influence upon its members, through constant teaching of Christian truth in ways that illuminate the historical conditions in which men live and the problems which they face. The church can be most effective in society when it inspires its members to ask in a new way what their Christian responsibility is whenever they vote, discharge the duties of public office, influence public opinion, or make decisions as employers or workers.[63]

On the problem of war the World Council found itself divided. Three broad positions were maintained: (1) Some held that even though entering a war may be a Christian's duty in particular circumstances, modern warfare, with its mass destruction, can never be an act of justice. (2) Others argued that war is never justified under any circumstances and argued that Christians should witness against war by refusing military service of all kinds. (3) Another group maintained that in the absence of impartial supranational institutions military action is the ultimate sanction of the rule of law and that citizens must be taught that it is their duty to defend the law by force if necessary.[64] All agreed that the causes of war should be attacked by promoting peaceful change and the pursuit of justice. The victors in the second world war were urged to hasten the making of just peace treaties with defeated nations allowing them to rebuild their political and economic systems for peaceable purposes.

The Council went on record as denouncing all forms of tyranny, economic, political, and religious. "We utterly oppose totalitarianism, wherever found, in which a state arrogates to itself the right of determining men's thoughts and actions instead of recognizing the rights of each individual to do God's will according to his conscience. In the same way, we oppose any church which seeks to use the power of the state to enforce religious conformity." [65] Although neither was mentioned specifically by name this denunciation was intended, presumably, both for Communist Russia and the Roman Catholic Church.

The Council urged the cultivation of respect for international law and the establishment of international institutions necessary to make that law effective. It commended the United Nations but urged the nations to surrender a greater measure of national sovereignty in the interest of the common good. It urged the adoption of an International Bill of Human Rights "making provision for the recognition, and national and international enforcement of all the essential freedoms of man, whether personal, political or social." [66]

Considerable attention was given by the Council to the problem of religious liberty. It enumerated as the basic rights of religious freedom (1) the right of every person to determine his own faith and creed, (2) the right of every person to express his religious beliefs in worship, teaching and practice and to proclaim the implications of his beliefs for relationships in a social or political community, (3) the right of every person to associate with others and to organize with them for religious purposes, and (4) the right of every religious organization, formed or maintained by action in accordance with the rights of individual persons, to determine its policies and practices for the accomplishment of its chosen purposes.[67]

## Roman Catholicism

THERE are many divergencies of opinion among individual Roman Catholics on problems of political and social order yet the Roman Catholic Church does have in the person and office of the Pope a spokesman for the Church on matters relating to the social order. The pronouncements of the Pope are considered infallible when he speaks *ex cathedra* on matters of faith and morals; his pronouncements on other matters are suggestive rather than binding. Since, however, they are suggestions which come from one who is regarded by Roman Catholics as the Vicar of Christ on earth they carry greater weight and authority than the pronouncements of any other individual or group.

It is impossible in the space available here to examine all of the papal pronouncements on matters of social importance even those of recent years. Instead we shall concentrate our attention upon three of the more important papal encyclicals: the *Libertas Praestantissimum* of Leo XIII (June 20, 1888), the *Rerum Novarum* of Leo XIII (May 15, 1891) and the *Quadragesimo Anno* of Pius XI (May 15, 1931).

In the encyclical *Libertas Praestantissimum* (1888) Pope Leo XIII examined the problem of human liberty and distinguished the Catholic conception of liberty from the conception held by Liberalism. The foundation of human liberty, he declared, rests upon the fact that man's soul is immortal and that he is endowed with reason; the object of liberty is that which reason approves as good. To be in harmony with reason is to be free. But the faculty of choosing the good is not perfect because of the sinful predisposition of man. Hence, human liberty stands in need of enlightenment and of law. Law is an ordinance of reason prescribing to the will what ought to be sought and what ought to be shunned. Pope Leo XIII goes on to define the law in the same way in which it was defined by St. Thomas Aquinas distinguishing between positive law, divine law, natural law and eternal law. Human liberty "does not consist in every man doing what he pleases" but by living his life "in accordance with the commands of the Eternal Law." [68] Human laws are binding when they have their origin in the eternal law and are in faithful correspondence with it. Similarly, the liberty of rulers "does not consist in the power to lay unreasonable and capricious commands upon their subjects" but consists in action conformable with "the principles of right reason." [69] In short, it is only by obedience to the authority of God that man can be truly free. Not only is the law necessary for the enlightenment of man's mind but also the grace of God which does not annul man's nature but perfects it. (Unlike orthodox Protestant theology which emphasizes the total depravity of man's nature, Roman Catholic theology declares that man's nature is imperfect but not totally depraved. Through the grace of God that nature may become more perfect and progress made toward perfection. While Protestant theology tends to emphasize the primary importance of faith as the means of salvation, Roman Catholic theology tends to emphasize the primary importance of good works.)

Extreme Liberalism, the Pope declared in *Libertas Praestantissimum*, denies the existence of any divine authority and thus, in effect, makes every man a law unto himself. The authority of the state is derived in liberal theory not from God but from the collective reason of the community, from the people, and whatever the majority decide, is right, is the source of rights and the source of obligations. This is wrong because it denies the sovereignty of the supreme law-giver, God, and because, by making human reason the ultimate and final judge of right and wrong, it makes goodness and wickedness a mere matter of opinion.

If liberty of conscience means, as some liberals interpret it to mean, that each man should have the liberty of worshipping God or not as he chooses this cannot be right. True liberty and true freedom of conscience means that each "may follow the will of God, and, from a consciousness of duty and free from every obstacle, obey His commands." [70] When the State commands what is contrary to God's laws "it is right not to obey." Those liberals who tend to make the state "absolute and omnipotent" deny that there can be such a thing as tyranny.

Freedom of speech, of press, and of teaching can never be, as some liberals suppose, unlimited. There is an obligation to uphold the truth and suppress the false when they are known but "in regard to all matters of opinion . . . full liberty of thought and speech is naturally within the right of every man; for such liberty never leads men to suppress the truth, but often to discover it and make it known." [71] Freedom of teaching consists of freedom to teach the truth and it is the Church which is the "greatest and most reliable teacher of mankind." This is no obstacle, as some believe, to intellectual progress, because "reason itself clearly teaches that the truths of divine revelation and those of nature cannot really be opposed to one another." [72] The Church, moreover, cannot agree that "every man is free to profess, as he may choose, any religion or none" for a State which adopted this principle would put all religions, irrespective of their truth, on an equal footing and would deny that the State itself owed homage to God. "Civil Society must acknowledge God as its Founder and Parent, and must obey and reverence His power and authority. Justice therefore forbids, and reason itself forbids, the State to be godless; or to adopt a line of action which would end in godlessness; namely to treat the various religions (as they call them) alike, and to bestow upon them promiscuously equal rights and privileges." [73] A State should profess the religion of Catholicism for only that is true.

In the encyclical *Rerum Novarum* (1891) Pope Leo XIII considered the economic condition of the working classes and the socialist solution. What is the cause of "the misery and wretchedness pressing so unjustly on the majority of the working class?" The working classes having become "isolated and helpless," have been forced to surrender "to the hard-heartedness of employers and the greed of unchecked competition." [74] Although disguised in form, the practice of usury has increased the trouble and "the hiring of labor, and the conduct of trade are concentrated in the hands of comparatively few; so that a small number of very rich men have been able to lay upon the teeming masses of the laboring poor a yoke little better than slavery itself." [75]

But Socialism, the Pope declares, is no remedy. It is not only contrary to justice but the worker would be the first to suffer if it were put into practice. It is unjust because "every man has, by nature, the right to possess property as his own" for as a rational animal "it must be within man's right to possess things, not merely for temporary and momentary use, as other living things do, but to hold them in stable and permanent possession." [76] God, it is true, "gave the earth for the use and enjoyment of the whole human race" but this does not mean that an individual cannot own a part of it, a part to be determined by his own industry. For, "even though apportioned among private owners, the earth ceases not to minister to the needs of all, inasmuch as there is no one who does not sustain life from what the land produces." [77] Further proof that private ownership is in accordance with the law of nature stems from the fact that a man has to exert labor in order to procure the fruits of nature and it is only just that he should possess the fruits of his own labor.

The right to own productive property derives, too, from the fact that every man as the head of a family has a duty to provide for the members of his family, to protect his children from want and misery, not only now but in the future. Private property is essential to the maintenance of the family and the family, as an older and more fundamental institution than the state, has "rights and duties peculiar to itself, which are quite independent of the State," and beyond the power of the State to modify. "Paternal authority can be neither abolished nor absorbed by the State, for it has the same source as human life itself." [78] Socialism tends to replace parental supervision with state supervision, it ascribes to the state duties and rights which properly belong to the family.

The inevitability of class conflict is false. Both employers and employees require each other, and as a consequence, each has duties to the other. It is the workers' obligation to carry out honestly all equitable agreements freely entered into, never to injure an employer's property or person, never to resort to violence in defending their own cause and to shun evil-principled agitators. It is the employers' obligation not to exploit labor, to respect the worker's dignity as a man and as a Christian to remember that "it is shameful and inhuman to treat men like chattels to make money by, or to look upon them merely as so much muscle and physical strength," to pay a just wage and "to refrain, religiously, from cutting down wages whether by force, by fraud or by usurious dealing." [79] The Pope reminds both employers and employees that they are alike children of God in need of redemption, that wealth is no passport to eternal happiness but a hindrance and that poverty is no disgrace nor a cause for shame. Only by a return to the Christian life can society be permanently healed.

In place of state ownership of the means of production the Pope urged the adoption of laws and policies which will encourage a more equitable distribution of wealth and "induce as many as possible of the people to become owners" of property. This will be possible, however, only if the worker is paid a wage that is not only "sufficient to enable him comfortably to support himself, his wife, and his children" but sufficient, with the practice of thrift, to accumulate some savings. [80] He favored the establishment of trade unions and urged especially the establishment of Catholic Trade Unions. The State should do its utmost, however, to forestall strikes by regulating the conditions and hours of work and by lending its "influence and authority to the removal in good time of the causes which lead to conflict between employers and employees." [81]

In 1931 Pope Pius XI issued an encyclical, *Quadragesimo Anno*, commemorating the encyclical *Rerum Novarum* and interpreting its principles in the light of the economic conditions then prevailing. Pius XI found the distribution of wealth "gravely defective," great wealth being held by the few while the many "live in destitution." [82] The wage system, he said, ought to be supplemented by some kind of partnership in which the workers participate either in management or in profits or in both. Social justice demands that a man be paid a wage adequate to meet normal domestic needs and reforms ought to be "introduced without delay which will guarantee such a wage to every adult working man." [83] Moreover, opportunities to work should be provided every man able and willing to work.

A large part of this encyclical is devoted to what the Pope refers to as "the reconstruction of the social order." The excessive "individualism" manifested in laissez-faire capitalism is, indeed, an evil which requires correction but there is a danger that in turning to the State to correct this evil we may create a colossus overburdened with duties which it cannot adequately discharge. Social efficiency requires the re-establishment of a graded hierarchy of associations between the individual and the State. These associations or vocational groups (*ordines*) should combine employers and employees engaged in the same trade or profession endowed with a certain power of self-government over matters of special concern to those engaged in the same trade or profession. We should strive in reconstituting the economy to avoid either the principle of unrestricted competition or the principle of economic dictatorship, relying rather upon the principles of Social Justice and Social Charity.

Some have seen in the corporations established under the aegis of Fascism in Italy a resemblance to the Pope's suggestion concerning the formation of vocational groups. There is a resemblance but not an identity. Speaking of these corporations the Pope declared "that the new . . . organization tends to have an excessively bureaucratic and political character, and that, notwithstanding the general advantage, it serves particular political aims rather than the establishment of a better social order." [84]

The Pope observed that economic power in modern capitalism is wielded less and less by the owners of property and more and more by the managers of property. By controlling credit, moreover, a few men are able to control "the life blood of the entire economic body." They "grasp in their hands the very soul of production, so that, against their will, no one can breathe." This accumulation of power is the direct result of unrestricted competition which fosters the strong and "those who fight most relentlessly, who pay less heed to the dictates of conscience." [85] This struggle for supremacy among the few economically powerful occurs not only within the domestic economy but between nations. Under the conditions of modern capitalism "the lust for profit" has been subordinated to "unbridled ambition to dominate." And the State which "should be the supreme arbiter, ruling . . . above all party contentions . . . has become instead a slave bound over to the service of human passion and greed." [86]

As to Socialism, as a remedy for these evils, Pope Pius XI declares that there "is a certain element of truth" in it but that, nevertheless, it is "founded upon a doctrine of human society, peculiarly its own, which is opposed to true Christianity." It is wrong when it "affirms that human society was instituted merely for the sake of material well-being" and to the extent that it denies the authority of God. Hence "Religious Socialism, Christian Socialism, are expressions that imply a contradiction in terms. No one can be at the same time a sincere Catholic and a Socialist properly so-called." The parent of Socialism was liberalism and its offspring will be Bolshevism.[87]

Christian social reconstruction requires primarily a renewal of the Christian way of life and a reaffirmation of the relationship of morality to economic activities. Essentially, the cure for our economic ills lies not so much in the reform of economic organization and structure as in moral and spiritual rebirth. If men are to overcome the "sordid selfishness which is the disgrace and the great sin of the present age" they must learn again "to seek first the kingdom of God and His justice." [88] And men must learn that justice alone is not enough, that it needs to be supplemented with charity, for without charity there can be no real brotherhood, for the brotherhood of man is born of the love of God.

In an encyclical issued in 1937 the Pope condemned the idolatrous worship of race, people, or State. In part he said:

He who takes the race, or the people, or the state, or the form of government, the bearers of the power of the State or any other fundamental element of human society—which in the temporal order of things have an essential and honorable place—out of the system of their earthly valuation, and make them the ultimate norm of all, even of religious, values, and deifies them with an idolatrous

worship, perverts and falsifies the order of things created and commanded by God . . .

It is part of the trend of today to sever more and more not only
morality, but also the foundation of law and jurisprudence, from
true belief in God and from His revealed commandments. Here we
have in mind particularly the so-called natural law, that is written
by the finger of the Creator Himself in the tables of the hearts of
men and which can be read on these tables by sound reason not
darkened by sin and passion. Every positive law, from whatever
lawgiver it may come, can be examined as to its moral implications,
and consequently as to its moral authority to bind in conscience,
in the light of the commandments of the natural law. The laws of
man that are in direct contradiction to the natural law bear an
initial defect, that no violent means, no outward display of power,
can remedy. By this standard must we judge the principle: "What
is of utility to the people is right." A right meaning may be given
to this sentence if it is understood as expressing that what is morally
illicit can never serve the true interests of the people. But even
ancient paganism recognized that the sentence to be perfectly accurate, should read: "Never is anything useful, if it is not at the same
time morally good. And not because it is useful is it morally good,
but, because it is morally good, it is also useful." (Cicero, *De Officiis*,
III, 30).

Cut loose from this rule of morality, that principle would mean,
in international life, a perpetual state of war between the different
nations. In political life within the state, since it confuses considerations of utility with those of right, it disregards the basic fact that
man as a person possesses God-given rights, which must be preserved
from all attacks aimed at denying, suppressing, or neglecting
them . . .[89]

Catholic social theory finds expression not only in papal
encyclicals but in the writings of individual Catholics and, in
recent years, notably in the writings of men like Jacques
Maritain and Christopher Dawson.[90] On the basis of Tho-
mistic philosophy Jacques Maritain has been particularly
active in formulating a philosophy of humanism which he
calls "personalism." We must recover, he insists, what modern
culture frequently denies: respect for human personality as
such. Society is not an entity in itself nor is it a mere collection
of individuals but it is a fellowship of human persons. No
social program or system which denies the dignity and needs

of individuals as human persons can or ought to survive. The "common good" which ought to be the aim of any social system must be conceived in terms of what is good for human persons.

The end of society is the good of the community, of the social body. But if the good of the social body is not understood to be a common good of *human persons*, just as the social body itself is a whole of human persons, this conception also would lead to other errors of a totalitarian type. The common good of the city is neither the mere collection of private goods, nor the proper good of a whole which, like the species with respect to its individuals or the hive with respect to the bees, relates the parts to itself alone and sacrifices them to itself. It is the good human life of the multitude, of a multitude of persons; it is their communion in good living. It is therefore common to both *the whole and the parts* into which it flows back and which, in turn, must benefit from it.[91]

This implies the recognition of fundamental rights belonging to individuals by virtue of their human personality. But the common good of human society is not a sum of temporal advantages and achievements for man is not only a material being but a spiritual being with an immortal soul, hence the common good must include values that are supra-temporal.

The human person is engaged in its entirety as a part of political society, but not a reason of everything that is in it and everything that belongs to it. By reason of other things which are in the person, it is also in its entirety above political society. For in the person there are some things—and they are the most important and sacred ones—which transcend political society and draw man in his entirety above political society—the very same whole man, who, by reason of another category of things, is a part of political society.[92]

Man's deficiencies as a material being require that he subordinate himself to the political community as a part of it, but his spiritual potentialities transcend political society and cannot be subordinated to it. Bourgeois individualism, communistic anti-individualism, and fascist anti-communism and anti-individualism all "disregard the human *person* in one way or another, and, in its place, consider, willingly or not, the *material individual* alone." [93]

In a book entitled *Christianity and Democracy* (1944) Maritain argues that democracy has its roots in the teachings of Christianity and that today democracy and Christianity have the same enemies. Christianity has taught the unity of the human race and the democratic conception of the natural equality of all men has its roots, not in any empirical evidence, but in the fact that all men are creatures of God and equal in His sight. The dignity of man stems from the fact that all men are created in the image of God. Christianity has taught that there is a law and a will greater than the law or will of any individual or group of individuals and that it is the obligation of rulers to govern justly and with compassion. "Under the often misunderstood but active inspiration of the Gospel, the secular conscience has understood the dignity of the human person and has understood that the person, while being a part of the State, yet transcends the State, because of the inviolable mystery of his spiritual freedom and because of his call to the attainment of supra-worldly possessions." [94] Because Christianity has taught that authority has its source in God and not in man the secular conscience has understood that "no man and no particular group of men has in itself the right to rule others." [95] Finally, "what has been gained for the secular conscience, if it does not veer to barbarism, is faith in the brotherhood of man, a sense of the social duty of compassion for mankind in the person of the weak and the suffering, the conviction that the political work par excellence is that of rendering common life better and more brotherly, and of working so as to make of the structure of laws, institutions and customs of this common life a house for brothers to live in." [96]

Christopher Dawson points out that there is no such thing as a completely Christian state or a Christian economic system, there are only states and social systems which "are more or less Christian." [97]

Today the world . . . is so convinced that economics are the only thing in the world that matter that it is difficult for Christians not to be affected by this prevalent mentality; so today we often find Christians, both Protestant and Catholic, who believe the evangelical maxims are inapplicable to our present circumstances and that we must first transform our economic system before we can begin to live a Christian life.

But this view seems to me to rest on a serious misunderstanding of Christian ethics and a fundamental misinterpretation of history. There has never been a time when society was completely Christian; Christianity has never been more than a leaven working in the world, and its work is never finished. . . .

The fact is that European civilization has been on the wrong road for so long that it is impossible to set it right by any obvious kind of political or economic reform. Protestantism, Liberalism, and Communism are the three successive stages by which our civilization has passed from Catholicism to complete secularism. The first eliminated the Church, the second eliminated Christianity, and the third eliminates the human soul. We cannot have a Christian society or a Christian economic life until our civilization has recovered its moral conscience, its faith in God and its membership of the Church. That may well be as slow and painful a process as the conversion of the Roman Empire.[98]

The Roman Catholic Church has frequently been criticized from without and sometimes from within for the pursuance of policies in practice which closely resemble political opportunism. Certainly the Church has frequently given the impression that it is more zealous in defense of ecclesiastical institutions and freedom than it is of individual freedom to apply the principles of Christianity in daily life. It has protested more vigorously in some notable instances in the recent past against the persecution of the Church as an institution and of Catholics in particular than it has against tyranny as such and the persecution of individuals irrespective of their faith. The Concordats which the Vatican concluded with the regimes established by Mussolini and Hitler, whatever their political justification, did much to strengthen those regimes. These actions although later repudiated in part by the encyclicals *Non Abbiamo Bisogno* (1931) and *Mit Brennender Sorge* (1937) have weakened the political strength of the Church by casting doubts on its motives. The close association of the Roman Catholic Church with the Franco regime in Spain and with reactionary regimes and policies in other parts of the world have seriously weakened the force of its pronouncements on social theory. The ambiguous terms, moreover, in which some of that theory has been expressed has led to various and conflicting interpretations among individual Catholics which the Church itself has not seen fit to resolve by a clear and decisive stand. It has resolutely and decisively taken a stand in opposition to Communism and in July, 1949, the Vatican announced that the Church would excommunicate all Catholics who knowingly and willingly profess, spread or defend Communism. The resolution of the Church in taking this stand is admirable but one cannot help wondering why similar action was not taken against Fascism.

If the Roman Catholic Church is criticized for its ambiguity in theory and practice it is also criticized, it must be said, for being too specific and too ready to distinguish right from wrong. This is the complaint lodged against it by neo-orthodox Protestants like Reinhold Niebuhr who insist that there is an essential ambiguity about political life which defies precise description in terms of absolute right and wrong. Thus it is said, on the one hand, and by the same critic, that the Roman Catholic Church has too precise a conception of "what the pattern of a Christian society should be," and, on the other, that is "far less united on great social decisions" than one would be led "to expect." [99]

It should be said in fairness that the Roman Catholic Church is probably no more ambiguous in theory or ambivalent in practice than Protestant churches. Protestantism has frequently allied itself with reactionary social policies and the maintenance of the social *status quo*. The disunity and lack of central organization that characterizes Protestantism obscures its ambivalence in a way in which the ambivalence of an organization as highly organized and centralized as the Roman Catholic Church cannot be obscured. But unless the Christian Church, Catholic and Protestant, is willing to risk martyrdom, to jeopardize its existence as an institution, if necessary, in order to proclaim the gospel of which it is the embodiment, it cannot hope for spiritual survival. The New Testament declares that those who seek to preserve their life shall lose it and only those who are willing to sacrifice their lives, if need be, shall preserve them. This is as true of institutions as it is of individuals. A Church that is more mindful of its existence as a social institution than it is of the gospel it has been called upon to proclaim to all who will hear it, has already begun to lose its *raison d'être*, namely, faith in God. It is true that the Church is inevitably enmeshed in the sins to which men are prone and not even it can escape the perversion of its aims by the rebellious wills of men. Yet, the Church must strive to attain as unequivocal a position as it is possible for human beings to attain by God's grace. The sinfulness of man should not be used as a cloak for indifference nor as an excuse for lack of thought, of effort or of courage. The disrepute in which Christianity stands in the modern world is at least in part the responsibility of Christians themselves, the betrayal of Christianity by Christendom. "Ye are the salt of the earth: but if the salt have lost his savour, wherewith shall it be salted?"

## *Anglicanism*

THE relationship between Christianity and the social order is represented in the modern world by a fourth movement known as Anglicanism which seeks to steer a middle course between Protestantism on the one hand and Roman Catholicism on the other. Its great spokesman on social questions was the late Archbishop of Canterbury, William Temple. Other influential spokesmen include V. A. Demant, Maurice Reckitt, Bernard I. Bell, Paul E. More and T. S. Eliot. The main task of the Church in social matters, William Temple declared, is to inculcate Christian principles and the power of the Christian spirit. It is not the task of the Church to provide specific remedies which require technical knowledge but to "announce Christian principles" and to "point out where the existing social order at any time is in conflict with them. It must then pass on to Christian citizens, acting in their civic capacity, the task of re-shaping the existing order in closer conformity to the principles." There can never be anything like a Christian solution to unemployment but the Church can and must say, although "I cannot tell you what is the

remedy . . . I can tell you that a society of which unemployment is a chronic feature is a diseased society, and that if you
are not doing all you can to find and administer the remedy,
you are guilty before God." [100] When features of the social
structure are clearly evil the Church can go further and point
these out. It is not the duty or function of the Church "to
sketch a perfect social order and urge men to establish it" for
men are not perfect and no social order, even if theoretically
perfect, could long remain so in practice. "The political problem is concerned with men as they are, not with men as
they ought to be. Part of the task is so to order life as to lead
them nearer to what they ought to be; but to assume that
they are already this will involve certain failure and disaster." [101] In fact "the art of government is the art of so ordering life that self-interest prompts what justice demands." [102]
We must accept as a fact of life that man is self-centered but,
at the same time, we must not lose sight of another fact that
man has "both capacities and achievements that could never
be derived from self-interest." For, although defaced, there
resides in man the image of God. Accordingly, man "must be
treated as what he actually is, but always with a view to what
in God's purpose he is destined to become." [103]

The first principle of Christian ethics and of Christian
politics is that every person must be respected as a person, as
a child of God, possessing "a worth absolutely independent of
all usefulness to society." [104] As a consequence, society should
be so constituted as to give every individual the maximum opportunity to realize his potentialities as a human being, "the
widest possible extension of personal responsibility." This is
what we mean by freedom. A Christian social order also emphasizes the need for social fellowship, the cooperation with
other persons for the satisfaction of mutual needs.

Liberty is actual in the various cultural and commercial and local
associations that men form. In each of these a man can feel that he
counts for something and that others depend on him as he on them.
The State which would serve and guard liberty will foster all such
groupings, giving them freedom to guide their own actions, provided these fall within the general order of the communal life and do
not injure the freedom of other similar associations.[105]

Freedom and fellowship issue in the obligation of Service.

> A man is a member of his family, of his nation, and of mankind. It is very seldom that any one can render a service directly to mankind as a whole. We serve mankind by serving those parts of it with which we are closely connected. . . .
>
> A man must chiefly serve his own most immediate community, accepting as the standard of its welfare that which its members are ready to accept (though trying it may be, to lead them nearer to a fully Christian view), but always checking this narrower service by the wider claims, so that in serving the smaller community he never injures the larger.[106]

The real crisis of our times, William Temple declared, is not primarily a moral or political but a cultural crisis. What he means is this:

> . . . man is not a being ruled wholly by his reason and conscious aims. His life is inextricably intertwined with nature and with the natural associations of family, livelihood, tradition and culture. When the connection with these sources from which the individual life derives nourishment and strength is broken, the whole life of society becomes enfeebled. The present plight of our society arises in large part from the breakdown of these natural forms of associations and of a cultural pattern formed to a great extent under Christian influences. New dogmas and assumptions about the nature of reality have taken the place of the old. New rituals of various kinds are giving shape to men's emotional life. The consequence is that while their aims still remain to a large extent Christian, their souls are moulded by alien influences.[107]

The same thing has been said more recently by Canon V. A. Demant.

> If we go on thinking and acting as if this civilization of ours is assured of its survival, or as if its strains could be cured by better political systems or economic methods or even more heroic morals, then—I contend—the breakdown will deepen into complete dissolution. On the other hand, if we frankly recognize that our western civilization is showing, on the largest scale ever known, all the signs which have marked the disintegration of cultures in the past, we may be able to plant the seeds of a renewal which will not have to wait until after a long period of utter decay. If men feel they are on

the right track, even if it is still very unpleasant, they will work for the future. Civilization dies when men do not anticipate the possibility of its death.[108]

## Conclusion

THE modern world has lived for many centuries off its Christian heritage but with the decline of Christianity as a religion, the Christian conscience has progressively deteriorated. To those moderns who declare that they would like to preserve the Christian ethics without the Christian religion, it must be replied that that experiment has already been tried and failed. Christianity is not, in any case, primarily or essentially a system of ethics. For it offers men, in its genuine, orthodox form, not moral advice, which is readily obtainable, but something even more valuable—assistance in doing that which men, for the most part, already know they ought to do. Christianity has a message not for men who are seeking moral advice but for men, who like St. Paul, cry out in despair: that which I would, I do not, but that which I hate, I do.

When I suggested at the beginning of this chapter that Christianity is a remedy for our individual and social evils I did not mean to imply that it is "like a patent medicine that is warranted to cure all diseases." It is not a political philosophy nor an economic program and it provides no short cuts to economic prosperity or social stability. It does not lessen the need to study our political, social and economic institutions or to formulate programs and to institute reforms which may improve our political and social structure but it will, indeed, give us a perspective and provide us with principles in terms of which we may accomplish these tasks better than we would without them. It will save us, moreover, from the illusion that we can establish a system which is perfect or make a reform which is final. We will realize that the task of achieving a just social order is an ever-continuing one and that justice is a goal to be striven after rather than finally obtained. It will place our political, social, and economic aspirations in proper perspective, subordinating them to an aspiration which should include but transcend them. For Christianity teaches us to seek a Kingdom which is not of this world yet, at the same time, to prepare for its advent by refusing to be conformed to this world.

This is a harsh saying to ears accustomed to the language of secularism. But Christian teaching supplements the harsh saying with a paradoxical one that reads: only by aiming above the world can we master the world. Only by aspiring to eternal life can we give meaning to temporal life. To be free *in* the world we must remember that we are not *of* the world. Christianity . . . is given us not to save our civilization but to save our souls. But it is also true that whatever welfare and prosperity and peace we shall be able to achieve in our civilization must flow from God's peace.[109]

It is a paradoxical truth that we never obtain the most important things in life by aiming at them directly. We do not obtain happiness by striving to be happy nor peace by trying to avoid conflict. Both happiness and peace are by-products of activities that have neither happiness nor peace as their immediate object. Happiness is the by-product of activity that has love, not happiness, as its object and peace is the by-product, not of the cessation of hostilities, but of justice. Some goods in the hierarchy of goods leading to God have priority over others and it is only by seeking the higher goods that we can obtain the lesser. Christ did not say: Seek ye first peace, or security, or happiness, but rather "Seek ye first the Kingdom of God and His righteousness" and these things (peace, security, and happiness) shall be added unto you. Christianity, therefore, claims to achieve as a by-product what "the secular physicians fail to achieve as a main work." [110]

We express no hyperbole in asserting that what is, humanly speaking, the greatest of all achievements, the rebuilding of a civilization, must yet, in the language of ultimate seriousness, be described as a by-work. It is true, as organizers of the peace of the world we must strain every nerve to push on in the direction in which the Charter of the United Nations points. As organizers of justice at home we must strive with might and main to discard the social evils created by the capitalist system. But in so doing we shall remember that except the Lord build the house, they labor in vain that build it. The very devotion which we give to the labor of construction must flow from a greater devotion, and all the self-giving love which we put into our handiwork must be a sacrifice and thank-offering. Organizing peace on earth is a gigantic task. To be successful in it, in a measure, we shall have to conceive of it not in the spirit of a giant world-builder (the giant might soon discover that he is a pygmy) but of a copyist, with the peace of God before us as a model.[111]

Christianity does not promise us an easy issue out of our afflictions, it does not promise to put an end to our suffering and pain but to make them meaningful. For Christ was crucified not that the world might be made safe for democracy; not that Western civilization might endure; not, indeed, that mankind might survive in this world; but rather, that following His example we should not shrink even before the Cross. As a Scottish divine, George MacDonald, has put it very aptly: "The Son of God suffered unto the death, not that men might not suffer, but that their sufferings might be like His." Christ's agony on the Cross was a prelude to His Resurrection, to the victory of life over death, and if our sufferings are like His we may look forward to the same eternal life of joy. This is the good news proclaimed in the New Testament—that God so "loved the world, that he gave his only-begotten Son, to the end that all that believe in him should not perish, but have everlasting life" (St. John iii. 16). When we pray to God, "Thy kingdom come . . . ," as one writer has expressed it very well: "We pray that God's external kingdom may be extended throughout the world, but also that our own submission to its claims may one day become unconditional, that the barriers of self-will may be broken down so that Christ may reign not only over us but in us. . . . So long as sin or any of its results remain, Christ's victory is incomplete. . . . Not until his own triumph over sin and death is reproduced in his followers, the members of his mystical Body, will Satan's kingdom at length be utterly vanquished. Only our own resurrection, our personal conquest of death, will cancel finally the dire results of Adam's sin, and so bring into being the Kingdom of God in its full splendor." [112] The same thing is said, in other words, in Scripture: "For as in Adam all die, so also in

Christ shall all be made alive. But each in his own order:
Christ the firstfruits; then they that are Christ's, at his coming.
Then cometh the end, when he shall deliver up the kindom to
God, even the Father; when he shall have abolished all rule
and all authority and power. For he must reign, till he hath
put all his enemies under his feet. The last enemy that shall be
abolished is death. . . . And when all things have been subjected unto him, then shall the Son himself be subjected to him
that did subject all things unto him, that God may be all in
all." (I Cor. 15:22–26, 28). Only if we are concerned about the
salvation of our souls shall we be of much use in saving the
world, only if our eyes are focused on the Kingdom of God
shall we see with clearer vision what needs to be done here
and now, only if we surrender our wills, as completely as men
can, to the will of God, will we be enabled by the power of
God to make the self-sacrifices which the salvation of the
world demands—in short, only by aiming above the world
shall we succeed in mastering the world.

# Notes

## CHAPTER 1

1. Some of this material appeared earlier in a symposium published in the *American Political Science Review* and is reprinted here with the permission of the editor of that publication. J. H. Hallowell, "Politics and Ethics," *American Political Science Review*, Vol. XXXVIII, No. 4 (August 1944), pp. 639 *ff*.; Gabriel Almond, Lewis Dexter, William Whyte and J. Hallowell, "Politics and Ethics—A Symposium," *ibid.*, Vol. XL, No. 2 (April 1946), pp. 283 *ff.*; Arnold Brecht, "Beyond Relativism in Political Theory," *ibid.*, Vol. XLI, No. 3 (June 1947), pp. 470 *ff.*; and Francis G. Wilson, "Research in Political Theory: A Symposium," *ibid.*, Vol. XXXVIII, No. 4 (August 1944), pp. 726 *ff.*

2. No government ever rested long upon force alone, for as Talleyrand once said to Napoleon: "You can do everything with bayonets, Sire, except sit on them." Rousseau put the matter succinctly when he said that, "The strongest is never strong enough to remain forever master unless he transforms force into law and obedience into duty." *Social Contract* (Everyman ed.), Bk. I, Ch. 3, p. 8.

3. For a more detailed discussion of compromise as a political ideal, see T. V. Smith, "Compromise: Its Context and Limits," *Ethics*, Vol. LIII, No. 1 (1942) and J. H. Hallowell, "Compromise as a Political Ideal," *Ethics*, Vol. LIV, No. 3 (April 1944), pp. 157 *ff*.

4. For an excellent introduction to the philosophy of Plato and Aristotle see John Wild, *Introduction to Realistic Philosophy* (New York, 1948). The best translation of Plato's *Republic* is the recent one by F. M. Cornford (New York, 1945) which is much superior to the older and more familiar translation of B. Jowett. A new translation of Aristotle's *Politics* by Ernest Barker has also recently appeared and is superior to older translations (Oxford, 1946).

5. R. G. Collingwood, *An Essay on Philosophical Method* (Oxford, 1933). For an excellent discussion of the nature and function of philosophy, a discussion to which the author is greatly indebted, see Helmut Kuhn, "Philosophy and Religion: The Humanity of Man" which appears as Chapter V in *A State University Surveys the Humanities* (Chapel Hill, 1945) and Helmut Kuhn, "Exhortatio ad Philosophiam," *Philosophy and Phenomenological Research*, Vol. VIII, No. 1 (Sept., 1947), pp. 83 *ff*.

6. Professor Elliott points out that "The philosophy of men is not automatically produced by the times. *It results from their efforts at understanding the times.* Quite as much it reshapes the times, as e.g., Benthamism did in England

through the first half at least of the nineteenth century. Economic interests themselves appear only through the conceptions which men have of them—more or less adequate." W. Y. Elliott, *The Pragmatic Revolt in Politics* (Macmillan, New York, 1928), p. 74. (Italics mine.) By permission of W. Y. Elliott.

7. For a discussion of the relationship between political thought and political action see Helmut Kuhn, "Thought and Action: A Meditation on the Principles of Political Science," *The Journal of Politics*, Vol. 8, No. 4 (November 1946), pp. 451 *ff*. For a discussion of the relationship between doctrines of man and politics see Francis G. Wilson, "Human Nature and Politics," *The Journal of Politics*, Vol. 8, No. 4 (November 1946), pp. 478 *ff*.; Nathaniel Micklem, *The Theology of Politics* (London, 1941); T. E. Jessop *et al.*, *The Christian Understanding of Man* (London, 1938); Benjamin F. Wright, "The Federalist on the Nature of Political Man," *Ethics*, Vol. LIX, No. 2, Part II (January 1949); Reinhold Niebuhr, *The Nature and Destiny of Man* (New York, 2 vols., 1941–43) and Jacques Maritain, *Scholasticism and Politics* (New York, 1939). For naturalistic points of view see Y. H. Krikorian (ed.), *Naturalism and the Human Spirit* (New York, 1944).

## CHAPTER 2

1. C. H. McIlwain, *The Growth of Political Thought in the West* (Macmillan, New York, 1932), pp. 3–4. Copyright 1932 by The Macmillan Company and used with their permission.

2. *Ethica Nic.*, Bk. I, Ch. 9. In opposition to the Sophists who contended that all restraint upon human desires is "unnatural" and bad, Plato argued that restraint is necessary to perfection. No one can become good at anything, whether it be boxing,

playing the piano, or carpentry, unless he is willing to submit himself to a discipline which restrains his natural impulses. What applies to the attainment of a particular skill applies equally to the attainment of human virtue itself. The development of human character, as such, necessitates the harmonizing of our desires in some orderly way, and, in the interest of harmony, we must, of necessity, impose limitations upon our particular desires and impulses. Plato further argued that it was this capacity to restrain one's self that made the existence of society possible. The discipline to which an individual must submit if he would be good is identical with the discipline to which he must submit if society is to exist. It is this identification of moral and social restraint that distinguishes Plato's thought from that of the Sophists and from that of many modern thinkers. In this connection, as M. B. Foster points out, "it is important to guard against misunderstanding of his doctrine. It is misunderstood by most of those critics who accuse him of 'idealizing' the state, or of 'sacrificing the individual' to it. This accusation would be true only if Plato had taught (as some subsequent philosophers have done) that there was a 'good' or an 'interest' of the state which might diverge from that of its individual members, and that in cases of divergence the latter should be sacrificed to the former. But Plato's theory is that there is no such divergence. Nature has established such a harmony between the individual and society (she has made him, as Aristotle said later, a 'political animal') that his individual good is attained and not sacrificed by submission to the requirements of social life. Nor must Plato be understood to mean that the laws and regulations imposed by any and every actual state necessarily conduce to the improvement of the individual subjects who are compelled to conform to them . . . In so far . . . as any state realizes its nature as a state, to that degree it must promote the good of its members. But any state may fall short to some degree of realizing its proper nature. There will be perversions and defective specimens among states, just as there are among plants and animals." *Masters of Political Thought: Plato to Machiavelli* (Houghton Mifflin Company, Boston, 1941), p. 42. By permission.

For an interpretation of the work of Plato and Aristotle see, in addition to Foster and the work cited earlier by McIlwain, F. M. Cornford's introduction to his translation of *The Republic of Plato* (New York, 1945); A. E. Taylor, *Plato: The Man and His Work* (New York, 1927); R. L. Nettleship, *Lectures on the Republic of Plato* (New York, 1936); John Wild, *Plato's Theory of Man* (Cambridge, Mass., 1946); Raphael Demos' introduction to *Plato: Selections* (New York, 1927); Werner Jaeger, *Paideia* (New York, 1943); Ernest Barker's introduction to his translation of *The Politics of Aristotle* (Oxford, 1946); A. C. Bradley, "Aristotle's Conception of the State," in *Hellenica*, edited by Evelyn Abbott (New York, 2d ed., 1898); Werner Jaeger, *Aristotle: Fundamentals of the History of his Development* (Oxford, 1934) and Ernst Cassirer, *The Myth of the State* (New Haven, 1946), Chs. V–VI. See also W. Y. Elliott and Neil A. McDonald, *Western Political Heritage* (New York, 1949).

3. McIlwain, *op. cit.*, p. 106.
4. *De Re Publica*, III, 22. Quoted by McIlwain, *ibid.*, pp. 111–112.
5. *De Re Publica*, I, 32. Quoted by McIlwain, *ibid.*, p. 116.
6. Quoted by McIlwain, *ibid.*, p. 125. For a discussion of medieval philosophy see Maurice de Wulf, *History of Mediaeval Philosophy* (London, 2 vols., 1926); Étienne

Gilson, *The Spirit of Mediaeval Philosophy* (New York, 1936) and other works by the same author; G. C. Crump and E. F. Jacob (eds.), *The Legacy of the Middle Ages*. For good illustrative material see R. L. Poole, *Illustrations of the History of Mediaeval Thought and Learning* (New York, rev. ed., 1920). For the political theory of the Middle Ages, in addition to the work cited by C. H. McIlwain, see R. W. and A. J. Carlyle, *History of Mediaeval Political Theory in the West* (London and New York, 6 vols., 1903–1936); W. A. Dunning, *A History of Political Theories: Ancient and Mediaeval* (New York, 1930); Otto F. Gierke, *Political Theories in the Middle Ages*, transl. with an Introduction by F. W. Maitland (Cambridge, 1900); and Heinrich A. Rommen, *The State in Catholic Thought* (St. Louis, 1945); and Alois Dempf, *Sacrum Imperium; Geschichts- und Staatsphilosophie des Mittelalters und der Politischen Renaissance* (Munich, 1929).

7. "The Christian religion is a religion of redemption, a gospel. It is good news, not good advice. The good news is that God, who is the source and end of the created world, is by an act of divine initiative restoring things to their true nature. In Jesus Christ, God the Son, the creative power of God pierces, purifies and transforms the creation. Redemption is always a restoration.

"Thus, while the Christian religion is primarily a gospel, it is also a philosophy. This Christian philosophy contains three axioms. The first is that in the actual world things are not true to their essential nature. There has been a Fall. The second is that 'the good' of anything is a recovery of its true nature, and that this recovery is made, not by any self-improvement, but by an act of God. There follows the third principle, that the true nature of any created thing is only sustained when it is held to its true end by supernatural direction and power.

"The good life is therefore in the Christian Faith something to be recovered rather than created by man. It is part of his essential being. Redemption through Christ effects a recognition rather than a discovery. Man's true nature is brought back with a price." V. A. Demant, *Theology of Society* (Faber & Faber, Ltd., London, 1947), p. 11. By permission.

8. A. J. Carlyle, *Property, Its Duties and Rights*, 2d ed., pp. 117–132. Quoted by McIlwain, *ibid.*, p. 162.

9. R. W. and A. J. Carlyle, *A History of Mediaeval Political Theory in the West*, Vol. I (New York, 1903), p. 192.

10. McIlwain, *op. cit.*, p. 197.

11. *Ibid.*, p. 197.

12. Quoted by H. O. Taylor, *The Mediaeval Mind* (Macmillan, 2 vols., 1925), Vol. II, p. 290. By permission of Harvard University Press, present holder of copyright.

13. Quoted by Taylor, *ibid.*, p. 293.

14. *Summa Theologica*, Prima Secundae Partis, Quaestic XC, art. iv. Quoted by McIlwain, *op. cit.*, p. 326.

15. See McIlwain, *ibid.*, p. 327.

16. Quoted by McIlwain, *ibid.*, p. 328.

CHAPTER 3

1. H. O. Taylor, *The Mediaeval Mind* (New York, 2 vols, 1925), Vol. II, p. 519. For a different interpretation see Maurice de Wulf, *History of Mediaeval Philosophy* (London, 2 vols., 1926), Vol. II, pp. 69 *ff.*

2. Taylor, *ibid.*, pp. 519–520.

3. Ernest Troeltsch, *The Social Teaching of the Christian Churches* (Macmillan, 2 vols., 1931), Vol. 2, p. 464. Used with the permission of The Macmillan Company.

4. Taylor, *op. cit.*, pp. 522–523.

5. Étienne Gilson, *The Spirit of Mediaeval Philosophy*. Transl. by A. H. C. Downes (Charles Scrib-

ner's Sons, New York, 1936), pp. 401–402. By permission.

6. Quoted by Preserved Smith, *History of Modern Culture* (New York, 2 vols., 1930).

7. Gilson, *op. cit.*, p. 402.

8. William Temple, *Nature, Man and God* (Macmillan, New York, 1934), pp. 62–63. Copyright 1934 by The Macmillan Company and used with their permission.

9. S. V. Keeling, *Descartes* (Oxford University Press, London, 1934), p. 32. By permission. Also E. Brehier, *Histoire de la Philosophie* (Paris, 1928), Vol. I, p. 759. See E. A. Burtt, *Metaphysical Foundations of Modern Physical Science* (New York, 1927), Ch. IV.

10. Francis Bacon, *Novum Organum*, Bk. I, Aphorism 69.

11. "Discourse on the Method of Rightly Conducting the Reason and Seeking for Truth in the Sciences," in *The Philosophical Works of Descartes*. Transl. by Haldane and Ross (Cambridge University Press, Cambridge, 1931), pp. 87, 89, 91 and 92. By permission.

12. William Temple, *op. cit.*, pp. 85–87.

13. *Discourse on Method*, *loc. cit.*, pp. 100–101.

14. Descartes, *Principles of Philosophy*, Part 1, Principle, vii. *Loc. cit.*, p. 221.

15. Von Hügel, *The Reality of God*, pp. 188–189. Quoted by William Temple, *op. cit.*, p. 79.

16. Quoted by J. H. Randall, Jr., *The Making of the Modern Mind*, rev. ed. (Houghton Mifflin, Boston, 1940), p. 237. By permission.

17. A. N. Whitehead, *Science and the Modern World* (Macmillan, New York, 1925), pp. 73 *ff.* (Italics mine.) Copyright 1925 by The Macmillan Company and used with their permission.

18. M. B. Foster, "Christian Theology and the Modern Science of Nature," *Mind*, Vol. 44, pp. 439–466; Vol. 45, pp. 1–27.

19. *Ibid.*, Vol. 45, pp. 13–14.

20. *Ibid.*, Vol. 45, pp. 19, 23–24.

21. According to Whitehead: "I do not think . . . that I have even brought out the greatest contribution of mediaevalism to the formation of the scientific movement. I mean the inexpugnable belief that every detailed occurrence can be correlated with its antecedents in a perfectly definite manner, exemplifying general principles. Without this belief the incredible labours of scientists would be without hope. It is this instinctive conviction, vividly poised before the imagination, which is the motive power of research: that there is a secret, a secret which can be unveiled. How has this conviction been so vividly implanted on the European mind? When we compare the tone of thought in Europe with the attitude of other civilizations when left to themselves, there seems but one source for its origin. It must come from the mediaeval insistence on the rationality of God, conceived as with the personal energy of Jehovah and with the rationality of a Greek philosopher." *Op. cit.*, p. 18. Whitehead is of the opinion, however, that "the faith in the possibility of science . . . is an unconscious derivative from mediaeval theology" and he is "not arguing that the European trust in the scrutability of nature was logically justified even by its own theology." *Ibid.*, p. 19.

22. Quoted by Randall, *op. cit.*, p. 220.

23. Whitehead, *op. cit.*, p. 83.

24. *Novum Organum*, Bk. I, Aphorism 81.

25. *Discourse on Method*, Part 6. By permission.

26. Burtt, *op. cit.*, pp. 10–11.

27. *The Prince*, Ch. XVIII, in Christian E. Detmold, *The Historical, Political, and Diplomatic Writings of Niccolo Machiavelli* (Boston, 4 vols., 1882), Vol. II, pp. 57–58. There is considerable difference of opinion among scholars as to what Machiavelli "really meant" and ever since he wrote he has been subjected both to extravagant condemnation and to equally extravagant praise. For a brief account of the major historical judgments which have been made of Machiavelli and for a very keen reappraisal of his significance see Ernst Cassirer, *The Myth of the State* (Yale University Press, New Haven, 1946), Chs. X–XII. The standard work on Machiavelli's life is P. Villari's *The Life and Times of Niccolo Machiavelli*. Eng. transl. by Linda Villari. (London, 2 vols., 1892). See also Jakob Burckhardt, *Die Kultur der Renaissance in Italien* for the background; English transl. by S. G. C. Middlemore (New York, 1937). See also Friedrich Meinecke's chapter on Machiavelli in *Die Idee der Staatsräson* (Munich, 3rd ed., 1929); Leonardo Olschki, *Machiavelli: The Scientist* (Berkeley, 1945); Charles N. R. McCoy, "The Place of Machiavelli in the History of Political Thought," *American Political Science Review* (August, 1943), pp. 626 *ff.;* G. H. Sabine, *A History of Political Theory* (New York, 1950), Ch. XVII; Michael B. Foster, *Masters of Political Thought: Plato to Machiavelli* (Boston, 1941), Ch. 8; and W. T. Jones, *Masters of Political Thought: Machiavelli to Bentham* (Boston, 1947), Ch. 2.

28. *Ibid.*, Ch. XXVI, *loc. cit.*, pp. 87–88. There is some controversy among scholars as to whether this concluding chapter of *The Prince* is an integral part of the work or a later addition to it but many scholars have seen in this concluding chapter a justification of all that preceded it. Professor Cassirer holds this view to be mistaken because he says "there are obvious differences between the book taken as a whole and the last chapter, differences of thought and differences of style. In the book itself Machiavelli speaks with an entirely detached mind. Everyone may hear him and make what use he will of his advice which is available not only to the Italians but also to

the most dangerous enemies of Italy. . . . In his analysis of political actions Machiavelli never gives vent to any personal feeling of sympathy or antipathy. To put it in the words of Spinoza he speaks of these things as if they were lines, planes, or solids. He did not attack the principles of morality; but he could find no use for these principles when engrossed in problems of political life. Machiavelli looked at political combats as if they were a game of chess. He had studied the rules of the game very thoroughly. But he had not the slightest intention of changing or criticizing these rules. His political experience had taught him that the political game never had been played without fraud, deception, treachery, and felony. He neither blamed nor recommended these things. His only concern was to find the best move —the move that wins the game." *Op. cit.*, p. 143.

29. *Discourses on the First Ten Books of Titus Livius*, Bk. I, Ch. LVIII, in Detmold, *op. cit.*, Vol. II, p. 217.
30. *Ibid.*, pp. 218–219.
31. Ernst Cassirer, *The Myth of the State* (Yale University Press, 1946), p. 138. By permission.
32. Detmold ed., p. 129.
33. *Discourses*, Bk. I, Ch. XI, *ibid.*, pp. 126 *ff*.
34. Cassirer, *op. cit.*, pp. 138–139.
35. *Ibid.*, p. 141.
36. Detmold ed., p. 421.
37. *Ibid.*, pp. 155–156.
38. *The Prince*, Ch. XXV, *ibid.*, pp. 82 *ff*.
39. "The difference between the Machiavellian and the Christian conceptions of the power by which human affairs are controlled," according to Michael Foster, "is the obverse side of the difference . . . between the Machiavellian and the Christian view of human virtue. According to Machiavelli, human virtue is displayed in the power to resist the force which governs the world; according to Christianity, in willing submission to the laws

and purposes of God." Foster, *op. cit.*, p. 283.
40. Martin Luther, *Works* (Erlangen ed.) Vol. XXII, p. 15.
41. Ernst Troeltsch, *op. cit.*, Vol. 2, pp. 468–469.
    Luther on one occasion declared that "there is no greater enemy of grace than Aristotle's ethics." Quoted by Gilson, *op. cit.*, p. 415. Gilson declares that, "For the first time, with the Reformation, there appeared this conception of grace that saves a man without changing him, of a justice that redeems corrupted nature without restoring it, of a Christ who pardons the sinner for self-inflicted wounds but does not heal them." *Ibid.*, p. 421. For another Catholic interpretation of Luther's thought see the essay on Luther by Jacques Maritain in *Three Reformers: Luther, Descartes, and Rousseau* (New York, 1936).
42. Quoted by T. M. Lindsay, *A History of the Reformation* (New York, 3rd ed., 1913), Vol. I, p. 443.
43. *Institutes*, Bk. I, Ch. VII, Sec. V.
44. Troeltsch, *op. cit.*, Vol. II, p. 471.
45. *Ibid.*, Vol. II, p. 472.
46. *Ibid.*, Vol. II, p. 475.
47. See the instructions issued by the Synod which met at Bern in 1532: Art. 3—"That God is revealed to the people in Christ alone"; Art. 5—"That the gracious God is perceived through Christ alone without any mediation." A very useful and convenient source of extracts from important documents illustrating the development of Christian doctrine is a book recently edited by Henry Bettenson entitled *Documents of the Christian Church* (London, 1942). An American edition is also available. It is published in the World's Classics series by the Oxford University Press.
48. *Works*, Vol. XII, p. 244.
49. *Ibid.*, Vol. X, p. 162.
50. H. O. Wakeman, *An Introduction to the History of the Church of England* (London, rev. ed., 1914).

51. William Haller, *The Rise of Puritanism* (New York, 1938), p. 89.

52. H. N. Fairchild, *Religious Trends in English Poetry*, (Columbia University Press, New York, 1939). Vol. I, pp. 546–547 and Vol. II, p. 475. By permission.

53. Max Shepard, "Sovereignty at the Crossroads," *Political Science Quarterly*, Vol. XLV (1930), pp. 580 *ff*. Reprinted by permission. The standard works on Bodin include: Roger Chauviré, *Jean Bodin, auteur de la République* (La Flèche, 1914); Roger Chauviré, *Colloque de Jean Bodin* (Paris, 1914); Henri Baudrillart, *Jean Bodin et son temps* (Paris, 1853); A. Garosci, *Jean Bodin politica e dritto nel rinascimento Francese* (Milan, 1934) and B. Reynolds, *Proponents of Limited Monarchy in Sixteenth Century France*.

54. Luther's position in this matter is unequivocal. "It is in no wise proper," he wrote, "for anyone who would be a Christian to set himself up against his government, whether it act justly or unjustly." Quoted by Preserved Smith, *The Age of the Reformation* (1920), p. 594. "There are no better works," Luther wrote, "than to obey and serve all those who are set over us as superiors. For this reason also disobedience is a greater sin than murder, unchastity, theft, and dishonesty, and all that these may include." "On Good Works," *Works*, Vol. VI, p. 250. Calvin's position is more ambiguous. For the most part he argues that it is as impossible to resist the magistrate as it is to resist God himself. (*Institutes*, Book IV, Ch. XX, sec. 23) "For, though the Lord testifies that the magistrate is an eminent gift of his liberality to preserve the safety of men, and prescribes to magistrates themselves the extent of their duty, yet he at the same time declares, that whatever be their characters, they have their government only from him; that those who govern for the public good are true specimens and mirrors of his beneficence; and that those who rule in an unjust and tyrannical manner are raised up by him to punish the iniquity of the people; that all equally possess that sacred majesty with which he has invested legitimate authority. . . . It is unnecessary . . . to labor much to evince an impious king to be a judgment of God's wrath upon the world, as I have no expectation that any one will deny it . . . But let us rather insist on the proof of that which the minds of men do not easily admit; that a man of the worst character, and most undeserving of all honor, who holds the sovereign power, really possesses that eminent and Divine authority, which the Lord has given by his word to the ministers of his justice and judgment; and, therefore, that he ought to be regarded by his subjects, as far as pertains to public obedience, with the same reverence and esteem which they would show to the best of kings. . . ." (*Ibid.*, Bk. IV, Ch. X, sec. 25) Although this is his general position there are statements in the *Institutes* which indicate that, under certain circumstances the overthrow of tyrants is justified. "But whatever opinion be formed of the acts of men, yet the Lord equally executed his work by them, when he broke the sanguinary sceptres of insolent kings, and overturned tyrannical governments. Let princes hear and fear." (Bk. IV, Ch. XX, sec. 31) "But in the obedience which we have shown to be due to the authority of governors, it is always necessary to make one exception . . . that it do not seduce us from obedience to him, to whose will the desires of all kings ought to be subject, to whose decrees all their commands ought to yield, to whose majesty all their sceptres ought to submit. And, indeed, how preposterous it would be for us, with a view to satisfy men, to incur the displeasure of him on

whose account we yield obedience to men! The Lord, therefore, is the King of kings. . . . If they command any thing against him, it ought not to have the least attention . . ." (Bk. IV, Ch. XX, sec. 32).

55. Quoted by W. A. Dunning, *A History of Political Theories: From Luther to Montesquieu* (New York, 1938), p. 54. For an excellent discussion of the political theory of the Huguenots see Guy Howard Dodge, *The Political Theory of the Huguenots of the Dispersion* (New York, 1947).

56. Quoted by F. J. C. Hearnshaw (ed.), *The Social and Political Ideas of Some Great Thinkers of the Sixteenth and Seventeenth Centuries* (London, 1926), p. 116.

57. *The Political Works of James I.* Intro. by C. H. McIlwain. (Cambridge, 1918), p. 333.

58. T. Hobbes, *Leviathan.* Edited with an introduction by Michael Oakeshott (Oxford University Press, New York, 1947), p. 5. By permission.

59. *Ibid.*, Part I, Ch. 1, p. 7.

60. *Ibid.*, Part I, Ch. 6, p. 32.

61. *Ibid.*, Part I, Ch. 13, p. 80.

62. *Ibid.*, Part I, Ch. 13, pp. 81–82.

63. *Ibid.*, Part I, Ch. 13, p. 82.

64. *Ibid.*, Part I, Ch. 13, p. 83.

65. *Ibid.*, Part I, Ch. 13, p. 84.

66. *Ibid.*, Part I, Ch. 14, p. 84.

67. *Ibid.*, Part I, Ch. 14, pp. 84, 85 and Ch. 15, p. 93.

68. George H. Sabine, *A History of Political Theory*, 2d. ed. (Henry Holt and Company, New York, 1950), p. 461. By permission.

69. *Leviathan*, Part I, Ch. 15, p. 94.

70. *Ibid.*, Part II, Ch. 17, p. 112.

71. *Ibid.*, Part II, Ch. 17, p. 112.

72. *Ibid.*, Part II, Ch. 18, p. 113.

73. *Ibid.*, Part II, Ch. 18, p. 114.

74. *Ibid.*, Part II, Ch. 18, p. 115.

75. *Ibid.*, Part II, Ch. 19, p. 121.

76. *Ibid.*, Part II, Ch. 21, p. 142.

77. *Ibid.*, Part II, Ch. 21, p. 143.

78. *Ibid.*, Part II, Ch. 26, pp. 172–174.

79. *Ibid.*, A Review and Conclusion, p. 463.

80. *Ibid.*, Part III, Ch. 39, pp. 305, 306.

81. *Ibid.*, Part III, Ch. 43, pp. 394–395.

82. *Ibid.*, Part III, Ch. 32, p. 243.

83. *Ibid.*, Part III, Ch. 33, pp. 254–255.

84. *Ibid.*, Introduction by Michael Oakeshott, p. liv.

85. *Ibid.*, pp. lv–lvi. (Italics mine.) For other interpretations of Hobbes's thought see: C. E. Vaughan, *Studies in the History of Political Philosophy* (Manchester, 2 vols., 1925), Vol. I, Ch. II; G. E. G. Catlin, *Thomas Hobbes as Philosopher, Publicist, and Man of Letters* (Oxford, 1922); John Laird, *Hobbes* (London, 1934); Leo Strauss, *The Political Philosophy of Hobbes* (Oxford, 1936) and Z. Lubienski, *Die Grundlagen des ethisch-politischen Systems von Hobbes* (Munich, 1932).

## CHAPTER 4

1. Reinhold Niebuhr, *Nature and Destiny of Man* (Charles Scribner's Sons, New York, 1941), Vol. I, p. 61. By permission.

2. George H. Sabine, *A History of Political Theory*, 2d ed. (Henry Holt and Company, New York, 1950), p. 432. By permission.

3. A. D. Lindsay, "Individualism," (In Seligman ed.) *Encyclopaedia of the Social Sciences* (8 vol. ed., 1932), Vol. IV. Copyright 1932 by The Macmillan Company and used with their permission.

4. *Ibid.*

5. *Ibid.*

6. Voltaire, *Pensées sur l'administration publique.* Quoted by H. Heller, *Europa und der Fascismus* (Berlin, 2d ed., 1931). The writings of Hermann Heller contain penetrating analyses of liberal thought and institutions in Europe and I am heavily indebted to them in my own analysis. In addition to the work cited see his *Politischen Ideenkrise der Gegenwart* (Breslau, 1926); *Die Souveranität: ein Beitrag zur Theorie des Staats- und Völkerrechts* (Berlin, 1927); *Rechtsstaat oder Diktatur?* (Tübingen, 1930); and his

*Staatslehre* edited by Gerhart Nie-
meyer (Leiden, 1934). I am also
heavily indebted to Gerhart Nie-
meyer's *Law Without Force*
(Princeton, 1941).

7. Jacobus Arminius (1560–1609)
was a Dutch theologian who took
issue with some of the tenets of
orthodox Calvinism and whose
followers were known as Arminians or Remonstrants. The Remonstrants formulated their departure from orthodox Calvinism
by declaring that: (1) the divine
decree of predestination is conditional, not absolute; (2) the
Atonement is in intention universal; (3) man cannot of himself exercise a saving faith; (4)
though the grace of God is a
necessary condition of human
effort it does not act irresistibly
in man; and (5) believers are
able to resist sin but are not beyond the possibility of falling
from grace. They were opposed
by the Gomarists who defended
the orthodox Calvinist position.
As chief magistrate to the city of
Rotterdam, Grotius issued an
edict recommending mutual toleration when the two groups
became embroiled in bitter controversy. The edict forbade ministers to discuss the disputed
doctrines in their pulpits. Grotius' personal preference was for
the position of the Arminians. In
1618 Grotius was arrested, sentenced to prison for life and had
his property confiscated. With
the aid of his wife he managed to
escape from prison and took
refuge in Antwerp and later in
Paris in 1621. It was while he
was in exile that he composed the
*De jure belli ac pacis*, the first draft
of which he had completed in
1604.

8. *The Law of War and Peace*, *Prolegomena*, sec. 28.
9. *Ibid.*, sec. 39.
10. *Ibid.*, sec. 39.
11. *Ibid.*, sec. 6.
12. *Ibid.*, sec. 8.
13. *Ibid.*, sec. 9.
14. *Ibid.*, sec. 12.
15. *Ibid.*, sec. 16.

16. *Ibid.*, sec. 15.
17. *Ibid.*, sec. 16.
18. *Law of War and Peace*, Bk. I, Ch.
1, sec. x, par. 1.
19. *Ibid.*, Bk. I, Ch. 1, sec. x, par. 5.
20. *Prolegomena*, sec. 39.
21. Sabine, *op. cit.*, p. 426.
22. *Law of War and Peace*, Bk. I, Ch.
1, sec. iv.
23. *Essay Concerning Human Understanding*, Bk. I, Ch. I, sec. 1.
24. *Ibid.*, Bk. II, Ch. I, sec. 9.
25. *Ibid.*, Bk. II, Ch. I, sec. 2.
26. *Ibid.*, Bk. II, Ch. VIII, secs. 14
and 15.
27. *Ibid.*, Bk. IV, Ch. I, secs. 1–2.
28. Reprinted from *A History of Western Philosophy* by permission of
Simon and Schuster, Publishers.
Copyright, 1945, by Bertrand
Russell. P. 612.
29. A. N. Whitehead, *Science and the
Modern World* (Macmillan, New
York, 1925), pp. 79–80. Copyright 1925 by The Macmillan
Company and used with their
permission.
30. *Ibid.*, p. 80.
31. *Ibid.*, pp. 81–82.
32. John Locke, *The Second Treatise
of Civil Government*, ed. by J. W.
Gough (Oxford, 1946), Ch.
VIII, sec. 95, p. 48.
33. T. Hobbes, *Leviathan*, Part I,
Ch. 13.
34. *Second Treatise*, Ch. II, sec. 4, p. 4.
35. *Ibid.*, Ch. II, sec. 6, p. 5.
36. *Ibid.*, Ch. IX, sec. 123, p. 62.
37. *Ibid.*, Ch. IX, sec. 124, p. 62.
38. *Ibid.*, Ch. IX, sec. 125, p. 63.
39. *Ibid.*, Ch. IX, sec. 126, p. 63.
40. *Ibid.*, Ch. VIII, sec. 95, p. 48.
41. *Ibid.*, Ch. VIII, sec. 98, p. 49.
42. *Ibid.*, Ch. XI, sec. 135, p. 67.
43. *Ibid.*, Ch. XI, sec. 135, p. 68.
44. *Ibid.*, Ch. XI, sec. 137, p. 69.
45. *Ibid.*, Ch. XI, sec. 142, p. 71.
46. *Ibid.*, Ch. XIX, sec. 222, p. 108.
47. *Ibid.*, Ch. XIX, secs. 228–229,
pp. 111–112.
48. *Ibid.*, Ch. V, sec. 27, p. 15.
49. *Ibid.*, Ch. V, sec. 27, p. 15.
50. *Ibid.*, Ch. V, sec. 31, p. 17.
51. *Ibid.*, Ch. V, sec. 31, p. 17.
52. *Ibid.*, Ch. V, sec. 45, p. 24.
53. *Ibid.*, Ch. V, sec. 47, p. 25.
54. *Ibid.*, Ch. V, sec. 48, p. 25.
55. *Ibid.*, Ch. V, sec. 50, p. 26.

56. Cook's introduction to *Two Treatises of Government*, Hafner Edition (Hafner Publishing Co., New York, 1947), pp. xxix–xxx. By permission.

57. For the purposes of comparison and for other interpretations of the meaning of liberalism see, among others: W. E. Lecky, *Democracy and Liberty* (London, 1896); J. M. Robertson, *The Meaning of Liberalism* (London, 1912); L. T. Hobhouse, *Liberalism* (New York, 1911); Guido de Ruggiero, *The History of European Liberalism.* Transl. by R. G. Collingwood (London, 1927); Julius Benda, *The Treason of the Intellectuals.* Transl. by R. Aldington (New York, 1928); Kingsley Martin, *French Liberal Thought in the Eighteenth Century* (Boston, 1929); Peter Drucker, *The End of Economic Man* (New York, 1939); E. J. Hughes, *The Church and the Liberal Society* (Princeton, 1944); Reinhold Niebuhr, *The Children of Light and the Children of Darkness* (New York, 1944); Hans J. Morgenthau, *Scientific Man vs. Power Politics* (Chicago, 1946); W. A. Orton, *The Liberal Tradition* (New Haven, 1945); F. M. Watkins, *The Political Tradition of the West: A Study in the Development of Modern Liberalism* (Cambridge, Mass., 1948); H. J. Laski, *The Rise of European Liberalism* (New York, 1936). Ruth Nanda Ashen (ed.), *Freedom: Its Meaning* (New York, 1940); Lord Acton, *The History of Freedom and Other Essays*, edited by J. M. Figgis and R. V. Laurence (London, 1907); Lord Acton, *Essays on Freedom and Power*, selected with an introduction by Gertrude Himmelfarb (Boston, 1948); Horace M. Kallen, *The Liberal Spirit* (Ithaca and New York, 1948); Rubin Gotesky, "Liberalism in Crisis," in Feliks Gross (ed.), *European Ideologies: A Survey of Twentieth Century Ideas* (New York, 1948). Walter Lippmann, *An Inquiry into the Principles of the Good Society* (Boston, 1937); F. W. Coker,

*Recent Political Thought* (New York, 1934); J. Salwyn Schapiro, *Liberalism and the Challenge of Fascism* (New York, 1949); Émile Faguet, *Le Liberalisme* (Paris, 1912); Ludwig von Mises, *Liberalismus* (Jena, 1927); Hermann Heller, *Die politischen Ideenkrise der Gegenwart* (Breslau, 1926); Salvador M. Dana Montaro, *Justicia Social y Reforma Constitucional* (Santa Fé, Argentina, 1948).

58. R. H. Tawney explains this conception in the following words: "Society is not a community of classes with varying functions united to each other by mutual obligations arising from their relations to a common end. It is a joint stock company rather than an organism, and the liabilities of the shareholders are strictly limited . . . The State, a matter of convenience, not of supernatural sanctions, exists for the protection of those rights, and fulfills its object in so far as by maintaining contractual freedom, it secures full scope for their unfettered exercise." *Religion and the Rise of Capitalism* (Harcourt, Brace and Company, Inc., New York, 1926), p. 189. By permission.

59. For a detailed analysis of the theory and practice of constitutional government see C. J. Friedrich, *Constitutional Government and Democracy* (Boston, 1941) and H. A. Finer, *The Theory and Practice of Modern Government*, one vol., rev. ed. (New York, 1949). For the meaning of constitutionalism in its historical context see C. H. McIlwain, *Constitutionalism: Ancient and Modern* (Ithaca, 1940) and his *Constitutionalism and the Changing World* (Cambridge, Mass., 1939). For an excellent discussion of the theoretical roots of American constitutional government see also E. S. Corwin, "The 'Higher Law' Background of American Constitutional Law," *Harvard Law Review*, Vol. XLII (1928), pp. 149–185 and pp. 365–409

and his *Liberty Against Government* (Baton Rouge, 1948).

60. C. H. McIlwain, *The Growth of Political Thought in the West* (Macmillan, New York, 1932), pp. 370–371. Copyright 1932 by The Macmillan Company and used with their permission.

61. E. P. Cheyney, *Readings in English History* (Ginn and Co., Boston, 1935), pp. 545–546. By permission.

62. The best work on the Declaration of Independence and the philosophical presuppositions underlying it, is Carl Becker's *The Declaration of Independence* (New York, rev. ed., 1942).

## CHAPTER 5

1. *Was ist Aufklärung?* (1784), *Werke*, Vol. 4, p. 169. Edited by E. Cassirer (Berlin, 1922).

2. *Was heisst: sich im Denken orientieren?* (1786) in *Werke*, Vol. 4, pp. 349.*ff*.

3. In the article on "Enlightenment" in the *Encyclopaedia of the Social Sciences* (1937 ed.), Vol. 5.

4. Carl Becker, *The Heavenly City of the Eighteenth-Century Philosophers* (Yale University Press, New Haven, 1932), pp. 50–51. By permission.

5. *The Reasonableness of Christianity* (Boston, 1811), pp. 234–235.

6. *Ibid.*, p. 170.

7. *Ibid.*, pp. 225–226.

8. Leslie Stephen, *History of English Thought in the Eighteenth Century* (London, 2 vols., 1881), Vol. I, p. 100.

9. *Op. cit.*, p. 240.

10. *Ibid.*, p. 242.

11. *Ibid.*, p. 243.

12. *Moral and Political Philosophy*, Bk. I, Ch. 7.

13. Samuel Clarke, *A Discourse Concerning the Unchangeable Obligations of Natural Religion and the Truth and Certainty of the Christian Revelation* (1705). Quoted by J. H. Randall, Jr., *The Making of the Modern Mind* (Houghton Mifflin Company, Boston, rev. ed., 1940), p. 290. By permission.

14. Randall, *ibid.*, p. 290.

15. Voltaire, *Bolingbroke*. Quoted by Randall, *ibid.*, p. 292.

16. *Letter to Damilaville* (1766) in *Oeuvres*, Ch. 19, p. 477.

17. *Treatise of Human Nature*, ed. by L. A. Selby-Biggs (London, 1896), Vol. II, p. 551.

18. Quoted by A. N. Whitehead, *Science and the Modern World* (Macmillan, New York, 1925), p. 5. Copyright 1925 by The Macmillan Company and used with their permission.

19. Whitehead, *ibid.*, p. 6.

20. *Système de la Nature*, Ch. IV. Quoted by Randall, *op. cit.*, p. 301.

21. *Le Bons-Sens*, sec. 22 in *ibid.*, p. 302.

22. *Système de la Nature*, Part II, Ch. XIV, in *ibid.*, p. 279.

23. *Essay on Man.*

24. Becker, *op. cit.*, p. 130.

25. *Sermons*. Preface to Sermons I and II.

26. *Enquiry Concerning the Principles of Morals*, Sec. 5, Pt. II.

27. *Op. cit.*, pp. 102–103.

28. *Outlines of an Historical View of the Progress of the Human Mind* (London, 1795), p. 317.

29. *Ibid.*, pp. 4–5.

30. *Ibid.*, pp. 316–317.

31. *Ibid.*, p. 327.

32. *Ibid.*, p. 344.

33. *Ibid.*, p. 368.

34. *Ibid.*, pp. 369.*ff*.

35. Karl Löwith, *Meaning in History: The Theological Implications of the Philosophy of History* (University of Chicago Press, Chicago: 1949), pp. 197–198. By permission. This is one of the best analyses of modern philosophies of history to appear in recent years. It subjects the idea of a "philosophy of history" itself to a searching and profound scrutiny in the light of Christian theology and is a welcome antidote to modern historicism.

36. *Ibid.*, p. 84. On the idea of progress see, in addition, F. J. Teggart, *The Idea of Progress* (Berkeley, 1925); J. B. Bury, *The Idea of Progress* (New York, 1932); W. R. Inge, *The Idea of Progress*

(Oxford, 1920); Carl Becker, *op. cit.;* A. Solomon, "The Religion of Progress," *Social Research* (December, 1946), and Christopher Dawson, *Progress and Religion* (London, 1945).

37. See Charles Gide and Charles Rist, *A History of Economic Doctrines*, 2d English ed. (G. G. Harrap and Co., London, 1948), p. 25 ff. By permission.

38. Gide and Rist, *ibid.*, p. 22.

39. *Maximes du Docteur Quesnay.* Quoted by Randall, *op. cit.*, p. 323.

40. Quoted by Gide and Rist, *op. cit.*, p. 27, footnote 3.

41. Mercier de la Rivière. Quoted by Gide and Rist, *ibid.*, p. 28, footnote 1.

42. *Origines et Progrès d'une Science nouvelle.* Quoted by Randall, *op. cit.*, p. 324.

43. Quoted by Gide and Rist, *op. cit.*, p. 52, footnote 1.

44. Quoted by Gide and Rist, *ibid.*, p. 54, footnote 1.

45. Quoted by Gide and Rist, *ibid.*, p. 54, footnote 4.

46. *Ibid.*, p. 105.

47. *Wealth of Nations*, Cannan's ed. (London, 1904), Vol. I, p. 421.

48. *Ibid.*, Vol. II, p. 304.

49. *Ibid.*, Vol. II, p. 308.

50. *Ibid.*, Vol. II, p. 185.

51. See *ibid.*, Vol. II, pp. 233 and 246.

52. Gide and Rist, *op. cit.*, p. 113.

53. Smith, *op. cit.*, Vol. I, p. 307.

54. Gide and Rist, *op. cit.*, pp. 118–119.

55. *The Spirit of the Laws*, transl. by T. Nugent (New York, 1899), p. 1.

56. *Ibid.*, p. 2.

57. *Ibid.*, p. 2.

58. *Ibid.*, pp. 4–5.

59. *Ibid.*, p. 5.

60. *Ibid.*, p. 6.

61. *Ibid.*, p. 8.

62. *Ibid.*, p. 10.

63. *Ibid.*, p. 21.

64. *Ibid.*, p. 41.

65. *Ibid.*, pp. 22–23.

66. *Ibid.*, p. 49.

67. *Ibid.*, p. 50.

68. *Ibid.*, pp. 25, 31 and 32.

69. *Ibid.*, p. 54.

70. *Ibid.*, p. 26.

71. *Ibid.*, pp. 58, 59 and 62.

72. See *ibid.*, Bks. XIV–XVII, pp. 221 ff.

73. *Ibid.*, p. 149.

74. *Ibid.*, p. 183.

75. *Ibid.*, p. 150.

76. *Ibid.*, pp. 151–152.

77. *Ibid.*, p. 155.

78. *Ibid.*, p. 156.

79. *Ibid.*, p. 153.

80. See V. L. Parrington, *Main Currents in American Thought: The Colonial Mind* (New York, 1927), Vol. I, pp. 53 ff. The best single source of the writings of the Puritans together with illuminating interpretative essays is a volume edited by Perry Miller and T. W. Johnson, *The Puritans* (New York, 1938). For these and later writings see also F. W. Coker, *Democracy, Liberty and Property: Readings in the American Political Tradition* (New York, 1942) and B. F. Wright, *A Source Book of American Political Theory* (New York, 1929). For an interesting thesis see R. B. Perry, *Puritanism and Democracy* (New York, 1944).

81. *Survey of the Summe of Church Discipline.*

82. Quoted by Parrington, *op. cit.*, Vol. I, p. 59.

83. "The Bloody Tenent Yet More Bloody" in *Publications of the Narragansett Club* (Providence, 1867), Vol. IV, p. 187.

84. "The Bloody Tenent," *ibid.*, Vol. III, p. 366.

85. Preface to "The Bloody Tenent," *ibid.*, Vol. III, p. 3.

86. *Vindication . . .* (Boston, 1860), pp. 54–55.

87. *Ibid.*, p. 50.

88. *Writings of Thomas Jefferson*, ed. by A. E. Bergh (Washington, 1903), Vol. XVI, p. 118.

89. For an excellent analysis of the philosophy of the Declaration see Carl Becker, *The Declaration of Independence* (New York, 1942). For a survey of American political theory see V. L. Parrington, *Main Currents in American Thought* (New York, 3 vols., 1927–1930); W. S. Carpenter, *The Develop-*

*ment of American Political Thought* (1930); J. M. Jacobson, *The Development of American Political Thought* (New York, 1932); E. R. Lewis, *A History of American Political Thought from the Civil War to the World War* (1937); C. E. Merriam, *American Political Ideas, 1865–1917* (1921); B. F. Wright, *American Interpretations of Natural Law* (1931); R. H. Gabriel, *The Course of American Democratic Thought* (New York, 1940); F. G. Wilson, *The American Political Mind* (New York, 1949); and Edward S. Corwin, *Liberty Against Government* (Baton Rouge, 1948). For more general intellectual and philosophical developments in America see Merle Curti, *The Growth of American Thought* (1943); L. M. Hacker, *The Shaping of the American Tradition* (New York, 1947); H. W. Schneider, *A History of American Philosophy* (New York, 1946); I. W. Riley, *American Thought from Puritanism to Pragmatism and Beyond* (New York, 2d ed., 1941); and for an evaluation of contemporary American civilization see John U. Nef, *The United States and Civilization* (Chicago, 1942); R. M. Weaver, *Ideas Have Consequences* (Chicago, 1948); and Peter F. Drucker, *The Future of Industrial Man* (New York, 1940).

90. H. N. Fairchild, *Religious Trends in English Poetry* (New York, 1942), Vol. II, pp. 372–373.

## CHAPTER 6

1. The most comprehensive study of Vico's philosophy is B. Croce's *The Philosophy of G. Vico*, transl. by R. G. Collingwood (New York, 1913). A sympathetic, profound and brief treatment can be found in Robert Flint's *Vico* (London, 1884). I have used an American edition of this work published with no date in Philadelphia. A more popular account is H. P. Adams, *The Life and Writings of Vico* (London, 1935). See also the excellent introduction by M. H. Fisch and T. G.

Bergin to Vico's *Autobiography*. A short but highly illuminating discussion of Vico's philosophy of history from the perspective of Christian theology will be found in Karl Löwith's *Meaning of History* (Chicago, 1949), Ch. VI.

2. *Opere*, Vol. II, pp. 63–64, quoted by Flint, *op. cit.*, pp. 86–87.

3. *Opere*, Vol. II, p. 64, quoted *ibid.*, p. 88.

4. *Opere*, Vol. II, pp. 67–68, quoted *ibid.*, p. 90.

5. Flint, *ibid.*, pp. 99–100.

6. Quoted *ibid.*, p. 118.

7. *The New Science of Gambattista Vico*, transl. by T. G. Bergin and M. H. Fisch (Cornell University Press, Ithaca, 1948), Par. 331. By permission.

8. *Ibid.*, par. 2.

9. *Ibid.*, par. 342.

10. Löwith, *op. cit.*, p. 124.

11. Flint, *op. cit.*, p. 195.

12. *New Science*, par. 1106.

13. Löwith, *op. cit.*, p. 134. According to Robert Flint, Vico's "whole attitude towards the future seems irreconcilable with the notion that he imagined that it would be a transcript of a page which had been already written. His belief in cycles or 'ricorsi' was, indeed, inconsistent with a belief in continuous progress in a straight line, but not with advance on the whole, not with a gradually ascending spiral movement, and still less did it imply that any cycle was perfectly like another, and that history merely repeated itself." *Op. cit.*, p. 228. Progress for Vico is real although he does not conceive of it as proceeding in a straight line.

14. A discussion of Hegel's philosophy will be found in Chap. 8. Savigny is given brief attention in Chap. 10.

15. Jacques Maritain, *Three Reformers: Luther—Descartes—Rousseau* (Sheed and Ward, Inc., London, 1936), p. 115, footnote. By permission.

16. Irving Babbitt, *Rousseau and Romanticism* (Houghton Mifflin, Boston, 1919), pp. 121–122. By permission.

17. Wordsworth, *The Tables Turned.*
18. Maritain, *op. cit.*, p. 96.
19. *Ibid.*, p. 98.
20. Quoted by Maritain, *ibid.*, pp. 109–110.
21. *Ibid.*, p. 98.
22. Quoted by Babbitt, *op. cit.*, p. 135.
23. Maritain, *op. cit.*, p. 100.
24. Quoted by Maritain, *ibid.*, p. 110, footnote.
25. *Ibid.*, pp. 115 *et seq.*
26. Rousseau, *Social Contract and Discourses* (Everyman's ed. 1938), p. 152.
27. *Ibid.*, pp. 214–215. (Italics mine.)
28. *Émile* in Romain Rolland (ed.), *The Living Thoughts of Rousseau* (New York, 1939), p. 86.
29. *Ibid.*, p. 88.
30. *Ibid.*, pp. 88 *et seq.*
31. *Social Contract, op. cit.*, p. 5.
32. *Ibid.*, p. 8.
33. *Ibid.*, p. 14.
34. *Ibid.*, p. 10.
35. *Ibid.*, p. 15.
36. *Ibid.*, p. 15.
37. *Ibid.*, pp. 15–16.
38. *Ibid.*, p. 18.
39. *Ibid.*, p. 17.
40. *Ibid.*, p. 25.
41. *Ibid.*, p. 25. (Italics mine.)
42. *Ibid.*, pp. 93–94. (Italics mine.) In an earlier passage, however, Rousseau had argued that "What makes the general will is less the number of votes than the common interest uniting them."
43. *Ibid.*, p. 33.
44. *Ibid.*, p. 34.
45. Maritain, *op. cit.*, pp. 139–140.
46. *Social Contract, op. cit.*, p. 35.
47. *Ibid.*, pp. 35–36.
48. Maritain, *op. cit.*, pp. 134–135.
49. *Ibid.*, p. 144.
50. *Ibid.*, p. 146. For other interpretations of Rousseau see the Introduction to *The Political Writings of Jean Jacques Rousseau* by C. E. Vaughan (Cambridge, 2 vols., 1915); Ernest H. Wright, *The Meaning of Rousseau* (Oxford, 1929); Albert Schinz, *La pensée de Jean Jacques Rousseau* (Paris, 1929); Charles W. Hendel, *Jean Jacques Rousseau, Moralist* (London, 2 vols., 1934); Émile Faguet, *La Politique comparée de*

*Montesquieu, Rousseau et Voltaire* (Paris, 1920).
51. Babbitt, *op. cit.*, pp. 135–136.
52. *Op. cit.*, pp. 117–118.
53. See Louis Madelin, *The French Revolution* (New York, 1931), pp. 387 *ff.*
54. *Ibid.*, p. 407.
55. Guido de Ruggiero, *History of European Liberalism* (Allen and Unwin, Ltd., London, 1927), p. 82. By permission.
56. Quoted in Introduction to *Edmund Burke Selections* (New York, 1925), p. viii.
57. Selections from Burke's writings are now easily obtainable in an excellent collection edited by Ross J. S. Hoffman and Paul Levack and entitled *Burke's Politics* (New York, 1949).
58. *An Appeal from the New to the Old Whigs* in *The Works of Edmund Burke* (Bohn ed., London, 1896). Vol. III, p. 16.
59. "Reflections on the Revolution in France," *Works*, Vol. II.
60. *Ibid.*
61. *Ibid.*
62. *Ibid.*
63. *Ibid.*
64. "Reform of Representation in the House of Commons," *Works*, Vol. VI, pp. 146 *ff.*
65. "Thoughts on the Causes of the Present Discontents," *Works*, Vol. I, p. 356.
66. *Ibid.*
67. Speech to the electors of Bristol, November 3, 1774. *Works*, Vol. I, p. 447.
68. *Ibid.*, pp. 446–447.
69. "Reflections on the Revolution in France."
70. "A Letter to a Noble Lord" (1796), *Works*, Vol. V, p. 120.
71. Speech on Moving his Resolutions for Conciliation with the Colonies, March 22, 1775. *Works*, Vol. I, pp. 450 *ff.*
72. "Reflections on the Revolution in France."
73. "A Letter to a Noble Lord."
74. "Reflections on the Revolution in France."
75. *History of Political Theory* (Henry Holt and Company, New York, 1950), pp. 618–619. Burke had

considerable influence in Germany in the development of conservatism there. See Reinhold Aris, *History of Political Thought in Germany from 1789 to 1815* (London, 1936).

## CHAPTER 7

1. *Hume's Moral and Political Philosophy.* Edited with an Introduction by Henry D. Aiken (Hafner Publishing Co., New York, 1948). *Treatise of Human Nature*, pp. 24–25. By permission.
2. *Ibid.*, p. 33.
3. *Ibid.*, p. 44.
4. *Ibid.*, p. 64.
5. *Ibid.*, p. 62.
6. *Ibid.*, p. 67. (Italics mine.)
7. *Ibid.*, p. 66. (Italics mine.)
8. Ernest Albee, *A History of English Utilitarianism* (Macmillan, New York, 1902), p. 96.
9. Hume, *Enquiry Concerning the Principles of Morals, loc. cit.*, p. 272, note 1.
10. *Ibid.*, p. 259.
11. *Ibid.*, p. 260.
12. *Ibid.*, p. 249.
13. *Ibid.*, p. 261.
14. Albee, *op. cit.*, p. 110.
15. *Principles of Moral and Political Philosophy* (1785). Quoted by Albee, *ibid.*, p. 170.
16. *De L'Homme* (1772), Chaps. IV, IX and X. Cf. the discussion of Helvetius' philosophy in Kingsley Martin, *French Liberal Thought in the Eighteenth Century* (Boston, 1929), pp. 177 *ff.*
17. *De L'Homme*, Vol. II, Sec. X, Ch. 1.
18. *De L'Esprit*, Essay III, Ch. XXII.
19. Martin, *op. cit.*, p. 183.
20. Quoted by Martin, *ibid.*, p. 183. (Italics mine.)
21. Martin, *op. cit.*, p. 184.
22. Quoted by Martin, *ibid.*, pp. 185–186.
23. *Ibid.*, p. 185.
24. *De L'Homme*, Sec. II, Ch. 2. (Italics mine.)
25. *An Introduction to the Principles of Morals and Legislation* (Oxford,

1879). The first edition was published in 1789.
26. See *ibid.*, pp. 17 *ff.* especially the footnote on p. 17.
27. *Ibid.*, p. 19, footnote.
28. *Ibid.*, p. 22, footnote.
29. *Ibid.*, p. 21.
30. *Ibid.*, p. 102.
31. *Ibid.*, p. 107.
32. *Ibid.*, pp. 29 *ff.*
33. *Ibid.*, p. 31.
34. *Ibid.*, pp. 33 *ff.*
35. *Ibid.*, pp. 44 *ff.*
36. *Ibid.*, p. 3.
37. The phrase "greatest happiness of the greatest number" does not actually appear in Bentham's *Introduction to the Principles of Morals and Legislation* but in the 1823 edition he added a note, on the first page, to the effect that "the greatest happiness or greatest felicity" principle might be preferable to the "principle of utility" since "the word *utility* does not so clearly point to the ideas of *pleasure* and *pain* as the words *happiness* and *felicity* do; nor does it lead us to the consideration of the *number*, of the interests affected." This lack, moreover, "of a sufficiently manifest connexion between the ideas of *happiness* and *pleasure* on the one hand, and the idea of *utility* on the other," he said, "I have now and then found operating, and with but too much efficiency, as a bar to the acceptance, that might otherwise have been given, to this principle." It is difficult to trace the origin of the phrase "greatest happiness of the greatest number" but it was used before Bentham by Hutcheson in his *Enquiry into our Ideas of Beauty and Virtue* (London, 5th ed., 1753), p. 185, and is also found in the introduction to Beccaria's *Treatise of Crimes and Punishments* (1764), a book which anticipates in many striking ways Bentham's theory.
38. *Theory of Legislation*. Translated and edited from the French of Étienne Dumont by C. M. Atkinson (London, 1914), 2 vols., Vol. I, p. 65.

39. *Ibid.*, Vol. I, p. 125.
40. *Manual of Political Economy. The Works of Jeremy Bentham* (Bowring ed., Edinburgh, 1839), Vol. III, Part IX, p. 33.
41. *Anarchical Fallacies, A Critical Examination of the Declaration of Rights, Works, ibid.*, Vol. II, Part VIII, pp. 500–501.
42. *Ibid.*, p. 501.
43. *A Fragment on Government.* Edited by F. C. Montague (London, 1931), p. 160.
44. *Ibid.*, p. 137.
45. *Ibid.*, p. 208, footnote. See also his *Introduction to the Principles of Morals and Legislation*, pp. 330 *ff.*
46. *A Fragment on Government*, p. 218.
47. *Ibid.*, p. 217.
48. Guido de Ruggiero, *Modern Philosophy.* Translated by A. H. Hannay and R. G. Collingwood (Macmillan, New York, 1921), p. 233. Used with the permission of The Macmillan Company.
49. *Ibid.*, pp. 235–236.
50. *Utilitarianism, Liberty, and Representative Government.* Everyman ed. Introduction by A. D. Lindsay (London, 1929), p. 6.
51. *Ibid.*, p. 7. (Italics mine.)
52. *Ibid.*, p. 7.
53. *Ibid.*, pp. 8 and 10.
54. *Ibid.*, pp. 32–33.
55. C. E. M. Joad, *Guide to the Philosophy of Morals and Politics*, pp. 334–335. Reprinted by permission of Random House, Inc.
56. *Utilitarianism, loc. cit.*, p. 16.
57. Joad, *op. cit.*, pp. 337–338.
58. *Op. cit.*, p. 60. (Italics mine.)
59. *On Liberty, loc. cit.*, p. 79 *et seq.*
60. *Ibid.*, p. 66.
61. *Ibid.*, p. 67.
62. *Ibid.*, pp. 67–68.
63. *Ibid.*, p. 68.
64. *Ibid.*, pp. 115–116.
65. *Ibid.*, p. 73.
66. *Ibid.*, p. 73.
67. *Ibid.*, pp. 164–165.
68. *Ibid.*, p. 75.
69. *Representative Government, loc. cit.*, p. 207.
70. *Ibid.*, p. 277.
71. *Ibid.*, p. 239.
72. *Ibid.*, pp. 231–232.
73. *Ibid.*, p. 237.
74. *Ibid.*, p. 241.

75. Gide and Rist, *History of Economic Doctrines*, 2d English ed. (George G. Harrap and Co., London, 1948); pp. 358–359. By permission.
76. *Ibid.*, p. 360.
77. For a detailed explanation of these see *ibid.*, pp. 360 *ff.*
78. *Principles of Political Economy*, Bk. IV, Ch. VII, par. 7.
79. *Ibid.*, Bk. IV, Ch. VII, par. 7.
80. *Ibid.*, Bk. II, Ch. XIII, par. 1.
81. *Liberty*, Ch. V (Everyman's ed. London, 1929), p. 163.
82. *Ibid.*, Ch. V, p. 157.
83. *Principles, op. cit.*, Bk. II, Ch. I, par. 1.
84. Gide and Rist, *op. cit.*, p. 373.
85. *Ibid.*, p. 374.
86. *Principles, op. cit.*, Bk. IV, Ch. VII, par. 4.
87. *Ibid.*, Bk. II, Ch. II, par. 4.

## CHAPTER 8

1. J. H. Randall, Jr., *Making of the Modern Mind* (Houghton Mifflin Company, New York, rev. ed., 1940), pp. 259–260. By permission.
2. *Ibid.*, pp. 266–267.
3. *Ibid.*, p. 270.
4. *The Critique of Pure Reason* in extracts from the *Philosophy of Kant* ed. by John Watson (New York, 1894), pp. 2–3.
5. A. D. Lindsay, *Kant* (Oxford University Press, London, 1934), pp. 48–49. By permission.
6. Kant, *Critique of Pure Reason, loc. cit.*, p. 3.
7. *Ibid.*, p. 6.

There is considerable confusion as to what Kant really meant by this statement and some caution is necessary in interpreting it. According to Lindsay: "For Kant, faith is not irrational or insufficiently grounded opinion. It is as much the product of reason as is knowledge, but it is reason in action as contrasted with knowledge. Reason dictates the moral law, and dictates that we should act as if we were free." Kant's position in

this matter, Lindsay says, has
been frequently misunderstood.
"Kant holds that we do not and
cannot begin with knowledge of,
or theoretical belief in, such
metaphysical truths [as freedom
of the will, immortality of the
soul, existence of God] and then
act in accordance with them.
The practical reason has primacy
over the theoretical. We begin
with the consciousness of the
moral law and of our obligation;
that is the unshakeable fact evident to all. A man may be a
conscious atheist, and yet recognize the moral law. Kant would
say of him that in his atheism he
denied the implications of his
own moral consciousness, and
that if he reflected rightly on
that moral consciousness, he
would realize that he was affirming practically what he denied
theoretically. So, on the other
hand, we may all by our practical wrongdoing act as if there
were no God in the world, however we may piously affirm that
there is. Yet this faith is not just
an unnecessary rationalization
of our action (in the modern bad
sense of the word rationalization). Moral action would be
unmeaning if we were not free, if
moral purposes did not transcend our finite existence, if they
were not the concern of the
nature of things; if, in short, the
intelligible world, as implied by
the practical reason, were not a
reality. The distinctive character
of Kant's position in the matter
is that we can affirm the reality
of something whose nature we
cannot understand. But this is
the distinctive character of his
conception of reason. For reason
. . . is the faculty of the unconditioned. All our judgments and
our actions, because they imply
truth and goodness, imply in
their ordinary everyday working
an infinite which transcends experience, and yet gives to experience all the meaning it has
for us." *Op. cit.*, pp. 197–198.
8. Lindsay, *ibid.*, pp. 290–291.

9. Kant, *Critique of Practical Reason.*
   Transl. by T. K. Abbott (London, 6th ed., 1909), p. 260.
10. William Temple, *Nature, Man
    and God* (Macmillan, New York,
    1934), p. 74. Used with the per-
    mission of The Macmillan Com-
    pany.
11. *Ibid.*, pp. 70–71.
12. *Ibid.*, p. 73.
13. *Fundamental Principles of the Meta-
    physic of Morals* in Watson, *op. cit.*,
    p. 225.
14. *Ibid.*, pp. 225–226.
15. *Ibid.*, p. 229.
16. *Ibid.*, p. 241.
17. *Ibid.*, p. 246.
18. *Ibid.*, p. 248.
19. *Ibid.*, pp. 248–249. The cate-
    gorical imperative, if one juxta-
    poses the several formulations,
    has the following content:
    (1) A society consists of equal,
        rational, human beings;
    (2) A society should continue
        to exist, preserving the
        existence of all of its mem-
        bers;
    (3) Hence the supreme rule of
        conduct: that the maxim
        of action must be com-
        patible with the continued
        existence of the society
        with all of its members.
    This is substantially the transfer
    of the idea of a mechanical sys-
    tem in equilibrium to society.
20. *Critique of Practical Reason*, Wat-
    son transl., p. 298.
21. *Philosophy of Law.* Transl. by
    W. Hastie (Edinburgh, 1887).
22. *Kant's Principles of Politics* (Edin-
    burgh, 1891). This book contains
    translations by W. Hastie of
    Kant's *The Natural Principle of
    the Political Order Considered in
    Connection with the Idea of Univer-
    sal History from the Cosmopolitan
    Point of View* (1784), *Relation of
    Theory to Practice in International
    Law* (1793) and *Eternal Peace*
    (1795).
23. *Ibid.*
24. *Ibid.*
25. *Ibid.*
26. Guido de Ruggiero, *History of
    European Liberalism* (George Allen

and Unwin, Ltd., London, 1927), p. 219. By permission.

27. *Kant's Principles of Politics, op. cit.*

28. *Eternal Peace* in an appendix to C. J. Friedrich, *Inevitable Peace* (Harvard University Press, Cambridge, 1948), p. 259.

29. *Ibid.*, p. 262.

30. *Ibid.*, pp. 263–264.

31. *Ibid.*, p. 254.

32. *Ibid.*, p. 281.

33. Friedrich, *ibid.*, pp. 37–38.

34. *Eternal Peace* in an edition transl. by M. C. Smith and entitled *Perpetual Peace* (London, 1903), pp. 153–154.

35. *Ibid.*, p. 154.

36. *Ibid.*, pp. 154–155.

37. *Ibid.*, p. 153.

38. Edward Caird, *Hegel* (Edinburgh, 1883), p. 89.

39. Preface to the *Philosophy of Right*, transl. by T. M. Knox (Oxford, 1942), p. 12.

40. Richard Kroner describes Hegel's Logic as a "logic of life." It has, he says, several aspects. "(a) It is a logic of spirit. The spirit is operative in its method. The intellect separates and objectifies, but the spirit reunites and resubjectifies. The intellect, however, is not a second power, opposed to spirit. It is itself a phase or moment of spirit, for it is spirit which divides itself and unifies itself. (b) The new Logic is also a logic of reason, for reason differs from the intellect or the understanding in being speculative. (c) And it is a logic of intuition, for intuition underlies the self as thinking and the self as thought; it is the power that unifies both. But . . . this intuition is not merely opposed to understanding; it is also at one with it in the living movement of logic. (d) This logic, finally, is a logic not only of knowledge, of thought, of the living self, but also of Being, Existence, and Reality. The movement of thought can no longer be opposed to its objects, since these objects themselves move in it." Introduction to Hegel's *Early Theological Writings*, transl. by

T. M. Knox (University of Chicago Press, Chicago, 1948), p. 31. By permission. There is a sense, I am told, in which Hegel's dialectic is a secularization of German mystical speculation, in particular that of Jacob Boehme. See Hans Urs von Balthasar, *Geschichte des eschatologischen problems in der modernen deutschen literatur* (Zurich, 1930).

41. J. Loewenberg, *Hegel: Selections* (Charles Scribner's Sons, New York, 1929). Introduction, pp. xvii–xviii. By permission.

42. *Ibid.*, pp. xviii–xix.

43. *Ibid.*, p. xxxii.

44. Hegel, *Philosophy of History* in *ibid.*, pp. 348–349.

45. Herbert Marcuse, *Reason and Revolution: Hegel and the Rise of Social Theory* (Oxford University Press, New York, 1941), pp. 9–10. For other interpretations of Hegel's philosophy see: Josiah Royce, *Spirit of Modern Philosophy* (Boston, 1899); W. T. Stace, *The Philosophy of Hegel* (London, 1924); G. P. Adams, *The Mystical Element in Hegel's Early Theological Writings* (Berkeley, 1910); J. G. Gray, *Hegel's Hellenic Ideal* (New York, 1941); H. A. Reyburn, *Hegel's Ethical Theory* (Oxford, 1921); M. B. Foster, *The Political Philosophies of Plato and Hegel* (Oxford University Press, Oxford, 1935); F. Rosenzweig, *Hegel und der Staat* (Munich, 1920); Wilhelm Dilthey, *Die Jugendgeschichte Hegels* (Berlin, 1906); T. L. Haering, *Hegel, sein Wollen und sein Werk* (Leipzig, 2 vols., 1929–1938).

46. *Philosophy of History, loc. cit.*, pp. 369–371.

47. *Ibid.*, p. 354.

48. *Ibid.*, p. 356.

49. *Ibid.*, p. 357.

50. M. B. Foster, *The Political Philosophies of Plato and Hegel* (Oxford University Press, New York, 1935), p. 204.

51. *Philosophy of Law* in Loewenberg, *Selections, op. cit.*, p. 468.

52. *Philosophy of Right*, transl. by T. M. Knox, *op. cit.*, par. 257 and

the addition to par. 258, pp. 155 and 279.

53. C. E. M. Joad, *Guide to the Philosophy of Morals and Politics* (Random House, Inc., New York, 1938), p. 587.
54. *Philosophy of Right* (Knox transl.), pars. 331 and 340, pp. 212 and 215–216.
55. *Ibid.*, par. 348, p. 218.
56. *Ibid.*, par. 324, p. 210.
57. *Ibid.*, par. 347, pp. 217–218.
58. *Ibid.*, pars. 333 and 338, pp. 213–214, 215.
59. Marcuse, *op. cit.*, pp. 204–205.
60. *Philosophy of Right*, *op. cit.*, pars. 243–244, pp. 149–150.
61. *Ibid.*, par. 203, p. 131.
62. *Ibid.*, par. 204, p. 132.
63. *Ibid.*, par. 205, p. 132.
64. *Ibid.*, par. 206, p. 132.
65. Marcuse, *op. cit.*, p. 211.
66. *Ibid.*, p. 218.
67. *Philosophy of Right*, *op. cit.*, addition to par. 280, p. 289.
68. *Ibid.*, par. 306, p. 199.
69. *Ibid.*, par. 302, p. 197.
70. Quoted by Marcuse, *op. cit.*, p. 235. In his Philosophy of Right, Hegel distinguishes *four* principles and four world-historical realms: (1) the Oriental, (2) the Greek, (3) the Roman, and (4) the Germanic. See pars. 353 ff.
71. Marcuse, *ibid.*, p. 236.
72. *Ibid.*, pp. 236–237.
73. Ernst Cassirer declares that "No other philosophical system has done so much for the preparation of fascism and imperialism as Hegel's doctrine of the state— this 'divine idea as it exists on earth.' Even the idea that, in every epoch of history, there is *one* and only one nation that is the real representation of the world spirit and that this nation has the right to rule all the others was first expressed by Hegel . . . Never before had a philosopher of the rank of Hegel spoken in this way. In the first decades of the nineteenth century we find the rise and ever-increasing influence of nationalistic ideals. It was, however, a new event in the history of political thought, an event pregnant with far-reaching and fearful consequences, when a system of *Ethics* and a philosophy of *Right* defended such a ruthless imperialistic nationalism, when Hegel declared the spirits of other nations to be 'absolutely without right' against the nation which, at a given historical moment, is to be regarded as the only 'agent of the world-spirit.' There is, however, one point in which the difference between Hegel's doctrine and modern theories of the totalitarian state becomes obvious. While it is true that Hegel exempted the state from all moral obligations and declared that the rules of morality lose their pretended universality when we proceed from the problems of private life and private conduct to the conduct of states, still there remain other bonds from which the state could not be released. In the Hegelian system the state belongs to the sphere of the 'objective mind.' But this sphere is only one element or moment in the self-actualization of the Idea. In the dialectic process it is transcended by that other sphere which, in Hegel's language, is called the realm of the 'Absolute Idea.' The Idea develops itself in three moments: Art, Religion, and Philosophy. It is clear that the state cannot treat these high cultural goods as mere means for its own purposes. They are ends in themselves that have to be respected and furthered . . . The state remains, as Hegel says, 'on the territory of finitude.' Hegel could not subordinate art, religion, and philosophy to it . . . 'The highest aim that the state can attain is that art and science are cultivated and come to a height corresponding to the spirit of the people. That is the principal end of the state—but an end that it must not bring about as an external work but that must arise from itself.' Hegel spoke not only of the power of the state but also of its 'truth'

. . . The guarantee of a constitution lies . . . 'in the indwelling spirit and the history of the nation by which constitutions have been made and are made.' To make this indwelling spirit subservient to the will of a political party or of an individual leader was impossible to Hegel. In this respect he would have rejected and abhorred the modern conceptions of the 'totalitarian' state." *The Myth of the State* (Yale University Press, New Haven, 1946), pp. 273 *ff*. By permission.

74. Loewenberg, *op. cit.*, p. xlii.
75. T. H. Green, *Lectures on the Principles of Political Obligation.* Introduction by A. D. Lindsay (London, 1941), p. 23.
76. *Ibid.*, pp. 20–21.
77. *Ibid.*, pp. 32–33.
78. *Ibid.*, pp. 124–125.
79. Quoted by Green, *ibid.*, p. 94.
80. *Ibid.*, p. 103.
81. *Ibid.*, p. 98.
82. *Ibid.*, p. 139.
83. *Ibid.*, p. 136.
84. *Ibid.*, p. 122.
85. *Ibid.*, p. 144.
86. *Ibid.*, p. 148.
87. *Ibid.*, pp. 148–149. (Italics mine.)
88. *Ibid.*, p. 207.
89. *Ibid.*, p. 216.
90. *Ibid.*, p. 153.
91. *Ibid.*, p. 220.
92. *Ibid.*, p. 220.
93. *Ibid.*, p. 221.
94. *Ibid.*, p. 222.
95. *Ibid.*, p. 224.
96. *Ibid.*, p. 224.
97. *Ibid.*, p. 225.
98. *Ibid.*, p. 225.
99. *Ibid.*, p. 226.
100. *Ibid.*, p. 226.
101. *Ibid.*, p. 228.
102. *Ibid.*, p. 229.
103. G. H. Sabine, *A History of Political Theory* (Henry Holt and Company, New York, 1937), p. 676.
104. F. H. Bradley, *Ethical Studies* Oxford, 2d ed., 1927), p. 184.
105. *Philosophical Theory of the State* (New York, 3d ed., 1920), Ch. VI, par. 5a.
106. *Ibid.*, Ch. V, par. 2.
107. *Ibid.*, Ch. XI, par. 7.
108. *Ibid.*, Ch. XI, par. 6.

## CHAPTER 9

1. Article on "Positivism," *Encyclopaedia of the Social Sciences*, Vol. VI.
2. Many of Comte's ideas were anticipated in the eighteenth century by the French statesman, Turgot (1727–1781) especially in his discourse *On the Successive Advances of the Human Mind* (1750). Turgot was of the opinion that "the same senses, the same organs, the spectacle of the same universe have everywhere given to men the same ideas, just as the same needs and the same propensities have everywhere taught them the same arts." Natural phenomena traverse certain fixed cycles of change. All things die but all things revive and time merely restores continually the likeness of what it has annihilated. Similarly all the ages of mankind are linked together by a chain of causes and effects. Turgot explicitly anticipates Comte's law of the three stages in these words: "Before knowing the connection of physical facts with one another, nothing was more natural than to suppose that they were produced by beings, intelligent, invisible, and like to ourselves. Everything which happened without man's own intervention had its god, to which fear or hope caused a worship to be paid conforming to the respect accorded to powerful men,—the gods being only men more or less powerful and perfect in proportion as the age which originated them was more or less enlightened as to what constitutes the true perfection of humanity. But when philosophers perceived the absurdity of these fables, without having attained to a real acquaintance with the history of nature, they fancifully accounted for phenomena by abstract expressions, by essences

and faculties, which indeed explained nothing, but were reasoned from as if they were real
existences. It was only very late
that from observing the mechanical action of bodies on one another, other hypotheses were inferred, which mathematics could
develop and experience verify."
Quoted by Robert Flint, *The
Philosophy of History in France and
Germany* (Edinburgh, 1874), p.
113. For an excellent discussion
of Comte's law of three stages see
Robert Flint, *ibid.*, Ch. XII. In
part he says: "There is, I think,
a certain measure of truth in this
alleged law. There are three
ways of looking at things,—a
religious, a metaphysical, and a
scientific. It is natural for the
mind to believe that things and
the succession of things tell something about a power in or beyond
them with faculties analogous to
those which itself possesses. It is
natural for it also to speculate on
the reason and mode of the
existence of things and to ask a
number of questions about them
which cannot be immediately
answered from observation of
their properties . . . It is natural for it no less to observe these
properties and study these relations. It is natural for it to do all
three, and even all three about
the same things; in other words,
things may be looked at in three
aspects. But three aspects are not
three successive states. From the
fact that it is natural for the
mind to look at things in all
these three ways, it in no wise
follows that it is necessary or even
natural to look at them one after
another . . . it is not natural to
suppose that the one mode will
be exhausted, gone through, before the other is entered on, but
that they will be simultaneous in
origin and parallel in development . . . ," pp. 268–269.

3. Auguste Comte, *A General View of
Positivism*. Translated by J. H.
Bridges (London, 1865), pp.
36–37.

4. *Ibid.*, p. 49.

5. Edward Caird, *The Social Philosophy and Religion of Comte*
(Glasgow, 1893), p. 21.

6. *Ibid.*, pp. 22–23.

7. Quoted by Caird, *ibid.*, p. 33.

8. Comte, *op. cit.*, p. 277.

9. *Ibid.*, p. 276.

10. Caird, *op. cit.*, pp. 137–138.

11. *Ibid.*, pp. 139–140.

12. Quoted by Caird, *ibid.*, pp. 140–141.

13. *Ibid.*, pp. 141–142.

14. J. S. Mill, *A System of Logic.* 8th
ed. (New York, 1890), pp. 607–608.

15. *Ibid.*, pp. 618–619.

16. *Ibid.*, p. 628.

17. *Ibid.*, p. 642.

18. *Ibid.*, p. 643.

19. *Ibid.*, p. 620.

20. See *ibid.*, pp. 596 *ff.*

21. *Ibid.*, p. 602.

22. *Ibid.*, p. 605.

23. Arthur O. Lovejoy, *The Great
Chain of Being* (Harvard University Press, Cambridge, Mass.,
1936), p. 144. By permission.

24. *Ibid.*, pp. 183–184. Some of those
who talked about the great
Chain of Being were Addison,
King, Bolingbroke, Pope, Haller, Thomson, Akenside, Buffon,
Bonnet, Goldsmith, Diderot,
Kant, Lambert, Herder and
Schiller. For a discussion of the
emergence of the idea of "evolution" see, in addition to the book
cited by Lovejoy, Erich Voegelin,
*Die Rassenidee in der geistesgeschichte
von Ray bis Carus* (Berlin, 1933).
Professor Voegelin points out
that the theory of evolution was
not only thoroughly developed
in the eighteenth century but
that its Darwinian form was
criticized before the event by
Kant in his *Kritik der Urteilskraft.*

25. *Fragments, or Minutes of Essays,
Works* (1809), Vol. VIII, p. 231.
Quoted by Lovejoy, *op. cit.*, p.
196.

26. *Disquisitions on Several Subjects*, I,
"On the Chain of Universal
Being," *Works* (1790), pp. 179–185. Quoted by Lovejoy, *ibid.*,
p. 197. ". . . it was not merely
that man's separation from the
lower order of things was thus

reduced to an almost inappreciable degree of difference," Professor Lovejoy declares, but "The definition of him as the 'middle link,' in the sense usually given to it, especially emphasized the peculiar duality of his constitution and the tragi-comic inner discord in him which results from this." *Ibid.*, p. 198. In Christian thought the inner discord was explained as a result of man's Fall from innocence but in the eighteenth century view man is "torn by conflicting desires and propensities . . . because of the requirements of the universal scheme of things; as a member of two orders of being at once, he wavers between both, and is not quite at home in either. He thus has, after all, a kind of uniqueness in nature; but it is an unhappy uniqueness. He is, in a sense in which no other link in the chain is, a strange hybrid monster; and if this gives him a certain pathetic sublimity, it also results in incongruities of feeling, inconsistencies of behavior, and disparities between his aspirations and his powers, which render him ridiculous." *Ibid.*, pp. 198–199. The poet Pope expressed this view of man's status in these lines from his *Essay on Man:*

Plac'd in this isthmus of a middle state,
A being darkly wise and rudely great,
With too much knowledge for the sceptic side,
With too much weakness for the stoic pride,
He hangs between; in doubt to act or rest;
In doubt to deem himself a god or beast;
In doubt his Mind or Body to prefer;
Born but to die, and reas'ning but to err; . . .
Chaos of Thought and Passion all confus'd,
Still by himself abus'd, or disabus'd;

Created half to rise, and half to fall,
Great lord of all things, yet a prey to all;
Sole judge of Truth, in endless error hurl'd;
The glory, jest and riddle of the world.

27. Quoted by Lovejoy, *op. cit.*, p. 234.

28. *Ibid.*, p. 287. "When the Chain of Being—in other words, the entire created universe—came to be explicitly conceived, no longer as complete once for all and everlastingly the same in the kind of its components, but as gradually evolving from a less to a greater degree of fullness and excellence," Professor Lovejoy declares, "the question inevitably arose whether a God eternally complete and immutable could be supposed to be manifested in such a universe. The question was not always, or at first, answered in the negative; there were numerous eighteenth-century attempts, . . . to combine the belief in a Creator . . . who could not generate a creation different at one time from what it is at another, with the conviction that the world, being expansive and progressive, *is* essentially different at one time from what it is at another, and that the general order of events in time is not a negligible feature of finite existence, irrelevant to those eternal aspects of things with which metaphysics has to do, but is an aspect of reality of profound significance for philosophy. So long as the two beliefs were held together, the seeming axiom to which I have referred—that the antecedent in a causal process cannot contain less than the consequent, or a higher type of being come from a lower—could still be precariously maintained. But with the end of that century and the opening decades of the nineteenth these assumptions of the traditional theology and metaphysics began to be reversed. God himself

was temporalized—was, indeed, identified with the process by which the whole creation slowly and painfully ascends the scale of possibility; or, if the name is to be reserved for the summit of the scale, God was conceived as the not yet realized final term of that process. Thus for emanationism and creationism came to be substituted what may best be called radical or absolute evolutionism—the typically Romantic evolutionism of which Bergson's *L'Évolution créatrice* is in great part a re-editing. The lower precedes the higher, not merely in the history of organic forms and functions, but universally; there is more in the effect than was contained, except as an abstract unrealized potentiality, in the cause." *Ibid.*, pp. 316–317.

29. Quoted in J. A. Thomson, *Biology for Everyman* (New York, 2 vols., 1935). Vol. II, p. 1002.
30. *Ibid.*, p. 1002.
31. *Ibid.*, p. 1008. The complete title of Darwin's book is *The Origin of Species by Means of Natural Selection, or the Preservation of Favored Races in the Struggle for Life.* In 1871 Darwin published *The Descent of Man* in which he argued that man was no exception to the hypothesis outlined in the *Origin of Species.* For a discussion of Darwin's theories and influence see among others: Jacques Barzun, *Darwin, Marx, Wagner* (Boston, 1941); Thomas P. Neill, *Makers of the Modern Mind* (Milwaukee, 1949), Ch. X; W. A. Locy, *Biology and Its Makers* (New York, 3rd ed., 1915); and Richard Hofstadter, *Social Darwinism in American Thought, 1860–1915* (New York, 1944).
32. *Darwin, Marx, Wagner, op. cit.*, p. 69.
33. Spencer, *First Principles* (New York, 1896), p. 48.
34. *Ibid.*, p. 68.
35. *Ibid.*, p. 163.
36. *Ibid.*, p. 164.
37. *Ibid.*, p. 284.
38. *Ibid.*, p. 407.

39. *Ibid.*, p. 559.
40. *Social Statics* (abbreviated ed. 1897), p. 43.
41. *Man Versus the State* (New York, 1884), p. 105.
42. *Ibid.*, p. 105.
43. *Through Nature to God* (Boston, 1899), p. 130.
44. *The Challenge of Facts* in the *Essays of William Graham Sumner*, ed. by A. G. Keller and M. R. Davie (New Haven, 2 vols. 1934), Vol. II, pp. 87 ff.
45. Whitehead, *Adventures of Ideas* (New York, 1933), p. 39.
46. *The Iconoclast* (August, 1870).
47. Lester F. Ward, *Pure Sociology* (Macmillan, New York, 1903),
48. *Ibid.*, pp. 19–20.
49. *Ibid.*, p. 135.
50. Lester F. Ward, *Applied Sociology* (Ginn and Company, New York, 1906), pp. 320–321.
51. Lester F. Ward, *Dynamic Sociology* (D. Appleton-Century Company, New York, 1903), Vol. II, p. 108.
52. Lester F. Ward, *Glimpses of the Cosmos*, 6 vols. (G. P. Putnam, New York, 1918), Vol. VI, pp. 62–63.
53. Lester F. Ward, *Outlines of Sociology* (New York, 1897), p. 258.
54. *Glimpses, op. cit.*, Vol. IV, p. 67.
55. *Applied Sociology*, p. 339.
56. *Outlines of Sociology* (Philadelphia, 1899), p. 157.
57. *Ibid.*, p. 7.
58. See Franz Oppenheimer, *The State* (New York, 1922), p. 15.
59. Gumplowicz, *op. cit.*, p. 179.
60. *Ibid.*, p. 180.
61. *Ibid.*, pp. 180–181.
62. *Ibid.*, p. 145.
63. *Ibid.*, p. 133.
64. *Ibid.*, p. 116.
65. *Ibid.*, p. 118.
66. *Ibid.*, p. 182.
67. Quoted by J. H. Randall, Jr., *Making of the Modern Mind* (Houghton Mifflin, Boston, 1940), p. 506.
68. A. N. Whitehead, *Science and the Modern World* (Macmillan, New York, 1925), p. 6. Copyright

1925 by The Macmillan Company and used with their permission.

69. Whitehead, *Adventures of Ideas* (New York, 1933), p. 157.

70. T. E. Jessop, "The Scientific Account of Man," in T. E. Jessop *et al.*, *The Christian Understanding of Man* (George Allen Unwin, Ltd., London, 1938), p. 40. By permission.

71. Morris R. Cohen, *Reason and Nature: An Essay on the Meaning of the Scientific Method* (New York, 1931), pp. 36–37.

72. *Ibid.*, p. 11.

73. Oswald Spengler, *The Decline of the West* (New York, 1928), Vol. II, p. 368.

74. Spengler, *Politische Schriften* (1934) pp. 85–86.

## CHAPTER 10

1. Roscoe Pound, "Jurisprudence," *E. S. S.* Vol. IV.

2. *Prolegomena*, Sec. 16.

3. Pound, *Interpretations of Legal History* (Harvard University Press, Cambridge, 1923), pp. 9–10. By permission.

4. Frederick von Savigny, *Of the Vocation of Our Age for Legislation and Jurisprudence*. Transl. by A. Hayward (London, 1831), p. 24.

5. Pound, *Spirit of the Common Law* (Marshall Jones Company, Francestown, N. H., 1921), pp. 153–154. By permission.

6. Savigny, *op. cit.*, p. 27.

7. *Ibid.*, p. 136.

8. *Ibid.*, p. 30. (Italics mine.)

9. G. F. Puchta, *Outlines of Jurisprudence as the Science of Right*. Transl. by Jartie (Edinburgh, 1887), pp. 30–31.

10. *Ibid.*, p. 57.

11. *Ibid.*, p. 58.

12. Pound, *Interpretations of Legal History*, pp. 12–13.

13. *Cursus der Institutionen* (1841). Quoted by Pound, *ibid.*, p. 47, note 1.

14. Beudant, *Le Droit individuel et l'état* (1891). Quoted by Pound, *ibid.*, p. 48.

15. Pound, *ibid.*, p. 54.

16. *Ancient Law* (London, 4th ed. 1870), p. 3.

17. J. T. Carter, *The Ideal and the Actual in Law* (1890), pp. 10–11.

18. J. T. Carter, *Law: Its Origin, Growth and Function* (New York, 1907), pp. 159–163.

19. A. N. Whitehead, *Adventures of Ideas* (New York, 1933), p. 41.

20. Talcott Parsons, "Society," *Encyclopedia of the Social Sciences*, Vol. VII, 1932. Copyright 1932 by The Macmillan Company and used with their permission.

21. Jeremy Bentham, *The Theory of Legislation*. Ogden ed. (London, 1931), p. 8.

22. John Austin, *Lectures on Jurisprudence* (London, 3d ed., 1869), Vol. I, pp. 182–183.

23. *Ibid.*, p. 227.

24. C. F. von Gerber, *Grundzüge eines Systems des deutschen Staatsrecht* (Leipzig, 1865), p. 3.

25. *Ibid.*, p. 19.

26. Paul Laband, *Das Staatsrecht des deutschen Reiches* (Tübingen, 5th ed., 4 vols. 1911–1914), Vol. II, p. 4.

27. *Ibid.*, pp. 29–30.

28. Philipp Zorn, *Das Staatsrecht des deutschen Reiches* (Berlin, 1880), Vol. I, pp. 111–112. (Italics mine.)

29. Laband, *op. cit.*, Vol. II, p. 186.

30. Laband, *Deutsches Reichsstaatsrecht* (Tübingen, 1907), p. 17.

31. Georg Jellinek, *Allgemeine Staatslehre* (Berlin, 3d ed., 1914), p. 386.

32. *Ibid.*, pp. 481–482.

33. *Ibid.*, p. 482.

34. Quoted by H. Heller, "Der Begriff des Gesetzes in der Reichsverfassung," *Veröffentlichungen der Vereinigung der deutschen Staatsrechtslehrer* (Heft 4, 1928), p. 116.

35. Kurt Pfeifer, *Die Idee der Grundrechte in der deutschen Literatur von 1790 bis Georg Jellinek* (Jena, 1930).

36. Georg Jellinek, *System der subjektiven öffentlichen Recht* (Tübingen, 2d ed., 1905), p. 82.

37. *Ibid.*, p. 103.

38. R. Stammler, "Fundamental Tendencies in Modern Jurispru-

dence," *Michigan Law Review*, Vol. 21, No. 6 (April, 1923), pp. 862 *ff*. By permission.

39. Stammler, *Theorie der Rechtswissenchaft* (Halle, 1911), p. 17. (Italics mine.)

40. Rubert Emerson, *State and Sovereignty in Modern Germany* (Yale University Press, New Haven, 1928), p. 163. By permission. An excellent analysis of nineteenth century German jurisprudence to which I am heavily indebted.

41. Stammler, "Fundamental Tendencies . . . ," *loc. cit.*, p. 863.

42. Stammler, *The Theory of Justice*. Transl. by I. Husik (New York, 1925), p. 40.

43. *Ibid.*, p. 89.

44. Emerson, *op. cit.*, p. 165.

45. Stammler, "Fundamental Tendencies . . . ," *loc. cit.*, p. 865.

46. *Theorie der Rechtswissenschaft*, p. 27.

47. W. E. Hocking, *Present Status of the Philosophy of Law and of Rights* (Yale University Press, New Haven, 1926), pp. 16–17. By permission.

48. Emerson, *op. cit.*, pp. 168–169.

49. Hans Kelsen, "Centralization and Decentralization," in *Authority and the Individual* (Harvard University Press, Cambridge, 1937), p. 212. By permission.

50. *Ibid.*, p. 213.

51. *Ibid.*, p. 213.

52. Hans Lauterpacht, "Kelsen's Pure Science of Law," *Modern Theories of Law* (Oxford University Press, London, 1933), pp. 111–112.

53. Kelsen, "The Pure Theory of Law," translated by C. H. Wilson. *Law Quarterly Review*, Vol. 51 (1935), pp. 517 *ff*. (Italics mine.)

54. *Ibid.* (Italics mine.)

55. *Ibid.*

56. Emerson, *op. cit.*, pp. 170–171.

57. Kelsen, *Hauptprobleme der Staatsrechtslehre* (1911), p. 465. Quoted by Emerson, *op. cit.*, p. 171. It should be pointed out in fairness to Kelsen that his motives in constructing this theory were more admirable than the consequences which flowed from it.

The theory was developed for the purpose of elucidating the structure of the continental administrative state and it had the *purpose* of eliminating the arbitrariness of political power, of binding it procedurally to the content of law as resolved upon by representative assemblies. That should not be forgotten in balancing the otherwise dark picture of the consequences. Moreover, in Kelsen's form, the theory has a significant function as *nomopoietics*, as a technique of law-making, which lawyers trained in the common-law tradition might well study.

58. *Moderne Rechtsprobleme* (1907), Par. 1.

59. Pound, *Interpretations of Legal History*, p. 143.

60. Kohler, *Philosophy of Law*. Translated by A. Albrecht (1914), p. 59.

61. *Ibid.*, p. 208.

62. *Ibid.*, p. 253.

63. Quoted by Hocking, *op. cit.*, p. 8.

64. *Philosophy of Law*, p. 36.

65. Hocking, *op. cit.*, p. 26.

66. *Ibid.*, p. 30.

67. Adolf Lasson, *System der Rechtsphilosophie* (Berlin, 1882), p. 288.

68. *Ibid.*, pp. 289–290.

69. Erich Kaufmann, *Das Wesen des Völkerrechts und die Clausala rebus sic stantibus* (Tübingen, 1911), p. 138.

70. *Ibid.*, p. 135.

71. See *ibid.*, pp. 151–152.

72. Carl Schmitt, *Der Begriff des Politischen* (1927). Translated by William Ebenstein in *Man and the State* (Rinehart and Company Inc., New York, 1947), pp. 299 *ff*. By permission. *Man and the State* is an excellent collection of extracts from some of the more important works in modern political theory.

73. I have not found it possible to include here a discussion of recent developments in French jurisprudence but the significance of the work of men like Esmein, Duguit, and Hauriou should not be overlooked. There is a development of thought

through the writings of these three jurists that leads directly to the kind of thinking exemplified by Carl Schmitt and embodied in practice in the Fascist state. For an extended discussion of Duguit's conception of the law and the relationship between that conception and Fascism, see W. Y. Elliott, *The Pragmatic Revolt in Politics* (New York, 1928). It is "inane" in Duguit's opinion to "wish to give a philosophical justification of political might. The truth is that political might is a fact which has in itself no character of legitimacy or illegitimacy. It is the product of social evolution." *Manuel de droit constitutionnel* (3d. ed.), p. 23. The authority of the state, according to Duguit, has neither legal nor moral justification, "The state is only the manifestation of a force and it may be defined as the man or the group of men who in fact in a given society are materially stronger than the others, or as the simple fact of the differentiation between the governor and the governed." *L'État, le droit objectif et la loi positive* (1901).

74. See W. W. Cook, "The Logical and Legal Bases of the Conflict of Laws," *Yale Law Review*, Vol. 33, pp. 457 *ff*; K. N. Llewellyn, "A Realistic Jurisprudence—The Next Step," *Columbia Law Review*, Vol. 30, pp. 431 *ff.*; Jerome Frank, *Law and the Modern Mind* (New York, 1930). See also "Law and the Modern Mind: A Symposium," by K. N. Llewellyn, Mortimer Adler and Jerome Frank in the *Columbia Law Review*, Vol. 31, pp. 82 *ff.* and Lon Fuller, *The Law in Quest of Itself* (Chicago, 1940).

75. "The Path of the Law," Max Lerner (ed.), *The Mind and Faith of Justice Holmes* (Little, Brown, Boston, 1943), pp. 78–79. Copyright 1943 by Little, Brown and Company and used with their permission.

76. "Natural Law," *ibid.*, p. 396.

77. *Ibid.*, pp. 396–397.

78. *Ibid.*, p. 398.

79. "The Soldier's Faith," *ibid.*, p. 21.

80. *Ibid.*, p. 20.

81. *Ibid.*, p. 19.

82. "Life as Joy, Duty, End," *ibid.*, pp. 42–43.

83. "The Path of the Law," *ibid.*, p. 82.

84. "The Common Law," *ibid.*, p. 57.

85. *Ibid.*, p. 58.

86. *Ibid.*, p. 59.

87. "Masters and Men: The Gas-Stokers Strike," *ibid.*, p. 51.

88. Ben W. Palmer, "Hobbes, Holmes, and Hitler," *American Bar Association Journal*, Vol. 31, pp. 569 *ff.*, p. 573. See also Ben W. Palmer, "Defense Against Leviathan," *ibid.*, Vol. 32, pp. 328 *ff.* For a contrary view see C. W. Briggs, "Justice Holmes Was Not on a Ladder to Hitler," *ibid.*, Vol. 32, pp. 631 *ff.* and T. V. Smith, "Justice Holmes: Voice of Democratic Evolution," *The Philosophy of American Democracy*, edited by Charner W. Perry (Chicago, 1943).

89. "The Path of the Law," Lerner, *op. cit.*, p. 75.

90. Roscoe Pound, *Contemporary Juristic Theory* (Claremont Colleges, 1940), pp. 15–16. By permission.

91. *Ibid.*, p. 16.

92. *Ibid.*, pp. 19–20.

93. W. W. Cook, *Yale Law Journal*, Vol. 13, pp. 457 *ff.*

94. Jerome Frank, *Law and the Modern Mind* (New York, 1930), p. 21.

95. *Ibid.*, p. 252.

96. For a penetrating review of Frank's book see Mortimer J. Adler's review in the *Columbia Law Review*, Vol. 31, pp. 91 *ff.*

97. Pound, *Contemporary Juristic Theory*, pp. 10–11.

### CHAPTER 11

1. For an excellent history of socialist thought see Alexander Gray, *The Socialist Tradition: Moses to Lenin* (London, 1946). For different interpretations of

that history see H. W. Laidler, *Social-Economic Movements* (New York, 1944), J. C. Hertzler, *The History of Utopian Thought* (New York, 1923), Max Beer, *History of British Socialism* (London, 1919), W. B. Guthrie, *Socialism before the French Revolution* (New York, 1907) and Edmund Wilson, *To the Finland Station* (New York, 1940).

2. Quoted by Gray, *op. cit.*, p. 48.
3. Plato, *Republic*. Translated by B. Jowett, 2 vols. (Oxford University Press, London, 3d ed., 1908), Vol. I. Book III, 416 c. By permission.
4. *The Politics of Aristotle*. Edited by Ernest Barker (Oxford University Press, London, 1946), p. 52, note 4.
5. *Ibid.*, pp. 55–56, note 4.
6. William Haller and Godfrey Davies (eds.) *The Leveller Tracts 1647–1653* (Columbia University Press, New York, 1944). By permission. Introduction by William Haller, pp. 35–36.
7. *Harleian Miscellany*, Vol. VIII, p. 590. Quoted by G. H. Sabine, *A History of Political Theory* (New York, 1937), p. 491.
8. *The True Leveller's Standard Advanced* (1649). Quoted by G. P. Gooch, *English Democratic Ideas in the Seventeenth Century* (Cambridge, 2d ed., 1927), p. 184.
9. *Law of Freedom* (1652), pp. 74–75. Quoted by M. Beer *History of British Socialism* (London, 1919), Vol. I, pp. 67–71.
10. *The Commonwealth of Oceana* (London, 1887).
11. Quoted by H. W. Laidler, *Social-Economic Movements* (New York, 1946), pp. 46–47.
12. C. Gide and C. Rist, *A History of Economic Doctrine* (George G. Harrap and Co., London, 2 Eng. ed., 1948), p. 214. By permission.
13. Quoted, *ibid.*, p. 218 note 5.
14. See *ibid.*, p. 218.
15. Quoted, *ibid.*, p. 218 note 6.
16. Quoted, *ibid.*, p. 232.
17. *Doctrine de Saint-Simon*. Edited by Bouglé and Halevy (Paris, 1924), p. 179.

18. Gide and Rist, *op. cit.*, pp. 239–241.
19. *Selections from the Works of Fourier*. Introduction by Charles Gide. Translated by J. Franklin (London, 1901), pp. 17–18.
20. *Ibid.*, p. 139.
21. *Ibid.*, p. 144.
22. *Ibid.*, pp. 147–148.
23. *Ibid.*, p. 152.
24. *Ibid.*, p. 153.
25. *Ibid.*, pp. 200–201.
26. *Ibid.*, p. 135.
27. Gide and Rist, *op. cit.*, p. 258.
28. For an account of some of these ventures see C. Nordhoff, *The Communistic Societies in the United States* (New York, 1875). See also Morris Hillquit, *History of Socialism in the United States* (New York, 1910), Charles Southeran, *Horace Greeley and other Pioneers of American Socialism* (New York, 1915), and G. B. Lockwood, *The New Harmony Movement* (New York, 1905).
29. *A New View of Society* (1st American Ed. New York, 1825), p. 16. See Frank Podmore, *Robert Owen*, 2 vols. (London, 1923), and Lloyd Jones, *The Life, Times, and Labors of Robert Owen* (London, 1919).
30. *Ibid.*, p. 22.
31. *Ibid.*, p. 46.
32. *Ibid.* Appendix, pp. 145–146 and 148.
33. *Ibid.*, pp. 154 ff.
34. Robert Owen, *Letters to the Human Race on the Coming Universal Revolution* (London, 1850), pp. 123–125.
35. *Ibid.*, pp. 42–43.
36. *Ibid.*, p. 45.
37. *Ibid.*, p. 45.
38. Gide and Rist, *op. cit.*, p. 252.
39. *What is Property*. Translated by B. R. Tucker (New York, n.d.), pp. 261–262.
40. *Ibid.*, p. 147.
41. *Ibid.*, p. 280.
42. *Ibid.*, pp. 285–286.
43. *Ibid.*, p. 278.
44. *Ibid.*, p. 278.
45. *Ibid.*, p. 288.
46. *Ibid.*, p. 293.
47. *System of Economical Contradictions or the Philosophy of Misery*. Trans-

lated by B. R. Tucker (Boston, 1888), pp. 446, 448–449.

CHAPTER 12

1. Quoted by Otto Rühle, *Karl Marx: His Life and Work* (London, 1929), p. 33. The literature on Marx and Marxism is of considerable volume and defies brief summarization but see, among others: Frank Mehring, *Karl Marx, the Story of his Life*, transl. by E. Fitzgerald (New York, 1935); Eugen von Böhm-Bawerk, *Karl Marx and the Close of His System: a Criticism*, transl. by A. M. McDonald (New York, 1898); M. M. Bober, *Karl Marx's Interpretation of History* (Cambridge, Mass., rev. ed., 1948); Werner Sombart, *Der proletarische Sozialismus* (Jena, 2 vols., 1924); Joseph A. Schumpeter, *Capitalism, Socialism and Democracy* (New York, 1942); the introduction by S. Landshut and J. P. Mayer to Karl Marx, *Der historische Materialismus: Die Frühschriften* (Leipzig, 2 vols., 1932); K. R. Popper, *The Open Society and Its Enemies* (London, 2 vols., 1945); Karl Löwith, *Von Hegel bis Nietzsche* (Zurich and New York, 1941); Sidney Hook, *Towards the Understanding of Karl Marx* (New York, 1933); Max Eastman, *Marxism: Is It Science?* (New York, 1940); F. J. Sheed, *Communism and Man* (New York, 1945); H. B. Parkes, *Marxism: An Autopsy* (Boston, 1939); Edmund Wilson, *To the Finland Station* (New York, 1940); Paul M. Sweezy, *The Theory of Capitalist Development* (New York, 1942) and Waldemar Gurian, *Bolshevism: Theory and Practice* (New York, 1932).

2. "Zur Kritik der Hegelschen Rechtsphilosophie," published in the *Deutsch-Französische Jahrbücher*. (1844). Quoted in Rühle, *op. cit.*, p. 57.

3. Quoted in *ibid.*, pp. 59–60.

4. Quoted in *ibid.*, pp. 81 *et seq.*

5. Quoted in *ibid.*, p. 85.

6. *Theses on Feuerbach* (1845). In Emile Burns (ed.), *A Handbook of Marxism* (Victor Gollancz, Ltd., London, 1935), pp. 228 *ff.* Used with the permission of Emile Burns.

7. Engels, *Herr Eugen Dühring's Revolution in Science* (1877) in Burns, *ibid.*, p. 237.

8. Engels, *ibid.*, pp. 256–257.

9. Engels, *Ludwig Feuerbach* (1886) in Burns, *ibid.*, p. 224.

10. Engels, *Anti-Dühring*, in *ibid.*, p. 266.

11. Marx, *Selected Works*, Vol. I, p. 16.

12. *Anti-Dühring*, in Burns, *op. cit.*, p. 279.

13. Marx, *A Contribution to the Critique of Political Economy* (1859) in Burns, *ibid.*, pp. 371–373.

14. Paul Barth, *Philosophie der Geschichte als Soziologie* (Leipzig, 1915), p. 633. The change of terminology in the *Critique* (from "conditioned" to "determined") is due to the fact that the original conception is "dialectical" and that Marx was at a loss to settle on a word for designating the dialectical relation. The change of terminology does not mean that we should accept the one or the other term as reflecting the "true meaning," but as an indication that the language implying causation is inadequate.

15. Paul Barth is of the opinion, as we saw in the passage quoted, that social phenomena for Marx are the product of technological developments alone. Werner Sombart, another close student of Marx, is of the same opinion. See *Der proletarische Sozialismus*, 2 vols. (Jena, 1924), Vol. I, pp. 209 *ff.* History, for Marx, is intelligible because it is a history of technology; tools are man-made and what is man-made is intelligible. Here there is an interesting connection between Marx's thought and that of Vico.

16. *The Poverty of Philosophy*. Translated by H. Quelch (Chicago, 1910), p. 119.

17. *Communist Manifesto*, in Burns, *op. cit.*
18. *Capital.* Translated by Moore and Aveling (London, 1909), Vol. I, p. 200.
19. *Ibid.*, p. 406 footnote.
20. *Anti-Dühring* in Burns, *op. cit.*, p. 279.
21. M. M. Bober, *Karl Marx's Interpretation of History* (Harvard University Press, Cambridge, Mass., 2d rev. ed., 1948), pp. 23–24. By permission.
22. F. Engels, *The Origin of the Family, Private Property and the State* (1884) in Burns (ed.) *op. cit.*, pp. 314–415.
23. *Ibid.*, p. 317.
24. *Ibid.*, p. 317.
25. *Ibid.*, p. 320.
26. *Ibid.*, p. 323.
27. *Ibid.*, p. 328.
28. *Ibid.*, p. 330.
29. *Communist Manifesto* (1848) in Burns *ibid.*, pp. 23–24.
30. *Ibid.*, p. 28.
31. *Ibid.*, p. 30.
32. *Ibid.*, p. 30.
33. *Capital.* Modern Library Ed. (New York, 1932), pp. 30–32.
34. *Ibid.*, p. 33.
35. *Ibid.*, pp. 44–45.
36. *Ibid.*, p. 48.
37. Gide and Rist, *op. cit.*, pp. 460–461.
38. *Capital*, *op. cit.*, pp. 181–182.
39. *Ibid.*, pp. 168–169.
40. *Ibid.*, pp. 203–204.
41. *Ibid.*, p. 204.
42. *Communist Manifesto*, *loc. cit.*, pp. 55–56.
43. *Ibid.*, pp. 37–38.
44. *Ibid.*, p. 59.
45. *Poverty of Philosophy.* Translated by H. Quelch (Chicago, 1910), pp. 190–191.
46. Quoted by Bober, *op. cit.*, pp. 264–265. Statements like the one quoted above are indicative of a genuine development within Marx's thought from an eschatological dialectic before 1848 to an evolutionary "softening" in the years after. It is these occasional "soft" utterances by Marx and Engels that were later to be seized upon by the Revionists.

47. Quoted by Bober, *ibid.*, p. 266.
48. *Introduction to the Civil War in France* (1891) in Burns (ed.) *op. cit.*, p. 171.
49. Bober, *op. cit.*, p. 271.
50. Burns, *loc. cit.*, p. 46.
51. *Communist Manifesto*, *ibid.*, pp. 42–43.
52. Engels, *Origin of the Family*, Burns, *loc. cit.*, pp. 303–304. Engels is inclined to be much more extreme in his views in these matters than is Marx. What Marx protested against, especially in his early writings, was not the institution of the family as such but what he thought the family had *degenerated* into under capitalism. Speaking of the dissolution of the "inner ties" of the family in the eighteenth century, Marx wrote: "The inner ties of the family, the individual parts out of which the concept of family life is made up, such as obedience, affection, conjugal fidelity, etc., had vanished; but the real body of the family, property relations, an exclusive attitude towards other families, an enforced life in common—the conditions that were determined by the existence of children, by the structure of modern towns, by the development of capital, etc.—these persisted, despite considerable modifications." Quoted by D. Ryazanoff (ed.), *The Communist Manifesto of Karl Marx and Friedrich Engles* (New York, 1930), p. 162. The aim of Communism, Marx frequently argued, was not to abolish the family but "to do away with the status of women as mere instruments of production."
53. *Ibid.*, p. 311.
54. *Ibid.*, p. 312.
55. Quoted by Bober, *op. cit.*, p. 149.
56. *Anti-Dühring*, Burns, *loc. cit.*, pp. 299 and 301.
57. *Ibid.*, p. 249.
58. *Ibid.*, pp. 248–249.
59. Quoted by Bober, *op. cit.*, p. 143.
60. *Anti-Dühring*, Burns, *loc. cit.*, p. 274.
61. Quoted by Bober, *op. cit.*, p. 138.
62. *Ibid.*, p. 138.

63. Engels, *Socialism, Utopian and Scientific*, pp. 76–77.
64. Marx, *Critique of the Gotlia Program*, p. 31.
65. Christopher Dawson, *Religion and the Modern State* (Sheed and Ward, London, 1935), pp. 86–88. Used with the permission of The Society of Authors.
66. Bober, *op. cit.*, p. 302.
67. *Ibid.*, p. 363.
68. H. B. Parkes, *Marxism: An Autopsy* (Houghton Mifflin Company, Boston, 1939), pp. 170–171. By permission.
69. *Ibid.*, pp. 177–178.
70. Christopher Dawson, *op. cit.*, pp. 95–96.
71. Reinhold Niebuhr, "Christian Politics and Communist Religion," in John Lewis (ed.) *Christianity and the Social Revolution* (Victor Gollancz, London, 1935), pp. 463 ff.
72. Dawson, *op. cit.*, p. 96.
73. *Ibid.*, p. 97. For an excellent discussion of Christianity and Marxism by both Catholic and Protestant writers see François Mauriac, Père Ducattillon, Alexandre Marc, Nicholas Berdyaev, Denis de Rougemont and Daniel-Rops, *Communism and Christians* (Westminster, Maryland, 1949).

CHAPTER 13

1. Quoted by H. W. Laidler, *Social-Economic Movements* (New York, 1946), p. 228.
2. Quoted by Victor Cathrein, *Socialism: Its Theoretical and Practical Application* (New York, 1904), p. 63. The texts of both the Gotha and Erfurt Programs can be found in this book, pp. 59 ff.
3. Bernstein, *Evolutionary Socialism* (New York, 1909), pp. xi, xii and xxii–xxiii.
4. *Ibid.*, p. 13.
5. *Ibid.*, pp. 38–39.
6. *Ibid.*, p. 39.
7. *Ibid.*, pp. 48–49.
8. *Ibid.*, p. 93.
9. *Ibid.*, p. 140.
10. *Ibid.*, p. 141.
11. *Ibid.*, pp. 144–145.
12. *Ibid.*, pp. 146–147.
13. *Ibid.*, pp. 164–165.
14. *Ibid.*, p. 218.
15. *Ibid.*, p. 224.
16. Kautsky, *Social Revolution* (Chicago, 1902), p. 84.
17. Kautsky, *The Labor Revolution* (London, 1925). p. 266.
18. Kautsky, *Road to Power* (Chicago, 1909), pp. 28, 52.
19. Kautsky, *Social Revolution*, pp. 82–83.
20. *Parliamentarismus und Demokratie* (Stuttgart, 1922), p. 133. Quoted by Francis W. Coker, *Recent Political Thought* (New York, 1934), pp. 80–81.
21. Emile Burns (ed.), *A Handbook of Marxism* (London, 1935), pp. 722 ff. Used with the permission of Emile Burns.
22. L. Lorwin, *Syndicalism in France* (Columbia University Press, New York, 1914), pp. 124–126. By permission.
23. *Ibid.*, pp. 126–127.
24. Quoted by Laidler, *op. cit.*, p. 297.
25. G. Sorel, *Reflections on Violence*. Translated by T. E. Hulme (Viking Press, New York, 1914), pp. 32 *et seq.*
26. *Ibid.*, pp. 88–89 and 90–91.
27. *Ibid.* Appendix entitled "Apology for Violence," pp. 297–298.
28. *Ibid.*, p. 290. For an excellent analysis of Sorel's theory and its relationship to Fascism see W. Y. Elliott, *The Pragmatic Revolt in Politics* (New York, 1928), especially Ch. IV.
29. E. R. Pease, *History of the Fabian Society* (New York, 1925), p. 269.
30. *Fabian Essays* (Boston, 1908), p. 27.
31. *Ibid.*, p. 22.
32. *Ibid.*, p. 96.
33. *Ibid.*, p. 116.
34. *Ibid.*, p. 113.
35. *Ibid.*, p. 152.
36. *Ibid.*, p. 151.
37. *Ibid.*, p. 185.
38. G. D. H. Cole, *Fabian Socialism* (Allen & Unwin, Ltd., London, 1943), p. 164. By permission of G. D. H. Cole and the Publishers.

39. Quoted by Laidler, *op. cit.*, p. 322.
40. Cole, *Guild Socialism* (Allen & Unwin, Ltd., London, 1920), pp. 36–37. By permission of G. D. H. Cole and the Publishers.
41. A. R. Orage, *An Alphabet of Economics* (London, 1917), p. 53.
42. Cole, *Guild Socialism*, p. 48.
43. *Ibid.*, p. 125.
44. *Ibid.*, pp. 121–122.
45. Cole, *The Simple Case for Socialism* (London, 1935), p. 156.
46. Cole, *The Intelligent Man's Guide to the Post-War World* (Oxford University Press, Inc., New York, 1948), pp. 269–270. By permission of G. D. H. Cole and the Publishers.
47. For a discussion of the parallels between English guild socialism, French syndicalism and Italian Fascism as variant solutions of a common problem and the connection between this whole complex and H. J. Laski's pluralism see W. Y. Elliott, *op. cit.* All represent an attack upon parliamentary, representative government and disillusionment with the idea that political conflict can best be solved by rational deliberation within the framework of a party system of government and under the rule of law. In part Professor Elliott points out: "Constitutional government represents the same effort at political synthesis that conceptual logic does for thought synthesis. It must shun alike pluralism and absolutism; it must admit the ideal character of its coherence, without abandoning logical coherence as a working method. A philosophy of constitutionalism is not so much a mere description of facts as it is a normative philosophy of the state . . . The coherent structure of law, shaped under a constitution, implies of necessity some accepted method of legal unification and determination for the solution of pluralistic forces which, if left to themselves, develop either the centrifugal tendencies of anarchy or the repressively centripetal tendencies of dictatorship. There is, wherever the organization of a people under law has achieved statehood, an habitual although not an absolute constitutional morality. This morality may be described as the active recognition of a relatively permanent community of purpose in the enforcement of law that has taken organic shape in a constitutional system. The constitutional system is accepted as the necessary presupposition of ordered human intercourse." But if the Marxian antithesis between classes is justified "then the persuasive methods of parliamentarism and constitutional responsibility are indeed vain. There is no basis for a community of purpose sufficiently strong to support the state. The solution is, indeed, force—whether that of Bolshevism or of Fascism." *Ibid.*, pp. 75–77. While inveighing against the idea of state sovereignty, the pluralist and the syndicalist, actually substitute a concept of *group* sovereignty for that of state sovereignty, thus attributing to the group authority and power they would deny to the state. "If the personality of individuals is to be attributed 'writ large' to corporate groups," moreover, "one may not stop short finally of the conception of an organic society, functioning with laws which are hardly a degree removed from those of biology—in short, with Duguit's final conception of solidarism, or Mussolini's fascism. 'Syndicalism'—in the broad sense in which Mr. Laski and Mr. Cole both accept the term to cover 'Trade Unionism in the light of the theory we have outlined, seeking in it the realization of the new group-personality which is the central fact of modern society'—can hardly evade the eventual development, dialectical or actual, into *Solidarisme* or *Organokratie.* Syndicalistic guild socialism is a

theoretical half-way house on the road towards those conceptions of society and government which appear most clearly in the theory of M. Duguit, and the practice of Fascism, just as M. Sorel's anarchistic Myth proved in application to be Sovietism in its development from group federalism to Leninism. Fascism is, *par excellence*, the result of this progress away from disintegration to absolute functionalism." *Ibid.*, pp. 213–214. For an interesting comparison of guild socialism and Fascism see Sidney and Beatrice Webb's projected *Constitution for the Socialist Commonwealth of Great Britain* (London, 1920).

48. In 1947 the Labor Party had a total membership of 5,040,299, of whom 4,386,074 were members of trade unions. Affiliated trade unions, Socialist and cooperative organizations pay annual dues of ten cents a member and the local Labor parties pay dues at the same rate. The Party is governed by an annual Conference and a National Executive Committee consisting of 27 members representing the various constituent bodies and elected by the Conference.

49. For a good brief account of the history and aims of the British Labor Party see C. R. Atlee, *The Labour Party in Perspective* (London, 1937). See also E. F. M. Durbin, *The Politics of Democratic Socialism* (London, 1940) which is an ardent plea for the compatibility of socialism and democracy.

50. C. R. Atlee, et al., *Labour's Aims in War and Peace* (London, 1940). Appendix, pp. 142–143.

51. H. J. Laski, "Great Britain Goes Socialist," *The Nation*, Vol. 161, p. 98 (August 4, 1945).

52. Cole, *The Intelligent Man's Guide to the Post-War World*, pp. 638–639.

53. Cole, *A Guide to Modern Politics*, (Alfred A. Knopf, New York, 1934), pp. 437, 443. Reprinted from *A Guide to Modern Politics*

by G. D. H. Cole and Margaret Cole by permission of Alfred A. Knopf, Inc., copyright 1934 by G. D. H. Cole and Margaret Cole.

54. Laski, "Plan or Perish," *The Nation*, Vol. 161, p. 651 (Dec. 15, 1945).

55. According to Max Kampelman, in an analysis of Laski's latest writings, "Mr. Laski now finds himself in the anomalous position of singing hosannas for democratic socialism in England and for totalitarian socialism in the Soviet Union at the same time, a basic contradiction from which his glib articulations cannot rescue him." "Harold J. Laski: A Current Analysis," *Journal of Politics*, Vol. 10, p. 154 (February, 1948). For an analysis of Laski's earlier writings and especially his theory of political pluralism see W. Y. Elliott, *op. cit.*, Ch. V.

56. H. J. Laski, *The State in Theory and Practice* (The Viking Press, Inc. New York, 1935), pp. 174 and 179. By permission.

57. *Ibid.*, pp. 251, 253–254 and 263.

58. V. Gollancz, *Our Threatened Values* (London, 1946), p. 19. By permission.

59. Francis W. Coker, *Recent Political Thought* (New York, 1934), p. 192.

60. W. Godwin, *An Enquiry Concerning Political Justice*. Edited by R. A. Preston (Appleton-Century-Crofts, Inc., New York, 1926), p. 11. By permission.

61. *Ibid.*, p. 55.

62. *Ibid.*, pp. 72–73.

63. *Ibid.*, p. 74.

64. *Ibid.*, p. 75.

65. *Ibid.*, p. 81.

66. Leslie Stephen, *English Thought in the Eighteenth Century*, Vol. II, p. 266.

67. Kropotkin, *The Conquest of Bread* (New York, 1906), pp. 10–11.

68. *Ibid.*, p. 29.

69. Kropotkin, *Anarchist Communism* (London, 1905), p. 4.

70. *Ibid.*, p. 35.

71. *Dieu et l'État, Oeuvres*, Vol. I, p. 288.

72. *Ibid.*
73. *Ibid.*
74. Quoted by George Catlin, *The Story of the Political Philosophers* (Whittlesey House, New York, 1939), p. 429.
75. Eric Voegelin, "Bakunin's Confession," *Journal of Politics*, Vol. 8, pp. 41–42 (February 1946). By permission.
76. Quoted by Voegelin, *ibid.*, p. 36.
77. *Ibid.*, pp. 36–37.

## CHAPTER 14

1. For an account of the Russian Revolution and the events leading up to it see: W. H. Chamberlin, *The Russian Revolution, 1917–1921* (New York, 2 vols., 1935); B. Pares, *A History of Russia* (New York, 3d ed., 1937); G. Vernadskii, *The Russian Revolution, 1917–1931* (New York, 1932); Leon Trotsky, *History of the Russian Revolution* (New York, 3 vols., 1932); Alexander Kerensky, *The Catastrophe* (New York, 1927), and V. I. Lenin, *The Revolution of 1917* (New York, 2 vols., 1932). For interesting material on Lenin and Trotsky see Edmund Wilson, *To the Finland Station* (New York, 1940).
2. Lenin, *What Is To Be Done?* in *Selected Works* (New York, 1935–38), Vol. II, p. 53. (Italics mine.)
3. Quoted by Max Eastman, *Marxism: Is it Science?* (New York, 1940), pp. 223–224.
4. *What Is To Be Done?*, *loc. cit.*, p. 139.
5. Lenin, *Imperialism: The State and Revolution* (Vanguard Press, New York, 1926), pp. 27–28. (Italics mine).
6. *Ibid.*, p. 91.
7. *Ibid.*, pp. 95–96. (Italics mine).
8. *Ibid.*, p. 95.
9. *Ibid.*, pp. 98–99, 100 and 102.
10. For an account of the Soviet economic system see: C. B. Hoover, *The Economic Life of Soviet Russia* (New York, 1931); L. E. Hubbard, *The Economics of Soviet Agriculture* (London, 1939); Hubbard, *Soviet Labor and Indus-

try* (London, 1942); Colin Clark, *A Critique of Russian Statistics* (London, 1939); N. Vosnesensky, *Economic Results of the USSR in 1940 and the Plan of National Economic Development for 1941* (Moscow, 1941) and A. Yugow, *Russia's Economic Front for War and Peace* (New York, 1942).
11. Lenin, *Selected Works*, Vol. VI, pp. 506–508.
12. On the first anniversary of the October Revolution, November 6, 1918, *Pravda* published an issue commemorating the event. In an inside page there is a short article by Stalin in which he declared: "All the work of practical organization of the insurrection was carried on under the direct leadership of the Chairman of the Petrograd Soviet, Comrade Trotsky. It may be said with certainty that for the speedy transition of the garrison over to the side of the Soviet and for the skilful organization of the work of the Military-Revolutionary Committee the Party was indebted most of all and principally to Comrade Trotsky." It is significant that volume four of Stalin's collected works (*Sochineniya*) reproduces this article from *Pravda* but completely deletes, without any indication of omission, the portion concerning Trotsky.
13. Manya Gordon, *Workers Before and After Lenin* (New York, 1941), p. 400. *Cf.* W. H. Chamberlin, *Russia's Iron Age* (Boston, 1934), pp. 66–92 and A. Yugow, *Russia's Economic Front for War and Peace* (New York, 1942), Ch. III.
14. Yugow, *op. cit.*, p. 11.
15. These figures and a discussion of their significance can be found in Yugow, *ibid.*, pp. 32 *ff.*
16. Professor Nicholas S. Timasheff shows in a recent study that the extrapolation of the production curve from 1890–1914 renders practically the same figures for the subsequent twenty-five years as the official Soviet statistics show. See N. S. Timasheff, *The Great Retreat: The Growth and Decline of Communism in Russia*

(E. P. Dutton and Co., New York, 1946) pp. 114–115 and 149–150.

17. *Pravda*, Feb. 19, 1941. Quoted by Yugow, *ibid.*, p. 21.
18. Quoted by Yugow, *ibid.*, p. 23.
19. *Ibid.*, p. 39.
20. L. E. Hubbard, *Soviet Labor and Industry* (London, 1942), p. 164. Cf. F. Forest, "An Analysis of Russian Economy" in *New International*, Jan.–Feb. 1943 and Peter Meyer, "The Soviet Union: A New Class Society," *Politics*, March, 1944.
21. *The* (London) *Economist*, July 3, 1943. Quoted by Arthur Koestler, *The Yogi and the Commissar* (Macmillan, New York, 1945), p. 159. Copyright 1945 by the Macmillan Company and used with their permission.
22. Quoted by Koestler, *ibid.*, pp. 159–160.
23. *Ibid.*, pp. 156–157.
24. For a detailed analysis of the class structure in present-day Russia see Timasheff, *op. cit.*, Ch. X. He estimates that "In 1937 there were 1,751,000 'enterprise managers,' 250,000 engineers, 80,000 agronomists, 80,000 scientists, 159,000 actors and artists, 297,000 journalists, 132,000 physicians, and 46,000 judges and prosecutors—a total of 2,800,000 persons eligible for membership in the two upper classes. An additional 2,500,000 were found in the bureaucracy. Assuming that their families consisted on the average of four persons, the size of the two classes may have been 20,000,000 or 13% of the population. This is, however, only a maximum; quite a few persons in the categories mentioned do not belong to the ruling or the Non-party Bolshevik groups, their income being insufficient. The upper class has been estimated to number 800,000 to 1,000,000 persons with the middle class consisting, perhaps, of 8,000,000 or 5% of the population. In 1939, the number of peasants (both collectivized and individual) was

found to be 78,600,000 or 46.4% of the population . . . The number of 'nontoilers' and persons of indeterminate occupation has appeared to be 1,200,000 or 7% of the population." *Ibid.*, pp. 310–311.
25. Professor Calvin B. Hoover informs me that most bonds now have lottery features in lieu of interest.
26. In Emile Burns (ed.), *A Handbook of Marxism* (London, 1935), pp. 937–938.
27. *Ibid.*, p. 940.
28. W. H. Chamberlin, *The Russian Enigma* (Charles Scribner's Sons, New York, 1943), p. 173. By permission.
29. Koestler, *op. cit.*, p. 161. See also Margaret Miller, *Labour in the USSR*, British Assoc. for Labour Legislation, 1942, pp. 19–21.
30. See David J. Dallin and Boris I. Nicholaevsky, *Forced Labor in Soviet Russia* (New Haven, 1947).
31. According to one account, that of Vladimir M. Petroff, now teaching at Yale University, and recorded in the petition of the A. F. of L. to the United Nations Economic and Social Council:

"At the age of 19 years, in February, 1935, I was arrested in Leningrad while I was studying at the Engineering Institute. My father was a high official in the Ministry of Domestic Commerce, and has a Socialist background. . . .

"After six months in jail I had a so-called trial. It took place behind closed doors, with no lawyer, no public, no prosecutor. I only had to answer questions and was declared guilty of Anti-Soviet propaganda. All evidence consisted of a schooltime diary, written by me at the age of 15 and which, I was told, contained criticisms. . . .

"The sentence was six years in prison . . . and I was sent to a concentration camp in northeastern Siberia. . . .

"I was sent to the goldmines as a worker where I stayed for two and a half years. Living conditions were terribly hard. We had to work in terrific cold—down to 70° below, F. Only when the temperature was 90 below did we not have to work. We lived in tents, and had only some stoves made from American gasoline barrels.

"Working hours were 12 hours a day in winter, and 14 to 15 hours in the summer. . . . Most of the prisoners were political prisoners.

"Mortality was high, and ran up to one-fourth of the inmates. Those who were too weak to work were shot. Others were accused of sabotage. Food was very poor, treatment cruel. We were frequently beaten. . . . We received no pay—only those who worked more than 100% of their assigned tasks received small amounts with which to buy tobacco, 85% of the workers, however, were unpaid.

"We had in our tent 40% intelligentsia (doctors, professors, engineers, etc.) and 60% peasants and workers. There were no criminals in our tent. The criminals were treated as an aristocracy and used as officials at the Camp. . . .

"From the information I received from people who came from other camps, I made up statistics to find out the number of prisoners on forced labor. Later on a Komsomol [a member of the Young Communist League] who came as a genuine NKVD official to the Magadan Camp, confirmed my statistics, namely, that there were, in 1941, between 8 and 10 million prisoners working."

There are innumerable firsthand accounts of conditions in Soviet Russia. See the following especially: Vladimir V. Tchernavin, *I Speak for the Silent Prisoners of the Soviets* (Boston, 1935); Markoosha Fischer, *My Lives in Russia* (New York, 1944); Freda Utley, *The Dream We Lost* (New York, 1940); Anton Ciliga, *The Russian Enigma* (1940); John

Scott, *Behind the Urals* (New York, 1942); Alexander Barmin, *One Who Survived* (New York, 1945); Victor Kravchenko, *I Chose Freedom: The Personal and Political Life of a Soviet Official* (New York, 1946). Compare these accounts with Hewlett Johnson, *The Soviet Power* (New York, 1940) and Sidney and Beatrice Webb, *Soviet Communism* (New York, 2 vols., 1936).

32. *Selected Works*, Vol. V, p. 295.

33. *Sovetskiye Finansy*, No. 9 (1947), p. 35.

34. One of the most recent accounts of Russian political institutions is Julian Towster's *Political Power in the U. S. S. R., 1917–1947; The Theory and Structure of Government in the Soviet State* (New York, 1948). A comprehensive but morally indifferent account will be found in Frederick L. Schuman, *Soviet Politics, At Home and Abroad* (New York, 1946). See also John N. Hazard, "The Soviet Government Organizes for Reconstruction," *Journal of Politics*, Vol. 8, No. 3, pp. 248 *ff.* (August, 1946); and Waldemar Gurian, *Bolshevism: Theory and Practice* (New York, 1932). For an account of Church and State relations in Russia see Paul B. Anderson, *People, Church and State in Modern Russia* (New York, 1944); John S. Curtiss, *Church and State in Russia* (New York, 1940) and Nicholas S. Timasheff, *Religion in Soviet Russia, 1917–1942* (New York, 1942). For an account of cultural developments see Max Eastman, *Artists in Uniform* (New York, 1934); Kurt London, *Seven Soviet Arts* (London, 1937); Dwight Macdonald, "The Russian Culture Purge," *Politics* (October 1948), pp. 297 *ff.*; and C. D. Darlington, "The Retreat from Science in Soviet Russia," *Nineteenth Century* (October 1947), pp. 157 *ff.*

35. *The Land of Socialism Today and Tomorrow.* Reports and Speeches at the 18th Congress of the Communist Party of the Soviet

Union, March 10–21, 1939. (Moscow, 1939), p. 465.

36. Chamberlin, *Russian Enigma*, p. 209.

37. Koestler, *op. cit.*, p. 172. See also Schwartz, "Heads of Russian Factories," *Social Research*, Sept., 1942.

38. One of the best accounts, in novel form, of the motivations which may have influenced those unjustly accused of treason is found in Arthur Koestler's, *Darkness at Noon* (New York, 1941).

39. A commission headed by Professor John Dewey has studied the "evidence" against Trotsky as presented in the Russian trials and reached the conclusion that most, if not all of it, was pure fabrication. See the study entitled: *Not Guilty: Report of the Commission of Inquiry into the Charges Made Against Leon Trotsky in the Moscow Trials*. (New York, 1938).

40. J. Stalin, "Report of the Work of the Central Committee to the 18th Congress of the C. P. S. U.," in *Land of Socialism, op. cit.*, pp. 43–44.

41. "Amendments to the Rules of the C. P. S. U.," *ibid.*, p. 447.

42. Stalin, "Report . . . to the 18th Congress," *loc. cit.*, pp. 44–45.

43. Stalin, *ibid.*, pp. 47–48.

44. Quoted in *East Europe*. A Weekly Bulletin of Seven East European Countries. London, March 19, 1947, p. 3.

45. *Pravda*, August 28, 1936. For an analysis of Stalin's life and role in the Soviet Union see Boris Souvarine, *Stalin* (New York, 1939).

46. The best history of the International is found in F. Borkenau, *World Communism: a History of the Communist International* (New York, 1939).

47. The complete text of the Program is found in Emile Burns, *op. cit.*, pp. 964 ff.

48. *Selected Works*, Vol. VI, p. 17.

49. *Bolshevik*, No. 18, 1947.

50. For an account of the techniques employed by the Communist parties in these countries see Vernon Van Dyke, "Communism in Eastern and Southeastern Europe," *Journal of Politics*, Vol. 9, No. 3, pp. 355–391 (August 1947). For an account by former Communists of their disillusionment, see R. H. S. Crossman *et al.*, *The God That Failed* (New York, 1950).

## CHAPTER 15

1. Étienne Gilson, *The Unity of Philosophical Experience* (Charles Scribner's Sons, New York, 1937), p. 274. By permission. In a similar manner Professor Helmut Kuhn points out that "the distinctive mark of humanity as over against materiality and animality" is not "a power of faculty residing in man as merely an additional endowment. Man, it is true, is capable of achievements beyond the reach of animals. Language and rational thought are given him alone. But if we understand the ancient definition of man as *animal rationale* in that sense (not the sense intended by its originators), it defines a hybrid rather than man. Nothing more monstrous than an animal, living, feeding, mating, perishing as an animal, but endowed with intelligence. Only a dehumanized man may approach this condition. Rather than being engrafted upon animality, the distinctively human element must inform and transfigure animality. Man is human not only by virtue of his ratiocinative power. He calls his matings marriage, his begetters parents, his feeding taking meals, and, conscious of life, he foresees the oncoming death. For better or for worse, he is an altogether unique being, projecting, as it were, into a dimension foreign to animality. All this is not said in confutation of the idea that rationality is the *differentia specifica* of our race. If only we fight shy of that emas-

culated idea of reason that infected post-Cartesian philosophy
(reason cut loose from passion
and debarred from vision), we
may find the ancient concept
still useful. Or rather it will
prove indispensable. It alone
meets a second requirement to be
fulfilled by any definition of man.
It assigns to him the place of a
potential spectator. As rational,
man does not live in an environment only, but in a world. He
is able to discover things as they
are by themselves, and he does
so for the sake of discovery. Im-
mersed as he is in the totality of
things, he may yet rise above
participation and face the world
(including himself) as a spectacle. Cosmology, not ecology,
describes his status. Only for a
philosophy which encompasses
man in the role of a rational
spectator do the elements of abstract knowledge acquired by the
natural sciences coalesce into a
concrete picture of reality. For
natural science presupposes a
fact which no natural science
will ever make intelligible; the
human observer. Only by virtue
of understanding himself can
man understand his sciences."
"Philosophy and Religion: The
Humanity of Man" in *A State
University Surveys the Humanities*
(University of North Carolina
Press, Chapel Hill) pp. 74–75. By
permission.

2. Gilson, *op. cit.*, p. 277.

3. To the extent that psychology
means the general description of
human conduct then it is at
least as old as the writings of
Plato and Aristotle. From the
earliest times men have specu-
lated about the relationship between the human body and the
soul (*psyche*). Both Plato and
Aristotle and the Christian philosophers regarded man as a
composite being, as a rational
life animating a material body.
It was not until Descartes declared that man is *two* substances,
an unextended mind and an extended matter that the essential
unity of man was challenged and
the mind-body problem emerged
in its modern form. Henceforth
there were attempts made to reduce the mental life of man to its
physical aspects or to reduce the
physical to the mental. One of
the first to attempt to explain
man's psychic life in terms of a
materialistic mechanism was
Thomas Hobbes (1588–1679)
and, as a consequence, he is
sometimes called the father of
modern psychology. And it was
John Locke in his *Essay Concerning the Human Understanding*
(1690) who suggested that the
principle of unity in man was
not the soul but a process of
association. This doctrine of the
association of ideas was developed by David Hume, James
Mill, and Maine de Biran. The
nineteenth century witnessed
the emergence of experimental
psychology, a kind of psychology
to which many modern psychologists would like to confine the
meaning of the word psychology
itself. The older psychology is
appropriately described as philosophical anthropology, modern
psychology differs from this older
form by its reliance solely upon
the concepts and methods of the
natural sciences. It is an attempt
to explain man's psychic life
wholly in terms of some immanent principle.

4. R. S. Woodworth, *Contemporary
Schools of Psychology* (Ronald
Press Company, New York, rev.
ed., 1948), p. 255. By permission.

5. J. B. Watson, *Behavior: An Introduction to Comparative Psychology*
(New York, 1914).

6. Edna Heidbreder, *Seven Psychol-
ogies* (Appleton-Century-Crofts,
Inc., New York, 1933), p. 417.
By permission.

7. *Ibid.*, p. 413.

8. *Ibid.*, p. 418.

9. *Ibid.*, p. 420.

10. Woodworth, *op. cit.*, p. 219.

11. *Ibid.*, p. 219.

12. *Ibid.*, p. 220.

13. McDougall, *Introduction to Social Psychology* (London, 1908), p. 44.
14. *Ibid.*, p. 18.
15. *Ibid.*, p. 26.
16. William McDougall, *The Group Mind* (New York, 1920), p. 6.
17. *Ibid.*, p. 20.
18. *Ibid.*, p. 78.
19. *Ibid.*, p. 53.
20. McDougall, *Psychoanalysis and Social Psychology* (London, 1936), p. 17. For an introduction to the theories of Sigmund Freud see *The Basic Writings of Sigmund Freud* translated and edited, with an introduction by Dr. A. A. Brill, Modern Library edition (New York, 1938). For a critical study of Freudian psychology from a Christian perspective see Rudolf Allers, *The Successful Error* (New York, 1940). The psychology of the unconscious is not wholly the product of Freud but has an ancestry which includes the writings of Herder, Baader, Schelling, Schopenhauer and Hartmann.
21. Woodworth, *op. cit.*, p. 174.
22. *Ibid.*, pp. 184 *ff.*
23. *Ibid.*, pp. 189 *ff.*
24. For a contrast between the Freudian and Christian conceptions of man see Reinhold Niebuhr, *The Nature and Destiny of Man*, Vol. I (New York, 1943), esp. Ch. II; Walter M. Horton, "The Christian Understanding of Man," in T. E. Jessop, *et al.*, *The Christian Understanding of Man* (London, 1938), pp. 215 *ff.* and Fulton J. Sheen, *Peace of Soul* (New York, 1949).
25. See Karen Horney, *The Neurotic Personality of Our Time* (New York, 1937); Erich Fromm, *Escape from Freedom* (New York, 1945) and J. C. Flügel, *Man, Morals and Society* (London, 1945).
26. H. D. Lasswell, *Psychopathology and Politics* (University of Chicago Press, Chicago, 1930), p. 125. By permission. See also H. D. Lasswell, *Politics: Who Gets What, When, How* (Chicago, 1936), and *The Analysis of Political Behavior* (New York, 1948).

27. Lasswell, *Psychopathology and Politics*, pp. 196–197.
28. *Ibid.*, p. 203. Another plea for a psychiatric approach to social problems will be found in Thurman W. Arnold's *The Folklore of Capitalism* (New Haven, 1937). His thesis is that we should try to mold principles to organizational needs rather than trying to mold organizations in terms of principles.
29. See Gabriel Tarde, *Social Laws* (New York, 1906) and *The Laws of Imitation* (New York, 1903).
30. E. Durkheim, *The Elementary Forms of Religious Life* (George Allen and Unwin, Ltd., London, 1915), p. 444. By permission.
31. *Ibid.*, pp. 10–17.
32. *Ibid.*, pp. 10–17. Probably the best analysis of Durkheim's work is to be found in Talcott Parsons, *The Structure of Social Action* (New York, 1937), esp. Chs. VIII–XI. The same book contains an analysis of Pareto's writings.
33. G. le Bon, *The Crowd* (Allen and Unwin, London, 1903), p. 30.
34. *Ibid.*, p. 41.
35. *Ibid.*, pp. 201–202.
36. *Ibid.*, p. 212.
37. Vilfredo Pareto, *The Mind and Society* (Harcourt Brace and Company, Inc., New York, 4 vols., 1935), Vol. II, par. 2060. By permission.
38. *Ibid.*, Vol. III, pp. 1241–1242.
39. *Ibid.*, Vol. II, par. 875.
40. *Ibid.*, Vol. II, par. 888.
41. *Ibid.*, Vol. III, p. 1401.
42. *Ibid.*, Vol. III, p. 1415.
43. *Ibid.*, Vol. III, par. 2274.
44. *Ibid.*, Vol. III, par. 2183.
45. *Ibid.*, Vol. III, par. 2053.
46. *Ibid.*, Vol. III, pp. 1281–1282.
47. *Ibid.*, Vol. III, p. 1293.
48. Melvin Rader, *No Compromise: The Conflict Between Two Worlds* (Macmillan, New York, 1939), p. 50. Copyright 1939 by The Macmillan Company and used with their permission. For other analyses of Pareto's writings see George C. Homans and Charles P. Curtis, Jr., *An Introduction to Pareto* (New York, 1934); Pitirim Sorokin, *Contemporary Sociological*

*Theories* (New York, 1928); William M. McGovern, *From Luther to Hitler* (Boston, 1941), pp. 434 ff.; L. J. Henderson, *Pareto's General Sociology* (Cambridge, Mass., 1935); F. Borkenau, *Pareto* (London, 1936), and James Burnham, *The Machiavellians* (New York, 1943).

49. C. S. Lewis, *Miracles* (Macmillan, New York, 1947), p. 27. Copyright 1947 by The Macmillan Company and used with their permission.

50. *Ibid.*, p. 28.

51. William James, *Pragmatism* (Longmans, Green and Company, New York, 1928), p. 8. Copyright 1928 by Longmans, Green & Company and used with their permission.

52. *Ibid.*, pp. 50 ff.

53. *Ibid.*, pp. 53–54.

54. *Ibid.*, p. 54.

55. *Ibid.*, p. 58.

56. *Ibid.*, pp. 222–223.

57. *Ibid.*, p. 230.

58. *Ibid.*, p. 201.

59. William James, *The Will to Believe* (New York, 1937), p. 11.

60. *Ibid.*, p. 22.

61. *Ibid.*, p. 29. (Italics mine.)

62. C. E. M. Joad, *Guide to Philosophy* (New York, 1937), p. 464. For an excellent discussion of Pragmatism from a Christian perspective see Robert L. Calhoun, "The Dilemma of Humanitarian Modernism," in T. E. Jessop, *et al.*, *The Christian Understanding of Man* (London, 1938). An eminent Italian philosopher, Guido de Ruggiero, uses harsh words in his description of pragmatism for, he says, with the emergence of Pragmatism "philosophy has vanished and we are on the brink of comedy, if not downright charlatanism." It is his contention that Pragmatism "solves" the perennial problems of philosophy by ignoring them. Speaking of William James' book on *Pragmatism* he says: "Here the pragmatist method is represented as a method of avoiding metaphysical discussions, or, better, of solving every problem by caprice. Is the world one or many? It is one if we look at it in one way, many if we look at it another. Let us say, then, that is at the same time one and many, and let us live in peace. Must we decide between theism and materialsm? The past does not tell us anything in favour of either the one or the other. Let us look within us. The world of materialism closes in tragedy and gloom: that of theism legitimizes our sublimest hopes. Is this latter in our interest? If so, let us accept it. This is magnificent reasoning; and the whole book is strewn with similar gems of logic. Truth is reduced to an economic fact, a form of wealth, a 'property' of our ideas; thought has an exchange value like that of a banknote which 'passes' so long as nobody rejects it; and so on through a series of ineptitudes that bring disgrace to the name of philosophy." *Modern Philosophy* (London, 1921), p. 256.

63. John Dewey, *The Influence of Darwin on Philosophy* (New York, 1910), p. 13.

64. Dewey, "The Need for Social Psychology, *Psychological Review* (July, 1917), p. 270.

65. Dewey, "Authority and Social Change," in the Harvard Tercentenary Publication, *Authority and the Individual* (Harvard University Press, Cambridge, 1937), p. 188. By permission.

66. *Ibid.*, pp. 183 and 184.

67. Bertrand Russell, *A History of Western Philosophy* (Simon and Schuster, New York, 1945), pp. 827–828. Reprinted from *A History of Western Philosophy* by permission of Simon and Schuster, Publishers. Copyright, 1945, by Bertrand Russell. See also George Santayana, "Dewey's Naturalistic Metaphysics" in P. A. Schilpp, *The Philosophy of John Dewey* (Evanston, 1939), pp. 243 ff. For an excellent analysis of the effect of pragmatism upon politics see W. Y. Elliott, *The Pragmatic Re-*

*volt in Politics* (New York, 1928). In part Professor Elliott says: "The Romanticist revolt against reason took philosophic form (if form it can be called) first in the protest philosophy of James. But reason has its revenge; because headlong rebellion against conceptual logic led him into urging the rights of belief where conviction could not be, James came in his later philosophy to destroy the very foundation upon which belief may rest with satisfaction. The effort of Instrumentalism to give some content to the practice of pragmatism has led to really useful experimentation in educational and social psychology . . . But Instrumentalism, in its constructive phase, is an economic interpretation of philosophy. It can talk only descriptively so long as its logic is that of psychology, or of a false interpretation of thinking in terms simply of supply and demand. Its test . . . must either be taken for granted from the beginning, or applied only when the act is a *fait accompli*. Even in the latter case, its method is apt to be a *post mortem* inquest which is prejudiced in favor of *de viventibus nil nisi bonum*, for survival value is all that Instrumentalism has as a check upon the interest value upon which judgment is to be passed. Nor can this *impasse* be escaped by an appeal to the method of science, unless that method be admitted to imply the necessity of something like a philosophy of science itself . . . The culmination of the pragmatic dialectic, where it leaves off being revolutionary Romanticism and becomes constructive, is a social theory that conceives individual relationships as simply organic, as functional, parts of a socially interdependent whole, a Fascist state in which the only divisions possible of determination are along the lines of the intensity of 'real' social forces. Purpose, having been omitted from the begin-

ning, purposeful society can never be." *Ibid.*, pp. 63–65.
68. *Die Fröhliche Wissenschaft.* Quoted by George A. Morgan, *What Nietzsche Means* (Cambridge, Mass., 1941), p. 38.
69. See Morgan, *ibid.*, pp. 324 *ff*.
70. John N. Figgis, *The Will to Freedom* or *The Gospel of Nietzsche and The Gospel of Christ* (Charles Scribner's Sons, New York, 1917), p. 290. By permission.
71. *Thus Spake Zarathustra.* Modern Library edition, p. 28.
72. Quoted by Figgis, *op. cit.*, pp. 75–77.
73. *Thus Spake Zarathustra, loc. cit.*, p. 149.
74. *Nachgelassene Werke.* Quoted by Morgan, *op. cit.*, p. 305.
75. Quoted by Morgan, *ibid.*, p. 376.
76. *Thus Spake Zarathustra, loc. cit.*, p. 195.
77. B. Russell, *op. cit.*, p. 767.
78. *Thus Spake Zarathustra, loc. cit.*, pp. 62–63.
79. Figgis, *op. cit.*, pp. 153–154.
80. *The Will to Power.* Quoted by Figgis, *ibid.*, pp. 276 *ff*.
81. Figgis, *ibid.*, p. 287.
82. *Ibid.*, p. 298.
83. *Ibid.*, pp. 312 *ff*. For other interpretations see Karl Jaspers, *Nietzsche; Einführung in das Verständnis seines Philosophierens* (Berlin, 1936); Karl Löwith, *Nietzsches philosophie der ewigen wiederkunft des gleichen* (Berlin, 1935); Ernst Bertram, *Nietzsche; Versuch einer Mythologie* (Berlin, 1918); C. P. T. Andler, *Nietzsche: Sa Vie et Sa Pensée* (Paris, 5 vols., 1920–1931); and H. A. Reyburn, *Nietzsche: The Story of a Human Philosopher* (London, 1948).

CHAPTER 16

1. C. J. H. Hayes, *Essays on Nationalism* (Macmillan, New York, 1926), p. 5. Copyright 1926 by The Macmillan Company and used with their permission. The French philosopher Ernest Renan (1823–1892) once described the characteristics of a nation in these words: "To have

common glories in the past, a common will in the present; to have done great things together; to wish to do greater; these are the essential conditions which make up a people . . . In the past, an inheritance of glories and regrets; in the future, one and the same program to carry out . . . The existence of a nation is a daily plebiscite." "Qu'est-ce qu'une nation?" in *Discours et Conferences* (Paris, 1922), pp. 227 ff.

2. *Ibid.*, p. 5.
3. Hans Kohn, *The Idea of Nationalism* (Macmillan, New York, 1944), pp. 18 and 19. Copyright 1944 by Hans Kohn. Used with the permission of The Macmillan Company.
4. *Ibid.*, p. 13.
5. Hayes, *op. cit.*, p. 6.
6. *Ibid.*, p. 31.
7. *Ibid.*, pp. 35–36.
8. *Ibid.*, p. 38.
9. *Ibid.*, pp. 38–39.
10. *Ibid.*, p. 40.
11. *Ibid.*, p. 49.
12. *Ibid.*, p. 72
13. Kohn, *op. cit.*, p. 429.
14. *Ibid.*, pp. 431–432.
15. Quoted by Kohn, *ibid.*, p. 431.
16. Quoted by Kohn, *ibid.*, p. 436.
17. Quoted by Kohn, *ibid.*, p. 439.
18. Quoted by Kohn, *ibid.*, p. 439.
19. Quoted by R. R. Ergang, *Herder and the Foundations of German Nationalism* (Columbia University Press, New York, 1931), pp. 243–244. By permission.
20. Quoted by Kohn, *op. cit.*, p. 448.
21. Quoted by Kohn, *ibid.*, p. 447.
22. Fichte, J. G., *Addresses to the German Nation.* Translated by Jones and Trumbull (Chicago, 1922), p. 113.
23. *Characteristics of the Present Age.* Translated by W. Smith (London, 1847), p. 33.
24. *Addresses, op. cit.*, p. 198.
25. It is in his *Addresses to the German Nation* especially that many writers have found evidence of Fichte's kinship to the Nazis. See among others, for example, W. H. McGovern, *From Luther to Hitler* (Boston, 1941), pp.

209 ff. But in opposition to such interpretations F. W. Kaufmann points out that Fichte is essentially a moral idealist and that "the most fervently nationalistic of Fichte's works is not a prophecy of German racial pre-eminence, but a challenge to take the lead in responsible world-citizenship. Its spirit is diametrically opposed to that of National Socialism." Fichte, he argues, represents not "another proof for an incorrigible warlike German mentality" but rather "the undeniable fact that National Socialism betrays the best German tradition and debases the German character." See his article entitled "Fichte and National Socialism," in the *American Political Science Review* (June 1942), pp. 460 ff.

26. See *Der Geschlossene Handelstaat* (Tübingen, 1800) in Fichte's *Werke* (Berlin, 1834–45). There is no English translation of this book.
27. *Guiseppe Mazzini: Selected Writings* edited by N. Gangulee (London, 1944), pp. 139–140. The passage quoted is from his *Autobiography.* For an excellent discussion of Mazzini's ideas see Hans Kohn, *Prophets and Peoples: Studies in Nineteenth Century Nationalism* (Macmillan, New York, 1946), pp. 78 ff. Copyright 1946 by The Macmillan Company and used with their permission. According to Professor Kohn: "The great war cries of the age, Fatherland, Liberty, Nationality, Equality, Progress, Fraternal Association, were to him holy and prophetic sounds of a new order of things, a complete translation of the words of Jesus, 'That all may be one.' He regarded the struggle of the peoples of Europe as a 'sacred struggle,' the logical consequence of the doctrine of the unity of God and therefore of the human race . . . For a man like Mazzini the true liberation of Italy could come only through ethical principles and religious enthusiasm

. . . He had no use for Machiavelli . . . A nation addicted to Machiavellianism, to immoral opportunism, would in spite of all outward successes and all its power, fall prey to inner decay and finally to foreign invasion." *Ibid.*, pp. 90–91.

28. In a letter to Melegari written in 1833. *Selected Writings, op. cit.*, p. 131.

29. From *The Duties of Man* (1858) in *Selected Writings*, p. 163.

30. *Selected Writings*, pp. 92–94. All the great nations at the time developed their nationalism under the guise of a universal mission.

31. Mazzini, *The Duties of Man and other Essays*. Translated by E. Noyes. Everyman edition (London, 1907), p. 55. *The Duties of Man* first appeared in 1844.

32. *Ibid.*, pp. 36–37.

33. *Ibid.*, pp. 49–50.

34. Hans J. Morgenthau, *Scientific Man vs. Power Politics* (University of Chicago Press, Chicago, 1946), p. 67. By permission.

35. F. M. Russell, *Theories of International Relations* (Appleton-Century-Crofts, Inc., New York, 1936), pp. 264–265. This book is unique in its scope. Much attention is given to the history and institutions of international relations but very little to theories of international relations. This book presents an excellent summary of most of those theories.

36. *Outlines of Sociology*. Translated by F. W. Moore (Philadelphia, 1899), p. 150. This book, as the *Grundriss der Soziologie*, first appeared in Vienna in 1885.

37. *Ibid.*, p. 151.

38. *Expansion of England* (London, 1883), p. 8.

39. See his *Reflections on the Origins and Destiny of Imperial Britain* (London, 1915).

40. *Ibid.*, p. 13.

41. *Ibid.*, p. 91. This theory of imperialism found practical embodiment in the life of Cecil J. Rhodes (1853–1902) and literary expression in the writings of Rudyard Kipling.

42. J. W. Burgess, *Political Science and Constitutional Law*. 2 vols. (Boston, 1890–91), Vol. I, p. 46.

43. *Democracy and Empire* (New York, 1901). Preface.

44. *Ibid.*, p. 270.

45. Von Treitschke, *Politics*. 2 vols. (New York, 1916), Vol. II, p. 13. Lectures first delivered in 1897–1898. For a discussion of Treitschke see Hans Kohn, *op. cit.*, pp. 106 *ff*.

46. *Politics*, Vol. I, p. 61.

47. *Ibid.*, Vol. I, pp. 74 and 75.

48. *Ibid.*, Vol. I, p. 66.

49. *Ibid.*, Vol. II, pp. 395–396.

50. *Ibid.*, Vol. I, p. 21.

51. *Ibid.*, Vol. II, p. 609.

52. *Ibid.*, Vol. II, p. 591.

53. *Ibid.*, Vol. I, p. 36.

54. *Ibid.*, Vol. I, pp. 19–21. Professor Kohn speaks of Treitschke as a prophet but a prophet who "held forth no generous promise to mankind . . . Unlike Mill, Michelet, or Mazzini, he had no universal message. He had no faith in the unity of law on earth nor in the triumph of justice over force. In spite of his Christian piety which grew on him with advancing age, he never, like the Hebrew prophets or Kipling's 'Recessional,' called his people to repentance and to the realization of the futility of might. His obsession with state, might and hero oversimplified human motives and relations as much as a naive faith in man's goodness or in exclusively economic incentives could do . . . Treitschke, like so many nationalists of modern times, confounded national independence and individual liberty under the one magic word "freedom." He thus made the essential—liberty in the human and universal sense—contingent upon something external and accidental—independence in the age of nationalism. The individual and the human suffered; the nation gained, but at the danger of becoming more and more self-contained, setting itself apart from the outside world, culti-

vating its own native culture, expecting the dawn of its day in history." *Op. cit.*, pp. 129–130.

55. Quoted by C. J. H. Hayes, *Historical Evolution of Modern Nationalism* (Macmillan, New York, 1930), p. 165. Copyright 1930 by The Macmillan Company and used with their permission.

56. *Ibid.*, p. 198.

57. *La Grand Pitié des Églises de France*, p. 7. Quoted by Hayes, *ibid.*, p. 196.

58. Hayes, *ibid.*, p. 202.

59. *Action Française*, June 10, 1908. Quoted by Hayes, *ibid.*, p. 204.

60. *La Politique Religieuse*, p. 184. Quoted by Hayes, *ibid.*, p. 205.

61. *Le Chemin de Paradis*. Quoted by Hayes, *ibid.*, p. 206.

62. *Ibid.*, p. 212.

63. For a discussion of pre-fascist Italian political thought see the article by that title written by Joseph Rossi in J. S. Roucek (ed.), *Twentieth Century Political Thought* (New York, 1946), pp. 553 *ff*. Also J. P. Mayer, *Political Thought: The European Tradition* (New York, 1939), Ch. IX and W. Y. Elliott, *The Pragmatic Revolt in Politics* (New York, 1928), esp. Ch. XI.

64. Benito Mussolini, "The Political and Social Doctrine of Fascism." This first appeared in the *Enciclopedia Italiana* in 1932. It has been translated and reprinted in various places including the periodical *International Conciliation* (Jan., 1935), No. 306.

65. Arthur de Gobineau, *The Inequality of Human Races*. Translated by A. Collins (New York, 1914). For a discussion of racial theories see Jacques Barzun, *Race: A Study in Modern Superstition* (New York, 1937); Franz Boas, *Race and Democratic Society* (New York, 1945); M. F. Ashley Montagu, *Man's Most Dangerous Myth: The Fallacy of Race* (New York, 1945); Ruth Benedict, *Race: Science and Politics* (New York, 1943) and F. H. Hankins, *Racial Basis of Civilization* (New York, 1926). For a more extended discussion of racism see

Erich Voegelin, *Die Rassenidee in der geistesgeschichte von Ray bis Carus* (Berlin, 1933) and his *Rasse und Staat* (Tübingen, 1933).

66. Gobineau, *op. cit.*, p. 209.

67. Hannah Arendt, "Race-Thinking before Racism," *Review of Politics* (Jan., 1944), Vol. 6, No. 1, pp. 36 *ff*., p. 58. This is an excellent discussion of the difference between "race-thinking" and "racism." The article points out that although "race-thinking" is old, "racism" is very new.

68. H. S. Chamberlain, *The Foundations of the Nineteenth Century*. 2 vols. (London, 1910), Vol. I, p. 247.

69. *Ibid.*, Vol. I, p. 345.

70. *Ibid.*, Vol. I, p. 491.

71. *Ibid.*, Vol. I, p. 331.

72. *Ibid.*, Vol. I, p. 257.

73. H. S. Chamberlain, *Auswahl aus seinen Werken* (Breslau, 1934), pp. 17 and 20.

74. Chamberlain, *Politische Ideale* (Munich, 1916), p. 88.

75. Frank H. Hankins, "Race as a Factor in Political Theory," in C. E. Merriam (ed.), *A History of Political Theories: Recent Times* (New York, 1924), pp. 522–523.

76. Franz Boas and others, *Aryan and Semite*, pamphlet (Cincinnati, 1934). For an excellent discussion of anti-Semitism see Jacques Maritain, *A Christian Looks at the Jewish Question* (New York, 1939) and the essays on that subject by the same author in *Pour La Justice: Articles et Discours 1940–1945* (New York, 1945). In part Maritain says: "If the Jewish people did not hear the call made to them by the dying Christ, yet do they remain ever summoned. If the Gentiles indeed heard the call, now racist paganism casts them away from it and from Him who is our peace. Anti-Semitic hatred is a directly anti-Christic frenzy to make vain the blood of Jesus and to make void His death. . . . To persecute the house of Israel is to persecute Christ, not in His mystical body as when the Church is persecuted, but in His

fleshly lineage and in His forget-
ful people whom He ceaselessly
loves and calls." *Pour la Justice*,
pp. 52 and 53. A highly provoca-
tive but illuminating analysis of
anti-Semitism will be found in
the essay by the French existentialist, Jean-Paul Sartre, entitled
"Portrait of the Anti-Semite."
Partisan Review Pamphlets,
No. 1.

77. Hans Gunther, *Racial Elements
of European History* (E. P. Dutton
& Company, Inc., New York,
1928), pp. 3 *ff*. By permission.
78. *Ibid.*, pp. 51 *ff*.
79. *Ibid.*, pp. 59 *ff*.
80. See, for example, Gunnar Myr-
dal, *An American Dilemma: The
Negro Problem and Modern Democracy*, 2 vols. (New York, 1944).
81. *Political Science and Comparative
Constitutional Law*, 2 vols. (Boston, 1890), Vol. I, p. 4.
82. *Ibid.*, Vol. I, p. 48.
83. Madison Grant, *The Passing of
the Great Race* (New York, 1916).
Preface.
84. *Ibid.*, pp. 150 and 198.
85. *Ibid.*, pp. 72 *ff*.
86. See, for example, Charles W.
Gould, *America: A Family Matter*
(New York, 1922); Carl C.
Brigham, *A Study of American Intelligence* (Princeton, 1923); Lo-
throp Stoddard, *The Rising Tide
of Color* (New York, 1920); Lo-
throp Stoddard, *The Revolt
Against Civilization* (New York,
1922); A. E. Wiggam, *The Fruit
of the Family Tree* (Indianapolis,
1924) and the writings of Thomas
Nixon Carver, Lawrence Dennis,
and Walter B. Pitkin.

87. See *Korematsu v. United States* 323
U. S. 214 (1944).
88. A. J. Toynbee, *A Study of History*. 6 vols. (Oxford University
Press, New York, 1934), Vol. I,
p. 245. From *A Study of History* by
Arnold J. Toynbee, published
under the auspices of the Royal
Institute of International Affairs.
Copyright 1946 by Oxford University Press, Inc.
89. Reinhold Niebuhr, *The Children
of Light and the Children of Dark-*

*ness* (Charles Scribner's Sons,
New York, 1944), pp. 139 *ff*.
90. Hayes, *Essays on Nationalism, op.
cit.*, p. 125.

## CHAPTER 17

1. See, for example, Robert A.
Brady, *The Spirit and Structure of
German Fascism* (New York,
1937).
2. Frieda Wunderlich, "Germany's
Defense Economy and the Decay
of Capitalism," *Quarterly Journal
of Economics*, Vol. LII, pp. 401 *ff*.
(May, 1938). By permission.
3. *Ibid.*, pp. 423–424.
4. *Ibid.*, p. 430.
5. Arnold Brecht, *Prelude to Silence*
(Oxford University Press, New
York, 1944), pp. 98–99. By per-
mission.
6. See, for example, John Dewey,
*German Philosophy and Politics*
(New York, 1942); William M.
McGovern, *From Luther to Hitler*
(Boston, 1941); William Ebenstein, *The German Record* (New
York, 1945), and the writings of
the Englishman, Lord Vansit-
tart. This theory of National
Socialism inspired the so-called
Morgenthau plan for Germany
immediately following World
War II.
7. See Guido de Ruggiero, *The
History of European Liberalism*
(London, 1927), esp. pp. 211 *ff*.
Also, J. H. Hallowell, *The De-
cline of Liberalism as an Ideology:
With Particular Reference to German
Politico-Legal Thought* (Berkeley,
1943), esp. Ch. II. Now available in the International Library
of Sociology and Social Reconstruction (London, 1946).
8. The best account of this revolt
and its history is Hans Rothfels',
*The German Opposition to Hitler*
(H. Regnery, Chicago, 1948).
Other accounts of varying accu-
racy are contained in F. von
Schlabrendorff, *They Almost Killed
Hitler* (New York, 1947); H. B.
Gisevius, *To the Bitter End* (Boston, 1947); *A German of the Resistance*, *The Last Letters of Count*

*Helmuth James von Moltke* (London, 1947); Allen W. Dulles, *Germany's Underground* (New York, 1947); and Gabriel A. Almond, "The German Resistance Movement," *Current History* (May–June 1946); on the opposition of Christians see N. Micklem, *National Socialism and Christianity* (Oxford, 1939) and *National Socialism and the Roman Catholic Church* (Oxford, 1938). See also Hugh Martin *et al.*, *Christian Counter Attack* (New York, 1944).

9. Benito Mussolini, "The Political and Social Doctrine of Fascism," reprinted in *International Conciliation* (Jan., 1935), No. 306. See also Alfred Rocco, "The Political Doctrine of Fascism," *International Conciliation* (1926), No. 223.

10. James Drennan, *B. U. F.: Oswald Mosley and British Fascism* (London, 1934), pp. 212–213.

11. Lawrence Dennis, *The Coming American Fascism* (New York, 1936), p. 105.

12. Quoted by Aurel Kolnai, *The War Against the West* (Victor Gollancz, Ltd., London, 1938), p. 299. By permission of Victor Gollancz, Ltd., and Viking Press, Inc., American Publishers.

13. Speech of Mussolini at Naples, Oct. 24, 1922. Quoted by H. Finer, *Mussolini's Italy* (New York, 1935), p. 218.

14. A. Rosenberg, *Der Mythus des 20. Jahrhunderts* (Munich, 1935), p. 114. "The myth of the twentieth century," according to the cover of this book, "is the myth of blood, which under the sign of the swastika unchains the racial world-revolution. It is the awakening of the race soul, which after long sleep victoriously ends the race chaos." Or, as Rosenberg states it in the opening pages of the book, "History no longer means war of class against class nor of church dogma and dogma, but blood and blood, race and race."

15. *Ibid.*, p. 117.

16. Joseph Goebbels, the Nazi Minister of Propaganda, described the Jews as "the world enemy, the destroyer of civilization, the parasite among nations, the son of chaos, the incarnation of evil, the germ of decomposition, the plastic demon of the decay of humanity" in a speech at the Nuremberg Party Congress in September, 1937.

17. Marinetti. Quoted by H. W. Schneider, *Making the Fascist State* (Chicago, 1928), pp. 261 *ff.*

18. Quoted in the *Mind and Face of Nazi Germany*, an anthology selected and edited by N. Gangulee (London, 1942), p. 129.

19. *Ibid.*, p. 1.

20. *Germany Reborn*, p. 79.

21. Hans J. Morgenthau, "Nazism," in J. S. Roucek (ed.), *Twentieth Century Political Thought* (New York, 1946), p. 132.

22. Hermann Rauschning, *The Revolution of Nihilism* (William Heinemann, Ltd., London, 1939). The best history of the the Nazi movement is Konrad Heiden's *A History of National Socialism* (London, 1934). See also his *Der Führer: Hitler's Rise to Power* (Boston, 1944). The best analysis of legal developments in Nazi Germany is Ernst Fraenkel, *The Dual State* (New York, 1941).

23. Rauschning, *ibid.*, p. 24.

24. *Ibid.*, p. 55.

25. *Ibid.*, pp. 59 *ff.* For an excellent study of the twentieth-century totalitarian dictatorship as the embodiment of "permanent revolution" see Sigmund Neumann, *Permanent Revolution* (New York, 1942). War, he says, is inseparable from Fascism and even "when power is won, the *permanent revolution*—even if renounced in foreign affairs, at least at times, for tactical reasons, has to go on in internal politics. Opposition groups have to be seized, the party has to be regularly purged, trials and expulsions have to take place. All this means stamina to a dictatorship, and even the most peaceful work of daily life must show the touch of warlike activity. There are a thousand battles going on:

the battle of grain, the battle for raw materials, the fight for joy after work, the battle of the birth rate. And they are all merely preparations for the supreme battle for world power." *Ibid.*, pp. 41–42.

26. Rauschning, *op. cit.*, pp. 87–88.

27. Peter Drucker, *The End of Economic Man* (The John Day Company, Inc., New York, 1939), pp. 227 *ff*. By permission.

28. *Cf.* José Ortega y Gasset, *The Revolt of the Masses* (W. W. Norton and Company, New York, 1932). By permission. I do not agree entirely with Ortega's analysis but it contains a great deal of truth. "Under the species of Syndicalism and Fascism," he declares, "there appears for the first time in Europe a type of man who does not want to give reasons or to be right, but simply shows himself resolved to impose his opinions. This is the new thing: the right not to be reasonable, the 'reason of unreason.'" *Ibid.*, p. 80.

29. "When German judges adjudicate . . . 'in National Socialist spirit' to the extent of twisting the letter of existing precepts, this is no mere subservience to a political upheaval," E. B. Ashton declares, "but an earnest and sincere fulfillment of judicial duty as it is now conceived . . . the vast majority of the highly conscientious and professionally proud German civil servants adjusted themselves to the new doctrine with surprising ease. . . . As a matter of fact, what we call 'misapplying the law,' to the Fascist simply means applying it in accordance with the principles that made it law. As a great German jurist put it: 'The will of the State is the soul of the law.'" *The Fascist: His State and His Mind* (London, 1939), pp. 131–132. For an account of how a degenerate liberalism paves the way for Fascism see Lewis Mumford, *Faith for Living* (New York, 1940).

30. Kolnai, op. cit., p. 15.

31. The same author quotes a Jesuit priest as saying, very aptly, that "The real problem is not Hitler, but the capacity to be infected by Hitler." The real problem is suggested by the title of a book by Max Picard, *Hitler in Our Selves* (H. Regnery, Chicago, 1947). Since the end of World War II many German intellectuals have begun a process of self-examination which has been fruitful in uncovering, in the words of one of them "the germ of evil which was planted long ago." See Karl Jaspers, *Die Schuldfrage* (Zurich, 1946); Friedrich Meinecke, *Die deutsche Katastrophe* (Wiesbaden, 1946); Julius Ebbinghaus, *Zu Deutschlands Schicksalswende* (Frankfurt, 1946); Gerd Tellenbach, *Die deutsche Not als Schuld und Schicksal* (Frankfurt, 1947) and Ernst Friedlander, *Von der inneren Not* (Hamburg, 1947).

32. *The New York Times*, October 15, 1933. Section V, pp. 1 and 24.

33. *Great Contemporaries* (London, 1935), p. 265.

34. London *Times*, November 7, 1938, p. 12.

35. Kolnai, *op. cit.*, p. 25.

36. Helmut Kuhn, *Freedom: Forgotten and Remembered* (University of North Carolina Press, Chapel Hill, 1943), pp. 7–8. By permission.

37. *Ibid.*, p. 25.

38. *Ibid.*, p. 110. Writing in 1930 Ortega y Gasset declared: "The whole world—nations and individuals—is demoralised. For a time this demoralisation rather amuses people, and even causes a vague illusion. The lower ranks think that a weight has been lifted off them. Decalogues retain from the time they were written on stone or bronze their character of heaviness . . . Lower ranks the world over . . . with holiday air take advantage of a period freed from burdensome imperatives. But the holiday does not last long. Without commandments obliging us to live after a certain fashion, our existence is that of the 'unem-

ployed.' This is the terrible
spiritual situation in which the
best youth of the world finds itself today. By dint of feeling itself
free, exempt from restrictions, it
feels itself empty. An 'unemployed' existence is a worse
negation of life than death itself.
Because to live means to have
something definite to do—a mission to fulfill—and in the measure in which we avoid setting
our life to something, we make it
empty. Before long there will be
heard throughout the planet a
formidable cry, rising like the
howling of innumerable dogs to
the stars, asking for someone or
something to take command, to
impose an occupation, a duty.
. . . Human life, by its very
nature, has to be dedicated to
something, an enterprise glorious
or humble, a destiny illustrious
or trivial. . . . In these years
we are witnessing the gigantic
spectacle of innumerable human
lives wandering about lost in
their own labyrinths, through
not having anything to which to
give themselves." *Op. cit.*, pp.
148 and 154.

39. Under the totalitarian dictatorship the State becomes the final
arbiter of all truth and all value.
"Man's supreme significance lies
in his citizenship. His art, science,
morals, religion are judged good
or bad in so far as they minister
to or hinder the absolute supremacy of political power. The
State's interest is the final arbiter
of all men's actions. But this
practical conception could never
have succeeded in generating the
mass following that it has if there
had been only hortatory injunctions to subordinate everything
to the supreme political end and
the plentiful oppressive coercion
that has accompanied these developments. This State absolutism is a going concern because
it is offered as an instrument for
implementing a much deeper
force which is not so much imposed as evoked—the hunger of
the soul of the man of today

which has been starved by the
agnostic empiricisms of secular humanism. It claims the
total loyalty of man and in
so doing restores to him the
sense of being purposive and recovers for him the consciousness
of social solidarity. But on a still
deeper level, these tendencies
give human beings the conviction
of being significant as conscious
agents in a process that is in the
sweep of the trend of all things.
This effect is gained by the shut-
ting out of much of reality or by
the distorting of it. But it is a
tremendous bait to the lacerated
soul of modern man, torn from
his spiritual and cosmic roots, to
be pushed back into what he is
taught to conceive as the purposive process of reality as a whole.
For the Communist the classless
society is the goal of history; for
the Fascist the national deed has
the force of a deity that generates
and judges men's actions and
thoughts; the German Nazi finds
himself the bearer of a racial
destiny that is the meaning of
existence." V. A. Demant, *Theology of Society* (Faber and Faber,
Ltd., London, 1947) p. 161. By
permission.

CHAPTER 18

1. G. K. Chesterton, *Orthodoxy*
(Dodd, Mead & Company, New
York, 1947), pp. 55–56. Reprinted by permission of Dodd,
Mead & Company from *Or-
thodoxy* by G. K. Chesterton.
Copyright, 1908, 1935, by G. K.
Chesterton. In the same book
Chesterton points out that with
the decline in religious faith
there is necessarily a decline of
faith in reason, "for they are
both of the same primary and
authoritative kind. They are
both methods of proof which
cannot themselves be proved.
And in the act of destroying
the idea of Divine authority
we have largely destroyed the
idea of that human authority

by which we do a long-division sum. With a long and sustained tug we have attempted to pull the mitre off pontifical man; and his head has come off with it." pp. 59–60.

2. B. Russell, "A Free Man's Worship" in *Mysticism and Logic* (W. W. Norton, New York, 1929). Reprinted from *Mysticism and Logic* by Bertrand Russell, by permission of W. W. Norton & Company, Inc. Copyright 1929 by W. W. Norton & Company, Inc.

3. Lewis Mumford, *Faith for Living* (Harcourt, Brace, New York, 1940), pp. 81–82. By permission.

4. Reinhold Niebuhr, *The Nature and Destiny of Man.* 2 vols. (Charles Scribner's Sons, New York, 1943), Vol. I, p. 273, note 4. By permission.

5. Romans 1: 18, 21–23.

6. Nicholas Berdyaev, *The Fate of Man in the Modern World* (Morehouse-Gorham & Company, London, 1935), pp. 28 ff. By permission.

7. Paul Tillich, *The Religious Situation.* Transl. by R. Niebuhr. (New York, 1932), pp. 19–20.

8. Berdyaev, *op. cit.*, pp. 34 ff.

9. An interesting, if somewhat extreme, interpretation of the discontinuity of modern culture will be found in Max Picard, *Hitler in Our Selves* (H. Regnery, Chicago, 1947). Another analysis of the same problem is found in T. S. Eliot, *Notes Towards a Definition of Culture* (New York, 1948).

10. Victor Gollancz, *Our Threatened Values* (Victor Gollancz, London, 1946). By permission. An American edition of this book is available through the publishing house of Henry Regnery, Chicago, Illinois.

11. *Ibid.*, p. 10.

12. *Ibid.*, pp. 15–16.

13. *Ibid.*, pp. 27–28.

14. *Ibid.*, p. 28.

15. *Ibid.*, p. 29.

16. Helmut Kuhn, *Encounter With Nothingness: An Essay on Existentialism* (H. Regnery Co., Chicago, 1949), pp. xii–xiii. By permission. For other accounts of existentialism see Werner Brock, *An Introduction to Contemporary German Philosophy* (Cambridge, 1947); Guido de Ruggiero, *Existentialism* (London, 1946); Marjorie Grene, *Dreadful Freedom: A Critique of Existentialism* (Chicago, 1948). Julien Benda, *Tradition de L'Existentialisme* (Paris, 1947); Jean Wahl, *A Short History of Existentialism* (New York, 1948). Among the writings of contemporary French existentialists now available in English are: Jean-Paul Sartre, *Existentialism* (New York, 1947); Sartre, *The Emotions: Outline of a Theory* (New York, 1948); Simone de Beauvoir, *The Blood of Others* (New York, 1948) and Gabriel Marcel, *The Philosophy of Existence* (New York, 1948). Among the numerous articles that have been written on existentialism the following might be especially mentioned: Hannah Arendt, "What is Existential Philosophy?" in *Partisan Review*, Vol. 13, pp. 34 ff. (Winter, 1946); Paul Tillich, "Existential Philosophy," *Journal of the History of Ideas*, Vol. 5, pp. 44 ff. (Jan., 1944) and Jean Wahl, "Existentialism: a Preface," *New Republic*, Vol. 113, pp. 142 ff. (Oct. 1, 1945). One of the first books to appear in the United States in the field of politics which strongly reflects the influence of existentialism is Hans J. Morgenthau, *Scientific Man v. Power Politics* (Chicago, 1946). A scholar who has read this manuscript, but prefers to remain anonymous, has suggested to me that existentialism found its first tentative crystallization in Montaigne's skepticism, especially in his *Apologie de Raimond Sebond* and its first full expression in Pascal's *Pensées*. According to the same scholar: "The 'problem' of existentialism is the attempt to withdraw from the plurality of discredited dogmatisms and to recover the existential experiences which ex-

press themselves in dogmatic symbols. It has, therefore, two principal manifestations: (1) the recovery of existential experiences, and (2) the understanding of dogmatic symbols as their historical expression. In the nineteenth century, the first type manifests itself in the work of Kierkegaard, the second type in Schelling's *Philosophie der Mythologie und der Offenbarung.* The German brand of the later development (Yorck, Jaspers, Heidegger), as well as the Spanish (Ortega y Gasset), and the French (Bergson), are part of the general Schelling-Renaissance and so far do not depend on Kierkegaard directly. The noisy development through Sartre, etc., is a symptom of the fact that the French complacent ideology of the Revolution has blown up and that France is moving into the situation of the 'crisis' in which the Germans found themselves already after Hegel." The word existentialism, was first coined by Friedrich H. Jacobi.

17. Kuhn, *op. cit.,* pp. xiii–xiv.
18. For an introduction to the writings of Kierkegaard which are voluminous see Robert Bretall (ed.) *A Kierkegaard Anthology* (Princeton, 1946). See also Walter Lowrie, *A Short Life of Kierkegaard* (Princeton, 1942); Walter Lowrie, *Kierkegaard* (New York, 1938); David F. Swenson, *Something About Kierkegaard* (Augsburg, rev. ed., 1945); M. Channing-Pearce, *The Terrible Chrystal: Kierkegaard and Modern Christianity* (London, 1940); John Wild, "Kierkegaard and Classical Philosophy," *Philosophical Review,* Vol. 49, pp. 536 *ff.*; Karl Löwith, "On the Historical Understanding of Kierkegaard," *Review of Religion,* Vol. 17, pp. 227 *ff.* (March, 1943); and Philip Merlan, "Toward the Understanding of Kierkegaard," *Journal of Religion,* Vol. 23, pp. 77 *ff.* (April, 1943).
19. *Philosophical Fragments* in Bretall (ed.) *op. cit.,* p. 154.

20. *Concluding Unscientific Postscript* (Princeton University Press, Princeton, 1944), pp. 179–180.
21. Kuhn, *op. cit.,* p. 68.
22. *Ibid.,* pp. 50–51.
23. Oswald Spengler, *Politische Schriften* (Munich, 1934), pp. 85–86.
24. Kuhn, *op. cit.,* p. 112.
25. *Ibid.,* pp. 75 *ff.*
26. *Ibid.,* pp. xix–xx.
27. *Ibid.,* p. xxii.
28. Helmut Kuhn, "The Classical Christian Tradition and the Emerging World," *Theology Today* (Jan., 1946), pp. 457–458. By permission.
29. One of the best analyses of representative "philosophies of history" with an analysis of the concept of "philosophy of history" itself is Karl Löwith's, *Meaning in History* (Chicago, 1949).
30. Spengler's idea of the growth and decay of civilizations was anticipated by Eduard Meyer in his *Geschichte des Altertums. Cf.* Spengler's philosophy of history with Pitirim A. Sorokin's *Social and Cultural Dynamics,* 6 vols. (1934–1939). There are several abridged versions of Sorokin's thesis available.
31. A one-volume abridged edition of Toynbee's *Study of History,* edited and abridged by D. C. Somervell is now available (Oxford University Press, New York, 1946). From *A Study of History* by Arnold J. Toynbee, published under the auspices of the Royal Institute of International Affairs. Copyright 1946 by Oxford University Press, Inc. Quotations are from that edition unless otherwise noted.
32. Says Toynbee: " . . . time is relative and . . . the spell of something less than six thousand years which bridges the interval between the emergence of the earliest known civilizations and our own day has to be measured for the purpose of our study on the relevant time-scale, that is in the terms of the time-spans of the civilizations themselves. Now, in surveying the relations of

civilizations in time, the highest number of successive generations that we have met with in any case is three, and in each case these three, between them, more than cover our span of six thousand years, since the last term in each series is a civilization that is still alive. The fact that, in our survey of civilizations, we have found in no case a higher number of successive generations than three means that this species is very young in terms of its own time-scale. . . . It goes without saying that some civilizations go back to the 'dawn of history' because what we call history is the history of man in a 'civilized' society, but if by history we meant the whole period of man's life on Earth, we should find that the period producing civilizations, far from being coeval with human history, covers only two per cent of it, one-fiftieth of the lifetime of mankind. Our civilizations may, then, be granted to be sufficiently contemporaneous with one another for our purpose." *Ibid.*, p. 42.

33. *Ibid.*, p. 56.
34. *Ibid.*, p. 60.
35. *Ibid.*, pp. 67–68.
36. *Ibid.*, p. 140.
37. *Ibid.*, p. 187.
38. *Ibid.*, p. 209.
39. *Ibid.*, p. 211.
40. *Ibid.*, p. 214.
41. *Ibid.*, p. 216.
42. *Love's Grave*. Quoted by Toynbee, *ibid.*, p. 275.
43. *A Study of History*, Vol. I, p. 41, note 3.
44. *Ibid.*, Vol. 5, p. 63.
45. *Ibid.*, Vol. 5, p. 25.
46. *Ibid.*, Somervell one-volume edition, p. 429.
47. *Ibid.*, p. 429.
48. *Ibid.*, p. 446.
49. *Ibid.*, p. 451.
50. *Ibid.*, p. 473.
51. *Ibid.*, p. 431.
52. *Ibid.*, p. 431.
53. *Ibid.*, p. 432.
54. *Ibid.*, p. 438.
55. *Ibid.*, p. 438.

56. Seneca, *De Clementia*, Bk. II, Ch. 5. Quoted by Toynbee, *ibid.*, p. 527.
57. I Cor. 1:27.
58. Toynbee, *op. cit.*, p. 529.

## CHAPTER 19

1. *The Case for Christianity* (New York, 1944), p. 24.
2. I am suggesting that the way back to personal sanity and social health lies in the recovery of the Hebrew-Greek-Christian tradition. This tradition provides the principles with which we can best understand ourselves and our society. Without "first principles" we can neither understand nor evaluate anything. Those who would do away with "first principles" must, of necessity, do away with explanation itself. C. S. Lewis points out that there is a kind of explanation which explains things by explaining them away, but, he says, "you cannot go on 'explaining away' for ever: you will find that you have explained explanation itself away. You cannot go on 'seeing through' things for ever. The whole point of seeing through something is to see something through it. It is good that the window should be transparent, because the street or garden beyond it is opaque. How if you saw through the garden too? It is no use trying to 'see through' first principles. If you see through everything, then everything is transparent. But a wholly transparent world is an invisible world. To 'see through' all things is the same as not to see." *The Abolition of Man* (New York, 1947), p. 50.
3. For an introduction to the Christian faith see: C. S. Lewis, *The Case for Christianity* (Macmillan, New York, 1944). Copyright 1944 by The Macmillan Company and used with their permission; C. S. Lewis, *The Problem of Pain* (New York, 1945); C. S. Lewis, *Miracles* (New York,

1947); A. E. Taylor, *Does God Exist?* (New York, 1947); G. K. Chesterton, *Orthodoxy* (New York, 1947); T. E. Jessop, *et al.*, *The Christian Understanding of Man* (London, 1938); H. N. Fairchild, *Towards Belief* (New York, 1935); J. H. Newman, *The Development of Christian Doctrine* (New York, 1949).

4. While liberal Protestantism is *primarily* an American movement it does have European roots, especially in the thought of the German theologians F. D. E. Schleiermacher (1768–1834), Albrecht Ritschl (1822–1889), and Adolf von Harnack (1851–1930).

5. Walter Rauschenbusch, *Christianity and the Social Crisis* (New York, 1907), pp. 59 and 61.

6. Rauschenbusch, *Christianizing the Social Order* (Macmillan, New York, 1912), p. 179. Copyright 1912 by The Macmillan Company and used with their permission.

7. *Ibid.*, p. 195.

8. *Ibid.*, p. 350.

9. *Ibid.*, p. 364.

10. *Ibid.*, p. 449.

11. Rauschenbusch, *A Theology for the Social Gospel* (Macmillan, New York, 1917), pp. 4–5. Copyright 1917 by The Macmillan Company and used with their permission.

12. *Ibid.*, p. 150.

13. *Ibid.*, p. 151.

14. *Ibid.*, p. 179.

15. *Ibid.*, p. 179.

16. *Ibid.*, p. 42.

17. *Ibid.*, p. 60.

18. *Ibid.*, p. 198.

19. *Ibid.*, p. 85.

20. *Ibid.*, p. 119.

21. *Christianity and the Social Crisis*, pp. 356–357.

22. *Ibid.*, p. 421.

23. *Ibid.*, p. 422. For a discussion of Rauschenbusch and the Social Gospel movement see: V. P. Bodein, *The Social Gospel of Walter Rauschenbusch* (New Haven, 1944); C. H. Hopkins, *The Rise of the Social Gospel in American Protestantism, 1865–1915* (New Haven, 1940); R. H. Gabriel,

*The Course of American Democratic Thought* (New York, 1940), Ch. 24 and W. M. Horton, *Realistic Theology* (New York, 1934).

24. For a recent statement of the pacifist position and argument see A. J. Muste, *Not by Might* (New York, 1947). For a critical analysis of this argument see J. H. Hallowell, "Pacifism: the Way to Peace?", in the *Crozer Quarterly*, Jan., 1949, pp. 30 ff.

25. See Karl Barth, *Church and State; The Knowledge of God and the Service of God* (New York, 1939); Emil Brunner, *The Divine Imperative* (New York, 1937) and *Justice and the Social Order* (London, 1945).

26. Reinhold Niebuhr, *The Nature and Destiny of Man*, 2 vols. (New York, 1943), Vol. I, p. 182.

27. *Ibid.*, Vol. I, pp. 183 ff.

28. Bertrand Russell, *Power, A New Social Analysis* (New York, 1938). Quoted by Niebuhr, *ibid.*, Vol. I, p. 189, note 6.

29. Niebuhr, *ibid.*, Vol. I, pp. 206–207.

30. *Ibid.*, Vol. I, p. 242.

31. *Ibid.*, Vol. I, p. 263.

32. Niebuhr, *Faith and History* (New York, 1949), p. 89.

33. *Christianity and Power Politics* (New York, 1940), p. 156.

34. *Ibid.*, p. 158.

35. *Faith and History*, p. 239.

36. *Ibid.*, p. 210.

37. *Ibid.*, pp. 135–136.

38. *Christianity and Power Politics*, p. 2.

39. *Ibid.*, p. 7.

40. *Ibid.*, pp. 22–23 *et seq.*

41. *Ibid.*, p. 25.

42. *The Children of Light and the Children of Darkness* (Charles Scribner's Sons, New York, 1944), p. xi. By permission.

43. *Ibid.*, p. xi.

44. *Ibid.*, p. 9.

45. *Ibid.*, pp. 11–12.

46. *Ibid.*, p. 59.

47. *Ibid.*, p. 61.

48. *Ibid.*, pp. 61–62.

49. *Ibid.*, p. 84.

50. *Ibid.*, p. 106.

51. *Ibid.*, p. 118.

52. *Ibid.*, pp. 164–165.

53. *Ibid.*, p. 166.

54. *Ibid.*, pp. 168 *ff*.
55. *Ibid.*, p. 170.
56. *Ibid.*, p. 174.
57. *Ibid.*, p. 181.
58. *Ibid.*, pp. 187–188.
59. *Ibid.*, pp. 188–189. For an excellent analysis of Niebuhr's position see Helmut Kuhn, "Charity and Contemplation," *Philosophy and Phenomenological Research*, Vol. IV, No. 3, pp. 420 *ff*. (March, 1944). By permission. In part, Professor Kuhn says, "We may unhesitatingly subscribe to 'Niebuhr's thesis' concerning the character of human knowledge and admit that it is (a) limited, (b) liable to errors resulting from a corruption of the will. This corruption is responsible for the ideological 'taint' that disfigures 'truths' as ordinarily advanced and believed in by the members of any human society. So far so good." But "the knowledge of the limitedness of the human intellect in general is, for the student of human nature, only the beginning of wisdom. Unless he is able to tell us to what extent, and with reference to what problems, human intelligence is limited, we shall obtain small enlightenment from what he has to tell us . . . Likewise it is true that human self-assertiveness perpetually imperils the objectivity of knowledge, especially in the field of social problems. But the correction of errors must come in the process of knowledge itself, through the ever-renewed effort to obtain a deeper insight into social truth, rather than through the scruple about human veracity in general.

"This, then, is the upshot of our critical remarks: in the chapter on truth, Niebuhr is concerned with the avoidance of error rather than with the attainment of truth. But fallacies cannot be avoided by general reflections on human fallibility. The Christian conscience, sounding a warning and reminding us of our frailty, appears as an intruder in the field of knowledge.

It is a nobler intruder, undoubtedly, than the materialistic *advocatus diaboli* who whispers into our ears that our alleged truth is a camouflaged interest and that we mean 'dollar' when we say 'soul'; nobler also than the psychoanalyst who, in his medico-mythological brogue, hints at 'repressions' and 'sublimations.' Nevertheless, the conscience voicing scruples about finitude is equally out of place. The passionate striving after truth (the truth that is God) must be its own check and corrective." Niebuhr's "portrayal shows man as the sinner groping along a hazardous path between precipices of error rather than as the ardent lover who presses on, divinely guided, toward an exuberance of light; and the Deity to Whom this finite and erring creature raises his eyes is the righteous God 'that trieth the hearts and reins' (Psalms 7, 9) rather than bounty without measure." *Loc. cit.*, p. 429 *et seq.*
60. The First Assembly of the World Council of Churches was held in Amsterdam, Holland, August 22–September 4, 1948. *Findings and Decisions*. A pamphlet published in Geneva, London and New York, pp. 44–45. The complete record of the First Assembly has been published in a volume entitled *Man's Disorder and God's Design* (New York, 1949).
61. *Findings and Decisions*, p. 45.
62. *Ibid.*, p. 46.
63. *Ibid.*, p. 47. The position of the World Council on the question of the formation of Christian political parties is somewhat confused and ambivalent. The question might well be asked: what alternative to Christian parties is there in countries in which all other parties are anti-Christian in program and practice?
64. *Ibid.*, pp. 54–55.
65. *Ibid.*, p. 56.
66. *Ibid.*, p. 61.
67. *Ibid.*, pp. 62–64.

68. Philip Hughes, *The Pope's New Order: A Systematic Summary of the Social Encyclicals and Addresses, from Leo XIII to Pius XII* (New York, 1944), p. 113. For other accounts of Catholic social theory see: J. A. Ryan and F. J. Boland, *Catholic Principles of Politics* (New York, 1940); J. A. Ryan and J. S. Husslein, *The Church and Labor* (New York, 1924); R. S. J. Corrogan, *The Church and the Nineteenth Century* (Milwaukee, 1938); H. E. Manning, *The Dignity and Rights of Labor* (London, 1934); F. S. Nitti, *Catholic Socialism* (New York, 1895) and E. J. Hughes, *The Church and the Liberal Society* (Princeton, 1944).

69. Philip Hughes, *op. cit.*, p. 113.

70. *Ibid.*, p. 118.

71. *Ibid.*, p. 117.

72. *Ibid.*, p. 117.

73. *Ibid.*, p. 116.

74. *Ibid.*, p. 208.

75. *Ibid.*, pp. 208–209.

76. *Ibid.*, pp. 209–210.

77. *Ibid.*, pp. 210–211.

78. *Ibid.*, p. 212.

79. *Ibid.*, pp. 214–215.

80. *Ibid.*, pp. 223.

81. *Ibid.*, p. 220.

82. *Ibid.*, p. 235.

83. *Ibid.*, p. 237.

84. *Ibid.*, p. 241.

85. *Ibid.*, p. 242.

86. *Ibid.*, p. 243.

87. *Ibid.*, p. 245.

88. *Ibid.*, p. 248.

89. The encyclical *Mit Brennender Sorge* of March 14, 1937.

90. See Jacques Maritain, *True Humanism* (London, 1938), *Scholasticism and Politics* (New York, 1939), *Christianity and Democracy* (New York, 1944), *The Rights of Man and Natural Law* (New York, 1943), *Education at the Crossroads* (New Haven, 1943), *Pour la Justice* (New York, 1945) and Christopher Dawson, *Religion and the Rise of Western Culture* (London, 1950).

91. Maritain, *The Person and the Common Good* (Charles Scribner's Sons, New York, 1947), pp. 40–41. By permission.

92. *Ibid.*, p. 63.

93. *Ibid.*, p. 81.

94. Maritain, *Christianity and Democracy* (Charles Scribner's Sons, New York, 1944), p. 47. By permission.

95. *Ibid.*, p. 50.

96. *Ibid.*, p. 56.

97. Dawson, *Religion and the Modern State*, (Sheed and Ward, London, 1935), p. 144. Used with the permission of The Society of Authors.

98. *Ibid.*, pp. 146–148.

99. John C. Bennett, *Christian Ethics and Social Policy* (New York, 1946), p. 37.

100. William Temple, *Christianity and the Social Order* (Penguin Publishers, Ltd., Middlesex, 1942), p. 37. By permission.

101. *Ibid.*, p. 38.

102. *Ibid.*, p. 43.

103. *Ibid.*, p. 44.

104. *Ibid.*, p. 45.

105. *Ibid.*, p. 49.

106. *Ibid.*, pp. 53–54.

107. *The Christian News-Letter*, No. 198. Dec. 29, 1943.

108. *The Listener.* June 26, 1947.

109. Helmut Kuhn, "The Classical Christian Tradition and the Emerging World," *Theology Today* (Jan., 1946), p. 448.

110. *Ibid.*, p. 448.

111. *Ibid.*, p. 449.

112. Dom Axel Graham, *The Christ of Catholicism: a Meditative Study* (New York, 1947), pp. 308–309.

# Index

749